ACTS OF THE APOSTLES

WISDOM COMMENTARY
Volume 45

Acts of the Apostles

Linda M. Maloney
with Ivoni Richter Reimer

Afterword by Willie James Jennings

Mary Ann Beavis
Volume Editor

Barbara E. Reid, OP
General Editor

A Michael Glazier Book

LITURGICAL PRESS
Collegeville, Minnesota

www.litpress.org

1	2	3	4	5	6	7	8	9

Library of Congress Cataloging-in-Publication Data

Names: Maloney, Linda M., author. | Reimer, Ivoni Richter, author. | Beavis, Mary Ann, editor. | Reid, Barbara E., editor.
Title: Acts of the Apostles / Linda M. Maloney with Ivoni Richter Reimer; afterword by Willie James Jennings, Mary Ann Beavis, volume editor, Barbara E. Reid, OP, general editor.
Description: Collegeville, Minnesota : Liturgical Press, [2022] | Series: Wisdom commentary ; volume 45 | "A Michael Glazier Book." | Includes bibliographical references and index. | Summary: "This commentary on Acts of the Apostles provides a feminist interpretation of Scripture in serious, scholarly engagement with the whole text, not only those texts that explicitly mention women. It addresses not only issues of gender but also those of power, authority, ethnicity, racism, and classism"— Provided by publisher.
Identifiers: LCCN 2022014786 (print) | LCCN 2022014787 (ebook) | ISBN 9780814681695 (hardcover) | ISBN 9780814669099 (pdf) | ISBN 9780814681947 (epub)
Subjects: LCSH: Bible. Acts—Feminist criticism.
Classification: LCC BS2625.52 .M35 2022 (print) | LCC BS2625.52 (ebook) | DDC 226.6/06—dc23/eng/20220624
LC record available at https://lccn.loc.gov/2022014786
LC ebook record available at https://lccn.loc.gov/2022014787

In loving memory of Luise Schottroff†,

and

For Bernadette, Bonnie, Irmgard, Eloise, and Elizabeth,
five Daughters of Wisdom who sustained me through it all.

—*Linda Maloney*

For my mother, Frida Richter†,
and for my friends and colleagues Marlene Crüsemann,
Erika Stückrath, Elsa Tamez, and Karin Volkwein.

—*Ivoni Richter Reimer*

Contents

Abbreviations

ANRW	*Aufstieg und Niedergang der Römischen Welt*
AUS	American University Studies
AV	Authorized Version (King James Bible)
BAFCS	The Book of Acts in its First Century Setting
BBR	*Bulletin for Biblical Research*
BDAG	Danker, Frederick W., Walter Bauer, William F. Arndt, and F. Wilbur Gingrich. *Greek-English Lexicon of the New Testament and Other Early Christian Literature*. 3rd ed. Chicago: University of Chicago Press, 2000.
BDB	Brown, Francis, S. R. Driver, and Charles A. Briggs. *A Hebrew and English Lexicon of the Old Testament*
BETL	Bibliotheca Ephemeridum Theologicarum Lovaniensis
BibInt	Biblical Interpretation Series
BJS	Brown Judaic Studies
BTS	Biblical Tools and Studies
CBQ	*Catholic Biblical Quarterly*
CD	Cairo Genizah copy of the Damascus Document
CIL	*Corpus Inscriptionum Latinarum*
CurTM	*Currents in Theology and Mission*

DBL	*Dictionary of Biblical Languages with Semantic Domains* (Swanson)
ECNT	Exegetical Commentary on the New Testament
EJL	Early Judaism and its Literature
ETL	*Ephemerides Theologicae Lovanienses*
FCB	Feminist Companion to the Bible
FCNTECW	Feminist Companion to the New Testament and Early Christian Writings
FOTL	Forms of the Old Testament Literature
GBS	Guides to Biblical Scholarship
HeyJ	*Heythrop Journal*
HTR	*Harvard Theological Review*
ICC	International Critical Commentary
IECOT	International Exegetical Commentary on the Old Testament
IFT	Introductions in Feminist Theology
IK	Inschriften griechischer Städte aus Kleinasien
JBL	*Journal of Biblical Literature*
JFSR	*Journal of Feminist Studies in Religion*
JRS	*Journal of Roman Studies*
JSJ	*Journal for the Study of Judaism in the Persian, Hellenistic, and Roman Periods*
JSOT	*Journal for the Study of the Old Testament*
JSOTSup	Journal for the Study of the Old Testament Supplement Series
JSNT	*Journal for the Study of the New Testament*
JSNTSup	Journal for the Study of the New Testament Supplement Series
JTS	*Journal of Theological Studies*
KNT	Kommentar zum Neuen Testament
LCL	Loeb Classical Library
LCR	*Lutheran Church Review*

LD	Lectio Divina
LNTS	The Library of New Testament Studies
LXX	The Septuagint
MT	Masoretic Text
NABRE	New American Bible, Revised Edition
Neot	*Neotestamentica*
NHL	*Nag Hammadi Library in English*. Edited by James M. Robinson. 4th rev. ed. Leiden: Brill, 1996.
NICNT	New International Commentary on the New Testament
NIV	New International Version
NovT	*Novum Testamentum*
NRSV	New Revised Standard Version
NTApoc	*New Testament Apocrypha*
NTOA	Novum Testamentum et Orbis Antiquus
NTS	*New Testament Studies*
NYRB	*New York Review of Books*
OBT	Overtures to Biblical Theology
PL	Patrologia Latina
PRSt	*Perspectives in Religious Studies*
RBL	*Review of Biblical Literature*
RSV	Revised Standard Version
SBL	Society of Biblical Literature
SBLDS	Society of Biblical Literature Dissertation Series
SBLSP	Society of Biblical Literature Seminar Papers
SBS	Stuttgarter Bibelstudien
SemeiaSt	Semeia Studies
SNTSMS	Studiorum Novi Testamenti Societas Monograph Series
SP	Sacra Pagina
SVTQ	*St. Vladimir's Theological Quarterly*
SymS	Symposium Series
TDNT	*Theological Dictionary of the New Testament*

TynBul	*Tyndale Bulletin*
WBC	Word Biblical Commentary
WCS	Wisdom Commentary Series
WGRWSup	Writings from the Greco-Roman World Supplement Series
WMANT	Wissenschaftliche Monographien zum Alten und Neuen Testament
WUNT	Wissenschaftliche Untersuchungen zum Neuen Testament
ZNW	*Zeitschrift für die neutestamentliche Wissenschaft und die Kunde der älteren Kirche*
ZPE	*Zeitschrift für Papyrologie und Epigraphik*

Contributors

Jo-Ann Badley has a PhD in New Testament from the Toronto School of Theology. She is currently dean of theology at Ambrose University where she also teaches New Testament and hermeneutics courses. Her long-standing research interest is reading the Bible for the life of the church, both as a theoretical question and in the interpretation of particular texts. She always works with the storied form of the biblical text to understand the significance of the text's details for the reader.

Sean D. Burke is an associate professor of religion at Luther College in Decorah, Iowa. He joined Luther's faculty in 2007 and currently serves the college in the role of associate provost. He is the author of *Queering the Ethiopian Eunuch: Strategies of Ambiguity in Acts* (Fortress Press, 2013) as well as the commentary on the Acts of the Apostles in the forthcoming new edition of *The Queer Bible Commentary* (SCM Press, 2006). He is also an Episcopal priest.

Teresa J. Calpino received her BS in communications from Northwestern University and her MA in biblical languages and literature and PhD in New Testament and early Christianity from Loyola University Chicago, where she is a lecturer. Her current research focuses on the use of violence in Acts and a reception history of why Marian apparitions highlight anger. Her book *Women, Work and Leadership in Acts* was published in 2014 by Mohr-Siebeck.

Willie James Jennings is associate professor of systematic theology and Africana studies at Yale University Divinity School. His specializations also include postcolonial and race theory. He received his BA from Calvin

College, his MDiv from Fuller Theological Seminary, and his PhD in systematic theology from Duke University. He is the author of prize-winning works, including *The Christian Imagination: Theology and the Origins of Race* (Yale University Press, 2010); *After Whiteness: An Education in Belonging* (Eerdmans), the 2020 Publishers Weekly book of the year; and *Acts* in the Belief series (Westminster John Knox, 2017). In 2015 he received the Grawemeyer Award in Religion for his groundbreaking work on race and Christianity. He pastored alongside his wife, the Rev. Joanne L. Browne Jennings, in a number of Baptist and Presbyterian churches during their years in North Carolina. Joanne and Willie Jennings are the parents of two daughters, Njeri and Safiya Jennings.

Ally Kateusz is a cultural historian specializing in the intersection of women and religion in early Christian art and texts. She is research associate at the Wijngaards Institute for Catholic Research, and her recent books are the illustrated *Mary and Early Christian Women: Hidden Leadership* (Palgrave Macmillan, 2019) and *Maria, Mariamne, and Miriam: Rediscovering the Marys* (Bloomsbury, 2020), coedited with Mary Ann Beavis. Her peer-reviewed articles have appeared in the *Journal of Feminist Studies in Religion*, the *Journal of Early Christian Studies*, *ΘΕΟΛΟΓΙΑ*, *The Priscilla Papers*, and other venues. An expanded investigation into Holy Spirit Mother is forthcoming in "Holy Spirit Mother and Intersex Jesus: Turning Point Nicene Creed," *S/HE: An International Journal of Goddess Studies* 1 (2022).

Hannah L. Lents holds masters of arts in ancient Greek and Roman studies from Brandeis University and religious studies from the University of Texas at Austin. She is currently pursuing a PhD in religious studies at UTA, with a concentration in religions of the ancient Mediterranean. Trained as an archaeologist, in her work she interrogates the historical relationships between literary spaces, landscapes, and characters with their material counterparts. She also sits on the student editorial board of *Religiology*, the Religious Studies department's blog.

Timothy Milinovich (PhD, Catholic University of America) is associate professor of theology and director of Catholic studies at Dominican University in River Forest, Illinois. His research interests have centered on rhetorical aspects of Paul's letters, including audience-oriented, structural, and political approaches, and the impact of Roman religion on the situations of early Christian communities. His books include *Now Is the Day of Salvation: An Audience-Oriented Study of 2 Corinthians 5:16–6:2* and

Beyond What Is Written: The Performative Structure of 1 Corinthians (both from Pickwick). His articles have appeared in *Catholic Biblical Quarterly*, *Biblical Theology Bulletin*, and *Biblica*.

Deborah Thompson Prince is an associate professor in the Theology and Religious Studies Department at Bellarmine University in Louisville, Kentucky. She received an MDiv from Louisville Presbyterian Seminary and a PhD in New Testament from the University of Notre Dame. She has published several journal articles on Luke-Acts and contributed to the commentary series Feasting on the Gospels: *Luke*, vol. 1 (Westminster John Knox, 2014). Her research interests include studying the nature and purpose of visionary narratives in biblical literature as well as exploring the significance of encounters with the divine in religious experience more broadly.

Joshua Paul Smith received his PhD in 2021 from the University of Denver and Iliff School of Theology Joint Doctoral Program in Religion. His dissertation, titled "Luke Was Not a Christian," approaches the question of Lukan authorship and socioethnic belonging from a consciously interdisciplinary perspective. Smith's research interests include cognitive sociolinguistics, the negotiation of early Jewish and Christian identities, and contemporary post-supersessionist biblical theology. He is an adjunct instructor in New Testament at Central Seminary in Shawnee, Kansas, and teaches world religions at Southeast Missouri State University. He lives in Cape Girardeau, Missouri, with his spouse Alyssa, their three cats, and eighty thousand honeybees.

Foreword

"Come Eat of My Bread . . . and Walk in the Ways of Wisdom"

Elisabeth Schüssler Fiorenza
Harvard University Divinity School

J ewish feminist writer Asphodel Long has likened the Bible to a magnificent garden of brilliant plants, some flowering, some fruiting, some in seed, some in bud, shaded by trees of age old, luxurious growth. Yet in the very soil which gives it life the poison has been inserted. . . . This poison is that of misogyny, the hatred of women, half the human race.[1]

To see Scripture as such a beautiful garden containing poisonous ivy requires that one identify and name this poison and place on all biblical texts the label "Caution! Could be dangerous to your health and survival!" As critical feminist interpretation for well-being this Wisdom Commentary seeks to elaborate the beauty and fecundity of this

---

1. Asphodel Long, *In a Chariot Drawn by Lions: The Search for the Female in the Deity* (London: Women's Press, 1992), 195.

Scripture-garden and at the same time points to the harm it can do when one submits to its world of vision. Thus, feminist biblical interpretation engages two seemingly contradictory insights: The Bible is written in kyriocentric (i.e., lord/master/father/husband-elite male) language, originated in the patri-kyriarchal cultures of antiquity, and has functioned to inculcate misogynist mind-sets and oppressive values. At the same time it also asserts that the Bible as Sacred Scripture has functioned to inspire and authorize wo/men[2] in our struggles against dehumanizing oppression. The hermeneutical lens of wisdom/Wisdom empowers the commentary writers to do so.

In biblical as well as in contemporary religious discourse the word *wisdom* has a double meaning: It can either refer to the quality of life and of people and/or it can refer to a figuration of the Divine. Wisdom in both senses of the word is not a prerogative of the biblical traditions but is found in the imagination and writings of all known religions. Wisdom is transcultural, international, and interreligious. Wisdom is practical knowledge gained through experience and daily living as well as through the study of creation and human nature. Both word meanings, that of capability (wisdom) and that of female personification (Wisdom), are crucial for this Wisdom Commentary series that seeks to enable biblical readers to become critical subjects of interpretation.

Wisdom is a state of the human mind and spirit characterized by deep understanding and profound insight. It is elaborated as a quality possessed by the sages but also treasured as folk wisdom and wit. Wisdom is the power of discernment, deeper understanding, and creativity; it is the ability to move and to dance, to make the connections, to savor life, and to learn from experience. Wisdom is intelligence shaped by experience and sharpened by critical analysis. It is the ability to make sound choices and incisive decisions. Its root meaning comes to the fore in its Latin form *sapientia*, which is derived from the verb *sapere*, to taste and to savor something. Hence, this series of commentaries invites readers to taste, to evaluate, and to imagine. In the figure of *Chokmah-Sophia-Sapientia-Wisdom*, ancient Jewish Scriptures seek to hold together belief in the "one" G*d[3] of Israel with both masculine and feminine language and metaphors of the Divine.

---

2. I use wo/man, s/he, fe/male and not the grammatical standard "man" as inclusive terms and make this visible by adding /.

3. I use the * asterisk in order to alert readers to a problem to explore and think about.

In distinction to traditional Scripture reading, which is often individualistic and privatized, the practice and space of Wisdom commentary is public. Wisdom's spiraling presence (*Shekhinah*) is global, embracing all creation. Her voice is a public, radical democratic voice rather than a "feminine," privatized one. To become one of Her justice-seeking friends, one needs to imagine the work of this feminist commentary series as the spiraling circle dance of wisdom/Wisdom,[4] as a Spirit/spiritual intellectual movement in the open space of wisdom/Wisdom who calls readers to critically analyze, debate, and reimagine biblical texts and their commentaries as wisdom/Wisdom texts inspired by visions of justice and well-being for everyone and everything. Wisdom-Sophia-imagination engenders a different understanding of Jesus and the movement around him. It understands him as the child and prophet of Divine Wisdom and as Wisdom herself instead of imagining him as ruling King and Lord who has only subalterns but not friends. To approach the N*T[5] and the whole Bible as Wisdom's invitation of cosmic dimensions means to acknowledge its multivalence and its openness to change. As bread—not stone.

In short, this commentary series is inspired by the feminist vision of the open cosmic house of Divine Wisdom-Sophia as it is found in biblical Wisdom literatures, which include the N*T:

> Wisdom has built Her house
> She has set up Her seven pillars . . .
> She has mixed Her wine,
> She also has set Her table.
> She has sent out Her wo/men ministers
> to call from the highest places in the town . . .
> "Come eat of my bread
> and drink of the wine I have mixed.
> Leave immaturity, and live,
> And walk in the way of Wisdom." (Prov 9:1-3, 5-6)

---

4. I have elaborated such a Wisdom dance in terms of biblical hermeneutics in my book *Wisdom Ways: Introducing Feminist Biblical Interpretation* (Maryknoll, NY: Orbis Books, 2001). Its seven steps are a hermeneutics of experience, of domination, of suspicion, of evaluation, of remembering or historical reconstruction, of imagination, and of transformation. However, such Wisdom strategies of meaning making are not restricted to the Bible. Rather, I have used them in workshops in Brazil and Ecuador to explore the workings of power, Condomblé, Christology, imagining a the*logical wo/men's center, or engaging the national icon of Mary.

5. See the discussion about nomenclature of the two testaments in the introduction, page xxxix.

Editor's Introduction to Wisdom Commentary

"She Is a Breath of the Power of God" (Wis 7:25)

Barbara E. Reid, OP

General Editor

Wisdom Commentary is the first series to offer detailed feminist interpretation of every book of the Bible. The fruit of collaborative work by an ecumenical and interreligious team of scholars, the volumes provide serious, scholarly engagement with the whole biblical text, not only those texts that explicitly mention women. The series is intended for clergy, teachers, ministers, and all serious students of the Bible. Designed to be both accessible and informed by the various approaches of biblical scholarship, it pays particular attention to the world in front of the text, that is, how the text is heard and appropriated. At the same time, this series aims to be faithful to the ancient text and its earliest audiences; thus the volumes also explicate the worlds behind the text and within it. While issues of gender are primary in this project, the volumes also address the intersecting issues of power, authority, ethnicity, race, class, and religious belief and practice. The fifty-eight volumes include the books regarded as canonical by Jews (i.e., the Tanakh); Protestants (the "Hebrew Bible" and the New Testament); and Roman Catholic, Anglican, and Eastern

Orthodox Communions (i.e., Tobit, Judith, 1 and 2 Maccabees, Wisdom of Solomon, Sirach/Ecclesiasticus, Baruch, including the Letter of Jeremiah, the additions to Esther, and Susanna and Bel and the Dragon in Daniel).

A Symphony of Diverse Voices

Included in the Wisdom Commentary series are voices from scholars of many different religious traditions, of diverse ages, differing sexual identities, and varying cultural, racial, ethnic, and social contexts. Some have been pioneers in feminist biblical interpretation; others are newer contributors from a younger generation. A further distinctive feature of this series is that each volume incorporates voices other than that of the lead author(s). These voices appear alongside the commentary of the lead author(s), in the grayscale inserts. At times, a contributor may offer an alternative interpretation or a critique of the position taken by the lead author(s). At other times, they may offer a complementary interpretation from a different cultural context or subject position. Occasionally, portions of previously published material bring in other views. The diverse voices are not intended to be contestants in a debate or a cacophony of discordant notes. The multiple voices reflect that there is no single definitive feminist interpretation of a text. In addition, they show the importance of subject position in the process of interpretation. In this regard, the Wisdom Commentary series takes inspiration from the Talmud and from *The Torah: A Women's Commentary* (ed. Tamara Cohn Eskenazi and Andrea L. Weiss; New York: URJ Press and Women of Reform Judaism, The Federation of Temple Sisterhoods, 2008), in which many voices, even conflicting ones, are included and not harmonized.

Contributors include biblical scholars, theologians, and readers of Scripture from outside the scholarly and religious guilds. At times, their comments pertain to a particular text. In some instances they address a theme or topic that arises from the text.

Another feature that highlights the collaborative nature of feminist biblical interpretation is that a number of the volumes have two lead authors who have worked in tandem from the inception of the project and whose voices interweave throughout the commentary.

Woman Wisdom

The title, Wisdom Commentary, reflects both the importance to feminists of the figure of Woman Wisdom in the Scriptures and the distinct wisdom that feminist women and men bring to the interpretive process. In the Scriptures, Woman Wisdom appears as "a breath of the power of God, and a pure emanation of the glory of the Almighty" (Wis 7:25), who was present and active in fashioning all that exists (Prov 8:22-31; Wis 8:6). She is a spirit who pervades and penetrates all things (Wis 7:22-23), and she provides guidance and nourishment at her all-inclusive table (Prov 9:1-5). In both postexilic biblical and nonbiblical Jewish sources, Woman Wisdom is often equated with Torah, e.g., Sirach 24:23-34; Baruch 3:9–4:4; 38:2; 46:4-5; 2 Baruch 48:33, 36; 4 Ezra 5:9-10; 13:55; 14:40; 1 Enoch 42.

The New Testament frequently portrays Jesus as Wisdom incarnate. He invites his followers, "take my yoke upon you and learn from me" (Matt 11:29), just as Ben Sira advises, "put your neck under her [Wisdom's] yoke and let your souls receive instruction" (Sir 51:26). Just as Wisdom experiences rejection (Prov 1:23-25; Sir 15:7-8; Wis 10:3; Bar 3:12), so too does Jesus (Mark 8:31; John 1:10-11). Only some accept his invitation to his all-inclusive banquet (Matt 22:1-14; Luke 14:15-24; compare Prov 1:20-21; 9:3-5). Yet, "wisdom is vindicated by her deeds" (Matt 11:19, speaking of Jesus and John the Baptist; in the Lukan parallel at 7:35 they are called "wisdom's children"). There are numerous parallels between what is said of Wisdom and of the *Logos* in the Prologue of the Fourth Gospel (John 1:1-18). These are only a few of many examples. This female embodiment of divine presence and power is an apt image to guide the work of this series.

Feminism

There are many different understandings of the term "feminism." The various meanings, aims, and methods have developed exponentially in recent decades. Feminism is a perspective and a movement that springs from a recognition of inequities toward women, and it advocates for changes in whatever structures prevent full flourishing of human beings and all creation. Three waves of feminism in the United States are commonly recognized. The first, arising in the mid-nineteenth century and lasting into the early twentieth, was sparked by women's efforts to be involved in the public sphere and to win the right to vote. In the 1960s and 1970s, the second wave focused on civil rights and equality for women. With the third wave, from the 1980s forward, came global feminism and the emphasis on the contextual nature of interpretation. Now a fourth wave may be emerging, with a stronger emphasis on the intersectionality of women's concerns with those of other marginalized groups and the increased use of the internet as a platform for discussion and activism.[1] As feminism has matured, it has recognized that inequities based on gender are interwoven with power imbalances based on race, class, ethnicity, religion, sexual identity, physical ability, and a host of other social markers.

Feminist Women and Men

Men as well as nonbinary people who choose to identify with and partner with feminist women in the work of deconstructing systems of domination and building structures of equality are rightly regarded as feminists. Some men readily identify with experiences of women who are discriminated against on the basis of sex/gender, having themselves had comparable experiences; others who may not have faced direct discrimination or stereotyping recognize that inequity and problematic characterization still occur, and they seek correction. This series is pleased to include feminist men both as lead authors and as contributing voices.

Feminist Biblical Interpretation

Women interpreting the Bible from the lenses of their own experience is nothing new. Throughout the ages women have recounted the biblical stories, teaching them to their children and others, all the while interpreting them afresh for their time and circumstances.[2] Following is a very brief sketch of select foremothers who laid the groundwork for contemporary feminist biblical interpretation.

One of the earliest known Christian women who challenged patriarchal interpretations of Scripture was a consecrated virgin named Helie, who lived in the second century CE. When she refused to marry, her

1. See Martha Rampton, "Four Waves of Feminism" (October 25, 2015), at http://www.pacificu.edu/about-us/news-events/four-waves-feminism; and Ealasaid Munro, "Feminism: A Fourth Wave?," *Political Insight* (September 2013), https://journals.sagepub.com/doi/pdf/10.1111/2041-9066.12021.

2. For fuller treatments of this history see chap. 7, "One Thousand Years of Feminist Bible Criticism," in Gerda Lerner, *Creation of Feminist Consciousness: From the Middle Ages to Eighteen-Seventy* (New York: Oxford University Press, 1993), 138–66; Susanne Scholz, "From the 'Woman's Bible' to the 'Women's Bible,' The History of Feminist Approaches to the Hebrew Bible," in *Introducing the Women's Hebrew Bible*, IFT 13 (New York: T&T Clark, 2007), 12–32; Marion Ann Taylor and Agnes Choi, eds., *Handbook of Women Biblical Interpreters: A Historical and Biographical Guide* (Grand Rapids: Baker Academic, 2012).

parents brought her before a judge, who quoted to her Paul's admonition, "It is better to marry than to be aflame with passion" (1 Cor 7:9). In response, Helie first acknowledges that this is what Scripture says, but then she retorts, "but not for everyone, that is, not for holy virgins."[3] She is one of the first to question the notion that a text has one meaning that is applicable in all situations.

A Jewish woman who also lived in the second century CE, Beruriah, is said to have had "profound knowledge of biblical exegesis and outstanding intelligence."[4] One story preserved in the Talmud (b. Ber. 10a) tells of how she challenged her husband, Rabbi Meir, when he prayed for the destruction of a sinner. Proffering an alternate interpretation, she argued that Psalm 104:35 advocated praying for the destruction of sin, not the sinner.

In medieval times the first written commentaries on Scripture from a critical feminist point of view emerge. While others may have been produced and passed on orally, they are for the most part lost to us now. Among the earliest preserved feminist writings are those of Hildegard of Bingen (1098–1179), German writer, mystic, and abbess of a Benedictine monastery. She reinterpreted the Genesis narratives in a way that presented women and men as complementary and interdependent. She frequently wrote about the Divine as feminine.[5] Along with other women mystics of the time, such as Julian of Norwich (1342–ca. 1416), she spoke authoritatively from her personal experiences of God's revelation in prayer.

In this era, women were also among the scribes who copied biblical manuscripts. Notable among them is Paula Dei Mansi of Verona, from a distinguished family of Jewish scribes. In 1288, she translated from Hebrew into Italian a collection of Bible commentaries written by her father and added her own explanations.[6]

Another pioneer, Christine de Pizan (1365–ca. 1430), was a French court writer and prolific poet. She used allegory and common sense

---

3. Madrid, Escorial MS, a II 9, f. 90 v., as cited in Lerner, *Feminist Consciousness*, 140.

4. See Judith R. Baskin, "Women and Post-Biblical Commentary," in *The Torah: A Women's Commentary*, ed. Tamara Cohn Eskenazi and Andrea L. Weiss (New York: URJ Press and Women of Reform Judaism, The Federation of Temple Sisterhoods, 2008), xlix–lv, at lii.

5. Hildegard of Bingen, *De Operatione Dei*, 1.4.100; PL 197:885bc, as cited in Lerner, *Feminist Consciousness*, 142–43. See also Barbara Newman, *Sister of Wisdom: St. Hildegard's Theology of the Feminine* (Berkeley: University of California Press, 1987).

6. Emily Taitz, Sondra Henry, Cheryl Tallan, eds., *JPS Guide to Jewish Women 600 B.C.E.–1900 C.E.* (Philadelphia: JPS, 2003), 110–11.

to subvert misogynist readings of Scripture and celebrated the accomplishments of female biblical figures to argue for women's active roles in building society.[7]

By the seventeenth century, there were women who asserted that the biblical text needs to be understood and interpreted in its historical context. For example, Rachel Speght (1597–ca. 1630), a Calvinist English poet, elaborates on the historical situation in first-century Corinth that prompted Paul to say, "It is well for a man not to touch a woman" (1 Cor 7:1). Her aim was to show that the biblical texts should not be applied in a literal fashion to all times and circumstances. Similarly, Margaret Fell (1614–1702), one of the founders of the Religious Society of Friends (Quakers) in Britain, addressed the Pauline prohibitions against women speaking in church by insisting that they do not have universal validity. Rather, they need to be understood in their historical context, as addressed to a local church in particular time-bound circumstances.[8]

Along with analyzing the historical context of the biblical writings, women in the eighteenth and nineteenth centuries began to attend to misogynistic interpretations based on faulty translations. One of the first to do so was British feminist Mary Astell (1666–1731).[9] In the United States, the Grimké sisters, Sarah (1792–1873) and Angelina (1805–1879), Quaker women from a slaveholding family in South Carolina, learned biblical Greek and Hebrew so that they could interpret the Bible for themselves. They were prompted to do so after men sought to silence them from speaking out against slavery and for women's rights by claiming that the Bible (e.g., 1 Cor 14:34) prevented women from speaking in public.[10] Another prominent abolitionist, Isabella Baumfree, was a former slave who adopted the name Sojourner Truth (ca. 1797–1883) and quoted the Bible liberally in her speeches[11] and in so doing challenged cultural assumptions and biblical interpretations that undergird gender inequities.

---

7. See further Taylor and Choi, *Handbook of Women Biblical Interpreters*, 127–32.

8. Her major work, *Women's Speaking Justified, Proved and Allowed by the Scriptures*, published in London in 1667, gave a systematic feminist reading of all biblical texts pertaining to women.

9. Mary Astell, *Some Reflections upon Marriage* (New York: Source Book Press, 1970, reprint of the 1730 edition; earliest edition of this work is 1700), 103–4.

10. See further Sarah Grimké, *Letters on the Equality of the Sexes and the Condition of Woman* (Boston: Isaac Knapp, 1838).

11. See, for example, her most famous speech, "Ain't I a Woman?," delivered in 1851 at the Ohio Women's Rights Convention in Akron, OH; Modern History Sourcebook, https://sourcebooks.fordham.edu/mod/sojtruth-woman.asp.

Another monumental work that emerged in nineteenth-century England was that of Jewish theologian Grace Aguilar (1816–1847), *The Women of Israel*,[12] published in 1845. Aguilar's approach was to make connections between the biblical women and contemporary Jewish women's concerns. She aimed to counter the widespread notion that women were degraded in Jewish law and that only in Christianity were women's dignity and value upheld. Her intent was to help Jewish women find strength and encouragement by seeing the evidence of God's compassionate love in the history of every woman in the Bible. While not a full commentary on the Bible, Aguilar's work stands out for its comprehensive treatment of every female biblical character, including even the most obscure references.[13]

 The first person to produce a full-blown feminist commentary on the Bible was Elizabeth Cady Stanton (1815–1902). A leading proponent in the United States for women's right to vote, she found that whenever women tried to make inroads into politics, education, or the work world, the Bible was quoted against them. Along with a team of like-minded women, she produced her own commentary on every text of the Bible that concerned women. Her pioneering two-volume project, *The Woman's Bible*, published in 1895 and 1898, urges women to recognize that texts that degrade women come from the men who wrote the texts, not from God, and to use their common sense to rethink what has been presented to them as sacred.

Nearly a century later, *The Women's Bible Commentary*, edited by Carol A. Newsom and Sharon H. Ringe (Louisville: Westminster John Knox, 1992), appeared. This one-volume commentary features North American feminist scholarship on each book of the Protestant canon. Like Cady Stanton's commentary, it does not contain comments on every section of the biblical text but only on those passages deemed relevant to women. It was revised and expanded in 1998 to include the Apocrypha/Deuterocanonical books, and the contributors to this new volume reflect the global face of contemporary feminist scholarship. The revisions made in the third edition, which appeared in 2012, represent the profound advances in feminist biblical scholarship and include newer voices (with Jacqueline E. Lapsley as an additional editor). In both the second and third editions, *The* has been dropped from the title.

---

12. The full title is *The Women of Israel or Characters and Sketches from the Holy Scriptures and Jewish History Illustrative of the Past History, Present Duty, and Future Destiny of the Hebrew Females, as Based on the Word of God.*

13. See further Eskenazi and Weiss, *The Torah: A Women's Commentary*, xxxviii; Taylor and Choi, *Handbook of Women Biblical Interpreters*, 31–37.

Also appearing at the centennial of Cady Stanton's *The Woman's Bible* were two volumes edited by Elisabeth Schüssler Fiorenza with the assistance of Shelly Matthews. The first, *Searching the Scriptures: A Feminist Introduction* (New York: Crossroad, 1993), charts a comprehensive approach to feminist interpretation from ecumenical, interreligious, and multicultural perspectives. The second volume, published in 1994, provides critical feminist commentary on each book of the New Testament as well as on three books of Jewish Pseudepigrapha and eleven other early Christian writings.

In Europe, similar endeavors have been undertaken, such as the one-volume *Kompendium Feministische Bibelauslegung*, edited by Luise Schottroff and Marie-Theres Wacker (Gütersloh: Gütersloher Verlagshaus, 2007), featuring German feminist biblical interpretation of each book of the Bible, along with apocryphal books, and several extrabiblical writings. This work, now in its third edition, was translated into English.[14] A multivolume project, *The Bible and Women: An Encyclopaedia of Exegesis and Cultural History*, edited by Mary Ann Beavis, Irmtraud Fischer, Mercedes Navarro Puerto, and Adriana Valerio, is currently in production. This project presents a history of the reception of the Bible as embedded in Western cultural history and focuses particularly on gender-relevant biblical themes, biblical female characters, and women recipients of the Bible. The volumes are published in English, Spanish, Italian, and German.[15]

Another groundbreaking work is the collection The Feminist Companion to the Bible Series, edited by Athalya Brenner (Sheffield: Sheffield Academic, 1993–2015), which comprises twenty volumes of commen-

14. *Feminist Biblical Interpretation: A Compendium of Critical Commentary on the Books of the Bible and Related Literature*, trans. Lisa E. Dahill, Everett R. Kalin, Nancy Lukens, Linda M. Maloney, Barbara Rumscheidt, Martin Rumscheidt, and Tina Steiner (Grand Rapids: Eerdmans, 2012). Another notable collection is the three volumes edited by Susanne Scholz, *Feminist Interpretation of the Hebrew Bible in Retrospect*, Recent Research in Biblical Studies 7, 8, 9 (Sheffield: Sheffield Phoenix, 2013, 2014, 2016).

15. The first volume, on the Torah, appeared in Spanish in 2009, in German and Italian in 2010, and in English in 2011 (Atlanta: SBL). The other available volumes are as follows: *Feminist Biblical Studies in the Twentieth Century*, ed. Elisabeth Schüssler Fiorenza (2014); *The Writings and Later Wisdom Books*, ed. Christl M. Maier and Nuria Calduch-Benages (2014); *Gospels: Narrative and History*, ed. Mercedes Navarro Puerto and Marinella Perroni; Amy-Jill Levine, English ed. (2015); *The High Middle Ages*, ed. Kari Elisabeth Børresen and Adriana Valerio (2015); *Early Jewish Writings*, ed. Eileen Schuller and Marie-Theres Wacker (2017); *Faith and Feminism in Nineteenth-Century Religious Communities*, ed. Michaela Sohn-Kronthaler and Ruth Albrecht (2019); *The Early Middle Ages*, ed. Franca Ela Consolino and Judith Herrin (2020); *Prophecy and Gender in the Hebrew Bible*, ed. L. Juliana Claasens and Irmtraud Fischer (2021); and *Rabbinic Literature*, ed. Tal Ilan, Lorena Miralles-Maciá, and Ronit Nikolsky (2022). For further information see https://www.bibleandwomen.org.

taries on the Old Testament. The parallel series, Feminist Companion to the New Testament and Early Christian Writings, edited by Amy-Jill Levine with Marianne Blickenstaff and Maria Mayo Robbins (Sheffield: Sheffield Academic, 2001–2010), contains thirteen volumes. These two series are not full commentaries on the biblical books but comprise collected essays on discrete biblical texts.

Works by individual feminist biblical scholars in all parts of the world abound, and they are now too numerous to list in this introduction. Feminist biblical interpretation has reached a level of maturity that now makes possible a commentary series on every book of the Bible. In recent decades, women have had greater access to formal theological education, have been able to learn critical analytical tools, have put their own interpretations into writing, and have developed new methods of biblical interpretation. Until recent decades the work of feminist biblical interpreters was largely unknown, both to other women and to their brothers in the synagogue, church, and academy. Feminists now have taken their place in the professional world of biblical scholars, where they build on the work of their foremothers and connect with one another across the globe in ways not previously possible. In a few short decades, feminist biblical criticism has become an integral part of the academy.

Methodologies

Feminist biblical scholars use a variety of methods and often employ a number of them together.[16] In the Wisdom Commentary series, the authors will explain their understanding of feminism and the feminist reading strategies used in their commentary. Each volume treats the biblical text in blocks of material, not an analysis verse by verse. The entire text is considered, not only those passages that feature female characters or that speak specifically about women. When women are not apparent in the narrative, feminist lenses are used to analyze the dynamics in the text between male characters, the models of power, binary ways of thinking, and the dynamics of imperialism. Attention is given to how the whole text functions and how it was and is heard, both in its original context and today. Issues of particular concern to women—e.g., poverty, food, health, the environment, water—come to the fore.

---

16. See the seventeen essays in Caroline Vander Stichele and Todd Penner, eds., *Her Master's Tools? Feminist and Postcolonial Engagements of Historical-Critical Discourse* (Atlanta: SBL, 2005), which show the complementarity of various approaches.

One of the approaches used by early feminists and still popular today is to lift up the overlooked and forgotten stories of women in the Bible. Studies of women in each of the Testaments have been done, and there are also studies on women in particular biblical books.[17] Feminists recognize that the examples of biblical characters can be both empowering and problematic. The point of the feminist enterprise is not to serve as an apologetic for women; it is rather, in part, to recover women's history and literary roles in all their complexity and to learn from that recovery.

Retrieving the submerged history of biblical women is a crucial step for constructing the story of the past so as to lead to liberative possibilities for the present and future. There are, however, some pitfalls to this approach. Sometimes depictions of biblical women have been naïve and romantic. Some commentators exalt the virtues of both biblical and contemporary women and paint women as superior to men. Such reverse discrimination inhibits movement toward equality for all. In addition, some feminists challenge the idea that one can "pluck positive images out of an admittedly androcentric text, separating literary characterizations from the androcentric interests they were created to serve."[18] Still other feminists find these images to have enormous value.

One other danger with seeking the submerged history of women is the tendency for Christian feminists to paint Jesus and even Paul as liberators of women in a way that demonizes Judaism.[19] Wisdom Commentary aims

---

17. See, e.g., Alice Bach, ed., *Women in the Hebrew Bible: A Reader* (New York: Routledge, 1999); Tikva Frymer-Kensky, *Reading the Women of the Bible* (New York: Schocken Books, 2002); Carol Meyers, Toni Craven, and Ross S. Kraemer, eds., *Women in Scripture* (Grand Rapids: Eerdmans, 2001); Irene Nowell, *Women in the Old Testament* (Collegeville, MN: Liturgical Press, 1997); Katharine Doob Sakenfeld, *Just Wives? Stories of Power and Survival in the Old Testament and Today* (Louisville: Westminster John Knox, 2003); Mary Ann Getty-Sullivan, *Women in the New Testament* (Collegeville, MN: Liturgical Press, 2001); Bonnie Thurston, *Women in the New Testament: Questions and Commentary*, Companions to the New Testament (New York: Crossroad, 1998).

18. J. Cheryl Exum, "Second Thoughts about Secondary Characters: Women in Exodus 1.8–2.10," in *A Feminist Companion to Exodus to Deuteronomy*, FCB 6, ed. Athalya Brenner (Sheffield: Sheffield Academic, 1994), 75–97, at 76.

19. See Judith Plaskow, "Anti-Judaism in Feminist Christian Interpretation," in *Searching the Scriptures: A Feminist Introduction*, vol. 1, ed. Elisabeth Schüssler Fiorenza with Shelly Matthews (New York: Crossroad, 1993), 117–29; Amy-Jill Levine, "The New Testament and Anti-Judaism," in *The Misunderstood Jew: The Church and the Scandal of the Jewish Jesus* (San Francisco: HarperSanFrancisco, 2006), 87–117.

to enhance understanding of Jesus as well as Paul as Jews of their day and to forge solidarity among Jewish and Christian feminists.

Feminist scholars who use historical-critical methods analyze the world behind the text; they seek to understand the historical context from which the text emerged and the circumstances of the communities to whom it was addressed. In bringing feminist lenses to this approach, the aim is not to impose modern expectations on ancient cultures but to unmask the ways that ideologically problematic mind-sets that produced the ancient texts are still promulgated through the text. Feminist biblical scholars aim not only to deconstruct but also to reclaim and reconstruct biblical history as women's history, in which women were central and active agents in creating religious heritage.[20] A further step is to construct meaning for contemporary women and men in a liberative movement toward transformation of social, political, economic, and religious structures.[21] In recent years, some feminists have embraced new historicism, which accents the creative role of the interpreter in any construction of history and exposes the power struggles to which the text witnesses.[22]

Literary critics analyze the world of the text: its form, language patterns, and rhetorical function.[23] They do not attempt to separate layers

20. See, for example, Phyllis A. Bird, *Missing Persons and Mistaken Identities: Women and Gender in Ancient Israel* (Minneapolis: Fortress, 1997); Elisabeth Schüssler Fiorenza, *In Memory of Her: A Feminist Theological Reconstruction of Christian Origins* (New York: Crossroad, 1994); Ross Shepard Kraemer and Mary Rose D'Angelo, eds., *Women and Christian Origins* (New York: Oxford University Press, 1999).

21. See, e.g., Sandra M. Schneiders, *The Revelatory Text: Interpreting the New Testament as Sacred Scripture*, rev. ed. (Collegeville, MN: Liturgical Press, 1999), whose aim is to engage in biblical interpretation not only for intellectual enlightenment but, even more important, for personal and communal transformation. Elisabeth Schüssler Fiorenza (*Wisdom Ways: Introducing Feminist Biblical Interpretation* [Maryknoll, NY: Orbis Books, 2001]) envisions the work of feminist biblical interpretation as a dance of Wisdom that consists of seven steps that interweave in spiral movements toward liberation, the final one being transformative action for change.

22. See Gina Hens-Piazza, *The New Historicism*, GBS, Old Testament Series (Minneapolis: Fortress, 2002).

23. Phyllis Trible was among the first to employ this method with texts from Genesis and Ruth in her groundbreaking book *God and the Rhetoric of Sexuality*, OBT (Philadelphia: Fortress, 1978). Another pioneer in feminist literary criticism is Mieke Bal (*Lethal Love: Feminist Literary Readings of Biblical Love Stories* [Bloomington: Indiana University Press, 1987]). For surveys of recent developments in literary methods see Terry Eagleton, *Literary Theory: An Introduction*, 3rd ed. (Minneapolis: University of

of tradition and redaction but focus on the text holistically, as it is in its present form. They examine how meaning is created in the interaction between the text and its reader in multiple contexts. Within the arena of literary approaches are reader-oriented approaches, narrative, rhetorical, structuralist, post-structuralist, deconstructive, ideological, autobiographical, and performance criticism.[24] Narrative critics study the interrelation among author, text, and audience through investigation of settings, both spatial and temporal; characters; plot; and narrative techniques (e.g., irony, parody, intertextual allusions). Reader-response critics attend to the impact that the text has on the reader or hearer. They recognize that when a text is detrimental toward women there is the choice either to affirm the text or to read against the grain toward a liberative end. Rhetorical criticism analyzes the style of argumentation and attends to how the author is attempting to shape the thinking or actions of the hearer. Structuralist critics analyze the complex patterns of binary oppositions in the text to derive its meaning.[25] Post-structuralist approaches challenge the notion that there are fixed meanings to any biblical text or that there is one universal truth. They engage in close readings of the text and often engage in intertextual analysis.[26] Within this approach is deconstructionist criticism, which views the text as a site of conflict, with competing narratives. The interpreter aims to expose the fault lines and overturn and reconfigure binaries by elevating the underling of a pair and foregrounding it.[27] Feminists also use other post-

Minnesota Press, 2008); Janice Capel Anderson and Stephen D. Moore, eds., *Mark and Method: New Approaches in Biblical Studies*, 2nd ed. (Minneapolis: Fortress, 2008); Michal Beth Dinkler, *Literary Theory and the New Testament*, AYBRL (New Haven: Yale University Press, 2019).

24. See, e.g., J. Cheryl Exum and David J. A. Clines, eds., *The New Literary Criticism and the Hebrew Bible* (Valley Forge, PA: Trinity Press International, 1993); Edgar V. McKnight and Elizabeth Struthers Malbon, eds., *The New Literary Criticism and the New Testament* (Valley Forge, PA: Trinity Press International, 1994).

25. See, e.g., David Jobling, *The Sense of Biblical Narrative: Three Structural Analyses in the Old Testament*, JSOTSup 7 (Sheffield: University of Sheffield Press, 1978).

26. See, e.g., Stephen D. Moore, *Poststructuralism and the New Testament: Derrida and Foucault at the Foot of the Cross* (Minneapolis: Fortress, 1994); *The Bible in Theory: Critical and Postcritical Essays* (Atlanta: SBL, 2010); Yvonne Sherwood, *A Biblical Text and Its Afterlives: The Survival of Jonah in Western Culture* (Cambridge: Cambridge University Press, 2000).

27. David Penchansky, "Deconstruction," in *The Oxford Encyclopedia of Biblical Interpretation*, ed. Steven McKenzie (New York: Oxford University Press, 2013), 196–205. See, for example, Danna Nolan Fewell and David M. Gunn, *Gender, Power, and Promise:*

modern approaches, such as ideological and autobiographical criticism. The former analyzes the system of ideas that underlies the power and values concealed in the text as well as that of the interpreter.[28] The latter involves deliberate self-disclosure while reading the text as a critical exegete.[29] Performance criticism attends to how the text was passed on orally, usually in communal settings, and to the verbal and nonverbal interactions between the performer and the audience.[30]

From the beginning, feminists have understood that interpreting the Bible is an act of power. In recent decades, feminist biblical scholars have developed hermeneutical theories of the ethics and politics of biblical interpretation to challenge the claims to value neutrality of most academic biblical scholarship. Feminist biblical scholars have also turned their attention to how some biblical writings were shaped by the power of empire and how this still shapes readers' self-understandings today. They have developed hermeneutical approaches that reveal, critique, and evaluate the interactions depicted in the text against the context of empire, and they consider implications for contemporary contexts.[31] Feminists also analyze the dynamics of colonization and the mentalities of colonized peoples in the exercise of biblical interpretation. As Kwok Pui-lan explains, "A postcolonial feminist interpretation of the Bible needs to investigate the deployment of gender in the narration of identity, the negotiation of power differentials between the colonizers and the colonized, and the reinforcement of patriarchal control over spheres

---

The Subject of the Bible's First Story (Nashville: Abingdon, 1993); David Rutledge, *Reading Marginally: Feminism, Deconstruction and the Bible,* BibInt 21 (Leiden: Brill, 1996).

28. See David Jobling and Tina Pippin, eds., *Semeia 59: Ideological Criticism of Biblical Texts* (Atlanta: Scholars Press, 1992); Terry Eagleton, *Ideology: An Introduction* (London: Verso, 2007).

29. See, e.g., Ingrid Rosa Kitzberger, ed., *Autobiographical Biblical Interpretation: Between Text and Self* (Leiden: Deo, 2002); P. J. W. Schutte, "When *They, We,* and the Passive Become *I*—Introducing Autobiographical Biblical Criticism," *HTS Teologiese Studies / Theological Studies* 61 (2005): 401–16.

30. See, e.g., Holly E. Hearon and Philip Ruge-Jones, eds., *The Bible in Ancient and Modern Media: Story and Performance* (Eugene, OR: Cascade Books, 2009).

31. E.g., Gale Yee, ed., *Judges and Method: New Approaches in Biblical Studies* (Minneapolis: Fortress, 1995); Warren Carter, *The Gospel of Matthew in Its Roman Imperial Context* (London: T&T Clark, 2005); *The Roman Empire and the New Testament: An Essential Guide* (Nashville: Abingdon, 2006); Elisabeth Schüssler Fiorenza, *The Power of the Word: Scripture and the Rhetoric of Empire* (Minneapolis: Fortress, 2007); Judith E. McKinlay, *Reframing Her: Biblical Women in Postcolonial Focus* (Sheffield: Sheffield Phoenix, 2004).

where these elites could exercise control."[32] Methods and models from sociology and cultural anthropology are used by feminists to investigate women's everyday lives, their experiences of marriage, childrearing, labor, money, illness, etc.[33]

As feminists have examined the construction of gender from varying cultural perspectives, they have become ever more cognizant that the way gender roles are defined within differing cultures varies radically. As Mary Ann Tolbert observes, "Attempts to isolate some universal role that cross-culturally defines 'woman' have run into contradictory evidence at every turn."[34] Some women have coined new terms to highlight the particularities of their socio-cultural context. Many African American feminists, for example, call themselves *womanists* to draw attention to the double oppression of racism and sexism they experience.[35] Similarly, many US Hispanic feminists speak of themselves as *mujeristas* (*mujer* is Spanish for "woman").[36] Others prefer to be called "Latina feminists."[37] As a gender-neutral or nonbinary alternative, many today use Latinx or Latine. *Mujeristas*, Latina and Latine feminists emphasize that the context for their

32. Kwok Pui-lan, *Postcolonial Imagination and Feminist Theology* (Louisville: Westminster John Knox, 2005), 9. See also Musa W. Dube, ed., *Postcolonial Feminist Interpretation of the Bible* (St. Louis: Chalice, 2000); Cristl M. Maier and Carolyn J. Sharp, *Prophecy and Power: Jeremiah in Feminist and Postcolonial Perspective* (London: Bloomsbury, 2013); L. Juliana Claassens and Carolyn J. Sharp, eds., *Feminist Frameworks and the Bible: Power, Ambiguity, and Intersectionality*, LHBOTS 630 (London: Bloomsbury T&T Clark, 2017).

33. See, for example, Carol Meyers, *Discovering Eve: Ancient Israelite Women in Context* (New York: Oxford University Press, 1991); Luise Schottroff, *Lydia's Impatient Sisters: A Feminist Social History of Early Christianity*, trans. Barbara and Martin Rumscheidt (Louisville: Westminster John Knox, 1995); Susan Niditch, *"My Brother Esau Is a Hairy Man": Hair and Identity in Ancient Israel* (Oxford: Oxford University Press, 2008).

34. Mary Ann Tolbert, "Social, Sociological, and Anthropological Methods," in *Searching the Scriptures*, 1:255–71, at 265.

35. Alice Walker coined the term (*In Search of Our Mothers' Gardens: Womanist Prose* [New York: Harcourt Brace Jovanovich, 1967, 1983]). See also Katie G. Cannon, "The Emergence of Black Feminist Consciousness," in *Feminist Interpretation of the Bible*, ed. Letty M. Russell (Philadelphia: Westminster, 1985), 30–40; Renita J. Weems, *Just a Sister Away: A Womanist Vision of Women's Relationships in the Bible* (San Diego: Lura Media, 1988); Nyasha Junior, *An Introduction to Womanist Biblical Interpretation* (Louisville: Westminster John Knox, 2015).

36. Ada María Isasi-Díaz (*Mujerista Theology: A Theology for the Twenty-First Century* [Maryknoll, NY: Orbis Books, 1996]) is credited with coining the term.

37. E.g., María Pilar Aquino, Daisy L. Machado, and Jeanette Rodríguez, eds., *A Reader in Latina Feminist Theology* (Austin: University of Texas Press, 2002).

theologizing is *mestizaje* and *mulatez* (racial and cultural mixture), done *en conjunto* (in community), with *lo cotidiano* (everyday lived experience) of Latina women as starting points for theological reflection and the encounter with the divine. Intercultural analysis has become an indispensable tool for working toward justice for women at the global level.[38]

Some feminists are among those who have developed lesbian, gay, bisexual, and transgender (LGBT) interpretation. This approach focuses on issues of sexual identity and uses various reading strategies. Some point out the ways in which categories that emerged in recent centuries are applied anachronistically to biblical texts to make modern-day judgments. Others show how the Bible is silent on contemporary issues about sexual identity. Still others examine same-sex relationships in the Bible by figures such as Ruth and Naomi or David and Jonathan. In recent years, queer theory has emerged; it emphasizes the blurriness of boundaries not just of sexual identity but also of gender roles. Queer critics often focus on texts in which figures transgress what is traditionally considered proper gender behavior.[39]

Feminists have also been engaged in studying the reception history of the text[40] and have engaged in studies in the emerging fields of disability theory and of children in the Bible.

---

38. See, e.g., María Pilar Aquino and María José Rosado-Nunes, eds., *Feminist Intercultural Theology: Latina Explorations for a Just World*, Studies in Latino/a Catholicism (Maryknoll, NY: Orbis Books, 2007). See also Michelle A. Gonzalez, "Latina Feminist Theology: Past, Present, and Future," *JFSR* 25 (2009): 150–55. See also Elisabeth Schüssler Fiorenza, ed., *Feminist Biblical Studies in the Twentieth Century: Scholarship and Movement*, The Bible and Women 9.1 (Atlanta: SBL Press, 2014), who charts feminist studies around the globe as well as emerging feminist methodologies.

39. See, e.g., Bernadette J. Brooten, *Love Between Women: Early Christian Responses to Female Homoeroticism* (Chicago: University of Chicago Press, 1996); Mary Rose D'Angelo, "Women Partners in the New Testament," *JFSR* 6 (1990): 65–86; Deirdre J. Good, "Reading Strategies for Biblical Passages on Same-Sex Relations," *Theology and Sexuality* 7 (1997): 70–82; Deryn Guest, *When Deborah Met Jael: Lesbian Feminist Hermeneutics* (London: SCM, 2011); Teresa Hornsby and Ken Stone, eds., *Bible Trouble: Queer Readings at the Boundaries of Biblical Scholarship* (Atlanta: SBL, 2011); Joseph A. Marchal, "Queer Studies and Critical Masculinity Studies in Feminist Biblical Studies," in *Feminist Biblical Studies in the Twentieth Century*, ed. Schüssler Fiorenza, 261–80.

40. See Sharon H. Ringe, "When Women Interpret the Bible," in *Women's Bible Commentary*, ed. Carol A. Newsom, Sharon H. Ringe, and Jacqueline E. Lapsley, 3rd ed. (Louisville: Westminster John Knox, 2012), 5; Marion Ann Taylor and Agnes Choi, eds., *Handbook of Women Biblical Interpreters: A Historical and Biographical Guide* (Grand Rapids: Baker Academic, 2012); Yvonne Sherwood, "Introduction," in *The Bible and Feminism: Remapping the Field* (New York: Oxford University Press, 2017).

Feminists also recognize that the struggle for women's equality and dignity is intimately connected with the struggle for respect for Earth and for the whole of the cosmos. Ecofeminists interpret Scripture in ways that highlight the link between human domination of nature and male subjugation of women. They show how anthropocentric ways of interpreting the Bible have overlooked or dismissed Earth and Earth community. They invite readers to identify not only with human characters in the biblical narrative but also with other Earth creatures and domains of nature, especially those that are the object of injustice. Some use creative imagination to retrieve the interests of Earth implicit in the narrative and enable Earth to speak.[41]

Biblical Authority

By the late nineteenth century, some feminists, such as Elizabeth Cady Stanton, began to question openly whether the Bible could continue to be regarded as authoritative for women. They viewed the Bible itself as the source of women's oppression, and some rejected its sacred origin and saving claims. Some decided that the Bible and the religious traditions that enshrine it are too thoroughly saturated with androcentrism and patriarchy to be redeemable.[42]

In the Wisdom Commentary series, questions such as these may be raised, but the aim of this series is not to lead readers to reject the authority of the biblical text. Rather, the aim is to promote better understanding of the contexts from which the text arose and of the rhetorical effects it has on people in contemporary contexts. Such understanding can lead to a deepening of faith, with the Bible serving as an aid to bring flourishing of life.

Language for God

Because of the ways in which the term "God" has been used to symbolize the divine in predominantly male, patriarchal, and monarchical modes, feminists have designed new ways of speaking of the divine. Some have called attention to the inadequacy of the term *God* by trying

41. E.g., Norman C. Habel and Peter Trudinger, *Exploring Ecological Hermeneutics*, SymS 46 (Atlanta: SBL, 2008); Mary Judith Ress, *Ecofeminism in Latin America*, Women from the Margins (Maryknoll, NY: Orbis Books, 2006).
42. E.g., Mary Daly, *Beyond God the Father: A Philosophy of Women's Liberation* (Boston: Beacon, 1973).

to visually destabilize our ways of thinking and speaking of the divine. Rosemary Radford Ruether proposed *God/ess*, as an unpronounceable term pointing to the unnameable understanding of the divine that transcends patriarchal limitations.[43] Some have followed traditional Jewish practice, writing *G-d*. Elisabeth Schüssler Fiorenza has adopted *G*d*.[44] Others draw on the biblical tradition to mine female and non-gender-specific metaphors and symbols.[45] In Wisdom Commentary, there is not one standard way of expressing the divine; each author will use her or his preferred ways. The one exception is that when the tetragrammaton, Yhwh, the name revealed to Moses in Exodus 3:14, is used, it will be without vowels, respecting the Jewish custom of avoiding pronouncing the divine name out of reverence.

Nomenclature for the Two Testaments

In recent decades, some biblical scholars have begun to call the two Testaments of the Bible by names other than the traditional nomenclature: Old and New Testament. Some regard "Old" as derogatory, implying that it is no longer relevant or that it has been superseded. Consequently, terms like Hebrew Bible, First Testament, and Jewish Scriptures and, correspondingly, Christian Scriptures or Second Testament have come into use. There are a number of difficulties with these designations. The term "Hebrew Bible" does not take into account that parts of the Old Testament are written not in Hebrew but in Aramaic.[46] Moreover, for Roman Catholics and Eastern Orthodox believers, the Old Testament includes books written in Greek—the Deuterocanonical books, considered Apocrypha by Protestants.[47] The term "Jewish Scriptures" is inadequate because these

---

43. Rosemary Radford Ruether, *Sexism and God-Talk: Toward a Feminist Theology* (Boston: Beacon, 1993).

44. Elisabeth Schüssler Fiorenza, *Jesus: Miriam's Child, Sophia's Prophet; Critical Issues in Feminist Christology* (New York: Continuum, 1994), 191n3.

45. E.g., Sallie McFague, *Models of God: Theology for an Ecological, Nuclear Age* (Philadelphia: Fortress, 1987); Catherine Mowry LaCugna, *God for Us: The Trinity and Christian Life* (San Francisco: HarperCollins, 1991); Elizabeth A. Johnson, *She Who Is: The Mystery of God in Feminist Theological Discourse* (New York: Crossroad, 1992). See further Elizabeth A. Johnson, "God," in *Dictionary of Feminist Theologies*, ed. Letty M. Russell and J. Shannon Clarkson (Louisville: Westminster John Knox, 1996), 128–30.

46. Gen 31:47; Jer 10:11; Ezra 4:7–6:18; 7:12-26; Dan 2:4–7:28.

47. Representing the *via media* between Catholic and reformed, Anglicans generally consider the Apocrypha to be profitable, if not canonical, and utilize select Wisdom texts liturgically.

books are also sacred to Christians. Conversely, "Christian Scriptures" is not an accurate designation for the New Testament, since the Old Testament is also part of the Christian Scriptures. Using "First and Second Testament" also has difficulties, in that it can imply a hierarchy and a value judgment.[48] Jews generally use the term Tanakh, an acronym for Torah (Pentateuch), Nevi'im (Prophets), and Ketuvim (Writings).

In Wisdom Commentary, if authors choose to use a designation other than Tanakh, Old Testament, and New Testament, they will explain how they mean the term.

Translation

Modern feminist scholars recognize the complexities connected with biblical translation, as they have delved into questions about philosophy of language, how meanings are produced, and how they are culturally situated. Today it is evident that simply translating into gender-neutral formulations cannot address all the challenges presented by androcentric texts. Efforts at feminist translation must also deal with issues around authority and canonicity.[49]

Because of these complexities, the editors of the Wisdom Commentary series have chosen to use an existing translation, the New Revised Standard Version (NRSV), which is provided for easy reference at the top of each page of commentary. The NRSV was produced by a team of ecumenical and interreligious scholars, is a fairly literal translation, and uses inclusive language for human beings. Brief discussions about problematic translations appear in the inserts labeled "Translation Matters." When more detailed discussions are available, these will be indicated in footnotes. In the commentary, wherever Hebrew or Greek words are used, English translation is provided. In cases where a wordplay is involved, transliteration is provided to enable understanding.

Art and Poetry

Artistic expression in poetry, music, sculpture, painting, and various other modes is very important to feminist interpretation. Where possible, art and poetry are included in the print volumes of the series. In

---

48. See Levine, *The Misunderstood Jew*, 193–99.

49. Elizabeth Castelli, "*Les Belles Infidèles*/Fidelity or Feminism? The Meanings of Feminist Biblical Translation," in *Searching the Scriptures*, 1:189–204, here 190.

a number of instances, these are original works created for this project. Regrettably, copyright and production costs prohibit the inclusion of color photographs and other artistic work.

Glossary

Because there are a number of excellent readily available resources that provide definitions and concise explanations of terms used in feminist theological and biblical studies, this series will not include a glossary. We refer you to works such as *Dictionary of Feminist Theologies*, edited by Letty M. Russell and J. Shannon Clarkson (Louisville: Westminster John Knox, 1996), and volume 1 of *Searching the Scriptures*, edited by Elisabeth Schüssler Fiorenza with the assistance of Shelly Matthews (New York: Crossroad, 1993). Individual authors in the Wisdom Commentary series will define the way they are using terms that may be unfamiliar.

A Concluding Word

In just a few short decades, feminist biblical studies has grown exponentially, both in the methods that have been developed and in the number of scholars who have embraced it. We realize that this series is limited and will soon need to be revised and updated. It is our hope that Wisdom Commentary, by making the best of current feminist biblical scholarship available in an accessible format to ministers, preachers, teachers, scholars, and students, will aid all readers in their advancement toward God's vision of dignity, equality, and justice for all.

Acknowledgments

There are a great many people who have made this series possible: first, Peter Dwyer, retired director of Liturgical Press, and Hans Christoffersen, editorial director of Liturgical Press, who have believed in this project and have shepherded it since it was conceived in 2008. Editorial consultants Athalya Brenner-Idan and Elisabeth Schüssler Fiorenza have not only been an inspiration with their pioneering work but have encouraged us all along the way with their personal involvement. Volume editors Mary Ann Beavis, Carol J. Dempsey, Gina Hens-Piazza, Amy-Jill Levine, Linda M. Maloney, Song-Mi Suzie Park, Ahida Pilarski, Sarah Tanzer, and Lauress Wilkins Lawrence have lent their extraordinary wisdom to the shaping of the series, have used their extensive networks of relationships to secure authors and contributors, and have worked tirelessly to guide their work to completion. Four others who have contributed greatly to the shaping of the project are Linda M. Day, Mignon Jacobs, Seung Ai Yang, and Barbara E. Bowe of blessed memory (d. 2010). Editorial and research assistant Susan M. Hickman provided invaluable support with administrative details and arrangements at the outset of the project. I am grateful to Brian Eisenschenk and Christine Henderson who assisted Susan Hickman with the Wiki. I am especially thankful to Lauren L. Murphy and Justin Howell for their work in copyediting; and to the staff at Liturgical Press, especially Colleen Stiller, production manager; Stephanie Lancour, production editor; Julie Surma, desktop publisher; Angie Steffens, production coordinator; and Tara Durheim, marketing director.

Authors' Acknowledgments

As I thought about what to write here, I went back to my Tübingen dissertation (published 1990) and discovered that nearly everyone I honored then is still at the top of my list! So to all my friends and companions in joy and sorrow from Tübingen until now, my unending gratitude. Special mention goes to those who have sheltered and sustained me along the way: Maria and Jochen, Lotte and Marius, Martha and Wolfgang, Hedi and Klaus, Rosemary and Mary, Judy and Mark, our friends at the Professor-Rebel-Haus in Tübingen, the people of Good Shepherd, Berkeley, my parishioners at St. Matthew's and Calvary, and, by no means least, my children—Vincent, who kept me company at home and abroad, David, my best cheerleader, and Sharon, daughter *nonpareil* in so many, many ways. Warm appreciation also to their spouses, Catherine, Jennifer, and Heidi, and to my amazing grandchildren, Andrew and Rachel. (Look for their names in lights!) A part of my heart remains always in Wavreumont in Belgium, where the monks of St. Remacle sheltered and uplifted me.

Special thanks to my colleagues, past and present, at Liturgical Press, with highest honor to Peter Dwyer as he retires, to Mark Twomey, and to Hans Christoffersen, who has made *my* retirement a busy time! Also to the untiring editorial and production staff, especially Lauren Murphy, Stephanie Lancour, Angela Steffens, and Colleen Stiller. I am especially grateful to Barbara Reid, who invited me to join the editorial board of Wisdom Commentary Series and to be lead author of this volume. And what can I say of the great company of scholars in the US, Canada, Germany, and Australia who have shown such leadership and dedication to the cause of feminist exegesis: Elisabeth Schüssler Fiorenza the first of so many—limited space allows me to write only that I have been infinitely lucky to know them.

Ivoni Richter Reimer wishes to pay loving tribute to the memory of Prof. Dr. Luise Schottroff, in which her coauthor also joins.

Dame Elizabeth Smith showed me new and interesting ways to think about Luke and Acts in her (alas, unpublished) "Deutero-Apocryphal Acts of Peter's Mother-in-Law"; her wit and wisdom have sparked my thinking over the years and inspired my preaching as well as my scholarship. I owe much as well to the amazing Dr. Amy-Jill Levine, whose comments on the draft Introduction helped me to analyze my arguments and focus throughout on what I wanted to say. Kudos likewise to my coauthors, all of whom have shown me different aspects of our shared topic and enriched this book so very much, and to my volume editor, Mary Ann Beavis, who tightened the screws and made it all shipshape.

Last but first, *die Gebrüder Lohfink*, Norbert and Gerhard: they have not only filled my head with Wisdom and my heart with the love of her; their enthusiasm for my first translations sparked my long engagement with that *metier*, which has sustained me through so many vocational changes.

Half a lifetime ago (in 1984!) Professor Gerhard Lohfink set me the task of studying the book of Acts to see what it can tell us about how to live in Christian community and testify to the world of all that God has done for and with us. I hope that readers of this book will find my conclusions helpful.

—Linda M. Maloney+
Enosburg Falls, VT
Summer 2022

Author's Introduction

Translating Worlds

The Acts of the Apostles is said to be the first church history. More precisely, Acts is the first work of its kind to have survived from Christian antiquity. But what is a "history" and what is, or was, "the church"?

History?

A history is not a "story of what happened at some time in the past." It is a story of what someone in a particular time and place, with a particular set of questions, wrote about what she or he discovered in answer to those questions and in relation to events in another time and place that was "past" from the author's point of view but was "present" to those within the story. The questions themselves are historically conditioned in every case by the circumstances of the one asking them. So in reading Acts we, in the twenty-first century, are approaching the book with our own questions, related to our own time and situation, and we are addressing those questions to an author whose time and whose world are only dimly known to us—an author who, in turn, was posing her or his own questions to a time and set of events still farther in the past. That author, moreover, had an explicit purpose in writing, and that intention shaped the events selected for the story and how they were interpreted. In the case of Acts, the character of the author and her or his intention have been subjects of profound dispute throughout the modern era and remain so today. It seems certain now that the author of Acts wrote for a community, or multiple communities, of Jesus-followers within a time frame around the end of the first and early decade(s) of the second centuries CE, probably in Ephesus and its neighborhood. The story was intended to help them shape their lives as followers of "the Way" of Jesus (not necessarily a fully defined group at the time, certainly not yet known, at least to themselves, as "Christians") in the face of the particular contemporary challenges in their life as a community. One set of questions the author most certainly did *not* pose overtly was the set with which we are most directly concerned: feminist questions about the roles and status and viewpoints of women and of other people marginalized in their society for various reasons. Part of our task will be to discover what is *not* in the text; another part will be to relate what *is* in the text to what we otherwise know about the political and social situation of the first and second centuries CE.

Still, we will do well to keep in mind that Acts, unlike the Gospels, is not concerned to teach Jesus' *message* or *ethics* or *morality* as such. It is not preaching for outsiders; it is instruction for insiders on how to be the community of Jesus, the people of the reign of God. The author evidently takes it for granted that people devoted to the Way of Jesus will not lord it over one another (Matt 20:25; Mark 10:42; Luke 22:25) because of gender or any other characteristic.

In *Caste: The Origins of Our Discontents*,[1] Isabel Wilkerson eloquently describes the invention of skin color, eye color, and other such features as ways of distinguishing "superior" from "inferior" groups of people, focusing especially on the Americas and particularly the United States. The "racialized" caste system she describes was created by Europeans in the "age of discovery" (!) to mark the persons they subjugated and/or enslaved as inferior. Such a system did not exist in the Roman world. Being "Roman" was superior to being "non-Roman," but the boundaries were fluid and not tied to specific physical features. There *was* a fixed caste system in that world, though, one that was created before the dawn of history and persists today: that of gender. At least since the moment when male human beings discovered that they played a role in reproduction, male has been accounted superior to female throughout

---

1. Isabel Wilkerson, *Caste: The Origins of Our Discontents* (New York: Random House, 2020).

the natural world (from a human, or at least a masculine, point of view), and a generous body of philosophy, physiology, and literature has developed and maintained the idea and its consequences. An awareness that the author of Acts, and almost all of its audience, regarded the situation as "natural" must inform our critique of the author's attitudes and language. Very much in the same way, enslaved persons were regarded as inferior, and the idea went virtually unquestioned. We will meet enslaved persons (all of them apparently young) in the Acts of the Apostles, but there is no overt critique of slavery, here or in the Gospels. Likewise we will meet women (and two of the three enslaved characters are women). Authors and scholars from antiquity to modern times have viewed their leadership activities as anomalous. In this commentary we will look at those matters differently.

While scientists in the twentieth and twenty-first centuries have shown that there is no physical difference between people of different "races" as defined by color or other forms of caste distinction, discrimination against women continues to be justified by the difference between women's and men's bodies. Now, however, even that barrier is being broken down, as transgender and nonbinary persons show us that gender is not based in physiology and can be altered, even without body-changing surgery. The reaction on the part of those for whom a necessary classification of persons as "better" or "worse," "superior" or "inferior" is a fundamental principle of their view of humanity and society has been swift, widespread, and often violent. Laws prohibiting transgender women and girls from participating in women's and girls' sports, and other laws forbidding any acknowledgment of "different" identities in schools, are an expression of the desperate need, on the part of some, to cling to immutable "difference" (that is, arbitrarily defined inferiority or superiority).

The author of Acts[2] is notably (and unusually in that time and place) *indifferent* to such ideas. In chapter 8 he includes a detailed story of the conversion of an Ethiopian, a man surely with dark skin, but not a word is said about color. The Ethiopian is also a eunuch, but that is not an issue either. This author accepts existing gender roles (in society at large), but he makes no effort to characterize any group of persons as inferior or "other." In fact, Acts 8 contains several nudges toward a more open community of worship—one that includes Samaritans and people with altered bodies (cf. Deut 23:1; Isa 56:3-4)—before the gentiles come into the picture at all.

---

2. Whom we will call "Lukas," for reasons explained below.

A central issue in *all* of our inquiries, in fact, will be that of "the other." The author of Acts seeks, by telling a story (or many stories), to construct an "us" for the audience—really a series of "us"es in different places, times, and circumstances, each of them defined over against a "them," a "not-us." One way of doing so is to put forward exemplary figures for imitation, by no means all from the same mold. We will see this repeatedly, and some of those exemplary figures are women—Tabitha, Lydia, Prisc[ill]a,[3] and others not named. One, Sapphira, is a counterexample: she illustrates how a woman ought *not* to behave. Another aspect of this "othering" process is the more subtle practice of "queering" individuals or groups, destabilizing their racial, gender, or national identities and thereby also undermining the caste system, the "us versus them" dichotomy. Our aim in such cases is to make room for ambiguity and ultimately to evaluate the claim that the Movement of Jesus-believers transcends social and gender/caste barriers and is open to all who choose it.[4]

That does *not* imply that all who join the Movement become *Jews* or that Jews within the Movement cease to be Jews. We must affirm with Jacob Milgrom that

> Israel's separation from the nations is the continuation (and climax) of the cosmic creation process. Just as Yhwh has separated mineral, vegetable, and animal species to create order in the *natural* world, so Israel must separate from the nations to create order in the *human* world. Israel, in its quest for holiness, is simultaneously manifesting the universal or primordial life process.[5]

The author of Acts tries to make that point while affirming the role of those who followed Jesus as an aspect of Israel's journey. That he was so understood in the early decades of the book's life is clear from the fact that the early apologists (Justin, Ignatius, et al.) who attacked "the Jews" and proclaimed separation from emergent Judaism made no use of Acts; it was only when Irenaeus applied his own interpretation to the

3. She is known in Acts by the diminutive "Priscilla" (18:2, 18, 26), but Paul, in his letters, calls her Prisca (see Rom 16:3; 1 Cor 16:19; 2 Tim 4:19).

4. See, e.g., Raimo Hakola, Nina Nikki, and Ulla Tervahauta, eds., *Others and the Construction of Early Christian Identities*, Publications of the Finnish Exegetical Society 106 (Helsinki: Finnish Exegetical Society, 2013).

5. Jacob Milgrom, *Leviticus: A Book of Ritual and Ethics*, Continental Commentary (Minneapolis: Fortress, 2004), 179, quoted in Matthew Thiessen, *Contesting Conversion: Genealogy, Circumcision, and Identity in Ancient Judaism and Christianity* (Oxford: Oxford University Press, 2011), 138.

politea

book in contending against Marcion (_Adversus Haereses_, ca. 180 CE) that it began to be read as anti-Jewish, an interpretation that has had fatal and long-lasting consequences.

A much more subtle aim of the text of Acts is to downgrade and condemn "pagan" religion, and with it the imperial cult. This appears mainly in the speeches placed in the mouth of Paul, but not only there. It was a dangerous move; later Christians criticized the cult of the emperor overtly, choosing the "witness" (_martys_) of martyrdom. We will note anti-imperialistic rhetoric at various points, but one thing should be clear from the outset: being anti-imperialistic did not involve being egalitarian. Whatever social changes the author of Acts envisioned, sweeping as they were and are, they did not include the elevation of the status of women in general (or slaves or others on the fringes of society). In that regard we have to continually read against the grain.

Church?

The other questionable word in our definition is "church." We need to understand at the outset that, at the time this author wrote, there was no such thing. In fact, it is a word the author uses sparingly, preferring to refer to "The Way," or "The Movement" (ἡ ὁδός). It is dynamic, not static. It is not what we think of as a church; it has no fixed structure other than that of individual communities with remembered ties to a "mother community" in Jerusalem. It was most certainly _not_ a "religion" as the Greco-Roman world understood that term, nor was its parent, the people of Israel.

As recent scholars have convincingly shown, the separation of the Jesus movement from the way(s) of the Jewish people was very gradual and highly disorganized, simply because neither movement was "organized" from the outset in the ways we are accustomed to seeing in what are now the "religions" of Christianity and Judaism. The various sects and movements among Jews—with the possible exception of the Jerusalem _politeia_ that, by the time Lukas wrote, was also a thing of the past—were just as varied and just as little organized as were those of the "Christians." There were even significant numbers of Jewish thinkers whose concept of God approached a _logos_ theology like that of the Fourth Gospel (minus the identification of the _logos_ or _memra_ with Jesus). It was not until a few decades after Acts was written that the Greek word _hairesis_ ceased to mean something like "sect" or what we now call "denomination" and began to mean "heresy" in the sense of "false teaching." That development awaited the establishment of some kind of regional or central authority that could say yes or no to a teaching or practice—that, in other words, was able to "other" certain groups and ultimately define them out of the Movement. Then, with the gradual establishment of the monepiscopacy in Christianity and of authoritative rabbinic teaching in Judaism after the Second Revolt in 132–136, real separation and "excommunication" could begin. The existence of a structure of authority was the precondition, in turn, for the recognition of Christianity, beginning with Constantine (ca. 313 CE, two full centuries after the composition of Acts), as a *religio licita*, an approved religion, and ultimately *the* official religion of the Roman Empire. That was the time when the two ways definitively began to part, with all the disastrous consequences (for both!) that we can now begin to understand.[6]

In spite of the fact that the author of Acts is not speaking of a "church" as such, he is interested primarily in ecclesiology, the formation of Jesus-believing communities, and not in a developed doctrine or theology like what emerged with the later apologists and "fathers" of the church. That is to say, he wants to gather, not to define, because *defining divides*. Identifying teaching as "ours" versus "theirs" is the beginning of heresiology: "we" have the true teaching; "they" don't belong with us. Lukas's Christology and ecclesiology are elastic, but his aim is inclusion. Since later apologists, notably Tertullian, personified heresy as a woman, we may say that Lukas's ecclesiology was much more "feminized," or at least inclusive of women, even though they remain for the most part invisible in the story.

Kyriocentrism

At the same time it was altogether true and taken for granted in this kyriocentric (lord-and-master-centered) world that, as the saying goes, "men are people; women are the female relatives of people." Men were the exemplary (indeed, the *real*) human beings. Discourse was likewise gendered: reason, piety, and control of the self and others were associated only with men, and men were measured by the degree to which they

6. For the development of this view of religious relationships in the first two centuries CE see especially Daniel Boyarin, *Border Lines: The Partition of Judaeo-Christianity* (Philadelphia: University of Pennsylvania Press, 2004), and Adam H. Becker and Annette Yoshiko Reed, eds., *The Ways That Never Parted: Jews and Christians in Late Antiquity and the Early Middle Ages* (Minneapolis: Fortress, 2007).

exhibited those qualities.[7] The next-generation apologist Justin would, indeed, insist that the fullness of *logos*, reason, could be attained only through Christ (who in the Fourth Gospel in fact embodies the *logos*). But while Acts also asserts that Jesus is Lord, he is never called "Word." What the apostles and other Jesus-believers preach is "the word of the Lord" or "the word of God." Still, he embodies the accepted male = human model, and the language of Acts is thoroughly phallogocentric;[8] that is to say, Lukas has no other language than the one he knows, and that language—Greek—"sees" the human landscape as made up of men, who are the paradigmatic human beings; women, people who do not fit the binary gender pattern, and slaves in general are only shadows or story props. Consequently, we are surprised to find at least two women characters in Acts who display the supposedly "male" characteristics of reason, piety, and self-control: namely, Lydia and Prisc[ill]a.

The feminist reader of Acts cannot help noticing that the author's presentation of three major issues that created a rupture between traditional Jews and Jesus-believers focuses on matters of primary concern only to men: the Jerusalem temple, table fellowship, and circumcision. The temple was a less divisive issue for Jewish women because they had only limited access to it and for gentile women because they had essentially none at all. Circumcision was obviously something that concerned only men.[9] Why was *that* tradition the make-or-break issue? Table fellowship was indeed of concern to women, as the battles between Paul and the women of Corinth reveal,[10] but we never read in Acts of any input on the subject from women. If a major obstacle in that context was the prohibition of meat offered to idols or improperly killed, it would surely have been a nonissue for the vast majority of women in the new communities, who were lucky if they tasted meat once a year. As for the elite women, they would not have had to sully themselves with food preparation:

---

7. See Jennifer Knust, "Enslaved to Demons: Sex, Violence and the Apologies of Justin Martyr," in *Mapping Gender in Ancient Religious Discourses*, ed. Todd Penner and Caroline Vander Stichele (Leiden: Brill, 2007), 431–55.

8. The term was coined by Jacques Derrida and has been examined in a feminist context by Luce Irigaray and others.

9. Female circumcision was not an issue in Mediterranean cultures; Western awareness of the practice is quite recent. See Shaye J. D. Cohen, *Why Aren't Jewish Women Circumcised? Gender and Covenant in Judaism* (Berkeley: University of California Press, 2005).

10. On this see especially Antoinette C. Wire, *The Corinthian Women Prophets: A Reconstruction through Paul's Rhetoric* (Minneapolis: Fortress, 1995); eadem, *2 Corinthians*, WCS 48 (Collegeville, MN: Liturgical Press, 2019).

that was for their slaves to perform. Slaves who joined the Movement might have had qualms, but we do not hear of them. And, by the way, why is there no discussion whatsoever of the slaves who appear in the text from time to time? Clearly, only a few decades after Acts was written, the authors of such New Testament texts as 1 Peter and the Pastoral Epistles found it necessary to insist on a code of household behavior that encompassed women, children, and slaves.[11]

The Jewish Lukas

In recent years a growing number of scholars have begun to question the conventional wisdom that the author of Acts was a gentile, suggesting instead that Lukas may have been raised and educated in a primarily Jewish setting, probably in the Greco-Roman diaspora. Several lines of evidence support this idea.

First, from a theoretical standpoint the last three decades of New Testament research have witnessed serious challenges to the notion that "Judaism" and "Christianity" were distinguishably separate religions in the first few centuries of the Common Era. While the so-called Parting of the Ways between Jews and Christians was once thought to have occurred around the time of the fall of the Jerusalem temple in 70 CE (or at the latest by the Bar Kokhba Revolt), recent analysis has pushed the date of final separation much later, perhaps even by centuries.[12] If Judaism and Christianity did not in fact coalesce into discrete "religions" until much later, this should compel readers of Acts to reconsider its status as a "Gentile Christian" text.[13]

Second, knowledge of Acts among early Christian writers is comparatively scarce, and few writers saw fit to comment on Lukas's ethnicity.[14] Irenaeus

---

11. A reader attuned to the gendered nature of these issues, especially circumcision, is first puzzled and then amused when reading many standard works on Acts that lavish gallons of ink on the reception or nonreception of the Torah doctrine on circumcision and the divisions it created between Jews and gentiles without once acknowledging that the subject does not concern women *at all*.

12. See nn. 4 and 6 above.

13. David Smith, "Luke, the Jews, and the Politics of Early Christian Identity" (PhD diss., Duke University, 2018). See, however, Jill Hicks-Keeton, Lori Baron, and Matthew Thiessen, eds., *The Ways That Often Parted: Essays in Honor of Joel Marcus* (Atlanta: SBL Press, 2018).

14. See Andrew Gregory, *The Reception of Luke and Acts in the Period before Irenaeus: Looking for Luke in the Second Century*, WUNT 169 (Tübingen: Mohr Siebeck, 2003).

is the earliest Christian writer to identify the author of the Third Gospel with Lukas, the physician and companion of Paul mentioned in Colossians 4:14 and 2 Timothy 4:11.[15] Since the author of Colossians does not include Lukas alongside Aristarchus, Mark, and Jesus Justus as "the only ones of the circumcision among [Paul's] co-workers for the kingdom of God" (Col 4:10–11), some early Christian writers reasonably assumed that this meant Lukas must have been a gentile.[16] Origen of Alexandria speculated that the author of the Third Gospel may have been the same as the *Loukios* (Lucius) whom Paul claims as a "relative" in Romans 16:21,[17] while Ephrem the Syrian attributed Acts to Lucius of Cyrene (Acts 13:1).[18] Still other traditions identify Lukas as one of the seventy (-two)—presumably Jewish—apostles commissioned by Jesus himself (Luke 10:1-20).[19] Intriguingly, the author of the Muratorian Fragment describes Lukas as "one zealous for the Law [i.e., Torah]," which would be a highly unusual designation for a gentile.[20]

Both Luke and Acts are also replete with internal literary evidence that strongly suggests Jewish authorship. The author of Acts is intimately familiar with the history, Scripture, and theology of Israel and weaves it throughout the narrative with the express aim of illustrating the means by which gentile followers of the Way have been "grafted" into Israel's grand narrative of salvation history. While not impossible, it is nonetheless highly unlikely that a gentile—even one who had become a Jewish proselyte—

15. Irenaeus, *Adversus haereses* 3.1.1; 3.10.1; 3.14.1-4. Curiously, Irenaeus makes no mention of Paul's reference to Lukas in Phlm 24.

16. It is unlikely that "ones of the circumcision" means simply "Jewish" here, since the three men mentioned in Col 4:10-11 are certainly not Paul's only Jewish coworkers!

17. Origen, *Commentary on the Epistle to the Romans* 10.39.1-2.

18. *Ephræm Syri: Commentarii in Epistolas D. Pauli: Nunc Primum Ex Armenio in Latinum Sermonem a Patribus Mekithartistis* (Venice: Typographia Sancti Lazari, 1893), 103.

19. Epiphanius, *Panarion* 1. *Anacephalaeosis* 1: *De Incarnatione* 4.3-6. ("Apostle" is used here in its root sense, "one who is sent," not in the specific Lukan usage that refers it to the Twelve.)

20. See the English translation in Bruce Metzger, *The Canon of the New Testament: Its Origin, Development, and Significance* (New York: Oxford University Press, 1987), 305–6. The Fragment (or "Canon") was traditionally dated ca. 170, a dating Metzger accepted, but some more recent scholars have objected, putting the date as late as the fourth century. See, e.g., Albert C. Sundberg Jr., "Canon Muratori: A Fourth-Century List," *HTR* 66 (1973): 1–41; Alan J. Hauser and Duane F. Watson, eds., *A History of Biblical Interpretation*, vol. 1: *The Ancient Period* (Grand Rapids: Eerdmans, 2003).

could have gained such a skilled mastery of Israel's Scriptures. Moreover, Lukas tenaciously defends both Jesus and Paul as consummate fulfillers of Torah, from Jesus' circumcision and purification in Luke 2:21-24 to Paul's insistence that even after his "conversion" to Christianity he nonetheless remains a Pharisee (Acts 23:6).[21]

The field of linguistic interpretation has also opened up new horizons in the reading of Acts. Albert Hogeterp and Adelbert Denaux have identified Semitic Greek in the vocabulary, syntax, and every level of narrative discourse in Luke and Acts.[22] In 1988 Marilyn Salmon raised an important question: If the term "gentiles" (τὰ ἔθνη) was Jewish "insider" language typically employed as a reference to non-Jewish "outsiders," why would Lukas be so fond of the term if the author was not Jewish himself?[23] Similarly, Lukas does not self-identify as a Christian (Χριστιανός), a term that appears twice in Acts and is used only by non-Christians, but rather speaks of "the Way" (ἡ ὁδός: Acts 9:2; 16:17; 18:26; 19:19, 23; 22:4; 24:14, 24), which recalls Jesus' speaking of the Way of Torah (Exod 32:8; Deut 9:12; Isa 30:21; cf. Luke 20:21; Acts 18:25, 26).

A major consequence of this understanding of Lukan authorship is that it produces a coherent and comprehensive reading of Luke and Acts in which the gentile mission is understood not as a *supersession* of Jewish belief and practice but rather as an *extension* of Israel's salvation history. Reading Luke and Acts as Jewish texts therefore reframes these narratives as accounts of intra-Jewish conflict rather than as a triumphalist story of the eclipse of Judaism by gentile Christianity. Given the sharp increase in anti-Semitic, white supremacist, and Christian nationalist violence in the United States and other Western countries in recent years, understanding the Jewish roots of Acts has seldom been more urgent than it is today.

Joshua Paul Smith

21. See Isaac Oliver, *Torah Praxis after 70 CE: Reading Matthew and Luke-Acts as Jewish Texts*, WUNT 2.355 (Tübingen: Mohr Siebeck, 2013); Matthew Thiessen, "Luke 2:22, Leviticus 22, and Parturient Impurity," *NovT* 54 (2012): 16–29.

22. Albert Hogeterp and Adelbert Denaux, *Semitisms in Luke's Greek*, WUNT 2.401 (Tübingen: Mohr Siebeck, 2018). See also Adelbert Denaux, Rita Corstjens, and Hellen Mardaga, *The Vocabulary of Luke*, BTS 10 (Leuven: Peeters, 2009).

23. Marilyn Salmon, "Insider or Outsider? Luke's Relationship with Judaism," in *Luke-Acts and the Jewish People*, ed. Joseph B. Tyson (Minneapolis: Augsburg, 1988), 76–82.

Lukas, the Author of Acts

Our author, then, is probably a male believer of Jewish descent writing in the first quarter of the second century. His use of the historical works of Flavius Josephus, both *The Jewish War* and the *Antiquities of the Jews*, and possibly *Against Apion* as well, makes an earlier dating at least questionable.[24] There is a near-consensus that he was the same person who wrote the Gospel of Luke, but there was probably a lapse of some thirty years between the two books (the Gospel is thought to have been produced around the year 90 CE),[25] and they never circulated together, nor does any manuscript of the New Testament, or of the Gospels and Acts, place them in sequence. So it seems legitimate not to rely on common authorship of the two books for our interpretation; certainly they were produced in very different times (and places?), with the result that the author's (or authors') points of view, experiences, and intent are different in the two books. In their *Rethinking the Unity of Luke and Acts*[26] Mikeal Parsons and Richard Pervo assented somewhat reluctantly to a single authorship, but they call the author "Lukas" to indicate an ambiguity, and so will we.

Why Was Acts Acknowledged So Late?

It is important to be aware that Acts, whether produced in the 90s of the first century or a decade or two or three later, did not achieve immediate recognition. It is first explicitly cited by Irenaeus in his *Adversus*

---

24. Many scholars dispute this author's use of Josephus, but Richard I. Pervo, *Dating Acts: Between the Evangelists and the Apologists* (Santa Rosa, CA: Polebridge, 2006), presents evidence that I find convincing.

25. Ibid. For a sharply divided debate on the dating of Acts see the essays in *Rethinking the Unity and Reception of Luke and Acts*, ed. Andrew F. Gregory and C. Kavin Rowe (Columbia: University of South Carolina Press, 2010).

26. Mikeal C. Parsons and Richard I. Pervo, *Rethinking the Unity of Luke and Acts* (Minneapolis: Fortress, 1993). For doubts about authorial unity see most recently Patricia Walters, *The Assumed Authorial Unity of Luke and Acts: A Reassessment of the Evidence*, SNTSMS 145 (Cambridge: Cambridge University Press, 2009), though her statistical method has met with much objection. On this see most recently the review by Mikeal Parsons and Heather Gorman (*Neot* 46 [2012]: 139–52) and Walters's response (*Neot* 52 [2018]: 489–95), citing D. Mealand, "The Seams and Summaries of Luke and Acts," *JSNT* 38 (2016): 482–502. In Walters's favor see Clare K. Rothschild, "Perfect Martyr? Dangerous Material in the Stoning of Stephen," in *Delightful Acts*, ed. Harold W. Attridge, Dennis R. MacDonald, and Clare K. Rothschild, WUNT 391 (Tübingen: Mohr Siebeck, 2017), 177–92.

Haereses (Against All the Heresies) in about 180—in other words, at least two generations after its composition. Irenaeus identified the author as a companion of Paul and the author both of the Gospel of Luke and of Acts—making it an extremely useful tool for combating Marcionism, since Marcion relied on an edited version of the Gospel of Luke, together with ten Pauline letters (excluding the Pastorals), as the basis for his anti-Jewish version of Christianity. Ironically, then, Lukas's account of the early church, with its powerful emphasis on the Jewish tradition as the root and ground of the new movement and its claim that Jesus was the son of *Israel*'s God, became a bulwark of an orthodoxy it did not really support (especially in its hierarchical manifestation).

The author of Acts is faced with two major tasks:

(1) The first is to establish the dignity and authority of Jesus in the eyes of "Jews and Greeks"—to argue to Jews for Jesus' identity as the promised end-time heir of David and to prove to both gentiles and Jews that this nobody from Galilee who died the death of a criminal traitor has been justified and exalted by the God of Israel *and* at the same time that he fits the Greco-Roman ideal of a superior man. That second aspect was less urgent in the Gospel, which therefore allowed for a greater presence and authority of certain women; those figures will recede significantly in the narrative of Acts. In fact, a major part of the program of Acts is to present the (male) leaders of the Movement as outstanding examples of Greco-Roman-Jewish manhood. "Jews and Greeks" (a phrase used only in diaspora contexts) means diaspora Jews first, and Hellenes (that is, people who consider themselves heirs to and participants in Greek culture) second. Lukas's anti-imperial rhetoric and his denunciation of idols are couched in the language of Hellenistic diaspora Judaism and tuned to those ears first of all.[27]

(2) The author's second task is to project onto the earliest beginnings of ἡ ὁδός (the Movement/the Way) a picture of what it *should be*, going forward—including how conflicts should be resolved. In the Lukan ideal the followers of the Way are (a) organized in communities (b) following the teaching of the apostles (c) under the guidance of the Holy Spirit. Moreover, those communities are not only called to seek to live in harmony but in essentials to exhibit *unanimity*.[28] Actions proposed to

---

27. See Drew J. Strait, *Hidden Criticism of the Angry Tyrant in Early Judaism and the Acts of the Apostles* (Lanham, MD: Lexington Books/Fortress Academic, 2019).

28. Ὁμοθυμαδόν, "with one accord," appears ten times in Acts, six times with regard to the Jesus-communities. The other four instances speak of the united hateful action of mobs against members of the Movement.

them by their leaders as the work of the Holy Spirit, when recognized as such, will be accepted by the assembled community. The picture Lukas paints is designed to counter the trend toward hierarchical authority—the apostles have no successors—but by the time the book circulated the pseudo-Pauline "Pastoral Epistles" had already been added to the Pauline corpus and soon after them the likewise pseudonymous letters of "Ignatius" began to circulate.[29] Both of those sets of "letters" were loud and strong—and ultimately dominant—voices for hierarchy and "orthodoxy." So Acts was read in that context.

Lukas's contemporary, the author of the Fourth Gospel, was of a similar mind, though for him the Twelve were not the real channels of Jesus' message; that was the Beloved Disciple. He has a similar community mind-set, and, as witnessed by the Johannine letters, the communities in that particular movement or *hairesis* were equally intent on love and unanimity, to the point of expelling some. The author of the Fourth Gospel makes the point quite tellingly in John 20, where Jesus has to appear to the disciples twice because Thomas is absent the first time; they must all see and affirm him lest there be any dissension among them.

Debating the Call, Subverting the Paradigm

It is tempting to try to novelize community life in Ephesus in the early second century, with "John," "Lukas," and the local disciples of Paul, Lydia, Prisca, and Apollos, together with Ephesian Jewish scholars of various lines of thought,[30] debating in anything but harmonious fashion, and each in turn writing his or her "history"—though in different genres. Perhaps the younger author-to-be of the Pastorals was listening and collecting ammunition for his defense of hierarchical authority. Of these, Lukas alone chose a literary form that is somewhere between popular romance and popular history, designed to appeal to an audience with some culture, though not to professional historians. Nowadays we might indeed compare Acts to a historical novel or one of those books or films said to be "based on real events." Shelly Matthews has proposed that the intended audience was, at least in part, made up of wealthy or well-

29. For the pseudonymity and late dating of the letters of Ignatius see Michael Theobald, *Israel-Vergessenheit in den Pastoralbriefen: ein neuer Vorschlag zu ihrer historisch- theologischen Verortung im 2. Jahrhundert n. Chr. unter besonderer Berücksichtigung der Ignatius-Briefe* (Stuttgart: Katholisches Bibelwerk, 2016).

30. As will be discussed later, there was a large and active Jewish community in Ephesus, with multiple synagogues.

to-do gentile women who would be attracted by the idea of harmonious and nonhierarchical community and who would offer their houses as bases for local communities. The literary genre of Acts was known to appeal to readers like these; the book showed them a way to be part of that new "us" without ceasing to be themselves.[31] Still, wealthy or prominent Hellene women are only silent figures in the background of a few scenes (see Acts 17:4, 12, 34; 24:24; 25:13).

We will therefore have an eye on locale, on politics contemporary to the story time and to the author's time, and especially on the gendered and hierarchical nature of discourse as Lukas seeks both to establish the authority of Jesus and the apostles and to model a Movement that can function without the immediate presence of either but is always guided by Sophia, the Holy Spirit.

In his *World Upside Down: Reading Acts in the Graeco-Roman Age*,[32] C. Kavin Rowe illustrates his premise that "Luke's second volume is a highly charged and theologically sophisticated political document that aims at nothing less than the construction of an alternative total way of life—a comprehensive pattern of being—one that runs counter to the life-patterns of the Graeco-Roman world." In short, to accept Jesus as *Kyrios*, "Lord of all" (cf. Acts 10:30), is to enter into a new way of being in a new community that is, in the author's vision, the beginning of the eschatological fulfillment of God's promises to Israel. Acts portrays the life of that community and its mission. But anything "new" in the world is new only in context; it can never be a completely "other" thing without becoming unrecognizable. So the new community of the Way turned its world upside down (Acts 17:6) without turning it inside out: it retained a social hierarchy that was soon solidified into a politico-religious one in which many people today can no longer discern the revolutionary movement of the first centuries. The male-female caste system remained unchallenged. It seems that feminist, womanist, mujerista, Asian-feminist, First Nations, and LGBTQIA+ theologians and persons acting out in society may indeed be once more overturning the established ways of thinking and doing: their identification with the movement to overturn "racial" caste is quite natural. This book is intended as a contribution to that earthshaking movement.

31. Shelly Matthews, *First Converts: Rich Pagan Women and the Rhetoric of Mission in Early Judaism and Christianity* (Stanford, CA: Stanford University Press, 2001).

32. C. Kavin Rowe, *World Upside Down: Reading Acts in the Graeco-Roman Age* (Oxford: Oxford University Press, 2010), 15.

One vital way in which Lukas subverts the dominant paradigm is his location of the ideal community of the beginnings *in the house.* In Lukas's milieu, the Jewish diaspora in a Greco-Roman world, the house was *the domain of women.* Men engaged in public discourse and debate (and so the leading male characters in Acts do); women taught at home, and the house was their sphere. So it should be no surprise that women like Tabitha, the mother of John Mark, Lydia, and Prisca (and perhaps the mother of Timothy?)[33] led communities of disciples and new converts in their homes; so must a great many other women have done. Their influence on the early development of what would become the church was no less significant than that of the men who worked in the public sphere, and, in portraying the house-church as the ideal, Lukas emphasizes that fact.

The paradigm for women's primary role in constituting and building up the new community is—and this may speak in favor of a unified authorship—Luke 10:38-42. In that story Martha is fulfilling the appointed duties of a woman in charge of a household while Mary is performing the role of a disciple, learning from Jesus. The meaning of the story has been too often turned on its head to prescribe passivity for women, but it teaches the opposite: women are not to limit themselves to the "traditional" housewifely role. Rather, now that Jesus has been exalted they should expand their sphere: now it is they, as those in charge of the house where the church gathers, who must take the lead—first learning the teaching of the apostles, then handing on that teaching to those who gather in their houses. In the new community women must be both evangelists and presiders in the house-church. So Adele Reinhartz has written: "Martha and Mary may have been seen as models of integration, according to which it was possible for women to view their belief in the Christ and active participation in the church as compatible with, and complementary to, other important elements of their lives."[34]

Seams, but Not Divisions

There have been nearly as many proposals for the outline and divisions in Acts as there are leaves on a tree, and we will not offer a new one. This is a story of the development of the Movement from its Jerusalem beginnings

33. Acts 16:1; cf. 2 Tim 1:5.
34. Adele Reinhartz, "From Narrative to History: The Resurrection of Mary and Martha," in *"Women Like This": New Perspectives on Jewish Women in the Greco-Roman World*, ed. Amy-Jill Levine, EJL 1 (Atlanta: Scholars Press, 1991), 161–84, at 184.

to the heart of the Roman world: a paradigmatic story intended to influence the shaping of that Movement's future. Most generally we may say
that Acts focuses first on the leadership of Peter and then on that of Paul,
with a considerable overlap in chapters 8–15. But Lukas's use of novelistic
techniques as a means of attracting his audience to this purported "history" overrides any rigid scheme of time or place. It is best simply to read
the story as it unfolds.

Acts in Our Time

It seems appropriate to be reflecting on Acts, a work crafted in a time
of violent upheaval and severe repression, in the weird postcolonial political and social world of the early twenty-first century. To speak only
of the world of biblical scholarship, postcolonial students of the Bible
and cultures are pushing the limits of colonial-era institutions, among
them the "learned societies" that were created in the late nineteenth
century to shape and shore up the image of a world sustained by imperial domination.[35] One effect of the COVID-19 crisis has been to prevent
those learned societies from holding the annual gatherings at which
members reinforce such received knowledge and status and admit to the
"guild" new scholars who have "mastered" the rules. Now, released into
the fresh air (even if masked), or communicating electronically across
vast distances, scholars who see the world with postcolonial vision are
seeking ways to find a solid footing outside the "guilds" and without
being dependent on them. They are gathering in virtual groups or small,
intimate ones, or they "mask" their new ideas in terms the guild thinks
it understands. They are heirs of the traditions of scholarship, but they
are a new thing, a new generation not bound by the old. Reading Acts
in this moment, as the portrait of a movement that is heir to one much
older yet adopting a new path that is incomprehensible to some and a
danger to others, should be a liberating experience.[36]

35. For a breathtaking analysis of the ways in which such institutions supported
and encouraged racial definition and hierarchy see Willie James Jennings, *The Christian Imagination: Theology and the Origins of Race* (New Haven: Yale University Press,
2010), esp. 150–55.

36. For ecofeminist observations in COVID-19 times see Ivoni Richter Reimer (org.),
with the participation of Ivone Gebara, Sandra Duarte de Souza, José Reinaldo Martins
Filho, Carolina Bezerra de Souza (Brazil), Maricel Mena Lopez (Colombia), Maria
Paula Meneses (Portugal), at https://www.youtube.com/watch?v=aHJbwFDBQgM
and https://www.youtube.com/watch?v=XZ9kQcpPm2k&t=584s.

Because I am a pastor and preacher whose work is rooted in biblical scholarship, my own preferred method of analysis is a form of reader-response criticism that I might call fact-based imaginative empathy. In other words: "Suppose it was not as we have always thought it was; suppose it was another way instead." What was the author, in that time and place, attempting to say to that audience, and how would they probably have responded, based on what we know of them? What, in turn, has been the impact over time of the "discourses of normativity that seek to project a linear and simplistic picture of the nature of early Christian history and identity,"[37] and what is their significance for us now, as attempts are being made to overthrow or undermine that normativity? Who have been the winners and losers in the struggle over that history and identity, and how do we relate to it, or what we can perceive of it, today? Lukas himself has long been projected as attempting just such a discourse, but in fact his skill is such that, appealing to those with eyes to see and ears to hear, he insinuates "subversive" viewpoints and "non-normative" circumstances, thus inviting "others" to identify with the Jesus movement. He does not define the "others" but invites them to find their own self-definition in relation to Judaism, the new movements within it, and the external pressures of the Roman imperial world.

Peeling back the layers of events and interpreting those events from a vastly different cultural perspective is a complicated archaeological, historical, even surgical enterprise, but a worthwhile and fascinating endeavor because "there is a crack in everything; that's how the light gets in."[38] So let us begin to peek through the cracks.

Linda M. Maloney

---

37. Caroline Vander Stichele and Todd Penner, *Contextualizing Gender in Early Christian Discourse: Thinking beyond Thecla* (London: T&T Clark, 2009), 96.
38. Leonard Cohen, "Anthem."

Acts 1:1-4a

Preface

Both the Gospel of Luke and the Acts of the Apostles have prefaces addressed to one "Theophilus," which is certainly a prime reason why the two books have been attributed to the same author. In fact, the only word the prefaces have in common is "Theophilus," the addressee. Theophilus may have been a historical person and the author's patron, but given the long time span between the composition of the two books (see the introduction), that seems improbable. We may instead consider "Theophilus" ("lover of God") to be a paradigmatic Christian, probably a gentile Christian, a collective person[1] representing the authorial audience[2] of Acts. The convention of subsuming the female grammatically within the male is operative here too: "Theophilus" is a Christian *person*, not limited to males in the audience. The author signals to readers that in this book gender will almost always have overtones of ambiguity.

---

1. See Ivoni Richter Reimer's exposition below.
2. This term refers to the ideal audience as the author imagines it and implicitly configures it in the text.

Acts 1:1-4a

1:1In the first book, Theophilus, I wrote about all that Jesus did and taught from the beginning ²until the day when he was taken up to heaven, after giving instructions through the Holy Spirit to the apostles whom he had chosen. ³After his suffering he presented himself alive to them by many convincing proofs, appearing to them during forty days and speaking about the kingdom of God. ⁴While staying with them, he ordered them not to leave Jerusalem, but to wait there for the promise of the Father.

Theophilus

We consider "Theophilus," to whom the two Lukan works[3] are addressed, to be a representative of a collective, of a community. The name itself can allude to a mostly gentile identity of this community and, as a representative of a diverse collective, it includes men and women of all ages, classes, and ethnicities who have been added to the Way/Movement. This is, therefore, also the audience the author addresses. The community is a "lover/friend of God" who knows the work of Jesus and now, in a new historical context, is called to continue his movement. This continuity is not a simple "repetition"; it is a process of rereading and reconstructing Jesus' work in other contexts. As a result it is marked simultaneously by discontinuities, new complexities, and ambiguities, all recorded narratively.

Ivoni Richter Reimer

This observation by Ivoni Richter Reimer is of crucial importance for understanding Acts in its original setting. This is not a "gospel," a portrayal of Jesus' life and teaching for the benefit of those outside or those newly gathered into the community and in need of instruction. Acts is a book for *insiders*, for women and men who have absorbed and accepted Jesus' teaching and who need support and encouragement in living the community life his teaching demands. Nowhere in Acts do we find a "doctrinal discourse"—no sermon on a mount or on a plain. It is not preaching but "signs and wonders" (cf. 2:22, 43; 4:30; 5:12; 6:8; 14:3; 15:12) that draw people; once they have "repented" (lit. "turned around"), been baptized, and received the Holy Spirit, they must learn a

---

3. See the introduction, also in relation to the authorship of Acts.

new way of life in which it will be the community itself that will instruct them in the ways of the reign of God. Lukas never proposes, anywhere in Acts, that women should behave in one way and men in another: quite the contrary, as the Sapphira and Ananias episode will show. This could be a counter to writings like the Pastorals[4] or even to some passages in Paul's authentic letters; however, the former are more likely to be later than, and a push-back against, the egalitarianism of Acts.

The scope of the preface to Acts is debated. Loveday Alexander, in her examination of the preface to Luke's Gospel,[5] devotes only four pages to Acts 1:1, which, as far as the comparison with Luke is concerned, constitutes the whole of the preface. She implicitly assigns Acts to a different genre than the Gospel(s); the burden of her analysis is that Luke's preface resembles those of popular scientific works, but the Acts preface, which fails to give any recapitulation of the previous book, is more like those of multivolume historical works. Obviously, Acts is of a different genre than any Gospel, but it implicitly claims at the outset to be a history as understood in the ancient mold.

In addition, Acts makes no claim to being definitive, something Luke's Gospel (1:1-4) emphatically does. The Gospel author's purpose in writing, "after investigating everything carefully," is that Theophilus "may know the truth" about Jesus' story—the implication being that the other accounts, however "orderly," are somehow deficient. In the preface to Acts, Lukas implies the same claim regarding the Gospel, but as far as this second work is concerned it is to be an account of how the apostles spread the teaching entrusted to them by Jesus both pre- and post-Easter. Moreover, unlike the Gospel, it is open-ended: in the course of the story we hear of the death of only one apostle (James), and at the end Paul, the great missionary, is very explicitly said still to be alive and teaching at his lodgings in Rome. "The Movement"[6] continues, and others will write about its further course.

The text here gives a first impression that during the forty days after Easter Jesus restricted his appearances to the Twelve. "While staying with them" (συνελθόντες ἠρώτων αὐτὸν) more properly means "while eating

---

4. 1 and 2 Timothy and Titus.

5. Loveday Alexander, *The Preface to Luke's Gospel: Literary Convention and Social Context in Luke 1.1-4 and Acts 1.1*, SNTSMS 78 (Cambridge: Cambridge University Press, 1993).

6. Or "the Way," ἡ ὁδος; see Acts 9:2; 19:23; 24:22. Lukas also uses the word ἐκκλησία, but in Acts it can refer to the assembly of Israel in the wilderness, to the gatherings of the Way, or to any public assembly (cf. Acts 7:38; 9:31; 11:26; 15:22; 19:32, 39).

with them," which seems to make these meals an extension of the Last
Supper account, in which (at least in the Synoptics) only "the twelve" or
"the apostles" figure—unlike many other meals recounted in the Gospels.[7]

Masculine Identifiers

The change from verse 2
to verse 3 marks a narrative
discontinuity: there is a break in
the narrative flow, a signal of the
complex literary composition
of the entire work. Verse 2 (in
Greek) ends by stating that Jesus
"was taken up [ἀνελήμφθη] to
heaven," and with this 1:1-2
has already forged the editorial
bridge with "the first book." It
is important, however, for the
author to give more information
about what happened before
Jesus' ascension, after his
resurrection. Thus verse 3 begins
with the relative pronoun "to
whom" in the dative masculine
plural, οἷς, referring to the
"apostles" (1:2). The author has
thus made efforts to connect his
preface (1:1-2) with an existing
tradition about the forty days[8]
of action of the Risen One with
his disciples. With this pronoun
the author directly identifies
the group of people gathered
(1:3-9) with the apostles. If we
understand the term "apostle"
in a reduced way as referring
to the Eleven/Twelve we have
here an androcentric authorial
characterization that deprives
women of their status as
evangelical witnesses of the
resurrection, but if we understand
the term "apostle" as symbolic
(twelve tribes of Israel) or in an
extended sense, then the narrative
includes women and men.

Ivoni Richter Reimer

Thus while the restriction of the title "apostle" to the Twelve[9] emphasizes the continuity of the new community with Israel of the twelve tribes
it is also understood by most interpreters as permanently masculinizing
the leadership of the Movement. The preface to Acts—and here it is distinctly discontinuous with the Gospels—stresses that it is the "apostles"
who are the witnesses to the resurrection and are commissioned to give

7. See, e.g., Luke 22:14; cf. Mark 14:3; Matt 26:6-7. Mark and Matthew refer to those
with Jesus at the Last Supper as "the twelve," the equivalent of Luke's "apostles."
John, who has no particular affection for the Twelve (and is averse to the term
"apostle") characterizes those at the Supper as "his own" (τοὺς ἰδίους).

8. This information appears only in Acts, which is an indication of efforts to connect the history of God open to "gentiles" with its Jewish liberation origins (exodus).

9. Paul and Barnabas are called "apostles" twice in chapter 14 (vv. 1, 14), but apparently
in their roles as "sent" by the community at Antioch. Lukas is not interested in applying
the cherished title to Paul in its primary sense, as if he were equal to one of the Twelve.

public testimony to it, in apparent contradiction to the accounts in all four Gospels, in which it is women who first receive that news and convey it to the Eleven. Insofar as future testimony is to be public—and Acts makes very little reference to nonpublic witness, as we will see—it is to be men's work, for the public sphere is theirs.

Whereas in the Gospel the "apostles" were only the Twelve, that ceases to be the case in Acts. The symbolic number twelve is restored by the election of Matthias, but that is the last we hear of him or of any others of the Twelve except Peter and (marginally) John and James (when he is killed).[10] The verb ἀποστέλλω, "send," is very prominent in Acts, and once the community moves beyond Jerusalem those who are ἀπόστολοι, "sent ones," are nearly always sent by a community, not by Jesus or any other individual figure.[11] The local community and not some central institution becomes the authority by whom people are sent on mission to spread the Movement.

Literary Aspects

The literary authorial effort is an important element in the construction of the work. Here verses 3-4 clearly summarize the narrative in Luke 24:13-43, highlighting that Jesus is alive and that he teaches and eats meals together with the group who had accompanied him from Galilee to Calvary and to the now empty tomb (cf. v. 21): Jesus lives! The narrative objective is to make the group remain in Jerusalem (Luke 24:47, 49, 52-53; Acts 1:4a) to reconfigure the history of God in the holy city. This is different from the tradition recorded in Mark 16:7; Matthew 28:7, 10, 16, which reconstruct history from Galilee. This literary and theological effort has to do with the objective of the work: starting from Jerusalem to take the gospel to all peoples (Acts 1:8) without breaking with the liberation origins of Israel.

Ivoni Richter Reimer

---

10. The "James" most prominent in Acts, Peter's ostensible successor as leader of the Jerusalem community, is the "brother of the Lord" and not either of the two Jameses in the Synoptic list or the one Lukas names at Acts 1:14.

11. The great exception is Saul/Paul, who regularly insists in his letters that he was called and sent by the risen Lord and not, e.g., by the church in Jerusalem. Lukas lets Paul affirm this twice in Acts as he tells of his encounter with the Risen One (cf. Acts 22:6-21; 26:12-23); the claim (for good or ill) was widely known. Still, it is apparent to the careful reader that Paul is first "vetted" and sent by the community at Damascus (9:19b-20, 27), then by that at Antioch (13:1-3), then *to* Antioch by the mother community in Jerusalem (15:22-30) and *by* the Antiochene community thereafter (15:40).

Acts 1:4b-14

Ascension

The author apparently means "they" throughout the passage to refer to "the apostles whom he had chosen" (v. 2), but "when they had come together" implies additional persons. Jesus' forty days of instruction have not shaken the ingrained expectations of at least some of his followers. They are still thinking in the paradigm of a restored (earthly?) "kingdom," presumably with Jesus at its head, wielding his messianic power confirmed by the resurrection.[1] Jesus' answer leaves the future open-ended (as the book of Acts will be). He does not even promise his followers wisdom or understanding, only "power" for witness. Lukas's apostles have authority, but they have to struggle for insight.

---

1. Here Jesus, in Lukas's portrayal, seems more in tune with currents in Jewish thought as regards messianic figures in the first centuries CE (and since) than are the apostles; see at Acts 2 below. As Paula Fredriksen has written, the focus on (eternal) salvation "never defined Second Temple Jewish culture or ideas of covenant, nor did it universally shape centuries of Jewish relationships with their non-Jewish neighbors in the cities of the diaspora. Jewish ancestral practices—inherited protocols for aligning heaven and earth—focused, rather, on the business of living Jewishly." (Review of Joshua D. Garroway, *The Beginning of the Gospel: Paul, Philippi, and the Origins of Christianity* [Cham, Switzerland: Palgrave Macmillan, 2018] in *RBL*, June 2020, online at https://www.bookreviews .org.) But Acts, whether we date it early or late, is contemporary with a wave of Jewish apocalyptic literature such as Jubilees, the Testaments of the Twelve Patriarchs, and 1 Enoch (which is explicitly quoted in the late first-century letter of Jude), and those writings were most definitely focused on the end time and the life beyond.

Acts 1:4b-14

⁴ᵇ"This," he said, "is what you have heard from me; ⁵for John baptized with water, but you will be baptized with the Holy Spirit not many days from now."

⁶So when they had come together, they asked him, "Lord, is this the time when you will restore the kingdom to Israel?" ⁷He replied, "It is not for you to know the times or periods that the Father has set by his own authority. ⁸But you will receive power when the Holy Spirit has come upon you; and you will be my witnesses in Jerusalem, in all Judea and Samaria, and to the ends of the earth." ⁹When he had said this, as they were watching, he was lifted up, and a cloud took him out of their sight. ¹⁰While he was going and they were gazing up toward heaven, suddenly two men in white robes stood by them.

What Did Jesus Really Say?

The obstinate adherence of the disciples to their familiar ways of thinking as pictured here, even after forty days of instruction from the Risen One, should recommend some caution about the received understanding of what Jesus actually said during his lifetime. The evangelists recorded what they heard him say, or what they were told by eye- and ear-witnesses that he had said, or what had been handed down, and the words, so far as they go, may well be authentic. But there is surely a surplus of meaning to which we ought to attend.

Almost no one in the twenty-first century affirms the institution of slavery as biblically warranted or commanded, but Scripture is still cited to affirm the subordination of women; the ostracizing of LGBTQIA+ persons; the establishment of class barriers based on color, immigration status, education, wealth and poverty, age, even body types—and, of course, religion (anti-Judaism, anti-Islamic prejudice, and on and on). A norm of full equality seems an ever-receding eschatological goal to many (a future horror to some for whom the prospect of a "majority-minority" population portends only a *reversal* of discriminatory norms). That does not absolve the rest of us from pursuing the goal.

We must be clear, however, that in citing a messianic expectation of the restoration of Israel's political independence—one of the common currents in apocalyptic thought contemporary to him—Lukas signals for the first and by no means the last time that he honors Israel's election and its faith; he uses language throughout Acts that coincides with first- and second-century CE Hellenistic Jewish polemic against the Roman

kyriarchy - In feminist theory is a social system or set of connecting social systems built around domination, oppression, and submission

[11]They said, "Men of Galilee, why do you stand looking up toward heaven? This Jesus, who has been taken up from you into heaven, will come in the same way as you saw him go into heaven." [12]Then they returned to Jerusalem from the mount called Olivet, which is near Jerusalem, a sabbath day's journey away. [13]When they had entered the city, they went to the room upstairs where they were staying, Peter, and John, and James, and Andrew, Philip and Thomas, Bartholomew and Matthew, James son of Alphaeus, and Simon the Zealot, and Judas son of James. [14]All these were constantly devoting themselves to prayer, together with certain women, including Mary the mother of Jesus, as well as his brothers.

usurpation. The assertion that the Way is in continuity with Israel can be read consistently as a counter to views like those of Marcion[2] (whose "New Testament" apparently included an edited version of Luke's Gospel together with the letters of Paul, but *not* Acts). Various currents in Jewish thought, including different views of the messiah, were still part of the active debates in which Lukas must have engaged.

In a larger sense the whole discourse of kingdom, and of Jesus' authority as subject to that of the "Father" God—in other words, the power structure of society writ large that is the background of Acts—continues and reinforces the kyriarchal pattern of power and dominance that is assumed as normative not only by Acts but by the biblical writings as a whole (though the New Testament and later writings vary in their desire to impose those norms on the Movement itself). Lukas writes in carefully nuanced language that challenges both the Greek and Roman power and its related cult,[3] but he never alludes to the kyriarchal structures of

2. All that we know about Marcion comes to us from his opponents. His dates are uncertain as well. He regarded the God of Israel as a false and vengeful deity unrelated to the God of Jesus Christ. (It seems that his version of Luke's Gospel omitted the early chapters describing Jesus' embeddedness in Israel, or it may be that Luke 1–2 were not yet part of the Third Gospel as known to Marcion. See Barbara E. Reid and Shelly Matthews, *Luke 1–9*, WCS 43A [Collegeville, MN: Liturgical Press, 2021], lv–lvi, with the works cited in n. 41 there.) Joseph B. Tyson, *Marcion and Luke-Acts: A Defining Struggle* (Columbia: University of South Carolina Press, 2006), sees Acts as a riposte to Marcion, which is possible, though that would push Acts to a very late date. More probably Acts is part of the ongoing debate, one side of which became a "movement" led by Marcion.

3. The word "cult," in this context, refers to a system of religious or quasi-religious veneration directed to symbolic or personified deities or to persons or things designated as holy or "divine," as in the case of the cult of the Roman emperors. Cultic

Kyrious: lord, master
a person exercising absolute ownership rights;
Acts of the Apostles lord (Lord)

society, let alone challenges them. The community he envisions is indeed kyriarchal: it has but one *Kyrios*, namely, Jesus. But the androcentrism of such a society on earth is simply taken as a matter of course. This observation should inform our reading as we proceed.[4]

The promise of the Spirit's power and the vocation to witness "to the ends of the earth" will be programmatic for the remainder of Acts; the first part of the promise will be seen to be fulfilled initially, in surprising fashion, in Acts 2, but there will be subsequent manifestations.[5] Jesus' words are a kind of compound of the commissions in Matthew 28 and Luke 24, though the Matthean scene takes place in Galilee; Matthew's depiction speaks of "authority" (ἐξουσία) and "teaching" (διδάσκοντες); Luke 24 and Acts 1 correspondingly emphasize "power" (δύναμις) and "witness" (μαρτύριον).

There are significant differences as well. Luke and Acts end and begin, respectively, with an "ascension" scene and are the only New Testament documents containing such an event or any reference to it. The two Lukan scenes take place, however, in different locations (though that news comes belatedly in Acts 1:12). In Luke the place is Bethany while in Acts the action plays out on the Mount of Olives. Both use a parallel with Elijah, but whereas in Luke the indeterminate "they" worship Jesus and, after his departure, immediately return rejoicing to Jerusalem, in Acts the "apostles," having displayed their misconception about what is to come next, stand gaping up at the cloud that has removed Jesus from their sight until they are jogged by the "two men in white robes" (cf. Luke 24:4; John 20:12). The message of the two passages inserts the notion of Jesus' parousia, which otherwise plays virtually no overt role in Acts. The book as a whole has nothing to say about an imminent return of Jesus, and its message is directed very much to the progress of the gospel in the here and now.

Another subtle but important difference concerns the scope of the mission. In Luke 24:47 the disciples were told that "repentance and forgiveness

veneration was an important mechanism for shoring up and sustaining Roman power, and violation of its norms could (and did) evoke severe punishment.

4. For this subject see especially Caroline Vander Stichele and Todd Penner, *Contextualizing Gender in Early Christian Discourse: Thinking Beyond Thecla* (London: T&T Clark, 2009), *passim*, as well as two other works edited by Vander Stichele and Penner, *Contextualizing Acts: Lukan Narrative and Greco-Roman Discourse*, SymS 20 (Atlanta: SBL, 2003), esp. Vander Stichele's essay, "Gender and Genre: Acts in/of Interpretation," 311–29; and *Mapping Gender in Ancient Religious Discourses*, BibInt 84 (Leiden: Brill, 2007): in this volume see especially the essay by the two editors, "Scripturing Gender in Acts: The Past and Present Power of *Imperium*," 231–66.

5. Cf. Acts 4:31; 6:3-5; 7:55; 8:15-17; 9:17; 10:44-47; 11:15-16; 13:2, 4, 9, 52; 15:8; 19:2, 6.

of sins is to be proclaimed in [Messiah's] name *to all nations*" (cf. Matt 28:19). At Acts 1:8 nothing is said of "nations"—a term with ethnic and political implications—or of messianic claims; the disciples will be empowered by the Holy Spirit to *be witnesses* "in Jerusalem, in all Judea and Samaria, and to the ends of the earth." It has been conventional for a very long time to see the spatial movement thus described as shaping the whole Acts narrative, with Rome representing "the ends of the earth." But while the real center of Acts is Jerusalem, the second-century audience and those who came after them would have regarded Rome as the *center* of the world, not its end. Augustus completed the conquest of the Iberian peninsula about 19 BCE. Julius Caesar had campaigned in Gaul, as every second-year student of Latin used to know ("*Gallia est omnis divisa in partes tres*"—Caesar's *Gallic Wars* was a standard text). Roman forces invaded Britain beginning in 43 CE, during the reign of Claudius, and that conquest was pretty well complete by 83. In other words, in the story-time of Acts "the ends of the earth" would have been represented in the west by the Atlantic Ocean and in the east by the Parthian Empire in what is now Iran, with the Sahara Desert limiting Roman expansion in North Africa. The Way of Jesus must cover at least that much territory and reach all the peoples within it before the end can come, and it is a calling to all people not to submit to a secular power, whether Roman or any other, but to be joined with Israel in its eschatological completion centered on Jerusalem (see Rev 21:2-4).

The Role of Baptism in the First Centuries

Beginning in the 70s CE and given the troubled state of diaspora synagogues after the destruction of the temple,[6] the debates and proposals about the "restoration of Israel" must have been intense and marked by conflicts.[7] According to the question in 1:6, Lukas, his apostles, and Theophilus (= the community) also took part in this discussion. In Acts 1:5 part of this debate is expressed through the understanding

---

6. See in this regard Ekkehard W. Stegemann and Wolfgang Stegemann, *The Jesus Movement: A Social History of Its First Century*, trans. O. C. Dean Jr. (Minneapolis: Fortress, 1999); Luise Schottroff, "Toward a Feminist Reconstruction of the History of Early Christianity," in *Feminist Interpretation: The Bible in Women's Perspective*, ed. Luise Schottroff, Silvia Schroer, and Marie-Theres Wacker, trans. Martin and Barbara Rumscheidt (Minneapolis: Fortress, 1998), 177–254.

7. The proposals were varied, as the letter to the Hebrews also demonstrates. These conflicts had a strong impact on Marcion's position with its anti-Jewish elements.

of the baptismal rite, here represented by two movements of socio-religious renewal: the followers of John the Baptist and the members of the Way; one baptized with water for repentance and the other "with the Holy Spirit."[8] This implies different identities:[9] to receive the Holy Spirit is henceforth to bear the name of Jesus, the Christ (2:36). The construction of this new identity, therefore, is marked by complexities and conflicts regarding the "restoration of Israel" and the character of the groups surviving the Great War of the 70s.

To be baptized "with the Holy Spirit" means to receive dynamic and transforming power (δύναμις) to testify about the life and work of Jesus Christ (1:8; 2:4, 32, and frequently). This involves a profound

conversion (2:38), reflected in the construction of community life through the experience of spirituality and solidarity (2:41-47). This is Lukas's proposal for "restoring" Israel.

The authorial hand is evident again in verses 9-11 with the second account of Jesus' ascension (cf. Luke 24:50-52). Variations include the apocalyptic elements of the "cloud" (Rev 11:12; 1 Thess 4:17) and the hierophany of the "two men in white robes" (see Luke 24:4),[10] who announce the future return (ἐλεύσαται) of this Jesus. The language is explicitly androcentric: here the two "angels" address the "men" (ἄνδρες, 1:11) who are staring up to heaven, parallel to the two "angels" who spoke to women in the resurrection of Jesus (Luke 24:4).

Ivoni Richter Reimer

Since the publication of *Die Himmelfahrt Jesu*[11] in 1971, Gerhard Lohfink's historical-critical analysis of the ascension scenes in Luke and Acts has been the starting point for all further analysis. He summarizes the several intentions behind Lukas's skillful composition in Acts 1:6-8:

- Continuity is established between the time of Jesus and the time of the church through the spatial symbol of continuity, "Jerusalem."

8. See Acts 18:35–19:6.

9. See below at Acts 2:4; 18:24–19:7.

10. In the narrative of the resurrection Mark 16:5 uses the term "young man" (in a white robe); Matt 28:2 speaks of an "angel" with a white robe, and John 20:12 has "two angels" in white robes; Luke 24:23 also speaks of "angels." This is the language of "epiphany," a profound religious experience of the sacred.

11. Gerhard Lohfink, *Die Himmelfahrt Jesu: Untersuchungen zu den Himmelfahrts- und Erhöhungstexte bei Lukas* (Munich: Kösel, 1971).

parousia - second coming
eschatologica = Theology - relating to death, judgment and the final destiny of the soul + mankind.

- Continuity is cemented between the time of Jesus and that of the church by means of a limited time framework. The Risen One appeared for only forty days, allowing little time for extensive secret revelations.

- Still, within those forty days the Risen One could have spoken of some new and secret things. But no!—Lukas emphasizes that he spoke about the "reign of God" (Acts 1:3), that is, precisely what he always talked about during his public activity before Easter, and nothing else.

The parousia question is also addressed. The disciples ask (1:6) about the time of Israel's restoration, but the Risen One instead points to the world mission in the power of the Spirit; the two "angels" are equally emphatic about that. It is the new Movement's mission to the world that will bring the triumph of the eschatological Israel.[12]

The note about the "mount called Olivet" (also an eschatological symbol, mentioned almost as an afterthought) and its being "a sabbath day's journey away" emphasizes the Torah observance of the Eleven and of the Movement as a whole. The distance was later established[13] as about three-quarters of a mile. Richard Pervo[14] translates σαββάτου ἔχον ὁδόν (lit. "having a Sabbath's journey") as "half a Sabbath day's journey," since presumably the group would have to have traveled there and back in one day.

---

12. Gerhard Lohfink, personal communication with Linda Maloney, March 11, 2020. Lohfink stresses that the doubling of the ascension scene and the continuance of the group of the Twelve represent continuity between the Gospel and Acts. That is certainly true, but in this author's opinion it does not prove single authorship.

13. Cf. m. 'Erub. 4:3 (second to third century CE). Lukas may know of it from Essene practice (see CD 10:21).

14. Richard I. Pervo, *Acts*, Hermeneia (Minneapolis: Fortress, 2009), 46n51, referring to C. K. Barrett, *A Critical and Exegetical Commentary on the Acts of the Apostles*, vol. 1, ICC (London: T&T Clark, 1994), 85–86. From Barrett's calculations it seems that Lukas probably derived his information from Josephus, who places the Mount of Olives five or six stadia (ca. 1,150 meters) from the city; rabbinic sources (e.g., m. 'Erub. 59a; y. Ber. 5.9a.40) set the length of a Sabbath's journey at two thousand cubits (= 1,120 meters). Since a date forty days after Easter would not be a Sabbath, the reference to "a sabbath day's journey" is almost surely another Lukan feature intended to establish the disciples' continued adherence to Jewish law.

Where Did the Movement Begin?

Because of our customary eliding of all differences among the Gospels (and Acts) it has seldom been questioned (until recently) that the Jesus Movement first coalesced in Jerusalem, but in fact Lukas is the only author who says so. According to Matthew and Mark the resurrection witnesses were told to go to Galilee, and it was there that the risen Jesus met them. John 20 breaks off after the scene in the "upper room" in Jerusalem, but the added chapter 21 places Jesus and the disciples back in Galilee, at the Sea of Tiberias.

The historical probability is that the Movement first coalesced in Galilee, where the "apostles" and at least some other believers had fled after Jesus' crucifixion and where a base of Jesus-followers remained. Experiences of the risen Jesus eventually led the Galilean leaders to return to Jerusalem, but certainly not within Lukas's programmatic "forty days."

Lukas has a different story to tell. Luke's Gospel begins and ends in the Jerusalem temple; Acts starts in Jerusalem, and its open ending is set in Rome. His Christology—Jesus as suffering prophet and Messiah-King of Israel, bringing about the opening to the gentiles—demands this scenario. This movement neither began nor will remain in a corner (cf. Acts 26:26); it goes forth from Zion.

Returning to the city, the group[15] repairs to the "room upstairs" and engages in prayer. The Eleven are now named, and we are explicitly told that they are with others, including "certain women" plus Jesus' mother and his brothers. Acts says nothing about disharmony between the apostles and Jesus' family; though none of Jesus' brothers is among the "apostles," one of them (James) will become the leader of the Jerusalem community after the departure of Peter.[16] "Mary" as the name of

15. The "they" who witness the ascension include but are not restricted to the Eleven: see vv. 6, 9. The angelic address, "Men of Galilee" (Ἄνδρες Γαλιλαῖοι), is conventional, like "Men of Judea" (Ἄνδρες Ἰουδαῖοι, 2:14), "Men of Israel (Ἄνδρες Ἰσραηλῖται, 2:22), and "Men, brothers" (Ἄνδρες ἀδελφοί, 1:16; 2:29, 37; 7:2, 26; 13:15, 26, 38; 15:7, 13; 22:1; 23:1, 6; 28:17). This address is reserved for Jewish audiences, and only in 7:2, 26; 22:1; 23:1, 6 can it be certainly assumed to be directed exclusively to men because in those passages Stephen and Paul are supposedly addressing the Sanhedrin.

16. In Luke's Gospel Jesus' brothers are mentioned only once (at 8:19-21) and not by name. In fact, the Lukan Jesus discourages inviting one's brothers to dinner (14:12) and approves "hating" one's family (14:26). See the interesting treatment of the link between Jesus' family (especially James) and strict Torah observance in the Jerusalem

Jesus' mother is traditional in the Synoptics; this is her final appearance. The names of all the rest of Jesus' female followers known from the Gospels have been "scrubbed," though clearly women make up a large portion of the Jerusalem community. One effect of the focus on Jerusalem and the location of the Movement's origins there is to effectively remove from the picture the group of women who followed Jesus in Galilee. The trajectory of Lukas's story is from Zion (= Jerusalem) through "all Judea and Samaria, and to the ends of the earth" (1:8). Galilee is not even a way station on that road.

What Is Mary Doing in Acts?

Mary, the mother of Jesus, is one of the women with the men of Galilee and Jesus' brothers in the upstairs room in Jerusalem. Lukas makes sure we know she is present here, but he never mentions her again in Acts. Even her witness to the identity of Jesus is underrepresented in this book: Peter chooses a replacement for Judas from among those who were with Jesus from the time of his baptism (Acts 1:22). If her witness to Jesus' prebaptismal life is superfluous to Acts, why does Lukas bother to mention her at all?

To suggest an answer to this question we need to follow Lukas's descriptor of this woman, the mother of Jesus, back into the Gospel. Mary's story begins powerfully with her assent to participate in the new work of God (Luke 1:38) and her witness to the constant character of the purposes of God (Luke 1:46-55). Luke depicts her as a prophet who speaks the mind and ways of the God of Israel.[17] She is a prototypical disciple, demonstrating power and vocation for witness. The new community, according to Lukas, embodies these ways: those who fear God are fearless before the powerful (Acts 4:19 and 24:10) and they care for the poor (Acts 2:45 and 4:32).

According to the Gospel, Mary and Jesus' brothers follow Jesus, but when they come to seek him Jesus dismisses them in favor of those who hear the word of God and do it (Luke 8:19-21).[18] The reader of the

---

community in Richard I. Pervo, "My Happy Home: The Role of Jerusalem in Acts 1–7," *Forum* 3 (Spring 2000): 31–55, esp. 36–39. See also the discussion at Acts 1:23 below.

17. Barbara E. Reid, "An Overture to the Gospel of Luke," *CurTM* 39 (2012): 428–34.

18. For an exposition of that story see Gerhard Lohfink, "Compliment and Return Compliment," in *Between Heaven and Earth: New Explorations of Great Biblical Texts*, trans. Linda M. Maloney (Collegeville, MN: Liturgical Press, 2022), 49–53.

Gospel knows, however, that this is an excellent description of the mother of Jesus. By naming Mary as present among the disciples in Acts, Lukas reminds the reader that a Jewish woman embodied (literally) a faithful witness to the works of God. Even briefly noting her presence in Acts affirms her faithfulness and closes her story in an orderly way, establishing her significance as an ideal follower.

Mary's narrative function is different from that of Peter or the other apostles who will carry the story from Jerusalem to the ends of the world. Where they move the story of the Movement across ethnic boundaries, Mary reminds us of the roots of the story in

Israel, through whom God acted for the life of the world. Like the ascension and the events of Pentecost, the accounts placed before and after the prayers in the upstairs room in Jerusalem, Mary draws us into reflection on the deepest mystery of the gospel, "the interface between heaven and earth," and provides a paradigm for living human life in a truly faithful way.[19] *This paradigm is a Jewish woman.* Thus Lukas indicates that the story of the Way is continuous with the story of Israel, as he will affirm again when Peter uses Israel's Scriptures to direct and interpret the nascent life of the community.

Jo-Ann Badley

It will appear in the next scene that the criterion for apostleship is having been a witness to Jesus from the time of his baptism by John until his resurrection. This makes Mary the proto-apostle, the original witness.[20]

19. J. D. G. Dunn, "The Ascension of Jesus: A Test Case for Hermeneutics," in *Auferstehung—Resurrection: The Fourth Durham-Tübingen Research Symposium: Resurrection, Transfiguration and Exaltation in Old Testament, Ancient Judaism and Early Christianity*, ed. Friedrich Avemarie and Hermann Lichtenberger, WUNT 135 (Tübingen: Mohr Siebeck, 2001), 302 and 313.

20. On Mary in Acts see especially Jo-Ann Badley, "What Is Mary Doing in Acts? Confessional Narratives and the Synoptic Tradition," in *Rediscovering the Marys: Maria, Mariamne, Miriam*, ed. Mary Ann Beavis and Ally Kateusz, LNTS (= JSNTSup) 620 (London: Bloomsbury T&T Clark, 2020), 47–58. The shift of community and worship from the temple to the synagogue and house assembly gave an important boost to women's leadership and participation. See Bernadette J. Brooten, *Women Leaders in the Ancient Synagogue: Inscriptional Evidence and Background Issues*, BJS 36 (Chico, CA: Scholars Press, 1982); on the ambiguities of women's status at this point in Acts and later see Turid Karlsen Seim, *The Double Message: Patterns of Gender in Luke-Acts* (Edinburgh: T&T Clark, 1994).

politcia ~ citizenship

What about the Temple?

One problem with positing joint authorship of Luke and Acts is their different treatments of the Jerusalem temple. It is not news that Luke's Gospel begins and ends in the temple (Luke 1:8; 24:52); Jesus is presented in the temple as an infant and greeted there by the prophets Simeon and Anna (2:22-38); in the temptation scene, the third and culminating test takes place "on the pinnacle of the temple" (4:9-12), and Jesus teaches in the temple even as a youth (2:46-50), calling it "my Father's house" (2:49); he returns there to teach at the end of his ministry (19:45–21:38). After the ascension his disciples return to Jerusalem, as instructed, "and they were continually in the temple blessing God" (24:52).

Contrast Acts: In 1:4, as in Luke 24:49, Jesus instructs the disciples to remain in Jerusalem. But in Acts they return from Olivet and go not to the temple but "to the room upstairs where they were staying" (1:13), and apparently that is where they remain, avoiding public notice, until after the Pentecost event; not until 2:46 do we learn that they are now spending "much time together in the temple." (Quite possibly "the room upstairs" is not in Jerusalem but in Galilee and represents the early stage of the Movement before its return to Jerusalem.) Concretely, Luke 21:38 tells us that "all the people would get up early in the morning to listen to [Jesus] in the temple," but the first temporal notice in Acts says that Peter and John were "going up to the temple at the hour of prayer, at three o'clock in the afternoon" (Acts 3:1). In the Gospel the sun is rising over the temple as Jesus teaches there; in Acts it is declining toward its setting.

What Luke and Acts do have in common in this regard is the characterization of Jesus' enemies. They are those officially associated with the temple and therefore with the Roman occupiers: the priesthood (now appointed by the secular authority), the scribes, the Sadducees—in other words, the Jerusalem *politeia*. In the Gospel the Pharisees are often critical of Jesus and his teaching and are criticized by him, though they also seek to protect him from Herod.[21] In Acts the portrayal of Pharisees is entirely positive, even though some of them are associated with the temple (Acts 5:34; 23:6-9; 26:5; see the analysis of 15:5 below).

The two texts appear to reflect two very different time periods and historical situations. The writer of the Gospel is still close to the soul-shattering destruction of Jerusalem and the temple, when conflicts

21. On Pharisees in Luke see Reid and Matthews, *Luke 1–9*, 180–82; Joseph Sievers and Amy-Jill Levine, eds., *The Pharisees* (Grand Rapids: Eerdmans, 2021).

and recriminations among Jewish groups and sects were especially painful; the temple, its significance and its glory, is a memory to be cherished and a hope to be retained. Acts shows a situation in which the temple is definitively a thing of the past. Dialogue between Pharisees and the Jesus movement is still cultivated, both in the homeland and in the diaspora, and both groups are uneasy about rising political-religious tensions with Rome that might (and very soon would) lead to further bloodshed and banishment. The early Movement and then Paul (himself a Pharisee: Acts 23:6; 26:5, and cf. Phil 3:5) are rejected by the Roman-collaborating temple authorities (though the Romans are portrayed as more benevolent than the Sadducees!). Acts bows to the past but looks to the future, as do the founders of rabbinic Judaism with whom its author is in dialogue.[22]

22. Nadav Sharon, *Judea under Roman Domination: The First Generation of Statelessness and Its Legacy*, EJL 46 (Atlanta: SBL Press, 2018), argues passionately that, from the time of the Hasmoneans onward, Judaism was living increasingly (even within Judea) in a diaspora situation that under Roman rule "significantly qualified the centrality of and all-encompassing reverence for the temple, thus setting the stage for the postdestruction era" (311). He points to Herod's choosing the high priests, who were, or were regarded as, his puppets, as well as the fact that in that era prophets (like John the Baptizer) led people into the "desert" and taught there, not in the temple. In addition he speaks of the rising importance of the diaspora institution of the synagogue (identified with the Pharisees, who emphasized teaching and keeping the Torah). Whether one accepts his basic thesis or not, Sharon has assembled important information about the period that is worthy of consideration. See also Lester L. Grabbe, *Judaic Religion in the Second Temple Period: Belief and Practice from the Exile to Yavneh* (London: Routledge, 2000).

Acts 1:15-26

Making Up the Twelve (Male) Apostles

" **I** n those days" (ἐν ταῖς ἡμέραις ταύταις) is a favorite phrase of this author (Acts 1:15; 6:1; 11:27; cf. Luke 24:18); as a narrative device it elides any gaps between events. The story moves rapidly here; what is important is that during the undefined period between Jesus' departure and the promised coming of the Spirit the number of the Twelve must be completed. By the time Acts was written, the theologians of the ἐκκλησία had already formulated the notion of "twelve apostles," matching the twelve tribes of Israel (cf. Matt 10:2; 19:28; Mark 3:14, 16; Luke 6:13; 22:30).[1]

Likewise, we first learn here that Peter is the leader of the postascension community. In the Gospels he is a denier of Jesus, just as Judas is the betrayer;[2] though there are some indications in Luke's Gospel that

---

1. It is interesting in this context that the phrase "one of the twelve" is applied *only* to Judas in the Synoptic Gospels (Mark 14:10, 43; *parr.* Matt 26:14, 47; Luke 22:3, 47). His sole other designation is "betrayer" (παραδιδοὺς, participle of παραδίδωμι, lit. "hand over," thus "one who hands over").

2. It appears that this man's name really was Ἰούδας, a common name with some variant spellings that English renders "Judah," "Judas," or "Jude." Though Israel's history had many honorable men of the name, from Judah son of Jacob to Judas Maccabaeus, "Judas" was reserved in Christian polemic for the disciple who allegedly

Acts 1:15-26

[15]In those days Peter stood up among the believers (together the crowd numbered about one hundred twenty persons) and said, [16]"Friends, the scripture had to be fulfilled, which the Holy Spirit through David foretold concerning Judas, who became a guide for those who arrested Jesus—[17]for he was numbered among us and was allotted his share in this ministry." [18](Now this man acquired a field with the reward of his wickedness; and falling headlong, he burst open in the middle and all his bowels gushed out. [19]This became known to all the residents of Jerusalem, so that the field was called in their language Hakeldama, that is, Field of Blood.) [20]"For it is written in the book of Psalms,

'Let his homestead become desolate,
    and let there be no one to live in it';

and

'Let another take his position of overseer.'

Peter will be restored to leadership, Luke 24 is ambiguous.[3] Peter visits Jesus' tomb and finds it empty but remains puzzled (the male disciples in Luke's account do not believe the women witnesses). Later we learn from others that "the Lord is risen indeed and has appeared to Simon" (Luke 24:34),[4] but we do not hear anything about the encounter. Nothing is said in either ascension account about Peter, though in Acts 1:13 he is (as always in the Synoptics) first in the list of apostles. Here in verse 15 he suddenly appears in the role of leader. While Peter is in one sense the model community leader in Acts, Lukas did not consider it possible

---

handed Jesus over to be killed. One fatal consequence was that, because someone named Ἰούδας was definitively a member of the Ἰουδαῖοι, he became a pejorative symbol for Jews in the minds of many Christians. Because of patristic and medieval usage, and especially because it is John's passion that is read on Good Friday in the Roman Catholic Church and others that share the Catholic tradition, the Johannine portrait of Judas is and has been the first image of him in most Christians' minds for many centuries.

3. It may be that Luke 24, like Luke 1–2, is an addition. See Barbara E. Reid and Shelly Matthews, *Luke 1–9*, WCS 43A (Collegeville, MN: Liturgical Press, 2021), lvi–lvii; Barbara E. Reid and Shelly Matthews, *Luke 10–24*, WCS 43B (Collegeville, MN: Liturgical Press, 2021), 626–27.

4. Luke's Gospel frequently refers to Simon Peter as "Simon" (Luke 4:38; 5:3-5, 8, 10; 6:14-15; 22:31; 24:34; the instances in chaps. 5, 22, and 24 are Luke's own material), but in Acts he is called "Simon" only in chaps. 10–11, the story of the conversion of Cornelius, which is thus clearly based on community tradition.

²¹So one of the men who have accompanied us during all the time that the Lord Jesus went in and out among us, ²²beginning from the baptism of John until the day when he was taken up from us—one of these must become a witness with us to his resurrection." ²³So they proposed two, Joseph called Barsabbas, who was also known as Justus, and Matthias. ²⁴Then they prayed and said, "Lord, you know everyone's heart. Show us which one of these two you have chosen ²⁵to take the place in this ministry and apostleship from which Judas turned aside to go to his own place." ²⁶And they cast lots for them, and the lot fell on Matthias; and he was added to the eleven apostles.

that subsequent leaders would have the apostolic charism[5] and role. The Twelve are unique.[6]

The story of Judas's end has almost nothing in common with Matthew's tradition[7] except for the "Field of Blood." The account in Acts 1 is shaped in accordance with a common preoccupation of Luke's Gospel as well as Acts, that love of money and possessions is the most insidious of sins; it even led Judas to the ultimate corrupt act: betrayal of the Lord.[8] The only thing worse than loving money for its own sake is trying to use it to buy spiritual power (cf. Acts 8:18-24). But the link to concern for the poor is absent from Acts: the word πτωχοί, so common in Luke's Gospel,[9] never appears. (Neither, indeed, does the word πλούσιος, "rich"![10]) There is only reference to the "needy," of whom there supposedly were none

5. A charism (from Greek χάρισμα "favor, grace"), in church parlance, is a divine gift bestowed on a person to enable her to act for the benefit of others, either in an office or through a special talent or character trait.

6. Acts is *kyriocentric* inasmuch as the Jesus movement has but a single *kyrios*: Jesus. Otherwise it is *androcentric* (male-centered): none of the church's leaders in Acts, not even the apostles, are depicted as figures of authority outside the community context.

7. Cf. Matt 26:31-56; 27:3-10; "Field of Blood" is at 27:8. The parenthesis in vv. 18-19 clashes blatantly with its context: Aramaic speakers would not need to have *Hakeldama* translated for them, nor would Peter refer to it as being "in their language"! This information is for the (mainly Greek-speaking) audience of Acts.

8. That money was Judas's motive is explicitly alleged in all three Synoptics. John goes still further, writing that Judas objected to Mary's anointing of Jesus (John 12:1-8) "not because he cared about the poor, but because he was a thief; he kept the common purse and used to steal what was put into it" (v. 6).

9. Ten appearances in Luke to zero in Acts.

10. Twelve appearances in Luke to zero in Acts.

among the disciples in Jerusalem(!),[11] and to those having possessions that, ideally, were placed at the service of the community.[12]

The choice of Judas's replacement presents some curious features as well as some characteristic Lukan themes. Readers and hearers of the Gospels would have been familiar with a whole list of followers of Jesus, both women and men. (In fact, in all the Gospel accounts it is *women*, not men, who are the first witnesses to the resurrection.) Yet no person known from the Gospels, female or male, is put forward to replace Judas. Peter states, as the first qualification, that the candidate is to be "one of the *men* [ἄνδρες] who have accompanied us" (v. 21)—even though the Gospel accounts (Matt 27:55; Mark 15:41; Luke 8:2; 23:55) repeatedly speak of *women* who traveled with Jesus from Galilee. The emphasis is clear: no woman can be an apostle in Lukas's sense of the word.[13]

Androcentric Language and Patriarchy

The first Christian "historiographical work" uses the apostolic authority of Peter narratively to set the criterion of male exclusivity in the exercise of hierarchical-institutional power. In this context the speech makes a point of presenting Judas's greed and sin as disqualifying him for the apostolate; however, the discourse likewise disqualifies women *because they are women* by simply ignoring them, thereby preventing them from officially being what they were and are: full participants in the life of discipleship and apostolic witnesses of the resurrection! The narrative is constructed in such a way as to legitimize the choice of the twelfth male apostle while simultaneously discriminating against and disqualifying women. In the same way it is necessary to reaffirm the full qualification of women in the

11. Acts 4:34; the obvious meaning there is that it was *because of* their community membership that none were needy.

12. The first such person mentioned is Barnabas (4:37), who serves as a counterfoil to Ananias and Sapphira; Tabitha (Acts 9:36-43) and Lydia (Acts 16:11-15, 40) are other upright examples.

13. Or of Paul's: his list of witnesses to the resurrection in 1 Cor 15:3-8 mentions no women, unless we are to assume that they are included among the "five hundred brothers." (The NRSV makes the inclusive move, calling them "brothers and sisters" with a note that the Greek has only "brothers," ἀδελφοί.) See Ivoni Richter Reimer, "Apostolado, diaconia e missão de mulheres nas origens do cristianismo: rever tradições para empoderar e promover cidadania plena," *Revista Pós-Escrito* 4 (2011): 110–26.

androcentrism - practice, conscious or otherwise, of placing a masculine point of view at the center of one's worldview, culture and history thereby marginalizing femininity

Jesus movement in order to perceive the conflict between the different traditions and the possibility, for that very reason, of constructing other forms for the Way, even today.

The androcentrism represented here may be linked to patriarchal/kyriarchal ideologies in Greco-Roman culture shared by some people of higher sociocultural status who joined the Way (among whom we may number the author of Acts).

Ivoni Richter Reimer

Still, why two otherwise-unknown men? Is it because the one chosen will be only a placeholder, a symbolic unit to make up the number twelve? A known person might have had various traditions attached to him, which would distract from the symbolic point. As it is, Matthias—as a name and nothing more—appears here and only here. The case is not quite the same with "Joseph [or: Joses] called Barsabbas, who was also known as Justus" (v. 23), who gets nine descriptive words to Matthias's none. Is "Joseph called Barsabbas" the same as the "Joseph, to whom the apostles gave the name Barnabas" in Acts 4:36? Or is he Joseph the brother of Jesus (cf. Matt 13:55; Mark 6:3)? Still a third possibility: is he a conflation of two brothers of Jesus, one named Joseph and the other named James? The latter is elsewhere called "the Just" (or "Justus") and is apparently the figure who succeeds Peter in the leadership of the community in Judea.[14] If this is the case there may be traces here of a leadership conflict in Jerusalem that Lukas smoothes over, as is his habit.[15]

The prayer reflects developing liturgical usage in the second-century church. God is the only one Scripture calls a "knower of hearts." The

14. Hegesippus, *Fragments* 1. John Painter, *Just James: The Brother of Jesus in History and Tradition* (Columbia: University of South Carolina Press, 1997), 44, asserts that "Acts explicitly names no single leader of the Jerusalem church" and that "Peter's prominence is in terms of his missionary activity in relation to the community at large rather than as leader of the church community." Acts 1 appears to contradict that position, since *before* any missionary outreach, and in the assembly that includes the whole community, Peter (at least according to Acts) takes the initiative in calling for the choice of a twelfth "apostle" and determines the qualifications for the office.

15. Richard I. Pervo, "My Happy Home: The Role of Jerusalem in Acts 1–7," *Forum* 3 (Spring 2000): 47 suggests another motive: "The criteria for an apostle . . . *are* in substance historical, but not early, for they represent the ultimate victory of those who would deny to Paul the title of apostle."

eaclesiastical - of or related to the church

Episcopal Church's eucharistic liturgy opens, even today, with a collect beginning "O God, to whom all hearts are open . . ."

Choosing by lot is good "biblical" practice (Lev 16:8-10; Num 26:55-56; 33:54; 34:13; 36:2, and frequently; see esp. Pss 16:5; 22:18 with Matt 27:35; Mark 15:24; Luke 23:34). Proverbs has two sayings: "The lot is cast into the lap, but the decision is the LORD's alone" (16:33); "Casting the lot puts an end to disputes and decides between powerful contenders" (18:18). If "canonical" Luke and Acts belong to the same author and/or are associated books, this scene may form an *inclusio* with the choosing of Zechariah by lot to serve in the temple (Luke 1:9), as in each case the lot is cast to choose a man for service to the Lord.

Thus the number of the "apostles" is completed—although, as Ivoni Richter Reimer writes, "it left indelible scars on the history of the church and in the history of Christian women, since ecclesiastical and political-social hierarchies have taken it as a model and have legitimized their structures of power and domination in speeches and narratives like the one presented here."

With the initial structure of the community of the Way in place, it remains only for the promise of the gift of the Spirit to be fulfilled.

theophany: used of any temporary, normally visible, manifestation of God

It is to be distinguished from that permanent manifestation of God in Jesus Christ, called the incarnation

Acts 2:1-13

Pentecost: The Spirit Falls on the Whole Company of Women and Men

The theophany in verses 1-4 echoes Old Testament models, in particular that at Sinai (Exod 19:16). Since Pentecost (Shavuot), the harvest festival occurring fifty days after Passover, was becoming identified in the second century with the celebration of the giving of the law at Sinai, Lukas's intention here is probably to make that connection. As Moses was on the mountain with the Lord for forty days and nights (Exod 34:28), so the disciples were instructed for forty days by the risen Jesus and are now anointed with the Holy Spirit to proclaim the messianic age to the people. The elements of wind and fire also reflect the Sinai event. (In fact, transferring fire is one of the "works" permitted on Shavuot; the Holy Spirit acts accordingly![1])

1. Whenever Lukas writes of the "Holy Spirit" it is in the context of Israel's experience and insights (as in, for example, Gen 1:2; Exod 31:3; Num 11:29; Ps 143:10). The idea of a triune God was far in the future, as was the maleness of all three Persons: the root of "Spirit" is "wind": Hebrew רוח (*ruaḥ*, feminine); Greek πνεῦμα (*pneuma*, neuter); Latin *spiritus* (masculine). See below, "Holy Spirit Mother in Early Christianity."

Acts 2:1-13

²˙¹When the day of Pentecost had come, they were all together in one place. ²And suddenly from heaven there came a sound like the rush of a violent wind, and it filled the entire house where they were sitting. ³Divided tongues, as of fire, appeared among them, and a tongue rested on each of them. ⁴All of them were filled with the Holy Spirit and began to speak in other languages, as the Spirit gave them ability.

⁵Now there were devout Jews from every nation under heaven living in Jerusalem. ⁶And at this sound the crowd gathered and was bewildered, because each one heard them speaking in the native language of each. ⁷Amazed and astonished, they asked, "Are not all these who are speaking Galileans? ⁸And how is it that we hear, each of us, in our own native language? ⁹Parthians, Medes, Elamites, and residents of Mesopotamia, Judea and Cappadocia, Pontus and Asia, ¹⁰Phrygia and Pamphylia, Egypt and the parts of Libya belonging to Cyrene, and visitors from Rome, both Jews and proselytes, ¹¹Cretans and Arabs—in our own languages we hear them speaking about God's deeds of power." ¹²All were amazed and perplexed, saying to one another, "What does this mean?" ¹³But others sneered and said, "They are filled with new wine."

Holy Spirit Mother in Early Christianity?

Acts mentions Holy Spirit forty-seven times but the Father only three. Today the trinitarian creed ties Father, Son, and Holy Spirit together as one, which makes Holy Spirit appear male too. In the early Christian era, however, Holy Spirit was sometimes remembered as female and mother.[2]

The most famous example is from the first- or second-century Gospel of the Hebrews. Origen of Caesarea (184–253) reported that this Hebrew gospel quoted Jesus himself after his baptism as speaking of "My mother, the Holy Spirit" (*Comm. Jo.* 2.6; *Hom. Jer.* 15.4). The second-century Greek Acts of Thomas 5.49 similarly describes the apostle Thomas after a baptism calling on Holy

2. Robert Murray, *Symbols of Church and Kingdom: A Study in Early Syriac Tradition* (Cambridge: Cambridge University Press, 1975), 312–20; Sebastian J. Brock, *Holy Spirit in the Syrian Baptismal Tradition*, Syrian Churches Series 9, 2nd ed. (Pune, India: Anita Printers, 1998), 16–36; Susan Ashbrook Harvey, "Feminine Imagery for the Divine: The Holy Spirit, the *Odes of Solomon*, and Early Syriac Tradition," *SVTQ* 37 (1993): 111–39; and Ally Kateusz, *Mary and Early Christian Women: Hidden Leadership* (New York: Palgrave Macmillan, 2019), 142–43.

Spirit as "Mother."[3] Irenaeus of Lyons, writing in Greek in Gaul around the year 180, recorded (disapprovingly) that some Christians spoke of their "Mother" Holy Spirit (*Adv. Haer.* 1.5.3). Several first- or second-century Coptic texts from the Nag Hammadi library appear to describe Holy Spirit as mother, including Gospel of Philip 55.24-26; Gospel of Thomas 101; and Apocryphon of John 10.17-19; also, the Gospel of the Egyptians (III 41.7-9; 42.4; 56.24; 58.3-4; 59.13-14) repeatedly describes a divine triad of Father, Mother, and Son.[4] Finally, the femininity of Holy Spirit appears to have been so important to some pre-Constantinian Latin Christians that on their epigraphs they changed the masculine-gendered *spiritus sanctus* to the feminine-gendered *spirita sancta*.[5] Around the year 410 Jerome argued that the motherhood of Holy Spirit was based on mere linguistic serendipity because "spirit" was feminine-gendered in Hebrew, neuter in Greek, and masculine in Latin (*Comm. Isa.* 11.24), yet the evidence demonstrates that the early Christian identification of Holy Spirit as Mother was accepted around the Mediterranean regardless of language.

What happened to her? Perhaps the Council of Constantinople in 380 is implicated, because its bishops are the ones who changed the creed to read that the Holy Spirit was identical in nature to the Father and Son—making her appear male. Consistent with this credal change as the proximate cause, Sebastian Brock says, "Towards the end of the fourth century Syriac [Aramaic] writers began to become wary about addressing Holy Spirit as Mother"; they began to change the feminine gender of "spirit" to masculine in their texts.[6] Susan Ashbrook Harvey adds that these scribes' grammatical changes "did violence to the fabric of the language."[7] Today we can be certain of one thing: the early Christian memory of Holy Spirit as Mother soon disappeared from view.

Ally Kateusz

3. Numbering from Han J. W. Drijvers, trans., "The Acts of Thomas," in *NTApoc* 2, ed. Wilhelm Schneemelcher, trans. R. McL. Wilson, rev. ed. (Cambridge: James Clark, 1992), 322–411, at 359–60.

4. Numbering from *NHL*.

5. Graydon F. Snyder, *Ante-Pacem: Archaeological Evidence of Church Life before Constantine* (Macon, GA: Mercer University Press, 1985), 126; Fernand Cabrol and Henri Leclercq, eds., *Dictionnaire d'archéologie chrétienne et de liturgie* (Paris: Letouzey et Ane, 1907–1953), 3.1, col. 1335; 7.1, col. 1006.

6. Brock, *Holy Spirit*, 19.

7. Harvey, "Feminine Imagery," 118.

The numbers of those who receive the Spirit in "the house" are uncertain. The text is ambiguous, perhaps deliberately so. For one thing, it would require a very large room to hold 120 people (see 1:15).[8] The focus immediately before this was on the Eleven and the choice of Matthias, but the action involved the whole community. There seems no good reason to think that in 2:1 "all together" (ὁμοῦ) refers only to a particular group. Certainly Lukas makes it seem that the subsequent audience for Peter's speech is entirely male (see commentary on 1:15-26 above), but in referring to the believers there in verse 15 Peter only speaks of "these" and avoids a gendered pronoun. While the likelihood that Lukas pictures women as speaking afterward to a supposedly all-male Jewish crowd in Jerusalem is very small, we should not doubt, in light of what follows, that he intends to say that the Spirit fell on the whole group of women and men gathered "together in one place."

Some commentators have observed that it is redundant to write that there were "Jews" living in Jerusalem. Apparently that was the opinion also of an early scribe, the writer of Codex Sinaiticus (א), who omitted the word. But Lukas is nailing down the point that this is a *Jewish* audience, belonging to the people Israel, now resident in Jerusalem (hence probably very devout),[9] but whose origins stretch throughout the diaspora, even "to the ends of the earth" (1:8). When the missionaries of the gospel travel to those places, the story sometimes implies that the people have already heard from their relatives in Jerusalem about this marvelous thing; perhaps envoys even discover that, as on this day, they are endowed by the Spirit with the ability to speak the local language (cf., e.g., 14:8-18). In any case Lukas means for the audience to know that the message is intended first and primarily for the people of Israel.

The earliest Christian authors were fascinated with the prophet Isaiah and the promise of a "pilgrimage of the nations" to Zion (Isa 2:2-5 = Mic 4:1-4). That vision is in the background of Matthew's account of the magi, and it underlies this passage in Acts as well, for these Israelites from the

---

8. In Lukas's time a roomy house-church might hold forty people; most houses would have been stretched by twenty or even fewer.

9. Diaspora Jews who moved their residence to Jerusalem, often referred to as "Hellenists"—see below at Acts 6—were in many cases submitting themselves to a life more economically and politically circumscribed than what they enjoyed in their homelands. Their choice to live in Jerusalem would often, at that time, have been motivated by apocalyptic expectations—though it was an apocalyptic belief that drove the Qumran Essenes *out* of Jerusalem.

diaspora are surely, in Lukas's view, a sign that their nations will follow, once the gospel has been preached to them.

The list of nations itself is peculiar: it contains some archaic ethnic designations ("Parthians, Medes, Elamites") and omits the whole of Greece, which is so central to Acts 17–20. Probably Lukas was using an older list and failed to modify it appropriately—for example, by omitting "Judea," which is the location of the scene itself. Richard Pervo writes of verses 10-11 that Ῥωμαῖοι designates citizens of Rome, not merely residents of the city itself. Apparently these include both "Jews by birth and Jews by choice/proselytes" as distinct from the "devout Jews . . . living in Jerusalem." Pervo writes that "the story symbolizes both the universality of the message . . . and the capacity of the gospel to address all sorts and conditions of people in their own terms,"[10] but the focus on the Jewish people should not be minimized.

"God's deeds of power" or "the mighty works of God" will be thematic in Acts (cf. 5:13; 10:46; 19:17). The essence of the apostolic proclamation is to bring to the attention of God's people, and through them to the whole world, that God is powerfully at work in the world in Jesus and now, after his exaltation, through the Holy Spirit. Reception of this knowledge, in Acts, is inevitably accompanied by acclamation and praise of God, as the gift of human freedom requires that God's gracious actions be freely accepted.[11] Proleptically, the Jerusalem crowd of Ἰουδαῖοι—except, of course, for the skeptics who chalk the utterances up to drunkenness—plays the role that will henceforth be assigned to the followers of the Way. The note in verse 13 about those who "sneered" is the first portent of a coming division between receptive hearers and scoffers and is a tribute to the author's skill in creating a narrative account.

10. Richard I. Pervo, *Acts*, Hermeneia (Minneapolis: Fortress, 2009), 58, 66. However, his equation of Ῥωμαῖοι with Roman citizens is questionable. See the excursus, "Did Paul Claim to be a Roman Citizen?" at pp. 236–38 below.

11. See Linda M. Maloney, *"All That God Had Done with Them": The Narration of the Works of God in the Early Christian Community as Described in the Acts of the Apostles*, AUS ser. 7: Theology and Religion 91 (New York: Lang, 1991), *passim*.

Acts 2:14-40

Peter's Pentecost Speech

Peter's initial speech closely resembles that of Paul in Acts 13:15-41, a key pairing of the two "apostles." Peter stands with "the eleven"; the remaining disciples are out of the picture. Ἄνδρες Ἰουδαῖοι (men of Judea) is a typical form of address, here emphasizing the Jewish character of the audience; Paul's ἄνδρες ἀδελφοί in 13:15, spoken in the synagogue in Pisidian Antioch, has the same function. Lukas emphasizes again and again in this chapter that the Movement is Jewish, its message directed to Jews. That message is shaped in terms of Jewish Scripture, retracing the history of Israel and ending with the powerful *peroratio*, "Therefore let *the entire house of Israel* know with certainty. . . ."[1]

Lukas makes no attempt at realism: how could a crowd of three thousand or more (cf. v. 41) have assembled in one place, and how could Peter have been heard by such a vast assembly?[2] Lukas had almost surely never

1. "Messiah" would not be a concept gentiles would readily understand at the time when this speech was supposedly given, though it would be familiar to later generations of the Movement who are Lukas's audience.

2. Much has been written about the speeches in Acts as Lukan compositions. The current consensus is that, whatever traditional theological material may underlie the speeches in Acts—which are much more numerous than in most historical works—they are thoroughly Lukan compositions and a feature of Lukan narrative that lends it a more "popular" and "novelistic" flavor than "straight history." Lukas's audience would have understood that.

¹⁴But Peter, standing with the eleven, raised his voice and addressed them, "Men of Judea and all who live in Jerusalem, let this be known to you, and listen to what I say. ¹⁵Indeed, these* are not drunk, as you suppose, for it is only nine o'clock in the morning. ¹⁶No, this is what was spoken through the prophet Joel:

¹⁷'In the last days it will be, God declares,
that I will pour out my Spirit upon all flesh,
and your sons and your daughters shall prophesy,
and your young men shall see visions,
and your old men shall dream dreams.
¹⁸Even upon my slaves, both men and women,
in those days I will pour out my Spirit;
and they shall prophesy.
¹⁹And I will show portents in the heaven above
and signs on the earth below,

* οὗτοι, "these" is ungendered.

blood, and fire, and smoky mist.
²⁰The sun shall be turned to darkness
and the moon to blood,
before the coming of the Lord's great and glorious day.
²¹Then everyone who calls on the name of the Lord shall be saved.'

²²"You that are Israelites, listen to what I have to say: Jesus of Nazareth, a man attested to you by God with deeds of power, wonders, and signs that God did through him among you, as you yourselves know—²³this man, handed over to you according to the definite plan and foreknowledge of God, you crucified and killed by the hands of those outside the law. ²⁴But God raised him up, having freed him from death, because it was impossible for him to be held in its power. ²⁵For David says concerning him,

'I saw the Lord always before me,
for he is at my right hand so that I will not be shaken;

seen Jerusalem, certainly not as it was before 70 CE; it is only a stage-set for the drama. At the same time, the language may be meant to convey that the Spirit has the power to enter and enliven "souls" even of those not physically present.

The scriptural citations reflect the rabbinic technique of *pesher*,[3] but in inverted fashion: instead of beginning with a scriptural passage and

3. *Pesher*, "interpretation" (in the Hebrew Bible only at Eccl 8:1), is found in its Aramaic form, *peshar*, thirty-one times in Daniel, mainly in reference to dream interpretation. It is especially frequent in the Qumran documents, which reflect a

²⁶therefore my heart was glad,
and my tongue rejoiced;
moreover my flesh will live in
hope.
²⁷For you will not abandon my
soul to Hades,
or let your Holy One
experience corruption.
²⁸You have made known to me the
ways of life;
you will make me full of
gladness with your
presence.'
²⁹"Fellow Israelites, I may say to you confidently of our ancestor David that he both died and was buried, and his tomb is with us to this day. ³⁰Since he was a prophet, he knew that God had sworn with an oath to him that he would put one of his descendants on his throne. ³¹Foreseeing this, David spoke of the resurrection of the Messiah, saying,

'He was not abandoned to Hades,
nor did his flesh experience
corruption.'
³²This Jesus God raised up, and of that all of us are witnesses. ³³Being therefore exalted at the right hand of God, and having received from the Father the promise of the Holy Spirit, he has poured out this that you both see and hear. ³⁴For David did not ascend into the heavens, but he himself says,

'The Lord said to my Lord,
"Sit at my right hand,
³⁵until I make your enemies
your footstool."'
³⁶Therefore let the entire house of Israel know with certainty that God has made him both Lord and Messiah, this Jesus whom you crucified."

³⁷Now when they heard this, they were cut to the heart and said to Peter and to the other apostles, "Brothers, what should we do?" ³⁸Peter said to them, "Repent, and be baptized every one of you in the name of Jesus Christ so that your sins may be forgiven; and you will receive the gift of the Holy Spirit. ³⁹For the promise is for you, for your children, and for all who are far away, everyone whom the Lord our God calls to him." ⁴⁰And he testified with many other arguments and exhorted them, saying, "Save yourselves from this corrupt generation."

seeking current application, the speaker here starts with current events and looks for Scripture to explain them.[4] The real intended audience is not the assembled "men of Judea" but Lukas's contemporaries; although the speech is crafted for its projected scene, the theology it expresses

---

technique of quoting the prophetic books verse by verse, with each verse followed by an interpretation designed to give the "plain meaning" of the prophet's words. See https://www.jewishvirtuallibrary.org/pesher.

4. This is a technique more familiar to modern audiences, who recognize it both from the New Testament text and from sermons.

overlaps with at least some part of intra-Jewish debate as Lukas knew it (and may have participated in it) in the early second century. Ultimately it says what Lukas believes the resulting conclusions should be!

Certainly these diverging ways of interpreting the Hebrew Scriptures are symptomatic of conflicting trends in theology and practice. Lukas is the "chronicler" of (what he hopes will be) a model story of the beginnings of the Jesus movement, resting on (some) traditions and (some) methods of interpretation projected as "real" and normative. They are, of course, reflective of the conflicts and developments of Lukas's own time and must be read in that context.

The reference to "my slaves, both men and women," in verse 18 is often taken to indicate universalism, encompassing even slaves, but in reality it has nothing to do with enslaved persons. These are τοὺς δούλους μου καὶ . . . τὰς δούλας μου—*my* (= *God*'s) slaves, male and female. This is an alteration of Joel 2:29 LXX (Hebrew 3:2), which refers simply to "the male and female slaves," עבדים ועל־השפחות‎ על־ה. The LXX text of Joel is mixed; it inserts μου after δούλους but not after δούλας. Lukas's usage is controlling here: δοῦλοι/δουλής are the servants of God; actual enslaved persons specifically mentioned as such in Acts (both of them female: Rhoda in 12:13-15 and the woman with the Pythonic spirit in 16:16) are referred to as παιδίσκη. This more closely reflects the Hebrew, which, as we see above, has very different words for male and female slaves.

Usage of *Δούλος, Δούλης, Παῖς, Παιδίσκη* in Acts

Παιδίσκη is the feminine form of παῖς, which can mean both "child" and "slave." The LXX routinely writes παῖς καὶ παιδίσκη for such expressions as "menservants and maidservants" or "male and female slaves." Matthew uses παῖς for the centurion's slave (8:6, 8, 13, *par.* John 4:51), for a boy who is healed (17:18), and in quoting the first Servant Song in Isaiah 42, making it a reference to Jesus (12:18). Luke's only uses are at 2:43 with reference to the "child" Jesus, at 7:7 for the centurion's slave, and at 8:54 to represent

Jesus' command to Jairus's daughter (a literal translation of Mark 5:41, Ταλιθα κουμ, "Talitha cum"; here, uniquely, παῖς is used as address to a female, and it is a change from Mark, who uses the common term for "little girl," κοράσιον). Luke's Gospel consistently refers to actual "slaves" as δοῦλοι, but Acts *never* does. In Acts, Jesus himself is called παῖς, but his followers are generally δοῦλοι, μαθηταί, πιστεύσοντες, ἀδελφοί ("servants," "disciples," "believers," "brothers" [the generic masculine in all cases but one: Tabitha alone is a μαθήτρια in 9:36]). In the Gospel the feminine δουλή is used only for Mary as "servant of the Lord" (1:38, 48). At Acts 20:12 the young man Eutychus, probably a slave, is called παῖς. As regards status in the community, this is a key observation. Enslaved persons in the audience for Acts, and especially women and girls, would surely have noticed that they alone are called παῖς or παιδίσκη, together with the παῖς Jesus, who thus ranks with the enslaved. Whatever status belongs to him is thus implicitly attributable to them. As we reflect in our own time on the implications and consequences of enslavement, would it not be appropriate to try reading terms like παῖς and δοῦλος with new eyes and analyzing the usage in Luke and Acts against that background?

TRANSLATION MATTERS

At Acts 2:24 the NRSV does a disservice to its readers by omitting any reference to the "pains" or "pangs" of death. It reads "but having freed him from death," with a note: "*Gk* the pains of death." The KJV has "having loosed the pains of death," which is a rather literal translation of the Greek λύσας τὰς ὠδῖνας τοῦ θανάτου. The NABRE has "the throes of death." This matters because the word for "pains" or "pangs" (or "throes") is ὠδῖνας, plural of ὠδίν, whose primary meaning is "experience of pains associated with childbirth." The secondary meaning is metaphorical but is tied to the primary one: "great pain (as in giving birth)" (BDAG, 1102). The word is used very frequently in the metaphorical sense, in both Greek and Jewish literature, especially with regard to the end-time crisis or messianic event (e.g., Mark 13:8 // Matt 24:8; 1QH xi.8-10) or in imagery like that in Revelation 12:2, where the verb (ὠδίνω) is used. The author of Acts, however, does not use the word anywhere but here.

In fact, this verse in Acts is the only one in the New Testament in which ὠδῖνας are experienced by an individual male. The background is most certainly Greek literature, in which heroes such as Herakles undergo such pains. Nicole Loraux writes: "Greek men . . . never cease in their suffering to imitate the woman in childbirth, whether by aping her with their bodies or borrowing her language of suffering. Thus the name for the labor of giving birth . . . becomes the generic designation for searing pain. . . . The model for suffering is feminine; women's physical suffering is used to express moral pain. It is also used to express—which is even more interesting—the suffering of men afflicted in body."[5] In summary, she writes, ὠδίν is "the feminine word for suffering."[6]

5. Nicole Loraux, *The Experiences of Tiresias: The Feminine and the Greek Man*, trans. Paula Wissing (Princeton: Princeton University Press, 1995), 34.
6. Ibid., 32.

TRANSLATION MATTERS (cont.)

The translators of the LXX had already begun the process of attaching Hebrew חִיל, the verb describing a woman in labor, only to humans and not to God: compare Psalm 89 [90]:2 LXX, "Before the mountains existed, and before the earth and the world were formed" with, e.g., Deuteronomy 32:18, "Thou hast forsaken the God that begot thee." English translators have tended to change the active form to a passive: e.g., the mountains "were brought forth" in Psalm 90:2 (with amazing consistency from AV to NRSV.[7]

Lukas, however, was very probably in dialogue with members of the emerging rabbinic movement and so could have been aware of their developing traditions, which attached this language to the "woes of the Messiah," that is, to apocalyptic. Rabbi Eliezer is said to have spoken in those terms around 90 CE.[8] Paul used it in a related sense with reference to the end-time sufferings of the community, but Lukas is determinedly nonapocalyptic; his thought develops in parallel, at least, to that of the rabbis: that the work of God's people is here on earth and they have no business speculating about the end (cf. Acts 1:6-8).

Characteristically, the postapostolic fathers and the apologists had little use for this language, except to disparage women: for example, 2 Clement 2:1-2 makes Isaiah 54:1 "Sing, O barren one" into "a warning against timorousness (in prayer) as in the case of women in labour" (!).[9]

Acts 2:24, then, serves especially well to point out the implications of gendered reading. When this passage was read in a first- or second-century context the male audience would probably have heard the metaphor on a secondary level, as an intense expression for a man's suffering.[10] But the female audience? They would most certainly have heard the author identifying Jesus' suffering with their own. In short, with this usage Lukas is "queering"[11] Jesus, freeing him

---

7. Other versions: AV, "Of the Rock *that* begat thee thou art unmindful, and hast forgotten God that formed thee"; NIV, "You deserted the Rock, who fathered [!] you, you forgot the God who gave you birth"; *Living Bible*, "They spurned the Rock who had made them, Forgetting it was God who had given them birth"; NRSV adds a footnote, "Or *that begot you*."

8. Cf. Georg Bertram, ὠδίν, ὠδίνω, TDNT 9 (1974): 667–74, esp. 671–73.

9. Ibid., 674. Clearly, anyone who describes a woman in labor as "timorous" has never seen one and needs to spend some hours viewing *Call the Midwife* (a TV series based on the memoirs of Jennifer Worth, set in the 1950s–60s in East End London).

10. See Mikeal C. Parsons and Martin M. Culy, *Acts: A Handbook on the Greek Text* (Waco, TX: Baylor University Press, 2003), 37: "The use of τὰς ὠδῖνας makes for a vivid expression: 'the childbirth-like/intense pains of death.'"

11. For an explanation of queer theory see, e.g., Sean D. Burke, *Queering the Ethiopian Eunuch: Strategies of Ambiguity in Acts*, Emerging Scholars (Minneapolis: Fortress, 2013); see also his essay on the Ethiopian eunuch at Acts 8 below. Very briefly, queer-

TRANSLATION MATTERS (cont.)

from stereotypical imagery that would define him as primarily or exclusively male rather than fully human. The same applies to the language for "child" and "slave" discussed above.

We may even go further: some interpreters of John 19:34-37 read the scene of blood and water issuing from Jesus' pierced side as representing the birth of renewed and redeemed Israel. The Fourth Gospel is supposed to have been composed in Ephesus, perhaps not long before Lukas was writing Acts in that city. The use of ὠδῖνας here, we propose, is part of a women's theology of Jesus' sufferings that reflects the experiences of women giving birth, and Lukas accepted that theology as part of his portrayal of Jesus' relationship to his redeemed community.

Lukas alters the Joel text in several ways.[12] Rabbinic exegesis did refer the prophecy of Joel to the end time, but Lukas's theology is anything but apocalyptic, so the change from the LXX "afterward" must be regarded as an alteration of Lukas's text. The citations from the Psalms do not prove that "David" was referring to Jesus, only that the psalmist was not speaking of himself, but they serve the purpose: to demonstrate that Jesus is the promised Messiah (χριστός, v. 36), anointed by God. The people of Jerusalem (i.e., the fictive audience) ignored the "deeds of power, wonders, and signs" he did in their midst and handed him over to be killed "by the hands of those outside the law." This phrase is partially exculpatory, since it may be taken as referring to the Romans—though without naming them, which would have been politically inexpedient. Nevertheless, all this took place according to the divine plan; moreover, as we learn in 3:17, the people "acted in ignorance" (despite the wonders and signs!).

---

ing is a strategy for shattering the illusion of normativity as regards gender, sexuality, and other social constructs taken to be "natural" or "essential."

12. Replacing "after this" with "in the last days" (v. 17) is not one of them. "In the last days" (ἐν ταῖς ἐσχάταις ἡμέραις) is probably a revision; it is not Lukan language, and the LXX reads μετὰ ταῦτα, "afterward" or "after these things," at Joel 2:28. Lukas's changes to the LXX Joel text include the insertion of "God declares" (λέγει ὁ θεός); reversing the order of "your young men . . . your old men . . ." (but keeping the same wording); the insertion of "and they shall prophesy" (καὶ προφητεύσουσιν) and the specifications "above" (ἄνω) and "below" (κάτω); he also improves the grammar by writing "before the coming" (πρὶν ἢ ἐλθεῖν) instead of "before [the . . . day of the Lord] come" (πρὶν ἐλθεῖν). An audience in the know would understand that what Peter is really saying is "in these days" or "today"—these things are happening *now*.

Jesus, having been raised by God and exalted, has poured out the Holy Spirit on believers: here at last we have the real answer to the charge that they are drunk! Peter ends by pointing out that the Spirit is the gift of "this Jesus whom you crucified," but when the audience is deeply moved by the speech and asks the Twelve, "what should we do?" there is a ready answer: repent ("turn," μετανοήσατε) and be baptized; your sins will be forgiven, and you too will receive the Holy Spirit. "For the promise is for you, for your children, and for all who are far away; everyone whom the Lord our God calls to him." This could later be read as a statement of universalism, but in the narrative context "all who are far away" could simply mean Jews in the diaspora, and those "whom the Lord *our* God calls to him" would mean the people of Israel before—and perhaps excluding—all others. In Lukas's conception, shared by many Jews of his era (see below on groupings within Judaism), gentiles could only be called to Israel's God through the life and example of the people Israel. "Everyone who calls on the name of the Lord will be saved" (v. 21), but being able to call on the name of the Lord is itself God's gift, mediated by those whom God has already called.

"Save yourselves from this corrupt generation [γενεᾶς σκολιᾶς ταύτης]" narrows the guilt to those of the fictive moment; Lukas's audience is off the hook, provided they respond to the call of "the Lord our God." The phrase γενεᾶς ταύτης in a pejorative sense is frequent in the LXX and in the Gospels,[13] but the added σκολιᾶς (in the metaphorical sense of "corrupt, morally crooked") is found only in late New Testament texts (and in Josephus).[14] Here we have another indicator of the social context of Lukas's audience.

---

13. Particularly in the "sign of Jonah" pericopes in the Synoptics (Matt 12:38-41; Luke 11:29-32; cf. Mark 8:11-12).

14. The LXX prefers the verb διαφθείρω and its cognates ("be depraved, corrupt"; see 1 Tim 6:5). Σκολιός has the primary meaning of "bent" and thus the metaphorical sense is "crooked," which by extension also means "corrupt," as in Acts 2:40; in 1 Peter 2:18 it is usually translated as "harsh" when applied to slavemasters. (See BDAG, 930.) *The Living Bible* deserves some respect here: it translates σκολιός in that verse as "tough and cruel"!

Acts 2:41-47

The Jerusalem Community: First Summary

The three major summaries in the Jerusalem section of Acts
(2:37-47; 4:32-37; 5:12-16) knit the story of the successful early
mission in Jerusalem together, smoothing transitions between conflict
situations that evoke speeches from Peter. These summaries act as "re-
volving doors" that sweep the audience from one scene to another, preventing a tedious sequence of "and then . . . and then." They also paint
a utopia (a popular literary form at least since Plato): in the beginning
was the model community, and all communities of Jesus' followers could
be such, if today's believers behaved like the first ones![1]

Different from many utopias, this one makes no mention of gender
relationships, hierarchies, and the like. Apparently the existing social
mores are preserved. Unlike what Plato describes in *Republic* 5, there is

---

1. The modern concept is derived from Thomas More's fifteenth-century *Utopia*
("Nowhere"). In general it refers to idealistic literary portrayals (including Plato's,
in his late work *Laws*, book 3) or real-life attempts to create self-sustaining, strife-free
communities based on religious or secular ideals. For the background in the ancient
world see Mary Ann Beavis, *Jesus & Utopia: Looking for the Kingdom of God in the Roman
World* (Minneapolis: Fortress, 2006). For contemporary examples see the website of
the Foundation for Intentional Community at https://www.ic.org.

Acts 2:41-47

⁴¹So those who welcomed his message were baptized, and that day about three thousand persons were added. ⁴²They devoted themselves to the apostles' teaching and fellowship, to the breaking of bread and the prayers.

⁴³Awe came upon everyone, because many wonders and signs were being done by the apostles. ⁴⁴All who believed were together and had all things in common; ⁴⁵they would sell their possessions and goods and distribute the proceeds to all, as any had need. ⁴⁶Day by day, as they spent much time together in the temple, they broke bread at home and ate their food with glad and generous hearts, ⁴⁷praising God and having the goodwill of all the people. And day by day the Lord added to their number those who were being saved.

evidently no idea that when "all who believed were together and had all things in common" this included women and children as common property, but neither is there any suggestion that the women who had been gifted with the Spirit, either in the Pentecost event indoors or by baptism subsequently, were called on to bear public witness. It is assumed that they continued in their domestic functions. One wonders whether the "things" (i.e., property) held in common included persons. If someone sold "possessions and goods" and distributed the proceeds, would that include human property as well? If fields were sold (cf. 4:34, 37), what happened to the laborers, free or slave, who worked them? If such questions even occurred to Lukas there is no evidence of it.[2]

In these scenes our author is certainly proposing a model for second-century Christian life in the urban centers of the empire as he knew them; he is not repeating traditions about first-century Jerusalem. Hence his picture is drawn with an extremely broad brush. The passage opens and closes with a phrase favored by our author in this first section of the book, ἐπὶ τὸ αὐτό, translated "together" in verse 44 and subsumed into "their number" in verse 47. More precisely, it means "in the same place," as clearly in 2:1, but it appears as "together" in NRSV here and in Acts 1:15; 4:26.[3] On the whole it seems that in these first chapters Lukas

2. Social justice as understood in different ages is ordinarily a basic presupposition of utopian communities; for example, those created in nineteenth-century North America were almost all aligned with the antislavery movement. There was no such movement in the ancient world.

3. Modern English translations are content with "added" to their number; the Authorized Version had "added" to the church.

thinks of it as a collective concept for belonging to the core Movement as it comes into being.[4]

The word translated "persons" in verse 41 is ψυχαί (Latin: *anima*, "souls, spirits"), and it is used again immediately afterward in verse 43 to refer to "everyone," apparently all those in Jerusalem who became aware of what was happening. The usage finesses any gender reference while also emphasizing the spiritual/pneumatic character of the events: the Spirit works where it wills. (See at 2:14 above.)

Another word to be noted is ὁμοθυμαδόν. Ten out of eleven New Testament verses containing this word are in Acts (1:14; 2:26; 4:24; 5:12; 7:57; 8:6; 12:20; 15:25; 18:12; 19:29; Rom 15:6). Though it can simply be another way of saying "together," the contexts in which Lukas uses it indicate that for him it signifies "being of one mind" or having a common purpose.[5] Lukas is not a fan of the monarchical episcopate, the modeling of church leadership on royal or imperial forms (as will appear), and so from time to time he makes a point of emphasizing that decisions and actions are taken by agreement of the whole group of believers—thus obliquely countering the strong contemporary (to him) emphasis on monarchical bishops as reflected in the writings of his contemporaries or near-contemporaries, including the letters of Ignatius and the Pastoral Epistles.[6]

The believers, under the apostles' leadership, spend their days in the temple (presumably in prayer and also in listening to the apostles' teaching) and their evenings "breaking bread" and "eating their food." Probably

4. Scribes had a very hard time with it in verse 47, as the mixed manuscript tradition reveals. For details on the text see Mikeal C. Parsons and Martin M. Culy, *Acts: A Handbook on the Greek Text* (Waco, TX: Baylor University Press, 2003), *ad loc.* The phrase is applied exclusively to the Jerusalem community in Acts; its last appearance is at 4:26, in the second summary.

5. For discussion see Linda M. Maloney, *"All That God Had Done with Them": The Narration of the Works of God in the Early Christian Community as Described in the Acts of the Apostles*, AUS ser. 7: Theology and Religion 91 (New York: Lang, 1991), 49; 61n37, with reference to Jacques Dupont, "L'Union Entre les Premiers Chrétiens dans les Actes des Apôtres," in *Nouvelles Études sur les Actes des Apôtres*, LD 118 (Paris: Cerf, 1984), 296–318. Despite his aversion to top-down leadership in the developing church, the author of Acts lived his whole life in the context of the Roman Empire, which necessarily shaped his overall worldview.

6. For the relative dating of Acts, the Pastorals, and the Letters of Ignatius see esp. Richard I. Pervo, *Dating Acts: Between the Evangelists and the Apologists* (Santa Rosa, CA: Polebridge, 2006); Michael Theobald, *Israel-Vergessenheit in den Pastoralbriefen: ein neuer Vorschlag zu ihrer historisch-theologischen Verortung im 2. Jahrhundert n. Chr. unter besonderer Berücksichtigung der Ignatius-Briefe* (Stuttgart: Katholisches Bibelwerk, 2016).

Lukas envisions the kinds of gatherings with which he is familiar or those Paul describes, e.g., in 1 Corinthians, in which the eucharistic celebration is integrated into a communal meal. The practice was early, but not *that* early. The Jerusalem community is still worshiping "day by day" in the temple. It seems that, in Lukas's interpretation, the public praise of God and apostolic teaching are instrumental in gaining public goodwill and drawing new converts to the Movement, but, as will appear in chapter 3, not every ψυχή in Jerusalem was equally impressed.

Acts 3:1–4:4

Peter and John in the Temple with a Man Who Cannot Walk

In Acts 1–2 all was sweetness, light, and harmony (except for the memory of Judas, of course). Beginning at Acts 3 the narrative is driven by conflict and persecution, even though such trouble in no way impedes the growth of the Movement but instead enhances it. But Acts 3 also continues the erasure of the women of the Jerusalem community as active subjects. Though women are implicitly present and active in various summaries and community scenes (e.g., 4:23-31), and though they are presumably as much in possession of the Holy Spirit as the community's men, the work of preaching, stated at the outset as the community's purpose, is reserved to men, primarily the apostles.

Giving credit where it is due, we must say that Lukas nowhere criticizes or diminishes women *as women*—despite the fact that pagan authors began very early to denigrate the Movement by saying that the behavior of its women revealed the illegitimacy of this "superstition." Thus Celsus (as quoted by Origen) dismissed the story of Jesus' resurrection by attributing it to "a hysterical female . . . and perhaps some other one of those who were deluded by the same sorcery."[1]

---

1. Origen, *Contra Celsum* 2.70. The reference is evidently to Mary Magdalene.

Acts 3:1–4:4

3:1One day Peter and John were going up to the temple at the hour of prayer, at three o'clock in the afternoon. 2And a man lame from birth was being carried in. People would lay him daily at the gate of the temple called the Beautiful Gate so that he could ask for alms from those entering the temple. 3When he saw Peter and John about to go into the temple, he asked them for alms. 4Peter looked intently at him, as did John, and said, "Look at us." 5And he fixed his attention on them, expecting to receive something from them. 6But Peter said, "I have no silver or gold, but what I have I give you; in the name of Jesus Christ of Nazareth, stand up and walk." 7And he took him by the right hand and raised him up; and immediately his feet and ankles were made strong. 8Jumping up, he stood and began to walk, and he entered the temple with them, walking and leaping and praising God. 9All the people saw him walking and praising God, 10and they recognized him as the one who used to sit and ask for alms at the Beautiful Gate of the temple; and they were filled with wonder and amazement at what had happened to him.

11While he clung to Peter and John, all the people ran together to them in

Knowing this makes it easier to understand (though still inexcusable) that early Christian men such as the author of the Pastorals (in, e.g., 1 Tim 5:3-16; 2 Tim 3:6-7), Justin (*Apology* 2.2), and Ignatius of Antioch (*Poly* 4, 5) wanted to make their church acceptable and unthreatening by confining women to "traditional" roles. Margaret Y. MacDonald summarizes accurately: "The end of the first century CE onward was characterized by an increased 'patriarchalization' of the church that manifested itself in an appeal for Christian wives to be model wives according to Greco-Roman ideals of fidelity and subjugation; such patriarchalization is said to have occurred as a direct result of early Christian concern for their public image in the face of growing societal hostility."[2] As she observes in her conclusion, the danger was that much greater because the women of the early communities of the Way *were* often unconventional and therefore threatening, to outsiders and insiders as well.

The scene of the healing of the man born lame, Peter's first miracle, is also a means of marginalizing women, even though in our culture and in English translation it appears to have nothing to do with women at all.

---

2. Margaret Y. MacDonald, *Early Christian Women and Pagan Opinion: The Power of the Hysterical Woman* (Cambridge: Cambridge University Press, 1996), 10.

the portico called Solomon's Portico, utterly astonished. [12]When Peter saw it, he addressed the people, "You Israelites, why do you wonder at this, or why do you stare at us, as though by our own power or piety we had made him walk? [13]The God of Abraham, the God of Isaac, and the God of Jacob, the God of our ancestors has glorified his servant Jesus, whom you handed over and rejected in the presence of Pilate, though he had decided to release him. [14]But you rejected the Holy and Righteous One and asked to have a murderer given to you, [15]and you killed the Author of life, whom God raised from the dead. To this we are witnesses. [16]And by faith in his name, his name itself has made this man strong, whom you see and know; and the faith that is through Jesus has given him this perfect health in the presence of all of you.

[17]"And now, friends, I know that you acted in ignorance, as did also your rulers. [18]In this way God fulfilled what he had foretold through all the prophets, that his Messiah would suffer. [19]Repent therefore, and turn to God so that your sins may be wiped out, [20]so that times of refreshing may come from the presence of the Lord, and that he may send

Mikeal Parsons[3] emphasizes the belief in the ancient world that external characteristics reveal inner qualities; thus the characteristics of the female body show the contours of the inner person (inferior), while those of the (ideal) male body show the man's personal superiority. Soul and body react on one another; changes in the body have corresponding effects on the soul, and vice versa. To the present case, Pseudo-Aristotle wrote that "those who have strong and well-jointed ankles are brave in character; witness the male sex. Those that have fleshy and ill-jointed ankles are weak in character; witness the female sex."[4] Similarly as to feet: "Those who have well-made, large feet, well-jointed and sinewy, are strong in character; witness the male sex. Those who have small, narrow, poorly-jointed feet, are rather attractive to look at than strong, being weak in character; witness the female sex."[5]

3. Mikeal C. Parsons and Martin M. Culy, *Acts: A Handbook on the Greek Text* (Waco, TX: Baylor University Press, 2003), *ad loc.*; see also Parsons, *Body and Character in Luke and Acts: The Subversion of Physiognomy in Early Christianity* (Waco, TX: Baylor University Press, 2011).

4. Pseudo-Aristotle, *Physiognomy* 810a.25-29.

5. *Physiognomy* 810a.15-22.

Acts 3:1–4:4 (cont.)

the Messiah appointed for you, that is, Jesus, [21]who must remain in heaven until the time of universal restoration that God announced long ago through his holy prophets. [22]Moses said, 'The Lord your God will raise up for you from your own people a prophet like me. You must listen to whatever he tells you. [23]And it will be that everyone who does not listen to that prophet will be utterly rooted out of the people.' [24]And all the prophets, as many as have spoken, from Samuel and those after him, also predicted these days. [25]You are the descendants of the prophets and of the covenant that God gave to your ancestors, saying to Abraham, 'And in your descendants all the families of the earth shall be blessed.' [26]When God raised up his servant, he sent him first to you, to bless you by turning each of you from your wicked ways."

[4:1]While Peter and John were speaking to the people, the priests, the captain of the temple, and the Sadducees came to them, [2]much annoyed because they were teaching the people and proclaiming that in Jesus there is the resurrection of the dead. [3]So they arrested them and put them in custody until the next day, for it was already evening. [4]But many of those who heard the word believed; and they numbered about five thousand.

The man at the Beautiful Gate has been, as it were, "feminized" from the womb; his useless and deformed feet and ankles would have marked him as "effeminate" and weak in character. He is an altogether negative figure whose only aim in life is to collect money; unlike persons with disabilities in the Gospels who look to Jesus for healing, this man has no expectation of it. His miraculous transformation is thus far more radical than those of the Gospel characters. His very nature is changed: he becomes a *man* as well as a believer and now stands (leaps, dances) alongside the apostles themselves. It is probably significant that nowhere in the Gospels or Acts do we read of the healing of a woman with weakened or nonfunctional limbs. The only similar healing is that of the bent-over woman in the synagogue, and in her case the healing is justified by the explicit statement that she is a "daughter of Abraham whom Satan held bound" (Luke 13:15).[6]

6. For the theme of salvation as release of the world from Satanic bondage see Susan R. Garrett, *The Demise of the Devil: Magic and the Demonic in Luke's Writings* (Minneapolis: Fortress, 1989).

Physiognomy

The ancient "science" of physiognomy purported to enable the analysis of character on the basis of external appearances and behavior. It related physical features to internal dispositions, either through the shape and character of the face and body (the anatomical method), through characteristics thought to be shared with certain animals (zoological), or by classification according to "race." (That these ideas are not really a thing of the past seems obvious enough.) All these were measured against the ideal, the "free man," or, by the time of Acts, specifically the Roman male citizen. Colonized peoples absorbed these ideas, especially when they were relatively congruent with their own social structures and attitudes.

In a recent study Cristiana Franco has shown that archaic Greek culture (as illustrated, for example, by Hesiod) had developed a "zoological" connection between dogs and women. Dogs associate with humans, share their food and houses, yet they are not human. Thus "dog" from an early time became shorthand for suggesting that a person so described might not be fully human. The insult was more often applied against women than men because women's humanity was more or less in doubt: they were far removed in shape and behavior from the free male. At that early period being κύνεος ("dog-like," metaphorically "shameless") was not exclusively a female trait, but its application to the character of Pandora was typical. It remained for later iterations of Western culture to specify "dogginess" as typical of "bitches."[7]

The author of Acts offers few physical descriptions of characters except where necessary to portray a healing. (While Acts, unlike the apocryphal Acts of Paul, never gives a physical description of Paul, it shows him being accepted as a Roman by other Romans, thus implying that his physical and mental features were ideal. The conflict of that portrayal with accounts of his having been beaten will be discussed in a later chapter.) We, in turn, are so accustomed to language that applies the

7. See Cristiana Franco, *Shameless: The Canine and the Feminine in Ancient Greece*, trans. Matthew Fox (Berkeley: University of California Press, 2014); cf. the reference to this work in Emily Wilson, "A Doggish Translation" (review of Barry B. Powell, *The Poems of Hesiod* [Berkeley: University of California Press, 2017]), *NYRB* 15 (January 18, 2018): 35–36.

assumptions of physiognomy (e.g., a man, but never a woman, has a "leonine" head) that careful reading is necessary.[8]

So the man at the temple gate is not only healed; he is "masculinized" and therefore "humanized" by his healing. No wonder he capers with such unbounded joy! For the first time in his life he has real status.

At 4:1 a new set of actors enters the scene.[9] The temple authorities have been alerted to the goings-on. It is entirely unlikely that the topmost officials of the temple would have come out personally to deal with such a trivial matter, but Lukas's plan demands that the onus for the tension between Christianity and Second Temple Judaism(s) must be placed first and above all on the religious authorities and not on the people as a whole. The "captain of the temple" would have been the highest-ranking person below the high priest. Both the Gospels and Josephus assert that the Sadducees, who were generally identified with the temple governance and were branded as collaborators with the Roman authority, were characterized religiously by their denial of a resurrection of the dead. Consequently, although the truly radical assertion in Peter's speech is that the Messiah had to suffer[10] and the language about resurrection is ambiguous, Lukas here has the officials zero in on the resurrection as the forbidden topic.

The scene ends with the coming of nightfall and the hearing is adjourned until morning, but not without a note that, in contrast to and in defiance of the officials, another five thousand men (ἄνδρες)[11] joined the Movement.

---

8. A useful exercise in preparation for "physiognomy-conscious" reading is to spend some time with a work such as Gerd Brantenberg, *Egalia's Daughters: A Satire of the Sexes*, trans. Louis Mackay (Emeryville, CA: Seal Press, 1985). Example: "Now physical strength, it is true, is reckoned to be a very feminine quality. That is why the wom, being smaller, does much harder physical training than the manwom" (99).

9. The division of the text into chapters and verses occurred much later and therefore should not control the way the text is read. Acts 4:1-4 continues and completes the account that began at 3:1.

10. There is no tradition in Judaism(s) of a suffering messiah, and the Isaiah texts about the "Suffering Servant" have almost always been read collectively, in reference to the Jewish people.

11. Although the NRSV renders ἄνδρες inclusively, "many . . . they," it denotes males, unlike ἄνθρωποι.

A Note on "Ableism"

Concern for preventing various forms of discrimination against those who are differently abled is relatively new in Western society. The texts of the New Testament generally regard disability (loss of sight, hearing, mobility) as an evil to be overcome and probably in some way the fault of the sufferer (see, e.g., John 9:1-2). The major concern is to free the person from her or his disability. So also here: the man born lame is restored to full health and function. There appears to be no concern for what happens after. Rehabilitation was not a "thing" in the ancient world. The man in this story, like others we encounter in the New Testament, has gained a livelihood by begging. Now he has no reason to beg, but how is he to live? He likely has never learned a trade; he obviously has no estate, perhaps not even a family. We learn at 4:22 that he is "more than forty years old," which was well past middle age in the first and second centuries. Lukas's underlying idea is surely that he will be accepted as a member of the Movement, where he can serve as a witness to God's mercy bestowed on him through Jesus. He will be worth remembering when we read that the group "had all things in common"—including, evidently, their possession of abilities or lack thereof—and each is valued equally with all others. That is the Lukan ideal of community.[12]

12. It is also the ideal of "Beloved Community" being sought by some churches in this century. See Stephanie Spellers, *The Church Cracked Open: Disruption, Decline, and New Hope for Beloved Community* (New York: Church Publishing, 2021), 30: "In beloved community, nobody is inferior or superior, of greater or lesser value. . . . Because the world has cast certain groups down, God provides the extra honor necessary to balance those wrongs and achieve equity. Their experiences become gifts to the whole."

Acts 4:5-22

The Apostles on Trial

Lukas now leads onto the stage the principal villains of the Movement's story about Jesus and his followers: the temple officialdom. Annas[1] and his son-in-law Caiaphas were familiar to readers/hearers of the Gospels. "John" is probably Jonathan, one of Annas's sons who succeeded Caiaphas and was high priest from 36 to 37 (thus either Caiaphas or Jonathan would be the active high priest in the story-world). "Alexander" is unknown. Lukas would have supplemented the information in the Gospels with further details from Josephus. This scene is the paradigm for all subsequent encounters in Acts between the Movement and "Jews": ordinary people, and even leading Pharisees, are awed by what they see and hear, but the leadership (central and local) remains obdurate and grows increasingly hostile.

In terms of physiognomy and the reigning interpretation of bodies and status this confrontation is perhaps even more revolutionary than

---

1. Annas's tenure as high priest ended in 15 CE when he was succeeded by his son-in-law, Caiaphas, who held the office until 36 CE, being then followed by Jonathan, the first of a succession of Annas's sons. (See Josephus, *Ant.* 18.95.) It appears, however, that Annas was regarded as somehow holding life tenure and so is regularly called high priest during the reigns of his son-in-law and sons. See Martin Goodman, *The Ruling Class of Judaea: The Origins of the Jewish Revolt against Rome A.D. 66–70* (Cambridge: Cambridge University Press, 1987).

Acts 4:5-22

[5]The next day their rulers, elders, and scribes assembled in Jerusalem, [6]with Annas the high priest, Caiaphas, John, and Alexander, and all who were of the high-priestly family. [7]When they had made the prisoners stand in their midst, they inquired, "By what power or by what name did you do this?" [8]Then Peter, filled with the Holy Spirit, said to them, "Rulers of the people and elders, [9]if we are questioned today because of a good deed done to someone who was sick and are asked how this man has been healed, [10]let it be known to all of you, and to all the people of Israel, that this man is standing before you in good health by the name of Jesus Christ of Nazareth, whom you crucified, whom God raised from the dead. [11]This Jesus is

'the stone that was rejected by
  you, the builders;
  it has become the
    cornerstone.'

[12]There is salvation in no one else, for there is no other name under heaven given among mortals by which we must be saved."

[13]Now when they saw the boldness of Peter and John and realized that

those between Jesus and the high-priestly family, for while in that case these ruling authorities were able to destroy their opponent (as they thought), here their efforts at punishment are futile. Their recognition of Peter and John as "uneducated and ordinary men" (and "companions of Jesus" as well) who nevertheless speak with eloquence is a status reversal of earthshaking proportions (quite literally, as the next scene will show). Moreover, the other despised body, that of the formerly lame man, stands beside them, and it is the apostles who have removed the defective character of that body, as the authorities think (since they reject the power of Jesus).

Elite men in antiquity were educated in rhetoric.[2] Contemporaries of Lukas would know that an orator was supposed to be a model of ideal

---

2. For a full treatment of the art of rhetoric as practiced by New Testament writers see Mikeal C. Parsons and Michael Wade Martin, *Ancient Rhetoric and the New Testament: The Influence of Early Greek Composition* (Waco, TX: Baylor University Press, 2018). Elite Greek and Roman boys (almost never girls) of what we would consider high school age moved from the elementary tasks of learning to write and read Greek (later, Latin as well) and followed a strict curriculum (the so-called *progymnasmata*) to achieve facility in written and oral expression, useful both for public speaking and for written composition: the summary term for the skill is rhetoric. See also George A. Kennedy, "The Speeches in Acts," in *New Testament Interpretation through Rhetorical Criticism* (Chapel Hill: University of North Carolina Press, 1984), 114–40.

they were uneducated and ordinary men, they were amazed and recognized them as companions of Jesus. [14]When they saw the man who had been cured standing beside them, they had nothing to say in opposition. [15]So they ordered them to leave the council while they discussed the matter with one another. [16]They said, "What will we do with them? For it is obvious to all who live in Jerusalem that a notable sign has been done through them; we cannot deny it. [17]But to keep it from spreading further among the people, let us warn them to speak no more to anyone in this name." [18]So they called them and ordered them not to speak or teach at all in the name of Jesus. [19]But Peter and John answered them, "Whether it is right in God's sight to listen to you rather than to God, you must judge; [20]for we cannot keep from speaking about what we have seen and heard." [21]After threatening them again, they let them go, finding no way to punish them because of the people, for all of them praised God for what had happened. [22]For the man on whom this sign of healing had been performed was more than forty years old.

masculinity, something simply unattainable by lower-class men (and, of course, enslaved men and all women). Because the orator's skills could be learned and imitated by those two groups, however, intense discipline was required. His speech, and the norms and values he presented, must "reflect the ideology of those in power, which, in turn, justifies the dominant social and moral order, thereby supporting its ideology."[3] That Peter and John, in the eyes of the ruling authorities of Judea, were certainly not doing that is glaringly obvious and deeply disturbing to the powerful. These are Galileans, after all, not only uneducated but probably illiterate, certainly not masters of Greek rhetoric! This confrontation is a potent example of Lukas's subversive technique. Here he critiques and even ridicules (in subtle fashion) a set of powerful men associated with the occupying power, but because these men are "Jews" it is less likely that the Roman authorities will perceive the criticism as relating to themselves.

Crucifixion was the ultimate device for shaming a body and therefore a person. That was a major reason why it was reserved for enslaved persons and traitors. Asked in what name they have healed, the apostles respond that they act "in the name of Jesus, whom you crucified," a

3. Caroline Vander Stichele and Todd Penner, *Contextualizing Gender in Early Christian Discourse: Thinking Beyond Thecla* (London: T&T Clark, 2009), 69.

direct blow at the canon of honor and shame, of right and wrong. These peasants are already "turning the world upside down" (Acts 17:6), presaging things to come.

If Lukas had Jewish readers/hearers who remembered events in Judea in the late first century they would not have harbored warm feelings toward the Annas family in any case. All the high priests of this period, including Annas, Caiaphas, and Jonathan, were appointed by the Roman governors or the Herodian ruler subject to Rome; thus the perception that the temple authorities, in the time before the Jewish Revolt of 66 to 70 CE, were working hand in glove with the occupiers was not in any way inaccurate. Upstart would-be religious and/or political authorities from the "peasantry" or other nonpriestly classes were all too frequent, from the aristocrats' point of view, and this Jesus movement was just one more. We can be certain of that because of the way the Jewish historian Flavius Josephus described the times in his *The Jewish War* and *Antiquities of the Jews*. Those works could have been familiar to Lukas[4] and possibly to at least some of his audience as well. Probably no one from Judea outside the ruling elite would have failed to hear the edge in the apostles' saying, "Whether it is right in God's sight to listen to you rather than God, you must judge." To members of the Movement, of course, the significance was all the more profound.

The elevation of "uneducated and ordinary men," as well as the healing of one formerly weak in the feet and ankles, had subversive significance for women and enslaved men also, in the longer run. The rise of one despised status group could not but cast doubt on the defined low status of others, and the disruptive effect of such perceptions intrudes here and there on the consciousness of readers of Acts. Lukas attempts to portray the early community as altogether harmonious, but contrary traditions surface in chapters 5 and 6. Still, this first clash with the religious authorities will be followed by a reassuring scene of unanimity (ὁμοθυμαδὸν) and the power it engenders.

We should note Lukas's soteriology as stated in verse 12: "there is no other name under heaven [except that of Jesus] given among mortals

---

4. The *Antiquities* was completed around 94 or 95 CE, and Lukas's apparent knowledge and use of it is one reason for dating Acts after 110 CE. See Richard I. Pervo, *Dating Acts: Between the Evangelists and the Apologists* (Santa Rosa, CA: Polebridge, 2006), 149–99, with table of correspondences between Luke/Acts and Josephus, especially the *Antiquities*, on p. 197. See also Joseph B. Tyson, *Marcion and Luke-Acts: A Defining Struggle* (Columbia: University of South Carolina Press, 2006), 14–15, echoing Pervo.

by which we must be saved." Is salvation therefore reserved for those who confess Jesus as Lord and Messiah? Μὴ γένοιτο![5] as Paul would say. Salvation is from the Lord, the God of Israel, who dwells above the heavens and whose true name is not to be uttered here below; either the letters of the tetragrammaton (Yʜᴡʜ) are recited individually or one refers simply to "Ha Shem" (The Name). Now, however, there is a Name below the heavens, among mortals, to which Jews and gentiles can appeal, namely, that of Jesus. That this name dwells "among mortals" also alludes to the mystery of the incarnation, something even most Christians have failed to grasp.

---

5. By no means! (Cf. Rom 3:3, 4.)

Acts 4:23-37

The Movement Gathered in Harmony

This scene is paradigmatic for what Lukas projects as the prophetic faith of the first community of believers. The apostles, having put the high priest and his coterie in their place, return to "their own" (τοὺς ἰδίους; NRSV "their friends" is too weak to express the intense nature of the community relationship) and report what has occurred. The account, with the community's response, is the most extended example of the pattern that will be established throughout Acts for a local community's reception and affirmation of the work of the Holy Spirit in its midst. The prayer is thoroughly oriented to biblical tradition.

Jesus here is "the one whom [the Lord] anointed," to match Psalm 2 LXX; he is also "your holy servant" (παῖς) in verses 27 and 30; the disciples are "your servants/slaves" (δοῦλοι).[1] When the disciples pray they receive exactly what they ask for—with additional *son et lumière*.[2] They pray that they may speak the word of God with boldness, and they are

---

1. See the discussion at 2:18 above. Δοῦλοι is used for the disciples in Acts only here (in prayer language) and at 16:17, where the slave woman (an outsider) calls Paul and Silas "servants [slaves] of the most high God." NRSV translates "Messiah," from the Hebrew of Ps 2, but Lukas is quoting the LXX: ὁ χριστός, "the anointed."

2. Visual, palpable effects.

Acts 4:23-37

²³After they were released, they went to their friends and reported what the chief priests and the elders had said to them. ²⁴When they heard it, they raised their voices together to God and said, "Sovereign Lord, who made the heaven and the earth, the sea, and everything in them, ²⁵it is you who said by the Holy Spirit through our ancestor David, your servant:

'Why did the Gentiles rage,
and the peoples imagine vain things?

²⁶The kings of the earth took their stand,
and the rulers have gathered together
against the Lord and
against his Messiah.'

²⁷For in this city, in fact, both Herod and Pontius Pilate, with the Gentiles and the peoples of Israel, gathered together against your holy servant Jesus, whom you anointed, ²⁸to do whatever your hand and your plan had predestined to take place. ²⁹And now, Lord, look at

granted the power to do so, along with an earthquake signaling that the requested "signs and wonders" (a favorite phrase in Acts)[3] will be forthcoming as well.

This divine response is to be expected because the disciples' reception of the apostles' report is carried out not just "together" (NRSV) but ὁμοθυμαδόν: "with one heart and soul,"[4] as will be repeated in the second summary of the nature of community life that follows immediately in 4:32-37.

The flow of the narrative is interrupted once more to describe the overall state of things in the growing community, again centering on its unanimity (ὁμοθυμαδόν), but a new element is introduced: common ownership of possessions. It is the apostles who continue to speak publicly; they are also the recipients of the members' liquidated property and managers of its distribution. Whereas in Luke's Gospel there was a great deal of attention paid to the "poor" and the "rich,"[5] Acts never uses those words. The reference here is, instead, to those who are "needy" (ἐνδεής). The Greek word is the remote ancestor of "indigent" and conveys a sense of lack or insufficiency, not just of things but in the person. Class status is creeping back into the picture, and it will have a special significance for women because the all-things-in-common system (administered by

3. "Signs and wonders," four times in Acts; "wonders and signs," four times; elsewhere in the New Testament, four times.

4. θυμός, the root word, is equivalent to Latin *anima*, "soul, spirit," etc.

5. See above at Acts 1:15-26, nn. 9–11.

their threats, and grant to your servants to speak your word with all boldness, [30]while you stretch out your hand to heal, and signs and wonders are performed through the name of your holy servant Jesus." [31]When they had prayed, the place in which they were gathered together was shaken; and they were all filled with the Holy Spirit and spoke the word of God with boldness.

[32]Now the whole group of those who believed were of one heart and soul, and no one claimed private ownership of any possessions, but everything they owned was held in common. [33]With great power the apostles gave their testimony to the resurrection of the Lord Jesus, and great grace was upon them all. [34]There was not a needy person among them, for as many as owned lands or houses sold them and brought the proceeds of what was sold. [35]They laid it at the apostles' feet, and it was distributed to each as any had need. [36]There was a Levite, a native of Cyprus, Joseph, to whom the apostles gave the name Barnabas (which means "son of encouragement"). [37]He sold a field that belonged to him, then brought the money, and laid it at the apostles' feet.

male leadership) deprives them of their rights under Jewish law to the property they bring to a marriage or are gifted with when they marry. Thus Barnabas's unilateral action in selling his field may be a violation of his wife's rights if she was not consulted. The legal question complicates the story told in the next chapter, as Ivoni Richter Reimer has shown.[6]

Also left unsaid is how the liquidation and sale of property relates to slaves. Was it the case, as John Chrysostom supposed,[7] that the believers would have manumitted them? In light of what follows[8] we may

6. Ivoni Richter Reimer, *Women in the Acts of the Apostles: A Feminist Liberation Perspective*, trans. Linda M. Maloney (Minneapolis: Fortress, 1995).

7. See Richard I. Pervo, *Acts*, Hermeneia (Minneapolis: Fortress, 2009), 127n14, citing Chrysostom, *Hom*. 11.

8. See also the attitude of the author of 1 Clement, who praised Christians who sold themselves into bondage and used the proceeds to feed others, and Ignatius, in the letter to Polycarp, who objects to the use of community property for manumitting slaves! Thus 1 Clem. 55.2: "Many among ourselves have given themselves to bondage that they might ransom others. Many have delivered themselves to slavery, and provided food for others with the price they received for themselves"; Ignatius, *Poly*. 4.3: "Let [slaves] not desire to be set free at the Church's expense, that they be not found the slaves of lust." (One wonders why being set free would make the person no longer legally enslaved "a slave of lust.") For whatever reason, the mind of the author of 1 Clement moves from the generosity of those who have enslaved themselves for others' sake to the observation that "Many women have received power through the grace of God and have performed many deeds of manly valour" (55.3), but goes on to speak of Judith and Esther, not his own contemporaries.

question whether that should be so easily assumed: after all, that would have meant subtracting value from the community's property.[9]

Barnabas will continue to play a prominent role in Acts. He is here introduced as an ideal Jewish Christian (he is a Levite, thus a religious official),[10] yet he is depicted as owning land (in theory Levites did not)[11] and as performing an action that (if it affected the rights of his wife) could be contrary to Jewish law but is praised as supporting the new, "ideal" system of community life.

9. Mary, the mother of John Mark, retained at least one slave, whom we meet at 12:13.

10. Flavius Josephus wrote that efforts by some Levites (nonpriestly members of the tribe of Levi) to elevate themselves to the status of priests (at a time shortly after the period depicted in Acts) "was contrary to the laws of our country" and was the sort of transgression that always brought punishment on his people (*Ant.* 20.9.6). (But see Malachi 2, which appears to equate priests and Levites.) In fact, the priests appointed by the Herodians were of the tribe of Levi but were no longer chosen from the descendants of Aaron, so the distinction between priests and Levites had become strictly functional by this time. Lukas may have thought of Barnabas as displaying humility and selflessness as a counter-example. At 6:7 we will read that "a great many of the priests became obedient to the faith," an unusual expression. The "chief priests" and "high priest," on the contrary, are consistent enemies of the Movement.

11. Cf., e.g., Num 18:24.

Acts 5:1-11

A Counter-Example: Ananias and Sapphira

In the continuing narrative Ananias and Sapphira furnish a direct counter-example to that of the pious Barnabas (4:36-37). Their story also dramatizes a point Lukas wishes to make about the nature of community life: being of one heart and soul necessarily means holding all things in common, since private ownership means private interest and a divided heart. Keeping property for oneself involves hedging the bet: in case the community fails, I can save myself. But that in itself is the seed of community failure, the opening for "Satan"[1] to corrupt the individual and thus the group.

---

1. This word appears in Acts only here and in Paul's speech to Agrippa II at 26:18. In Luke's Gospel the tempter is ὁ διάβολος, "the devil," contrary to the other Synoptics; for Luke, Satan is a power in conflict with God and master of an otherworldly realm who overpowers people rather than tempting them (cf. Luke 10:18; 11:18; 22:3, 31). Peter's usage here is more akin to that of Matthew and Mark, while the speech in Acts 26 is more Lukan.

Acts 5:1-11

⁵:¹But a man named Ananias, with the consent of his wife Sapphira, sold a piece of property; ²with his wife's knowledge, he kept back some of the proceeds, and brought only a part and laid it at the apostles' feet. ³"Ananias," Peter asked, "why has Satan filled your heart to lie to the Holy Spirit and to keep back part of the proceeds of the land? ⁴While it remained unsold, did it not remain your own? And after it was sold, were not the proceeds at your disposal? How is it that you have contrived this deed in your heart? You did not lie to us but to God!" ⁵Now when Ananias heard these words, he fell down and died. And great fear seized all who heard of it. ⁶The young men came and wrapped up his body, then carried him out and buried him.

Because the husband's whole property, in Jewish law, was security for his wife's *kethuba*,² Sapphira had to consent³ to the sale, as Lukas correctly notes. He treats it as a free decision on her part; given the kyriarchal marriage institution we may wonder about the extent to which she felt pressure to comply with her husband's wishes. She had nothing to gain by it, as in becoming part of the community she had already implicitly surrendered her right to the property—unless the agreement between her and Ananias was to hold back an amount equivalent to her *kethuba* for her protection. In the framework of the story, however, there is no reflection on the motives of the character "Sapphira"; she simply participates in and suffers the consequences of the concealment along with the character "Ananias." Lukas treats the story as if it reflects equal responsibility on the part of Sapphira: she is accorded equal status with her husband in decision making, unfortunately in this case to a bad end.

Lukas appears to present the interaction with Peter as taking place in a community gathering. It seems likely (especially in light of Acts 6:2-5) that decisions about the liquidation of property were made "in common" and not by the leadership; the corollary is that entering the community meant voluntarily surrendering one's right to one's property, consenting

2. What we loosely translate "dowry." See Ivoni Richter Reimer, *Women in the Acts of the Apostles: A Feminist Liberation Perspective*, trans. Linda M. Maloney (Minneapolis: Fortress, 1995), 2–6.

3. In v. 1 the NRSV translators have supplied "the consent of." The Greek text reads Ἀνὴρ δέ τις Ἀνανίας ὀνόματι σὺν Σαπφίρῃ τῇ γυναικὶ αὐτοῦ (a certain man called Ananias with Sapphira his wife). The use of σύν ("with") rather than καί ("and") renders the subject singular rather than plural. Lukas's usage here subtly underlines the fact that the couple are acting together as one; this is agreement, collusion, not merely "consent"!

⁷After an interval of about three hours his wife came in, not knowing what had happened. ⁸Peter said to her, "Tell me whether you and your husband sold the land for such and such a price." And she said, "Yes, that was the price." ⁹Then Peter said to her, "How is it that you have agreed together to put the Spirit of the Lord to the test? Look, the feet of those who have buried your husband are at the door, and they will carry you out." ¹⁰Immediately she fell down at his feet and died. When the young men came in they found her dead, so they carried her out and buried her beside her husband. ¹¹And great fear seized the whole church and all who heard of these things.

in advance to its sale when the community decided it was needed for common use. The individual owner(s) would have been responsible for the actual sale, and they would have known what price was received. Peter's questions in verse 3 imply that the community had requested the sale but not stipulated what sum was to be donated; the evil deed is the concealment, the "lie" to the Holy Spirit (ψεύσασθαί σε τὸ πνεῦμα τὸ ἅγιον) involved in the "keeping back" (νοσφίζομαι).

The use of Greek νοσφίζομαι is significant in the biblical and contemporary Greek context: it represents the action of an insider who retains property that belongs to a whole community or, by transference, to God and is therefore a kind of blasphemy. The precise term is "embezzlement." It is further important to notice that Ananias and Sapphira's "deed" is a πρᾶγμα, a word always used in the New Testament in a negative sense as something wicked.[4] The interests of God and the community are firmly fused here, though we will learn in Acts 6 that they are beginning to come apart.

The "punishment miracle" first strikes Ananias; it then falls also on Sapphira when she repeats her husband's lie.[5] It is important to see that it is not Peter who orders or executes the punishment; he only makes public the sin, and it is the sin itself that slays. This is therefore not a contradiction to Lukas's hostility to hierarchical authority; it is not an exercise of the "Petrine office." Sapphira continues to be complicit in her husband's actions.[6] Lukas implies that she had a choice about whether to lie or not,

4. Cf. 2 Cor 7:11; Jas 3:16; see Richter Reimer, *Women,* 10–11.
5. Leviticus 5:1 demands that anyone who has knowledge of false testimony is required to speak the truth about it.
6. Lukas is not a fan of kyriarchal marriage. Acts portrays only four couples in which the woman is visibly present in the text; three of them are of this type (Ananias

but as the story is told she is in fact led into a trap: only after affirming what she supposed her husband had said is she condemned. For all she knows, Ananias might have had a change of heart and confessed; in that case the whole punishment would fall on her. But in reality she has laid the trap for herself by consenting to the lie in the first place, and she should not be stripped of responsibility and made a victim.[7]

It has been suggested that Sapphira's primary offense was her refusal to define herself over against Ananias and her surrender to his choice,[8] but that is too narrow a view of self-definition in the first- or second-century context. The autonomous individual is a child of the Enlightenment; for eons before that, human beings had defined themselves as part of a "collective person."[9] Sapphira's complicity lay in her rejecting the self-definition she (and Ananias) had already accepted, namely, as members of the Movement. Instead, she reverted to her identity as part of a marital "self" of spouses and family. She thus betrayed her "true" identity in the eyes of the community and of the Holy Spirit.[10]

Kerstin Schiffner, in her essay "Solidarität" (Solidarity),[11] writes that this text is "situated in Lukas's description of the common life of the first Christ-believing Jewish community in Jerusalem." She continues: "Lukas is again and again concerned to explore the nature of dealings with material possessions and what a common life including poor and rich would look like. . . . Thus the question is repeatedly one of a common

---

and Sapphira; Felix and Drusilla; Agrippa and Berenice [brother and sister]). In none of them is the woman (or the man, for that matter) portrayed favorably; Drusilla and Berenice seem to be mentioned as links to history rather than for themselves. The only married woman who shines in this story is Prisca ("Priscilla" to Lukas), and her marriage is quite evidently *not* of the kyriarchal type.

7. This interpretation presupposes that Sapphira in the story knew the false amount that was to be presented to the apostles. We should emphasize (as Peter does in vv. 3-4) that it is not the retention of the property (to part of which, at least, Sapphira herself was entitled) but the *lie* that is the offense.

8. See Richter Reimer, *Women*, 22.

9. See ibid., 19.

10. The couple's "deaths" represent expulsion from the community, the place in which true "life" was now to be lived. In the projected historical context, social ostracism such as that imposed on "lepers" could indeed lead to physical death, but clearly the nascent Jerusalem community of the Way had no such influence on the wider society. This is simply one of the most dramatic of Lukas's instructive narratives on how the Jesus community should live.

11. Kerstin Schiffner, "Solidarität," in *Entdeckungen. Ungewöhnliche Texte aus dem Neuen Testament*, ed. Dietlinde Jessen and Stefanie Müller (Stuttgart: Katholisches Bibelwerk, 2003), 83–92.

life in solidarity such as the one Lukas paints in vivid terms especially in the first chapters of Acts."[12]

Schiffner also links verses 3 and 9, with their accusation that Ananias and Sapphira have "lied to" and "put to the test" God's Spirit. They have broken solidarity not only with the mortal members of the community but with the Spirit who is within them (severally and as a whole); they have attempted to serve two masters (cf. Matt 6:24 // Luke 16:13). By that very act they have severed their connection with the source of life: they have "given up [lit. "breathed out"] the Spirit" (ἐξέψυχεν, vv. 5, 10). Peter has described their deed, but it is the act itself that has killed them; physical death is only the outward sign of their spiritual perishing.[13]

At the end of the story Lukas for the first time refers to those of the Movement gathered in Jerusalem as "the church/the assembly" (ἡ ἐκκλησία). He distinguishes, it seems, between the Movement in general and those gathered in a particular place (he uses the same word for the "assembly" of citizens in Ephesus).[14]

We may rightly see the story of Ananias and Sapphira as a fable, much like the story of Adam and Eve in Genesis 3; there the offense was acting contrary to Yhwh Elohim's plan for the world, while here it is striking a blow at Jesus' plan for community. In the larger sense the story has implications for us all. While we citizens of earth do not practice community of goods, we do ultimately "share all things in common." When we damage or destroy any part of the earth we are reducing the common property. "Keeping back" what belongs to all—for example, by selling public lands for private profit or polluting common waters—is a sin against the community of earth's dwellers, and pretending it is an expression of our God-given "freedom" is a defiance of the Holy Spirit who cares for all creation (Gen 1:2; Wis 7:22; 8:1). There is a price to be paid for even that narrower degree of community we call "civilization," and it is due to the whole society from all holders of property, according as any have need.

12. Ibid., 84–85 (trans. Linda M. Maloney).

13. Ibid., 88–90 (trans. Linda M. Maloney).

14. For ἐκκλησία as members of local communities see also 8:1, 3; 11:22; 12:5; 15:4, 22; 18:22 (Jerusalem); 11:26; 13:1; 14:27; 15:3 (Antioch); 20:17 (Ephesus); 14:23; 15:41; 16:5 (other local places); 9:31 (throughout Judea). Once (in 7:38) it refers to "the congregation [of Israel] in the wilderness." Only in 20:28, in Paul's farewell to the Ephesian elders (πρεσβύτεροι) does it refer to "the church of God" in general.

Acts 5:12-42

Peter and the Apostles Confront the Authorities for the Last Time

The author's plan for Acts develops with an eye to the audience. Having demonstrated in the first chapters that the Movement is rooted and embedded in the history of Israel, Lukas moves to show that it is also a "philosophy" as the Hellenistic world understands such a school or way of thinking. The Movement now has a place of its own, not the temple as such but again "Solomon's Portico" (cf. 3:11), which Josephus identifies as a colonnade on the east side of the temple.[1] Philosophical schools usually had a special meeting place and were sometimes defined by it; the working of "signs and wonders" was also associated with leading philosophers, as it was with prophets in Israel.[2]

This lofty presentation of the apostles at the beginning of the story is ironically coupled, at the end, with the statement that "they rejoiced that they were considered worthy to suffer dishonor for the sake of the

---

1. *J.W.* 5.185; *Ant.* 20.221. Josephus's work is the probable source for Lukas's knowledge of Jerusalem, especially the temple.

2. So, for example, the followers of Aristotle were called "Peripatetics" because they strolled about the *peripatoi* of their meeting place, the Lyceum in Athens. "Signs and wonders" are never attributed to Jesus in the Gospels. (In John 4:48 he rejects them.) For Lukas they are emblematic of the life and work of the Movement: the phrase occurs eight times in Acts, with only slight variations (see at 4:30 above).

Acts 5:12-42

¹²Now many signs and wonders were done among the people through the apostles. And they were all together in Solomon's Portico. ¹³None of the rest dared to join them, but the people held them in high esteem. ¹⁴Yet more than ever believers were added to the Lord, great numbers of both men and women, ¹⁵so that they even carried out the sick into the streets, and laid them on cots and mats, in order that Peter's shadow might fall on some of them as he came by. ¹⁶A great number of people would also gather from the towns around Jerusalem, bringing the sick and those tormented by unclean spirits, and they were all cured.

¹⁷Then the high priest took action; he and all who were with him (that is, the sect of the Sadducees), being filled with jealousy, ¹⁸arrested the apostles and put them in the public prison. ¹⁹But during the night an angel of the Lord opened the prison doors, brought them out, and said, ²⁰"Go, stand in the temple and tell the people the whole message about this life." ²¹When they heard this, they entered the temple at daybreak and went on with their teaching.

When the high priest and those with him arrived, they called together the council and the whole body of the elders of Israel, and sent to the prison to have them brought. ²²But when the temple police went there, they did not find them in the prison; so they returned and reported, ²³"We found the prison securely locked and the guards standing at the doors, but when we opened them, we found no one inside." ²⁴Now

name," something so shocking in a society governed by an ethos of honor and shame that it signals again to the audience that their world is being "turned upside down" (cf. 17:6). It is also an implicit attack on the kinds of persons who dishonor others to exalt themselves—emperors and their agents, for example—here disguised as the temple authorities.

We learn in verse 14 that the new believers being added to the Movement include both women and men; Lukas insistently keeps that fact before his readers' minds. Peter's noncontact miracle working ("look, no hands!") both echoes that of Jesus, for example, in the case of the centurion's slave (Luke 7:1-10), and foreshadows that of Paul (see Acts 14:9; 19:12).

Lukas has constructed a richly comic one-act play, largely replicating the pattern established in Acts 3–4 but expanding on it. Again the chief priest(s) and the "council" and "elders" are the villains; again they are identified with the Sadducees, who are this time called a "sect" (αἵρεσις). While Lukas will on several occasions refer to the Pharisees or to the Movement as a αἵρεσις (Pharisees: 15:5; 26:5; the Way/Nazarenes: 24:5,

when the captain of the temple and the chief priests heard these words, they were perplexed about them, wondering what might be going on. [25]Then someone arrived and announced, "Look, the men whom you put in prison are standing in the temple and teaching the people!" [26]Then the captain went with the temple police and brought them, but without violence, for they were afraid of being stoned by the people.

[27]When they had brought them, they had them stand before the council. The high priest questioned them, [28]saying, "We gave you strict orders not to teach in this name, yet here you have filled Jerusalem with your teaching and you are determined to bring this man's blood on us." [29]But Peter and the apostles answered, "We must obey God rather than any human authority. [30]The God of our ancestors raised up Jesus, whom you had killed by hanging him on a tree. [31]God exalted him at his right hand as Leader and Savior that he might give repentance to Israel and forgiveness of sins. [32]And we are witnesses to these things, and so is the Holy Spirit whom God has given to those who obey him."

[33]When they heard this, they were enraged and wanted to kill them. [34]But a Pharisee in the council named Gamaliel, a teacher of the law, respected by all the people, stood up and ordered the men to be put outside for a short time. [35]Then he said to them, "Fellow Israelites, consider carefully what you propose to do to these men. [36]For some time ago Theudas rose up, claiming to be somebody, and a

14; 28:22),[3] this is the only instance in which he speaks of the Sadducees as such. Sadducees appear, though less frequently than Pharisees, in all three Synoptic Gospels, where their significant characteristic is that they deny the resurrection. Matthew otherwise equates the two groups, but Lukas does not. In Luke's Gospel the Pharisees engage in discussions with Jesus and are not his implacable foes; in Luke 13:31 some of them even warn him of a threat from Herod. (Of course, if a Pharisee or any other character in Luke's story is "rich," that's another matter.) Lukas will make good use of the fact that the Sadducees deny the resurrection in Acts 23, where Paul claims to belong both to the Movement and to the αἵρεσις of the Pharisees, thus setting off a quarrel between the Sadducee and Pharisee factions. Evidently his audience is aware of the distinction; in Acts 15 we read that some Pharisees were members of the Movement

3. All references to the Movement as a αἵρεσις are by outsiders, often hostile ones; the usage with regard to the Pharisees is essentially neutral.

Acts 5:12-42 (cont.)

number of men, about four hundred, joined him; but he was killed, and all who followed him were dispersed and disappeared. [37]After him Judas the Galilean rose up at the time of the census and got people to follow him; he also perished, and all who followed him were scattered. [38]So in the present case, I tell you, keep away from these men and let them alone; because if this plan or this undertaking is of human origin, it will fail; [39]but if it is of God, you will not be able to overthrow them—in that case you may even be found fighting against God!"

They were convinced by him, [40]and when they had called in the apostles, they had them flogged. Then they ordered them not to speak in the name of Jesus, and let them go. [41]As they left the council, they rejoiced that they were considered worthy to suffer dishonor for the sake of the name. [42]And every day in the temple and at home they did not cease to teach and proclaim Jesus as the Messiah.

and demanded a strict application of the law, which in the real world was *a*, if not *the*, defining characteristic of Pharisees in general.[4]

A Pharisee appears in Acts for the first time here, in the person of Gamaliel. This man (Gamaliel I) was a semi-legendary figure of the period being described; his descendants would be involved in a complicated battle—in progress at the time Lukas was writing—over the "succession" to rabbinic leadership in emergent Judaism. Making him a spokesman here for an irenic attitude toward the Movement, emphasizing that its success or failure would be determinative, was highly strategic in the atmosphere of the early second century—by which time, of course, the Movement had spread widely (thanks in large part to the Pharisee Paul) and enjoyed some success.[5] To put the frosting on the cake, Gamaliel opens his address to the Sadducees with a phrase (προσέχετε ἑαυτοῖς ["consider carefully"; lit. "take heed to yourselves"]) very familiar from the LXX but used in the New Testament only in the Lukan corpus.[6] Taken together

---

4. The Pharisees' devotion to Torah is stressed in all the Synoptic Gospels and in Acts; see Josephus, *J.W.* 2.161-62.

5. Readers or hearers of Acts would learn, at the beginning of Paul's final battle with the Jewish leaders in Jerusalem (Acts 22:3), that Gamaliel was Paul's teacher (a statement that finds no support in Paul's writings). Rereaders/hearers would already know this and would relish the irony here.

6. Luke 12:1; 17:3; 21:34; Acts 5:35; 20:28. See Mikeal C. Parsons and Martin M. Culy, *Acts: A Handbook on the Greek Text* (Waco, TX: Baylor University Press, 2003), *ad loc.* They write that the phrase is "fairly common in the LXX"; see, e.g., Gen 24:6;

with Peter's statement in verse 30 that "the God of our ancestors raised up Jesus, whom you had killed by hanging him on a tree,"[7] this was rubbing salt in Sadducean wounds, since the reason for their denial of the resurrection was that it is not in the Torah (= Pentateuch)—the books written by and about those they claimed, above all, as their ancestors.

The story ends where it began, in the temple and "at home" (the phrase means "in the houses," plural, or "from house to house"). "Proclaim" (εὐαγγελίζομαι, lit. "spread [the] good news") appears here for the first time in Acts; it will recur no fewer than fifteen times.[8] The text could be taken to imply that all the "proclaiming" was done by the apostles, but there is no explicit subject for the verbs in this clause, and if the Movement was large and rapidly growing (as Lukas pictures it), it is more probable than not that some of the teaching and proclaiming in the houses was done by the women members.[9] The passage that immediately follows will posit that the work of caring for the house churches was too much for the apostles, who needed to delegate. Is their assignment of that work to seven men to be read as a measure for suppressing women's teaching and proclamation? The continuing story will make that question still more urgent.[10]

Exod 19:12; 34:6; Deut 4:23. The context is almost always "taking care to" hold to the covenant, to Torah.

7. "Hanging on a tree" is likewise a Hebrew Bible/LXX reference; cf. esp. Deut 21:22-23.

8. The word is used fifty-four times in the New Testament, twenty-five of them in Luke and Acts.

9. Cf. 1 Tim 5:13, where the (post-Lukan) author complains about "younger widows" as "gossips and busybodies," "gadding about from house to house." For that author any teaching activity by women that was not about obedience to male authority would fall into the category of gossip (cf. 2 Tim 3:6).

10. We must always remember that this is the story of the beginnings as Lukas *thinks they must have or should have been* (in God's plan); at best what he relates is based on three or four generations of oral tradition. The numbers of believers in Jerusalem are hugely exaggerated.

Acts 6:1-7

The Widows' Crisis
and the Choosing of the Seven

For such a short passage, this story presents a plethora of confusions. Feminist scholars in particular have proposed that the διακονίᾳ τῇ καθημερινῇ (wrongly translated "daily distribution of food" in the NRSV; more properly "everyday ministry")[1] is a reference to those community members charged with service, including but not limited to serving the daily communal (and eucharistic) meal, and that the persons whose service is being downgraded here were "widows" (an order of service in the Christian community in Lukas's own time; cf. 1 Tim 5:3-16).[2] Alternatively, Peter's claiming the "service of the word"

---

1. The Greek is τῇ διακονίᾳ τῇ καθημερινῇ ("the daily service"), and the Vulgate follows: *ministerio quotidiano*. Nothing is said about food. Apparently that idea has entered because of the reference in the next verse to "serving at table," διακονεῖν τραπέζαις (Latin: *ministrare mensis*). See Ivoni Richter Reimer, "Acts," trans. Nancy Lukens, in *Feminist Biblical Interpretation: A Compendium of Critical Commentary on the Books of the Bible and Related Literature*, ed. Luise Schottroff and Marie-Theres Wacker (Grand Rapids: Eerdmans, 2012), 688.

2. That this was a conflict over ministerial responsibilities (though not the later order of "deacons") was suggested already by Elisabeth Schüssler Fiorenza, *In Memory of Her: A Feminist Theological Reconstruction of Christian Origins* (New York: Crossroad, 1983), e.g.: "It is possible, therefore, that the conflict between the Hellenists and the

Acts 6:1-7

⁶:¹Now during those days, when the disciples were increasing in number, the Hellenists complained against the Hebrews because their widows were being neglected in the daily distribution of food. ²And the twelve called together the whole community of the disciples and said, "It is not right that we should neglect the word of God in order to wait on tables. ³Therefore, friends, select from among yourselves seven men of good standing, full of the Spirit and of wisdom, whom we may appoint to this task, ⁴while we, for our part, will devote ourselves to prayer and to serving the word." ⁵What they said pleased the whole community, and they chose Stephen, a man full of faith and the Holy Spirit, together with Philip, Prochorus, Nicanor, Timon, Parmenas, and Nicolaus, a proselyte of Antioch. ⁶They had these men stand before the apostles, who prayed and laid their hands on them.

⁷The word of God continued to spread; the number of the disciples increased greatly in Jerusalem, and a great many of the priests became obedient to the faith.

for the apostles (and, as appears subsequently, the Seven) can be read as an androcentric claim to that office for males only. Both or either may be so, but given Lukas's aversion to an established hierarchy and preference for a synagogal model of leadership by "presbyters/elders" (some of whom would certainly have been women), it would be an intrusion here.[3] The intent, in line with his overall program, would rather be to depict an orderly growth of the community and a delegation of authority as needed.

As stated above, Lukas would not have had much, if any, direct knowledge of the original Jerusalem community. Because he is concerned throughout his writing to depict an orderly development of the Jesus movement it is not likely that he would have wanted to stress here the kind of official rankings of which the author(s) of the Pastorals and the

---

Hebrews involved the role and participation of women at the eucharistic meal. The expression that they were 'overlooked' or 'passed over' in the daily *diakonia* or ministry could indicate either that they were not assigned their turn in the table service or that they were not properly served" (166). See also Barbara E. Reid, "The Power of Widows and How to Suppress It (Acts 6:1-7)," in *A Feminist Companion to the Acts of the Apostles*, ed. Amy-Jill Levine with Marianne Blickenstaff, FCNTECW 9 (New York: T&T Clark, 2004), 71–88.

3. For women's leadership in the synagogues of the period see Bernadette J. Brooten, *Women Leaders in the Ancient Synagogue: Inscriptional Evidence and Background Issues*, BJS 36 (Chico, CA: Scholars Press, 1982).

apostolic fathers after him are so fond. At the same time we should note that this author would not have used a story, or created one, that did not speak to his second-century audience, which means he could not have invented the idea of a distinct group (or distinct groups) of widows in the community. He had to work with a familiar picture (however imaginary) of a Jesus community to establish his image of the Jerusalem community as the ideal.

Widows

Widows are far more present in Luke-Acts than in the other Gospels or Paul's letters, but the difference between Luke and Acts is striking. In the Gospel widows appear singly, not as part of a distinct group, and they are often assertive.[4] Others are representative of the plight of widows in that time and place: the widow at Nain who has lost her son (Luke 7:11-15), the hypothetical widow who has to marry all her late husband's brothers (Luke 20:27-33), and the widows whose houses are "devoured" (Luke 20:46-47).

The case is altogether different in Acts, where widows appear in only two scenes: this one in Acts 6 and in Acts 9 as a group associated with Tabitha. No individual women are called widows (with the momentary exception of Sapphira, who is a widow for a few hours, though unbeknownst to her):

not Tabitha, not Lydia, not even the mother of John Mark (12:12), who is evidently the head of her own household.

There is probable cause for this: the Gospel of Luke reflects a still-remembered Palestinian Jewish milieu in which village women and members of the artisan classes were an active part of society. Acts, written decades later and in a diaspora milieu, comes from the hand of an author who was familiar with institutionalized groups of widows such as are reflected in the Pastorals. Lukas's reconstruction of the Jerusalem community makes use of such a group as a narrative device to move the story forward by demonstrating how well the Jesus community handled disputes—by contrast with the picture of the Jerusalem Jewish leadership. Both the Jerusalem widows and those at Joppa are imagined to be poor

---

4. Thus Anna the prophet (Luke 2:36-38), the widow at Zarephath to whom Elijah was sent and who was herself an interesting character (1 Kgs 17:8-24; Luke 4:25-26), the widow who got the better of the judge (Luke 18:1-8), and the widow giving her two copper coins to the temple that were worth more than all that the rich people offered (Luke 21:1-4).

and dependent, objects of the community's charity—unlike those combatted by the author of the Pastorals, who found them uppity and needing to be put in their place.

Throughout the Lukan corpus the response to widows, whether individually or as a group, marks the responder either positively or negatively in the narrative. Widows are especially prominent in the Torah in Deuteronomy (10:18; 14:29; 16:11, 14; 24:17, 19-21; 26:12-13; 27:19).[5] David Moessner,[6] among others, has pointed to Luke's intention to depict Jesus and his disciples as mirroring the Moses of Deuteronomy 18:18 ("I will raise up for them a prophet like you from among their own people; I will put my words in the mouth of the prophet, who shall speak to them everything that I command"). Care for outcasts (widows, orphans, lepers, aliens, etc.) defines righteousness in Deuteronomy. Thus care for widows is a prominent positive characteristic attributed to the new community. Not only that: it is a *model*. Contrasting the response to the plight of a group of women in the community, as Lukas pictures it, with the attitude displayed, for example, in 1 Timothy 5:3-16 or 2 Timothy 3:6 reveals that Lukas understands far better than male leaders who came after him that concern for the well-being of *all* community members is vital to the Movement's success—and he singles out a group of women as the paradigm.

All in all, as we have already seen, women in Acts, both singly and in groups, are for the most part plot devices with no claim to individuality other than what (as in the case of Lydia) Lukas has constructed for them to suit his narrative purpose. The one exception is Prisca (or "Priscilla") in chapter 18. She was less easily manipulated in Lukas's text because she was a real person (see the references to her in Rom 16:3; 1 Cor 16:19; 2 Tim 4:19). Prisca/Priscilla will play an important role later on.

5. See Todd Penner, *In Praise of Christian Origins: Stephen and the Hellenists in Lukan Apologetic Historiography*, Emory Studies in Early Christianity 10 (New York: T&T Clark, 2004), 265.

6. David Moessner, *Lord of the Banquet: The Literary and Theological Significance of the Lukan Travel Narrative* (Minneapolis: Fortress, 1989), 259–88; also Luke Timothy Johnson, *The Literary Function of Possessions in Luke-Acts*, SBLDS 39 (Missoula: Scholars Press, 1977), 60–76; F. Scott Spencer, "Neglected Widows in Acts 6:1-7," *CBQ* 56 (1994): 715–33.

We should notice that Lukas never uses the title διάκονος for anyone, female or male. Instead, he writes of διακονία, "service," here in a twofold sense: "service at table" (v. 2; cf. v. 1) and "service of the word" (v. 4). His word for all the community members is "disciple" (μαθητής, feminine μαθήτρια).

Words for Members of the Movement in Acts

Lukas uses μαθητής ("disciple") here for the first time in Acts and employs it three times in seven verses. Mark (followed by Luke) had abandoned that designation for Jesus' followers when they fled from him after his arrest; Lukas restores it here and continues to use it for Christians in a particular place. Of all the designations for followers of the Way, this is the only one to appear in the feminine form, μαθήτρια (of Tabitha in 9:36). That is the only break in the verbal androcentrism of the text whereby women are concealed under the "generic masculine." Ἀδελφοί (siblings, lit. "brothers") at first applies to Jewish members of the Movement, but after the "apostolic council" it is extended to gentile members as well. As Paul Trebilco observes, "For Luke the key background context of usage of ἀδελφοί is the OT and Jewish usage for members of God's people."[7]

Similarly, ἐκκλησία ("assembly") is used to emphasize the community character of the Movement; once (at 7:38) it designates the assembly of Israel in the wilderness, which for Lukas is the prototype of his ἐκκλησία. It is used only once (at 5:11) for the Jerusalem Jesus community. Lukas is not fond of the term ἅγιοι, "saints," but his use of it (at 9:13, 32, 41; 26:10) implies that he knows it was an early designation for members of the Jerusalem church. Other uses in participial form and applying to gentiles indicate that they are *incorporated among* the "saints/those who are sanctified." That says, once again, that sanctification belongs to the people of God, beginning with Israel and now including gentiles.[8]

The designation "believer" (in various forms based on the verb πιστεύω) seems to be an early usage in Greek-speaking settings and does not bear all the community weight of other terms; its emphasis is instead on faith as the foundation of the Movement's life.

---

7. Paul Trebilco, "The Significance of the Distribution of Self-Designations in Acts," *NovT* 54 (2012): 30–49, at 36.
8. Ibid., 47–48.

The separation of the Seven (evidently part of the tradition Lukas is following; cf. 21:8) as a group of missionaries distinct from the Twelve[9] obviously has nothing to do with table service. The two who are subsequently mentioned, Stephen and Philip, are clearly "evangelists" (Philip explicitly at 21:8).

In fact, Lukas is not downgrading the women of the community here specifically by denying them the right to engage in table service (if that is the meaning intended) but rather in general by cementing the social distinctions of his time and place: women cook and serve (and clean up!); men teach and preach in public. That is the picture he paints. If the community widows had surrendered all their property for the use of the community they certainly expected to be cared for by their sisters and brothers in the Movement, so the story of the widows here is the positive foil to the Ananias and Sapphira example in chapter 5.

In his book on Stephen, John J. Pilch proposed yet another interpretation of the community's problem: that it derived from a linguistic and cultural divide. The Twelve are portrayed as Galileans and evidently their leadership, at least (Peter, James, and John, as well as Jesus' brother James, who will assume leadership of the Jerusalem community after Peter's departure), are Aramaic speakers. Pilch proposes that it was not ordinary food but the bread of the Word that was not reaching the Hellenist widows on equal terms because no Greek speakers had been appointed to teach them. Be it noted also that "Hellenists" include women as well as men; we may not exclude the possibility—or probability—that those who complained of the neglect of Hellenist widows were their sisters, daughters, aunts, or mothers! The selection of seven Hellenist *men* who do not "serve at tables" any more than the Twelve but who, as represented by Stephen, become evangelists and wonder-workers in the Greek-speaking community effectively conceals the presence and activity of Hellenist women.[10] Perhaps the Seven did begin their ministry by serving at the communal meals alongside the women and there learned from the widows the wisdom they (or some of them) subsequently applied in preaching.

Clearly, in Lukas's conception of the event, the choice of the Seven is made by the whole community (παντὸς τοῦ πλήθους), in contrast to

9. This is the only passage in Acts that refers to the apostles as "the Twelve."

10. John J. Pilch, *Stephen: Paul and the Hellenist Israelites* (Collegeville, MN: Liturgical Press, 2008). Pilch is very clear that the Seven are *not* "deacons"; they perform διακονία, but so do many other characters in the story, women included.

the casting of lots by which Matthias was added to the Eleven (1:26). Throughout the remainder of Acts no major decision affecting the life of the community will be made without the action, or at least the affirmation, of all the members.

TRANSLATION MATTERS

A subtlety in the language of verses 1-2 may suggest that the Hellenist widows were being denied their roles not as table servers but as distributors of the community cash. Verse 1 speaks of διακονίᾳ τῇ καθημερινῇ (daily service) while verse 2 specifies διακονία τραπέζαις (service at tables). The daily service could be "works of mercy" in general but, then as now, "table" in many languages, including English, is closely related to the word for "bank" (cf. English "bench," and Mark 11:15 *parr.* Matt 21:12; John 2:15; Luke omits).[11] Denying them the right to the office of managing the community's finances, or perhaps at least the part related to food distribution, would be a more serious downgrading of women's responsibility, and we cannot rule out the idea that Lukas was thinking of it since, as Ute Eisen has shown, there were women money managers ("stewards," οἰκονόμεισσαι) among Christians in Asia Minor in the fourth century, by which time the office had been institutionalized, if it was not so earlier.[12] The Pastorals, as is typical of them, push toward institutionalizing the duties of the οἰκονόμοι and assigning them to the bishop/overseer (ἐπίσκοπος). In the second-century context this portrayal by Lukas could be read as a push-back against just that: here Peter renounces the work of the οἰκονόμος in favor of the διακονία τοῦ λόγου.

At the same time the relationship of "Hebrews" to "Hellenists" appears fraught. It is usually said that the "Hebrews" spoke Hebrew or Aramaic and that "Hellenists" spoke Greek. It is often further presumed that the latter were the more "progressive" or "cosmopolitan" group, the "Hebrews" more the old guard. In fact, as subsequent events will show, it will be the "Hellenists" in Jerusalem (other than those who have joined the Movement) who are most outraged at Stephen's preaching. As Richard Pervo observes, "The 'Hellenists' would have been Diaspora Jews who

11. Richard I. Pervo, *Acts*, Hermeneia (Minneapolis: Fortress, 2009), 159n66. He adds that F. F. Bruce advocated this interpretation but Ernst Haenchen "rightly" rejects it.

12. Ute E. Eisen, *Women Officeholders in Early Christianity: Epigraphical and Literary Studies*, trans. Linda M. Maloney (Collegeville, MN: Liturgical Press, 2000), 217–22. She points out (219–20) that Paul speaks of himself and his coworkers as "stewards" (οἰκονόμοι) in reference to their apostolic office (cf. 1 Cor 4:1-2).

settled in 'the Holy City.' Such persons were intrinsically unlikely to have been predisposed to take a relaxed approach to Torah-observance."[13] To see the "Hebrews" as somehow equivalent in their views to the Sanhedrin and the "Hellenists" as the progressive faction is to succumb to anti-Judaism—as if exposure to Hellenistic culture made Jews more "open" or "modern" in their thinking! Lukas repudiates that idea.

The social situation of the Hellenists should also be noted: having moved from their original homes to Jerusalem, they were much more socially exposed than those native to the city. (The Galileans were somewhere in between: Aramaic speakers, but at some remove from their native social milieu.) Both groups were at a distance from their families and their home synagogues or worship groups. Feelings of mistrust and of being put at a disadvantage because of their status, culture, or color were not unnatural in such a situation, and for widows the isolation from family must have been particularly painful and even desperate.[14]

Group Identifications in Early Judaism[15]

Acts was written in a time of major social disruption when, after the destruction of the Jerusalem temple, the groupings within Judaism that had developed since the Hasmonean era were being forced to realign and rethink their identities. The Sadducees (and the Qumran sectarians)

---

13. Pervo, *Acts*, 154. For a modern parallel see Dani Shapiro, *Devotion: A Memoir* (New York: HarperCollins, 2010), 101–2, speaking of American cousins who have moved to Jerusalem and become *Haredim*: "They lived in insular communities, cut off from the outside world. . . . They spent their lives—literally every waking minute of their lives—studying Torah. . . . The word itself—*haredi*—derives from the Hebrew word for fear. 'One who trembles in awe of God.' In their eyes, I doubt I would even qualify as Jewish."

14. See Gerhard Lohfink, "How the Church Grows," in *Between Heaven and Earth: New Explorations of Great Biblical Texts*, trans. Linda M. Maloney (Collegeville, MN: Liturgical Press, 2022), 326–30.

15. For a full (though contested) exposition of this subject see Craig C. Hill, *Hellenists and Hebrews* (Minneapolis: Fortress, 1992). The most recent, and most illuminating, discussion of the distinctions between Sadducees and Pharisees, and between Hellenists and "Hebrews," is Daniel R. Schwartz, "Jewish Movements of the New Testament Period," in *The Jewish Annotated New Testament*, ed. Amy-Jill Levine and Marc Zvi Brettler, 2nd ed. (Oxford: Oxford University Press, 2017), 526–30. Much of the following information is derived from that essay.

were closely identified with the hereditary priesthood and the temple; Lukas would have known of them almost entirely from traditions and through Josephus's writings. The Pharisees were to the "left" of the Sadducees, and the Hellenists were, generally speaking, the "left wing" of the Pharisees. The signal difference between Sadducees and Pharisees, as Daniel R. Schwartz describes it, was that the former "would tend to assume that the rules dealing with the sacred and with binding obligations are established by nature, whereas Pharisaic and rabbinic Jews would tend to think that human decisions play a much more important role."[16] The implications of that distinction for conflicts within and among the Jesus communities, especially as regards the status of gentile converts, should be kept in mind as the story in Acts unfolds. As Schwartz writes: "The whole premise of Hellenism—a universalist movement, which allowed people everywhere to become 'Greeks' by virtue of their education and culture—is that what makes people what they are is their culture, i.e., their values and commitments, not their birth or their location." Significantly for a feminist viewpoint is his further observation that "the Greek gymnasia around the East were schools that turned barbarians into Greeks."[17] Since the gymnasia were male-only places, women were excluded from that acculturation process.

While Lukas's knowledge of the history of the period is evidently derived in large part from Josephus (or Josephus's sources), his work also reflects a thorough knowledge of the books of Maccabees, in which the Hellenists are anything but heroic figures: quite the contrary. Lukas's Hellenists (like the diaspora Jews, including members of the Movement, among whom he lived) are not like the villains of Maccabees; they are as opposed to the Roman co-optation of the Jewish religious leadership as the Maccabeans had been in the past. Still, as Greek speakers (and it seems that for Lukas "Hellenist" primarily means "Greek-speaking Jew") they are "not quite authentic" in the eyes of Jerusalemites in particular, and for that reason have to assert their Jewishness all the more. Paul will prove to be the prime example.

16. Schwartz, "Jewish Movements," 528.
17. Ibid., 529.

Conflict and Growth

Quite a few exegetes believe that Lukas romanticized the early Jerusalem community. Evidently they have not read Acts very carefully, because the beginning of chapter 6 reveals no such glorifying romanticism. The young Jerusalem community repeats the sins that the Old Testament attributes to the Exodus generation: mistrust, complaining, rebellion.
. . .

Lukas means to say that it is especially in crisis, in the profound distress of the young community and the response forced by that distress, that the community is able to grow. The strife between the Hellenists and the Hebrews was not eliminated by people softening their feelings and speaking politely to each other but by all joining together in taking a new step.

Gerhard Lohfink[18]

This is certainly Lukas's creation, based on little or no evidence from the time he describes, but for that very reason we can read in it his purpose in writing. The choice of the Seven is not about installing seven *men* to deal with the needs of a group of *women* but about the common action of women and men. A surface reading shows men acting and being appointed to serve, but Lohfink's analysis emphasizes that it is the *whole* group of women and men who must consent to the arrangement and incorporate it in their lives if it is to succeed. The Twelve (who make their last appearance here) are the *center* of the community, not its head. Their concern is not to impose their own solution but to make sure that all members have a stake in the resolution of the problem and are satisfied.

18. From Lohfink, "How the Church Grows," a reflection on the readings for the Fifth Sunday of Easter, Year A, 326–30.

Acts 6:8-15

Stephen's Ministry

Lukas's shaping of the first part of Acts on the pattern of the Gospels is never more obvious than here.[1] Stephen's public activity and his trial are obviously modeled on those of Jesus, although this time it is Jews from the diaspora who are the instigators of conflict, and there is no involvement of the Roman authorities. The idea in John 18:31 (not in the Synoptics) that the Jewish authorities were not allowed to put someone to death is seemingly unknown to Lukas, or else he is aware that lynching was not unusual; condemnation by the Sanhedrin ("council") and mob execution are clearly in order, and when the Romans are reluctant to railroad Paul (chaps. 23–25) a similar lynching will be attempted, but unsuccessfully.

From what we now understand about the "Hellenists" (see above, pp. 28n9, 78–82), we can see why it is they who are first enraged at Stephen's preaching and why it is Hellenist members of the Movement who are drummed out of Jerusalem after his death. Lukas may have had a source for his account of Stephen's death (though not for his speech, which is

---

1. See the table in Richard I. Pervo, *Acts*, Hermeneia (Minneapolis: Fortress, 2009), 168 for a comparison between the trials of Stephen and Jesus; Lukas has made use of Mark as well.

[8]Stephen, full of grace and power, did great wonders and signs among the people. [9]Then some of those who belonged to the synagogue of the Freedmen (as it was called), Cyrenians, Alexandrians, and others of those from Cilicia and Asia, stood up and argued with Stephen. [10]But they could not withstand the wisdom and the Spirit with which he spoke. [11]Then they secretly instigated some men to say, "We have heard him speak blasphemous words against Moses and God." [12]They stirred up the people as well as the elders and the scribes; then they suddenly confronted him, seized him, and brought him before the council. [13]They set up false witnesses who said, "This man never stops saying things against this holy place and the law; [14]for we have heard him say that this Jesus of Nazareth will destroy this place and will change the customs that Moses handed on to us." [15]And all who sat in the council looked intently at him, and they saw that his face was like the face of an angel.

altogether Lukan). Whatever tradition Lukas had about parties in Jerusalem apparently came from Josephus.

In his commentary Richard I. Pervo translates "synagogue of the Freedmen" and what follows as "Synagogue of Former Slaves, whose members came from Cyrene and Alexandria."[2] This sheds more light on their possible perspective. If these men (apparently only men are in view) had been enslaved, probably in Roman service, they would be all the more jealous of the ancestral traditions they cherished so much that they had resettled in Judea rather than in Rome or one of the Roman *coloniae*. They, more than others, would be outraged by Stephen's accusations that the people had been unfaithful to the Torah in their moral conduct and also by creating a "house made with hands" for YHWH to live in. Though they may gather in "synagogues" organized on the basis of ethnicity or social status, their ultimate devotion is to the temple, the magnet that has drawn them to Jerusalem. This would be all the more true of Jews from Alexandria, who had suffered humiliation at the hands of the Romans despite their wealth and education.

---

2. See ibid., 164–67. The audience for Acts would be reminded that people from Egypt and Cyrene were among those who heard Peter's speech at Pentecost; "Jews from Asia" will also be the instigators of the attack on Paul in the temple in Acts 21.

Synagogues

It is anachronistic to imagine (as Lukas may, in fact, do) that Jerusalem was home to a number of "synagogues" in the sense of buildings dedicated to that purpose.[3] While the Talmud asserts that there were a hundred synagogues in Jerusalem before its destruction, archaeologists have found evidence of only one, and that one is questionable.[4] Flavius Josephus, who was a primary source for Lukas's historical knowledge, rarely refers to synagogues, and then most often to those in Caesarea and Antioch. Synagogues, as fixed locations partly or solely dedicated to Jewish assembly for study (and prayer?),[5] were almost entirely a diaspora phenomenon. We should think of synagogues in Judea almost always as gatherings rather than gathering places. So the "synagogue of the Freedmen" would have been a distinct group of people, and the household gatherings of the Movement would have been "synagogues" in the same sense.[6] Reading Acts 2:46 again, we can picture the communities both attending the temple for worship and gathering in homes for "the breaking of bread" (a favorite Lukan expression for the community meal; cf. Luke 24:35) and instruction in the Way—the "service of tables" and the service of the Word—both undoubtedly performed by women as well as men and possibly by (formerly or currently) enslaved persons as well.[7]

---

3. See Judith Lieu, " 'The Parting of the Ways': Theological Construct or Historical Reality?" in *Neither Jew Nor Greek? Constructing Early Christianity* (London: Bloomsbury T&T Clark, 2003; 2016). Citations are from the 2nd ed. She writes: "The synagogue was not the only focal institution for the Jewish community nor need it always have been a physical structure" (45).

4. The "Theodotus inscription," discovered in the City of David in 1913 and now in the Rockefeller Museum, refers to a synagogue and hostels, but the synagogue remains have not been found.

5. Judith Lieu ("Parting," 46) refers to Stefan Reif's study of Jewish prayer: "The apparently long-standing tradition of assembly on the sabbath was also related as much, if not more, to study than to prayer" (Stefan C. Reif, *Judaism and Hebrew Prayer* [Cambridge: Cambridge University Press, 1993], 47).

6. When we read, in the second half of Acts, that Paul's first action on entering a new place of mission is to go to the synagogue, we should keep in mind that it is quite natural he would go first to the house of study in order to preach. His continued participation in prayer with his fellow Jews is evidently assumed as quite natural, since it is never explicitly mentioned.

7. See further Lee I. Levine, "The Synagogue," in *The Jewish Annotated New Testament*, ed. Amy-Jill Levine and Marc Zvi Brettler, 2nd ed. (New York: Oxford University

It is important to the narrative that Stephen himself be a Hellenist, a representative of Greek-speaking Judaism, because his story marks the break point when part of the Movement is forced out of Jerusalem to spread the gospel to Jews elsewhere and ultimately to gentiles. Hence Stephen will be painted in the colors of a Greek-style hero, and that model will be enlarged and augmented in the figure of Paul. The "face of an angel" or "shining" face is a *topos* familiar to readers of Greek literature (including the LXX) and signals a brilliant orator or an "athlete of virtue."[8]

This is a major step forward in the plot because Stephen (representatively for the Seven, perhaps) here takes on the role of an apostle. It is necessary at this point that preaching and wonder working be taken up by a Greek speaker because the Way is about to move out from Jerusalem, beyond Judea and Samaria, and onward, to places where the *lingua franca* is Greek.

Also, just as the apostles are exemplary Aramaic-speaking Jewish men, so Stephen is a paragon of Hellenistic Judaism. He performs "signs and wonders" as Moses (cf. 7:36), Jesus, and the apostles had done and as Philip (cf. 8:13) and Paul and Barnabas will do after him. In his speech before the Sanhedrin he will lay claim to the whole heritage of Israel and accuse his hearers as the prophets did and as Jesus is portrayed in the Gospels as doing: of disobedience to the law and perversion of Israel's faith. Unlike most (though not all) biblical prophets, however, he will speak no words of comfort, only of condemnation. Lukas wrote Acts at a time when the debate among Jews, members of the Movement, and spokespersons for the imperial power and cult was becoming more and more rancorous. Jewish revolts were erupting in the diaspora, to be followed within a decade or two by the final Roman seizure and clearance of the land of Israel and its renaming as *Palestina* for the ancient foes, the

---

Press, 2017), 662–66; Jordan J. Ryan, *The Role of the Synagogue in the Aims of Jesus* (Minneapolis: Fortress, 2017).

8. See Pervo, *Acts*, 170n48: "Transfiguration of leading characters is common in popular literature." He notes, *inter alia*, Dan 3:92; Joseph and Aseneth 18:7-9; Martyrdom of Polycarp 12–14 (12.1: "his countenance was full of grace"); Acts of Paul and Thecla 1, where Paul "sometimes had the countenance of an angel." Novels like *Ethiopian Story* (8.9.13) have such scenes as well. For a rabbinic example see Qoh. Rab 8.2, "a man's wisdom lights up his face." (See David H. Aaron, "Shedding Light on God's Body in Rabbinic Midrashim: Reflections on the Theory of a Luminous Adam," *HTR* 90 [1997]: 299–314, at 306.)

Philistines. At about that time, too, *hairesis* would become heresy (among both Jews and those coming to be called Christians as well as mutually). The storm clouds are gathering, and Lukas projects that storm backward into the earliest years of the Movement.

The women of the Movement, insistently mentioned throughout the first five chapters, will from this point on be of only incidental interest, at least until Paul enters Greek territory. In Lukas's story it is an all-male crowd that challenges and does away with Stephen, though in chapter 8 women will be equal victims of the persecution that follows.

This chapter is a *crux interpretum* and in recent years has been read as definitive proof that Lukas is anti-Jewish.[9] I believe we should read it instead as a brilliant narrative exposition of the tensions and sorrows of diaspora existence. Lukas lived and wrote in the diaspora; he knew it well. Here he projects the controversies in his own context backward to the beginnings in Jerusalem, where he can bring together the key opponents in his scenario: the Sanhedrin and Hellenist Jews from the diaspora (two mutually exclusive groups). One of his aims is to illustrate clearly for his gentile audience that there is no longer (if there ever was) a unified "Judaism" any more than there is a unified "Jesus movement." The boundaries are porous and the debates ongoing, though the goal is the same: to gather "a people for [God's] name" (15:14). For the Jewish opponents as pictured in Acts, that people is and remains the people Israel. For Lukas it is the people Israel that welcomes gentiles who have accepted Israel's message conveyed through Messiah Jesus. The danger of violent conflict (and of provoking the Roman power) is real, which is one reason why the account of the Movement in the first part of Acts is (at least on the surface) so irenic, so sunshine-and-light. There have been difficulties within the community and with the Jerusalem elite, as pictured in chapters 3–5. The story looks back to the death of Jesus as paradigmatic and forward to the strains and struggles of existence in a diaspora that will prove to be permanent.

We may read the shape of Acts 1–7, especially 6–7, as a progressive exposition of the tension between the "household" of the community of

---

9. The most prominent and thorough treatment of the story of Stephen as an expression of anti-Judaism in Acts is Shelly Matthews, *Perfect Martyr: The Stoning of Stephen and the Construction of Christian Identity* (New York: Oxford University Press, 2010).

the Way and the temple as the domain of the official Jewish leadership.[10] The audience is shown a contrast between the two groups in terms of the value of φιλία (love, friendship) and φιλανθροπία (fellow-feeling, hospitality; cf. 28:2). In Acts 6:1-7 we witness a threat to φιλία through internal division over the status and rights of the widows. Despite the apparently pacific resolution, a fissure has developed that will continue to expand, climaxing in the "apostolic council" in Acts 15 and clearly remaining unresolved (see below on Acts 21 and beyond). At the same time φιλία between the Jewish religious establishment and the leadership of the Movement erodes rapidly. As Todd Penner writes, "The entire narrative framework sets the two entities side by side, initiating a comparison of the respective groups based on their responses to the narrative tensions: One will escalate the breakdown of *philanthropia*, while the other will attempt to resolve it."[11] This also ties to what has been called the "persecution motif" in Acts, in which spokespersons for the Movement such as Stephen are identified with God's prophets in the past, speaking God's word and suffering for it, and thereby offering a model of perseverance for believers: as the words of God spoken through the prophets of old have been fulfilled, so it will ultimately be with those spoken today—but in the meantime believers must endure trials.

From this point forward we will encounter repeated instances of violence in Acts, both verbal and physical and perpetrated not only by "them."[12] In such conflicts the members of the Way who either undertake aggression or are its noble victims are portrayed according to the "cardinal virtues of male comportment. . . . [T]he Greek civic values of the *polis* . . . are represented most forcefully by those characters who not only exhibit such values, but who also embody the fullest possible ex-

10. See Todd Penner, *In Praise of Christian Origins: Stephen and the Hellenists in Lukan Apologetic Historiography*, Emory Studies in Early Christianity 10 (New York: T&T Clark, 2004), 263–65.

11. Ibid., 264–65.

12. For this subject see esp. Todd Penner and Caroline Vander Stichele, "Gendering Violence: Patterns of Power and Constructs of Masculinity in the Acts of the Apostles," in *A Feminist Companion to the Acts of the Apostles*, ed. Amy-Jill Levine with Marianne Blickenstaff, FCNTECW 9 (Cleveland: Pilgrim, 2004), 193–209. It is important to be aware that most elite Jews, in Judea and in the diaspora, would have absorbed and attempted to embody Greek and Roman *civic* values.

pression of masculine power and control as a result."[13] The domestication
of women and their reduction in status are the inevitable counterpart.
Lukas probably had reservations (in light of his experience) about the
kinds of restrictions imposed on women by the author of the Pastorals,
but his glorification of masculine ideals certainly lays the foundation for
the house in which they are soon to be confined.[14]

13. Ibid., 203. They also note how the expansion of the Movement is what triggers
violence and mirrors imperial Roman politics, offering "an extreme disjunction between the *pax* that is proclaimed and the 'history' that unfolds" (204).

14. Of first importance for this topic are the writings of Mary Rose D'Angelo, especially "The *ANHP* Question in Luke-Acts: Imperial Masculinity and the Deployment
of Women in the Early Second Century," in *A Feminist Companion to Luke*, ed. Amy-Jill
Levine with Marianne Blickenstaff, FCNTECW 3 (London: Sheffield Academic, 2002),
44–69; eadem, " 'Knowing How to Preside over His Own Household': Imperial Masculinity and Christian Asceticism in the Pastorals, *Hermas*, and Luke-Acts," in *New
Testament Masculinities*, ed. Stephen D. Moore and Janice Capel Anderson, SemeiaSt
45 (Atlanta: SBL Press, 2003), 265–95.

Acts 7:1–8:1a

Stephen's Defense and Martyrdom

The speech is entirely Lukas's composition, and the whole account of Stephen is modeled on the life and death of Jesus. In turn, both Jesus and Stephen reflect the history of Israel's prophets as known to Lukas: the prophets preached repentance to Israel and were condemned, often killed, for it.[1] Lukas's Christology is above all prophetic: Jesus Messiah is the "prophet like Moses" whom God had promised and whom, in this author's opinion, all Jews should be expecting and should recognize as having come.[2]

---

1. Gary Gilbert, in his commentary on Acts in *The Jewish Annotated New Testament* (ed. Amy-Jill Levine and Marc Zvi Brettler, 2nd ed. [Oxford: Oxford University Press, 2017], 234), notes with regard to v. 52 that this is a possible reference to 2 Chr 24:20-21 and the killing of Zechariah son of Jehoiada, as well as a common motif in the Jewish *Lives of the Prophets* (see Charles C. Torrey, *The Lives of the Prophets*, Greek Text and Translation [Eugene, OR: Wipf & Stock, 2020]).

2. Todd Penner emphasizes that the Jerusalem apostles as well as Stephen, Philip, and Paul follow a Mosaic paradigm: "Stephen is both contrasted with his opponents and compared to Moses." Todd Penner, *In Praise of Christian Origins: Stephen and the Hellenists in Lukan Apologetic Historiography*, Emory Studies in Early Christianity 10 (New York: T&T Clark, 2004), 288–89.

Acts 7:1–8:1a

⁷:¹Then the high priest asked him, "Are these things so?" ²And Stephen replied: "Brothers and fathers, listen to me. The God of glory appeared to our ancestor Abraham when he was in Mesopotamia, before he lived in Haran, ³and said to him, 'Leave your country and your relatives and go to the land that I will show you.' ⁴Then he left the country of the Chaldeans and settled in Haran. After his father died, God had him move from there to this country in which you are now living. ⁵He did not give him any of it as a heritage, not even a foot's length, but promised to give it to him as his possession and to his descendants after him, even though he had no child. ⁶And God spoke in these terms, that his descendants would be resident aliens in a country belonging to others, who would enslave them and mistreat them during four hundred years. ⁷'But I will judge the nation that they serve,' said God, 'and after that they shall come out and worship me in this place.' ⁸Then he gave him the covenant of circum-

cision. And so Abraham became the father of Isaac and circumcised him on the eighth day; and Isaac became the father of Jacob, and Jacob of the twelve patriarchs.

⁹"The patriarchs, jealous of Joseph, sold him into Egypt; but God was with him, ¹⁰and rescued him from all his afflictions, and enabled him to win favor and to show wisdom when he stood before Pharaoh, king of Egypt, who appointed him ruler over Egypt and over all his household. ¹¹Now there came a famine throughout Egypt and Canaan, and great suffering, and our ancestors could find no food. ¹²But when Jacob heard that there was grain in Egypt, he sent our ancestors there on their first visit. ¹³On the second visit Joseph made himself known to his brothers, and Joseph's family became known to Pharaoh. ¹⁴Then Joseph sent and invited his father Jacob and all his relatives to come to him, seventy-five in all; ¹⁵so Jacob went down to Egypt. He himself died there as well as our ancestors, ¹⁶and their bodies were

Israel's prophets had denounced their people in the harshest possible terms, threatening utter destruction in order to turn the people to repentance, and suffering for doing so.[3] Lukas is fully aware of this and uses the same kind of language, often drawn directly from the prophetic books, in Stephen's speech[4] and notably also in Paul's words at the end of Acts. That was dangerous for the future, because his gentile audience probably lacked awareness of Israel's past, and in later generations the prophets' polemic was read as a rejection of the Jewish people.

3. See esp. Jer 26:20-23.
4. Compare the accusation "uncircumcised in heart and ears!" in Acts 7:51 with Jeremiah 9:26: "all the house of Israel is uncircumcised in heart."

brought back to Shechem and laid in the tomb that Abraham had bought for a sum of silver from the sons of Hamor in Shechem.

¹⁷"But as the time drew near for the fulfillment of the promise that God had made to Abraham, our people in Egypt increased and multiplied ¹⁸until another king who had not known Joseph ruled over Egypt. ¹⁹He dealt craftily with our race and forced our ancestors to abandon their infants so that they would die. ²⁰At this time Moses was born, and he was beautiful before God. For three months he was brought up in his father's house; ²¹and when he was abandoned, Pharaoh's daughter adopted him and brought him up as her own son. ²²So Moses was instructed in all the wisdom of the Egyptians and was powerful in his words and deeds.

²³"When he was forty years old, it came into his heart to visit his relatives, the Israelites. ²⁴When he saw one of them being wronged, he defended the oppressed man and avenged him by striking down the Egyptian. ²⁵He supposed that his kinsfolk would understand that God through him was rescuing them, but they did not understand. ²⁶The next day he came to some of them as they were quarreling and tried to reconcile them, saying, 'Men, you are brothers; why do you wrong each other?' ²⁷But the man who was wronging his neighbor pushed Moses aside, saying, 'Who made you a ruler and a judge over us? ²⁸Do you want to kill me as you killed the Egyptian yesterday?' ²⁹When he heard this, Moses fled and became a resident alien in the land of Midian. There he became the father of two sons.

³⁰"Now when forty years had passed, an angel appeared to him in the wilderness of Mount Sinai, in the flame of a burning bush. ³¹When Moses saw it, he was amazed at the sight; and as he approached to look, there came the voice of the Lord: ³²'I am the God of your ancestors, the God of Abraham, Isaac, and Jacob.' Moses began to tremble and did not dare to look. ³³Then the Lord said to him, 'Take off the sandals from your feet, for the place where you are standing is holy ground. ³⁴I

Accused (vv. 13-14) of speaking against the temple and the law—but by false witnesses!—Stephen offers a lengthy (though edited) history of God's promises to Israel and Israel's infidelity, asserting that it is his accusers who are unfaithful to the law, not he. Consider just Psalm 78 (worth reading in its entirety):

> They tested the Most High God,
> and rebelled against him.
> They did not observe his decrees,
> but turned away and were faithless like their ancestors;
> they twisted like a treacherous bow. (Ps 78:56-57)

have surely seen the mistreatment of my people who are in Egypt and have heard their groaning, and I have come down to rescue them. Come now, I will send you to Egypt.'

35"It was this Moses whom they rejected when they said, 'Who made you a ruler and a judge?' and whom God now sent as both ruler and liberator through the angel who appeared to him in the bush. 36He led them out, having performed wonders and signs in Egypt, at the Red Sea, and in the wilderness for forty years. 37This is the Moses who said to the Israelites, 'God will raise up a prophet for you from your own people as he raised me up.' 38He is the one who was in the congregation in the wilderness with the angel who spoke to him at Mount Sinai, and with our ancestors; and he received living oracles to give to us. 39Our ancestors were unwilling to obey him; instead, they pushed him aside, and in their hearts they turned back to Egypt, 40saying to Aaron, 'Make gods for us

who will lead the way for us; as for this Moses who led us out of the land of Egypt, we do not know what has happened to him.' 41At that time they made a calf, offered a sacrifice to the idol, and reveled in the works of their hands. 42But God turned away from them and handed them over to worship the host of heaven, as it is written in the book of the prophets:

'Did you offer to me slain victims
    and sacrifices
   forty years in the wilderness, O
      house of Israel?
43No; you took along the tent of
   Moloch,
   and the star of your god
      Rephan,
   the images that you made
      to worship;
so I will remove you beyond
   Babylon.'

44"Our ancestors had the tent of testimony in the wilderness, as God directed when he spoke to Moses, ordering him to make it according to the pattern

Lukas surely has in mind the account of Jeremiah's trial:

Thus says the LORD: Stand in the court of the LORD's house, and speak to all the cities of Judah that come to worship in the house of the Lord; speak to them all the words that I command you; do not hold back a word. It may be that they will listen, all of them, and will turn from their evil way, that I may change my mind about the disaster that I intend to bring on them because of their evil doings. . . .

The priests and the prophets and all the people heard Jeremiah speaking these words in the house of the LORD. And when Jeremiah had finished speaking all that the LORD had commanded him to speak to all the people, then the priests and the prophets and all the people laid hold of him, saying, "You shall die! Why have you prophesied in the name of the LORD, saying, 'This house shall be like Shiloh, and this city

he had seen. ⁴⁵Our ancestors in turn brought it in with Joshua when they dispossessed the nations that God drove out before our ancestors. And it was there until the time of David, ⁴⁶who found favor with God and asked that he might find a dwelling place for the house of Jacob. ⁴⁷But it was Solomon who built a house for him. ⁴⁸Yet the Most High does not dwell in houses made with human hands; as the prophet says,

⁴⁹"Heaven is my throne,
　　and the earth is my footstool.
What kind of house will you build
　　for me, says the Lord,
　　or what is the place of my
　　　　rest?
⁵⁰Did not my hand make all these
　　things?'

⁵¹"You stiff-necked people, uncircumcised in heart and ears, you are forever opposing the Holy Spirit, just as your ancestors used to do. ⁵²Which of the prophets did your ancestors not persecute? They killed those who foretold the coming of the Righteous One, and now you have become his betrayers and murderers. ⁵³You are the ones that received the law as ordained by angels, and yet you have not kept it."

⁵⁴When they heard these things, they became enraged and ground their teeth at Stephen. ⁵⁵But filled with the Holy Spirit, he gazed into heaven and saw the glory of God and Jesus standing at the right hand of God. ⁵⁶"Look," he said, "I see the heavens opened and the Son of Man standing at the right hand of God!" ⁵⁷But they covered their ears, and with a loud shout all rushed together against him. ⁵⁸Then they dragged him out of the city and began to stone him; and the witnesses laid their coats at the feet of a young man named Saul. ⁵⁹While they were stoning Stephen, he prayed, "Lord Jesus, receive my spirit." ⁶⁰Then he knelt down and cried out in a loud voice, "Lord, do not hold this sin against them." When he had said this, he died. ⁸:¹And Saul approved of their killing him.

shall be desolate, without inhabitant'?" And all the people gathered around Jeremiah in the house of the LORD.

When the officials of Judah heard these things, they came up from the king's house to the house of the LORD and took their seat in the entry of the New Gate of the house of the LORD. Then the priests and the prophets said to the officials and to all the people, "This man deserves the sentence of death because he has prophesied against this city, as you have heard with your own ears." (Jer 26:2-3, 7-11)

Subsequent prophets continued to rail against the people's disobedience. For example, the last prophet in the book of the Nevi'im, known as Malachi, bitterly charged the levitical priesthood with corruption and failure to listen (thus "heart and *ears*"). "If you will not listen, if you will not lay it to heart to give glory to my name, says the LORD of hosts, then

I will send the curse on you and I will curse your blessings. . . . I will rebuke your offspring, and spread dung on your faces, the dung of your offerings, and I will put you out of my presence" (Mal 2:2-3).[5]

Stephen's recitation of Israel's history through the time of Moses is straightforward and follows the story as Torah relates it (warts and all). But when he comes to speak of the temple he strongly implies that it is another in Israel's series of idolatrous works, a "house made by human hands," and not willed by God. According to the traditions recorded in the historical books God had forbidden David to build a temple;[6] while Solomon's later action is celebrated,[7] in 1 Kings 8:27 Solomon himself is made to acknowledge that "even heaven and the highest heaven cannot contain you, much less this house that I have built!" The historical books themselves are ambivalent about it and about Solomon, who enslaved his people to build the temple and then married foreign wives (who brought their pagan cults with them) to enhance his power. In the next generation after Solomon the kingdom was divided because the people rebelled against his and his successor's oppression. Solomon's temple was destroyed by the Babylonians in 587 BCE, and there were ambivalent feelings about its rebuilding, as reflected, for example, in 1 Esdras. That late book (from the second century BCE), now found among the "apocrypha," revealed uneasiness with a restoration of Israel and rebuilding of the temple by anyone other than a descendant of David (contrary to the celebratory story in the canonical books of Ezra-Nehemiah) and so invented a Davidide character, Zerubbabel, to lead the rebuilding. The book is a critique of the Hasmonean rulers and their successors, thus also of the temple cult as governed by them. It makes its own use of Ezra-Nehemiah by letting Ezra appear in the story to insist on full observance of Torah (including the dismissal of "foreign" wives and children!). Rebuilding the temple is not enough: obedience to Torah is the temple's *raison d'être*.[8]

Jewish tradition, by the time of Stephen, held firmly that God is both universal and can be worshiped in a single place. Lukas was familiar

---

5. This book was probably composed after the building of the "Second Temple," ca. 500 BCE.

6. At least according to Solomon: see 1 Kgs 8:17-19; 1 Chr 22.

7. The account in 1 Kings probably rests on the "Book of the Acts of Solomon" (see 1 Kgs 11:41). For a wry fictional treatment of Solomon's politics see Stefan Heym, *The King David Report* (London: Hodder & Stoughton, 1973).

8. See esp. 1 Esdras 5, 7–9, *par.* Ezra 3:8-13; 5–6, 9. For an excellent analysis of 1 Esdras see Dieter Böhler, *1 Esdras*, trans. Linda M. Maloney, IECOT (Stuttgart: Kohlhammer, 2016).

with that tradition,[9] yet he wrote in a time when Herod's temple building had been destroyed by the Romans, and it seemed to him that the cycle that had brought down Solomon's temple was repeating itself: infidelity to the covenant (above all, in his eyes, the rejection of Jesus), divine condemnation, exile or suppression of the population. Violent resistance, and the rise of other messianic claimants, was already stirring and would lead, within a decade or two after the composition of Acts, to the Bar Kokhba revolt and the expulsion of Jews from Jerusalem, which the Romans then renamed Aelia Capitolina.

What Lukas wrote was used by Christians after him to condemn and dismiss and persecute Jewish people, but we now know that such division was long in developing. Lukas's contemporaries, and possibly he himself, were certainly in dialogue with the rabbinic movement (Pharisees and others) that was struggling to establish a Judaism that could continue without the temple. In Lukas's view Israel's salvation had already come, and the only way forward was to live in that light. His desire was not "Christianity" as a separate entity but a Judaism on Jesus' model, as he understood it.

Debate continues over whether Lukas's quotations of the Scriptures, as here in Stephen's speech and elsewhere in Acts, are to be read as a final condemnation of Judaism. This is the opinion of many scholars, both Jewish and non-Jewish.[10] Similarly, they see Paul's last words in Acts 28:27-28 (quoting Isa 6:9-10) as a final rejection of the Jews in the persons of their leaders at Rome. Others, however, myself included, read the ending of Acts as open: Paul does not die, and hope for reconciliation persists. Stephen speaks, as does Paul, in the spirit of Israel's prophets, railing against the people's failure to live according to Torah. The prophets always held out hope for restoration, but sometimes it is hard to hear; certainly Stephen's words are not very hopeful, and yet he ends his speech with "You are the ones that received the law as ordained by angels, and yet you have not kept it" (v. 53).[11] Is there hope there?

---

9. See 2 Macc 14:35; Josephus, *Ant.* 8.107.

10. See, e.g., Gary Gilbert's short essay, "Stephen's Speech," in *The Annotated Jewish New Testament* (2nd ed.), 234: "Similar rehearsals of Israel's past, such as Neh 9 and Ps 78, also combine historical review with rebuke of the people's rebellious nature, yet these texts, unlike Stephen's speech, ultimately assert that God is merciful and faithful to the covenant with the people of Israel. Stephen's speech, in contrast, ends on a note of condemnation, without any hope for Israel's future." The "contrast" may be less than Gilbert implies.

11. Matthew Thiessen, *Contesting Conversion: Genealogy, Circumcision, and Identity in Ancient Judaism and Christianity* (Oxford: Oxford University Press, 2011), contends that in vv. 8-9 Stephen in fact affirms circumcision "on the eighth day" as a part of the

Indeed, there is: turning back to the law is, after all, the key to renewal and restoration; listening to prophets instead of attacking them will ultimately bring the reign of God. Moreover, Lukas would have intended his audience to hear in Stephen's vision ("I see the heavens opened and the Son of Man standing at the right hand of God!"; v. 56) the introduction to the "turn" in the prophetic books when, after a scouring denunciation of the people's infidelity to the law, the prophet tells what he or she sees "in the days to come" (cf. Isa 2:2 // Mic 4:1; 27:6). But Stephen is shouted down before he can tell the vision to the full.

Nonetheless, the scene depicted is traumatic for all concerned. Stephen is vindicated by a heavenly vision; his accusers refuse to acknowledge it; they rush him outside the city and lynch him by stoning. (Where are the Roman authorities, here and in the next chapter? Compare the similar attempt on Paul's life at 21:27-35.) The Lukan Gospel hedges on Roman responsibility, but in general the Gospels agree that it was the Romans who killed Jesus, though the impetus may have come from the Sanhedrin and their allies. This account in Acts leaves the Romans completely out of the picture and places the whole onus on—well, whom exactly? Supposedly Stephen has been speaking in the presence of the high priest (6:1) and the "council" (6:12, 15) as well as those (the Freedmen and Hellenists in 6:9?) who had first confronted him and who had "stirred up the people as well as the elders and the scribes." Which of these are the "they" in verses 54, 57-59? All of them or only some? Certainly the Pharisees are conspicuously absent; after all, Stephen's stress on keeping Torah would have been quite compatible with their belief. In any case the pattern replicates that of the condemnation of Jesus, and Stephen (like Jesus in the disputed verse Luke 23:34a), dies asking God to forgive his enemies. His plea, "Lord, do not hold this sin against them," should be included in discussions of the "finality" (or not) of Israel's condemnation. Certainly Stephen—like Jesus—does not condemn even those directly responsible for his death but instead holds out hope that they may "understand with their heart and turn—and I would heal them" (Isa 6:10, quoted by Paul at Acts 28:27).[12]

---

covenant that Israel has indeed kept, and must continue to keep. "If Luke believed that the rite of circumcision was no longer necessary, Stephen's reference to it would be inexplicable" (118).

12. Shelly Matthews, *Perfect Martyr: The Stoning of Stephen and the Construction of Christian Identity* (New York: Oxford University Press, 2010) has argued vigorously and eloquently that the story of Stephen is key to Lukas's construction of nascent Christianity *in opposition to* Judaism. I disagree.

Several recent authors have noted that, literarily speaking, "Stephen the first martyr" did not exist before Irenaeus introduced Acts to the reading public in about 180, more than a century after the purported time (ca. 36 CE) of the events in which he figures. The meaning of his name (*stephanos* = "crown"), so often associated in early Christianity with martyrdom (cf. Heb 2:9; 1 Pet 5:4; Rev 2:10), may at least imply that he is Lukas's own invention, based on the first name in the list of those chosen to perform διακονία (6:1-6). The audience is prepared for him to be singled out because he is the only one in the list who is characterized by more than his name or place of origin; he is "a man full of faith and the Holy Spirit," as he demonstrates thereafter.[13] Clare K. Rothschild has even proposed that Stephen may have been invented "in response to the political-theological climate of the time during which he was 'discovered.'"[14] In my opinion he is far too Lukan a character to be removed from Acts, and his emphasis on the law makes him an eloquent spokesman for the continuity of Judaism and the Jesus movement.

Coded Language[15]

There are at least three points in Stephen's speech at which he seems to be using expressions similar to those employed by both Hellenized Jews and gentiles in Rome's orbit to reject the religion of idols and the Roman rulers who identified themselves with the gods. These are in verse 2, "the God of glory"; verse 48, "the Most High"; and verse 52, "the Righteous One." These, and in particular the description of oppression in Egypt by Pharaoh, would have been highly intelligible especially to the "Alexandrians" (cf. 6:9), whose lives and culture in that sophisticated city had been brutally attacked, first by Augustus's assertion of supremacy through the building of the Sebasteion[16] in his own

---

13. For the rapid growth of Stephen's popularity after his appearance in *Adversus Haereses* see François Bovon, "Beyond the Book of Acts: Stephen, the First Christian Martyr, in Traditions Outside the New Testament Canon of Scripture," *PRSt* 32 (2005): 93–107.

14. Clare K. Rothschild, "Perfect Martyr? Dangerous Material in the Stoning of Stephen," in *Delightful Acts*, ed. Harold W. Attridge, Dennis R. MacDonald, and Clare K. Rothschild, WUNT 391 (Tübingen: Mohr Siebeck, 2017), 177–91, at 191.

15. On the subject of coded language see Drew J. Strait, *Hidden Criticism of the Angry Tyrant in Early Judaism and the Acts of the Apostles* (Lanham, MD: Lexington Books/Fortress Academic, 2019), and C. Kavin Rowe, *World Upside Down: Reading Acts in the Graeco-Roman Age* (Oxford: Oxford University Press, 2009).

16. *Augustus* in Latin corresponds to *Sebastos* in Greek.

honor and his imposition of a special tax, the *laographia*,[17] and then by Gaius Caligula, who demanded to be worshiped as a god. Jews who had fled Alexandria for provincial Jerusalem were probably more devout and more resentful of Roman usurpation of religious claims than most of those long resident in Judea, with the exception of separatist groups like the Essenes.

The phrase "the God of glory [Ὁ θεὸς τῆς δόξης]" is itself unique in the Bible.[18] Lukas uses it in this context as coded language critical of idol worship and of any concession whatever to honoring human beings as divine.[19] The LXX[20] makes it plain that "glory" as such belongs only to the God of Israel (e.g., "I am the LORD, that is my name; my glory I give to no other, nor my praise to idols" [Isa 42:8]). Human glory is perishable, and if it is not the glory given by God (e.g., to Israel, or to the "one like a human being" in Dan

7:14, whom Lukas would have identified with the risen Lord), it is pernicious. For Israel to glorify any but YHWH is even more wicked than for the nations to do so, since the gentiles do not know better, but Israel does: "If you will not listen, if you will not lay it to heart to give glory to my name, says the LORD of hosts, then I will send the curse on you and I will curse your blessings; indeed I have already cursed them, because you do not lay it to heart" (Mal 2:2). The implication of Stephen's speech is clear: for Israel this is a time to repent of any behavior that accords to the emperor the glory that belongs to YHWH. Likewise, Lukas's gentile audience is called to repent of its attachment to idols and join with repentant Israel in its future course.

"The Most High [ὁ ὕψιστος]" is an epithet for God greatly favored in the Apocrypha, and in the New Testament primarily in Luke-Acts.[21] It is drawn especially from the LXX polemic against idols and emperor

---

17. This tax was imposed on Jews and native Egyptians, thus reducing both to subordinate status as *peregrini* ("foreigners" in their own land!); previously the Jews of Alexandria had enjoyed superior rank and even had their own ethnarch (see Josephus, *Ant.* 14.114–18).

18. Cf. 1 Cor 2:8, "the Lord of glory"; Eph 1:17, "the Father of glory."

19. See Strait, *Hidden Criticism*, 266: "By the mid-first century it is notable that eleven imperial family members received cultus."

20. Reference in this context is to the biblical translation used by Lukas and familiar to his characters.

21. Luke 1:32, 35, 76; 6:35; 8:28; Acts 7:48; 16:17; otherwise only Mark 5:7 // Luke 8:28 and Heb 7:1, there alluding to Gen 14:18-22.

worship. So especially the book of Daniel, and Wisdom of Solomon (written most probably in Egypt in reaction to Augustan oppression and hence reflecting the thinking of Alexandrian Jews); the latter conceals anti-imperial polemic by painting an image of the ideal king. There the king is addressed directly: "For your dominion was given you from the Lord, and your sovereignty from the Most High; he will search out your works and inquire into your plans" (Wis 6:3). Previously Ben Sira had described Wisdom herself as the emanation of the Most High (Sir 24:1-22); the author of the book of Wisdom embraces her as the ideal to be honored and clung to (and not some earthly ruler, even one like Solomon who was supposedly God's anointed).

"The Righteous One [ὁ δίκαιος]" is a title for YHWH in Isaiah 24:16, and righteousness is of God. "The righteous one, my servant" is the subject of the Servant Songs (cf. Isa 53:11). Wisdom of Solomon begins "Love righteousness, you rulers of the earth" (Wis 1:1) and goes on to emphasize that it is wicked to oppress righteous persons. Again this is veiled criticism of Roman authorities who claimed to be righteous/just (δίκαιος) but oppressed the Jewish people. Lukas uses "the Righteous One" three times in Acts[22] in accusations against opponents in Jerusalem, and only there.

Two other points should be noted: Lukas does not expect Jesus' return in anything like the near future, and he discourages the idea with scenes like this one. Stephen's vision is of "the Son of Man standing at the right hand of God" (v. 56) in "the heavens," and it is there that he asks to be received. "Son of Man," derived from Daniel 7:13-14,[23] is a messianic title in the Gospels and other early Jewish literature,[24] but this is the only New Testament appearance of the title outside the Gospels. Despite the messianic reference (comprehensible only to Jews and those very familiar with Jewish literature), nothing is said about Jesus returning, either to destroy or to save. This serves to counter official fears (in Lukas's own time) that might have been aroused by the speech itself; Lukas is executing a delicate balancing act. Insiders understand that the mission of the

22. Acts 3:14; 7:52; 22:14.
23. Where NRSV now appropriately renders it "human being."
24. E.g., Ezek 8:2; 4 Ezra 13. See the discussion in John J. Collins, *Daniel, with an Introduction to Apocalyptic Literature*, FOTL 20 (Grand Rapids: Eerdmans, 1984).

Movement is "to the ends of the earth." By the end of Acts it has only got as far as Rome, but there is no hint that it will stop there.

Second, Lukas uses this occasion to introduce the hero of the second half of Acts, "a young man named Saul." This youth, later known as Paul, will be the main protagonist of the rest of the book. A strict Pharisee, a student of Gamaliel (according to Acts 23:3), and a persecutor of the Way, he will be overcome by divine power and his whole life will be changed. If it can happen to Saul, Lukas more than implies, it can happen to anyone.

But there is one more thing: It is only in Acts that Paul is referred to as Saul; Paul himself, in his letters, seems to be ignorant of the appellation. As Richard Pervo has pointed out, "The grecized form of 'Saul,' Σαῦλος, had the connotation of an exaggerated form of walking, particularly of males who wiggled their hips in an 'effeminate' manner."[25] In other words, Lukas queers his hero, Saul/Paul, from the moment of his introduction. Unlike, for example, the Acts of Thecla, which describes Paul's appearance,[26] Lukas offers no description of Paul except to call him, and have him refer to himself as, Saul.[27] The use of "Saul" drops out when Paul's mission to the gentiles begins. Interpreters have read this as a switch from a Jewish form of the name to a Greek one, but the form Σαῦλος is Greek and is never used by the LXX or Josephus for King Saul.[28] Evidently the original audience of Acts was supposed to understand that Saul/Paul was in every way more than met the eye.

---

25. Richard I. Pervo, *Acts*, Hermeneia (Minneapolis: Fortress, 2009), 198n25, citing Anacreon, frg. 66b; 113; Aristophanes, *Wasps* 1173; Lucian, *Lex.* 10; and Clement, *Paed.* 3.11.69, and noting that Josephus does not use Σαῦλος for King Saul.

26. "A man small of stature, with a bald head and crooked legs, in a good state of body, with eyebrows meeting and nose somewhat hooked, full of friendliness; for now he appeared like a man, and now he had the face of an angel" (Acts of Thecla 3). János Bollók, "The Description of Paul in the Acta Pauli," in *The Apocryphal Acts of Paul and Thecla*, ed. Jan N. Bremmer (Kampen: Kok Pharos, 1996), 1–15, argues that most of these features were viewed negatively in ancient texts on physiognomy. Crooked legs, for example, could be associated with immorality and enslavement to wicked desires; baldness could connote intelligence but also sensuality. For a full explanation of queer theory see "The Ethiopian," pp. 111–21, esp. 113–14.

27. Paul is called or refers to himself as "Saul" in Acts 7:58; 8:1, 3; 9:1, 4, 8, 11, 17, 22, 24; 11:25, 30; 12:25; 13:1, 2, 7, 9, and is referred to as "Saul, also known as Paul" in 22:7, 13; 26:14. He is "Paul" some 145 times, all of them after 13:9. The uses of "Saul" in chaps. 22 and 26 are Paul's quoting of Jesus' words to him at the time of his vision on the Damascus road.

28. The LXX transliterates the name, calling the king Σαούλ.

Acts 8:1b-25

The Mission Begins

The killing of Stephen sets off a paroxysm in Jerusalem (where, once again, are the Roman authorities?),[1] and Saul the coat-check boy rockets to the role of chief persecutor. No respecter of persons, he seizes women and men indiscriminately and thrusts them into prison. We are not told what percentage of the "thousands of believers" (cf. 2:41; 4:4) were seized and what portion fled. As the story continues we learn that it is primarily the "Hebrews" (represented by "the apostles") who remain in Jerusalem and the "Hellenists" who scatter through Judea and Samaria. Again we may wonder: what about Galilee and the communities of the Movement that (historically speaking) must have been growing there under the leadership of the women and men who had followed Jesus and ministered to him and his disciples? (See Luke 8:1-3.) They were key factors in the Gospels. Surely Galilee would have been the appropriate place for the refugees from Jerusalem to seek shelter, but

1. Those authorities are remarkably absent from the first nine chapters of Acts, in contrast to their key roles in the rest of the book. Lukas is very guarded in his treatment of the Romans. Acts 1–9 depict events primarily in Jerusalem and could be viewed by outsiders as an interreligious squabble of no interest to them as long as those involved didn't do it in the streets and frighten the horses, as Queen Elizabeth I is alleged to have said. Once the scene moves outside Judea, interaction with Roman authorities becomes inevitable and has to be described and evaluated—still most often in "coded language."

Acts 8:1b-25

[1b]That day a severe persecution began against the church in Jerusalem, and all except the apostles were scattered throughout the countryside of Judea and Samaria. [2]Devout men buried Stephen and made loud lamentation over him. [3]But Saul was ravaging the church by entering house after house; dragging off both men and women, he committed them to prison.

[4]Now those who were scattered went from place to place, proclaiming the word. [5]Philip went down to the city of Samaria and proclaimed the Messiah to them. [6]The crowds with one accord listened eagerly to what was said by Philip, hearing and seeing the signs that he did, [7]for unclean spirits, crying with loud shrieks, came out of many who were possessed; and many others who were paralyzed or lame were cured. [8]So there was great joy in that city.

[9]Now a certain man named Simon had previously practiced magic in the city and amazed the people of Samaria, saying that he was someone great. [10]All of them, from the least to the greatest, listened to him eagerly, saying, "This man is the power of God that is called Great." [11]And they listened eagerly to him because for a long time he had amazed them with his magic. [12]But when they believed Philip, who was proclaiming the good news about

the Galilean part of the Movement (possibly dominated by women?) has no role in the story being told in Acts.

Those who flee Jerusalem are evidently not silenced or cowed: they proceed to spread the word (ὁ λόγος). The representative teacher is Philip, one of the Seven; here we see the development of the ministry for which that group was commissioned. We have heard only of Stephen preaching and performing wonders in Jerusalem (cf. 6:8-10); now Philip is the first (and only) one of the group to represent the work of the remaining six outside the capital city. Philip is the leading figure of chapter 8, and he will reappear in an incidental role in chapter 21. Evidently those commissioned by the "apostles" (i.e., the Twelve) are empowered to preach, baptize, and work wonders, but they lack the authority to convey the Holy Spirit, so Peter and John have to come from Jerusalem to lay hands on the new converts.

Later, in chapter 19, we learn that Paul is also able to convey the Spirit; it appears that he can do so because he (with Barnabas) has been commissioned not by members of the Twelve but by the community at Antioch (13:1-4). It is the community there who lay hands on their missionaries, making them "apostles" in the sense of persons who are sent with authority. In Acts the "apostolic succession" is conveyed by the Spirit *acting through the community* and those sent *by the community*.

the kingdom of God and the name of Jesus Christ, they were baptized, both men and women. [13]Even Simon himself believed. After being baptized, he stayed constantly with Philip and was amazed when he saw the signs and great miracles that took place.

[14]Now when the apostles at Jerusalem heard that Samaria had accepted the word of God, they sent Peter and John to them. [15]The two went down and prayed for them that they might receive the Holy Spirit [16](for as yet the Spirit had not come upon any of them; they had only been baptized in the name of the Lord Jesus). [17]Then Peter and John laid their hands on them, and they received the Holy Spirit. [18]Now when Simon saw that the Spirit was given through the laying on of the apostles' hands, he offered them money, [19]saying, "Give me also this power so that anyone on whom I lay my hands may receive the Holy Spirit." [20]But Peter said to him, "May your silver perish with you, because you thought you could obtain God's gift with money! [21]You have no part or share in this, for your heart is not right before God. [22]Repent therefore of this wickedness of yours, and pray to the Lord that, if possible, the intent of your heart may be forgiven you. [23]For I see that you are in the gall of bitterness and the chains of wickedness." [24]Simon answered, "Pray for me to the Lord, that nothing of what you have said may happen to me."

[25]Now after Peter and John had testified and spoken the word of the Lord, they returned to Jerusalem, proclaiming the good news to many villages of the Samaritans.

Samaritans

The author of Luke's Gospel appears to have a particular fondness for Samaritans (see Luke 10:25-37; 17:11-19). The author of Acts treats them as the first "outsider" converts to the Way and seems less favorably inclined toward them; their admiration of Simon marks them as credulous and of questionable fidelity to the one God. Hostility between the people of Judah and those of Samaria was centuries-old and deeply embittered. Nowadays we would see Samaritans as one among many Jewish groups until the second or first century BCE, at which point Samaritan scholars introduced some variant readings into their Pentateuch to support worship on Mount Gerizim rather than in Jerusalem. The division continues even today. Lukas papers over it; to him all the peoples of the Covenant, even deviants like the Samaritans, are part of the nation called by God, and the word of salvation belongs to them too. This is one of the passages that may reflect dialogue in Ephesus between the authors of the Fourth Gospel and of Acts (see especially John 4).

At verse 9 we meet the first real "outsider" to be attracted to the Move-ment in the person of Simon, who may or may not be a Samaritan. (Lukas is very fond of the expression "[a] certain . . . [τίς]"; it appears a dozen times in Acts in this mildly distancing sense.) Simon is not called a μάγος although he does "practice magic," and the people accept his assurance that he is someone great. But here for the first time in Acts, and by no means the last, Lukas addresses a favorite theme: magic is devilish, corrupting, and infinitely inferior to the message of Jesus and his Movement. Philip overtrumps Simon; on hearing Philip's preach-ing and seeing his "signs" (*not* magic), many believe and are baptized, including Simon himself.

Still, all is not well with Simon; when Peter and John come from Jeru-salem to pray for the newly baptized and bestow the Holy Spirit, Simon offers to purchase the power from them, thus becoming eternally infa-mous for committing the sin that will be named for him: simony (= at-tempting to purchase sacred office or power). Evidently Simon seeks to retain his position as a wonder-worker by buying a portion of the Spirit above and beyond what others receive—clear evidence that he has not grasped the nature of the Way. Peter rebukes him in the most violent fashion, and Simon asks penitently that Peter will pray "that nothing of what you have said may happen to me." It appears that Simon retains a magical idea of divine power that would not be out of the mainstream of ancient Near Eastern thinking: those with power to summon a spirit receive, or become able to effect, what they ask that power to do. Peter's reaction reinforces the point that the Spirit is not in the power of the in-dividual apostles to convey, while also implying the consistent Lukan aversion to the misuse of wealth.

Magic and Magicians in Acts

Three times in Acts we read of magicians in confrontation with leaders of the Movement: Simon "Magus" in 8:9-24; Bar-Jesus/Elymas in 13:6-12; the seven sons of Sceva in 19:11-29. Susan R. Garrett[2] has argued that Lukas's point in these encounters is to show that (a) practicing "magic" is serving Satan; (b) Jesus has conquered Satan, as shown in Luke's Gospel; (c) those who continue to serve Satan are doomed together with him, because the victorious Jesus will

2. Susan R. Garrett, *The Demise of the Devil: Magic and the Demonic in Luke's Writings* (Minneapolis: Fortress, 1989).

judge them all. The defeat of each of the three practitioners or sets of practitioners demonstrates this, and at the end of the third episode some, at least, of those practicing magic in Ephesus burn their valuable books of spells.

For Lukas, Garrett writes, there are only two powers at war in the world: Jesus, the anointed of Israel's God, and Satan. Heretofore Satan has held sway in the world and has often seduced even God's own people away from God, but now God has conquered through the Son, and Satan's ultimate doom is sure. The sooner everyone comes to recognize that, the sooner the reign of God will come throughout the world. Israel is anointed to bring the word of God's sovereignty to the nations (which by definition are servants of Satan because they worship other gods). But Lukas's view of Israel's history is strongly influenced by his reading of Isaiah: God's people have continually fallen into idolatry, serving other gods. YHWH has also continually forgiven them. Now that YHWH's anointed, Jesus, has won the final victory it is vital that Israel assume its role as example and messenger to the nations. The first part of Acts has shown how that should be done. All this history—as Lukas understands it—has been summarized in Stephen's speech. Now is the time for action. It will be necessary to oppose the unrepentant, as personified in the practitioners of magic (who act in the power and person of Satan), because they pollute the community and resist the power of the One who has conquered in Jesus' death and resurrection.

Mitzi J. Smith analyzes the story of Simon as part of her demonstration of "how characters are constructed as internal and external others in the book of Acts."[3] Her literary analysis focuses on how Lukas uses characters' interactions to show the differences between "approved" mediators of teaching and those who are portrayed as "others," whether inside or outside the Movement group. She finds Simon to be an "external other," distinguished by his magical practices (and thinking) from Philip and Peter and showing that, despite his baptism, he is an outsider. It is not clear whether he receives the Spirit together with the other converts. Peter's authoritative denunciation renders him powerless, deprived even of the authority he had previously exercised, and thus a "nobody" in the Samaritan community. We hear nothing further of his fate, but Christian imagination was more than equal to the task of

---

3. Mitzi J. Smith, *The Literary Construction of the Other in the Acts of the Apostles: Charismatics, the Jews, and Women* (Eugene, OR: Pickwick, 2011), 21. In Garrett's terms, "others" are constructed as servants of Satan, from whom Simon's "authority" came.

demonizing him, making him the arch-heretic, the pattern for all others.

Hans-Josef Klauck has detailed the way Simon was condemned. The Acts of Peter depict him competing with Peter in Rome and dying ignominiously. This is contrary to Lukas's intent, as revealed in his leaving the story open-ended both here and in chapter 28. Simon's reaction in verse 24 reveals his repentance, and Codex D makes this more emphatic by adding "he did not cease to shed many tears." By presenting this warning in narrative form to those still attached to or backsliding into pagan practices, or those abusing church offices, Lukas offers hope to the repentant in all generations. Conversion, he says, is not once-for-all; it is a lifetime task.[4]

A queering analysis is appropriate for this and the stories of encounters between Paul and practitioners of magic at 13:6-12 and 19:11-20. Simon is portrayed as neither altogether an insider nor completely an outsider: before his baptism he is doing magic in Samaria, but we are not told that he is a Samaritan; after his baptism he has apparently surrendered his previous power and cannot obtain a new one. Moreover, he is someone who does magic but is not a Magus (despite the postbiblical traditions in which he becomes "Simon Magus"). He calls himself "Great" (μέγας), yet he is rendered powerless and fearful by men who make no such claims.

The other two sets of characters, the ones Paul encounters, are portrayed (apparently) as Jews but outsiders to the Movement: either hostile to it or, like Simon, hoping to take advantage of it. In both those cases, as we will see, their defeat and humiliation benefits the Movement; that is not said of Simon and may be the reason why he was made the subject of attacks in later tradition. The destiny of all three sets of characters is left open; their punishment invites (and perhaps causes) repentance. Not so with the only two "heretics" from within the Movement, Ananias and Sapphira: their internal betrayal of the community is punished immediately and irrevocably.

Magic was itself an ambiguous phenomenon in the world of Acts. In the circles of philosophers and religious thinkers in which Lukas moved

---

4. Hans-Josef Klauck, *Magic and Paganism in Early Christianity: The World of the Acts of the Apostles*, trans. Brian McNeil (Minneapolis: Fortress, 2003), 22–23.

it was looked down on as superstition and manipulation, but it was a major component of popular religion. It was frequently associated—negatively—with women, so that the gender identity of a man specializing in magic was implicitly suspect. As we are beginning to see, there is virtually no significant character in Acts, certainly none who moves the plot forward, who is not somehow queered. The next person we meet on the page is the paradigmatic example of what that can mean.

Acts 8:26-40

The Ethiopian

This story, which seems to stand like a dolmen in the landscape of Acts, unrelated to anything else, is in fact of enormous significance. It shows Philip completing his independent mission,
quite beyond anything he might have planned, by being confronted
with someone utterly strange to his milieu, exotic and singular. Philip
is plopped down beside him and then summarily removed as soon as
he has completed his task of introducing the Ethiopian to faith in Jesus
and initiating him through baptism. The Ethiopian "went on his way
rejoicing," most certainly not meaning to keep his experience to himself.
It seems that, in the Lukan scheme, this person has been chosen by the
Holy Spirit to evangelize the whole of Africa, at least. He is, in Lukas's
telling, the very first missionary to Jews and gentiles outside the land
of Israel and implicitly to the whole world. As the whole human race
(we now know) sprang from an African woman, so the whole of the
Jesus movement outside the Mediterranean world emanates first from
an African eunuch.

The presence of the Ethiopian in the story (or on the margins of the narrative proper) opens up a range of topics that interest us very much in our
century, though for Lukas some are peripheral. Hans-Josef Klauck gave
a brilliant summary of most of the issues in his book *Magic and Paganism
in Early Christianity*, though neither magic nor paganism plays any role
here. As he writes: "Luke's presentation at vv. 27-28 displays all his skill

111

Acts 8:26-40

[26]Then an angel of the Lord said to Philip, "Get up and go toward the south to the road that goes down from Jerusalem to Gaza." (This is a wilderness road.) [27]So he got up and went. Now there was an Ethiopian eunuch, a court official of the Candace, queen of the Ethiopians, in charge of her entire treasury*. He had come to Jerusalem to worship [28]and was returning home; seated in his chariot, he was reading the prophet Isaiah. [29]Then the Spirit said to Philip, "Go over to this chariot and join it." [30]So Philip ran up to it and heard him reading the prophet Isaiah. He asked, "Do you understand what you are reading?" [31]He replied, "How can I, unless someone guides me?" And he invited Philip to get in and sit beside him. [32]Now the passage of the scripture that he was reading was this:
"Like a sheep he was led to the
    slaughter,
    and like a lamb silent before its
        shearer,
    so he does not open his
        mouth.
[33]In his humiliation justice was
    denied him.
    Who can describe his generation?
    For his life is taken away
        from the earth."

* A nice wordplay: the man traveling in Γάζα is in charge of the queen's γάζης.—LM

in the narrative description of persons. Using only a few attributes and relative clauses, he lets us see the picture of a living personality."[1] In those two verses we learn that the man is an *Ethiopian* (i.e., from today's northern Sudan), a *eunuch*, *treasurer* or *chancellor* to the Candace (queen mother), and therefore of high *social status* and, evidently, *wealthy*. He is also an adherent of Israel's religion although, as a eunuch, he could not be a full member but would have been treated as a "God-fearer."

The Eunuch

In Acts 8:27 the reader is introduced to a character with multiple identities: ἀνὴρ Αἰθίοψ εὐνοῦχος δυνάστης Κανδάκης βασιλίσσης Αἰθιόπων, ὃς ἦν ἐπὶ πάσης τῆς γάζης αὐτῆς. Out of all these ways of identifying the character, the only one that the author uses throughout the rest of the story is εὐνοῦχος, "eunuch" (8:34, 36, 38, and 39). This eunuch from Ethiopia was reading the prophet Isaiah on his way home from Jerusalem when he was joined by Philip, one of the seven men appointed by the apostles to the task of service in 6:1-6. Philip proclaims the good news to him, and then the

1. Hans-Josef Klauck, *Magic and Paganism in Early Christianity: The World of the Acts of the Apostles*, trans. Brian McNeil (Minneapolis: Fortress, 2003), 24.

34The eunuch asked Philip, "About whom, may I ask you, does the prophet say this, about himself or about someone else?" 35Then Philip began to speak, and starting with this scripture, he proclaimed to him the good news about Jesus. 36As they were going along the road, they came to some water; and the eunuch said, "Look, here is water! What is to prevent me from being baptized?"* 38He commanded the chariot to stop, and both of them, Philip and the eunuch, went down into the water, and Philip baptized him. 39When they came up out of the water, the Spirit of the Lord snatched Philip away; the eunuch saw him no more, and went on his way rejoicing. 40But Philip found himself at Azotus, and as he was passing through the region, he proclaimed the good news to all the towns until he came to Caesarea.

* NRSV: Other ancient authorities add all or most of verse 37. "And Philip said, 'If you believe with all your heart, you may.' And he replied, 'I believe that Jesus Christ is the Son of God.'"

---

eunuch asks the central question of the narrative: "Behold, water; what is preventing me from being baptized?" (8:36).[2] In his first sermon Peter told the audience how to respond properly to the gospel: "Repent and be baptized each of you in the name of Jesus Christ for the forgiveness of your sins, and you will receive the gift of the Holy Spirit" (2:38). Those who were baptized "devoted themselves to the teaching of the apostles and to the community, to the breaking of bread and to the prayers" (2:42). So may this eunuch from Ethiopia be baptized, receive the gift of the Holy Spirit, and devote himself to the community?

I come to the interpretation of Acts 8:26-40 with particular questions and interests. First, how would a narrative about a eunuch have been read in the social context of the early audiences of Acts? Second, how does this narrative fit into the larger narrative of the book as a whole? I am also interested in identifying biblical materials that can enable a more inclusive vision of community among contemporary Christians, especially in relation to the diversity of genders and sexualities. I have found that queer theory can be very helpful in pursuing this final interest.

Throughout history, cultural groups have tended to naturalize and essentialize their culturally specific explanations of gender and sexuality. In other words, although gender and sexuality

---

2. Translations of biblical and classical literature are my own.—SDB

are social constructions, people have understood and explained them as being determined by nature (biology) in such a way as to create stable essences as a core feature of human identity. This kind of thinking leads to the claim, long opposed by feminists, that "biology is destiny." One way to resist such problematic dominant social constructions of gender and sexuality—including patriarchy, hegemonic masculinity, and heteronormativity—is to deconstruct, or queer, cultural texts, to pull back the curtain in order to reveal that they are indeed social constructions and not the natural order of the world.[3]

No one knows exactly when the first human males were castrated, although it was probably after the first cattle were castrated around 2300 BCE.[4] Castration usually involved the crushing or removal of the testicles (while leaving the penis intact), thus rendering those males incapable of reproduction. Two different types of eunuchs were probably familiar to the early audiences of Acts: the *galli*, devotees of the goddess Cybele who castrated themselves, and the court eunuchs who served rulers or imperial officials.

The social role of the court eunuch probably developed from rulers' need to guard the women (and children) of their harems. Over time some rulers began to employ the eunuchs in their households as royal and imperial administrators, perhaps to counterbalance the power of the nobility. The employment of eunuchs is well documented for the courts of Mesopotamia, Persia, China, India, Rome, and Byzantium, and if one accepts my argument that the relevant Akkadian, Hebrew, and Greek words for "eunuch" should always be read as "a castrated male," then eunuchs were also employed in the royal courts of Israel and Judah.[5]

The very existence of court eunuchs troubled the multiple, intersecting, foundational binary oppositions on which the dominant Greco-Roman construction of masculinity was built: hairy/smooth, active/passive, sexually insertive/sexually receptive, impenetrable/penetrable, inviolable/violable, free/enslaved, and citizen (or native)/foreigner. As characters in Greco-Roman texts, therefore, eunuchs have the potential to queer ancient masculinity, that is, to reveal its constructedness, contingency, and instability.

---

3. For more on queer theory see Sean D. Burke, *Queering the Ethiopian Eunuch: Strategies of Ambiguity in Acts*, Emerging Scholars (Minneapolis: Fortress, 2013), 39–65.

4. Gary Taylor, *Castration: An Abbreviated History of Western Manhood* (New York: Routledge, 2000), 167–69.

5. For the full argument see Burke, *Queering the Ethiopian Eunuch*, 19–38.

Most court eunuchs were castrated before puberty. The embodied results of castration included a mixture of features normatively coded as masculine and feminine. Compared to normatively embodied adult males, such eunuchs lacked facial and body hair, had wider hips and higher voices, and tended to have less developed musculature. In addition, the distribution of body fat was more characteristic of adult females, tending to produce an enlargement of the breasts and buttocks. That their ambiguous bodies troubled distinctions of gender is reflected in the inability of ancient authors to agree on their gender identity: they variously gendered eunuchs as effeminate males, half-men/half-males, girls, beings that have changed (or are in the process of changing) from male to female, hybrids of male and female, neither male nor female, and even as not human. How secure a foundation for ancient masculinity could gender be if a human being that began life as a normative male could relatively easily be transformed into something else?

It was generally believed in the Greco-Roman world that eunuchs castrated before puberty lacked sexual desire, but that did not prevent ancient authors from speculating on their sexuality. It was perfectly acceptable for eunuchs to be penetrated by those socially recognized as men. Given their proximity to the women of the royal court, however, it was feared that they were also penetrated by women (through oral sex), which upset the foundational sexual distinctions on which masculinity depended.[6] In addition, ancient authors feared that some eunuchs could still achieve erections and hence could usurp a man's role as the penetrator of his wife without ever leaving evidence in the form of pregnancy. How secure, then, were the foundational distinctions between activity and passivity, sexual insertiveness and receptiveness, and impenetrability and penetrability on which the dominant Greco-Roman construction of masculinity depended?

One could not achieve masculinity, meaning one could not be socially recognized as a man in the Greco-Roman world, unless one were freeborn. Most eunuchs were slaves or freedmen, so they would seem to have been disqualified. Aristotle famously argued that some human beings were by nature rulers while others were by nature slaves.[7] The problem is that the sources of enslaved persons included freeborn boys who had been kidnapped, captured in war, or exposed to die. Did their

6. On the understanding of oral sex within a construction of sexuality defined by penetration see ibid., 73–75.
7. See Aristotle, *Politics* 1.1-2.

enslavement demonstrate that they were slaves by nature, or did it point to the fragility and instability of the distinction between free and enslaved? In addition, eunuchs—slaves or freedmen who had been castrated involuntarily—rose to positions of power, including in some cases power over those who were socially recognized as men. Xenophon offered an explanation as to why rulers like Cyrus of Persia chose eunuchs as their most intimate servants:

> And [Cyrus] held that no one would ever be faithful who loved another more than the one who required his guarding. He believed, therefore, that those who had children or agreeable wives or boyfriends were by nature constrained to love these ones most. But as he saw that eunuchs lacked all these things, he held that they would esteem most highly such ones as could best make them rich, stand by them if they were wronged, and place them in offices of honor; and he held that no one could sur-pass him in bestowing such favors. Besides these things, as eunuchs are disreputable among other people, on account of this as well they need a master and defender; for there is no man who would not think himself worthy to have more than a eunuch in everything unless there were someone more powerful to prevent his doing so; but there is noth-ing to prevent even a eunuch from being superior to all in faithfulness to his master.[8]

Paradoxically, the power of eunuchs depended on their alienation from their natal families, their inability to father children, and their absolute dependence on their masters.

Finally, one had to be born a citizen (or a native) in order to have the possibility of achieving social recognition as a man in the Greco-Roman world. Eunuchs were identified as foreigners in this world, even in contexts where (as scholars now know) a significant number of them were citizens (or natives) who had been provided to the royal court by their families. Eunuchs were especially associated with Persians, an "Asiatic" people to whom Greco-Roman authors attributed characteristics of effeminacy and slavishness.[9] How secure was masculinity when those perceived as effeminate, slavish, foreign eunuchs could exercise power over them precisely *because* they were effeminate, slavish, and foreign?

The juxtapositions of identities in the character introduced

8. Xenophon, *Cyropaedia* 7.5.58-65.
9. On Roman views of the Persians/Parthians see Benjamin Isaac, *The Invention of Racism in Classical Antiquity* (Princeton: Princeton University Press, 2004), 371–80.

in Acts 8:27 highlights all the ways in which eunuchs could destabilize the foundational distinctions on which the dominant Greco-Roman construction of masculinity depended. This person is both a eunuch (εὐνοῦχος) and an ἀνὴρ (the gendered term for a "man") rather than ἄνθρωπος (the generic term for a "human being"). He is both a eunuch and a powerful official (δυνάστης) whose possession of a chariot and a scroll suggests that he owned or had access to wealth (and could read!). He is both a eunuch and an Ethiopian (Αἰθίοψ), and he is the Ethiopian queen mother's servant, which might have raised uncomfortable questions around sexuality.

The entrance of the Ethiopian eunuch into the narrative can be read as a drag performance. "Drag" is a term that is typically used to describe a performance in which the assigned sex of a performer is not the same as the gender being performed. Judith Butler argues that "in imitating gender, drag implicitly reveals the imitative structure of gender itself—as well as its contingency," for rather than parodying an original, drag reveals that all gender is "imitation without an origin."[10] While not all drag performances queer normative constructions of gender and sexuality, I think that the Ethiopian eunuch's has the potential to do so because ultimately an audience cannot determine which of his identities are natural and which are performed. Such a drag performance pulls back the curtain and reveals the constructedness, contingency, and instability of ancient masculinity.

It is this drag performer who now wants to be baptized into the community of the Way. Baptism is connected with "religious" identity in the first half of Acts. Those who are baptized in 2:42 are identified as Jews and proselytes (2:9-11), and those who are baptized in 8:12 are identified as Samaritans. Thus far, then, only the children of Israel have been baptized. But the identity of the Ethiopian eunuch is a collection of ambiguities, and this extends to his "religious" identity as well. Reception history demonstrates that over the centuries various interpreters have argued that the Ethiopian eunuch must be read as a Jew, as a proselyte, and as a gentile.[11] Some have even suggested that the author of Acts knew that he was a gentile but introduced ambiguity into his identity because he wanted him to be read as a figure on the periphery of the children of Israel, perhaps to cover up the conflict between this narrative

---

10. Judith Butler, *Gender Trouble: Feminism and the Subversion of Identity* (New York: Routledge, 1990), 137–38.

11. See Burke, *Queering the Ethiopian Eunuch*, 1–5.

and the narrative of Cornelius regarding the first baptism of a gentile.[12]

Deuteronomy 23:1 prohibited the admission of one whose testicles have been crushed to the assembly of YHWH. Nevertheless, according to the author of Acts the Ethiopian eunuch had come to Jerusalem to worship (v. 27), he was reading the prophet Isaiah (vv. 34-35), he heard Philip's proclamation of the gospel (vv. 34-35), and he asked to be baptized (v. 36). Are these the actions of a Jew, a proselyte, or a gentile? Are these the actions of a God-fearer, a construction of identity that itself destabilizes the distinction between Jew and gentile? If his "religious" identity is indeterminable, should this prevent him from being baptized? In the narrative it does not.

How, then, does this narrative of the baptism of a eunuch from Ethiopia fit into the book's story as a whole? At the beginning of this narrative an angel of the Lord tells Philip to get up and go where the angel directs (8:26). An angel of the Lord speaks to other characters in

Acts as well, to tell them what to do at key moments in the narrative (see 5:19-20; 10:3-6; 27:23-24). In the midst of the narrative the Spirit tells Philip to join the eunuch's chariot (8:29), just as the Spirit tells other characters in Acts what to do at key moments (see 10:19-20; 13:2; 16:6-7; 20:23; 21:11). At the end of the narrative the Spirit snatches Philip away (8:39-40). There is only one other story in Acts in which an angel speaks at the beginning, the Spirit speaks in the midst, and the Spirit acts at the end, and that is the narrative of Cornelius. The key question is how to understand the relationship between the narratives of the eunuch from Ethiopia and Cornelius.

Elsewhere I have proposed what I might now call a maximal interpretation.[13] If we read the quotation from Joel 3:1-5 in Acts 2:17-21 as a programmatic statement, the book of Acts is the narrative of the expansion of a small community of Jewish followers of the Way of Jesus with the goal that the Spirit be poured out on all flesh and everyone who calls on the name of the Lord be saved.

12. These include Hans Conzelmann (*Acts of the Apostles: A Commentary*, trans. James Limburg, A. Thomas Kraabel, and Donald H. Juel, Hermeneia [Philadelphia: Fortress, 1987], 68), Luke Timothy Johnson (*The Acts of the Apostles*, SP 5 [Collegeville, MN: Liturgical Press, 1992], 159), Howard Clark Kee (*To Every Nation under Heaven: The Acts of the Apostles*, New Testament in Context [Harrisburg, PA: Trinity Press International, 1997], 110), and Ben Witherington III (*The Acts of the Apostles: A Socio-Rhetorical Commentary* [Grand Rapids: Eerdmans, 1998], 292–93). For a full discussion see Burke, *Queering the Ethiopian Eunuch*, 7–10.

13. See Burke, *Queering the Ethiopian Eunuch*, 138–41.

The narrative begins with the baptism of Jews and proselytes in chapter 2, continues with the baptism of Samaritans in the first part of chapter 8, and then the baptism of the eunuch from Ethiopia in the second part of that chapter. The eunuch's ambiguity serves to disqualify "religious" identity as a basis for inclusion or exclusion from baptism, and thus there is nothing to prevent the baptism of the unambiguously gentile Cornelius and his household in chapter 10. The focus in the narrative of Cornelius, then, shifts to the issue of table fellowship between Jewish and gentile followers of the Way, which is gradually resolved in chapters 11–15, and the rest of Acts narrates Paul's ongoing mission to the gentiles.

One thing I like about this maximal interpretation is that it queers Acts itself by taking a narrative that has traditionally been identified as marginal to the book and demonstrating that it is rhetorically productive to read it as central. I am mindful, however, that in contemporary English Bibles the narrative of the Ethiopian eunuch consists of fourteen or fifteen verses (depending on whether or not one includes 8:37), while the narrative of Cornelius contains sixty-six verses, including both the narration and its repetition in summary form in the words of Peter to the community in Jerusalem. I am more and more open, therefore, to the more "minimal" interpretation of the many scholars who argue that the narrative is indeed loosely connected to the rest of the book and primarily serves the purpose of fulfilling the promise of Isaiah 56:3-8 that Y_HWH_ will gather eunuchs and foreigners into the restored Israel. With the restoration of Israel completed in chapter 8, then, the author of Acts moves on to the mission to the gentiles.

It is entirely possible that the author's interest in the narrative of the eunuch from Ethiopia was limited to the issue of "religious" identity and inclusion within a restored Israel. In choosing a narrative about a eunuch, however, the author (unknowingly) produced a surplus of meaning that could be activated in new ways in new contexts. Contemporary Christians can read this as a narrative of inclusion in the community of the Way regardless of whether one is free or enslaved, citizen/native or foreigner, sexually insertive or sexually receptive, male, female, or anything in between. Such a reading is especially liberating for contemporary Christians who identify as lesbian, gay, bisexual, trans, queer, intersexed, asexual, or others defined in some way by gender and/or sexuality (LGBTQIA+ persons).

I describe the Ethiopian eunuch of Acts 8:26-40 as a queering figure. I am not thereby suggesting that eunuchs were the "direct ancestors" of gay, transgender, or queer persons as those identities are constructed today, nor am I proposing that an ancient eunuch would have possessed some sort of "queer consciousness." Instead I am proposing that ancient eunuchs queered the foundational distinctions of gender, sexuality, freedom, and citizenship on which the dominant Greco-Roman construction of masculinity depended. Likewise, today's LGBTQIA+ persons share this potential for queering the contemporary dominant constructions that perpetuate patriarchy, hegemonic masculinity, and heteronormativity.

Many LGBTQIA+ Christians today are asking questions similar to the one asked by the eunuch from Ethiopia: "Behold, water; what is preventing me from being baptized?" (8:36). We are asking not only what bars us from baptism but what prevents us from full membership in the community, from full inclusion at the table, from presiding at the table, and from receiving God's and the community's blessing on our relationships. In light of Acts 8:26-40 the answer should be, "Nothing at all," and I am glad to say that some churches and other religious bodies have heeded this word and taken the next step in expanding the circle of inclusion to more followers of the Way. It is my hope that more churches will follow their lead.

Sean D. Burke

I, personally, favor a maximalist interpretation: this is *not* the beginning of the gentile mission or simply an expansion of the Movement that is not defined by religious or national identity. Instead, it is the fulfillment of the vision of Trito-Isaiah. Having learned from Philip who is the subject of Isaiah 53, the Ethiopian can indeed rejoice in reading, three chapters later, a promise that when

> my salvation will come,
>   and my deliverance be revealed . . .
>   . . .
> Do not let the foreigner joined to the Lord say,
>   "The Lord will surely separate me from his people";
> and do not let the eunuch say,
>   "I am just a dry tree."
> For thus says the Lord:
> To the eunuchs who keep my sabbaths,
>   who choose the things that please me
>   and hold fast my covenant,
> I will give, in my house and within my walls,
>   a monument and a name
>   better than sons and daughters;

I will give them an everlasting name
   that shall not be cut off.
  . . .
all who keep the sabbath, and do not profane it,
   and hold fast my covenant—
these I will bring to my holy mountain,
   and make them joyful in my house of prayer;
their burnt offerings and their sacrifices
   will be accepted on my altar;
for my house shall be called a house of prayer
   for all peoples. (Isa 56:1, 3-7)

This time of salvation, Lukas believes, is a time when God will break down all barriers *within* the people of God, a unity that will then lead to the "pilgrimage of the nations" (cf. Isa 47, *inter alia*). If the end of the passage above seems familiar, it should: the Synoptic evangelists all quote it, in whole or in part, at the climax of the scene in which Jesus expels the merchants and money-changers from the temple (Mark 11:17; Matt 21:13; Luke 19:46), thus preparing for the fulfillment of this end-time prophecy.

The inclusion of the Ethiopian is the final action that signals the all-inclusive nature of the people of God and so sets the stage for welcoming even gentiles (foreigners) into God's family.

Acts 9:1-31

The Calling of Saul

The first seven chapters of Acts have Peter, the apostles, and the Jerusalem community as their setting and binding characters. Chapters 16–28 are a chronicle of Paul and his activities. The middle chapters, 8–15, are less unified because they describe transitions, conversions, and crucial decisions that will drive the rest of the action. Lukas is not adept at changes between places and leading characters; he tends to park certain characters offstage until they are next needed. So Philip, having played his role in chapter 8, is stationed at Caesarea until he reappears to play a minor part in chapter 21. Barnabas was introduced in 4:36, and, given his description, one would have expected him to be chosen as one of the Seven, but he was not. He resurfaces at 9:27 to reassure the "disciples" at Jerusalem that Saul is a changed man; he seems to know what had happened at Damascus though we are never told he was there. Barnabas will continue to be a significant mediator between Antioch and Jerusalem, as well as a missionary companion of Paul, until the end of Acts 15.

Saul was introduced as a zealous persecutor of the Jerusalem community in 8:1-3, thus providing a reason for the community's partial dispersal, and consequent mission, to Samaria and beyond. He now reappears at the beginning of chapter 9. His zeal is undiminished; the Greek text more than implies that he believed a violent persecution of

9:1Meanwhile Saul, still breathing threats and murder against the disciples of the Lord, went to the high priest 2and asked him for letters to the synagogues at Damascus, so that if he found any who belonged to the Way, men or women, he might bring them bound to Jerusalem. 3Now as he was going along and approaching Damascus, suddenly a light from heaven flashed around him. 4He fell to the ground and heard a voice saying to him, "Saul, Saul, why do you persecute me?" 5He asked, "Who are you, Lord?" The reply came, "I am Jesus, whom you are persecuting. 6But get up and enter the city, and you will be told what you are to do." 7The men who were traveling with him stood speechless because they heard the voice but saw no one. 8Saul got up from the ground, and though his eyes were open, he could see nothing; so they led him by the hand and brought him into Damascus. 9For three days he was without sight, and neither ate nor drank.

10Now there was a disciple in Damascus named Ananias. The Lord said to him in a vision, "Ananias." He answered, "Here I am, Lord." 11The Lord said to him, "Get up and go to the street called Straight, and at the house of Judas look for a man of Tarsus named Saul. At this moment he is praying, 12and he has seen in a vision a man named Ananias come in and lay his hands on him so that he might re-

the Movement would work to his advantage in Jerusalem.[1] "Breathing" (threats and murder) is a mild translation of the Greek ἐμπνέω, which in the LXX described the "snorting" of Yʜwʜ, like a stormy wind (Isa 40:24), or the vicious behavior of the ungodly.[2] Saul is "snorting fire" against members of the Way. His journey to Damascus does bestow on him the utmost benefit, but it does so by reversing his plans and expectations. Acts 9:3-18 narrates his call for the first time (he will tell it again himself in chapters 22 and 26) and describes his acceptance into the Jesus movement, but there is other important business to be dealt with in chapters 10–12, so at the end of the episode Saul, like Philip, is "parked" at a distance in Tarsus (9:30); Barnabas will retrieve him from there in 11:25.

Why Tarsus? Because it was Paul's home town, of course. Really? Paul himself never mentions the place in his letters. We only "know" that Paul

1. Thus Mikeal C. Parsons and Martin M. Culy, *Acts: A Handbook on the Greek Text* (Waco, TX: Baylor University Press, 2003), 170, on Acts 9:2: "ᾐτήσατο . . . The middle [voice] denotes personal benefit to the one asking."

2. In 2 Macc 9:7 Antiochus was "breathing fire in his rage against the Jews." See also Josephus, *J.W.* 5.458.

gain his sight." [13]But Ananias answered, "Lord, I have heard from many about this man, how much evil he has done to your saints in Jerusalem; [14]and here he has authority from the chief priests to bind all who invoke your name." [15]But the Lord said to him, "Go, for he is an instrument whom I have chosen to bring my name before Gentiles and kings and before the people of Israel; [16]I myself will show him how much he must suffer for the sake of my name." [17]So Ananias went and entered the house. He laid his hands on Saul and said, "Brother Saul, the Lord Jesus, who appeared to you on your way here, has sent me so that you may regain your sight and be filled with the Holy Spirit." [18]And immediately something like scales fell from his eyes, and his sight was restored. Then he got up and was baptized, [19]and after taking some food, he regained his strength.

For several days he was with the disciples in Damascus, [20]and immediately he began to proclaim Jesus in the synagogues, saying, "He is the Son of God." [21]All who heard him were amazed and said, "Is not this the man who made havoc in Jerusalem among those who invoked this name? And has he not come here for the purpose of bringing them bound before the chief priests?" [22]Saul became increasingly more powerful and confounded the Jews who lived in Damascus by proving that Jesus was the Messiah.

was from Tarsus because Lukas says so in Acts (at 9:11; 21:39; 22:3), each time in connection with the call story. This may be based on tradition, but commentators take it as fact and use it as a basis for asserting that Paul was a "Hellenist Jew." Paul himself says no such thing (cf. his self-description in Phil 3:5),[3] but at his initial appearance in Acts 8 he appears to be a leader among the Hellenists in Jerusalem who are opposed to Stephen. This is plausible because when he returns to Jerusalem in his new role as a preacher of the Way (9:28-30) it is the Hellenists who are enraged at the turncoat and attempt to kill him. Later, at 22:3, Lukas has him say: "I am a Jew, born in Tarsus in Cilicia, but brought up in this city at the feet of Gamaliel, educated strictly according to our ancestral law, being zealous for God." The education in the law and the zeal, as well as his role as a persecutor, are things Paul attributes to himself in his letters; the rest we "know" only from Acts.

3. ". . . circumcised on the eighth day, a member of the people of Israel, of the tribe of Benjamin, a Hebrew born of Hebrews; as to the law, a Pharisee; as to zeal, a persecutor of the church; as to righteousness under the law, blameless."

[23]After some time had passed, the Jews plotted to kill him, [24]but their plot became known to Saul. They were watching the gates day and night so that they might kill him; [25]but his disciples took him by night and let him down through an opening in the wall, lowering him in a basket.

[26]When he had come to Jerusalem, he attempted to join the disciples; and they were all afraid of him, for they did not believe that he was a disciple. [27]But Barnabas took him, brought him to the apostles, and described for them how on the road he had seen the Lord, who had spoken to him, and how in Damascus he had spoken boldly in the name of Jesus. [28]So he went in and out among them in Jerusalem, speaking boldly in the name of the Lord. [29]He spoke and argued with the Hellenists; but they were attempting to kill him. [30]When the believers learned of it, they brought him down to Caesarea and sent him off to Tarsus.

[31]Meanwhile the church throughout Judea, Galilee, and Samaria had peace and was built up. Living in the fear of the Lord and in the comfort of the Holy Spirit, it increased in numbers.

This question is customarily dismissed by proposing that Lukas is using a well-known tradition here.[4] If so, where did he find it? Rainer Riesner's observation about the lack of interest shown in this by critical scholars is apt, but it appears only in a footnote.[5] Making Paul a Jew of the diaspora is convenient for a portrayal of him as called to missionize the gentiles and may also help to explain why (despite Lukas's efforts to conceal the fact) he was from this point onward the object of suspicion by Jews of all sects and persuasions at Jerusalem (and elsewhere)—members of the Way included.[6] It is also helpful to Lukas's portrayal of

4. For the most cogent analysis of Lukas's (non)use of traditional material in describing Paul's calling see Gerhard Lohfink, *Paulus vor Damaskus*, SBS 4 (Stuttgart: Katholisches Bibelwerk, 1966). I am grateful to Professor Lohfink for this and many other insights into the accounts of Paul's calling.

5. Rainer Riesner, *Paul's Early Period: Chronology, Mission Strategy, Theology*, trans. Douglass Stott (Grand Rapids: Eerdmans, 1998), 265n8: "The apostle's origin in Tarsus is also supported by G. Lüdemann, *Early Christianity according to the Traditions in Acts* (Eng. Trans., 1989), 241. It is striking in the larger sense how seldom this bit of Lukan information has been doubted by skeptical scholarship. [!] Has this also had something to do with a certain theological preference for the diaspora Jew Paul, to whom syncretic tendencies might sooner be attributed?"

6. See below at Acts 15 and 21.

Paul's mission: this Paul is a citizen of Tarsus, the capital of Cilicia and "no mean city" (Acts 21:39).[7]

Here again, however, Lukas's (deliberate or inadvertent) queering of Saul/Paul intrudes. In all three accounts of the scene outside Damascus the voice from heaven addresses Saul as Σαούλ, the transliteration of the Hebrew name. We have already noted that until Acts 13 and the beginning of his participation in the gentile mission Saul is always referred to in the *narrative* text as Σαῦλος, yet in 9:4; 22:7; 26:14 he is addressed as Σαούλ, echoing the name of Israel's first king as given in the LXX. (Lukas hammers the point home in 13:21, when he has Paul refer to King Σαούλ in his first missionary speech, in the synagogue at Pisidian Antioch.) The disciple Ananias addresses him in the same way in response to his own vision in 9:17; 22:13, calling him "Brother Saul" (Σαοὺλ ἀδελφέ). This usage signals that the heavenly voice addressed Saul in Hebrew (and so, perhaps, did Ananias) and thus underscores the point that Saul/Paul is first, last, and always a *Jew*. It also reminds readers that Paul identified himself in his own letters as being, like King Σαούλ, "a member of the tribe of Benjamin" (Rom 11:1; Phil 3:5).[8]

We are so used to attributing the double name Saul/Paul to this figure in history that we generally overlook the fact that Paul never refers to himself, in past or present tense, as "Saul," nor does anyone else. Only the author of Acts ever calls him "Saul."[9] Since there is no historical basis for the appellation, its purpose may be to enable the address "Σαούλ, Σαούλ" in the Damascus scene (v. 4). Lukas's audience should understand that the character in Acts may differ in many ways from the Paul they know from the letters, even to the point of bearing a different name (or more than one), yet he is the same complicated person; what one says of oneself and what others report about one are often at variance, yet the different accounts, if sincere, represent the same human reality in different ways.

In that vein it is important to compare and contrast Lukas's account of Saul/Paul with what Paul himself wrote in Galatians (especially chap. 1).

---

7. Thus the AV, which captures the irony in the litotes, οὐκ ἀσήμου πόλεως πολίτης, the rhetorical eloquence of which is completely deflated by the NRSV's "an important city."

8. Contrary to popular interpretation, he does not become "Paul" when he accepts Jesus as Savior; the voice of Jesus always addresses him as Σαούλ. Lukas glides over the change of name at the beginning of Paul's first missionary journey, mentioning it only in an aside.

9. There are a dozen occurrences in the Apocryphal Acts, but those are clearly dependent on the canonical Acts.

Both agree that Paul was deeply learned in and zealous for the law and an eager persecutor of the church. Both say that Jesus was revealed to Paul and that the revelation effected a thorough change in his life.[10] But here (and even in the telling of it) the stories diverge. The description of the scene of his calling is found only in Acts. Paul speaks of it, in his letters, in abstract terms as an event: for example, "when God . . . was pleased to reveal his Son to me" (Gal 1:15-16). He gives much more detail about his travels after that revelation and his encounters with the apostles in Jerusalem and Antioch than about the vision itself (Gal 1:17-19; 2:1-14).

The parallel/contrast will resume with the events of Acts 15. But one other major difference between Paul's and Lukas's version of the effect of Saul/Paul's joining the Way needs to be emphasized. Paul asserts in Galatians (which Lukas certainly knew) that God's purpose in calling him was "so that I might proclaim him [the Son] among the Gentiles" (Gal 1:16). For Lukas the gentile mission will be initiated by God, to be sure, but at Acts 9:30 he removes Saul from the scene so that he can show in Acts 10 how God called *Peter* to begin the gentile mission with the household of the centurion Cornelius.[11]

The Saul of Acts first preaches Jesus *in the synagogues* in Damascus but (as always in Acts) arouses enmity from "the Jews"; he then settles in Jerusalem and takes up Stephen's former role, sparring with the Hellenists. (Purportedly from the diaspora himself, and certainly learned in Greek, he is well-suited to that role.) This is in continuity with his having "confounded the Jews who lived in Damascus." God knows that Paul will be sent to the gentiles, "and kings and . . . the people of Israel," as the narrative of Acts will show, and God confides that fact to Ananias (v. 15), but did Ananias tell Saul? The only hint that a gentile mission is in view is that here, for the first time in Acts, οἱ Ἰουδαῖοι are named as a group separate from the disciples of the Way.

Ananias himself is of interest as an agent in the story. He is clearly a Jewish believer; when the Lord speaks to him in a vision (v. 10), he answers Ἰδοὺ ἐγώ, κύριε ("Here I am, Lord"), the LXX translation of הנני (*hinnēnî*), the proper response when one is addressed by YHWH Elohim, as shown by Abraham in Genesis 22:1.[12] Saul responds to the

---

10. Lukas shapes all three accounts of Saul's/Paul's calling almost word for word according to the pattern of the calling of Jacob in Gen 46:2-3.

11. The scene of Cornelius's call in 10:3-5 parallels Paul's call scene in chaps. 9, 22, and 26.

12. The expression occurs a total of 175 times in the Hebrew Bible, from Abraham in Genesis to Malachi, often merely as a demonstrative, "See . . . ," but it is very

"voice" in 9:5 simply with a polite "Who are you, Lord?" (Τίς εἶ, κύριε; more properly, "Who are you, sir?"). The different expressions show that Ananias recognizes the one speaking to him as *the* Lord (Jesus); ironically, Saul is also being addressed by *the* Lord (Jesus), but does not know him.

Saul begins his imitation of Jesus by remaining in darkness (as Jesus remained in the tomb), not eating or drinking, for three days and nights before Ananias comes to heal and baptize him. Ananias has been told that Saul "is an instrument whom I have chosen to bring my name before Gentiles and kings" as well as before Israel, but he does not tell Saul that, only that he has been sent so Saul may regain his sight and be filled with the Holy Spirit (= baptized). Was Ananias taking things one step at a time, given his apprehension about Saul's character as a persecutor of the Way? Lukas's audience would have known what Saul/Paul's mission was to be, but he himself may not learn it now because the gentile mission will begin with Peter, in Acts 10.

Paul's account in Galatians goes on to show him as *the* apostle to the gentiles, and indeed the messenger of a gospel that entirely abrogates the law of Moses as far as gentiles are concerned.[13] His whole focus is to be on converting gentiles, and he will seldom appeal to his fellow Jews (though he may mourn over them in the letter to the Romans). Lukas's Saul/Paul is an altogether different character, and his Jesus movement is very unlike Paul's mission. The gentile mission will be inaugurated by God, through Peter, in chapter 10 and defended by Peter in Jerusalem in Acts 11. It will be seen bearing fruit later in that chapter and will burst into bloom in Acts 13–14 with the first "foreign" mission of Barnabas and Paul. In Acts 15 Lukas will show the Jerusalem community, led by James and Peter, coming together in council to affirm a rule of life in accord with Torah precedent that makes room for Jews who observe the law and gentiles who keep the rules prescribed in Genesis for non-Jews. His

---

familiar in the above sense from its repeated use in 1 Sam 3:4-16 when Yhwh calls Samuel and from Isaiah's response to his call vision in Isa 6:8: "Here am I; send me!"

13. For Paul's references to his calling see Gal 1:11-17; 1 Cor 15:5-9. His account differs from that of Lukas in three significant ways: (1) Paul insistently calls himself an "apostle"; he sees that as the legitimation of his mission (cf. Rom 1:1; 1 Cor 1:1; 9:1-3; 15:9-11; 2 Cor 1:1; Gal 1:1–2:14). For Lukas only the Twelve are "the apostles" and the definition is given in Acts 1:21-22 at the election of Matthias. (2) Paul links his calling to the Easter events; Lukas sets it clearly apart from them, which has to do with his plot-scheme: Paul is called to the gentile mission, and he is not part of the beginnings. (3) In Paul's version he is called directly by Jesus (cf. Gal 1:1); Lukas focuses on the mediation of the call through the community (represented by Ananias and Barnabas). For details see Lohfink, *Paulus vor Damaskus*, esp. 85–89.

Paul thereafter conducts mission trips throughout Asia Minor and parts of Greece, but wherever he goes he starts in the synagogue, only leaving it when he is chased out. We are supposed to surmise that Lukas's Paul preaches the rule of life assented to by the Jerusalem council, relaxing the precept of male circumcision for gentile members but retaining the dietary and ethical commandments.

Paul writes in the heat of battle, defending his understanding of what the message is to be and of the way he should conduct his mission. He is "zealous" for the law and for the gospel, remaining a firebrand throughout his life. Lukas writes in retrospect; he knows what Paul wrote but he reads his character and activity in accord with the purposes of his own narrative, which is still intent on persuading both Jewish believers in the diaspora and gentile potential believers there that Jesus is the prophet foretold, the last and definitive word of God to God's people, and the Savior of the world, though hints of the "historical" Paul leak through here and there, as will appear.

We may note that Acts is full of visions and dreams and encounters with the risen Jesus, but they all happen to men—even men who are not yet part of the Movement, like Saul and Cornelius.[14] In chapter 16 we will meet Lydia, a "God-fearer," and learn that "the Lord opened her heart to listen eagerly to what was said by Paul." Hers is surely no less a revelation of the Lord than that of Cornelius, but it is said to be through human agency and not a direct encounter with Jesus or an angel. (Are Lukas's women more rational than men?)

A brief account of Saul's work among the Jews in Damascus shows that he has not ceased to be a troublemaker, though now by haranguing ("confounding") the Jewish population of the city, who soon have enough of him. A comic scene—an intertextual reminiscence of the escape of the Israelite spies from Jericho in Joshua 2:15-23—gives a light touch to the first of Saul/Paul's many escapes from the hands of enemies both Jewish and gentile. In the book of Joshua, Israel's spies were "let down by a rope through the window" by Rahab, whose house was part of the city wall (v. 15). Lukas knows the story, but he eschews any characterization of "his [Paul's] disciples." A Jewish audience, at least, would have appreciated the parallel and perhaps pictured a scene involving the local Rahab. Paul then goes to Jerusalem, where he is distrusted (for good reason!) by both

14. Contrast this program in Acts with Mary's angelic encounter in the infancy narrative in Luke (Luke 1:26-38).

the people of the Way and his erstwhile companions, the "Hellenists."
Barnabas reappears to vouch for him to the Jerusalem Jesus community,
but there is no appeasing his former Hellenist allies; a second attempt is
made on Saul's life, and he is dispatched via Caesarea to Tarsus.

The account of Saul's entry into the Movement concludes with the
last of the Lukan "summaries" in verse 31 (cf. 2:43-47; 4:32-35; 5:12-16;
5:42; 6:7). Repeatedly throughout the first part of his work Lukas has
used these summaries to point out the way of life of the believers in Jerusalem and the growth of house communities there. This last summary
expands the picture to include "the church throughout Judea, Galilee,
and Samaria"[15]—still Jewish/Samaritan territory, still fully embedded in
historic Israel. That is about to change. The transition is subtly marked:
here, for the first time in Acts, Lukas refers to the Movement as "the
church," ἡ ἐκκλησία (v. 31). He previously used the term only once (in
Stephen's speech), there in reference to Israel. The next use will be for
the church in Antioch, in the diaspora (11:26); it will appear once more
for the "mother church" in Jerusalem (15:22). Then it drops out of this
specialized use again and reverts to its basic meaning as "assembly"
during the riots in Ephesus (19:32, 39), its last appearance in Acts.

15. Galilee emerges from the shadows!—but only here, and only in reference to
the early period—and this despite the fact that "Galilee of the Gentiles" (Matt 4:15)
had a very mixed population.

Acts 9:32-43

Peter on Mission: Tabitha Is Raised

The summary in verse 31 wrapped up the story of the Movement in Israel's land (Judea, Galilee, and Samaria). We know from the account at the beginning of chapter 8 that Peter is one of the people who were not subject to Saul's persecution and had remained in Jerusalem. Evidently at this point the observance of the Jerusalem community, including worship in the temple, remained acceptable to the temple leadership and the non-Movement Hellenists. There is no hint of Hellenist opposition to that community; persecution will come only—briefly—from Agrippa I in chapter 12.[1] Peter and John go out into the hinterlands (as in 8:14-25) to receive new adherents and bestow the Holy Spirit. What we read in 9:32-43 seems like a similar apostolic visit, this time by Peter alone and to the coastal region. He is traveling here and there as the Spirit directs (or to the extent that believers' hospitality is available). Eventually he comes to Lydda.[2]

---

1. Even later, when Paul is attacked in the temple and then arrested, there is no hint of friction between the community of the Way in Jerusalem (now led by James) and the other Jews in the city. In fact, Paul's only defenders will be the Pharisees. See esp. Acts 21:20-24; 23:6-9.

2. Lydda and Joppa are on the coast road south of Caesarea and are thus to some degree liminal territory. Joppa was the port of Jerusalem at this period. The Jewish

³²Now as Peter went here and there among all the believers, he came down also to the saints living in Lydda. ³³There he found a man named Aeneas, who had been bedridden for eight years, for he was paralyzed. ³⁴Peter said to him, "Aeneas, Jesus Christ heals you; get up and make your bed!" And immediately he got up. ³⁵And all the residents of Lydda and Sharon saw him and turned to the Lord.

³⁶Now in Joppa there was a disciple whose name was Tabitha, which in Greek is Dorcas. She was devoted to good works and acts of charity. ³⁷At that time she became ill and died. When they had washed her, they laid her in a room upstairs. ³⁸Since Lydda was near Joppa, the disciples, who heard that Peter was there, sent two men to him with the request, "Please come to us without delay." ³⁹So Peter

The history of Lydda (Lod) could shed some light on the date of Acts. At the time depicted in the story Lydda was a town of no great significance. It was destroyed (not for the first time) in an early phase of the Jewish War and was then resettled with Jewish refugees from other places. In the period after 70 CE it became a rabbinic center second only to Yavneh, and Lukas could have known of its scholarship.[3] But the years 115 to 117 saw uprisings among the Jewish populations in Cyrenaica, Cyprus, and Egypt, at a time when the imperial armies were occupied by war with the Parthians. Within two years the rebellions were crushed, and the leaders of the Judeans fled to Lydda, which was captured and became the site of mass slaughter, so that "the slain of Lydda" found a reverential place in the Talmud.[4]

Thus Lydda was "in the news" in the years when we think Acts was written, and it made a good backdrop for the first act of this missionary journey.[5] Lukas uses "saints" for believers only four times in Acts; three of them are in chapter 9, including one each for Lydda and Joppa. The

---

residents there had frequent contact with gentiles in the course of commerce; relations with the Romans were often hostile. See Ivoni Richter Reimer, *Women in the Acts of the Apostles: A Feminist Liberation Perspective*, trans. Linda M. Maloney (Minneapolis: Fortress, 1995), 33.

3. See Ben-Zion Rosenfeld, *Torah Centers and Rabbinic Activity in Palestine, 70–400 CE: History and Geographic Distribution*, trans. Chava Cassel (Leiden: Brill, 2010), 41–44.

4. This conflict is sometimes called the "Kitos War" for the Roman general Lusius Quietus, who besieged and captured Lydda.

5. See Martin Goodman, *Rome and Jerusalem: The Clash of Ancient Civilizations* (New York: Vintage, 2008). Ironically, Lydda (now called Lod) was the scene of a mass deportation of Palestinians in 1948 and was resettled mainly by Jews from Arab countries.

got up and went with them; and when he arrived, they took him to the room upstairs. All the widows stood beside him, weeping and showing tunics and other clothing that Dorcas had made while she was with them. [40]Peter put all of them outside, and then he knelt down and prayed. He turned to the body and said, "Tabitha, get up." Then she opened her eyes, and seeing Peter, she sat up. [41]He gave her his hand and helped her up. Then calling the saints and widows, he showed her to be alive. [42]This became known throughout Joppa, and many believed in the Lord. [43]Meanwhile he stayed in Joppa for some time with a certain Simon, a tanner.

other two (at 9:13 and 26:10) refer to the community in Jerusalem. The term is apparently reserved for Jewish Jesus-followers in the land of Israel. Whether Aeneas is one of the "saints" or not we do not learn. His story closely resembles Peter's first healing, of the man who begged at the temple and whose disability seems also to have rendered him bedridden. Both are healed through the name of Jesus Christ (which in Acts is mainly pronounced in the context of healing and/or baptism). Both get up immediately; Aeneas is not allowed to go hopping about like the man in chapter 3 because he is ordered first: "make your bed!" (Modern parents will identify with this, but in the historical context it raises the question: was Aeneas enslaved?) As in chapter 3, the event makes a big impression and leads to many conversions.

Lukas is known to like pairs of people and of stories, and the story of Aeneas is commonly paired with that of Tabitha in 9:36-42, but in fact the Aeneas story really matches the one in Acts 3. Tabitha's story is instead paired with that of Cornelius: both she and he are "raised from the dead." Tabitha's physical raising (she already being a believer and therefore having been raised in baptism previously) matches Cornelius's deliverance from the Satanic hold of paganism, represented here by the Roman military occupation; both characters are known for their good works, which show that they deserve to be blessed with a mighty work of God.

Ivoni Richter Reimer devoted much study to the story of Tabitha over several years. The following contribution was written especially for this volume.

For an account see Benny Morris, *The Birth of the Palestinian Refugee Problem, 1947–1949*, Cambridge Middle East Library (Cambridge: Cambridge University Press, 1987).

The Disciple Tabitha (9:36-43)[6]

Acts 9:36-43 presents and reconstructs part of the history of the Christian community in Joppa and introduces a new scene with another space/city and new characters. The ending (9:43) is not part of the story but is the author's characteristic elaboration, marking the "bridge" to the next narrative (Acts 10:5-8).

While Peter was working in and around Lydda, a nearby community in the port city of Joppa was going through a situation of suffering and loss: the disciple Tabitha has fallen ill and died, and the community is organizing for her burial. Some terms of the narrative indicate that this is a community of the Way: Peter was known, and there were disciples (v. 38), saints (v. 41), and, most strikingly, *a disciple* named Tabitha (v. 36). The term μαθήτρια appears in the New Testament only here, probably because it is a relevant aspect of mission that is highlighted in the Lukan work. This is significant, since we know that the term μαθηταί ("disciples," plural; cf. 9:38) generally includes men and women.[7] Here we have scriptural testimony to this understanding.

This is the first narrative in Acts that highlights the leadership of a female disciple in an existing Christian community. Being a disciple implies teaching what you have learned, organizing the group for which you are responsible and the activities developed there, announcing the good news, and therefore performing mission. One of the characteristics of Tabitha's work is highlighted in the text: "she was full of good works and the mercies that she practiced" (v. 36, my translation). Published translations soften the force of this expression and make it difficult to visualize what Tabitha was doing when they say "she was devoted to good works and acts of charity," implying that ἐλεεμοσύνη[8] is what we would call "giving alms." These attributes, however, added to the name Tabitha,[9] indicate the Aramaic-Jewish origin and spirituality of this disciple and her community: there are many texts in the Old and New Testaments that show what the works practiced by

---

6. Translated by Mariosan de Sousa Marques.

7. Thus consistently in Acts; see, e.g., 6:1-2, 7; 9:1, 26, etc. Lukas refuses to admit that there had been a rupture between Paul and the communities of more traditional Jewish believers in the land of Israel, but the abrupt disappearance of "disciples" from the text after 21:16 spoke volumes to the original audience.—LMM

8. Ἐλεεμοσύνη has a broader meaning than "alms," being derived from the term ἐλεήμων, "compassionate, merciful."

9. Ταβιθά, "gazelle." Cf. Song of Solomon 4:5.

Tabitha are. Such "good works" performed by people are a sign and expression of God's love.[10] We understand the ἐλεεμοσύναι as "works of mercy," which may include alms but also encompass actions such as those that are mentioned in Matthew 25:35-36 and refer to the practice of justice. The LXX repeatedly translates the Hebrew words חסד (*hesed*, "mercy") as ἔλεος and צדקה (*tsedekah*, "justice, righteousness") as ἐλεεμοσύνη: God is on the side of those who suffer violence and oppression and will grant them justice and good things (Jer 1:27; 59:16; Pss 23:5; 102:6; Deut 6:24-25; 24:13, etc.). Those who practice this mercy are people motivated by God's own mercy! Mercy and justice are sisters and are manifested in works of love and care for vulnerable people (cf. Matt 23:23)!

Luke 11:41 and 12:33 can help us better understand the use of ἐλεεμοσύνη ποιεῖν ("do justice/mercy"), because the term ἐλεεμοσύνη διδόναι, "giving alms," is used there, the difference being in the verbs "do" and "give." "Doing ἐλεεμοσύνη" is more than "giving," as also expressed in Matthew 6:1-4, which links the expression with δικαιοσύνη, "justice." Ancient Jewish practice, also known by the rabbis, understands ἐλεεμοσύνη ποιεῖν as a human response to the love of God expressed as works of mercy, among which are giving alms, visiting the sick, hosting migrants, providing food and clothing for needy people, etcetera (Matt 25:35-36).[11]

Acts 9:39 shows one aspect of Tabitha's good works and merciful practices: all the widows wept and showed the tunics and robes[12] she made when she was with them. The preposition μετά with the genitive indicates an existing relationship between people, specifically μετά τινος εἶναι, to be beside someone/together with

---

10. See Luke 6:9 *par.*; John 5:29; Rom 2:7; 13:3; 2 Cor 9:8; Phil 1:6; Eph 2:10; Col 1:10; 1 Tim 2:10; 5:10; 2 Tim 2:21; 3:17; Titus 1:16; 3:1.

11. See details, discussion, and bibliography in Richter Reimer, *Women in the Acts of the Apostles*, 36–41, emphasizing the embeddedness of these practices in Judaism, *contra* earlier authors such as Paul Billerbeck. See also Egon Brandenburger, "Taten der Barmherzigkeit als Dienst gegenüber dem königlichem Herrn (Mt 25,31-46)," in *Diakonie: biblische Grundlagen und Orientierungen. Ein Arbeitsbuch*, ed. Gerhard K. Schäfer and Theodor Strohm, 2nd ed. (Heidelberg: HVA, 1994), 297–325. The author presents sources that demonstrate the existence of catalogues of practices of mercy to guarantee right and justice for the poor, which, in the case of the Old and New Testaments, are conditions for entering the royal realm of God-King and King-Messiah Jesus (311–12).

12. The terms χιτών and ἱμάτιον describe the common set of garments worn in antiquity; the χιτών was worn under the ἱμάτιον and was generally sleeveless.

someone.[13] This formulation carries with it a deep meaning of belonging, of community. The imperfect of ποιεῖν indicates repeated action, continuity in the work Tabitha did with this group of widows. The diaconal center of the community may have been working with widows, which would be in line with Jewish and Christian spirituality, which requires caring for orphans and widows (Deut 10:18; 24:17-22; Luke 18:1-8; Jas 1:27).

The narrative shows that the community is confronted with Tabitha's death and is preparing for her burial, since the rite of washing the body has already been done. It is said that she had fallen ill but not what disease or infirmity caused her death. The community is ready for the final farewell when they learn of Peter's presence in Lydda. They send two men to call Peter, asking him to come without delay (9:38), to which Peter reacts positively. The narrative says nothing about the community's expectations regarding Peter: why did they call him? What did they expect from him? Was he known to the community?

Peter acts as a leader in relation to the Joppa community, which may be a direct or indirect result of his previous missionary work. He has the freedom and authority to enter and leave the upper part of the house (ὑπερῷον, cf. Acts 1:13; 2:1), in which religious activities including the funeral vigil were commonly carried out, and to order everyone to leave that space. The Greek term for this action is ἐκβάλλω, "expel, send people out" (9:40),[14] and to us it can feel alienating: Was Peter rude to the community that was in mourning for the loss of their disciple-leader? Why did he have to act like that?

Narratively the space is prepared for the demonstration of the extraordinary power that manifests itself through Peter, in a clear allusion to the power that also acted through Elisha in the story of the Shunammite woman and her son (2 Kgs 4:32-37), a structural and thematic model for this one. Like Elisha, Peter is left alone with the corpse; Elisha and Peter pray; both narratives highlight the body with which Elisha and Peter interact, with Peter addressing the body/corpse: "Tabitha, get up!" (9:40;

---

13. See interpretive details in Richter Reimer, *Women in the Acts of the Apostles*, 42–43.

14. In Matt 9:25 // Mark 5:40 Jesus also "expels" people from a space but calls the girl's father and mother to be with him. In the parallel story Luke avoids that "rough" language (cf. Luke 8:51). Still, it is evident that stories of Jesus' miracles of healing/raising the dead are the model here.

see Mark 5:41). The result in both narratives is similar: the boy and Tabitha open their eyes, and Acts 9:40 highlights that Tabitha, "seeing Peter," recognizes him and sits up. Only then does he reach out to her and lift her from the place where she was being prepared for burial. He then calls "the saints and widows" and presents Tabitha to them, alive (9:41).[15]

Some highlights:

(a) The narrative presents three terms to characterize the people who made up that community: ἡ μαθήτρια and οἱ μαθηταὶ (9:36, 38), "woman disciple; fe/male disciples"; αἱ χῆραι, "the widows" (9:39, 41); and οἱ ἅγιοι, "the saints" (9:41), in addition to the δύο ἄνδρες, "two men" (9:38) who went to fetch Peter and who may be among the saints or disciples. We understand that there is an interdependence among the groups mentioned, all of them being part of and participating in the community with different functions. The widows' group is perhaps the most vulnerable and according to Jewish tradition needs greater care; however,

we must be careful not to see them as dependent and solely the objects of action by other members of the community. In 9:39 the relationship of belonging between Tabitha and all widows is expressed; it is quite possible that they worked together in the diaconal task of making clothes and that widows were not merely recipients of the benefit (see Acts 6:1). The mention of these groups, especially widows and saints, indicates similarities with the historical contexts of the Pastoral Letters, hence a later period in the constitution of communities. In this context widows are also an active and organized group (1 Tim 5:1-16): they not only receive community aid but exercise community leadership functions with or alongside elders and administrators.[16] Their *diakonia* constituted a recognized position in the churches even during the second century, but under the influence of the apologists and later church "fathers" (Tertullian, Ignatius of Antioch, Basil of Caesarea) and according to the Apostolic Constitutions (fourth century), widowhood as an

15. "Saints" (ἅγιοι) is a word reserved in the LXX for God's people (Israel) and appears only four times in Acts, always in reference to Jewish members of the Way. Is the usage here meant to tell us that the community in Joppa is made up mainly or entirely of refugees from the persecution in Jerusalem? See "Words for Members of the Movement in Acts" at Acts 6:1-7 above.

16. Ἐπίσκοποι. See also Luise Schottroff, "'Holy in Body and Spirit' (1 Cor. 7:34): The Forms of Women's Lives in Early Christianity," in Luise Schottroff, Silvia Schroer, and Marie-Theres Wacker, eds., *Feminist Interpretation: The Bible in Women's Perspective*, trans. Martin and Barbara Rumscheidt (Minneapolis: Fortress, 1998), 190–96.

office gave way to the diaconal model of virgins.[17] In Acts 9:36-42 Tabitha appears as the leader of this house and of the work carried out with the widows; her house was a domestic church (like that of Prisca: Acts 18:1-3; Rom 16:3-5).

(b) The earliest communities in the region of Sharon, Lydda, and Joppa are remembered through the prominence given to the disciple Tabitha and the missionary work of Peter. The community in Joppa already knew Peter (9:38), and Tabitha recognized him (9:40), which indicates that the community arose through the missionary work done previously by Peter and/or his group.[18] Peter is given authority that puts him at the service of the community, the revival of Tabitha serving as a prime example. This revival is the result of Peter's spirituality, expressed through kneeling, praying, turning to the body/corpse, and ordering Tabitha to stand up: Peter is an instrument of the miracle, not its author. Even though the expression "in the name of Jesus Christ"[19] is lacking, that element is presupposed (see 9:34); it is the reason why "many people believed in the Lord." This is the Lord Jesus who acts through Peter and who in Acts takes on a powerful miraculous function as a θεῖος ἀνήρ, a "divine man." The narrative illustrates this power in such a way that it could compete with Philostratus's accounts (second century) of Apollonius of Tyana's miracles: he healed the blind and lame, cast out demons, and revived the dead.[20] Therefore this Peter connects, on the one hand, with

---

17. For further information see Ruth Albrecht, "Jungfrau/Witwe," in *Wörterbuch der Feministischen Theologie*, ed. Elisabeth Gössmann and Beate Wehn (Gütersloh: Mohn, 1991), 207–10; Luise Schottroff, "DienerInnen der Heiligen: der Diakonat der Frauen im Neuen Testament," in *Diakonie: biblische Grundlagen und Orientierungen. Ein Arbeitsbuch*, ed. Gerhard K. Schäfer and Theodor Strohm, 2nd ed. (Heidelberg: HVA, 1994), 222–42; Lucinda A. Brown, "Tabitha," in *Women in Scripture: A Dictionary of Named and Unnamed Women in the Hebrew Bible, the Apocryphal/Deuterocanonical Books, and the New Testament*, ed. Carol Meyers, Toni Craven, and Ross S. Kraemer (Grand Rapids: Eerdmans, 2001), 159–60.

18. It may also be that these are original members of the Jerusalem community; see n. 15 above.—LMM

19. Frequent in Acts and associated in the first part especially with Peter: see Acts 2:38; 3:6, 16; 4:10. It then becomes a baptismal formula: thus Acts 8:16 (cf. 2:38); 10:48; 1 Cor 1:13; 6:11.

20. See Philostratus, *The Life of Apollonius of Tyana*, LCL 16 (Cambridge, MA: Harvard University Press, 1912). For details and sources see Ivoni Richter Reimer, *Milagre das Mãos: curas e exorcismos de Jesus em seu contexto histórico-cultural* (Goiânia: Ed.da UCG; São Leopoldo: Oikos, 2008), 26–30.

the healing prophet Elisha in Jewish tradition and, on the other, with Greco-Roman stories of "divine men" who competed in words, healings, and miracles with the apostles of the Lord Jesus Christ (see Acts 14:8-18). This shows that the objective of the narrative is the expansion of the Christian faith among people of Jewish and gentile origin.

(c) One of the objectives of the narrative is to demonstrate the extraordinary power of Peter, who in addition to preaching the gospel and healing the sick even has the power to revive the dead with a word. The result of this demonstration of power is shown first to the community (as Tabitha is presented alive) and then to the whole city. The subsequent adherence of the local population to the Lord Jesus through faith (9:42) is characteristic of healings and miracles in the New Testament.

As a theologian and pastor I have given many courses and much assistance in communities, social movements, and groups of pastoral formation. When we work on this text the people always ask: "Has Tabitha *really* risen?" It was from this restlessness and interaction with several hermeneutical subjects that we came to understand this narrative as a mythical reconstruction of the origins of that Christian community in Joppa.[21] The power of gestures and words, *diakonia* as a testimony to the love of God, and the merciful praxis of Tabitha as well as the community groups gathered around the same objective: these are the center of the narrative whose "object" of articulation is the disciple Tabitha. As ancient historiography the narrative would then have the function of "making history" of this community built from the diaconal praxis of Tabitha and the group of widows who met at her home. This reconstruction of origins involves community memory, selective and reconstituted, as well as authorial intent. Tabitha's "resurrection" is understood as symbolic in the plot of the mythical narrative, whose function is to reorganize the diaconal community as had the leader Tabitha, who, though dead, continues to live in the community through her exemplary liberative and

---

21. See arguments and theoretical references in Ivoni Richter Reimer, "A Discípula Tabita Vive! O poder do mito na reorganização da vida comunitária," in *Anais do III Congresso Internacional em Ciências da Religião. Mitologia e Literatura Sagrada*, ed. Ivoni Richter Reimer, Haroldo Reimer, and Joel Antônio Ferreira (Goiânia: Ed. da PUC Goiás, 2010), 173–82. In terms of literary criticism Martin Dibelius viewed this narrative in Acts 9:36-42 as a "paradigmatic *legend*," that is, a narrative that aims to motivate people to act like the protagonist, in this case Tabitha. Martin Dibelius, *Studies in the Acts of the Apostles*, ed. Heinrich Greeven, trans. Mary Ling (London: SCM, 1973).

> supportive praxis. We thus realize
> that this way of reading frees
> the narrative from the shackles
> of the letter and allows it to
> receive the power of the Spirit to
> embolden women and men even
> today to (re)build communities
> of solidarity, many of which are
> called "Tabithas."
> *Ivoni Richter Reimer*

Mary Ann Beavis has proposed that, apart from symbolic and theological considerations, the concrete reason why the male disciples at Joppa were so disturbed by Tabitha's death was that she was an economic mainstay of the community of widows—and, indeed, of the community as a whole.[22] Without her, the men might be called on to support the widows, something that male leaders of the Movement in Lukas's time were increasingly reluctant to do (see 1 Tim 5:3-16; contrast Jas 1:27).[23] Lukas's story, however, would never depict members of the Movement in that way!

The dual miracle stories in Acts 9:32-43 both separate and act as a bridge between two vision narratives: those of Paul and Ananias in the earlier part of chapter 9 and those of Peter and Cornelius in chapter 10. The combination illustrates how the growth of the Way is accomplished both through internal experiences that drive external events and through public manifestations that attract attention from outsiders, who then become insiders or, as also in the accounts of Jesus' work, enemies.

22. See Teresa J. Calpino, "Crafting Gender in Acts: Tabitha and Lydia," at Acts 16:6-34 below.

23. For more on this subject see Mary Ann Beavis, "'If Anyone Will Not Work, Let Them Not Eat': 2 Thessalonians 3.10 and the Social Support of Women," in *A Feminist Companion to Paul: Deutero-Pauline Writings*, ed. Amy-Jill Levine and Marianne Blickenstaff, FCNTECW 7 (London: T&T Clark, 2003), 29–36.

Acts 10:1–11:18

God Shows No Partiality

Now for the first time Peter, and the Movement with him, crosses the line: he enters gentile territory—the Roman-built city of Caesarea Maritima, administrative capital of the Roman provincial government and seat also of (Herod) Agrippa I—and extends the mission to gentile persons. This is the major turning point in Acts and, as it turns out, in the history of the Jesus movement that would become the *ekklēsia*.

As befits its importance, this composite scene is the longest in Acts. Together with the subsequent account of Peter's report to the Jerusalem community it is longer even than the account of Paul's journey to Rome. In a sense there is another parallel here: we find Peter, the leading apostle, making the long journey not just from Joppa to Caesarea but from a Movement located entirely within nascent Judaism to one that extends to gentiles. Soon Paul, whom Lukas portrays as the super-missionary, will travel farther and farther through gentile territory until at last he reaches their capital city, Rome, but Lukas is emphatic that the gentile mission begins with Peter, the chief apostle.

10:1In Caesarea there was a man named Cornelius, a centurion of the Italian Cohort, as it was called. 2He was a devout man who feared God with all his household; he gave alms generously to the people and prayed constantly to God. 3One afternoon at about three o'clock he had a vision in which he clearly saw an angel of God coming in and saying to him, "Cornelius." 4He stared at him in terror and said, "What is it, Lord?" He answered, "Your prayers and your alms have ascended as a memorial before God. 5Now send men to Joppa for a certain Simon who is called Peter; 6he is lodging with Simon, a tanner, whose house is by the seaside." 7When the angel who spoke to him had left, he called two of his slaves and a devout soldier from the ranks of those who served him, 8and after telling them everything, he sent them to Joppa.

9About noon the next day, as they were on their journey and approaching the city, Peter went up on the roof to pray. 10He became hungry and wanted something to eat; and while it was being prepared, he fell into a trance. 11He saw the heaven opened and something like a large sheet coming down, being lowered to the ground by its four corners. 12In it were all kinds of four-footed creatures and reptiles and birds of the air. 13Then he heard a voice saying, "Get up, Peter; kill and eat." 14But Peter said, "By no means, Lord; for I have never eaten anything that is profane or unclean." 15The voice said to him again, a second time, "What God has made clean, you must not call profane." 16This happened three times, and the thing was suddenly taken up to heaven.

17Now while Peter was greatly puzzled about what to make of the vision that he had seen, suddenly the men sent by Cornelius appeared. They were asking for Simon's house and were standing by the gate. 18They called out to ask whether Simon, who was called Peter, was staying there. 19While Peter was still thinking about the vision, the Spirit said to him, "Look, three men are searching for you. 20Now get up, go down, and go with them without hesitation; for I have sent them." 21So Peter went down to the men and said, "I am the one you are looking for; what is the reason for your coming?" 22They answered, "Cornelius, a centurion, an upright and God-fearing man, who is well spoken of by the whole Jewish nation, was directed by a holy angel to send for you to come to his house and to hear what you have to say." 23So Peter invited them in and gave them lodging.

The next day he got up and went with them, and some of the believers from Joppa accompanied him. 24The following day they came to Caesarea. Cornelius was expecting them and had called together his relatives and close friends. 25On Peter's arrival Cornelius met him, and falling at his feet, worshiped him. 26But Peter made him get up, saying, "Stand up; I am only a mortal." 27And as he talked with him, he went in and found that many had assembled; 28and he said to them, "You yourselves know that it is unlawful for a Jew to associate with or to visit a Gentile; but God has shown me that I should not call anyone profane or unclean. [29]So when I was sent for, I came without objection. Now may I ask why you sent for me?"

[30]Cornelius replied, "Four days ago at this very hour, at three o'clock, I was praying in my house when suddenly a man in dazzling clothes stood before me. [31]He said, 'Cornelius, your prayer has been heard and your alms have been remembered before God. [32]Send therefore to Joppa and ask for Simon, who is called Peter; he is staying in the home of Simon, a tanner, by the sea.' [33]Therefore I sent for you immediately, and you have been kind enough to come. So now all of us are here in the presence of God to listen to all that the Lord has commanded you to say."

[34]Then Peter began to speak to them: "I truly understand that God shows no partiality, [35]but in every nation anyone who fears him and does what is right is acceptable to him. [36]You know the message he sent to the people of Israel, preaching peace by Jesus Christ—he is Lord of all. [37]That message spread throughout Judea, beginning in Galilee after the baptism that John announced: [38]how God anointed Jesus of Nazareth with the Holy Spirit and with power; how he went about doing good and healing all who were oppressed by the devil, for God was with him. [39]We are witnesses to all that he did both in Judea and in Jerusalem. They put him to death by hanging him on a tree; [40]but God raised him on the third day and allowed him to appear, [41]not to all the people but to us who were chosen by God as witnesses, and who ate and drank

with him after he rose from the dead. [42]He commanded us to preach to the people and to testify that he is the one ordained by God as judge of the living and the dead. [43]All the prophets testify about him that everyone who believes in him receives forgiveness of sins through his name."

[44]While Peter was still speaking, the Holy Spirit fell upon all who heard the word. [45]The circumcised believers who had come with Peter were astounded that the gift of the Holy Spirit had been poured out even on the Gentiles, [46]for they heard them speaking in tongues and extolling God. Then Peter said, [47]"Can anyone withhold the water for baptizing these people who have received the Holy Spirit just as we have?" [48]So he ordered them to be baptized in the name of Jesus Christ. Then they invited him to stay for several days.

[11:1]Now the apostles and the believers who were in Judea heard that the Gentiles had also accepted the word of God. [2]So when Peter went up to Jerusalem, the circumcised believers criticized him, [3]saying, "Why did you go to uncircumcised men and eat with them?" [4]Then Peter began to explain it to them, step by step, saying, [5]"I was in the city of Joppa praying, and in a trance I saw a vision. There was something like a large sheet coming down from heaven, being lowered by its four corners; and it came close to me. [6]As I looked at it closely I saw four-footed animals, beasts of prey, reptiles, and birds of the air. [7]I also heard a voice saying to me, 'Get up, Peter; kill and eat.' [8]But I replied, 'By no means, Lord; for nothing profane or unclean has ever entered my mouth.' [9]But a second time the voice answered from heaven, 'What God has made clean, you must not call profane.' [10]This happened three times; then everything was pulled up again to heaven. [11]At that very moment three men, sent to me from Caesarea, arrived at the house where we were. [12]The Spirit told me to go with them and not to make a distinction between them and us. These six brothers also accompanied me, and we entered the man's house. [13]He told us how he had seen the angel standing in his house and saying, 'Send to Joppa and bring Simon, who is called Peter; [14]he will give you a message by which you and your entire household will be saved.' [15]And as I began to speak, the Holy Spirit fell upon them just as it had upon us at the beginning. [16]And I remembered the word of the Lord, how he had said, 'John baptized with water, but you will be baptized with the Holy Spirit.' [17]If then God gave them the same gift that he gave us when we believed in the Lord Jesus Christ, who was I that I could hinder God?" [18]When they heard this, they were silenced. And they praised God, saying, "Then God has given even to the Gentiles the repentance that leads to life."

Visions in Acts 9 and 10[1]

The book of Acts is known by scholars and lay readers alike for its speeches. Less often noted are its many visions, surpassed in quantity in the New Testament only by the book of Revelation. One cannot read Acts, therefore, without recognizing the centrality of visions.

A vision narrative recounts a revelatory encounter with the divine in which the divine presence is distinctly manifested to a person or group of people. By this definition there are eighteen vision narratives in Acts: thirteen original narratives (1:9-11; 2:2-4; 5:19-20; 7:55-56; 8:26; 9:3-7; 9:10-16; 10:3-6; 10:10-16; 12:7-10; 16:9; 22:17-21; 27:23-24) and five that recount previously narrated visions (10:30-32; 11:4-10; 11:13-14; 22:6-10; 26:13-18). The visions in Acts are significantly more numerous in the first twelve chapters (thirteen) than in the whole last half of the book (five), and the greatest concentration of visions, including the longest and most complex, is found in chapters 9–10. These chapters relate two pairs of visions and subsequent retellings: Saul and Ananias (9:1-19) and

1. This contribution is based on Deborah Thompson Prince, "Exploring the Visions of Acts in Their Narrative Context," in *Bible as Never Seen Before: Analyzing Dreams and Visions in Ancient Religious Literature*, SemeiaSt (Atlanta: SBL Press, forthcoming).

Cornelius and Peter (10:1-33). Each visionary encounters the divine presence in a different way, which exemplifies the wide range of experiences considered to be visionary in Acts. Saul's and Peter's visions incorporate visual stimuli, although Saul's involves a bright light that blinds while Peter's incorporates visual symbols. Ananias hears the voice of the Lord but does not "see" anything, while Cornelius is visited by an angel of the Lord.

Each pair can be identified as a "double vision," which refers to the visions or dreams of two separate characters narrated in conjunction with each other so that a pair of interdependent visions is formed. The pair functions to provide "a resolution of some sort . . . particularly . . . for purposes such as the advancement of plot."[2] The visions in Acts 9 and 10 fit this description well. Neither Saul's nor Peter's vision is complete in and of itself. Each depends on its counterpart vision—those of Ananias and Cornelius, respectively—to develop or interpret the divine message. Saul's commission to preach "before Gentiles and kings" is only revealed through Ananias's vision (9:15), and Peter is left in doubt about the meaning of his vision until he meets Cornelius's men (10:17-23), who are sent to Peter in response to the angel's message to Cornelius (10:5).

Furthermore, both pairs of visions advance the plot by providing divine authorization and legitimation for the gentile mission. This is the key debate in Acts 9–15. In the visions in Acts 9 and 10 this mission is supported by divine manifestations to multiple witnesses. First, Saul's commission to preach to gentiles is asserted in one of the paired visions in chapter 9 (to Ananias), and then Peter's and Cornelius's visions, as interpreted in Peter's speech (10:34-48), support the inclusion of gentiles into the Jesus community. This inclusion is first questioned (11:1-4) and then accepted by the "circumcised believers" in Jerusalem (11:18), but it is again at issue at the "Jerusalem Council" in Acts 15. Interestingly, the divine authorization provided through the visions is not absolute. In each case the message of the vision must be clarified and corroborated by other reliable sources and must be explained to and accepted by the larger community and its leaders (11:1-18; 15:1-35).

Deborah Thompson Prince

---

2. John Hanson, "Dreams and Visions in the Graeco-Roman World and Early Christianity," *ANRW* 2, *Principat*, ed. Wolfgang Haase, 23.2 (1980): 1395–1427, at 1415. Hanson elsewhere describes this as a resolution of "actual or potential conflict" ("The Dream/Vision Report and Acts 10:1–11:18: A Form-Critical Study" [PhD diss., Harvard University, 1978], 47).

The several "scenes" that make up the account appear to be mis-matched. Peter's vision is about clean and unclean animals as food, but at Cornelius's house he interprets it as being about not dividing *people* into clean and unclean. As the story develops we learn that there are two key elements to the Jewish/gentile distinction, and the most neuralgic point is not the food laws but male circumcision—or the relationship between the two, since circumcised and noncircumcised males were not supposed to eat at the same table. (No woman is mentioned throughout this sequence, even though we necessarily assume women's presence in both Simon's and Cornelius's households as well as in the community at Jerusalem. That there were enslaved persons in Cornelius's household is made clear, however, in v. 7.) Or can it be that there are bookends, with Tabitha's community in Joppa representing an ideal to which the resistant elements in Jerusalem (11:1-18; 15:5) are contrasted? Lukas goes out of his way to emphasize that the resistance comes from "circumcised believers" and that Peter's companions were all male (see 10:45; 11:2). The issue of male circumcision affects men, and they alone will deal with it. We never hear a woman's voice on the issue, and those who agitate it are all specified as male. It will reappear in chapter 15 in a way that threatens to break the Movement apart. There it is resolved by the decree proposed by James: that gentile converts, if male, may be excused from the requirement of circumcision, but certain food laws will continue to apply to everyone. A careful reading of the text will show that the male circumcision issue never *was* resolved. "Circumcised" (i.e., Jewish male) believers continued to insist on it, but, as Paul's letter to the Galatians shows,[3] Paul rebelled against it and refused to impose it on any of his male *gentile* converts. The divisive issue in his later communities, as witnessed in his correspondence, was in fact the question of clean and unclean foods (specifically, meat offered to idols). Only in the early letter to the Galatians do we read of the history of Paul's clashes with believers still insisting on circumcision for all males, as well as customs related to the Jewish calendar.

Peter himself appears as a firm adherent to the law; he resists the voice he hears in his trance, steadily refusing to "kill and eat" lest he transgress Torah. His entering Cornelius's house is not in itself defiling; though he says that "God has shown me that I should not call any*one* profane or unclean" (κοινὸν καὶ ἀκάθαρτον, 10:28) that is still a far cry from wel-coming such persons into the community of Jesus' followers. After all,

---

3. See especially Gal 2:11-14; 5:2-6, 12(!).

he would not *eat* anything "profane or unclean" (κοινὸν καὶ ἀκάθαρτον, 10:14). He has simply concluded from the heavenly voice's instruction that he is not to regard *persons to whom he has been sent* as off limits to him.

Israel's Mission

Is it Israel's mission to be missionary? The answer to that question divides Christians from Jews to this day. Acts says yes; rabbinic Judaism and its daughters say emphatically no. Christianity's claim to be the missionary-messianic heir of Judaism has led to a pernicious form of supersessionism that many Christians and many Jews are seeking to combat. Still, the question of mission and inclusion remains insoluble in our time. One Orthodox Jewish position that bears great authority was stated recently by the chief rabbi of Vienna, Arie Folger:

> Judaism, as we know, is a non-missionary religion. In our view it is not necessary that humanity become Jewish in order to find the soul's salvation; it is sufficient that it see itself as part of the Noachide covenant[4] and hold to it. Only Jews are obligated to keep the law of Torah in its entirety. In that way we create space for many who think otherwise. . . . [W]e are intended to live our values precisely in *this* land, where we are in large part to build up our Jewish utopia: a land that lives according to Jewish values, a land in which love of G*d, love of humanity, and justice among one another are united. . . . Many Jews see in the renewal of a Jewish society in the Holy Land a process of a pre-messianic return that has already begun.[5]

What Rabbi Folger describes is, in fact, very close to the program of Acts: the community decision in chapter 15 does indeed require of gentile

---

4. The "Noachide covenant" or "Seven Laws of Noah" as defined by the rabbis prohibits the worship of idols and cursing God and requires keeping the commandments not to kill, commit adultery, or steal and not eating the limb of a live animal (a paradigm for cruelty). This last is a constraint on the killing of animals for food, which was not permitted before the flood. The seventh command is to create courts of justice. The biblical basis is Gen 9:1-17. Cf. b. Sanh. 56a-b and t. 'Abod. Zar. 8:4. These commandments are obligatory for all gentiles, whereas the 613 commandments of Torah apply only to Jews.

5. Rabbi Arie Folger, "Eine unwahrscheinliche Reise," in *Ebrei e Cristiani: Eine jüdisch-christliche Begegnung an der Lateran-Universität in Rom am 16. Mai 2019. Theologica* 7/2.3 (2019): 9–21, at 11, 17, 14. Translation Linda M. Maloney. As Westerners seek to repent of the evil of colonialism and to reject the "Doctrine of Discovery" we would do well to reflect on the relationship between "mission" and colonial expansion and domination. See esp. Willie James Jennings, *The Christian Imagination: Theology and the Origins of Race* (New Haven & London: Yale University Press, 2010).

converts only that they keep the Noachide covenant. But the vision of the author of Acts is that members of the Jesus movement would be part of one community living out Jewish values and not divided between a "truly Jewish" center and a "Noachide" periphery.

When Acts was written there was still at least a scintilla of hope for such a community life; within two decades that hope had vanished along with Jewish presence in the land now renamed by the Romans for its former Philistine inhabitants: Palestine.

Two passages from the Gospels have features in common with Acts 10. At Matthew 8:5-13 and Luke 7:1-10 Jesus heals the slave of a centurion in Capernaum. The healing is done at the request of a gentile but not necessarily *for* a gentile, since the slave may well be Jewish. Luke adds some embellishments to the story to embed it firmly in a Jewish context: he has the centurion employ Jewish elders to make the request to Jesus, and they praise the centurion: "He is worthy of having you do this for him, for he loves our people, and it is he who built our synagogue for us" (Luke 7:4-5). Both versions emphasize that, at the centurion's request, Jesus does not enter his house but heals the slave from a distance.

There is a distinct parallel between the centurion of Luke 7:1-10 and Cornelius in Acts 10. Both are worthy men and somehow connected to their Jewish neighbors: the character in Luke is "worthy" (ἄξιος) because of his demonstrated love for the Jewish people; Cornelius is "a devout man who feared God [εὐσεβὴς καὶ φοβούμενος τὸν θεὸν] with all his household." We are to infer that this Roman officer, as a God-fearer, was following Torah in some fashion—perhaps by observing the Noachide laws in general, though avoiding nonkosher meat could have been difficult—and had convinced or compelled his family and slaves to do likewise. His office would have prevented him from embracing Torah completely, so Peter will show him a way to be part of a community of faith whose requirements will be compatible with his calling.

The Italic cohort (six detachments of one hundred men, each headed by a centurion) was an auxiliary unit composed of freedmen and was stationed in Syria at this period. Were the freedmen under Cornelius's command gentiles or Jews, or some of each? If there were Jews under his command his contact with those men could have influenced him to act generously toward the Jewish community, but that would make him an unusual Roman in his time, one who treated "common soldiers" as worthy of respect. The fact that he sends "a devout soldier" to find Peter suggests, however, that (in the story, at least) this may be the case.[6]

There is some ambiguity in the narrative that follows. We learn at 10:24 that Cornelius "had called together his relatives and close friends." Is it exclusively these upper-rank persons who constitute the "many" who assemble to hear Peter preach, or is the rest of the household also present when the Holy Spirit falls on "all who heard the word" (10:44)? In Lukas's telling, the Holy Spirit is not given to people who are not prepared to receive it, who are unable to distinguish God's Spirit from the many other spirits of the various religions. So the centurion in the Gospel is a friend to the Jews, but Cornelius is evidently much more than that. How it happens that his relatives and close friends, and perhaps his whole household, are prepared to receive the Spirit is unclear; the "household," slaves included, are supposedly God-fearers (10:2), but the relatives and friends? How is it that a Roman centurion has relatives in this place, on what were from the Roman point of view the fringes of civilization?

Probably Lukas simply wants to paint the scene as involving a relatively large number of people because at 10:44-48 he portrays the coming of the Spirit in direct parallel to the Pentecost event. Those assembled receive the Holy Spirit and speak in tongues, extolling God (cf. 2:1-4). The astonishment of the "circumcised believers" accompanying Peter resembles that of the crowds in Jerusalem. Peter orders that those who have thus received the Spirit should be baptized (cf. 2:38, 41) and reinforces the parallel by saying they "have received the Holy Spirit just as we have." That Peter and his fellow Jews (who are evidently members of Tabitha's community at Joppa, so v. 23) "stay for several days" at Cornelius's house affirms the fact that community and table fellowship are now open to all believers, gentile as well as Jew.

This makes it all the more curious that Cornelius and his household appear in Acts 10 and nowhere else. Peter leaves at 11:2, and we hear no more about these new members of the Movement; in his account to the Jerusalem community Peter speaks only of "the man" (no name or military rank) and his "household." In Acts 21:10 Paul will spend "several days" at Philip's house in Caesarea on his way to Jerusalem, and "some of the disciples from Caesarea" (21:16) accompany him from there to the capital city, but we never learn whether those disciples were among

---

6. See Hans-Josef Klauck, *Magic and Paganism in Early Christianity: The World of the Acts of the Apostles*, trans. Brian McNeil (Minneapolis: Fortress, 2003), 31.

the persons baptized by Peter and his companions. Within a few weeks Paul is back in Caesarea, this time as a prisoner lodged in the Roman praetorium, and there he remains for more than two years; although the governor specifies that Paul is "to have some liberty" and that the centurion (evidently not Cornelius!) is "not to prevent any of his friends from taking care of his needs" (24:23), there is no description of any further interaction between Paul and the believers at Caesarea.

All this goes to show that Acts 10:1–11:18 is a Lukan composition structured for a particular purpose and without incidentals or "local color." Its purpose is to show Peter, the leading apostle, as inaugurating, and then defending, the gentile mission, on direct orders from God. But we need to notice also that there is a difference between a mission to gentiles, with the possible formation of gentile communities of Jesus-believers, and the integration of gentiles into communities formerly made up only of Jewish believers. Nothing in Peter's action, or in his subsequent explanation of it to the leadership in Jerusalem, proposes or even suggests such an integration. That issue will come later, and Acts is unclear about its resolution.

In his reflections on this passage Willie James Jennings takes us even deeper into its significance, showing how the vision of the living creatures links the reader back to Genesis, when God saw all creation together and pronounced it very good.[7] Later, God's Torah had distinguished "clean" and "unclean" foods in a way particular to Israel's context in the land and among pagan peoples, but now that salvation is being offered to those "foreign" peoples the separating factors will be called into question. As Jennings writes, Peter "is not being asked to possess as much as he is being asked to enter in, become through eating a part of something that he did not imagine himself a part of before the eating."[8] All creation is to be made one again in the reign of God, and Lukas views the evangelization of the gentiles as another sign of the inbreaking of that reign. Now that all the nations are being called to come to Israel for instruction, the barriers that might hold them back must be torn down. So Peter first invites Cornelius's emissaries into a house not his own, the house of a family practicing an "unclean" profession; he will then go with them to the home of a gentile, a Roman officer (hence not merely a gentile but an enemy occupier). This is "outreach" at an extreme. But we should never lose sight of the fact that it is a preaching of Israel's God to non-Jews, an invitation to believe in the God of Israel.

---

7. Willie James Jennings, *Acts*, Belief: A Theological Commentary on the Bible (Louisville: Westminster John Knox, 2017), 105–7.

8. Ibid., 107.

The action is not well received by the mother community in Jerusalem (11:1-18). In fact, we can quickly see that Peter has lost his former authority there because of his actions. Previously the unquestioned leader of the Jerusalem community, he is now called on the carpet and required to justify what he has done. In this scene the circumcision issue is front and center; the hostile voices come exclusively from men, and the focus is not on table fellowship with gentiles (female and male) but solely on eating with "uncircumcised men" (ἄνδρας ἀκροβυστίαν ἔχοντας).

Matthew Thiessen emphasizes that this scene underscores Lukas's attitude toward the issue of circumcision, writing that "Luke does not believe that circumcision is no longer a valid or significant rite; rather he demonstrates that gentiles do not have to adopt the law." He quotes Michael Wyschogrod:

> Had the thought that with the coming of Christ the Law had been abolished entered anyone's mind in Jerusalem, there could clearly not have ensued a long discussion, settled with some difficulty, as to whether circumcision and the Law ought to be made obligatory for gentiles. If it was no longer obligatory for Jews, how could it possibly become so for others? The only possible explanation dictated by the facts is that the possibility of the Torah not remaining binding for Jews never occurred to anyone in Jerusalem.[9]

Still, the status of male gentile proselytes[10] remains iffy. Peter's dilemma is that, as Jennings writes, "he must give witness to the witnesses of Jesus and try to convince them that God transgresses."[11] He does so by relating his experience; only after doing so does he reference Jesus' words as given at Acts 1:5, thus drawing the circle from Pentecost to the narrative present. That clinches the argument; his hearers "were silenced." They (the same they as in the previous verses?) praise God and affirm, "Then God has given even to the Gentiles the repentance that leads to life" (11:18).

---

9. Matthew Thiessen, *Contesting Conversion: Genealogy, Circumcision, and Identity in Ancient Judaism and Christianity* (Oxford: Oxford University Press, 2011), 140, quoting Michael Wyschogrod, *Abraham's Promise: Judaism and Jewish-Christian Relations*, ed. R. Kendall Soulen (Grand Rapids: Eerdmans, 2004), 194.

10. For Luke/Lukas it seems clear that proselytes (προσήλυτοι) are not Jews. Two of the three occurrences of this word (Acts 2:11; 13:43) distinguish such persons from Jews or Israelites. Thiessen (*Contesting Conversion*, 135) points out that recent translations of the LXX (e.g., *New English Translation of the Septuagint* and *La Bible d'Alexandrie*) read προσήλυτος as "guest" and "étranger," interpreting "proselyte" or "convert" as "an overreading of the text." See further discussion there, pp. 135–37.

11. Jennings, *Acts*, 115.

Curiously, in his speech to his Jerusalem brothers Peter tells the story of his vision in detail, with the same vocabulary, but he skips the application, summarizing it simply as "the Spirit told me . . . not to make a distinction between them and us" (11:12). (What is the scope of "them" and "us"?) He omits his preaching, saying that the Holy Spirit fell upon "them" as he began to speak. Evidently the point that this is *God's* doing and not Peter's is what needs to be brought home to the men of Jerusalem: "God did it; nothing I said made any difference. Don't blame me." This is clearly a Peter who no longer exercises much, if any, authority in Jerusalem; he will very soon disappear from Acts altogether.

The fact that Peter does not tell his fellow Jews in Jerusalem any details of his speech is surely no accident. What would they make of "I truly understand that God shows no partiality, but in every nation anyone who fears him and does what is right is acceptable to him" (10:34-35)? The faith that has sustained Israel through every horror visited upon it throughout history is the conviction that God *is* partial to Israel, that the Jews are God's own chosen people and therefore God will ultimately vindicate them: the favorite image is that of the other nations making pilgrimage to Zion.[12] The author of Acts must posit (and does) that what is now happening is precisely the beginning of that pilgrimage and in no way the replacement of Israel as first in God's heart. But there is too little evidence of that reality in the time about which he writes and even in his own time (or ours!) for him to show Peter making an issue of it.

The telling of stories from the mission, affirmed as the work of God and ratified by the community as such, will be a recurrent scene in Acts (cf. 12:17; 14:27-28; 15:6-22; 21:17-20).[13] These scenes represent Lukas's vision of how the emergent church should make major decisions, discerning God's will in their lives together. The fact that in several of these scenes the decision apparently did not "take," that it was contested soon afterward, probably shows us that Lukas's audience was all too aware that the scenes he was painting were more prescriptive than descriptive; they represent an ideal that is seldom attained, especially in hierarchical institutions such as most Christian churches have proven to be.

12. Isaiah 2:3; 60:14.

13. For a detailed study see Linda M. Maloney, *"All That God Had Done with Them": The Narration of the Works of God in the Early Christian Community as Described in the Acts of the Apostles*, AUS ser. 7, Theology and Religion 91 (New York: Lang, 1991).

Acts 11:19-30

Peace and Growth

The scene shifts abruptly from Jerusalem to Antioch. This passage belongs logically after 9:25 or 9:31, but because it hints at the conversion of gentiles at Antioch, the episode of Peter and Cornelius had to be inserted in order to affirm that the gentile mission originated with the apostle appointed by Jesus to shepherd the Movement's continuation on earth. In fact, the text speaks somewhat gingerly of gentile proselytes, having first emphasized (v. 19) that those scattered from Jerusalem after Stephen's death spoke *to no one except Jews*. In any case it is not really clear that "Hellenists" in verse 20 would refer to non-Jews; in Acts 6 we encountered Hellenists in Jerusalem who were violent opponents of any change in Jewish customs (6:14), and in 21:27 it will be "Jews from Asia"[1] (therefore most certainly "Hellenists") who stir up the Jerusalem crowd against Paul for allegedly violating the temple precincts by bringing in gentiles. The time-location is reinforced by the mention of the emperor Claudius (who ruled 41–54 CE).

The Greek text speaks of "Hellenists," but some manuscripts have "Greeks." Richard Pervo cut the Gordian knot by translating "those who spoke Greek,"[2] which could refer to Jews, especially in the diaspora, as

---

1. That is, Asia Minor.
2. Richard I. Pervo, *Acts*, Hermeneia (Minneapolis: Fortress, 2009), 289.

Acts 11:19-30

¹⁹Now those who were scattered because of the persecution that took place
over Stephen traveled as far as Phoenicia, Cyprus, and Antioch, and they
spoke the word to no one except Jews.
²⁰But among them were some men of
Cyprus and Cyrene who, on coming to
Antioch, spoke to the Hellenists also,
proclaiming the Lord Jesus. ²¹The hand
of the Lord was with them, and a great
number became believers and turned
to the Lord. ²²News of this came to the
ears of the church in Jerusalem, and
they sent Barnabas to Antioch. ²³When
he came and saw the grace of God, he
rejoiced, and he exhorted them all to
remain faithful to the Lord with stead-
fast devotion; ²⁴for he was a good man,
full of the Holy Spirit and of faith. And
a great many people were brought to

well as to gentiles. It is not really Lukas's plan to have a mission to the
gentiles carried out independently of (and prior to) the work of Peter and
especially Paul, but he evidently has traditions to account for. Antioch,
the third most important city of the empire (after Rome and Alexandria),
would be the first great center of the gentile mission, though Paul would
not retain his base there. Still, Lukas once again emphasizes that the
mission is to Jews first. It was Antioch that saw communities now called
"Christian" (v. 26)[3] grow in a metropolitan, urban environment, and
the church would retain its urban character into the early Middle Ages.

This time when good news reaches Jerusalem about conversions elsewhere (cf. 8:14) it is not apostles who are sent to the new location; it is
Barnabas. This may aid the chronological relocation of the events to follow those at Caesarea by suggesting that those who have heard Peter's
justification for having baptized Cornelius and his household are still in
"wait and see" mode regarding the admission of gentiles.

Barnabas we have already met (4:36-37; 9:27). He appeared first as a
Levite from Cyprus, a man of property who shared his wealth with the
Jerusalem community. Later he befriended the newly obedient Saul and
spoke on his behalf before the apostles. We would expect him to have
been one of the Cypriots (v. 20) who preached the word in Antioch, but
in Lukas's story he has remained in Jerusalem and is now dispatched
by the church there to assess the situation. (Note that it is "the church in

---

3. The term was originally demeaning. John H. Elliott translates it "Christ-lackeys"
in his *A Home for the Homeless: A Social-Scientific Criticism of 1 Peter, Its Situation and
Strategy* (Minneapolis: Fortress, 1990), 73–74, 95–96. It became a legal designation in
the second century CE.

the Lord. [25]Then Barnabas went to Tarsus to look for Saul, [26]and when he had found him, he brought him to Antioch. So it was that for an entire year they met with the church and taught a great many people, and it was in Antioch that the disciples were first called "Christians."

[27]At that time prophets came down from Jerusalem to Antioch. [28]One of them named Agabus stood up and predicted by the Spirit that there would be a severe famine over all the world; and this took place during the reign of Claudius. [29]The disciples determined that according to their ability, each would send relief to the believers living in Judea; [30]this they did, sending it to the elders by Barnabas and Saul.

Jerusalem," not its leadership alone, that sends Barnabas. This remains a community effort.) Lukas eulogizes Barnabas, "who combines the qualities of Joseph of Arimathea, Cornelius, and the Seven."[4] We would expect him to continue in his pioneering role as a missionary, but once he has fulfilled his function of integrating Paul into the community at Antioch and helping him to display his missionary qualities in chapters 13 and 14 he is sent away at the end of chapter 15, never to reappear.

Χριστιάνοι

This hybrid Latin-Greek word appears only twice in Acts: here and at 26:28. The second use, in the mouth of Herod Agrippa, confirms that the word, if not an outright pejorative, at least has a negative implication, like similar terms referring to someone as belonging to or associated with a group adherent to some leader. Lukas generally avoids it and uses it here probably because his source makes a point of it: Antioch is the mother church of "Christians." It seems

significant that the earliest documentation of Χριστιάνος is in the letters attributed to Ignatius (of Antioch!), probably written after the Bar Kokhba revolt, when the introduction of a tax on Jews made it useful to distinguish Jews from non-Jews.

Calling themselves Χριστιάνοι represented a distancing of the group from the Ἰουδαίοι—a move abhorrent to Lukas, who is still insisting on the Jewish identity of the Jesus movement. He acknowledges the circulation of the term by others but makes no use of it himself.

4. Pervo, *Acts*, 291.

It seems that Barnabas was never entirely in accord with Paul's full acceptance of gentiles without condition. Perhaps it was because he was a Levite and thus "professionally," by birth, dedicated to Torah. He had probably studied the words of the prophet Malachi, whose whole writing was a sharp critique of the infidelity of the priests and Levites of the Second Temple (ca. 500 BCE), citing the "messenger of the Covenant"—who in later Christian interpretation would be identified with Jesus. Certainly in the witness of Acts, Barnabas embodied the qualities Malachi ("my messenger") demanded of a servant of YHWH: reverence, integrity, teaching truth, turning people from their sins, and acting as the messenger of the Lord (see Mal 2:5-7).[5] Barnabas may not have been ready to act as radically as Paul proposed to do.

The chronology is slippery here: according to Paul's own testimony he worked in Asia for fourteen years before returning to Jerusalem, evidently via Antioch (Gal 2:1). The author of Acts makes it seem as if events flow smoothly along without interruption, as a storyteller must. In fact these were years of slow growth, setbacks, differences over how to proceed and how to relate to "others." Antioch was a key nodal point. Its large Jewish community survived the First Revolt (66–73/74 CE), and the Jewish and Christian communities remained competitive there for centuries to come. Antioch's "progressive" approach to relations between members of the two communities would not be welcome in Jerusalem, as chapter 15 will show.

The new community at Antioch reveals its character when Agabus arrives and prophesies famine.[6] There were, in fact, a number of severe grain shortages during Claudius's reign because of the failure of the harvests in Egypt, North Africa, and the Levant, Rome's breadbasket. The use of "prophecy" here plants the idea that the shortage must have been foreseen for the immediate future, because the Jesus-people in Antioch spring into action. The reference is probably borrowed from Josephus (*Ant.* 20.2.5, 49-53), who describes a famine *in Judea* some time in the 40s CE. It serves Lukas's purpose because it allows him to stretch the time frame to allow for Peter's supposedly previous action in converting the

---

5. Note how well these characteristics fit John the Baptizer, also a member of the tribe of Levi, as he is portrayed in the Gospels. The Gospel writers knew their Septuagint.

6. That there would be famine "all over the world" is an exaggeration, to say the least, but it is good biblical language: Noah's flood, after all, was supposed to destroy "everything that is on the earth" (Gen 6:17).

first gentiles and at the same time to write of Paul's bringing a "collection" to Jerusalem—hoping his readers will identify this collection with the one from gentile communities that Paul speaks of so ardently in his letters. Lukas does not want to have to explain how and why that collection from gentiles was rejected by Jerusalem. By inserting a collection from Antioch here he can posit that Paul's statement in Galatians 2:10 that "they [the Jerusalem leaders of the Movement] asked only one thing, that we remember the poor, which was actually what I was eager to do" refers to this incident and explains his solicitude for the "poor" of Jerusalem.

"Bread and Circuses"

We inherit the phrase "bread and circuses" (*panem et circenses*) from Lukas's younger contemporary Juvenal in his seventh *Satire*. His jibe was directed at the Roman method of keeping the urban poor subdued, especially in times of hardship. The economy of the city of Rome was not geared to producing goods for export; its population, nearing a million by the second century, was altogether dependent on imported food (as are twenty-first-century cities). Rome needed its empire to survive. It gave the provinces "law and order" and demanded grain in return. The grain ration, regarded as a hereditary right of the descendants of those who had conquered the world for Rome, dated back to the early republic, but it was due only to those who resided in the city of Rome. It began in the late second century BCE as a provision of grain at a reduced price, but after 62 BCE it was free of any charge. Each recipient was issued a square wooden "voucher" into which were measured five *modii* (about seventy-three pounds) of wheat per month. The Roman equivalent of "food stamps," it was not sufficient for life and was considered a supplement. Since the grain supply from abroad was contingent on weather in the exporting regions and on the navigability of the sea between them and Rome, this means of quelling unrest could instead become a significant cause of it.[7] The emperor Claudius himself suffered the indignity of being "stoned" with breadcrusts by an angry Roman mob during a grain shortage.

In times of famine it was traditional for communities to appeal to local "benefactors." It was regarded as the duty of the wealthy (especially landowners)

7. For details on the grain ration see Linda Ellis, "A Brief Look at the Juvenal's 'Bread & Circuses,'" at https://drlindaellis.net.

to provide aid to their tenants and neighbors in distress—and of course it was likewise in their own interest if they didn't wish to see their barns burned down. So we would expect that the community in Antioch would solicit its wealthier members for donations to alleviate suffering in Judea. The "subscription list" was open to the whole community, "according to their ability" (Acts 11:29)—which means more was expected of those with greater means. Bruce Winter takes a more idealistic view:

> All were to do good. When the secular clients who did not engage in work became Christians they were required to give up their patronal relationship and work in order to have the wherewithal to give to those in need. The whole Christian community was commanded to do good to [all], especially those of the household of faith. The response of the Christians in Antioch may have been guided by the role of benefactor borrowed from the Graeco-Roman world but its application to all Christians represents a radical reshaping of the underlying concept.[8]

Richard Pervo points out[9] that what we know of the Movement in Antioch in the late first and early second centuries CE reflects a shifting pattern of ecclesiastical organization. Acts seems to show Barnabas (?) or Barnabas and Saul together developing what Pervo calls the "community organizer" model of urban mission later pursued by Paul. Matthew's Gospel, usually assigned to Antioch, shows a preference for teachers and possibly prophets as community officers; the letters of Ignatius[10] plead

8. Bruce Winter, "Acts and Food Shortages," in *The Book of Acts in Its Graeco-Roman Setting*, ed. David W. J. Gill and Conrad Gempf, BAFCS 2 (Grand Rapids: Eerdmans, 1994), 59–78, at 76. This describes the situation in Jerusalem as Lukas idealizes it in the first chapters of Acts.

9. Pervo, *Acts*, 292–93, citing Gerd Theissen, *The Social Setting of Pauline Christianity: Essays on Corinth*, trans. and ed. J. Schütz (Philadelphia: Fortress, 1982).

10. These should now be dated post-Acts and not ca. 115 as previously. See Pervo, *Dating Acts: Between the Evangelists and the Apologists* (Santa Rosa, CA: Polebridge, 2006), 366. Michael Theobald (*Israel-Vergessenheit in den Pastoralbriefen: ein neuer Vorschlag zu ihrer historisch-theologischen Verortung im 2. Jahrhundert n. Chr. unter besonderer Berücksichtigung der Ignatius-Briefe* [Stuttgart: Katholisches Bibelwerk, 2016)] makes a vigorous and well-documented argument that the "letters of Ignatius" are pseudonymous and belong to a time around 160 CE.

for a tight overarching hierarchy of bishop, deacons, and presbyters; the *Didachē*, which could reasonably be located in or near Antioch,[11] reflects ongoing conflict between "itinerant charismatic prophets and the resident bishops and deacons."[12] But Lukas's insistence on attributing the origins of the gentile mission to the Jerusalem leaders (the apostles and the *presbyteroi* who succeed them there) has rendered the influence of Antioch murky. He refers in this passage to prophets and elders at Jerusalem and at 13:1 to prophets and teachers at Antioch. Since we know there were women prophets in Israel, and since Paul knows of women who prophesy in Corinth (e.g., 1 Cor 11:5), there is good reason to suppose there would have been women prophets in the Antioch community. We also know that women taught, the prime example in Acts being Prisca (18:26). Bishops (or "overseers") are unknown, presbyters are equivalently "elders," as in the synagogue, and though there is plenty of *diakonia* being practiced, there is no such thing as "a deacon."

Another change is simply described without remark: the communal organization that supposedly characterized the Jerusalem community is unknown in Antioch, where the prophecy of famine leads believers there to send "relief" (διακονία) to those in Judea "according to their ability" (v. 30). The resources of the well-to-do members are theirs to use as the Spirit moves them, and they thus become benefactors of the poor in Judea and, presumably, in Antioch as well. Economic stratification, it seems, goes hand in hand with the gentile mission.

It turns out that in reality Paul's "I alone know God's will because it was revealed to me" approach to deciding the delicate questions raised by the mission to non-Jews proved unpopular at Antioch, while Peter's more moderate and gradual program prevailed there (see Gal 2:11-14). Lukas does not show us Peter at Antioch, only Saul (later Paul) and Barnabas. He has the Antioch community anoint these two for mission and shows them returning there to loud acclaim. He makes the Jerusalem community decision in Acts 15 the universal rule, and he depicts the subsequent separation of Paul and Barnabas as based on their disagreement over whether to take Mark with them on their next missionary tour—not on Barnabas's supposed "hypocrisy" in siding with other "Jews" in the Antioch community about table fellowship with the gentile members, as depicted in Galatians (2:13).

11. See Kurt Niederwimmer, *The Didachē*, trans. Linda M. Maloney, Hermeneia (Minneapolis: Fortress, 1998), 53–54.
12. Pervo, *Acts*, 292.

In such a setting it was possible (at least in the beginning) to rethink the roles of all community members, female and male, free and enslaved, proprietor and handworker. Was that part of the reason why in the second century the hierarchy-minded Ignatius found himself no longer welcome in the place where he claimed the title of bishop?[13]

13. Supporters of a monarchical episcopate—something "Ignatius" adamantly advocates—have steadfastly defended the authenticity of the "Letters of Ignatius," while, since the Reformation, those advocating a nonhierarchical church order have rejected them. In the twenty-first century some scholars have addressed the difficulty by arguing for a later date for the letters and possible pseudonymity. See n. 10 above.

Acts 12:1-25

Exit Peter, and Also Agrippa; Rhoda Remains

This chapter is one of Lukas's best literary creations.[1] It is a novella in the ancient style with a typical set of characters, periods of suspense, and moments of comedy, and yet it is based on and intertwines biblical parallels and precedents. It gives Peter an exciting "send-off" (apart from a cameo in chap. 15) and chronicles, without comment, the change of leadership in Jerusalem. The author has constructed a tale of Peter's arrest and rescue, in the Passover night, that echoes both the exodus and Jesus' passion. The story seems dropped into the book at this point for no particular reason, but what we have seen about the food shortage in Judea (11:28-30) could very well suggest why the local ruler would want to distract the hungry mob with bloody spectacles,[2] and the tension over food supply returns to the fore in the account of the death of "Herod" at the end (v. 23).

1. Richard I. Pervo, *Acts*, Hermeneia (Minneapolis: Fortress, 2009), 315, calls it "a literary triumph."
2. This ruler is the third of four "King Herods" to appear in Luke-Acts: Herod the Great at Luke 1–2; his son Herod Antipater, known by the nickname "Antipas," whom Jesus called "that fox" and who was tetrarch of Judea but never held the title "king"; Aristobulus's son Marcus Julius Agrippa (this one); and *his* son, also named Marcus Julius Agrippa, who will appear in the final chapters of Acts.

Acts 12:1-25

12:1About that time King Herod laid violent hands upon some who belonged to the church. 2He had James, the brother of John, killed with the sword. 3After he saw that it pleased the Jews, he proceeded to arrest Peter also. (This was during the festival of Unleavened Bread.) 4When he had seized him, he put him in prison and handed him over to four squads of soldiers to guard him, intending to bring him out to the people after the Passover. 5While Peter was kept in prison, the church prayed fervently to God for him.

6The very night before Herod was going to bring him out, Peter, bound with two chains, was sleeping between two soldiers, while guards in front of the door were keeping watch over the prison. 7Suddenly an angel of the Lord appeared and a light shone in the cell. He tapped Peter on the side and woke him, saying, "Get up quickly." And the chains fell off his wrists. 8The angel said to him, "Fasten your belt and put on your sandals." He did so. Then he said to him, "Wrap your cloak around you and follow me." 9Peter went out and followed him; he did not realize that what was happening with the angel's help was real; he thought he was seeing a vision. 10After they had passed the first

The body of the chapter (vv. 1-23) is framed by accounts of the wicked deeds of Agrippa I (= "Herod"). Evidently Lukas's audience in the second century, far distant from Judea, were as clueless about the Herodian family as an Introduction to New Testament class I once stymied with an exam question asking them to name three Herods. Lukas is not interested in such details, since all "Herods" are stock villains in his story. The account of Peter's escape from prison is counter-paralleled with the story of Agrippa's actions and attitudes: as Peter, aided by God, escapes from the threat of death and regains his freedom, so Herod, making *himself* divine, is cast down from the height of his autonomy and becomes captive to a deadly disease.

Susan R. Garrett has written eloquently about Acts 12 in connection with her work on how the story of Israel and that of Jesus and his followers represent the liberation of the world from the power of Satan; the key verse for her is Luke 9:31, where, during the "transfiguration" scene, Jesus speaks with Moses and Elijah about his coming ἔξοδος ("exodus").[3] The timing at Passover also suggests connections with early Christian

3. See Susan R. Garrett, *The Demise of the Devil: Magic and the Demonic in Luke's Writings* (Minneapolis: Fortress, 1989), and in particular her "Exodus from Bondage: Luke 9:31 and Acts 12:1-4," *CBQ* 52 (1990): 656–89.

and the second guard, they came before the iron gate leading into the city. It opened for them of its own accord, and they went outside and walked along a lane, when suddenly the angel left him. [11]Then Peter came to himself and said, "Now I am sure that the Lord has sent his angel and rescued me from the hands of Herod and from all that the Jewish people were expecting."

[12]As soon as he realized this, he went to the house of Mary, the mother of John whose other name was Mark, where many had gathered and were praying. [13]When he knocked at the outer gate, a maid named Rhoda came to answer. [14]On recognizing Peter's voice, she was so overjoyed that, instead of opening the gate, she ran in and announced that Peter was standing at the gate. [15]They said to her, "You are out of your mind!" But she insisted that it was so. They said, "It is his angel." [16]Meanwhile Peter continued knocking; and when they opened the gate, they saw him and were amazed. [17]He motioned to them with his hand to be silent, and described for them how the Lord had brought him out of the prison. And he added, "Tell this to James and to the believers." Then he left and went to another place.

liturgical actions, specifically baptism, with its death-to-life theme.[4] Imprisonment was a familiar figure for death in the ancient world, and liberation from prison—rare as it was—was viewed almost as a return from the dead. So Peter's miraculous escape is seen here as an echo both of Israel's liberation from Egypt and of Jesus' liberation from the bonds of death: these are the heritage of his followers and the fulfillment of the promise to Israel.

The ancient world was unfamiliar with the horror of mass prolonged incarceration as inflicted on the world in the twentieth century and beyond. Wrongdoers (or supposed wrongdoers) were seized, tried, sentenced, and executed within a very short time: in Jesus' case, no more than twenty-four hours, according to the Gospels.[5] Supposedly this was

4. See, e.g., Col 3:13; Eph 5:14, post-Pauline writings very familiar to Lukas.
5. See, e.g., James S. Jeffers, *The Greco-Roman World of the New Testament Era: Exploring the Background of Early Christianity* (Downers Grove: IVP, 1999), 157: "Romans, like most ancients, did not punish people with imprisonment. Prisons were used simply as places of detention while awaiting trial or punishment. The Roman equivalent of long incarceration was exile, in which the convicted person was exiled to an island or remote city for an indefinite period (or for life). This punishment usually was reserved for the upper classes." See also Edward M. Peters, "Prison before the Prison: The Ancient and Medieval Worlds," in Norval Morris and David J. Rothman, eds., *The*

Acts 12:1-25 (cont.)

[18]When morning came, there was no small commotion among the soldiers over what had become of Peter. [19]When Herod had searched for him and could not find him, he examined the guards and ordered them to be put to death. Then he went down from Judea to Caesarea and stayed there.

[20]Now Herod was angry with the people of Tyre and Sidon. So they came to him in a body; and after winning over Blastus, the king's chamberlain, they asked for a reconciliation, because their country depended on the king's country for food. [21]On an appointed day Herod put on his royal robes, took his seat on the platform, and delivered a public address to them. [22]The people kept shouting, "The voice of a god, and not of a mortal!" [23]And immediately, because he had not given the glory to God, an angel of the Lord struck him down, and he was eaten by worms and died.

[24]But the word of God continued to advance and gain adherents. [25]Then after completing their mission Barnabas and Saul returned to Jerusalem and brought with them John, whose other name was Mark.

a rushed proceeding because of the approach of the Passover Sabbath, but the prisons of the time were not equipped to house and feed prisoners over many days or weeks. Paul's lengthy imprisonment as described in Acts is highly unusual and therefore very likely to be unhistorical. In Acts 12, Agrippa has disposed of James very swiftly, and Peter is only spared for a day or two because of the Passover.[6] His deep sleep in the castle dungeon, chained between two guards, represents his death.[7] His deliverance more than symbolizes resurrection; thus the rejection of Rhoda's message by the community of disciples and their awe at Peter's appearance. Peter himself has so little expectation of being released alive that he firmly believes he is dreaming; only finding himself alone in the dark street makes him aware that this may be reality after all.

Oxford History of the Prison: The Practice of Punishment in Western Society, ed. Norval Morris and David J. Rothman (New York: Oxford University Press, 1998), 3–43, at 19, referring to the imperial period: "punitive imprisonment for any length of time seems to have been infrequent."

6. The Passover feast furnishes a convenient reason for accelerating execution in the case of Jesus (cf. John 18:28; 19:31) and delaying it in the case of Peter.

7. Questions have been raised about whether Peter was, in fact, executed in Jerusalem, possibly together with James, since there is no record of where he went afterward, although tradition has consistently connected his death with Rome.

The "angel of the Lord" who effects Peter's escape in verses 7-11 is a character not to be dismissed as merely a stock figure. This ἄγγελος ("messenger") may be the same one who opened the doors of the prison to free Peter and John at 5:19. If so, this is the only such "messenger" in the story who *acts* by opening prison doors. Otherwise *angels* (including this one) direct *characters* (Peter and John, Philip, Cornelius, Paul) to act ("go," 5:19; 8:26; "send," 10:22; 11:13; "don't be afraid," 23:27). The angel who acts (5:19; 12:7-10) may well be the same in both places because the angel who "strikes down" (ἐπάταξεν) Herod in 12:23 behaves, verbally speaking, much like the angel who in 12:7 taps (kicks!) Peter in the ribs (πατάξας δὲ τὴν πλευρὰν) to wake him up![8]

We also note the presence in the story of two women—something unique in Acts. Both are apparently members of the same household, but one is clearly wealthy since she has, evidently in her own right, a house with a courtyard. (Peter knocks at the "outer gate" in v. 13.) This woman is surely a widow; she is identified in relation not to her husband but to her son, as "Mary, the mother of John whose other name was Mark."

The household includes at least one enslaved person, the woman Rose ("Rhoda" in Greek means "rose"), who bears a common slave name; almost certainly she is not the only such person present. This wealthy household was a good place for believers to assemble for prayer, since even in times of famine it was probably better supplied with food than most homes, but it was in all likelihood a group of not more than twenty or so.[9] Even large houses could not accommodate many more persons than that in their public rooms.

Mary herself remains offstage, but Rose is front and center. Ivoni Richter Reimer has argued that Rose has escaped her servile status to become a trusted member of the household. Would that it were so, but modern scholars have seen Rose as essentially a comic figure, the stock character in ancient comedy whom no one will believe.[10] At the same time Lukas makes her the one person in the story who believes without seeing. She thus parallels the women in Luke's Gospel who believed in Jesus' resurrection without having seen him and who testified of it to the other disciples, who regarded their words as "an idle tale" and "did not believe them" (Luke 24:8-11).

---

8. The verb πατάσσω means "beat, knock, strike, smite"—definitely not "tap."

9. See above at Acts 2:1-13, n. 3.

10. See J. Albert Harrill, "The Dramatic Function of the Running Slave Rhoda (Acts 12.13-16): A Piece of Greco-Roman Comedy," *NTS* 46 (2000): 150–57.

Comic Interlude?

For feminist readers the scene at Mary's house is contrary to the supposedly "triumphal" character of the chapter[11] because this interlude seems to come at the expense of the two women. We are somewhat prepared for the comedy by the account of the angel's actions in the prison: she kicks Peter in the ribs to wake him (or maybe pokes him with a shepherd's staff), then instructs him about getting dressed as if she were his nanny: "Fasten your belt and put on your sandals. Now put on your cloak and follow me."

Rose is properly a heroine in the tradition, but the original audience for the story would have recognized her as a stereotypical comic figure: the "running slave."[12] Her running from the gate to announce the good news of Peter's arrival leaves him standing in the street, a prey to the watch or, we would expect, to the now-aroused guards from the palace. This makes for terrific suspense in the telling, but it does not reflect well on the assembled community. Perhaps the episode is meant to remind the audience that Peter had once before encountered a slave woman in a courtyard (Luke 22:54-62), and demonstrated his weak character at the time, before his encounter with the risen Jesus. We would like to suppose that Rose is a full member of the house-church community, but the fact that she is dismissed as "out of her mind" (v. 15) says that on the surface of the story she is nothing but a stupid slave.

Enslavement

Rhoda/Rose represents an enormous class of persons imprisoned for life by the institution(s) of slavery, an accepted fact of life through most of history. As Jennifer Glancy writes, "Slavery was so basic a structure in the ancient world that challenging it might have seemed as odd as asking why water was wet or ice

11. See n. 1 above.

12. This figure appears in two catalogues of stock comedic characters compiled by Terence (see Pervo, *Acts*, 306n61). See also Kathy Chambers, " 'Knock, Knock—Who's There?' Acts 12:6-17 as a Comedy of Errors," in *A Feminist Companion to the Acts of the Apostles*, ed. Amy-Jill Levine with Marianne Blickenstaff, FCNTECW 9 (Cleveland: Pilgrim Press, 2004), 89–97.

cold."[13] Rose, doorkeeper in a Jewish woman's household, may have been better treated than most, but not necessarily. After all, early Christian writers were quite comfortable with enslavement, and even with cruelty toward those enslaved. Apologists in the early centuries defended against the accusation that Christians disrupted society by, among other things, appealing to slaves and women; no such thing! they claimed. The protection of social order became a standard argument among pagans and Christians alike for maintaining slavery and harsh discipline—with regard to women in general as well as to female and male slaves. Augustine claimed that violence was necessary to support the social hierarchy, which represented God's will, and agreed with Ambrose and others that enslaved persons in particular had to be kept in line. John Chrysostom considered physical discipline of the enslaved an inevitable part of keeping good order in the household but also as serving the moral improvement of those persons and providing an example to others of what could happen to them if they stepped out of line.

We cannot be content to condemn past attitudes. As Glancy writes: "Rather than wondering why it took so long for ancient Christians to recognize slavery as incompatible with the gospel, Christians today might better ask what contemporary structures we take for granted are in fact inconsistent with the good news we proclaim."[14] Moreover, "it is easy to recognize the moral compromises of the first and second century. Much harder to discern are the moral compromises Christians make today for personal or institutional advancement."[15] Persons enslaved in the twenty-first century by sex trafficking are mainly, though not exclusively, women; many are still children. We are also witnesses, across the world, to wage slavery whereby people are kept bound to a place and an occupation by economic pressure. One vicious prototype in the United States was the sharecropping

---

13. Jennifer A. Glancy, *Slavery as Moral Problem in the Early Church and Today* (Minneapolis: Fortress, 2011), 54. This 113-page volume is a stunningly succinct presentation of an enormous subject. For the legacy of slavery in Judaism, Christianity, and Islam see the essays in Bernadette J. Brooten, ed., with Jacqueline L. Hazelton, *Beyond Slavery: Overcoming Its Religious and Sexual Legacies*, Black Religion/Womanist Thought/Social Justice (New York: Palgrave Macmillan, 2010).

14. Consider, e.g., mass homelessness in the United States and vast refugee camps elsewhere.

15. Glancy, *Slavery as Moral Problem*, 54, 61.

system in the Southern states, which in the nineteenth and twentieth centuries (and still, in pockets, today) bound people to the land by means of steadily accumulating debt, ultimately stripping them of the right to own anything. In prior centuries Native Americans were coerced into indebtedness so that their lands could be seized "peacefully."

Angela Y. Davis wrote in 1998 that "one has a greater chance of going to jail or prison if one is a young black man than if one is actually a law-breaker."[16] Some two decades later we might rewrite the first part of her statement to read: "in the United States of America one has a far greater chance of being shot to death. . . ." Many of us know this in our bones, and if we are unaware, the daily and hourly newscasts are there to remind us. We are much less often reminded that young Black women who are the victims of crime are far less likely than white women to receive justice. Likewise, the vicious treatment of immigrants and refugees, documented by some media, is trivialized and even celebrated by others—at least when those persons are "non-white."

Some of us profit from this system by achieving a mendacious "peace of mind" about supposed lawbreakers being barred from "roaming our streets." More insidious still is our acquiescence in, even profiting from, the obsession with imprisonment. Willie James Jennings writes: "We would do well to remember . . . v. 19 as more and more people are being invited to participate in the ever-expanding prison industrial complex as a robust site for the expansion of capital and the growth of new markets. Could it be that the church must now seek the deliverance of not just the prisoner but also the guards?"[17] Indeed, those who earn their livelihood by imprisoning others are themselves as much victims as Herod's guards.[18] Herod sought public approval through egregious executions and "graciously relenting" from extortion of the people of Tyre and Sidon. Who are the angels today who will dethrone them

---

16. Angela Y. Davis, "Racialized Punishment and Prison Abolition," in *The Angela Y. Davis Reader*, ed. Joy James (Malden, MA: Blackwell, 1998), 105, cited in Willie James Jennings, *Acts*, Belief: A Theological Commentary on the Bible (Louisville: Westminster John Knox, 2017), 126.

17. Jennings, *Acts*, 130–31. For full documentation see Michelle Alexander, *The New Jim Crow: Mass Incarceration in the Age of Colorblindness*, 10th anniv. ed. (New York: New Press, 2020).

18. For a first-person account of life in a "for-profit" prison see Shane Bauer, *American Prison: A Reporter's Undercover Journey into the Business of Punishment* (New York: Penguin, 2018).

and their policies—and not by replicating their violence? The United Methodist Church resolved in 2012 to divest from its stock ownership in private prisons, while other churches, notably the United Church of Christ, have called for the abolition of such institutions; it is difficult to see them as anything other than the use of persons for profit—something we are too delicate, it seems, to call slavery.

Ronald Charles has concluded that "by silencing slaves and using a rhetoric of violence, the authors of these [ancient] texts contributed to the construction of myths in which slaves functioned as a useful trope to support the combined power of religion and empire."[19] In Lukas's account in Acts 12 we hear the the loud voices of the assembly in verse 15 telling Rose, "You are out of your mind!"—language that not only demeans but effectively denies the full humanity of its object. We do not hear the voice of Rose herself. Still, her actions speak for her, and she comes off better than the other characters in the story; she "recognizes" Peter's voice (v. 14), and she stands firm against dismissal and ridicule: "she insisted that it was so" (v. 15). Her persistent voice cannot be ignored, and she is vindicated. She is a second "angel" who acts to rescue Peter from Herod's forces. Because she is not silenced, even though she is not quoted, Acts 12 does not "support the combined power of religion and empire" but demolishes it, clearly revealing the wickedness of the royal/imperial power and illustrating God's judgment in Herod's gruesome death.

Eventually, then, the group concedes that it may be Peter's "angel" (or ghost?) who has come to inform them of his death. This echoes the story of John the Baptizer's execution in prison by Herod Antipas, Agrippa's predecessor. Clearly these believers had no real confidence in their prayers being heard.[20]

The eventual encounter with Peter at the gate is not calculated to alleviate the sense that he is not really alive. Once the gate is finally opened to him we would expect him to enter the courtyard and take refuge in

19. Ronald Charles, *The Silencing of Slaves in Early Jewish and Christian Texts*, Routledge Studies in the Early Christian World (London: Routledge, 2020), 3. This book will be a vital source for anyone examining the treatment of slaves in the Bible and pseudepigrapha.

20. We may speculate why there was earnest prayer for Peter when he was imprisoned while evidently no prayers were offered for Paul during his long incarceration—at least we do not read about any.

Mary's house. Not so. He does not even pass through the gate but holds up his hand for silence and delivers a farewell message: after describing his release from prison he instructs his hearers to report to "James"[21] and "to the believers," which is odd, since this group are surely believers themselves. Are they being chided for having doubted (as Rose did not)?

Acts 12 brings together, one last time, the trio of Peter, James, and John, so familiar from the Gospels, but only to dismiss them: James is executed, John is mentioned only as his brother, and Peter, after his release, leaves Jerusalem. The apostolic period is effectively over; except for the artificial scene in Acts 15 none of the Twelve will appear in this work again. Leadership of the Jerusalem church now lies with the "elders," headed by James. Lukas's audience were evidently supposed to understand who this James was. If they knew Paul's letter to the Galatians (as Lukas certainly did), they had learned there that he was "the Lord's brother." We might think that this succession (or revolution?) in the leadership of the mother community in Jerusalem—evidently with the claim that James has assumed at least the titular headship of the Movement, if not more—would be described. The inference must be that it was not as matter-of-fact as Lukas makes it seem—which fits the author's inclination to smooth out differences and clashes within the community when possible.

Lukas has crafted the chapter to remove Peter from the story in a glorious manner. He has no reliable report of Peter's execution in Jerusalem, and he needs him to reappear in chapter 15 at the "apostolic council"— the artificial nature of which is made clear by the fact that Peter vanishes to "another place," reappears in chapter 15, and then disappears for good without any indication as to where he has been in the meantime or where he goes afterward. Perhaps the audience was expected to know, from Galatians 2:11-14, that Peter had gone to Antioch, but that is not part of Lukas's story. He simply needs to get Peter off the stage in a dignified way so the rest of the narrative can be about Paul.

There is another shift in the story here, in the Movement's relations with "the Jews." These are now in collusion with Agrippa, who is killing those belonging to "the church" (ἐκκλησία) not only because he is a bloodthirsty tyrant but because it pleases "the Jews" (v. 3). Parallels in Acts 24:27 and 25:9 show the Roman governors Felix and Festus similarly currying favor with "the Jews." In each instance "the Jews" (in the internal context of the story) refers to the Jerusalem Jewish leadership.

---

21. Not the James who was executed in v. 2.

To this point opposition to the Movement has come only from that group and briefly from "the Jews" at Antioch (9:23), who initially opposed Paul but seem to have lost their animus in the meantime. Is this because the Jesus-followers in Antioch are now called "Christians" (11:26) and are not intent on proclaiming themselves part of Judaism? It seems, rather, that Lukas has located the nexus of Jewish opposition in the temple leadership and their followers. Stephen's speech in chapter 7 has laid out the reason for that: supposed upholders of the law, those leaders are (in Lukas's eyes) violators of the law like those described by the prophet Malachi.[22] Everywhere outside Jerusalem, as we now begin to follow Paul's missionary activity, the reaction is mixed: sometimes "the Jews" stir up opposition to Paul and his companions; at other times the missionaries are in hot water because they *are* "Jews." Lukas is adept at holding the audience's attention and keeping suspense alive.

Finally, the narrative returns to Agrippa. On discovering Peter's escape he has the guards tortured and executed, thus affirming our impression of his character.[23] Then, the Passover being completed, he swans off to Caesarea. The food shortage reenters the picture in oblique fashion. The cities of Tyre and Sidon were biblical tropes for wicked places: see Ezekiel 28, where the prince of Tyre is accused of amassing wealth (the ultimate Lukan horror) and Sidon of treating Israel with contempt, and Luke 10:13-14, "Woe to you, Chorazin! Woe to you, Bethsaida! . . . at the judgment it will be more tolerable for Tyre and Sidon than for you."

In the face of starvation the leaders of Tyre and Sidon have evidently bribed Agrippa's chamberlain to intercede for them. Supposedly Agrippa accedes graciously to their petition and on an appointed day appears in his silver-threaded royal robes[24] to receive their homage.[25] He oversteps

22. Cf. *inter alia* Mal 1:6-13; 2:1-9.
23. Lukas hates the Herodians in general; the only possible exception is Agrippa II, who is an ineffectual prop in Acts 25–26. Susan Garrett (*The Demise of the Devil*) regards the Herodians as, so to speak, Satanic figures. The execution of guards was common practice when prisoners had escaped—*pour encourager les autres*, no doubt. For an example from ancient literature see Chariton, *Callirhoe* 3.4.18.
24. Pervo cites a similar scene, this one featuring a queen: "Arsake gave orders for a pavilion to be erected beneath a canopy of purple embroidered with gold. Then, exquisitely arrayed, she took her seat on an elevated throne, encircled by her body-guard in their gilded armor. Holding aloft a herald's staff to signify that she wished to negotiate peace . . ." (*Ethiopian Story* 7.3, quoted in Pervo, *Acts*, 314n133).
25. The "them" who is addressed is peculiar: surely no more than a few envoys would have traveled the long distance to Caesarea, and the mob reaction seems to come from the locals.

himself, failing to rebuke the crowds that blaspheme by honoring him as a god. An angel (cf. vv. 7-10) steps in and slays him.[26] He suffers a death worthy of a tyrant, as—in Lukas's opinion—a Herod should.

For Lukas's audience this chapter in Acts may have offered welcome entertainment (while also conveying a message about the progress of the Word). For us in the twenty-first century it is a kick in the ribs: a powerful reminder that if we continue to put ourselves in the place of God in our treatment of our fellow human beings we will suffer severe consequences. Second-century audiences were inured to the social realities of enslavement and imprisonment. We dare not be.

Chapter 12 of Acts concludes with the last of Lukas's summaries of the peaceful growth of the Movement. Paul and Barnabas (who were evidently supposed to have been in Jerusalem during the episode of James's execution and Peter's imprisonment but were somehow not involved in the action, even though they have recruited John Mark and perhaps were staying at his mother's house) are safely returned to Antioch, which will now become the hub of missionary action.

---

26. The source of the story may be Josephus, *Ant.* 19.343-50; see Richard I. Pervo, *Dating Acts: Between the Evangelists and the Apologists* (Santa Rosa, CA: Polebridge, 2006), 170–78. The Herodians have remained a source of reference (and entertainment) through the millennia. I confess my favorite member of the clan is Herod Herdman. (See Barbara Robinson, *The Best Christmas Pageant Ever* [New York: Scholastic, 1972], 66.)—LMM

Acts 13:1–14:28

Barnabas and Paul on Mission

The apostolic ministry of Peter and the other Eleven ends, and the focus shifts entirely to the missional ministry of Saul, who within nine verses becomes Paul, the name by which he was already known to most if not all of Lukas's audience and, evidently, to himself. This queering of Saul/Paul's identity functions, in part, to reinforce his rootedness in and identification with the heritage of Israel as he moves into the diaspora and then to pagan contexts. It is an important aspect of Lukas's "Jews first" program: as noted, the Lukan work reserves the mission to the gentiles for the time after the end of apostolic leadership. The mission is initiated by the Spirit through Peter but will be extended through Barnabas and Paul, starting from Antioch, where the disciples (μαθηταὶ), according to 11:26, began to be called Χριστιανοί, "Christians."

The audience is probably meant to understand, then, that Paul really was a νεανίας, a "young man" (7:58), when he first appeared in the text and that the time he supposedly spent in Tarsus extended over more than a decade, during which he achieved maturity. (The "fourteen years" of Gal 2:1 may be correct.) Peter's going "to another place" in 12:17 essentially represents his death as far as the community in Jerusalem is concerned; the association with the death of Agrippa I in 44 CE is anachronistic and may simply serve as a useful frame.

The house churches of the ἐκκλησία at Antioch (κατὰ τὴν οὖσαν means either "locally" or "at that time," or both) are led by "prophets and

175

^{13:1}Now in the church at Antioch there were prophets and teachers: Barnabas, Simeon who was called Niger, Lucius of Cyrene, Manaen a member of the court of Herod the ruler, and Saul. ²While they were worshiping the Lord and fasting, the Holy Spirit said, "Set apart for me Barnabas and Saul for the work to which I have called them." ³Then after fasting and praying they laid their hands on them and sent them off.

⁴So, being sent out by the Holy Spirit, they went down to Seleucia; and from there they sailed to Cyprus. ⁵When they arrived at Salamis, they proclaimed the word of God in the synagogues of the Jews. And they had John also to assist them. ⁶When they had gone through the whole island as far as Paphos, they met a certain magician, a Jewish false prophet, named ⁷Bar-Jesus. He was with the proconsul, Sergius Paulus, an intelligent man, who summoned Barnabas and Saul and wanted to hear the word of God. ⁸But the magician Elymas (for that is the translation of his name) opposed them and tried to turn the proconsul away from the faith. ⁹But Saul, also known as Paul, filled with the Holy Spirit, looked intently at him ¹⁰and said, "You son of the devil, you enemy of all righteousness, full of all deceit and villainy, will you not stop making crooked the straight paths of the Lord? ¹¹And now listen—the hand of the Lord is against you, and you will be blind for a while, unable to see the sun." Immediately mist and darkness came over him, and he went about groping for someone to lead him by the hand. ¹²When the proconsul saw what had happened,

he believed, for he was astonished at the teaching about the Lord.

¹³Then Paul and his companions set sail from Paphos and came to Perga in Pamphylia. John, however, left them and returned to Jerusalem; ¹⁴but they went on from Perga and came to Antioch in Pisidia. And on the sabbath day they went into the synagogue and sat down. ¹⁵After the reading of the law and the prophets, the officials of the synagogue sent them a message, saying, "Brothers, if you have any word of exhortation for the people, give it." ¹⁶So Paul stood up and with a gesture began to speak:

"You Israelites, and others who fear God, listen. ¹⁷The God of this people Israel chose our ancestors and made the people great during their stay in the land of Egypt, and with uplifted arm he led them out of it. ¹⁸For about forty years he put up with them in the wilderness. ¹⁹After he had destroyed seven nations in the land of Canaan, he gave them their land as an inheritance ²⁰for about four hundred fifty years. After that he gave them judges until the time of the prophet Samuel. ²¹Then they asked for a king; and God gave them Saul son of Kish, a man of the tribe of Benjamin, who reigned for forty years. ²²When he had removed him, he made David their king. In his testimony about him he said, 'I have found David, son of Jesse, to be a man after my heart, who will carry out all my wishes.' ²³Of this man's posterity God has brought to Israel a Savior, Jesus, as he promised; ²⁴before his coming John had already proclaimed a baptism of repentance to all the people of Israel. ²⁵And as John was finishing his work, he said, 'What do you suppose that I am? I am not he. No, but one is coming after me; I am not worthy to untie the thong of the sandals on his feet.'

²⁶"Brothers and sisters, you descendants of Abraham's family, and others who fear God, to us the message of this salvation has been sent. ²⁷Because the residents of Jerusalem and their leaders did not recognize him or understand the words of the prophets that are read every sabbath, they fulfilled those words by condemning him. ²⁸Even though they found no cause for a sentence of death, they asked Pilate to have him killed. ²⁹When they had carried out everything that was written about him, they took him down from the tree and laid him in a tomb. ³⁰But God raised him from the dead; ³¹and for many days he appeared to those who came up with him from Galilee to Jerusalem, and they are now his witnesses to the people. ³²And we bring you the good news that what God promised to our ancestors ³³he has fulfilled for us, their children, by raising Jesus; as also it is written in the second psalm,

'You are my Son;
today I have begotten you.'
³⁴As to his raising him from the dead, no more to return to corruption, he has spoken in this way,

'I will give you the holy promises made to David.'
³⁵Therefore he has also said in another psalm,

'You will not let your Holy One experience corruption.'

³⁶For David, after he had served the purpose of God in his own generation, died, was laid beside his ancestors, and experienced corruption; ³⁷but he whom God raised up experienced no corruption. ³⁸Let it be known to you therefore, my brothers, that through this man forgiveness of sins is proclaimed to you; ³⁹by this Jesus everyone who believes is set free from all those sins from which you could not be freed by the law of Moses. ⁴⁰Beware, therefore, that what the prophets said does not happen to you:

⁴¹'Look, you scoffers!
Be amazed and perish,
for in your days I am doing a
work,
a work that you will never
believe, even if
someone tells you.'"

⁴²As Paul and Barnabas were going out, the people urged them to speak about these things again the next sabbath. ⁴³When the meeting of the synagogue broke up, many Jews and devout converts to Judaism followed Paul and Barnabas, who spoke to them and urged them to continue in the grace of God.

⁴⁴The next sabbath almost the whole city gathered to hear the word of the Lord. ⁴⁵But when the Jews saw the crowds, they were filled with jealousy; and blaspheming, they contradicted what was spoken by Paul. ⁴⁶Then both Paul and Barnabas spoke out boldly, saying, "It was necessary that the word of God should be spoken first to you. Since you reject it and judge yourselves to be unworthy of eternal life, we are

now turning to the Gentiles. [47]For so the Lord has commanded us, saying,

'I have set you to be a light for the Gentiles,
so that you may bring salvation to the ends of the earth.'"

[48]When the Gentiles heard this, they were glad and praised the word of the Lord; and as many as had been destined for eternal life became believers. [49]Thus the word of the Lord spread throughout the region. [50]But the Jews incited the devout women of high standing and the leading men of the city, and stirred up persecution against Paul and Barnabas, and drove them out of their region. [51]So they shook the dust off their feet in protest against them, and went to Iconium. [52]And the disciples were filled with joy and with the Holy Spirit.

[14:1]The same thing occurred in Iconium, where Paul and Barnabas went into the Jewish synagogue and spoke in such a way that a great number of both Jews and Greeks became believers. [2]But the unbelieving Jews stirred up the Gentiles and poisoned their minds against the brothers. [3]So they re-mained for a long time, speaking boldly for the Lord, who testified to the word of his grace by granting signs and wonders to be done through them. [4]But the residents of the city were divided; some sided with the Jews, and some with the apostles. [5]And when an attempt was made by both Gentiles and Jews, with their rulers, to mistreat them and to stone them, [6]the apostles learned of it and fled to Lystra and Derbe, cities of Lycaonia, and to the surrounding country; [7]and there they continued proclaiming the good news.

[8]In Lystra there was a man sitting who could not use his feet and had never walked, for he had been crippled from birth. [9]He listened to Paul as he was speaking. And Paul, looking at him intently and seeing that he had faith to be healed, [10]said in a loud voice, "Stand upright on your feet." And the man sprang up and began to walk. [11]When the crowds saw what Paul had done, they shouted in the Lycaonian language, "The gods have come down to us in human form!" [12]Barnabas they called Zeus, and Paul they called Hermes, be-

teachers," very much like the situation reflected in the *Didachē*, a work roughly contemporary with or slightly previous to Acts and probably from western Syria, possibly even from Antioch.[1] The (partial) list framed by the names of Barnabas and Saul is representative; Simeon, Lucius,[2] and Manaen are otherwise unknown. Again Lukas makes no issue about race: Simeon, a "prophet and teacher" is "called Niger (Νίγερ, black),"

---

1. See Kurt Niederwimmer, *The Didachē*, trans. Linda M. Maloney, Hermeneia (Minneapolis: Fortress, 1998); Aaron Milavec, *The Didachē: Text, Translation, Analysis, and Commentary* (Collegeville, MN: Liturgical Press, 2003).

2. Origen identified Lucius with Lukas himself.

cause he was the chief speaker. ¹³The priest of Zeus, whose temple was just outside the city, brought oxen and garlands to the gates; he and the crowds wanted to offer sacrifice. ¹⁴When the apostles Barnabas and Paul heard of it, they tore their clothes and rushed out into the crowd, shouting, ¹⁵"Friends, why are you doing this? We are mortals just like you, and we bring you good news, that you should turn from these worthless things to the living God, who made the heaven and the earth and the sea and all that is in them. ¹⁶In past generations he allowed all the nations to follow their own ways; ¹⁷yet he has not left himself without a witness in doing good— giving you rains from heaven and fruitful seasons, and filling you with food and your hearts with joy." ¹⁸Even with these words, they scarcely restrained the crowds from offering sacrifice to them.

¹⁹But Jews came there from Antioch and Iconium and won over the crowds. Then they stoned Paul and dragged him out of the city, supposing that he was dead. ²⁰But when the disciples surrounded him, he got up and went into the city. The next day he went on with Barnabas to Derbe.

²¹After they had proclaimed the good news to that city and had made many disciples, they returned to Lystra, then on to Iconium and Antioch. ²²There they strengthened the souls of the disciples and encouraged them to continue in the faith, saying, "It is through many persecutions that we must enter the kingdom of God." ²³And after they had appointed elders for them in each church, with prayer and fasting they entrusted them to the Lord in whom they had come to believe.

²⁴Then they passed through Pisidia and came to Pamphylia. ²⁵When they had spoken the word in Perga, they went down to Attalia. ²⁶From there they sailed back to Antioch, where they had been commended to the grace of God for the work that they had completed. ²⁷When they arrived, they called the church together and related all that God had done with them, and how he had opened a door of faith for the Gentiles. ²⁸And they stayed there with the disciples for some time.

and that's that. It is Barnabas and Saul who are the focus of attention. The ἐκκλησία holds worship services and practices fasting, a discipline familiar to Judaism. Λειτουργέω (NRSV: "worshiping") refers to the work of the assembly, but its common use in Judaism described duties performed by priests and Levites in the temple;[3] the Antioch community understands itself as in continuity with Judaism and the cult at Jerusalem.

3. See BDAG, 590, λειτουργέω. The reference, as also for the modern English form "liturgy," is always to *public* worship or service by or on behalf of a society or community.

The "they" in verses 2 and 3 is unclear: Does it refer only to the four "prophets and teachers" or to their respective communities or (improbably) to the whole ἐκκλησία at Antioch? Did the Spirit speak only to the four men, or only to Barnabas and Saul, or to the gathered group? In any case a further period of prayer and fasting follows in order to confirm that the message of the Spirit has been correctly understood and is genuine; then "they" lay hands on the two designated missionaries and send them forth.

There seems no reason to restrict the "they" who laid hands on (= ordained?) the missionaries to the community leadership. The mission is initiated by the Holy Spirit through the community (whether house churches or a full gathering such as 14:27 implies) and is completed by a report to the community and its approval of what has been done. We know from Paul's own letters that he and his "team" were not the only missionaries in the field; they are simply Lukas's paradigm, and their sending—by the local community—is intended to be paradigmatic for all missions.

The "idealized" character of this mission should be clear enough from its peculiar itinerary, which seems to be a more or less random list of places that, given the state of roads and harbors at the time, no one would visit in this sequence. The initial voyage to Cyprus is a standard beginning (cf. 15:39; 21:3; 27:4), but beyond that the sequence is confused. Did Barnabas and Saul cross Cyprus on foot to reach the capital at Paphos (see "when they had gone through the whole island," v. 6) or did they sail along the coast? From Paphos they sail to Perga, which is not an appropriate landing place if one is aiming for Antioch "in Pisidia," and the sequence of cities visited in chapter 14 is altogether random. This journey is a construct throughout.

In fact, Lukas has no interest in Cyprus except as a stage for the encounter between Paul and Bar-Jesus (or "Elymas"—the Greek text is too poorly preserved or corrupt to allow us to make much of the double name). That Cyprus had long since been missionized is made abundantly clear by the presence of Barnabas throughout the early narrative as well as the statement in 11:20 that believers were coming *from* Cyprus to preach in Syria. As Peter had confronted and denounced Simon in Samaria, so now Paul meets a man whom Lukas this time labels both a magician and (emphatically) a "Jewish false prophet" (v. 6). Lukas uses this episode to drive home the point that Jews, who now have access to the triumphant power of Jesus over Satan, have no business serving as

Satan's magicians and emulating the false prophets of Israel's past. Such practices may impress the gentiles because they are idolators, but no Jew should fall for it or be an agent of it. The fact that the proconsul, Sergius Paulus (the highest Roman official to appear in Acts), is intrigued by Bar-Jesus/Elymas is rather the cherry on the cake: here is an exemplary and "intelligent" gentile, but he can't see through the works of the magician until Paul confronts this "false prophet" and demonstrates his greater authority by blinding him. Then the proconsul "believed"—surely a major breakthrough, much more significant than the conversion of a centurion—but evidently the event is of no importance to Lukas since he makes nothing of it. Being "astonished at the teaching about the Lord" (v. 12) is not the right reaction; belief should lead to repentance and turning away from idols, but nothing is said of Sergius Paulus's doing that.

Who, exactly, did Lukas conceive Bar-Jesus to be? He is "queer," to begin with: he has a Jewish name, then a Greek name that supposedly translates it,[4] but these are mentioned in passing; afterward he is only "son of the devil" and "enemy of all righteousness" (v. 10) in Paul's accusation. He is "with" Sergius Paulus, who summons Paul and Barnabas to debate him. What does his being "with" the proconsul mean? We should consider, I think, that Bar-Jesus may well have been enslaved. Such persons often had two names, especially if they were "foreigners" in Greco-Roman society.[5] Having a magician in one's household would be a proper perquisite for a high official in a foreign land, and the enslaved person would be a valuable possession. It may be that Sergius Paulus was not only "astonished" at having his pet magician stripped of his powers but mightily chagrined. Perhaps in Lukas's imagination he "adopted" Saul as a replacement for his lost magician, changing his name to Paul to match his own. After all, Saul/Paul seems to exhibit magical powers of his own, being capable of blinding Bar-Jesus and rendering him helpless.

4. It is in this passage that "Saul" becomes "Paul" as well. Is it accidental that this happens in the presence of a high official named "Paulus"? Does Lukas think of Sergius Paulus as choosing to be Paul's "patron" during his stay in Paphos?

5. See Kostas Vlassopoulos, "Athenian Slave Names and Athenian Social History," *ZPE* 175 (2010): 113–44. It was usual for enslaved persons in large households to be given an additional name to distinguish among those bearing very common names.

TRANSLATION MATTERS

"Astonished" is much too mild a translation for the participle of ἐκπλήσσομαι; grammarians have rendered it "to be so amazed as to be practically overwhelmed."[6] (We might say he was "blown away.") The root verb πλήσσω, meaning "strike," was used of "divinely-administered blows or disasters that come to persons or things."[7] If Sergius Paulus's reaction is not like that of the slaveowners in Acts 16 who are enraged at Paul's rendering their slave girl useless to them, it may be because he is "astonished at the teaching about the Lord"; that is, he attributes the event to some kind of divine power—which Lukas certainly thinks he should!—but as he disappears from the story, we will never know.

The remainder of the chapter deals with Paul and Barnabas's visit to Antioch in Pisidia. Mark (here referred to as "John") "defects" or "retreats" from the leading missionaries and returns to Jerusalem; no reason is given, and describing his departure as a "defection"[8] sets up the break with Barnabas in 15:37-39 (where NRSV describes his action as "desertion"). Barnabas is already receding behind Paul: he was not mentioned in the Elymas story, and the subsequent portion of the journey begins with "Then Paul and his companions set sail" (v. 13).

The first order of business in Pisidian Antioch is for Paul to deliver his "inaugural address." A pattern of events is also established that will be followed through the rest of Acts:[9] Paul arrives in a place with his entourage; he goes to the local synagogue on the Sabbath; he testifies to the message about Jesus as savior of Israel; he is at first well received, but then the Jewish leaders and/or the gentile leadership in the place turn against him, and he and his companions are driven out.

Paul's speech likewise follows a model established by Peter and then Stephen: he rehearses the history of God's care for Israel, speaks of how the ancestors failed to listen to the prophets and so were punished, and then of how God has not abandoned this people but has sent one last

6. Johannes P. Louw and Eugene A. Nida, eds., *Greek-English Lexicon of the New Testament Based on Semantic Domains*, 2 vols. (New York: United Bible Societies, 1988), 25.219, as quoted in Mikeal C. Parsons and Martin M. Culy, *Acts: A Handbook on the Greek Text* (Waco, TX: Baylor University Press, 2003), 249.
7. BDAG, 830.
8. See Parsons and Culy, *Acts*, 251.
9. See 14:1-6, 8-30; 16:11-40; 17:1-8, 11-14; 18:1-17; 19:8-20.

prophet, Jesus.[10] Following in the footsteps of their forebears, the Jewish leaders rejected him and brought about his death, but God raised him up, and his chosen witnesses testify to this. The speaker then appeals to the listeners to accept the message about Jesus and be set free.

Lukas's portrayal of Jesus consistently focuses on his character as the last of Israel's prophets and thus its Messiah. It tiptoes around questions of the Christ's divinity; at no time does Lukas propose that Jesus' executioners were "killing God" or attempting to do so. They were simply prophet-killers like their ancestors before them, with similar initial results, but God would not let them win this time. Lukas wrote in an age when emergent Judaism was splintered, ousted from its center in Jerusalem, and riven by repeated eruptions of messianism, at least according to Josephus. Revolts were breaking out in the diaspora, especially in Egypt. Within a decade after the probable completion of Acts one such messianic leader, Simon Bar-Kosiba (aka "Bar Kokhba"), even brought off a serious revolt and won the support of at least one leading rabbi, Akiva. The smashing of his movement led to the expulsion of Jews from Judea as well as savage reprisals by the Romans in the unruly parts of the diaspora. The members of the Movement, who now began to call themselves "Christians" if only to distinguish themselves from the people the Romans were out to exterminate (and to avoid paying the tax levied on Jews for the upkeep of pagan temples in Rome), were particularly convinced that Jesus' preaching of peace was something to be proclaimed and adhered to—which it was, at least until Christianity became the official religion of the empire, whereupon (and thereafter) swords were blessed and the emperor revered.

It is also in the context of this first missionary journey of Paul and Barnabas that Lukas begins to speak of "the Jews" as a hostile group *outside* Jerusalem, signaling that the rest of Acts will be designed to appeal especially to a gentile audience. Lukas hopes that the beginnings of what he interprets as the promised gathering of the nations to Zion (see esp. Isa 60:14) will cause his own people, who are meant to govern and teach those foreign peoples, to grasp what God is still offering. Here Lukas is

---

10. Paul's speech, like that of Peter, especially emphasizes the positive: the fulfillment of God's promises to Israel. Stephen's speech, on the other hand, stresses Israel's constant defection, culminating in the rejection of Jesus, and almost says that the people will never repent. Only his dying "do not hold this sin against them" (7:60) offers a shred of hope similar to those proffered by Israel's prophets to soften their denunciations.

clearly influenced by Paul's letter to the Romans.[11] Lukas did not know Paul in person; he reshaped (or invented?) the facts of Paul's life to suit his own plot line and to depict the kind of character who would drive his story in the right direction. But it would not be right to say that Lukas's Paul is not the "real" Paul, any more than it would be to say that the Paul who wrote the letters attributed to him *was* the "real" Paul. The latter is a character projected onto the page by the author—and so is the former.

Following the established pattern of rejection of the message by the Jerusalem leadership, Lukas portrays the Jewish leadership in the diaspora cities as likewise jealous and hostile. Here he is undoubtedly drawing on his own experience. Still, it is *never* only "the Jews" in any place who make trouble for the missionaries; they are equally persecuted by gentile authorities (or mobs) for being Jews themselves.

As will be the case throughout, the missionaries and their message are at first received with joy by *all* who hear them. (At 13:16 these are limited to Jews and "God-fearers."[12]) But word gets around. By the next Sabbath "the Jews" have two reasons for opposing the missionaries: first, "many Jews and devout converts to Judaism followed Paul and Barnabas" (13:43), and second, they are now drawing a huge crowd ("almost the whole city," v. 44). How is the leadership supposed to keep order, and who is going to instruct all these people after Paul and Barnabas have hit the road to the next place? There is a prospect of chaos, with various factions claiming to be "real Jews" clashing in the streets, and when the Roman authorities come down on the rioters, You Know Who will get the blame.[13]

It gets even worse when Paul and Barnabas declare that, since the Jewish leadership is rejecting them, they will now turn "to the Gentiles" (v. 46) and "as many as had been destined for eternal life became believers" (v. 48). Lukas deliberately leaves their number as vague as can be imagined; still "the word of the Lord spread throughout the region" (v. 49). How did that happen? Was this message being spread by something

---

11. See esp. Romans 11.

12. Here Lukas appears to envision as "God-fearers" only gentiles who are serious enough about their interest in Jewish teaching to attend synagogue. Again, we should keep in mind that the "synagogue," whether a private home or a public building of some kind, would not have held more than two or three dozen people at most.

13. Today's readers are probably familiar enough with the rivalry among "Christian" denominations—at least until the end of the twentieth century, before the ascendancy of the "nones"—to appreciate that "stealing sheep" from a local synagogue would not have been welcomed.

like a game of "telephone"?[14] No wonder the people in charge of keeping order are worried. They turn to the upper classes, those whose interest in peace and good order is strongest and who are best able to enforce it. This is the only time that "devout women of high standing" are drawn into opposing the missionaries (v. 50). They would have as great an interest as the "leading men" in keeping order, and indeed they are the first group mentioned; still, the class lines in Pisidian Antioch must have been drawn more sharply than those in, say, Thessalonica (cf. 17:4). In the end Paul and Barnabas "shook the dust off their feet in protest against them" (v. 51), as Jesus had instructed,[15] and departed for Iconium.[16]

In Iconium the pattern repeats itself: preaching in the synagogue; acceptance by both women and men, Jews and gentiles (proselytes or "God-fearers"); opposition from "unbelieving Jews" (14:2), who now stir up gentile opposition. Even so, the missionaries remain "for a long time," continuing to preach and to be the instruments of God's "signs and wonders" until the combined hostility of Jewish and gentile factions, and a plot to stone them, causes them to move on (v. 3). Lukas's calling the missionaries "apostles" in verse 4 is unique in Acts. It may be taken from a source or it may be used here (and *only* here for any but the Twelve) to emphasize that Paul and Barnabas have been chosen and "sent" by the community at Antioch in the same way the Twelve were chosen and sent by Jesus. While all four Gospels frequently use the underlying verb, ἀποστέλλω, for Jesus' sending or being sent, Lukas is sparing in his use of it in Acts, preferring forms of πέμπω. For him the missionaries are better characterized as "angels/messengers," as indicated by his consistent use

14. It seems odd that in the whole account of the mission in Acts 13–14 there is no mention of baptism. The willing Jewish recipients of the message in Pisidian Antioch are instructed to "continue in the grace of God" (13:43). Eager gentiles subsequently "became believers" (13:48) as do both Jews and gentiles in Iconium (14:1). Is this another difference between the Petrine and Pauline missions? Was it at one time the case that only certain persons could baptize, or that baptism was optional for Jews? See Paul's protest (1 Cor 1:14-17) that his role is preaching, not baptizing.

15. Cf. Luke 9:5; 10:11. Parsons and Culy remark that "This idiom referred to a symbolic action . . . that served as a public demonstration" of breaking communication and also rejecting further responsibility. They add that "the action may well have been somewhat inflammatory in this context" (*Acts*, 270), which qualifies as a major understatement.

16. As already mentioned, Iconium is not a logical next stop, but we are moving into the territory that would be celebrated in the Acts of Paul and Thecla and about which no doubt legends already abounded.

of forms of the verb ἀγγέλλω ("send") for their reports to their originating communities or other assemblies of followers of the Way (cf. 4:23; 12:17; 14:27; 15:4). The one time Acts speaks of "mission" (at 12:25 NRSV) the word used is διακονία.[17]

Paul and Barnabas thus flee to "Lystra and Derbe, cities of Lycaonia, and to the surrounding country" (v. 6)—which is to say, to the back of beyond. It was still the case when Acts was written that Romans in general considered the "Christians" to be rabble-rousers and their natural public the great unwashed. Lukas, rather than refuting such charges, makes use of them by creating a semi-comic scene in Lystra that he will later counter with a dramatic tableau in Athens, still the intellectual and cultural capital of the world.[18] But to get a true picture we will need to connect Acts 14:6-20 with 16:1-5.

This is the only time Lukas depicts Paul among "simple" people and country folk.[19] But the original audience would have understood much more; like us, they found themselves in "an increasingly diverse and multicultural world" and filled in the layers of background: "Two Jewish-Christian missionaries arrive in a Roman colony in the middle of the seemingly long-Hellenized but still barbarian region of Lycaonia, preach in Greek about the Jewish God-Man Jesus, and are promptly

17. Authorized Version: "ministry." The word διακονία is virtually unknown to the LXX, appearing once in 1 Maccabees in reference to a "table service" (i.e., dinnerware). Where the NRSV writes "mission" (Judg 18:5-6; 1 Sam 15:18, 20), the underlying Hebrew word is דרך and the LXX writes ἡ ὁδός; both words mean "the way," the very expression Lukas has chosen to designate the Jesus movement. Διακονία in Acts refers primarily to service within or on behalf of the communities of the Way, thus at Acts 6:1, 4 (cf. Luke 10:40: Martha) and in 12:25, where (with 11:29) it frames the work of Barnabas and Saul in bringing the collection to the "poor" (i.e., the Jesus community) in Jerusalem. Only once, at Acts 20:24, is it a reference to external "mission." There it appears on the lips of Paul, who was well known to have employed it frequently in that sense. Hence the "mission" of the nascent church in the second century, according to Lukas, is primarily *service* to and solidarity with those who have committed to the Way; they will serve as a shining example to those outside and thus a "draw" (cf. Isa 49:11; Matt 5:16). In Lukas's vision women and men together performed such service, in solidarity.

18. See Dean P. Béchard, "Paul among the Rustics: The Lystran Episode (Acts 14:8-20) and Lucan Apologetic," *CBQ* 63 (2001): 84–101.

19. For an insightful summary and interpretation of Acts 14:6-20 in context see Glen L. Thompson, "What We Have Here Is a Failure to Communicate: Paul and Barnabas at Lystra—Seen from Wauwatosa," in *Heritage and Hope: Essays in Honor of the 150th Anniversary of Wisconsin Lutheran Seminary*, ed. Kenneth A. Cherney (Milwaukee: Wisconsin Lutheran Seminary Press, 2013), 105–34.

acclaimed as Olympian gods by Lycaonian-speaking Gentiles."[20] The "first missionary journey" is built around a set of examples of Pauline ministry among different groups of Jews and gentiles, from the educated in Pisidian Antioch to the "barbarians" in Lystra.

The language barrier is all but insurmountable in Lystra, as it will also be in Malta (28:1-10). In both cases the cultural clash is presented as a failure of understanding on the part of the "barbarians" because they do not speak Greek and they identify the strangers with their own gods—not as a failure of the missionaries to try to understand these people who are "foreign" to them.

Lukas's audience would have known that veterans of two Roman legions had been granted land in Lystra and that they and their families (numbering perhaps three thousand) would probably have made up a substantial part of the "urban" population (having exchanged their farm-land for city "condos")[21] with the Lycaonians mainly farming outside the center. The healed man evidently understood Greek and may have been part of the urban elite. The "crowds" (present in the market) saw the healing and interpreted it in their own terms: as the work of gods. Paul and Barnabas are apparently caught unawares by the joyous cele-bration and the plan to sacrifice to them; the only message they succeed in conveying is so bland that it could be understood as inoffensive to Lycaonians, Greeks, Jews, and Romans.

Evidently the Greek-speaking Jews of Lystra listened longer and were impressed; word reaches Iconium and Antioch of what is going on, and Jewish believers from there—who probably speak Lycaonian—swing the crowd back to their side. Paul is stoned and left for dead but "the disciples surrounded him" (v. 20)—in other words, there are an indeterminate number of believers in Lystra by this time—and he and Barnabas depart.

Who, then, was left to carry on the mission in Lystra? Why, Eunice and Lois, of course![22] At the beginning of chapter 16 the story returns to Lystra, and lo! there is a "disciple" there named Timothy who is "well spoken of by the believers in Lystra and Iconium" (16:2). More on that anon.

The rest of the mission is quickly summarized (vv. 21-25). The most significant statement is that, having made many disciples in Derbe, the missionaries retraced their circuitous route through Lystra, Iconium, and

20. Ibid., 106.

21. Ibid., 117–18, n. 25.

22. See 2 Tim 1:5. Given the character of Lystra, the audience may be shocked to learn, in Acts 16, that it is the home of Timothy and his mother!

Antioch of Pisidia, and in each of these four "churches" they appointed elders (πρεσβύτεροι). This speaks of organization and hoped-for continuity. The elders are plural, as was customary in Jewish practice; there is nothing to say that they were all men. The appointment of the elders takes place "with prayer and fasting" (v. 23), mirroring the sending of Paul and Barnabas. These will be the shepherds of the local flocks, but all the members are entrusted to "the Lord."

The chapter concludes with the missionaries' return to the community that had commissioned and sent them. Verse 27 is intended as a typical conclusion to a missionary journey but also as characteristic of the infant church's life: "When they arrived, they called the church together and related *all that God had done with them.*" The actions of leaders must be ratified by the whole community if they are to be taken as valid examples and acknowledged as the work of God. Such acknowledgment affirms the church's belief that God is at work in it, and that such important developments as "opening a door of faith for the Gentiles" are in fact the work of God and not human work.[23] Lukas thus gives voice to an important principle for discernment illustrated in this chapter: to seek in and from the text (written, spoken, or lived) what is of God and what is of human making.

"And they stayed there with the disciples for some time" (v. 28) is one of the statements that serve to pause the action for an indeterminate period and cover chronological gaps.[24] The action of chapter 15 in fact belongs chronologically before this first missionary journey into gentile territory, as we know from Paul's outline in Galatians, but evidently Lukas wants to give Paul special status before that great turning point is reached.

---

23. See Linda M. Maloney, *"All That God Had Done with Them": The Narration of the Works of God in the Early Christian Community as Described in the Acts of the Apostles,* AUS ser. 7, Theology and Religion 91 (New York: Lang, 1991), esp. chap. 6.

24. See, *inter alia*, Acts 9:43; 12:19; 14:3; 15:32-33; 18:20, 23; 19:22; 20:18; cf. 10:48; 16:15; 18:3, 11, 18; 28:14. The verb διατρίβω, generally translated "stay," is one of Lukas's favorites; he uses it at least twenty-one times in Acts, but it does not appear in Luke's Gospel, where, as in most of the New Testament apart from a few uses in John, the favored verb for "remaining" is μένω. The basic meaning of διατρίβω is "rub through, wear away," sometimes with an undertone of "endure," even "toil," as when Josephus (*Ant.* 6.297) uses it of Joseph's indenture to Laban. Even while "staying" in a place the messengers of the gospel are not idle.

Acts 15:1-35

The Great Council

L ukas has fashioned here a climax and a turning point in Acts: the center of action shifts from Jerusalem to the gentile mission field, and the central focus moves from Peter to Paul. At the same time Jerusalem's centrality (in the narrative) is lost. In the remaining chapters Paul will revisit Jerusalem twice, but the coolness toward him there (to the point of open hostility) that Lukas suppresses in chapter 15 will be evident by chapter 21, when Paul's arrest merits no notice or resistance from the Jerusalem community. That Jerusalem was, by Lukas's time, almost nothing but a historical memory for the gentile church is clear from the fact that the Deutero-Pauline letters never speak of it at all.[1]

The background text for the action depicted in Acts 15 is Galatians 2, but the chronology in that letter is displaced to suit Lukas's purpose. The heart of both Galatians 2 and Acts 15 is the controversy over the circumcision of male gentiles who wish to join the Movement. That question had been settled decades before Acts was written and was by no means an issue for its projected audience. So why bring it up at all? Lukas uses it to insist, once and for all, that the Movement welcomes all believers; the key issue for him is table fellowship. Jews are the first believers, and if they continue to observe *halakah* they cannot eat with

---

1. See Michael Theobald, *Israel-Vergessenheit in den Pastoralbriefen: ein neuer Vorschlag zu ihrer historisch-theologischen Verortung im 2. Jahrhundert n. Chr. unter besonderer Berücksichtigung der Ignatius-Briefe* (Stuttgart: Katholisches Bibelwerk, 2016).

15:1Then certain individuals came down from Judea and were teaching the brothers, "Unless you are circumcised according to the custom of Moses, you cannot be saved." 2And after Paul and Barnabas had no small dissension and debate with them, Paul and Barnabas and some of the others were appointed to go up to Jerusalem to discuss this question with the apostles and the elders. 3So they were sent on their way by the church, and as they passed through both Phoenicia and Samaria, they reported the conversion of the Gentiles, and brought great joy to all the believers. 4When they came to Jerusalem, they were welcomed by the church and the apostles and the elders, and they reported all that God had done with them. 5But some believers who belonged to the sect of the Pharisees stood up and said, "It is necessary for them to be circumcised and ordered to keep the law of Moses."

6The apostles and the elders met together to consider this matter. 7After there had been much debate, Peter stood up and said to them, "My brothers, you know that in the early days God made a choice among you, that I should be the one through whom the Gentiles would hear the message of the good news and become believers. 8And God, who knows the human heart, testified to them by giving them the Holy Spirit, just as he did to us; 9and in cleansing their hearts by faith he has made no distinction between them and us. 10Now therefore why are you putting God to the test by placing on the neck of the disciples a yoke that neither our ancestors nor we have been able to bear? 11On the contrary, we believe that we will be saved through the grace of the Lord Jesus, just as they will."

12The whole assembly kept silence, and listened to Barnabas and Paul as they told of all the signs and wonders that God had done through them among the Gentiles. 13After they finished speaking, James replied, "My brothers, listen to me. 14Simeon has related how God first looked favorably on the Gentiles, to take from among them a people for his

impure gentile men. But the Eucharist, in the context of shared meals, is central to the life of the Movement. The Jerusalem decree says nothing at all about circumcision; it speaks only of the rules regarding clean foods and thus ties together with Peter's vision in chapter 10. The episode climaxes not with Paul's denunciation of Peter, as in Galatians 2:14, but with the triumphant return of Paul, Barnabas, and their companions to Antioch and the community's rejoicing.

It should be made clear that the issue of circumcision in no way affected Jewish (or gentile) women. There was some debate in antiquity about whether women were excluded from the covenant because they were not circumcised (no Jewish women were ever circumcised, unlike Egyp-

name. [15]This agrees with the words of the prophets, as it is written,

[16]'After this I will return,
and I will rebuild the dwelling of
David, which has fallen;
from its ruins I will rebuild it,
and I will set it up,
[17]so that all other peoples may
seek the Lord—
even all the Gentiles over
whom my name has
been called.
Thus says the Lord, who has
been making these
things [18]known from
long ago.'

[19]Therefore I have reached the decision that we should not trouble those Gentiles who are turning to God, [20]but we should write to them to abstain only from things polluted by idols and from fornication and from whatever has been strangled and from blood. [21]For in every city, for generations past, Moses has had those who proclaim him, for he has been read aloud every sabbath in the synagogues."

[22]Then the apostles and the elders, with the consent of the whole church, decided to choose men from among their members and to send them to Antioch with Paul and Barnabas. They sent Judas called Barsabbas, and Silas, leaders among the brothers, [23]with the following letter: "The brothers, both the apostles and the elders, to the believers of Gentile origin in Antioch and Syria and Cilicia, greetings. [24]Since we have heard that certain persons who have gone out from us, though with no instructions from us, have said things to disturb you and have unsettled your minds, [25]we have decided unanimously to choose representatives and send them to you, along with our beloved Barnabas and Paul, [26]who have risked their lives for the sake of our Lord Jesus Christ. [27]We have therefore sent Judas and Silas, who themselves will tell you the same things by word of mouth. [28]For

tian women, who at one period were[2]) or whether they were somehow included (by menstruation or by other means) but only as second-class Jews. Both because of that and because in the upper classes of the gentile world women were generally excluded from banquets and other public meals, the issue of bodily purity did not touch them in such contexts. In making this long-dead issue so central to his story Lukas betrays his indifference to the interests of women. Despite his desire to appeal to well-to-do women,[3] he reveals his real interest by the way he discusses issues that

2. See Shaye J. D. Cohen, *Why Aren't Jewish Women Circumcised? Gender and Covenant in Judaism* (Berkeley: University of California Press, 2005), 56–57.

3. See Shelly Matthews, *First Converts: Rich Pagan Women and the Rhetoric of Mission in Early Judaism and Christianity* (Stanford, CA: Stanford University Press, 2001); on the circumcision issue see esp. pp. 69–70.

Acts 15:1-35 (cont.)

it has seemed good to the Holy Spirit and to us to impose on you no further burden than these essentials: [29]that you abstain from what has been sacrificed to idols and from blood and from what is strangled and from fornication. If you keep yourselves from these, you will do well. Farewell."

[30]So they were sent off and went down to Antioch. When they gathered the congregation together, they delivered the letter. [31]When its members read it, they rejoiced at the exhortation.

[32]Judas and Silas, who were themselves prophets, said much to encourage and strengthen the believers. [33]After they had been there for some time, they were sent off in peace by the believers to those who had sent them.* [35]But Paul and Barnabas remained in Antioch, and there, with many others, they taught and proclaimed the word of the Lord.

* Some mss. (notably the D-text) insert v. 34: "But it seemed good to Silas to remain there."

were important to women (such as their inclusion in community meals and governance),[4] which is to say: hardly at all. The only woman who speaks of her own volition in Acts (Lydia, at 16:15) does so to ask for acceptance into the community and, by inference, into its table fellowship.[5]

Circumcision and Jewish Identity[6]

For as long as women were considered lesser human beings by those who controlled society and its norms (if they were full persons at all), their lack of circumcision was a nonissue. The rabbis did not bother even to discuss it.[7] The requirement of circumcision for males was likewise a settled matter in emergent Judaism, but it was a problem for the Movement as it opened itself to gentile men. Jews were perceived in

---

4. See Antoinette C. Wire, *The Corinthian Women Prophets: A Reconstruction through Paul's Rhetoric* (Minneapolis: Fortress, 1990); Kathleen E. Corley, *Private Women, Public Meals: Social Conflict in the Synoptic Tradition* (Peabody, MA: Hendrickson, 1993).

5. Sapphira speaks two words (ναί, τοσούτου) at 5:8, responding to what Peter has just asked (εἰ τοσούτου). The unnamed woman with a Pythonic spirit speaks at 16:17, but the voice is that of her oracle, not her own.

6. For a full treatment of this subject see especially Cohen, *Why Aren't Jewish Women Circumcised?*

7. The tractate b.Yeb. 46a deals with whether a (male) proselyte is such without circumcision: "Our Rabbis taught: 'If a proselyte was circumcised but had not per-

the ancient world as a people "set apart." Their uniqueness attracted the respect of some; from others it evoked distrust and fear—and, consequently, ridicule.[8] For the people of Israel, however, uniqueness was a treasured gift. The books of Maccabees reflect how sharply the people of Judah rejected the attempt by the Seleucid ruler Antiochus IV Epiphanes to make the population of his realm uniform. "The king wrote to his whole kingdom that everyone should be one people, and that all should give up their particular customs. All the gentiles accepted the command of the king. . . . And the king sent letters [*biblia*] by messengers to Jerusalem and the towns of Judah; he directed them to follow customs strange to the land . . . to leave their sons uncircumcised. They were to make themselves abominable by everything unclean and profane, so that they would forget the law

and change all the ordinances" (1 Macc 1:41-49). The result was the Maccabean revolt, never forgotten; Lukas's debt to those books has long been remarked by scholars.

Gentile observers were especially puzzled by Jewish (and, later, Christian) monotheism, which they considered exclusivist and intolerant; they were especially put off by attitudes like those expressed in the Letter of Aristeas (second century BCE): "To prevent our being perverted by contact with others or by mixing with bad influences, [the Lawgiver] hedged us in on all sides with strict observances connected with meat and drink and touch and hearing and sight, after the manner of the Law."[9]

The issue might have been resolved in the manner depicted by Lukas in Acts 15 except for one factor: Paul. His insistence that the continued practice amounted

---

formed the prescribed ritual ablution, R. Eliezer said, "Behold he is a proper proselyte; for so we find that our forefathers were circumcised and had not performed ritual ablution." If he performed the prescribed ablution but had not been circumcised, R. Joshua said, "Behold he is a proper proselyte; for so we find that the mothers had performed ritual ablution but had not been circumcised." The Sages, however, said, "Whether he had performed ritual ablution but had not been circumcised or whether he had been circumcised but had not performed the prescribed ritual ablution, he is not a proper proselyte, unless he has been circumcised and has also performed the prescribed ritual ablution." " See https://halakhah.com/yebamoth/yebamoth_46.html. This is probably spelled out in order to counter Christians' insistence that baptism is sufficient for all, but the use of the example of the "mothers" of Israel is significant.

8. See, e.g., Tacitus, *Histories* 5.5.

9. *Letter of Aristeas* 142. For a very readable treatment of these issues see Daniel Lynwood Smith, *Into the World of the New Testament: Greco-Roman and Jewish Texts and Contexts* (London: Bloomsbury, 2015).

to a rejection of God's salvation extended in Jesus[10] created an estrangement between members of the Movement who regarded themselves, and behaved as, faithful Jews and the growing contingent of male gentile believers; this was further exacerbated by the destruction of the temple in 70 CE and cemented by the Second Revolt from 132 to 136.

Marcion's embrace of Paul and rejection of the Hebrew Bible and its God seemed logical enough to many, and the apologists'[11] response, which reinterpreted Israel's Scriptures as a foreshadowing of Jesus and of Jesus as the only Son of God (rather than Israel itself), pushed Christians and Jews farther apart. The medieval church maintained a system of required practices, so that the acts of Jewish observance were not altogether strange to it, but at the beginning of the modern era the Reformation, with its repudiation of "works-righteousness," rekindled hostility and kept it alive.

From then until now Jewish love of and rejoicing in Torah and its commandments remains a puzzle to Christians, at least to those who are convinced they are "saved" once and for all by faith (and/or baptism) and that therefore admitting any kind of *required* religious practice is nothing short of blasphemous. What, then, to make of Psalm 119, an unrestrained paean to the law and the pleasures of observing it?

The author of Acts lifts up Paul as his hero in the gentile mission—after all, his target audience is mainly gentile—but he is unwilling to repudiate Jewish believers in Jesus Messiah. Indeed, he maintains his conviction that the covenant continues in its full form for Jews within the Movement as well as outside it. Paul may think that his fellow Jews will be gathered in at the end of the ages (Romans 11), but Lukas wants to hold the Movement together in the present. Therefore he makes Paul an irenic partner in the decision of the Jerusalem Council: to preserve table fellowship on the basis of the food laws and leave the issue of circumcision aside. That decision was already prefigured in Peter's dream and his interpretation of it in Acts 10–11. Lukas knows better, as his account of Paul's break with Barnabas (at 15:36-40) and the evident hostility to Paul at Jerusalem in Acts 21 reveal, but he does his best to soften the

---

10. Cf. Gal 5:2: "Listen! I, Paul, am telling you that if you let yourselves be circumcised, Christ will be of no benefit to you." Paul's insistence on his own authority in the question is telling.

11. The "apologists" include such figures as Justin, Tatian, Minucius Felix, Tertullian, and Clement of Alexandria. They are so called because they are known for their vigorous defense of ("apology" for) Christians as a separate religious group.

account, and at the end of his book he still has Paul preaching to, and persuading, his fellow Jews.

In sum: for the actual Paul it's either/or; for Lukas it's (he hopes) both/and.

We ourselves, the heirs of nearly two thousand years of the tragic estrangement between Christians and Jews, must inevitably ask: How would things have been different if women had been running the show? What if the women disciples of Moses and of Jesus had been asked for their opinion? Would they have seen male circumcision as *the* make-or-break issue? That seems unlikely. They might well have had ideas about the rules for common meals,[12] but the condition of men's sexual organs would probably not have played much of a role in their thinking about who might or might not participate. Willingness to come together and to respect the presence and the voices of *all* participants would surely have governed their choice of those with whom they desired table fellowship. The openness of some modern Jewish movements[13] and of some Christian churches[14] to the participation and leadership of people of all genders, sexualities, and ethnicities gives us a glimpse of what might have been.

Acts 15 begins and ends in Antioch. That early center of the Jesus movement, with its multiple communities of Aramaic-speaking Jewish believers, Hellenistic Jewish believers, and former gentiles, has been home base for Paul and Barnabas since Acts 11:19 and was the sending church for their mission in chapters 13–14. At 14:27-28 the missionaries had reported to the whole of the Antioch community what great deeds God had done with them, and they had settled back into life in the city "for some time."

Chapter 15 takes up the story again with "then"—which is to say, Lukas's chronology is extremely vague. Has news of the Antioch mission

12. See Wire, *Corinthian Women Prophets, passim.*

13. Reform Judaism as well as the organizations that are heirs to the New Jewish Agenda (1980–1992).

14. Most non-Evangelical churches—with the glaring omission of the Roman Catholic Church, the biggest of them all, and, of course, the Orthodox churches—now welcome ordained and nonordained leadership from both women and men, as well as all ethnicities. The battle for LGBTQIA+ equality has seen significant victories, though much remains to be done. Prominent in this movement within the United States and Canada have been the United Church of Christ and the churches of the Anglican Communion (ECUSA and the Anglican Church of Canada).

to the gentiles reached Jerusalem and—despite Peter's defense of his baptism of Cornelius and his household—met with disapproval there? We were never informed about the precise resolution of the Cornelius episode: Were he and his male household members required, after the fact, to be circumcised? Has a delegation like the one described in 15:1 been sent to Caesarea, or is it the practice at Antioch that is especially objectionable to the leaders in Jerusalem? In any case it will turn out that the life of the community at Antioch is key to understanding both the historical context of Acts 15 and Lukas's handling of it.

Lukas's composition in chapter 15 is very much to his purpose in writing Acts: to show that the Jesus movement began in Jerusalem, was organized as Jesus had wished, and remained within Judea until scattered by opposition from the temple authorities. Acts 11:19 emphasizes that those dispersed by the persecution after Stephen's death proselytized as far as Phoenicia, Cyprus, and Antioch "and they spoke the word to no one except Jews." At Antioch (11:20) that extended likewise to "Hellenists," the erstwhile enemies of Stephen in Jerusalem, but Jews all the same.

But the Hellenists at Antioch seem to be somehow the camel's nose under the tent flap, because we learned at 11:26 that "it was in Antioch that the disciples were first called Christians"—in other words, outsiders began to realize that their practice was somehow different from that of other synagogues; specifically, they allowed full participation by "gentiles" as variously defined. The sneering term "Christians" might even have been invented by pious Hellenists, since it is a Latinized Greek word and was unlikely to have been coined by insiders.

The stories about Peter in Acts 10–12 portray him as having been brought to accept the Antiochene practice, not without difficulty. He is shown receiving a vision and understanding it as mandating the baptism, and thus the inclusion, of gentiles in the new community without the imposition of prior requirements such as male circumcision. That in itself apparently reduced his status at Jerusalem, as we saw. The fact that he had to answer to the community for his conduct implicitly told us that he is no longer its leader and guide. His explanation is said to silence the objections and evoke praise of God for giving "repentance" to the gentiles (11:18), but that still leaves gentiles in a separate "box"—nothing is said of integrating them into the core communities. Moreover, Peter's arrest, imprisonment, miraculous release, and departure from Jerusalem "to another place" in Acts 12 in fact represent his rejection by the Jerusalem leadership (James is now its head, 12:17) and may imply his removal to Antioch (cf. Gal 2:11-14).

It was at Antioch (home to a large and long-standing Jewish colony) that Paul was schooled at length by Barnabas and others, and it was from Antioch that those two were dispatched as (in Lukas's story) the first missionaries sent into gentile territory. The audience is probably meant to understand that it was Paul's experiences on that journey that fully convinced him that God had "opened a door of faith for the Gentiles" (14:27) and they should not be excluded from full participation in the Movement and its eucharistic table fellowship. That was the message he (and, perhaps, Barnabas) preached at Antioch "for some time" (14:28).

"Then"—breaking suddenly into this peaceful scene—"certain individuals" (τινες; nothing could be vaguer) come "down"[15] from Judea and begin teaching the "brothers"[16] that circumcision "according to the custom of Moses"[17] is necessary for salvation (15:1): that is, that full observance of the Jewish law is a requirement for men to be members of the Jesus communities as well. This amounts to a denial that the mission of Paul and Barnabas, just acknowledged by the Antioch community as the work of God (14:27), was really from God at all. Naturally the two missionaries speak up in defense of their actions, and those two are dispatched at the head of a group from Antioch to take up the matter with the apostles and elders (i.e., the Jerusalem leadership of the Movement). Lukas is careful not to say that the disruptive Judeans were sent by the Jerusalem community officially.

In 15:3-4 Lukas fashions another link to the missionary journey and the pivotal statement in 14:27: again Paul and Barnabas (and company) are sent by the church, report on the results of their work, and bring joy to believers en route (cf. 13:52); arriving in Jerusalem, they report there, as they had done in Antioch, "all that God had done with them."[18] But the joy in Jerusalem is immediately interrupted by the reintroduction of the issues of circumcision and law observance, this time by "believers who belonged to the sect of the Pharisees" (v. 5; cf. 21:17-21). This introduction of hostile Pharisees seems an anomaly: everywhere else in Acts the Pharisees are on the side of the Jesus-believers, and of course Paul insists

---

15. The primacy of Jerusalem ("the mountain of the LORD's house" is "the highest of the mountains" [Isa 2:2]) is reflected in "geographic" language.

16. The NRSV here translates the plural of ἀδελφοί logically as "brothers" instead of its usual generic usage; cf. "believers" in 15:3.

17. The language subtly reflects the Antiochene and Jerusalemite points of view. At v. 1 circumcision is called a "custom" (ἔθος); at v. 5 it is a "law" (νόμος).

18. See the resource cited above at 14:27.

in his defense speeches that he himself is (not *was*) a Pharisee. It seems, though, that "Pharisee" is a cipher here for exclusionary Jesus-believers who want to integrate all members of the new movement into Jewish practice as defined by the Pharisees, that is, strict observance of the law. It is a question whether this would have allowed for gentile converts at all or whether those not born Jews would have remained in a permanent proselyte status.

The initial description of the subsequent assembly is inconsistent. It seems that, first of all, there is a council of the leadership ("the apostles and the elders," v. 6) at which there is "much debate," suggesting at the very least a lack of the supposedly usual unanimity. Then Peter addresses the group, beginning (as in 2:29) with "Men, brothers" (ἄνδρες ἀδελφοί), which could indicate he is speaking only to the apostles and elders, not to the whole community, but at verse 12 "the whole assembly kept silence, and listened to Barnabas and Paul." Did they hear Peter's speech or not? And are they still present when James "replies," in the next verse, again beginning ἄνδρες ἀδελφοί?

In fact, ἄνδρες ἀδελφοί is Lukas's favored opening for an address to a group of *Jews*: 1:16 to the Jesus-believers assembled in the "upper room"; 2:29, 37 to and from the Pentecost crowds; 7:2 in Stephen's speech to the Sanhedrin; 13:15, 26, 38 as Paul addresses the synagogue in Pisidian Antioch; 22:1, Paul to the people of Jerusalem; 23:1, 6, Paul to the San-hedrin; 28:17, Paul to the local Jewish leaders in Rome. Some of those groups (the Sanhedrin, for example) might be presumed to be all male; others are most certainly not, though the language ignores the women among them. Here in 15:7, 13 the "whole assembly" certainly included both women and men; the debaters in verse 7—Peter, Paul, Barnabas, and James—may do all the talking, but the whole assembled community in Jerusalem is listening throughout.

What—in the projected chronology of Acts—would that assembly at Jerusalem have made of Peter's statement that "in the early days" God had chosen him to evangelize the gentiles? In the story as we have heard it thus far, Peter's encounter with Cornelius's household did not take place until after the development of the Jerusalem community, the crisis surrounding the death of Stephen, and the scattering of the believers as a result of persecution. In all that time, as far as the story goes, the word had been preached only to Jews and Samaritans. When, in chapter 10, Peter is ordered to visit Cornelius he is both shocked and resistant. There is no indication at all that from "the early days" he has known himself called to speak to gentiles. In Paul's view (see Gal 2:7-9) the mission to the gentiles had always been his own, by God's design; Peter's mission had always been and still was to "the circumcised," and that, according to Paul, was agreed upon at their meeting in Jerusalem (of which Acts is unaware).

Peter's words reiterate in substance his speech at Acts 11:4-17, but with a subtle difference. While he had previously said of the gentiles receiving the Holy Spirit that "God gave them the same gift that he gave us when we believed in the Lord Jesus Christ" (11:17), now he adds, "and in cleansing their hearts by faith he has made no distinction between them and us" (15:9). "Making no distinction" is a step beyond conveying a gift. Here Lukas has Peter argue that all believers, through the gift of the Holy Spirit, are equal in dignity and not to be categorized by their past character, their race, or (implicitly) their gender. It is grace that saves both Jew and gentile (v. 11). (Here Peter sounds much like Paul!)

Verse 10 is a clever turn. Lukas has Peter accuse his fellow Jews of "putting God to the test," echoing Moses' lament in the Torah (Deut 6:16; cf. Ps 106:14; Mal 3:15). Commentators have seized on the assertion that requiring everyone to keep the whole law is "a yoke that neither our ancestors nor we have been able to bear," writing that this is language from a time when Christianity had broken away from Judaism. That is a misreading. Lukas is reminding readers of Stephen's impassioned accusation: "You are the ones that received the law as ordained by angels, *and yet you have not kept it*" (7:51, 53). The argument is that God gave the precious gift of Torah to Israel, but history shows the people have seldom or never kept it—present company not excepted! How, then, can they demand that people ignorant of the law, yet whom God has called, must do what Israel has never been able to do?

Paul and Barnabas then take the stage and tell of "all the signs and wonders that God had done through them among the Gentiles" (v. 12). The "rule of three" is in place: the pair have announced in 14:27 and 15:4 "all that God had done with them." Now, in the third repetition, the expression is expanded by the addition of Lukas's favorite phrase, "signs and wonders," and by the emphasis that these were done "among the Gentiles." The missionaries also step back a pace from saying that God has been their partner, doing things "with" them, acknowledging instead that God is the sole agent and has acted "through" them.

Finally, James steps forward to give his assessment. He is depicted as the leader in Jerusalem.[19] His group is clearly opposed to the acceptance of gentiles without their being fully incorporated into the practice of

19. James may be, indeed probably was, the leader of a faction that had displaced the "Petrines" in the Jerusalem leadership, but to admit that is contrary to Lukas's intent to portray unanimity there.

Judaism.[20] Lukas knows this and so walks a fine line in the narrative; he dare not deny what people know about James and his group, but he will not surrender his plea for gentile inclusion.

So James begins with a reference to Peter's experience in the house of Cornelius. To make clear that Peter is and remains a Jew, Lukas has James call him "Simeon," not "Simon" or "Simon Peter" or even "Cephas" as found elsewhere in the New Testament.[21] (The author of the late letter called 2 Peter also uses "Simeon," presumably to authenticate his writing.) In Genesis, Simeon son of Jacob was noted for violence and cruelty toward the Shechemites in revenge for Shechem's taking his sister Dinah; Simeon in Luke's Gospel is an old and wise prophet. It is possible that both those features of Peter's character—his volatility in the Gospel accounts and his wisdom and leadership in Acts—are alluded to here. Given the violent hatred displayed by the biblical Simeon toward non-Israelites,[22] there is heavy irony in the statement that "Simeon has related how God first looked favorably on the Gentiles, to take from among them a people for his name" (v. 14).

Then James interprets Peter's message. Nothing is said about incorporating gentiles into the Jewish people; rather, God will form a "people for his name" from among the gentiles, a people distinct from the people Israel. Thus James reinterprets Peter's report of his experience in the house of Cornelius to mean that God calls gentiles but does not call them into the original and enduring people of God. There is plenty of good precedent for this in the Hebrew Scriptures,[23] but Lukas chooses to craft a basis out of texts that speak only of the rescue and planting of Israel in its own land (Amos 9:11-12; Jer 12:15).

The speech concludes with James's "decision"—in the first-person singular—that "those Gentiles who are turning to God" should not be

20. By the time Acts was written, rabbinic opinion was moving toward the conclusion that Jews are born not made, so that no proselyte would have been acknowledged, in that period at least, as being fully a Jew. See Cohen, *Why Aren't Women Circumcised?* That Lukas knew this is clear from Acts 21.

21. At John 1:42 (explaining "Cephas" as the Aramaic equivalent of "Peter"); Paul consistently refers to him as "Cephas," never "Peter" (thus 1 Cor 1:12; 3:22; 9:5; 15:5; Gal 1:18; 2:9, 11, 14).

22. See Genesis 34. The irony is compounded by the fact that in that chapter circumcision is demanded of gentiles (and accepted by them!), but their doing so does not alleviate the rage of Simeon and Levi, who take advantage of their weakened state to slaughter them.

23. Cf. Isa 2:2; 11:10; 49:6; 55:5; 60:3; Jer 3:17; 4:2; Mic 4:2-3; Mal 1:11.

asked to observe any commandments other than those prescribed in the Torah for aliens in the land of Israel (cf. Lev 17–18). A major difficulty, of course, is that the situation is reversed: it is now the people of Israel who are dispersed into the lands of those "aliens." In such a situation concessions must be made, but the law can be applied here also: just as aliens who desired to celebrate Passover were to be admitted on the same conditions as Israelites (Num 9:14), so now admission to *table fellowship* is subject to similar conditions that here are left somewhat vague to allow for local application. Paul's concessions on this subject in 1 Corinthians 8 show that, contrary to Lukas's portrait of him, he advocated an entirely law-free participation, his only reservation being that care should be taken to ensure that more observant believers will not be scandalized. James's conclusion, that "Moses" (that is, Torah) has long been proclaimed in every city on every Sabbath, is another way of saying that gentiles have no excuse for ignorance about the law; the implication is that if they want to be part of this new Jewish community they should be aware of its fundamental rules and prepared to obey them.

The choosing of messengers "with the consent of the whole church" implies universal affirmation of James's decision without explicitly stating the fact. The sending of members from Jerusalem (Judas and Silas) together with Paul and Barnabas to carry the letter announcing the decision more than implies that James and his associates did not trust the Antiochene messengers to give an accurate report of what had been decided. The letter itself is ambiguous. It is pointedly addressed "to the believers [ἀδελφοὶ, lit.: "brothers"] of Gentile origin in Antioch and Syria and Cilicia" (v. 23). As in the Ananias and Sapphira case in chapter 5, we learn that the decisions of the Jerusalem community (or its leaders) coincide with the will of the Holy Spirit. Whereas in the earlier instance the participation of the larger community is emphasized, at this stage the members are playing a distinctly subordinate role; the development toward "church" is underway.

Notably, no message is sent to the Jewish believers in Antioch, Syria, and Cilicia. It appears that they are free to associate with gentile believers on the conditions stated in the letter, or not. If gentiles are accepted into Jewish or mixed communities of Jesus-believers they should not be expected to follow Jewish customs other than those specified in the letter, but there is nothing here that says they cannot simply be refused entrance.

Antioch will continue to be a place that goes its own way, with Jewish believers maintaining a strong presence and authority even in "mixed" communities. It appears that, a generation after Lukas wrote, the Antioch community was profoundly disturbed by the hostility of its "bishop,"[24] Ignatius, to the inclusion of any "Jewish" practices whatsoever in what was now "Christian" life. They had him arrested for causing upheaval in the city, resulting in his being sent to Rome for judgment (and execution).[25] In letters supposedly written at various stops on his journey to Rome their author reveals his continued hostility to anything "Jewish"—symptomatic of the much-deteriorated situation between Jewish and gentile believers that, over centuries, resulted in a "parting of the ways."[26]

24. *Episkopos,* "overseer," was not yet a separately defined office in the second century.

25. The traditional story of Ignatius is remarkably congruent with the story of Paul in Acts.

26. For Ignatius's attitudes see Shaye J. D. Cohen, "Judaism without Circumcision and 'Judaism' without 'Circumcision' in Ignatius," *HTR* 95 (2002): 395–415. For dating see n. 1 above.

Acts 15:36–16:5

Paul on His Own;
Eunice and Timothy

Lukas and Paul provide different, though overlapping, accounts of what transpired at Antioch after the meetings in Jerusalem, as a comparison of Acts with Paul's letter to the Galatians reveals:

Acts 15:36-41	Galatians 2:11-14
³⁶After some days Paul said to Barnabas, "Come, let us return and visit the believers in every city where we proclaimed the word of the Lord and see how they are doing." ³⁷Barnabas wanted to take with them John called Mark. ³⁸But Paul decided not to take with them one who had deserted them in Pamphylia and had not accompanied them in the work. ³⁹The disagreement became so sharp that they parted company; Barnabas took Mark with him and sailed away to Cyprus. ⁴⁰But Paul chose Silas and set out, the believers commending him to the grace of the Lord. ⁴¹He went through Syria and Cilicia, strengthening the churches.	But when Cephas came to Antioch, I opposed him to his face, because he stood self-condemned; for until certain people came from James, he used to eat with the Gentiles. But after they came, he drew back and kept himself separate for fear of the circumcision faction. And the other Jews joined him in this hypocrisy, so that *even Barnabas was led astray by their hypocrisy*. But when I saw that they were not acting consistently with the truth of the gospel, I said to Cephas before them all, "If you, though a Jew, live like a Gentile and not like a Jew, how can you compel the Gentiles to live like Jews?"

^{16:1}Paul went on also to Derbe and to Lystra, where there was a disciple named Timothy, the son of a Jewish woman who was a believer; but his father was a Greek. ²He was well spoken of by the believers in Lystra and Iconium. ³Paul wanted Timothy to accompany him; and he took him and had him circumcised because of the Jews who were in those places, for they all knew that his father was a Greek. ⁴As they went from town to town, they delivered to them for observance the decisions that had been reached by the apostles and elders who were in Jerusalem. ⁵So the churches were strengthened in the faith and increased in numbers daily.

Eunice and Timothy (upper left) by Henry Lejeune. Lois and Timothy (lower right) by Rembrandt. Creative Commons (CC BY-SA 3.0).

The substance of the scene is the ongoing conflict at Antioch (*contra* Acts 15:31), and, as far as Lukas is concerned, the key outcome is a split between Paul and Barnabas, something apparently known and requiring explanation. But the reason given is altogether different. In Paul's nearly contemporary and probably more accurate version, with allowance being made for Paul's own bias, the quarrel is still over the conditions for admission of gentile men to the Lord's table. Paul calls the Jerusalem attitude (represented here by "Cephas") *hypocrisy* and says that "even Barnabas" was "led astray" by it. Lukas would never, ever characterize behavior within the earliest communities in such terms, and he makes the split between Barnabas and Paul revolve around their attitudes toward Mark.

Willie James Jennings examines the quarrel over Mark in terms of trust: Paul does not trust Mark, but Barnabas does. Why the difference? Barnabas and Paul have heretofore been paired, but "Barnabas always seems to be ahead of Paul, drawing Paul to where he should be" (cf. 4:36-37; 9:27; 11:25), bridging, for Paul, the old to the new. This "son of encouragement" (4:36) is, in Lukas's narrative, a "risk-taker, because Barnabas seemed to always make heavy wager on people," and this situation is no different. Having previously taken a risk with Paul, Barnabas is now likewise willing to trust Mark. He and Paul see Mark from different angles and both perspectives are valid, but they do not promise equal returns.

Risking trust in someone may bring disaster (as Paul sees it), but it can hold even greater promise. Jennings concludes that "the risks of ministry are inseparable from the risks of relationship. Yet it seems that Barnabas was still ahead of Paul, trying to bring him where he needed to be in that inescapable struggle of trusting those who have or might or will fail us."[1]

It may also be that Barnabas's being "led astray" is related to his choice of Mark as missionary companion. Lukas has laid the groundwork for connecting Mark with the Jerusalem faction: according to Acts 12:12 his mother, Mary, was the head of her own household in the city and it was a customary gathering place for Jesus-followers. The naming of this person is peculiar: in 12:12 he is "John whose other name was Mark." When next encountered, apparently in Cyprus (where he surfaces unannounced in an aside at 13:5), he is simply "John," and so again at 13:13, where he "left them and returned to Jerusalem," allegedly the action that causes Paul to dismiss him as a traveling companion at 15:38, where he regains his original appellation, "John called Mark." All this may be an echo of Paul's attitude in Galatians, which was certainly familiar to Lukas: Paul wants nothing more to do with Jerusalem or with any kind of residual separation of ethnicities in his mission. The tension with the Jerusalem community will remain evident in the rest of the story.

Paul in the Letters and Acts: Another View

Comparing the writings of historical figures to later biographical works about them can create new sets of questions. This scenario arises with the portraits of Paul in his own letters and in Acts. On the one hand, consistency abounds: Paul is a Pharisee who persecuted Christians before his mystical encounter with Christ. He proclaimed the gospel throughout the Mediterranean region and worked to support his own ministry. His public preaching style led to numerous imprisonments and, finally, to Rome.

There are also, however, major discrepancies. Paul inveighs against gentile circumcision in the letters but circumcises Timothy, his half-gentile lieutenant, in Acts (16:3). Paul claims adamantly that he had minimal connection with Jerusalem and met with no Judean churches in his first fourteen years (Gal 1–2), but in Acts Paul receives the Jerusalem leaders' approval before he and

---

1. Willie James Jennings, *Acts*, Belief: A Theological Commentary on the Bible (Louisville: Westminster John Knox, 2017), 150–51.

Barnabas preach for an unknown period of time in Judea (Acts 9:28-29). One of the more tendentious issues involves Paul's visits to Jerusalem. In Galatians, Paul speaks of a meeting with Peter and James three years after his encounter with Christ (1:18-20) and a meeting fourteen years later in which he, Barnabas, and Titus presented his gospel to the "Pillars" in the face of opposition. Acts also relates a visit of Paul and Barnabas to Jerusalem after Paul's mystical encounter (Acts 9:26-30) that aligns with Galatians 1:18-20, but it also includes visits to Jerusalem to deliver the collection for the poor (11:30 + 12:25), the so-called council regarding circumcision of male gentiles (15:2-29), and a final visit before his arrest in 21:15–23:22.

The visit in Galatians 1:18-20 corresponds with Acts 9:26-30, but questions surround how the remaining visits align. The traditional model holds that Galatians 2:1-10 reflects Paul's view of the so-called council in Acts 15. The value of this model is that it corroborates the significant decision to expand the gospel to gentiles with minimal requirements. Proponents point to the issue of circumcision in both accounts. This model (Gal 2 = Acts 15) creates a new problem, however, due to the intervening visit for the collection in Acts 11–12 and Paul's clear claims in Galatians that he had not been in Jerusalem more than these two times to meet with the Pillars.[2]

Some scholars have tried to minimize the problem by claiming that either Paul or the author of Acts had a particular interest in shaping the story as he did.[3] These positions range along a spectrum with some claiming the changes to the chronology do not nullify the theological truth of the text (e.g., Raymond E. Brown and John Meier),[4] while others see the credibility of Acts (as history) taking a hit, at best.[5]

But drawing into question the historical accuracy of a canonical work has evoked questions from several scholars: examples include Richard Longenecker and David A. deSilva,[6] who claim that another

---

2. Craig S. Keener, *Acts: An Exegetical Commentary, 15:1–23:35* (Grand Rapids: Baker, 2014), 2194–2215; Loveday C. A. Alexander, "Chronology of Paul," in *Dictionary of Paul and His Letters: A Compendium of Contemporary Biblical Scholarship*, ed. Gerald F. Hawthorne, Ralph P. Martin, and Daniel G. Reid, IVP Bible Dictionary Series (Downers Grove: IVP, 2015), 115–23.

3. See Thomas R. Schreiner, *Galatians*, ECNT 9 (Grand Rapids: Zondervan, 2010), 28–29; Peter Oakes, *Galatians*, Paideia (Grand Rapids: Baker, 2015), 20–21.

4. Raymond E. Brown and John Meier, *Antioch and Rome: New Testament Cradles of Catholic Christianity* (Mahwah, NJ: Paulist Press, 1983), 29.

5. A prominent example is Richard I. Pervo, *Acts*, Hermeneia (Minneapolis: Fortress, 2009), 369n10: "All of the arguments demonstrating that Acts 15 and Galatians 2 treat

model (Gal 2 = Acts 11) resolves the literary tension and retains credibility for Paul and Luke-Acts. For example, both those accounts mention Barnabas and a collection for the poor in Jerusalem. The setting of Acts 11, which portrays a more intimate meeting between Paul and the Pillars, fits the description of Galatians 2 better than the larger council envisioned in Acts 15. Also, it is not clear that circumcision as it is discussed in Acts 15 is really the focus of Galatians 2. In fact, without Acts 15 it would be difficult to discern in Galatians 2 any major statement by the Pillars regarding circumcision in general. This setting requires an early date for Galatians that precedes the so-called council, but such a date would explain why Paul only mentions two visits in Galatians while Acts lists as many as five: when Galatians was written Paul had made only two of these visits, and the remaining visits described in Acts occurred after the letter's dispatch to the Galatian communities.

Although some commentators have migrated from the traditional model to the other model (Gal 2 = Acts 11), key voices maintain a cautious tone. The contentious situation in Galatia creates the possibility that the narrative of Acts might be more reliable if Paul were reporting only specific visits with Peter or the Pillars to support his argument. Moreover, any reading of Luke-Acts reveals a remarkable literary talent capable of modifying sources to produce a smooth narrative rather than a list of chronological events. The Third Gospel's rearrangement of the call of the disciples or the parables in the teaching discourses (Luke 9–16) are but a few examples. Just as disagreements among the Gospels do not invalidate the texts, so too can the variations regarding Paul in his letters and Acts stand without significant controversy.

Timothy Milinovich

Paul now goes his own way, accompanied by Silas (who supposedly had returned to Jerusalem in 15:32 but is somehow again present in Antioch). Barnabas and Mark also go on mission, retracing the previous route via Cyprus, and so they sail over the horizon, never to return to the

the same meeting and the elaborate source hypotheses needed to account for these show how much effort can be expended in avoiding the simplest and most probable solution," with further reference to Richard I. Pervo, *Dating Acts: Between the Evangelists and the Apologists* (Santa Rosa, CA: Polebridge, 2006), 79–96.

6. Richard N. Longenecker, *Galatians*, WBC 41 (Dallas: Word Books, 1990), 46; David A. deSilva, *The Letter to the Galatians*, NICNT (Grand Rapids: Eerdmans, 2018), 48–60.

story. "Cephas," too, is missing; in Acts he gave his last word at 15:7-11, and he does not appear in Antioch at all.

Clearly Lukas wants to establish that Paul is now *the* head of all new missionary efforts, and it is Paul's teaching that will be the Christian standard. Barnabas and Mark may cultivate the already-plowed ground in Cyprus (Barnabas's home);[7] Philip and his prophetic daughters may continue the work in Caesarea—and beyond (see below at Acts 21:8-9). Paul will "keep his feet on the ground," pursuing his journey by land through Syria and Cilicia, revisiting Derbe and Lystra (cf. 14:6-21), and then pressing on into Phrygia and Galatia. The community at Antioch commends Paul and Silas to the grace of God (v. 40), a commendation not said to be accorded to Barnabas and Mark (v. 39). From now on the focus will be entirely on Paul.

As Paul (the Greek text simply says "he"; Silas is not mentioned) revisits Derbe and Lystra, the audience will inevitably think of the troubles he and Barnabas experienced in those places because of the intervention of "Jews from Antioch and Iconium." Lukas says not a word about any of that here, but in Lystra Paul encounters "a disciple named Timothy" (16:1). Paul chooses him as a traveling companion—a fact very well known to Lukas's audience, as Timothy is probably the most prominent figure, next to Paul, in the genuine Pauline letters and is the supposed addressee of two pseudonymous ones.

Willie James Jennings writes: "Timothy appears, the mulatto child," calling him also "the in-between disciple."[8] We tend to think of multiple ethnicities in one person as an anachronistic concept in the Graeco-Roman world, but the pseudo-reality of "race" (really ethnicity) was beginning to establish itself in Greek thought and practice and was only solidified by ever-broadening Roman conquests. Jewish-Greek intermarriage was certainly possible, but some of Israel's prophets had railed against it, and it was not well regarded by the leadership of Judaism as it was shaping itself in Lukas's time.

Timothy is indeed burdened by the ambiguities of ethnic mixing. He is a hybrid, both Jew and Hellene.[9] Then, thanks to Paul, he becomes queer as well. Paul circumcises Timothy, a grown man, supposedly "be-

7. Legend says that Mark evangelized Egypt; that supposedly happened before the projected date of this incident, and it is not part of Lukas's story.

8. Jennings, *Acts*, 152.

9. "Hellene" is a better descriptor for the multi-ethnic communities of Greek-speakers in Asia Minor and Macedonia than "Greek."

cause of the Jews," but that did not make Timothy a Jew. Lukas takes care to point out that his mother was a Jew, but in the projected time of Acts both Jewish and Greek societies were patrilineal.[10] Timothy would be regarded as a gentile, and gentile proselytes or "converts" who frequented the synagogue remained just that, which is what makes the reported attempts of some Jewish Jesus-believers to require circumcision of gentile male believers so bizarre; such a move amounted to queering the gentile men who became Jesus-believers, making them appear to be Jews in every sense while really they were Jewish proselytes who were followers of the Way.[11]

So Paul's action as described in Acts renders Timothy a person of ambiguous status besides being a hybrid. Contrast this with Paul's real attitude, as expressed in Galatians: in Jerusalem "even Titus, who was with me, was not compelled to be circumcised, though he was a Greek" (Gal 2:3). Later in the letter he tells his gentile male audience that if they accept circumcision "Christ will be of no benefit to you" (Gal 5:2).[12]

Mitzi J. Smith has analyzed Timothy's situation in terms of "respectability politics," referring to

> the notion that if a member of a subordinated, marginalized, or oppressed group exhibits acceptable and submissive behaviors, is socially compliant in her appearance and ways of being (e.g., attire, hair style, language, voice, sexuality, marital status, and so on), achieves some

10. The question is disputed, but the weight of evidence seems to say this. See Shaye J. D. Cohen, "Was Timothy Jewish (Acts 16:1-3)? Patristic Exegesis, Rabbinic Law, and Matrilineal Descent," *JBL* 105 (1986): 251–68, where he concludes: "Was Timothy Jewish? In all likelihood Luke did not think so. The vast majority of ancient and medieval exegetes did not think so. There is no evidence that Paul or the Jews of Asia Minor thought so. . . . [T]here is no evidence that any Jew in premishnaic times thought that the child of an intermarriage followed the status of the mother. Was Timothy Jewish? The answer must be no."

11. For a thorough discussion of the complexities of Timothy's circumcision see Matthew Thiessen, "An Anomalous Circumcision for an Anomalous Situation (Acts 16:1-3)," in *Contesting Conversion: Genealogy, Circumcision, and Identity in Ancient Judaism and Christianity* (Oxford: Oxford University Press, 2011), 120–23. Consider also that Lystra is in Galatia, and it is in his letter to the Galatians that Paul rails violently against the circumcision of gentile men.

12. See above, "The Great Council," n. 7. It remains possible that Lukas, living in a Greco-Roman city in the early second century, thought that the Roman law of status applied: the citizenship status (not the ethnicity) of the parents determined that of the children; he may also have been familiar with rabbinic debates on the subject. This would be another argument for a late dating of Acts.

> measure of success regardless of any systemic obstacles, and according to the standards of the dominant culture, she will be accepted by the dominant group. . . . In Acts, Paul, as a member of the dominant race [Jews], succumbs to and imposes the burden of respectability on Timothy when he has him circumcised after the Jerusalem Council had ruled, under the leadership of James, the brother of Jesus, that the burden of circumcision should not be hoisted on the backs of Gentile believers.[13]

In this interpretive context Jews are the dominant race. Smith affirms that for the author of Acts the Jesus movement "is still a sect within Judaism with Jewish leaders who do not cease to be Jewish or to call the shots."[14]

It is the circumstances of diaspora politics, where ethnicity and gender are problematic categories, that seem to compel Timothy's circumcision. It is not said that Timothy willingly submitted to it. Evidently neither he nor his mother, who was already a Jesus-believer (as, presumably, was he), had considered it necessary. This is an act that challenges the "rules" of Roman order: it creates an ethnically bifurcated person. Bureaucratic "rules" in our own time are not very different. "Mulatto," Willie James Jennings's descriptive term, is not a category permitted by the US census: only one race per person is allowed.[15]

Tat-Siong Benny Liew has written that Acts has an "ethnicity problem," and so does Paul, as portrayed here. "Acts contains many references to the community's successful mission to Gentiles, but the work of mission and evangelism is restricted to Jews (Palestinian and Hellenistic)." He suggests that the ethnic monopoly constitutes a kind of "glass ceiling" for gentile Christ-followers.[16] But according to Eric Barreto it is the shattering of that glass that is at stake here. "Ethnic negotiations" are Lukas's concern in this chapter, but not only here. Lukas has a theology of ethnicity that is vital to his vision of the church now coming to be:

---

13. Mitzi J. Smith, "Paul, Timothy, and the Respectability Politics of Race: A Womanist Inter(con)textual Reading of Acts 16:1-5," *Religions* 10 (March 13, 2019), 1. Introduction (available at https://www.mdpi.com/2077-1444/10/3/190/htm).

14. Ibid., 1n2.

15. This has the (intended) result of undercounting some minority groups as assimilated second, third, and later generations descended from immigrants or enslaved persons, given no choice, in many cases list their ethnicity as "white." I myself now regard my "race" as *human*, and so mark myself as "other" when "human" is not an option.—LMM

16. Tat-Siong Benny Liew, "Acts of the Apostles," in *Global Bible Commentary* (Nashville: Abingdon, 2004), 419–28, as quoted in Smith, "Paul, Timothy, and Respectability Politics," part 4.

Luke does not imagine a church stripped of ethnic distinctives but a movement that embraces such differences as endemic to the cultures of antiquity and the ambiguities surrounding ethnic reasoning as a valuable discursive space within which to portray a movement that invites all peoples.[17]

But if Lukas is sensitive to ethnic differences and inclusion of all peoples, he is for the most part oblivious to members of the "other" gender. Women appear in the text as needed but never for long and almost always in service to the needs of men.

We need to consider that Timothy's mother, Eunice,[18] was not just a random "Jewish woman who was a believer." In all likelihood she was the head of the household of the Way in Lystra, having assumed leadership there after Paul and Barnabas's departure. Then it would seem that she, at home in her diaspora setting, was not concerned that her son with a gentile father was not circumcised. It was only the Paul of Acts who had a problem. Reading between the lines, should we suppose that—having been pretty much left out of the discussion of this painful male-only problem—she and her diaspora Jewish sisters had concluded that it was not something they needed to worry about and had told their menfolk "just get over it already"?

"Salvation Is from the Jews" (John 4:22)

The words the author of the Fourth Gospel places in the mouth of Jesus closely reflect the conviction of the author of Acts and may be the echo of a discussion between the two writers in Ephesus. Lukas remains convinced that, while people of Jewish and gentile descent belong together in the Movement, it remains the calling of Israel to be the instrument of salvation for all humanity. By their faithful keeping of the covenant (as the heart of the Way, Lukas hopes) they will, ultimately, lead the whole human world to the banquet in Jerusalem. The decree of the council in Acts 15 does not deny that. Gentile believers are obligated only to keep the laws for "foreigners," but there is no relaxation of the duties of Jews, whether within or outside the Movement. (Lukas's vision is

---

17. Eric D. Barreto, *Ethnic Negotiations*, WUNT 294 (Tübingen: Mohr Siebeck, 2010), 185.

18. 2 Tim 1:5.

212 Acts of the Apostles

that such divisions among Jews will soon cease.) In Lukas's eyes Timothy is a Jew and must keep the whole law, including the rite of circumcision; Paul is depicted as recognizing that. (In Galatians 2 he speaks repeatedly of a "gospel for the uncircumcised" and a "gospel for the circumcised," supposedly assigned to different missionaries, even though later in the letter he insists—to his gentile audience—that the law is obsolete and circumcision with it.) By the time he wrote Romans he had clearly reconsidered:

Then what advantage has the Jew? Or what is the value of circumcision? Much, in every way. For in the first place the Jews were entrusted with the oracles of God . . . for the gifts and the calling of God are irrevocable. (Rom 3:1-2; 11:29)

Christians' taking Paul's talk of "two covenants" literally, and reading Galatians to say that Jesus has fulfilled the "old covenant" by his death, so that it no longer obliges anyone (Jew or Greek), has been the source of infinite agony for Jewish people throughout subsequent history. Paul had second thoughts; Lukas rejected the idea, and so should we, his readers.[19]

Despite Paul's supposed desire to have Timothy as a companion, in the rest of Acts they are seldom together; Timothy seems to work primarily in Macedonia (cf. 17:14-15; 19:22). He is not said to accompany Paul and Silas when they leave Lystra, and Smith proposes that this was because of the circumcision, a dangerous procedure for an adult male and requiring two to three weeks for recovery. Evidently the Paul of Acts regarded the need for Timothy to be identified by diaspora Jewish men as a member of Israel as more important than the physical danger to Timothy.[20] Paul has rendered Timothy "respectable," but at what cost? As Smith sees it, "[Paul] operates from a position of racial bias and as the one with the authority and power, his bias is oppressive, harmful, consequential, and impacts Timothy's quality of life. . . . [T]he circumcision of Timothy was no microaggression."[21] Barreto views the scene

---

19. See especially Norbert Lohfink, *The Covenant Never Revoked: Biblical Reflections on Christian-Jewish Dialogue*, trans. John J. Scullion (Mahwah, NJ: Paulist Press, 1991).

20. For a graphic biblical description of the effects of circumcision on adult males see Gen 34:25-31.

21. Smith, "Paul, Timothy, and Respectability Politics," part 5.

instead as demonstrating the pliability of ethnic constructions and as collapsing exclusive categories. "The story of Timothy demonstrates that the conclusions of the apostolic council required application in the midst of complex ethnic negotiations; that is, how Jews and Hellenes would relate to one another was not entirely self-evident even in the wake of Acts 15."[22] That will be abundantly clear when Paul and his companions return to Jerusalem in Acts 21.

We might wish that Lukas had dealt openly with Timothy's ambiguous status, but Acts is a narrative, not a theological treatise. We are left to deal with these realities ourselves, in our own time. Willie James Jennings writes:

> Inter-existence, bicultural or biracial [or intergender] could be held softly or strongly, be acknowledged or denied, be actively resisted or passionately affirmed. . . . To live in between presents a possibility of turning a question on peoples that has rarely been asked: Could you imagine a new way of seeing and being yourself?[23]

In fact, that seems to be the question Lukas really proposes to his audience.

From Lystra the missionary team proceeds "from town to town" (evidently without Timothy, who does not reappear until 17:14, in Beroea). Their sole purpose is supposedly to convey the Jerusalem decree of the "apostles and elders." The participating Jerusalem community has been erased from the picture and with it, as far as the language is concerned, its women leaders and members.[24] Readers and hearers are assured, in the last of the Lukan "summaries," that the "churches" (ἐκκλησίαι) are growing both in faith and in numbers (cf. 14:23).

22. Barreto, *Ethnic Negotiations*, 71, 117–18, at 118.
23. Jennings, *Acts*, 156.
24. In reality the group of "elders" probably included women, but the masculine form πρεσβύτεροι conceals them.

Acts 16:6-34

A Drama in Three Acts Featuring Lydia and a Woman Prophet

The party's route evidently takes them on a diagonal across Asia Minor (the Roman province of Asia). Mysia lay in the northwest portion of the province and Bithynia-Pontus to the east of Mysia, so the Spirit's guidance keeps the group pointed toward Troas, forbidding them to enter the northern reaches. Focusing now entirely on Paul, Lukas avoids any mention of the traditions of Peter's ministry in Bithynia-Pontus; the pseudonymous Petrine letters come from that region, and it had certainly been missionized by the end of the first century, as 1 Peter is addressed to the believers in "Pontus, Galatia, Cappadocia, Asia, and Bithynia," and Pliny's correspondence with Trajan describes his dealings with "Christians" there during his governorship.[1]

The Spirit-guided journey culminates in a night vision in the port of Troas. Paul sees a "man of Macedonia" pleading that the missionaries come there "and help us" (16:9). Alexandra Gruca-Macaulay posits that the man in the vision is a military figure since the next stop, Philippi,

---

1. See 1 Pet 1:1; also *The Letters of Pliny*, ed. Adrian N. Sherwin-White (Oxford: Oxford University Press, 1966). The letters to the emperor Trajan were written while Pliny was governor of Bithynia, 109–110 CE.

Acts 16:6-34

⁶They went through the region of Phrygia and Galatia, having been forbidden by the Holy Spirit to speak the word in Asia. ⁷When they had come opposite Mysia, they attempted to go into Bithynia, but the Spirit of Jesus did not allow them; ⁸so, passing by Mysia, they went down to Troas. ⁹During the night Paul had a vision: there stood a man of Macedonia pleading with him and saying, "Come over to Macedonia and help us." ¹⁰When he had seen the vision, we immediately tried to cross over to Macedonia, being convinced that God had called us to proclaim the good news to them.

¹¹We set sail from Troas and took a straight course to Samothrace, the following day to Neapolis, ¹²and from there to Philippi, which is a leading city of the district of Macedonia and a Roman colony. We remained in this city for some days. ¹³On the sabbath day we went outside the gate by the river, where we supposed there was a place of prayer; and we sat down and spoke to the women who had gathered there. ¹⁴A certain woman named Lydia, a worshiper of God, was listening to us; she was from the city of Thyatira and a dealer in purple cloth. The Lord opened her heart to listen eagerly to what was said by Paul. ¹⁵When she and her household were baptized, she urged us, saying, "If you have judged me to be faithful to the Lord, come and stay at my home." And she prevailed upon us.

was a Roman *colonia*, a settlement of retired Roman veterans.[2] Such colonies enjoyed the privileges of freedom from taxation and the use of Roman legal procedures (which are only marginally visible when Paul and Silas are in Philippi).

More probably the "man of Macedonia" is an angelic representation, the counterpart to Peter's vision in Acts 10:10-16. In each case this is the only vision (ὅραμα) received by Paul and Peter that urges them to new action.[3] What is really striking is that in the very next sentence the narration shifts abruptly to the first-person plural: "*we* immediately tried to cross over to Macedonia." The "we" passages in Acts are a notorious point of contention, especially as regards the identity of the author and

2. But so was Lystra (14:8-20), where Roman "law and order" are not in evidence either.

3. A second vision granted Paul at Acts 18:9 is a message of consolation encouraging him to keep on doing what he has been doing. Peter "thinks" he is having a vision when the angel leads him out of prison in chap. 12, but in the story world it is "real" on the material level. Paul describes his Damascus road encounter as a "vision" only once, in his defense before Agrippa.

¹⁶One day, as we were going to the place of prayer, we met a slave-girl who had a spirit of divination and brought her owners a great deal of money by fortune-telling. ¹⁷While she followed Paul and us, she would cry out, "These men are slaves of the Most High God, who proclaim to you a way of salvation." ¹⁸She kept doing this for many days. But Paul, very much annoyed, turned and said to the spirit, "I order you in the name of Jesus Christ to come out of her." And it came out that very hour.

¹⁹But when her owners saw that their hope of making money was gone, they seized Paul and Silas and dragged them into the marketplace before the authorities. ²⁰When they had brought them before the magistrates, they said, "These men are disturbing our city; they are Jews ²¹and are advocating customs that are not lawful for us as Romans to adopt or observe." ²²The crowd joined in attacking them, and the magistrates had them stripped of their clothing and ordered them to be beaten with rods. ²³After they had given them a severe flogging, they threw them into prison and ordered the jailer to keep them securely. ²⁴Following these instructions, he put them in the innermost cell and fastened their feet in the stocks.

²⁵About midnight Paul and Silas were praying and singing hymns to God, and the prisoners were listening to them. ²⁶Suddenly there was an earthquake,

the dating of the material,[4] but most modern commentators see them as a literary device. This first "we" passage seems to contain only 16:10-18. There is nothing to suggest we should read the account of Paul's and Silas's imprisonment and release as first-person narrative. We are certainly back to third-person narrative by the end of chapter 16, unless the "we" narrator is not among those who depart the city.

---

4. Irenaeus (*Haer.* 3.14.1), the first author to note the existence of Acts, also inaugurated the theory that the "we" passages prove the author of Acts was a companion of Paul—a very useful position for combating his chief doctrinal enemy, Marcion. Modern research on the problem essentially began in the mid-twentieth century, and at present only the most conservative scholars still maintain that "we" = Lukas and other companions of Paul. For a concise discussion and references see Richard I. Pervo, excursus "'We' in Acts," in his Hermeneia commentary (*Acts* [Minneapolis: Fortress, 2009]), 392–96, where he concludes: "The use of 'we' does not identify the author of Acts. It does serve to enhance the credibility of the narrative and to associate the narrator with the person of Paul. It is a bid to be recognized as an exponent of authentic Paulinism and to authenticate the Paulinism of Acts. 'We' is to Acts as the letter form is to the Deutero-Pauline epistles."

Acts 16:6-34 (cont.)

so violent that the foundations of the prison were shaken; and immediately all the doors were opened and everyone's chains were unfastened. [27]When the jailer woke up and saw the prison doors wide open, he drew his sword and was about to kill himself, since he supposed that the prisoners had escaped. [28]But Paul shouted in a loud voice, "Do not harm yourself, for we are all here." [29]The jailer called for lights, and rushing in, he fell down trembling before Paul and Silas. [30]Then he brought them outside and said, "Sirs, what must I do to be saved?" [31]They answered, "Believe in the Lord Jesus, and you will be saved, you and your household." [32]They spoke the word of the Lord to him and to all who were in his house. [33]At the same hour of the night he took them and washed their wounds; then he and his entire family were baptized without delay. [34]He brought them up into the house and set food before them; and he and his entire household rejoiced that he had become a believer in God.

The first episode in Philippi has drawn the attention of feminist commentators in particular. The star of verses 16-18 is a remarkable woman named Lydia who, according to this text, essentially founds and assumes leadership over the first group of Jesus-followers in Philippi. She not only requests baptism for herself and her household; she insists that the missionaries take up residence in her house. "She prevailed upon us," παρεβιάσατο (v. 15), from παραβιάζομαι, is the same word used for the disciples' urging the stranger to remain with them at Emmaus in Luke 24:29; they too are successful in their entreaty. The root verb βιάζω in fact means "to force," and the prefix παρα- intensifies it; there is an *inclusio* with the first active verb in verse 15, παρεκάλεσεν, from παρακαλέω, "she urged us," in which παρα- intensifies the root verb καλέω, "call, invite." In other words, Lydia's entreaties are so urgent and powerful that the missionaries really have no choice but to assent to her wishes. Baptism has conferred on Lydia the power of the Spirit, and in that Spirit she exerts her authority as host and leader of the new community; the missionaries are now dependent on her hospitality.

When instructing his disciples (according to the Sayings Source, Q; cf. Matt 10:5-16; Luke 10:2-12), Jesus emphasized that they must stay in whatever house was open to them; they were not to pick and choose. (Thus Luke 10:7, "do not move about from house to house!") Here Lydia insists that Jesus' rule be followed in succeeding generations, and in the diaspora as well.

There has been much discussion about whether the "place of prayer" (vv. 13, 16) was a synagogue. In light of recent analysis, as noted in the excursus on the synagogue at Acts 6, I think we may infer that

Lukas envisions two types of Jewish gatherings in this diaspora setting: "synagogues" for teaching and study (6:9; 9:2, 20; 13:5, 14-15, 43;
14:1; 15:21; 17:1, 10, 17; 18:4, 7-26; 19:8; 22:19; 24:12; 26:11), and "places of
prayer" specifically for that purpose.[5] Since Lukas depicts the προσευχή
in Philippi as a gathering only of women, it is at least possible that the
Jewish community in Philippi had no synagogue building or designated
gathering place or that in that city it was customary for Jewish women
and men to pray separately. If there was such a division, it had resulted
in the rise of one woman, Lydia, to a position of leadership and influence.

Since in the long history of the Jewish diaspora the home has become
a primary place for prayer—the Passover celebration, the greatest of all
feasts, takes place there—the hints about the situation in Philippi may
also open a window on the lives of Jewish proselyte women in the gentile
world. If they were the wives or slaves of pagan men they would probably
have had no place for prayer and worship at home; if they were lucky
they found a Lydia or a Prisca who could create a safe space for them to
pray and learn. With the arrival of Paul and his companions the "place of
prayer" in fact becomes a synagogue as well: a place of study and teaching.

What sort of woman is this Lydia, who has received the charism of
community leadership through the Spirit? Her portrait has varied widely
over the centuries. Earlier interpreters almost universally saw Lydia as
a wealthy purple-dealer who gave hospitality to the missionaries. Ivoni
Richter Reimer's careful analysis[6] has overturned that idea, showing
Lydia as a working woman associated with others in her trade. Lillian
Portefaix[7] has analyzed Acts 16 in conjunction with Paul's letter to the
Philippians, positing the viewpoint first of the recipients of the letter and
then of Acts. Alexandra Gruca-Macaulay[8] has employed sophisticated
socio-rhetorical methods to conclude that Lydia was a "huckster," a
socially dubious character, and one of a series of persons "called" in
this chapter. The most recent and succinct treatment of the chapter as a
whole is by Angela Standhartinger; her focus is on the portrayal of Paul
in the Roman *Colonia Philippi*, and her suggestion is that his sojourn in

5. Cf. 1 Macc 3:46 (Mizpah); 3 Macc 7:20 (Ptolemais), τόπος προσευχῆς for "place of
prayer" outside Jerusalem.
6. Ivoni Richter Reimer, *Women in the Acts of the Apostles: A Feminist Liberation Perspective*, trans. Linda M. Maloney (Minneapolis: Fortress, 1995), 71–150.
7. Lillian Portefaix, *Sisters Rejoice: Paul's Letter to the Philippians and Luke-Acts as Seen
by First-Century Women* (Stockholm: Almqvist & Wiksell, 1988).
8. Alexandra Gruca-Macaulay, *Lydia as a Rhetorical Construct in Acts* (Atlanta: SBL
Press, 2016). If we accept this characterization we have to conclude that Lydia's adherence to the Way elevated her social status (see v. 40).

that "miniature copy of Rome" is a preview of his last visit (as depicted in his letter); Lukas has supplied this version with a better ending.[9]

Recent analyses of the Philippi chapter in Acts have in common that they have abandoned the attempt to seek a historical basis for it. We are interested, instead, in what Lukas was doing here: what did he hope to accomplish by telling the stories of Lydia, the enslaved girl, and the jailer, and having Paul present himself as a Roman? My view of the chapter is that it is Lukas's move, at this point, to both lighten and expand the narrative while still moving the story forward. His gentile audience may be getting restless after the ordeal of chapter 15 and the seemingly endless wrangling about their own place in the new community, which by the time Acts reached them had been firmly established for decades. So Lukas offers them some scenes with which they are familiar and comfortable because they resemble typical events in contemporary Greek novels. At the same time the introduction of two seemingly different women opens the narrative to a "third space," a "constructed common past"[10] such as novels, in fact, present.

Richard Pervo was the first to propose in detail that the Lukan writings owe much to the ancient novel.[11] Lillian Portefaix also suggests more than once in her book on Philippi, which is based on reader-response criticism, that these scenes have reference to that form of popular writing. Angela Standhartinger speaks of the motifs of prison escape, door-opening miracles, and last-minute rescues in that genre, while pointing to the symbolic character of some features as well.[12]

Directions given in visions or dreams are a common feature of the ancient novel,[13] so that the appearance of the "Macedonian man" is an appropriate starting point for the European mission. "Paul, like Alexander and Caesar, experienced the vision of a personified province or

---

9. Angela Standhartinger, "Better Ending: Paul in the Roman *Colonia Philippi* in Acts 16," in *Delightful Acts: New Essays on Canonical and Non-canonical Acts*, ed. Harold W. Attridge, Dennis R. MacDonald, and Clare K. Rothschild, WUNT 391 (Tübingen: Mohr Siebeck, 2017), 227–43, here at 243. For an analysis of such scenes in "Third Space" see Hannah Lents's essay on Damaris in Athens (with further references), at Acts 17 below.

10. See Hannah Lents's essay below for definition of terms.

11. Richard I. Pervo, *Profit with Delight: The Literary Genre of the Acts of the Apostles* (Philadelphia: Fortress, 1987).

12. Standhartinger, "Better Ending," 241–43 and nn. 93, 101, 112. See also the narratological study by Ute E. Eisen, *Die Poetik der Apostelgeschichte: Eine narratologische Studie*, NTOA 58 (Fribourg: Academic Press; Göttingen: Vandenhoeck & Ruprecht, 2006), 97, with reference, *inter alia*, to Pervo, *Profit with Delight*.

13. See above at Acts 10.

nation."[14] This signifies a dramatic move from one cultural context to another. We will have more to say about Lukas's use of ethnicity later.

Dreams often posit divine intervention in the storyline; similarly, chance encounters are divinely arranged. In Chariton's *Callirhoe*, for example, the lovers meet only because the sheltered Callirhoe participates in a public festival of Aphrodite, and Chaireas is walking home from the gymnasium. "So by chance they ran into one another at a narrow bend in the road and met, the god orchestrating this encounter so that each could see the other."[15] So also the mission of Paul and Silas leads them to seek out a "place of prayer," a public space where they encounter Lydia, and everything follows from that.

While in previous centuries Lydia was regarded as a stock character (even if posited as historical), more recently liberation theology and the development of the study of ethnicity have pointed to a more complicated and significant conception on Lukas's part. Lydia's role is that of the "other Cornelius," which is to say that her real "counterpart" in the typical Lukan male-female pairing is the Roman centurion, the first gentile convert, who is likewise displaced from his homeland. Lydia, commonly labeled the "first convert in Europe," is in fact not European: her origins are in Asia Minor (Thyatira), and her ethnic and status origins are indefinite. For the purposes of the "novel" she can be read as a woman of high standing, but on a deeper level she is a "hybrid,"[16] possibly a freedwoman or the daughter of freedpersons, a dealer in purple cloth—which may mean she was a wealthy merchant or that she was only a local dealer, even someone who, together with her household, engaged in the dirty, smelly business of cloth-dying involving marine creatures, so that she was routinely to be found near the river. She is head of a household, possibly made up of her coworkers and fellow members of this προσευχή and so resembling Tabitha's community. She may have been enslaved in the past; she may be an enslaver in the story's present. Lukas makes her an enigma, offering broad scope for interpretation.

---

14. Pervo, *Profit with Delight*, 73, referring to Quintus Curtius Rufus, *Historia Alexandri Magni* 4.2.16; Suetonius, *The Life of Julius Caesar* 7, 81, as well as *The Life of Apollonius of Tyana* 4.34: "While he was reflecting on these things, he had the following dream: a very tall and aged woman appeared, embraced him and beseeched him to visit her before sailing to Italy."

15. Chariton, *Callirhoe*, in *Callirhoe and an Ephesian Story: Two Novels from Ancient Greece*, trans. with introduction and notes by Stephen M. Trzaskoma (Indianapolis: Hackett, 2010), 1.1.

16. See Eric D. Barreto, *Ethnic Negotiations*, WUNT 294 (Tübingen: Mohr Siebeck, 2010). We might well say that Lydia is one more character who is queered by Lukas.

Crafting Gender in Acts: Tabitha and Lydia

The stories of Tabitha and Lydia have always been studied individually, but due to similarities in both their presentation and their social contexts they invite analysis as a pair. One important lens for this exploration is that of occupation: the women are depicted as a seamstress and a dealer in purple cloth, respectively. Although there is no inscriptional or material evidence for a historical Tabitha or Lydia, readers and hearers of Lukas's story would have recognized them as types familiar throughout the Roman Empire. They represent a class of women who have been largely ignored because of their absence from the literary sources and because past scholarship could not conceive of the possibility that women in the Greco-Roman world operated as independent heads of households, business leaders, and religious authorities. Nevertheless, numerous inscriptions reveal women displaying their job titles and leadership roles with pride and memorializing their contributions to their communities. Acts "crafts" Tabitha and Lydia as working, independent heads of household, exemplars of their gender, and ideal followers of the risen Christ, showing that without the business resources and hospitality of such women the gospel would never have reached so wide an audience. The literary evidence on which many studies have relied gives only one perspective, namely, that of elite males who held women and work in equal disdain. Although elite authors may have looked down on workers involved in the trades, the portraits of Tabitha and Lydia in Acts, taken together with inscriptional and material evidence, tell a different story.

The elite male perspective is on full display in Cicero's and Martial's evaluations of the working class. Both *De Officiis* 1.150-51 and Martial's more colorful comments in *Epigrams* 12.59 suggest to many scholars that these views were widely held by people at all socioeconomic levels, but Martial skewered the farmer, cobbler, and fuller for exaggerated comic effect while Cicero denigrates tradespersons and glorifies agricultural landownership and his own lifestyle as a gentleman farmer. To make wider assumptions based solely on this type of self-serving literary evidence can lead one down a very narrow and contrived garden path.

In contrast, the tomb of Marcus Vergilius Eurysaces and his wife Antistia, discovered in the Porta Maggiore region of Rome, publicly identifies the couple as bakers, eulogizing one of the very trades Cicero denigrates.[17] The tomb itself is quite large and ornate. A memorial of this type tells us that the couple had a good deal of money and wanted to spend it to memorialize not only themselves but also their profession. The couple style themselves as aristocrats through the depiction of their dress and Antistia's hairstyle. The grave inscription prominently describes their occupation; the couple are proud of their success, display their job title (*pistoris redemptoris*) prominently, and do not seem concerned that elite citizens like Cicero might make fun of their stylized dress or their occupation. Whatever humble origins lay in the past, the couple's poses, the tomb, and the inscription reveal that Vergilius and Antistia were bakers who wanted to be seen.

In Pompeii, Naevoleia Tyche commissioned a very elaborate and expensive tomb for herself and her husband.[18] Although the husband is mentioned along with his job title as an officer of the imperial cult, Naevoleia's likeness and occupation take center stage. The inscription explicitly states that she paid for the family's tomb from her own family funds (ἐκ τῶν ἰδίων).

She states that she was a freed slave and that she gained her fortune through involvement in the shipping industry; the ornate tomb decoration even includes her likeness on the prow of a ship. In another example, one of the largest and most impressive buildings in Pompeii was a uniquely designed structure donated to the city by Eumachia.[19] The inscription on the building, which suggests her donation is for civic benefit, bears only her name and also designates her as a priestess of the cult of Ceres. Archaeologists have concluded that the size of the building and its placement in the center of the largest marketplace indicate that it served as a business center for foreign and domestic merchants involved in various trades while in the city. Even if women as a group were held in lesser esteem in Roman society, individuals like Naevoleia and Eumachia functioned prominently as business, civic, and religious patrons who displayed their titles and their contributions to the community in public dedicatory inscriptions. Such examples provide a background for Tabitha's characterization as a businesswoman, patron, and religious leader in Joppa.

---

17. The inscriptions for the tomb are found in *Corpus Inscriptionum Latinarum* = *CIL* (Berlin: De Gruyter, 1931; repr. 1976) 1.2, 1203–5. Most scholars date this tomb to the late-Republican to early Imperial period, most likely during the reign of Augustus.

18. *CIL* 10.1030. First century CE.

19. *CIL* 10.813. First century CE.

In another important example of female civic patronage, five inscriptions found at Corinth and dated to the late first century CE all name Junia Theodora as a civic patron and ambassador.[20] These same five inscriptions, with the identical text, were found in Lycia, thus indicating her prominence in both cities. Junia was probably a Greek woman who was a citizen of the city of Corinth and also of Rome. In spite of the fact that the inscriptions do not mention the usual public works projects found in other dedicatory inscriptions, Junia's do contain all the characteristic elements of the genre. She is honored for commercial and political patronage to her native Lycia, and not just to a single city but to a federation of some thirty-six cities called "the Lycian league." According to the text she welcomed ambassadors, exiles, and citizens of the Lycian league into her home and advocated for their concerns while in Corinth. Junia used her wealth and influence to ensure that the needs and concerns of her native land were heard within the Roman political system and that its citizens could find refuge within her walls. This type of hospitality and advocacy is paralleled in Lydia's characterization in Acts 16. Further, Junia's goodwill and generosity in drawing on her own substance for the benefit of her community recall Tabitha's commemoration in Acts 9:36.

Recent archaeological excavations at Ostia Antica show that, far from being a small port of entry to Rome, the city covered approximately seventy thousand square kilometers and included warehouses and docks for large ships carrying goods from ports throughout the empire and beyond.[21] Numerous reliefs name women working in such trades as shoemaking and vegetable sales and as owners of public houses and cafeterias. In each case their trade is portrayed prominently both in pictures and in words. Because there are also many reliefs in Ostia that advertise only the type of commerce—such as a picture of a food pot marking a public cafeteria—we may surmise that these female shop owners went to extra effort and expense to put their likeness and job title on the public signage, as much to advertise their business as to visibly display their work.

In Rome approximately 78.8 percent of the female occupational inscriptions identify women working in the cloth trade and/or clothing

---

20. Hans-Josef Klauck, "Junia Theodora und die Gemeinde von Korinth," in *Religion und Gesellschaft im frühen Christentum*, WUNT 152 (Tübingen: Mohr Siebeck, 2003), 232–50.

21. Carlo Pavolini, "A Survey of Excavations and Studies on Ostia (2004–2014)," *JRS* 106 (November 2016): 199–236.

manufacture.[22] Some of the titles they list are "silkworker, spinner, woolworker, purple dyer, tailor of clothing with gold leaf (*auri vestrix*) and managers of the workshop (*officianatrix*)." They also identify women with titles such as jewelry maker, ironsmith, manufacturer of gold leaf, and dealer (*negotiatrix*) in various grains, foodstuffs, and cloth. One must guard against the kind of stereotyped assumption about gender dynamics in the ancient world that has led past scholars to conclude that women could not have held high-level managerial or ownership positions. While it may be true that the women who held these jobs were underappreciated and even oppressed, that need not mean they did not take pride in their work as a contribution to their community and as an important part of their identity.

The parallels between the women in the epigraphic sources and the characters of Lydia and Tabitha go even further. Tabitha, whose home is the hub of clothmaking activity, is representative of women who acted as managers, apprentices, and profit-sharers in textile businesses. Inscriptions both from the Greek East and from Rome show that women worked in collectives where they performed specialized tasks within the supply chain such as carding, spinning, dyeing, or sewing the cloth into clothing. Occupational inscriptions from Rome and many other places[23] indicate that enslaved or formerly enslaved women also used these trades as a path to manumission for themselves, family members, and associates. Jobs that might have been held in low esteem could also promise increased rights and freedom. The loss of Tabitha seems to have been significant to her community; her title of "disciple" shows that she was both an economic and a spiritual benefactor. The women who gather in her home mourn the death of their patron, coworker, religious leader, and liberator in one.

Lydia's narrative also centers around a household, workshop, and spiritual community. The women are gathered on the Sabbath to pray together, and they probably also work together in the purple cloth trade. Although some have argued that Lydia's name suggests that she was a former slave, her designation as a Thyatiran could also indicate that she was a citizen of the city of Thyatira who was doing business in Philippi as a trader

22. Sandra Joshel, *Work, Identity, and Legal Status at Rome: A Study of the Occupational Inscriptions at Rome* (Norman: Oklahoma University Press, 1992). This remains the signal work on this material.

23. See the inscriptional evidence found in *Sources Bibliques* 18. One example of this is inscription no. 13305.

in purple cloth, much like Junia Theodora. When Lydia demands that Paul and his companions stay in her home she does so on her own authority. She also requests baptism for herself and her entire household, further reinforcing that she is acting as head of the household. Although it is true that evidence indicates that most free women in the Greco-Roman world were either married, widowed, or divorced, the text of Acts makes no such designation for either Tabitha or Lydia. Sometimes silence speaks very loudly.

What seems clear from the inscriptional and material data is that both Tabitha and Lydia bear certain resemblances to the women in those sources. While I make no claim for a historical Tabitha or Lydia, there is sociocultural plausibility for both stories. Tabitha and Lydia act as female heads of household who are employed in a trade, not independently but as part of a cooperative network of women. They work in cities with active markets and within diverse ethnic and religious communities, and they have responsibilities in both spheres. Acts highlights traits in its female characters that mirror and celebrate the situations and aspirations of its audience. Studying Tabitha and Lydia as a pair allows us an alternative way to craft our view of the gender roles of women in the Greco-Roman world. It also provides us the means of recognizing the many nameless, forgotten women who labored for the benefit of their households, civic communities, and the Jesus movement. Without them we might never have heard the stories of Peter, Paul, and the other male figures in Acts.

Teresa J. Calpino

Certainly Lukas could have made a more intriguing figure of Lydia if he had wanted to. He is careful to state that she came from Thyatira. If, as is currently proposed, Lukas had his base in Ephesus, he may have been acquainted with the Johannine writings, including Revelation. That book (supposedly composed around 96 CE) begins with a series of letters to seven churches that may have circulated independently. Lukas, writing in the early second century, could surely have read the letter to the church at Thyatira that says in part: "you tolerate that woman Jezebel, who calls herself a prophet and is teaching and beguiling my servants to practice fornication and to eat food sacrificed to idols" (Rev 2:20).[24]

24. This is a biblical passage unsurpassed in its violent misogyny. It continues: "I gave her time to repent, but she refuses to repent of her fornication. Beware, I am

Thyatira was known in the early second century not only as a center of commercial manufacturing but as a place where women were prominent. Iulia Iuliana and Iulia Menogensis held public offices, and others had priestly or high priestly duties in the numerous cults of the gods, Apollo and Artemis prominent among them.[25] It is highly probable that there was a sizeable Jewish community in Thyatira also, since two thousand Jewish families from Mesopotamia had been settled in the region by Antiochus III around 210 BCE.[26]

Lydia could have been a Jewish proselyte, an adherent of one of the Greek gods, or something more: Thyatira had a long tradition of ecstatic religion and prophecy. One author remarks regarding an early third-century inscription that "[i]t is remarkable that a century before Christianity is legalized, Christians around Thyatira are publicly declaring their faith."[27] But the evidence of such commitment, and enthusiasm, is far older than that. In the latter part of the second century the prophetic spirit in Phrygia and environs burst into full bloom with the arrival of the New Prophecy, whose leaders were women.[28] The New Prophecy dominated the region for more than a century and spread abroad, even as far as North Africa, where the apologist Tertullian was drawn to it. So powerful was the movement that Tertullian, a noted misogynist, praised its women prophets fulsomely and even joined that woman-led manifestation of Christianity. It is against that Phrygian/Lydian background that we should view Lydia, daughter of Thyatira.

---

throwing her on a bed, and those who commit adultery with her I am throwing into great distress, unless they repent of her doings; and I will strike her children dead" (vv. 21-23). The author of Revelation was clearly in a fury at the female leadership in public life and religious expression at Thyatira; the rape threat is scarcely veiled.

25. See Svlatoslav Dmitriev, *City Government in Hellenistic and Roman Asia Minor* (Oxford: Oxford University Press, 2005), 180, with references: "In Thyatira, Iulia Iuliana held the *agonothesia* [a liturgical civic office that involved organizing (and funding) public spectacles, including athletic contests] and Iulia Menogensis occupied not only the *agonothesia* but also the *stephanephoria* [she wore a garland as symbol of sacred and magisterial dignity] and *prytaneia* [presiding office, held in rotation]. . . . Women also held the *demiourgiai* [long-term civic offices], priesthoods and high priesthoods, and various other offices."

26. Josephus, *Ant.* 12.148-53. Lydia may, indeed, have been a Jewish woman, not a gentile at all!

27. Mark Wilson, "The Social and Geographical World of Thyatira," *Lexham Geographic Commentary on Acts through Revelation* (Bellingham, WA: Lexham, 2019), 655–64, at 662.

28. The New Prophecy is commonly and wrongly called "Montanism," after Montanus, the male member of the leadership group. Surprise.

In the novelistic portrayal in Acts it is "love at first sight" as Lydia responds immediately to Paul's (and Silas's?) preaching, just as Thecla will do.[29] "The Lord opened her heart," much as Aphrodite touched Callirhoe's, and she seeks baptism for herself and her whole household. (Typically the "religious" or cultural choice of the mistress or master becomes the fate of the whole family of relatives, adherents, and enslaved persons: see 10:44-48; 16:33.) Lydia's next words: "If you have judged me to be faithful to the Lord, come and stay at my home," appear to suggest that the whole process lasts longer than a single day: probably Lydia shows herself faithful and advances in her faith over a period of time, after which she (forcefully![30]) requests that her faithfulness be rewarded by the missionaries' taking up residence with her. So the "lovers" are joined.

The vague time-scheme continues: "One day, as we were going to the place of prayer" (v. 16). There may be overlap here: Paul, Silas, and company are regularly (perhaps daily?) going to the "place of prayer," and the mantic woman begins to follow them (for "many days"). Their move to Lydia's house may take place during this period; perhaps it is achieving that solid footing for the group that allows Paul, at last, to take action against this disrupter of his mission. Exasperated, he exorcises the mantic spirit: "I order you in the name of Jesus Christ to come out of her" (v. 18). It does, and the enslaved young woman (παιδίσκη) vanishes from the story along with it, but with her goes her considerable earning power, and that is distinctly unpleasing to her owners.

---

29. See *Acts of Paul* II, "The Acts of Paul and Thecla," §7: "And as Paul was saying these things in the midst of the assembly in the house of Onesiphorus, a certain virgin, Thecla . . . sat at the window hard by, and hearkened night and day unto the word concerning chastity which was spoken by Paul: and she stirred not from the window, but was led onward by faith, rejoicing exceedingly: and further, when she saw many women and virgins entering in to Paul, she also desired earnestly to be accounted worthy to stand before Paul's face and to hear the word of Christ." (M. R. James, *The Apocryphal New Testament* [Oxford: Clarendon, 1924], available at https://www.earlychristianwritings.com/text/actspaul.html.)

30. See above for παρεβιάσατο (v. 15). As usual, the AV is more forthright: "she constrained us." In biblical writings the reference is usually to moral force (thus 2 Kgs 2:17, "they [the company of prophets] urged him [Elisha] until he was ashamed"; Josephus, *C. Ap.* 2.233, "to be compelled to do or to speak anything contrary to their own laws"). See BDAG, 759. Is there a suggestion that Paul and company considered Lydia's house "unclean" in some way and were somewhat reluctantly persuaded to see it differently by her submission to baptism, together with her whole household? That would be another parallel with the story of Cornelius (see 10:27, 48).

Saundra Schwartz[31] has explored the use of the "adultery type-scene," a stock feature of ancient novels and plays, in the Apocryphal Acts (where the sex was laundered out, but not the violence). Here Lukas plays on this very familiar scene to emphasize the purity of Paul's motives and the venality of the woman's enslavers. Like Andrew in the apocryphal Acts of Andrew, our hero engages with a woman to her immediate benefit (releasing her from enslavement both to the spirit and to her owners), but in doing so he robs her "master(s)" of something they value very highly—so much so that they will take Paul to court and name him as co-respondent (= thief of their woman).[32]

Violence follows, but only the violence visited on men is acknowledged: Paul and Silas are beaten and not only jailed but put in a kind of "stocks." That same night they, like Peter in chapter 12, are miraculously freed (not by an angel but by an earthquake), and afterward, having converted the jailer and his household, Paul at last presents his defense and reveals his accusers' venal motives. Interpreters have puzzled over why he did not do so when he was first accused and so avoid the beating and jailing, but that would have interrupted the "novel," which has to reach its satisfactory resolution. It is evident from the narrator's tone that such commerce in prophecy is contemptible from Paul's point of view, and putting its practitioners out of business is a service to the community.[33]

The most recent and, in my view, the best in-depth analysis of the scene involving the enslaved παιδίσκη with her prophetic gift is that of Ronald Charles.[34] He treats the scene(s) in verses 16-18 as a "mirror story" corresponding in many ways to the account of Rhoda in Acts 12:12-17 and clarifying aspects of that scene that were left ambiguous. Both women are prophets; "both are able to perceive or to recognize particular voices."[35] Both are insistent in announcing their message; both stories contain an element of excitement, and the public perception of both these enslaved women by observers is the same: they are mad!

---

31. Saundra Schwartz, "From Bedroom to Courtroom: The Adultery Type-Scene and the *Acts of Andrew*," in *Mapping Gender in Ancient Religious Discourses*, ed. Todd Penner and Caroline Vander Stichele (Leiden: Brill, 2007), 267–311.

32. Pervo wryly observes (*Acts*, 406n55) that "this exorcism would arouse considerable critical contempt if found in Apocryphal Acts."

33. See ibid., 405.

34. Ronald Charles, *The Silencing of Slaves in Early Jewish and Christian Texts*, Routledge Studies in the Early Christian World (London: Routledge, 2020), esp. chap. 5, "Slaves in the Book of Acts," 215–65.

35. Ibid., 229.

Rhoda's role is played out in a single scene, but the prophetic woman in Philippi is at work over a longer period; though she first follows Paul and his group "one day" as they are on their way to the προσευχή and shouts her message (vv. 16-17), she keeps it up over "many days" (v. 18) until Paul silences her. Charles raises the interesting question whether she follows them into the "place of prayer," in which case she would also be paralleled with Rhoda, who interrupted the gathering in Mary's house (12:14).

Prophesying women are "crazy"—that is a common stereotype in the early Common Era, and not only then. But Lukas evidently has more in mind here. Readers are often puzzled about why Paul is so angry at the woman for saying exactly what the group are about: "These men are slaves of the Most High God, who proclaim to you a way of salvation" (v. 17). A slave (παιδίσκη) announces to the world that Paul and his companions too are *slaves* (δοῦλοι), though whereas she is enslaved to earthly κύριοι (masters, owners), these others are slaves of the Most High God, supreme among the gods.[36]

How did she know that? Quite possibly she has been part of the group that gathers in the προσευχή for morning and evening prayer and instruction. She has not accepted baptism because she fears that would deprive her of her mantic gift, as Paul's exorcism now does, thus rendering her worthless to her owners (v. 19)—but she knows who they are, and in her prophetic state she cannot hold back from proclaiming it.

Clearly, Paul is enraged. Why, when the woman speaks the truth? It can only be because being proclaimed a "slave" by a woman who is indeed enslaved in the flesh, a social "nobody," is not a good way to begin a mission among free Romans, to say the least. First, he finds himself in a synagogal assembly headed by, and largely populated by, women, and now an *enslaved* female has put him on her level. The rest of the story serves to rehabilitate Paul, at least to a degree, by bonding him with a Roman jailer and his household. Ronald Charles sees this as a parallel to Cornelius, but as indicated above I see the real parallel to Peter's mission in the story of Lydia. The jailer in chapter 16 is terrified, suicidal, and subservient, not noble like Cornelius.

The enslaved woman, once drained of her value (to men), is simply dropped from the story. That "her subsequent life would not have been enviable"[37] is the understatement of the ages. Was she simply abandoned

36. The enslaved girl/woman (παιδίσκη) has been demeaned by men; the "slaves [δοῦλοι] of the Most High God" have been raised beyond human measure.
37. Pervo, *Acts*, 406n57.

by her owners, or did they sell her for whatever they could get, retain her as a menial, or place her in a brothel?[38] Lukas is no more interested in her fate than are the men in the story world.

The woman's vanishing from the story is equivalent to her disappearance from social reality. We see the same sequence enacted over and over again today, as prisoners are released from jails and patients are discharged from mental institutions: they are thrown onto the streets with no means of sustaining themselves or integrating into society and so become "nonpersons."

Scorning a woman's religious practice would also have been useful in warding off suspicion that the missionaries of the Way were spreading a "new religion" or introducing "new gods," which in Rome (and presumably in the "little Rome" of Philippi) was a capital offense.[39] Charles observes that

> Luke's socio-political work in the second-century Roman world was filled with ambiguities that required him to live and negotiate various tensions. . . . He needed to portray the Most High God as the Jewish God without alienating any Roman who would like to be part of the movement, or without pushing Roman authorities that value order and stability to consider this growing and diverse movement of which he was a part any threat to the proper functioning of the empire; he did not want the movement of the Way to be seen as suspicious of manufacturing any subversive social and political activities.[40]

Under Domitian, in the last decade of the first century,[41] Roman xenophobia, misogyny, and especially anti-Judaism were at a peak, as witnessed by the writings of such eminences as Juvenal and Martial,

---

38. Ronald Charles writes that "we can consider the maid slave with the spirit of divination in Acts 16 as someone at the margin of society but serving those firmly established at its center" (*Silencing*, 234). Losing one's usefulness to powerful men is always perilous.

39. Introducing "alien deities" was the capital charge on which Socrates was condemned. Still, Lukas's subtlety is remarkable. He has the enslaved girl call Paul and companions καταγγελέως, "proclaimers, heralds," and at 17:16 some Athenians will dub Paul himself "a *proclaimer* of foreign divinities" (ξένων δαιμονίων δοκεῖ καταγγελεὺς). The noun is relatively uncommon, but Lukas is extremely fond of words built on the root αγγελ-. See, *inter alia*, Linda M. Maloney, *"All That God Had Done with Them": The Narration of the Works of God in the Early Christian Community as Described in the Acts of the Apostles*, AUS ser. 7, Theology and Religion 91 (New York: Lang, 1990), *passim*.

40. Charles, *Silencing*, 231–32.

41. Usually assumed to be the time when Acts was written; Lukas would in any event have been familiar with what took place then.

among others. Shelly Matthews notes the prominence of "a common Roman *topos* that linked religious and sexual misconduct as twin perils of the state."[42] Thus the idea of applying sexual innuendo to the activities of "foreign" prophets, seers, and missionaries was by no means far-fetched. Ronald Charles observes that "Paul preached to the jailer; he preached to the 'proper' women, but not to the 'nagging-then-exorcised' nameless slave woman. She is silenced instead."[43]

The last scene of the romance takes place in a prison. Prison scenes are ubiquitous in the Apocryphal Acts, as also in the novels. So in Chariton's *Callirhoe*, Chaireas and his companion are imprisoned by pirates, then sold; after some other laborers stage an escape he is nearly executed; later, Callirhoe is captured but is rescued by Chaireas. In *An Ephesian Tale* both spouses suffer captivity, but only the man, Habrocomes, is imprisoned. The Acts of Paul and Thecla has the sequence of Acts 16: the "adultery" scene leads to Paul's being accused, imprisoned, and beaten (in that order), while an unavailing attempt is made to execute Thecla; from that point on Thecla has all the adventures.

Here in Acts 16:21-34 we instead have an all-male sequence (apart from the presumed but unnamed female members of the jailer's "entire family" in v. 33). Paul and Silas are stripped and beaten with rods, then thrown into prison; the jailer is ordered to keep them secure, and so they are put in "the hole" with their feet in stocks. No problem! The pair take to singing hymns and praying, thus entertaining their fellow prisoners (though in this case neither the missionaries nor the prisoners seem to think that conversion might follow). In Acts (both canonical and apocryphal) the imprisoned believers are models of character; like prophets and sages before them, they pray and sing.[44] The earthquake at midnight[45] shakes the prison's foundations but apparently without bringing down

---

42. Shelly Matthews, *First Converts: Rich Pagan Women and the Rhetoric of Mission in Early Judaism and Christianity* (Stanford, CA: Stanford University Press, 2001), 10–15; at 10.

43. Charles, *Silencing*, 231. Moreover, "as far as the narrative goes, [she] did not enter into any salvation offered by Paul and his people. A Roman soldier and his household will (16:33)" (236).

44. E.g., Daniel (Dan 3:16-24 LXX); Joseph (T. Jos. 8:5); Socrates (Plato, *Phaid.* 60d). See Standhartinger, "Better Ending," 237n64.

45. A favored time for rescues (cf. Acts 5:29; 9:24; 12:6; 27:27, but also Philostratus, *Vit. Apoll.* 8:30); cf. Pervo, *Acts*, 411n95. Philippi was, in fact, all but destroyed by an earthquake in 619 CE, but there is no record, or evidence, of a severe quake in the first century.

the walls; only the doors fly open and all chains are unfastened. We expect an immediate exodus of everyone inside (and so does the jailer), but Paul and Silas are more like Chaireas and his friend in *Callirhoe*;[46] they remain where they are—and in this case they somehow persuade the other prisoners to remain as well, which seems more than improbable, but verisimilitude is not a priority for Lukas at this point. After all, how does it happen that an earthquake has not awakened anyone in Philippi except the jailer?[47]

The jailer's response echoes the promise of the mantic woman: "These men . . . proclaim to you a way of salvation" (v. 17). Like Lydia, now the jailer is baptized (after having demonstrated, by washing the wounds of his former captives, that he is a changed man), and so is his family.[48] A meal then follows (cf. 10:48),[49] but the missionaries' stay with the jailer and his family is cut short the following morning.

46. 4.2. Here some of those chained together escape but are captured and executed, whereupon those who remain (having slept through the escape?) are ordered crucified.

47. This is one of the points at which exegetes have often pointed out strong parallels with Euripides's *Bacchae*: "Chains fell off their feet, just dropping on their own. Keys opened doors not turned by human hands" (*Bacchae* 557–59). In that case the persons freed were Bacchic women! But while doors popping open is not improbable, chains falling off is, and so what we are looking at here is a miracle story: the prayers and hymns of the missionaries have brought liberation.

48. It seems probable that, since the "entire household" rejoices with the jailer at his becoming a believer (v. 34), we are to suppose that they all believed as well.

49. Matthews, *First Converts*, 88–89, observes that this is the first instance of Paul's being *said* to share a table with a gentile (convert); readers must infer for themselves that "staying at Lydia's house" involved eating!

Acts 16:35–40

Denouement

The closing scene appears somewhat anticlimactic: after having beaten and imprisoned the missionaries, why do the magistrates order them released without explanation (to them or to the audience)? Is it because of the earthquake? Nothing is said about it. It is as if the whole scene in verses 25-34 had never happened; it is a foreign body within the text. Consider that in verse 34 Paul and Silas are in the jailer's house, sharing a meal, but in verse 36 he reports their release to them by saying: "come out now and go in peace." Had he chained them in the depths of the prison again after breakfast?

It appears that, as we observed above, the prison scene was needed to round off the "Philippi novel," for which reason Paul's claim to Romanness, and thus the release, had to wait until after it had been told. The placement also adds weight to Lukas's point in this chapter: that ethnicity is no barrier to following Jesus. Paul is both Ἰουδαῖος and Ῥωμαίους.[1] So (apparently) is Silas. Furthermore, Philippi's proud "Romanness" need not be threatened by the presence of multiethnic persons and their participation in its civic and religious life.

Paul's apparent and sudden claim to be a "Roman citizen" is startling, and yet it has been accepted by readers and students of Acts over the centuries, despite the fact that in neither the extant Pauline nor the pseudo-Pauline letters does the word "Roman" even appear. "Rome" is referred to as a place, nothing more.

---

1. This corresponds to Lukas's interpretation of the missionary's dual name: "Saul, also known as Paul" (13:9).

³⁵When morning came, the magistrates sent the police, saying, "Let those men go." ³⁶And the jailer reported the message to Paul, saying, "The magistrates sent word to let you go; therefore come out now and go in peace." ³⁷But Paul replied, "They have beaten us in public, uncondemned, men who are Roman [citizens], and have thrown us into prison; and now are they going to discharge us in secret? Certainly not! Let them come and take us out themselves." ³⁸The police reported these words to the magistrates, and they were afraid when they heard that they were Roman citizens; ³⁹so they came and apologized to them. And they took them out and asked them to leave the city. ⁴⁰After leaving the prison they went to Lydia's home; and when they had seen and encouraged the brothers and sisters there, they departed.

Did Paul Claim to Be a Roman Citizen?

Nowhere in his extant letters does Paul lay claim to Roman citizenship; he does not even claim to be a native of Tarsus, yet both are asserted quite forcefully in Acts. Or are they? The association with Tarsus may well be traditional, though not necessarily as used in Acts. The assumption that Paul claimed Roman citizenship, however, appears to rest on a (wishful?) misreading of Acts.

Reading a modern translation like the NRSV, we find Paul claiming Roman citizenship at Acts 16:37; 22:25, 27-28; in 16:38; 22:26, 29; 23:27 other characters in the story make that assertion about him. At *every point* where the text reads "Roman," the NRSV inserts "citizen." But as

Eric Barreto has most recently pointed out,² that is not what the original document says. At 16:37 the text says ἀνθρώπους Ῥωμαίους ὑπάρχοντας, "people who are Romans," and the same is true (in the singular) at 22:25 (ἄνθρωπον Ῥωμαῖον); only at 21:39 does Paul claim to be a "citizen" (πολίτης), not of Rome but of Tarsus. In fact, his statement there is "I am a Jew, from Tarsus in Cilicia, a citizen of an important city."³ Likewise in 22:26-28 the dialogue actually reads:

" 'What are you about to do? This man is a Roman.' The tribune came and asked Paul, 'Tell me, are you a Roman?' And he said, 'Yes.' The tribune answered, 'It cost me a large sum of money to get my citizenship [πολιτείαν].' Paul said, 'But I was born so.' Immediately those who

2. Eric D. Barreto, *Ethnic Negotiations*, WUNT 294 (Tübingen: Mohr Siebeck, 2010), 139–80.
3. The AV translation "no mean city" was more accurate as well as more eloquent.

were about to examine him drew back from him; and the tribune also was afraid, for he realized that Paul was a Roman and that he had bound him."

The last such statement is at 23:27, and again Paul is called Ῥωμαῖός, not πολίτης. Interestingly, the Vulgate followed the Greek text except in 22:26, 29, and the Authorized Version never uses "citizen" except where Paul claims to be a citizen of Tarsus.

Acts	Greek	Vulgate (Jerome)	Authorized Version (KJV)	NRSV	Speaker
16:37	ἀνθρώπους Ῥωμαίους	*homines romanos*	Romans	Roman citizens	Paul
16:38	Ῥωμαῖοί	*Romani*	Romans	Roman citizens	Narrator
22:25	ἄνθρωπον Ῥωμαῖον	*hominem romanum*	Roman	Roman citizen	Paul
22:26	ἄνθρωπος Ῥωμαῖός	*civis romanus*	Roman	Roman citizen	Centurion
22:27	Ῥωμαῖος	*Romanus*	Roman	Roman citizen	Tribune
22:29	Ῥωμαῖός	*civis romanus*	Roman	Roman citizen	Narrator
23:27	Ῥωμαῖός	*Romanus*	Roman	Roman citizen	Claudius Lysias

Certainly Lukas knew that Paul never claimed in his letters to be a Roman citizen, and so he never has him say it; it is equally certain that he wanted his readers to infer it, especially from "But I was born so."[4] Such an assumption suits the plot very well, but modern focus on it subverts Lukas's larger point: that Paul (and Silas) were both Jews and Romans, people of mixed ethnicity but loyal both to Judaism and Jewish nationality and to Rome and its governing institutions. They were "hybrids," and hybridity was as appropriate for followers of Jesus as was a supposedly "pure" ethnicity.

4. The sequence, as noted, is actually that the tribune says he paid a lot for his πολιτεία and Paul's "but I was born so" refers to his own πολιτεία, i.e., as a citizen of Tarsus. Being "freeborn" was also one of the necessary preconditions for citizenship; it is possible the tribune was not born free and had to purchase an exemption.

By pointing out that he is Ῥωμαῖος, Paul undercuts the enslavers' accusation that he and Silas are disrupting civil order "because they are Jews" (Ἰουδαῖοι ὑπάρχοντες). He thus refutes the accusers' charge that the missionaries are disrupting the Roman colonial life of Philippi, and the reason for their wrath is implicitly (though not explicitly) laid bare: they are greedy enslavers. Their greed condemns them; their former slave, on the other hand, having been "freed from her infirmity," her "bondage to Satan" (cf. Luke 8:2; 13:12), has the opportunity to become part of the new movement if she can somehow escape the clutches of her enslavers.[5] The missionaries themselves could have collected funds to free the enslaved girl, but nothing is said of that. She is instrumental to the story, but she is "freed" only from what makes her valuable to others; her new status leaves her worse off than ever.

Having thus cast scorn on the enslavers and forced the city magistrates to come to *him* to beg forgiveness for their actions, Paul agrees to leave Philippi on condition that he be protected by an escort. A farewell visit to Lydia and her household[6] rounds off the apocryphal romance, and the missionaries depart—at least, Paul and Silas do (cf. 17:1). The narrative focus is on Paul, and his associates come and go as suits the narrative.

A final note on Lydia: the one point on which I differ strongly with Ronald Charles[7] concerns his characterization of Lydia as purely a "listener." "Lydia," he writes, "behaves herself well within the bounds of expected societal norms."[8] Not so, in my reading! Lydia is a breaker of all manner of social and religious boundaries, as we have seen in the previous chapter, and she is anything but silent: "When she and her household were baptized" she speaks:[9] "If you have judged me to be faithful to the Lord, come and stay at my home" (16:15). Both her words and her actions prove her fidelity and status, "and she prevailed." She is anything but "the good/ideal woman, the true Pauline line" whom "the

---

5. Throughout Acts, Lukas shows nothing but contempt for "pagan" cults and practices.

6. NRSV "brothers and sisters" for ἀδελφοὺς, "brothers," clearly illustrates the effects of androcentric language. The likelihood that the community of the Way in Lydia's house was made up solely (or even primarily) of "brothers" is zero.

7. Ronald Charles, *The Silencing of Slaves in Early Jewish and Christian Texts*, Routledge Studies in the Early Christian World (London: Routledge, 2020), chap. 5.5, "The Tale of Three Women."

8. Ibid., 239, 231.

9. Lydia appears, in fact, to be the only woman in Acts who speaks on her own initiative.

narrative uses . . . and then discards," one of "the 'proper' women."[10] He is right, however, to quote Maia Kotrosits's summary: "As a diasporic story, Acts charts the meager and finite agencies, strange bedfellows and, most poignantly, the incessant journeying from romance to disillusionment that comprise imperial and colonial life."[11] That life, as original hearers and readers of Acts would have known from experience, was lived not only by males.

10. Charles, *Silencing*, 240.

11. Maia Kotrosits, *Rethinking Early Christian Identity: Affect, Violence, and Belonging* (Minneapolis: Fortress, 2015), 107.

Acts 17:1-34

Ascending through Macedonia to the Areopagus

The next stop on the missionary tour is Thessalonica, the capital city of Macedonia and two to four times the size of Philippi. It seems on the surface that Paul and his company will repeat the same pattern, already established on the first missionary journey, by going first to the synagogue and remaining there until expelled (cf. 13:5 [Salamis]; 13:14 [Antioch in Pisidia]; 14:1 [Iconium]), but in fact Paul will henceforth use the synagogue merely as a starting point; his real aim is the public square, where he will have a larger gentile audience. In this way Lukas accommodates his narrative both to what his audience knew about Paul from his letters and to his own desire to depict the openness of the Jesus movement to the gentiles, especially those who identify as not only Greek but also Roman.

We need to appreciate the political and social environment within which the mission is transpiring. The provinces of Macedonia (represented in Acts by Philippi, Thessalonica, and Beroea) and Achaia (represented by Athens and Corinth) were in competition for prestige and status within the Roman Empire. Augustus, on gaining control of the nascent empire, had reserved to himself the governance of the outlying regions (including Judea and Syria) but returned the internal provinces (which included Asia as well as Achaia and Macedonia) to the jurisdiction of the Roman

Acts 17:1-34

17:1After Paul and Silas had passed through Amphipolis and Apollonia, they came to Thessalonica, where there was a synagogue of the Jews. 2And Paul went in, as was his custom, and on three sabbath days argued with them from the scriptures, 3explaining and proving that it was necessary for the Messiah to suffer and to rise from the dead, and saying, "This is the Messiah, Jesus whom I am proclaiming to you." 4Some of them were persuaded and joined Paul and Silas, as did a great many of the devout Greeks and not a few of the leading women. 5But the Jews became jealous, and with the help of some ruffians in the marketplaces they formed a mob and set the city in an uproar. While they were searching for Paul and Silas to bring them out to the assembly, they attacked Jason's house. 6When they could not find them, they dragged Jason and some believers before the city authorities, shouting, "These people who have been turning the world upside down have come here also, 7and Jason has entertained them as guests. They are all acting contrary to the decrees of the emperor, saying that there is another king named Jesus." 8The people and the city officials were disturbed when they heard this, 9and after they had taken bail from Jason and the others, they let them go.

10That very night the believers sent Paul and Silas off to Beroea; and when they arrived, they went to the Jewish synagogue. 11These Jews were more receptive than those in Thessalonica, for they welcomed the message very eagerly and examined the scriptures every day to see whether these things were so. 12Many of them therefore believed, including not a few Greek women and

Senate. These "pacified provinces" enjoyed a much greater degree of control over their own resources and governance and did not have to suffer the presence of Roman legions. Tiberius took back control of Macedonia and Achaia as a means to putting down revolts in the north, but Claudius restored their status as senatorial provinces in 44 CE. There must still have been some jitters among the commercial and governing classes when Paul showed up.[1]

For a long time Paul has been compared (or rather, contrasted) by scholars with traveling "philosophers" and charlatans seeking gain. But considering that the areas he was visiting enjoyed only a veneer of autonomy and, as Tiberius's action illustrates, could be deprived of their rights by Roman authority for any reason or none, they might well

1. This description relies on Antoinette Clark Wire, *2 Corinthians*, WCS 48 (Collegeville, MN: Liturgical Press, 2019), 26–27.

men of high standing. [13]But when the Jews of Thessalonica learned that the word of God had been proclaimed by Paul in Beroea as well, they came there too, to stir up and incite the crowds. [14]Then the believers immediately sent Paul away to the coast, but Silas and Timothy remained behind. [15]Those who conducted Paul brought him as far as Athens; and after receiving instructions to have Silas and Timothy join him as soon as possible, they left him.

[16]While Paul was waiting for them in Athens, he was deeply distressed to see that the city was full of idols. [17]So he argued in the synagogue with the Jews and the devout persons, and also in the marketplace every day with those who happened to be there. [18]Also some Epicurean and Stoic philosophers debated with him. Some said, "What does this babbler want to say?" Others said, "He seems to be a proclaimer of foreign divinities." (This was because he was telling the good news about Jesus and the resurrection.) [19]So they took him and brought him to the Areopagus and asked him, "May we know what this new teaching is that you are presenting? [20]It sounds rather strange to us, so we would like to know what it means." [21]Now all the Athenians and the foreigners living there would spend their time in nothing but telling or hearing something new.

[22]Then Paul stood in front of the Areopagus and said, "Athenians, I see how extremely religious you are in every way. [23]For as I went through the city and looked carefully at the objects of your worship, I found among them an altar with the inscription, 'To an unknown god.' What therefore you worship as unknown, this I proclaim to you. [24]The

have been inclined to look with suspicion on anyone proposing himself or herself as a "traveling dignitary." Such itinerants might well be bent on exploitation when they proposed an agenda of their own for the provinces they visited. What holds for the governing and commercial classes was all the more true for the representatives of diaspora Judaism in those places.[2]

Willie James Jennings gives us the best direction for reading Acts 17, showing how, at Thessalonica, Paul and Silas invade the sacred space of Jewish people already confronted with the tensions of diaspora existence. They are struggling against the threat of identity loss and a fear of infidelity toward Israel's God as they accommodate themselves to their surroundings. Paul tries to batter these troubled people into submission with words; in three Sabbaths in the synagogue he does no works of

2. See ibid., 28, with source references.

Acts 17:1-34 (cont.)

God who made the world and everything in it, he who is Lord of heaven and earth, does not live in shrines made by human hands, ^{25}nor is he served by human hands, as though he needed anything, since he himself gives to all mortals life and breath and all things. ^{26}From one ancestor he made all nations to inhabit the whole earth, and he allotted the times of their existence and the boundaries of the places where they would live, ^{27}so that they would search for God and perhaps grope for him and find him—though indeed he is not far from each one of us. ^{28}For 'In him we live and move and have our being'; as even some of your own poets have said,

'For we too are his offspring.'

^{29}Since we are God's offspring, we ought not to think that the deity is like gold, or silver, or stone, an image formed by the art and imagination of mortals. ^{30}While God has overlooked the times of human ignorance, now he commands all people everywhere to repent, ^{31}because he has fixed a day on which he will have the world judged in righteousness by a man whom he has appointed, and of this he has given assurance to all by raising him from the dead."

^{32}When they heard of the resurrection of the dead, some scoffed; but others said, "We will hear you again about this." ^{33}At that point Paul left them. ^{34}But some of them joined him and became believers, including Dionysius the Areopagite and a woman named Damaris, and others with them.

healing or exorcism. It is all talk. Jennings writes: "We must never glorify argument as the engine that moves the thinking of a community forward. Such a way of thinking reflects a profoundly chivalric and masculine vision of progress where truth wins out through combat and violence, and in the end power begets more power."[3]

Lukas is convinced that the message of Jesus will (or should!) resolve all ethnic conflicts and shows little sensitivity to the tensions inherent in communities in which not all members, or even most, belong to the privileged, educated (male) elite. He seems convinced that the new form of Judaism that his character Paul preaches will overcome Greek and Roman prejudice against Jews (a prejudice that was especially virulent and mortally dangerous at the time Acts was written). He is blind to "how a gospel vision of humanity might be eclipsed by the desire to overcome opposition."[4]

3. Willie James Jennings, *Acts*, Belief: A Theological Commentary on the Bible (Louisville: Westminster John Knox, 2017), 170. In this vein see also C. Kavin Rowe, *World Upside Down: Reading Acts in the Graeco-Roman Age* (Oxford: Oxford University Press, 2009).
4. Jennings, *Acts*, 171.

The action from now on implicitly moves more and more outside the "house" that has been the center of the Movement heretofore. In the household, whether Jewish, Greek, or Roman, women were always part of the gathering, sometimes as leaders, sometimes as hosts, always as active participants. The public sphere belonged to men—especially in Greek society, much less so in Egypt and in Asia Minor, the region now left behind. (Consider what was said above about Thyatira.) Lukas underscores the change by emphasizing that "a great many of the devout Greeks and not a few of the leading women" were attracted to Paul's teaching (17:4). "Leading women" must be understood also to be Greeks and members of a class in which women had some access to the public sphere as well as control of dwellings suitable for housing communities of Jesus-followers. Lukas takes it for granted that his audience knows how such house-communities formed in the wake of missionaries' preaching, but here the action is still public: Paul's opponents are depicted as "jealous" people who resort to collecting "ruffians" from the streets to use against the missionaries.

The mob in Thessalonica attacks the house where they believe Paul and his companions are staying, but the missionaries are not to be found so they seize the householder, Jason, and a few other "believers" instead and haul them before the magistrates to answer for the charges laid against Paul. "Turning the world upside down" has become a famous phrase, but as Richard Pervo observes,[5] it deprives the words of their intended political significance: the only other occurrence of the verb ἀναστατόω in Acts is at 21:38 in reference to "the Egyptian" who supposedly "stirred up a revolt." Creating a revolution and making Jesus equal or superior to the emperor were capital crimes; Lukas uses such charges to emphasize the supposedly dramatic and universal effect of the missionaries' preaching. But he wants to get on with the story, so (as so often) money settles the matter: Jason and "the others" (the other believers? the mob? the instigators of the riot?) have to post bond. After that, under cover of darkness, Paul and Silas are smuggled out of town.

The pair immediately surface in Beroea, a town about a week's journey to the west and far more auspicious for their work. The Jews of Beroea are a studious lot; evidently they are highly literate, and no wonder: they include "not a few Greek *women and men* of high standing" (v. 12)[6]—even though the initial reference of the statement is "these Jews"

5. Richard I. Pervo, *Acts*, Hermeneia (Minneapolis: Fortress, 2009), 420n23.
6. Or are only the women "of high standing"? The Greek is γυναικῶν τῶν εὐσχημόνων καὶ ἀνδρῶν οὐκ ὀλίγοι (women of high standing and men not a few).

(v. 11). Perhaps the synagogue at Beroea is the intellectual center of the town and attracts an ecumenical congregation. Of course, the villains from Thessalonica are hot on the heels of the miscreants, so Paul is again bundled out of town—this time alone. Silas and Timothy (who suddenly resurfaces) remain behind. Paul is shipped to Athens and sends word by his escort that the men left behind should join him "as soon as possible," which turns out to be not until he reaches Corinth.

For Lukas's purposes Paul is in Athens only to give a speech and be arraigned before the council of the Areopagus. There is no missionary purpose; Athens, the summit of learning, is a box to be checked. Over the years this speech (composed, of course, by Lukas in and for his own time) has been read as favorable to Rome, or as subversive of empire, or simply as a critique of idolatry. Most recently Drew J. Strait has interpreted the speech in its cultural and political context in Hellenistic Judaism[7] and in dialogue with other scholars seeking to locate the Lukan Paul (and especially the Areopagus speech)[8] in the politics of Paul's time or, more properly, Lukas's. In concluding his book Strait summarizes three possible descriptors for the speech's political attitude.

The first of these comes from Karl Galinsky,[9] who calls the speech's tone "*supra*-imperial," a "critique of any object of divine and/or royal power that distracts the auditor from acknowledging the 'superior' and 'surpassing' Lordship of the resurrected and ascended Christ."[10] This also suits Lukas's apologetic purposes in that he alludes to Greek philosophers in order to exalt the crucified Lord above all Roman religions. A second descriptor, from Anathea Portier-Young, is "counter-cosmology." In this view the speech is a direct confrontation between two opposing

---

7. Drew J. Strait, *Hidden Criticism of the Angry Tyrant in Early Judaism and the Acts of the Apostles* (Lanham, MD: Lexington Books/Fortress Academic, 2019).

8. Anathea E. Portier-Young, *Apocalypse against Empire: Theologies of Resistance in Early Judaism* (Grand Rapids: Eerdmans, 2011); Rowe, *World Upside Down*; Ramsay Macmullen, *Enemies of the Roman Order: Treason, Unrest, and Alienation in the Empire* (London: Routledge, 1992); Neil Elliot, "The 'Patience of the Jews': Strategies of Resistance and Accommodation to Imperial Cultures," in *Pauline Conversations in Context: Essays in Honor of Calvin J. Roetzel*, ed. Janice Capel Anderson, Philip Sellew, and Claudia Setzer, JSNTSup 221 (Sheffield: Sheffield Academic, 2002), 32–41. See also Todd C. Penner, *In Praise of Christian Origins: Stephen and the Hellenists in Lukan Apologetic Historiography*, Emory Studies in Early Christianity 10 (New York: T&T Clark, 2004).

9. Karl Galinsky, "The Cult of the Roman Emperor: Uniter or Divider?," in *Rome and Religion: A Cross-Disciplinary Dialogue on the Imperial Cult*, ed. Jeffrey Brodd and Jonathan L. Reed (Atlanta: SBL, 2012), 1–22.

10. Cited in Strait, *Hidden Criticism*, 355.

cosmological positions: that the cosmos is ruled by Jesus Messiah, crucified and ascended, or that it is under the rule of Satan, gods, *and imperial authorities*. This position also takes into account certain "noncultic objects of resistance," as when the new community's cosmology ran athwart that of the ruling elite on issues of social status and economic redistribution (as Lukas describes the practices of the early Jerusalem community).[11]

The third descriptor Strait offers is called "alter-cultural," placing the conflict between the Jesus movement and the ruling powers on the level of traditional cultural values, texts, rituals, and ideologies. Summarizing, Strait writes: "The political attitude of the Areopagus speech can be described, then, as a counter-cosmology, wherein the *Weltanschauung* of early Christianity confronts Greco-Roman conceptions of euergetism [benevolence or benefaction], monotheism, and cosmic hierarchy with an alter-cultural vision of politics and religion."[12] Yet he concludes that Lukas's strategy in the Areopagus speech has to be called "allusive." Lukas, he says, writes "with a paintbrush," but the rulers (as Lukas probably hopes) will perceive only "shades of grey." The audience Lukas seeks, the "active readers," will be able to enter into the narrative to identify Athens's idols for what they really are.

Reading Acts 17 through a feminist critical lens, Hannah Lents gives us another view, directly relevant to our study, of what the episode would have meant for Lukas's audience and what it means for us.

Third Space in Paul's Areopagus Speech

The feminist critical lens invites interpretive entry into Paul's Acts 17 Areopagus speech at the very end, with "a woman named Damaris." Feminist criticism considers what in Paul's speech attracted her to faith in Jesus. A postcolonial framework recognizes her as a doubly colonized person marked by her status as both a Roman subject living in Athens and a woman under Greco-Roman patriarchy. Thus Damaris invites the reader to engage the text as Musa Dube's "hesitant traveller, an alert companion" who is attentive to unequal power.[13]

11. See Portier-Young, *Apocalypse against Empire*, 383; Strait's description is in *Hidden Criticism*, 355–56.

12. Strait, *Hidden Criticism*, 356.

13. Musa W. Dube, "Batswakwa: Which Traveller Are You (John 1:1-18)?," in *The Bible in Africa: Transactions, Trajectories and Trends*, ed. Gerald O. West and Musa W. Dube (Leiden: Brill, 2000), 150–62, at 157.

If we attend to Damaris's colonized perspective, Paul's Areopagus speech emerges as Third Space, a moment that creates the possibility of radically unmarked status by breaking down the subjugator/subjugated binary. After introducing Third Space, I demonstrate how the speech interacts with Greco-Roman concepts of euergetism and ancestry. I then show how the Areopagus speech first challenges and then reinscribes these norms through Third Space, highlighting how reading as Damaris's alert companion reveals unequal power.

Third Space, as theorized by postcolonial literature scholar Homi Bhabha, serves to suspend normal power relationships to create a space where the speaker and audience are equal conversation partners. This mutually unmarked status emerges when the speaker fuses distinctive pasts imagined by different communities to construct a single, shared human past: Thus "to dwell 'in the beyond' is . . . to be part of a revisionary time, a return to the present to redescribe our cultural contemporaneity; to reinscribe our human, historic commonality. . . . [T]he intervening space 'beyond' becomes a space of intervention in the here and now."[14] This constructed common past creates space for change in the present. On equal footing, conversation partners can envision a future of collaborative possibilities grounded in the altered present. Third Space, as an in-between space, is impossible to maintain. It is a moment that quickly collapses into itself and reinscribes extant power by imagining alternate structures. Paul's Areopagus speech reconstructs normative power relations in the Roman Empire by recasting God as the head of a heavenly empire.[15]

The Roman Empire is the normative power structure that Paul seeks to deconstruct for his audience. The system of euergetism, or benefaction, had characterized power relationships between individuals, institutions, and cities in the Aegean before the Roman Empire. Elites donated money, buildings, and gifts to demonstrate the giver's power over the receiver. The surplus resources implied by the gift ingratiate the recipient into a position of subordination. The Roman emperor assumed the role of universal benefactor following the conquest of the Greek East. Imperial cults concretely illustrate this ideology. Emperors, their families, and Rome (personified by the goddess Roma) provided the peace and security necessary

---

14. Homi Bhabha, *The Location of Culture* (New York: Routledge, 1994), 10.

15. For a discussion of how the historical Paul used imperial patronage in his rhetoric in Romans see Neil Elliott, *The Arrogance of Nations: Reading Romans in the Shadow of Empire* (Minneapolis: Fortress, 2008), 44–47.

for daily life to operate in an orderly fashion.[16] Thus they received thank-offerings and the right to impose laws, taxes, and military might on the dependent provinces to ensure the maintenance of cosmic order. Imperial subjecthood permeated all aspects of life. Every home contributed imperial taxes, neighbors engaged in disputes might appeal to the Roman governor, and the emperor could deploy his armies to deflect barbarians or quell provincial dissent. The communities Paul addressed could define themselves by their location in this power structure.

Ancient Mediterranean people also used ancestry to claim power and distinction over other groups. Thus Greeks, Romans, and Judeans kept records of their family trees as well as strictly regulating customs and laws regarding the legitimacy of children and inheritance.[17] The Roman emperors exploited these cultural values by constructing divine lineages for themselves. The Julio-Claudian emperors traced their lineage from the goddess Aphrodite, and the poet Virgil wrote his epic *Aeneid* to cast Romans as descendants of exiled Trojans. Ancestry was a powerful tool for constructing barriers and bridges between peoples.

Acts 17 identifies Jews, Epicureans, Stoics, and Areopagites as specific communities whom Paul addressed during his gospel proclamation in Athens. Each located itself within the systems of benefaction and ancestry within the Roman Empire. As the story progresses, so does the social status of groups Paul encounters. Diaspora Jews had marginalized status and often occupied ambiguous positions with respect to imperial patronage and traditional ancestry. They only recognized divine benefaction from their God, although they accommodated imperial euergetism by praying to their God for the health of the emperor. Their ancestor Abraham remained completely outside of Greco-Roman lineages.[18] Epicureans and Stoics might occupy several positions within the euergetism system, and their philosophies encouraged benefaction. Both defined their communities by descent from intellectual ancestors. Still, their lifestyles

---

16. L. Michael White, *From Jesus to Christianity: How Four Generations of Visionaries and Storytellers Created the New Testament and Christian Faith* (New York: HarperCollins, 2004), 49–50.

17. Lin Foxhall, *Studying Gender in Classical Antiquity* (New York: Cambridge University Press, 2013), 45–67, esp. 46–50.

18. Some Jewish apologists, however, integrated other Old Testament figures into those lineages. For example, Josephus claimed that Moses was the intellectual father of Greek philosophers (*C. Ap.* 2.168).

and commitment to alternative lineages occasionally resulted in banishments and executions. Areopagites received imperial benefactions on behalf of Athens, and they themselves bestowed gifts on cities, local institutions, and individuals. Admittance to serve on the Areopagus council required ancestral purity; only free Athenian citizens descended from three generations of free fathers qualified for office. Paul had to transcend these boundaries to proclaim the gospel message successfully.

The author of Acts strategically employs the ἀγορά, translated in the NRSV as "marketplace," as the setting to introduce Paul's transgression of group boundaries. Acts 17 presents Paul's primary audience as "those who happened to be in the marketplace." The marketplace gathered all Athenians together.[19] Therefore locating Paul in the marketplace broadens his audience to the entire city of Athens, composed of Jews, philosophers, Areopagites, and all other inhabitants and visitors. Despite the crowds that populated the marketplace, individuals still interacted with each other as prescribed by their position in the imperial hierarchy.

Consider Damaris: whatever her socioeconomic status, her actions were restricted by her gender. She might worship at any number of the marketplace's temples, but not as a priest; she might buy and sell goods, but elite men far removed from production regulated prices; she might stroll through the square, but rarely alone. The marketplace both invited those gathered to commune with each other and reinforced social boundaries. Paul's speech activates the possibility of a marketplace community without such limitations.

Having set Paul's audience as diverse marketplace frequenters, the author places the trial in an in-between space. In the story world a woman named Damaris shares the same space as the Areopagite Dionysius, and an itinerant preacher from Tarsus is a powerful traveler who can assert his right to speak among his hosts.[20] The language describing the occasion for the speech is ambiguous and the ordinary functioning of social relations is not operative in this scene. Unnamed persons bring Paul before the highest court, yet they seem to ask him to explain his teaching rather than demanding a criminal defense.

19. Sara Mills discusses how architectural space both regulates social relationships and offers arenas for resistance and disruption: "Gender and Colonial Space," in *Feminist Postcolonial Theory: A Reader*, ed. Reina Lewis and Sara Mills (Edinburgh: Edinburgh University Press, 2010), 692–719, at 705.

20. Musa Dube considers the power relationships at work in traveling in "Batswakwa: Which Traveller Are You?"

Elite Athenian men invite a Jewish man to explain his image of God; this might be typical behavior for philosophers, but not for government officials. Paul's first utterance continues, gently, to dislodge his audience from the normative power structure.

Paul begins his speech by subtly undermining Athenian claims to correct worship. He first recognizes the elite status of his audience by addressing them as Ἄνδρες Ἀθηναῖοι, or "Athenian men." Indeed, Areopagites were exclusively men with citizenship in Athens. He observes that they are "extremely religious in every way." The Greek word translated as "religious," δεισίδαιμον, is not necessarily a compliment. It can mean either positive piety or negative superstition, depending on the context. As indicated above, the context of this speech is ambiguous; Paul is neither accuser nor accused. The use of δεισίδαιμον at this moment functions to unsettle his listeners' self-assurance and is both an accolade of Athenian piety and a condemnation of their misplaced worship. Even the next sentences do not characterize the Athenians as superstitious, however, but maintain their in-betweenness.

Acts 17:23 further disrupts this audience's self-understanding by attributing their worship to a God revealed to them by Paul, an itinerant foreign Jewish preacher. The author characterizes Paul as transgressing cultural boundaries when he relates that in his exploration of their city he encountered an altar dedicated "to an unknown god." In the next verse he reveals that this unknown god is the God of Israel. Thus by the beginning of verse 24 the Athenians remain δεισίδαιμον, both pious and superstitious. They are superstitious because they worship many gods but pious because one of these gods is the true God. Having unsettled their religious position, Paul then dismantles the Athenians' political position.

Paul's description of the true God in 17:24-25 reconstructs the imperial benefaction system. He reveals that God is the greatest benefactor because the Deity created all things and reigns over this creation independent of humanity. Although Paul's speech directly contrasts his God with those of the Athenians he also implicitly contrasts this God with the emperor. The emperor and other gods must live in stone buildings and eat what their subjects produce, but the one God does not require such support. Therefore Israel's God alone bestows pure benefactions; because God requires nothing, humans can never put God in their debt. The construction of humanity as equally indebted to God flattens the Greco-Roman hierarchy. Third Space finally comes to fruition in the next moment when Paul erases ancestry.

Third Space erupts into Paul's speech with the utterance

"From one ancestor he made." The Greek literally translates "from one he made." The emperor claimed ancestry from Aphrodite, Jews from Abraham, philosophers from their teachers, and Areopagites from pure Athenians. Paul makes these lineages irrelevant. This ancestor is nationless, genderless, classless—lacking all identity markers that condition social relationships. If all descend from one, there can be no pure Athenian stock to fill Areopagite seats, no reason to create intellectual lineages, no people exclusively worshiping God, no person more divine than the rest. A woman named Damaris could occupy this space with as much right and dignity as Areopagites, Jews, and philosophers. She could imagine a life unconstrained by her gendered status. But only for a moment.

The next words, "all nations," collapse the Third Space. Entering the in-between and beyond is always temporary. "From one ancestor he made all nations to inhabit the whole earth, and he allotted the times of their existence and the boundaries of the places where they would live." Perhaps all people descend from one, but they descend in closed-off groups with boundaries ordained by God. An "alert companion" of Damaris hears that the radical equality suggested by descent from one is instantly resigned to a world governed by natural divisions.

Paul explains that God intended these divisions to foster the peoples' search for the divine. Incongruously, the divisions prove his earlier claim in 17:29 that human artistry does not form God.

The claim that God is not made of gold or silver casts Athenians as superstitiously, rather than piously, δεισίδαιμον and serves to locate Paul's audience as thorough outsiders to God's people. To become insiders they must repent: their accidental worship of the true God no longer gives them in-between status but fully defines them as Other. His final statement, the closest Paul comes to naming Jesus, promises judgment, not benefaction. The result recasts the Roman Empire as the kingdom of God. God replaces the emperor as the ultimate judge who will divide humanity into those who have and those who have not obtained citizenship in the kingdom.

Damaris felt compelled by Paul's words to become one of the few Athenian believers. Why? The speech is explicitly addressed to men, ἄνδρες ἀθηναῖοι. The emergence of Third Space, however, erases gendered distinction. In the moments when Paul suspends normal social order Damaris glimpses herself outside of patriarchy. As for what exactly such a life would look like, Paul says nothing beyond equal dependence on divine benefaction. Third Space opens possibilities and changes the present. Damaris, accepting the vague promise of possibility, becomes an agent of change through her choice to follow Paul, perhaps as a "hesitant traveller" seeking the promises of Third Space.

Damaris's choice of discipleship is closed to further analysis. The author of Acts invoked womanhood when it suited him, for his rhetorical purposes. It would be disappointing, since we opened with the promise of considering a particular woman's perspective, to conclude that this woman is a man's literary device. But that is not the case. Naming Damaris injects women back into the entire chapter, back into Athens. Her name and her womanhood juxtaposed with the name Dionysius and his august male office, that of

Areopagite, force readers to ask where Damaris and her sisters fit into the narrative of Paul's speech. Damaris invites all her companions to notice the reinscription of power in Paul's speech.

None of the named places in Acts 17 comfortably accommodates a woman with interests in philosophy, yet the author names Damaris along with Dionysius "and others with them." She was there. So were her friends, sisters, aunts, cousins, women she knew from shops, and women she had never met. Women inhabited the ancient world, but our male sources (and predominantly male scholarly tradition) write women out of space. Third Space creates a wedge for ancient women to assert themselves into narrative space.

Hannah Lents

Verse 32 ties the story back to 2:12-13,[21] thus again paralleling Paul with Peter. At the same time it looks forward to 23:6-12, linking the scoffers in Athens (presumably Epicureans) with the Sanhedrin in their disbelief in resurrection. The lack of any genuine opposition (and the lack of much interest) reinforces the sneers at Athens and its culture inserted previously ("Now all the Athenians and the foreigners living there would spend their time in nothing but telling or hearing something new," v. 21) and underscores the irony and ambiguity of Paul's opening words ("Athenians, I see how very religious you are in every way," v. 22). Paul, still without his companions, moves on to Corinth.

21. "All were amazed and perplexed, saying to one another, 'What does this mean?' But others sneered and said, 'They are filled with new wine.'" See also the forward link to 28:24 and Paul's Jewish listeners at Rome: "Some were convinced by what he had said, while others refused to believe."

Acts 18:1-28

Prisca and Aquila,
Corinth and Ephesus

Having failed to make much of a mark in Athens, Paul moves on—without explanation, and without Silas and Timothy—to the more prosaic commercial city of Corinth. His usual pattern of synagogue visit, controversy, public preaching, trouble with the law, and departure is framed by a new element: the establishment of a missionary partnership with a couple who were there before him, namely, Prisca and her husband Aquila.[1] Supposedly their partnership begins because Prisca and Aquila work in the textile trade[2] (as do all the artisans Lukas mentions in Acts), but it becomes clear that their primary activity is mission and that they are well-versed in Scripture and in the Way of Jesus.[3]

---

1. The couple were certainly known to most of Lukas's audience, at least through Paul's letters (see Rom 16:3; 1 Cor 16:19; also 2 Tim 4:19) and probably through the memories of their contemporaries in Corinth, Ephesus, and Rome. Paul consistently calls this woman "Prisca," as does 2 Timothy, which is post-Pauline. Lukas has a penchant for using diminutive forms of names: Priscilla for Prisca, Silas for Silvanus. Here it may represent a (vain!) attempt to reduce Prisca to secondary status since she is almost an afterthought at her first appearance in v. 2, but by v. 18 she is in first place, and there she remains (cf. 18:26).

2. The word σκηνοποιός, rendered by NRSV as "tentmakers" in v. 3, connotes more generally "craft with fabrics."

3. "Way of God" (τὴν ὁδὸν τοῦ θεοῦ) in v. 26 has strong textual support and may be original, but it is suspect because Lukas's normal usage is simply "the Way" or "the

Acts 18:1-28

18:1After this Paul left Athens and went to Corinth. 2There he found a Jew named Aquila, a native of Pontus, who had recently come from Italy with his wife Priscilla, because Claudius had ordered all Jews to leave Rome. Paul went to see them, 3and, because he was of the same trade, he stayed with them, and they worked together—by trade they were tentmakers. 4Every sabbath he would argue in the synagogue and would try to convince Jews and Greeks.

5When Silas and Timothy arrived from Macedonia, Paul was occupied with proclaiming the word, testifying to the Jews that the Messiah was Jesus.

6When they opposed and reviled him, in protest he shook the dust from his clothes and said to them, "Your blood be on your own heads! I am innocent. From now on I will go to the Gentiles." 7Then he left the synagogue and went to the house of a man named Titius Justus, a worshiper of God; his house was next door to the synagogue. 8Crispus, the official of the synagogue, became a believer in the Lord, together with all his household; and many of the Corinthians who heard Paul became believers and were baptized. 9One night the Lord said to Paul in a vision, "Do not be afraid, but speak and do not be silent; 10for I

Moving from Macedonia to Achaia and from Thessalonica to Corinth was not calculated to win Paul any friends in the latter place because there was intense rivalry between Corinth and the cities of Macedonia. Paul is therefore fortunate to find shelter in Corinth with an experienced missionary couple. They are diaspora Jews with a wider experience of the Roman world than Paul has. Aquila is said to be a native of Pontus in Asia Minor, which at the time of the action in Acts 18 was a client kingdom of Rome that incorporated Armenia Minor. Aquila, therefore, may have had a mixed ethnicity. By about the time Acts was written, Bithynia-Pontus had become a Roman senatorial province. It is not clear whether Prisca also came from the Black Sea coast or whether she was a native of Rome. Both were members of the Jesus movement at an early date, since according to Acts they were among the Jews expelled from Rome by Claudius for creating an uproar over "Chrestus."[4] This prob-

---

Movement" (ἡ ὁδός): so 9:19; 19:9, 23; 22:4; 24:14, 22. The D-text, as usual, downplays the contributions of women by deleting "Priscilla" here.

4. Suetonius, *Claudius* 25.4. For a discussion of probable dates see Richard I. Pervo, *Acts*, Hermeneia (Minneapolis: Fortress, 2009), 446–47; he rejects the conventional dating to 49. Pervo points out that by no means "all the Jews" were expelled from Rome at any time.

am with you, and no one will lay a hand on you to harm you, for there are many in this city who are my people." [11]He stayed there a year and six months, teaching the word of God among them.

[12]But when Gallio was proconsul of Achaia, the Jews made a united attack on Paul and brought him before the tribunal. [13]They said, "This man is persuading people to worship God in ways that are contrary to the law." [14]Just as Paul was about to speak, Gallio said to the Jews, "If it were a matter of crime or serious villainy, I would be justified in accepting the complaint of you Jews; [15]but since it is a matter of questions about words and names and your own law, see to it yourselves; I do not wish to be a judge of these matters." [16]And he dismissed them from the tribunal. [17]Then all of them seized Sosthenes, the official of the synagogue, and beat him in front of the tribunal. But Gallio paid no attention to any of these things.

[18]After staying there for a considerable time, Paul said farewell to the believers and sailed for Syria, accompanied by Priscilla and Aquila. At Cenchreae he had his hair cut, for he was under a vow. [19]When they reached Ephesus, he left them there, but first he himself went into the synagogue and

ably took place in 41/42 CE. If Prisca and Aquila went directly to Corinth they could have been in residence and preaching the message of the Jesus movement for a minimum of seven or eight years before Paul's arrival.

It is the case, certainly, that we must read this section as one of Lukas's "chronological" compositions, similar to (or patterned on) Luke 2:1-5; 3:1-2. The figure of the proconsul Gallio is inserted as an anchor, though the dates of his proconsulship are obscure to us now. They may fall within a span of years between 49 and 54 or belong to a documented period around the year 52.[5] Either way, it would seem that Prisca and Aquila could have been resident in Corinth for a decade or more when Paul came there.[6] The fact that Paul insists in 1 Corinthians (3:6-8) that he "planted" the Corinthian church does not make it so, and in other places he concedes that he was not the sole founder.[7]

It is very likely that Prisca and Aquila had started a "house church," gathering Jews whom they encountered at their place of business or elsewhere and who were interested in hearing their message. They did

5. See Pervo, *Acts*, excursus "Acts 18 and Chronology," 445–47.

6. Ibid., 445–46; only Paul's "mission to Corinth" counts, it seems.

7. See the rather obscure language (e.g., in 1 Cor 1:12-16) referring to rival factions in Corinth "belonging" to Apollos, Paul, and Cephas.

Acts 18:1-28 (cont.)

had a discussion with the Jews. [20]When they asked him to stay longer, he declined; [21]but on taking leave of them, he said, "I will return to you, if God wills." Then he set sail from Ephesus.

[22]When he had landed at Caesarea, he went up to Jerusalem and greeted the church, and then went down to Antioch. [23]After spending some time there he departed and went from place to place through the region of Galatia and Phrygia, strengthening all the disciples.

[24]Now there came to Ephesus a Jew named Apollos, a native of Alexandria. He was an eloquent man, well-versed in the scriptures. [25]He had been instructed in the Way of the Lord; and he spoke with burning enthusiasm and taught accurately the things concerning Jesus, though he knew only the baptism of John. [26]He began to speak boldly in the synagogue; but when Priscilla and Aquila heard him, they took him aside and explained the Way of God to him more accurately. [27]And when he wished to cross over to Achaia, the believers encouraged him and wrote to the disciples to welcome him. On his arrival he greatly helped those who through grace had become believers, [28]for he powerfully refuted the Jews in public, showing by the scriptures that the Messiah is Jesus.

not undertake to preach in the synagogue, though they may well have attended. They were certainly "practicing" Jews, but they enriched their Judaism and that of others with the message of Jesus. They are continuing the pattern of the church in the house, and in Lukas's story Prisca's role is to emphasize to the audience, once and for all, that the house is the woman's domain and at the same time the true home of the church as Lukas idealizes it. Moreover, as Willie James Jennings has pointed out, we have in Prisca and Aquila a counter-couple to Ananias and Sapphira and an example—the sole example in Acts—of a married pair working in harmony to advance the gospel, a model that authors of the next generation would seek (successfully, in the long run) to erase.

Lukas's established pattern for his depiction of Paul in action is repeated once again: Paul arrives in a new place, goes to the synagogue, preaches, stirs up a riot, then moves on, either to a different base of operations or out of the city entirely.[8] Paul's letters offer a good deal of evidence of his ability to make himself unpopular in many places—as much with the Roman authorities as with his fellow believers—but the pattern is a Lukan creation.

---

8. See, e.g., 9:19-25, 28-30; 13:14-51; 14:1-6; 17:1-10; 19:8-10.

To break the monotony of this model Lukas inserts another comic scene, this time starring the Roman proconsul. Paul, having (as always) made trouble in the synagogue (v. 6), renders himself even more obnoxious by proclaiming "from now on I will go to the Gentiles"—but he doesn't. He moves to a house next door to the synagogue, supposedly belonging to Titius Justus, a "worshiper of God" (σεβομένη τὸν θεόν, the same phrase as was used of Lydia at 16:14), and there he goes on persuading not just any Jews but Crispus, "the official of the synagogue," and his household, as well as "many of the Corinthians"—whether Jews or Hellenes is unspecified.

Evidently unable to dislodge Paul by ordinary means, the synagogue leaders approach the freshly minted proconsul Gallio with their plea, and the comedy plays out. The Roman official has not the slightest interest in the petty affairs of ethnic and religious minorities, especially "words and names and your own law," and dismisses them, whereupon "all of them" turn on Sosthenes, who evidently has replaced Crispus as "official of the synagogue" since Crispus has joined the Movement. Not waiting to move outside, they beat Sosthenes right in front of the bench. Lukas reinforces the point: "Gallio paid no attention to any of these things."

Such scenes were stock elements of Roman comedy and contemporary novels, and Lukas makes the most of this one both for entertainment and to emphasize to any Romans who might have doubts about the Movement that (as far as they are concerned!) it is nothing to worry about, being a purely internal matter among Jews and their hangers-on.

Paul's stay in Corinth is extended "for a considerable time," but we learn nothing of what transpired. Lukas almost certainly knew at least 1 Corinthians and has no interest in reporting what kind of turmoil Paul left in his wake. That it was considerable, and involved many of the Corinthian women, is clear from Antoinette Wire's careful expositions.[9]

The women of the Way in Corinth had developed powerful prophetic gifts. Paul did not appreciate that kind of rivalry, and in his first letter back to Corinth, written from Ephesus, he gave officious commands about what women were and were not allowed to do. It is hard to imagine that he did not realize such wielding of the whip would not be effective, but the reaction to his letter was apparently vehement. Paul had not taken the Corinthian women seriously. It may be that his primary association

9. For a full treatment see Antoinette C. Wire, *The Corinthian Women Prophets: A Reconstruction through Paul's Rhetoric* (Minneapolis: Fortress, 1990) and her *2 Corinthians*, WCS 48 (Collegeville, MN: Liturgical Press, 2019).

with fellow Jews had led him to ignore the cultural milieu from which
local gentiles came: Corinth was a
Roman colony dating back to the
first century BCE; it had an amphi-
theater and other public buildings
displaying scenes from Roman my-
thology, notably Dionysian themes
featuring maenads. David Balch argues that "such Dionysian amphi-
theater art would have been painted
on the domestic walls of Corinthian
domus."[10] Maenads were the pagan
Greek equivalent of female prophets,
and seeing them daily on the walls
of their houses must have furnished
much food for thought on the part of
the women within, mistresses and
enslaved alike.

Dancing Maenad
Metropolitan Museum of Art,
CC BY 2.5.[11]

In his second letter to the Corinthians Paul shows that he is taken aback
and that he will no longer attempt to enforce his "rules." He may have
had good reason to worry: the communities of the Way in Corinth were
evidently "recruiting women and slaves independently of their husbands
and/or masters."[12] In his second letter he shifts to a defensive mode,
describing the hardships he and his fellow missionaries are suffering and
trying to convince the Corinthians that their burgeoning life "in Christ"
and acquisition of higher social status through their prophetic activity
are purchased at the price of his own loss of status—accepting beatings,
for example. He concedes that they are enjoying the fruits of their faith,

10. David L. Balch, "Women Prophets / Maenads Visually Represented in Two
Roman Colonies: Pompeii and Corinth," in *Contested Ethnicities and Images: Studies in
Acts and Art*, WUNT 345 (Tübingen: Mohr Siebeck, 2015), 259–78 , at 259.
11. <https://creativecommons.org/licenses/by /2.5>, via Wikimedia Commons
https://commons.wikimedia.org/wiki/File:Dancing_Maenad_Met_35.11.3.jpg
12. Wire, *2 Corinthians*, 85–86, citing 1 Cor 7:12-24.

communicating with God in prayer, prophecy, and speaking in tongues, but he fears that this may be too easily interpreted as the kind of oracular speech by women that was part of Greek culture—and why not? Paul himself had insisted (in Galatians, for example) that membership in the Movement did not call for deculturation! Whatever the resolution—or lack thereof—the Corinthian community remained vibrant and contentious, as the letter known as 1 Clement shows.[13]

Lukas speaks instead of Priscilla and Aquila's accompanying Paul as far as Ephesus, where a good many of his own audience probably resided and where traditions about that time, some half-century in the past, were certainly vivid. It seems likely that Paul's mixed success in Corinth made him want an advance party in the even greater city of Ephesus who would again gather the initial community and perhaps prepare the new believers for what was likely to happen when Paul arrived. Lukas depicts Paul as making a single visit to "the synagogue" in Ephesus and holding a "discussion"[14] there, but quickly departing on his whirlwind tour of Jerusalem, Antioch, and his former successful mission field in eastern Asia Minor.

For feminist readers 18:24-28 is probably the high point of Acts. At some time after Prisca and Aquila have established a home in Ephesus, but while Paul is elsewhere, a learned Jew of Alexandria appears in the city. Alexandria was the intellectual hub of the extended Roman world. It contained the most significant Jewish settlement outside the land of Israel; it was supposedly the place where the Septuagint was written; it was home to the greatest first-century Jewish thinker whose works have survived: Philo.[15] Apollos is the only person described in Acts as "eloquent," and there may be a reflection of his reputation in Corinth in Paul's assertion at the very beginning of his self-defense before the

13. The date of 1 Clement is disputed, but the document may well be contemporary with Acts (early second century). Its author scolds the Corinthians for deposing their presbyters.

14. Greek διελέξατο, from διαλέγομαι, the source of English "dialogue." The Greek word had a broader scope and in Hellenistic Greek usage could refer also to an address or debate, but Lukas's penchant for using Septuagintal language might favor simply "speaking with." Cf. Gottlob Schrenk, "διαλέγομαι, διαλογίζομαι, διαλογισμός," *TDNT* 2 (1964): 93–98.

15. Philo lived ca. 25 BCE to 50 CE, so Apollos could well have been his student. We have Philo's works because they were preserved by Christians, mainly on account of their use of allegory, a feature that (together with Philo's use of the LXX) made his works unpalatable to the later rabbis.

Corinthian audience that "Christ did not send me to baptize but to proclaim the gospel, and not with eloquent wisdom, so that the cross of
Christ might not be emptied of its power" (1 Cor 1:17).[16]

Apollos, as depicted, takes the Jewish community of Ephesus by storm
with his "burning enthusiasm," but his learning is deficient. He has accurate knowledge about Jesus but "he knew only the baptism of John." In
other words, he knew of the Jewish practice of "baptism for repentance"
or for purification (see 19:4), but he was unaware of the new baptism into
the Way, which confers the Holy Spirit.[17] Prisca and Aquila took him
under their wing and described how the Jesus movement had developed
post-Easter and what the Pentecost events signified.[18]

It is not clear how long Apollos was under instruction, but at some time
his teachers, with the assent of the whole community, judged him ready for
the mission field and supported his desire to go to Achaia, beginning with
Corinth. Evidently his eloquence, supported by his new knowledge, made
a great impression there, in contrast to Paul's inferior oratorical gifts.[19] It
does not appear that Apollos taught a different message, but that he did
it better is highly probable. Knowing Prisca would certainly have given
him a better sense of how to communicate with the women of the Way!

In chapter 19 we will read of how Paul, on his return to Ephesus, found
some disciples there who had not received the Spirit in baptism because
they knew only John's baptism. Lukas may think of them as disciples of
Apollos (pre-Prisca and Aquila). Paul baptizes these disciples and they
receive the Spirit. In the case of Apollos nothing is said about Prisca
and Aquila having rebaptized him or his receiving the Spirit, but from
the description of his subsequent activity in Corinth and the power of
his preaching we have to suppose either that the Spirit had fallen on
him independently of another baptism (as in the case of Cornelius and
his household) or that Prisca and Aquila had been instrumental in the
Spirit's coming upon him. Without his having received the Spirit, they
and the Ephesus community would not have encouraged him to go
to Achaia, nor would his mission have been so effective among those

16. Paul mentions Apollos no fewer than six times in the first four chapters of
1 Corinthians, sometimes together with "Cephas" as his apparent rivals for the Corinthians' allegiance.

17. See above at Acts 13:1–14:28, n. 14.

18. Lukas's knowledge of this episode may be seen as additional evidence that
Ephesus was his home, or at least the place of Acts' composition.

19. Cf. 2 Cor 10:10: "For they [evidently Paul's opponents in Corinth] say, 'His
[i.e., Paul's] letters are weighty and strong, but his bodily presence is weak, and his
speech contemptible.'"

who "through grace had become believers." That expression itself is interesting, since it leaves open the question of how "grace" had been conferred on the Corinthians: whether through Prisca's and Aquila's teaching, Paul's preaching, or as a result of their incorporation into the community of believers.

Willie James Jennings has written of how this snippet portrays Prisca and Aquila as something new, a pair gifted with "a pedagogy . . . powerful enough to teach the powerful, and bring clarity and precision to faith where there had been great zeal but fragmentary knowledge. . . . [They] show what a couple can do joined to Jesus. They can speak truth to power and instruct the powerful." They exhibit "a microcell of insurgency."[20] And it is Prisca who is the teacher. Lukas had tried putting her in second place (at 18:2), but that attitude could not be maintained in view of her reputation. The couple work in tandem, and she takes the lead. Previously we have seen women community leaders (Tabitha, the mother of John Mark, and Lydia) who are evidently single. Here we have a woman who is married and yet preeminent. She is a new model alongside the others: the church in her house depicts what other such household communities should strive to be, whether one member of the household or another is the "head."

I am reminded here of a couple of our own time, Ruth Bader Ginsburg and her husband Martin, whose partnership and wisdom are a blessing and encouragement to so many, especially of the disenfranchised. They too lived a reversal of many conventional roles: Martin pursued a successful legal career, but he also took charge of the cooking (and became a gourmet chef!) when his wife evinced no interest in or aptitude for it; she instead became a justice of the Supreme Court and a historic champion of equality for all persons.

We wish we could know more about Prisca and Aquila. Did they accept Paul's version of the "Way of God"? Is that why they became his companions and advocates? Was Prisca the founder of the "Pauline School" in Ephesus? Paul's ardent admiration of them (cf. Rom 16:3-4) would favor that position, but it could also support the idea that Romans 16:1-24, which does not appear as part of Romans in some early manuscripts, was part of a letter written to the community at Ephesus that was later copied into Romans. On the other hand, the Ephesian "Pauline School" was responsible for post-Pauline letters (Colossians and

---

20. Willie James Jennings, *Acts*, Belief: A Theological Commentary on the Bible (Louisville: Westminster John Knox, 2017), 183.

Ephesians) that contain a "household code" prescribing subordination for married women ("Wives, be subject to your husbands," Col 3:18; Eph 5:22). It is hard indeed to imagine Prisca accepting as "gospel" the idea that women should be silent and subservient—though that elaboration of "subordination" first appears in the still later "Pastorals." Perhaps she did indeed leave Ephesus and return to Rome, due to disagreement with the way the "School" was going or for missionary reasons.

A final note: where there is a "school" there must be teachers. There has been renewed discussion in the last few years about whether there was an office of teacher in the Movement and whether teachers continued active after the writing of the Gospels. Lukas only uses the word for teachers (διδάσκαλοι) once, at 13:1, where he lists "prophets and teachers" at Antioch without specifying whether the men he names were one or the other or both. Paul evidently knew of "teachers" in Corinth, and it was in Corinth that he met Prisca and Aquila. From the description of their activities in Corinth and in Ephesus we may well posit that they were prominent διδάσκαλοι in both places, perhaps the first such among the members of the Movement in Ephesus. That would explain why it was they who instructed Apollos. Who but a διδάσκαλος would be qualified to "explain the way of God more accurately" to that talented preacher?[21]

---

21. For women as teachers in the early church see Ute E. Eisen, *Women Office-holders in Early Christianity: Epigraphical and Literary Studies*, trans. Linda M. Maloney (Collegeville, MN: Liturgical Press, 2000), chap. IV, "Teachers of Theology," 89–115.

Acts 19:1-20

Paul's Work in Ephesus

Lukas reintegrates Paul into the story of the mission by relating his encounter with some disciples who, like Apollos, "know only the baptism of John" (18:25). It is important to the story that Paul appear to be better than, or at least the equal of, Apollos, especially since the latter seems at this point to be having greater success in Corinth than Paul had enjoyed. Lukas would like to portray a seamless Movement (though one subject to disruption from within, as in Acts 6), but other evidence shows that, given cultural differences and distance, a number of branching "Ways" developed early.

The next pericope, in fact, reflects some such development.[1] As usual, Paul preaches first in the synagogue, arouses opposition, and this time

---

1. For a helpful outline of and commentary on Acts 19 see Elisabeth Schüssler Fiorenza, "Miracles, Mission, and Apologetics: An Introduction," in *Aspects of Religious Propaganda in Judaism and Early Christianity*, ed. Elisabeth Schüssler Fiorenza (Notre Dame, IN: University of Notre Dame Press, 1976), 1–25; portions are quoted in Pervo, *Acts*, 465–66. She divides the chapter into three parts: I. (vv. 1-10), "Christianity *vis-à-vis* Judaism"; II. (vv. 11-20), "The Miraculous Powers of the Christian Missionary"; III. (vv. 21[3]-40), "Polytheist Competition."

¹⁹:¹While Apollos was in Corinth, Paul passed through the interior regions and came to Ephesus, where he found some disciples. ²He said to them, "Did you receive the Holy Spirit when you became believers?" They replied, "No, we have not even heard that there is a Holy Spirit." ³Then he said, "Into what then were you baptized?" They answered, "Into John's baptism." ⁴Paul said, "John baptized with the baptism of repentance, telling the people to believe in the one who was to come after him, that is, in Jesus." ⁵On hearing this, they were baptized in the name of the Lord Jesus. ⁶When Paul had laid his hands on them, the Holy Spirit came upon them, and they spoke in tongues and prophesied—⁷altogether there were about twelve of them.

⁸He entered the synagogue and for three months spoke out boldly, and argued persuasively about the kingdom of God. ⁹When some stubbornly refused to believe and spoke evil of the Way before the congregation, he left them, taking the disciples with him, and argued daily in the lecture hall of Tyrannus. ¹⁰This continued for two years, so that all the residents of Asia, both Jews and Greeks, heard the word of the Lord.

actually splits the synagogue community, "taking the [i.e., his] disciples with him" and moving to a public lecture hall. There he preaches for two years, with the remarkable result that "all the residents of Asia [Minor], both Jews and Greeks, heard the word of the Lord." Given the absence of mass media in the first century, Lukas must mean us to understand that those who heard Paul's preaching carried it throughout the region. It is still the same message for "Jews and Greeks," but inevitably it would have been heard differently and elaborated differently in different cultural milieux.

It is worth noting that Lukas says nothing of Paul's having converted (or been in conflict with) prominent women—or any women— in Ephesus, as previously in Philippi, Beroea, and Athens. The twelve "disciples" of verses 1-12 are *men*, ἄνδρες. There may be good reason for that, as will appear.

Verses 11-19 are a section on magic and exorcism, showing how God's power was manifested through Paul by the application of mere "second-class relics"[2]—sweat bands or loincloths—without his needing so much

2. First-class relics are actual fragments or remnants of a saint's person; second-class relics are things that have touched the saint.

¹¹God did extraordinary miracles through Paul, ¹²so that when the handkerchiefs or aprons that had touched his skin were brought to the sick, their diseases left them, and the evil spirits came out of them. ¹³Then some itinerant Jewish exorcists tried to use the name of the Lord Jesus over those who had evil spirits, saying, "I adjure you by the Jesus whom Paul proclaims." ¹⁴Seven sons of a Jewish high priest named Sceva were doing this. ¹⁵But the evil spirit said to them in reply, "Jesus I know, and Paul I know; but who are you?" ¹⁶Then the man with the evil spirit leaped on them, mastered them all, and so overpowered them that they fled out of the house naked and wounded. ¹⁷When this became known to all residents of Ephesus, both Jews and Greeks, everyone was awestruck; and the name of the Lord Jesus was praised. ¹⁸Also many of those who became believers confessed and disclosed their practices. ¹⁹A number of those who practiced magic collected their books and burned them publicly; when the value of these books was calculated, it was found to come to fifty thousand silver coins. ²⁰So the word of the Lord grew mightily and prevailed.

as to say a word or raise his hand. This section is Lukas's "last word" on the subject: Jewish miracles (including those of Jesus and his disciples) are *good*; pagan magic and exorcism are *bad*. Usurping the name and power of Jesus is *worse than bad*! Damnable!

That people were supposedly healed or exorcised by the mere touch of Paul's dirty laundry has troubled many interpreters (as well it should!). Some have excused the practice by saying or hinting that it was something women did: the eminent German exegete Theodor Zahn, for example, wrote, "The relatives of the sick will have succeeded in persuading Priscilla, in whose house Paul was staying, to lend them some head-cloth or handkerchief or other, which they would have returned immediately."[3] Prisca, in the renowned exegete's mind, is a proper housewife who does her lodger's laundry while he is out converting the world, and she thoughtfully provides his soiled sweat-cloths and loincloths (politely rendered "handkerchiefs" in Zahn's version and "aprons" in NRSV) to other women to use for working "Christian magic."[4]

3. Theodor Zahn, *Die Apostelgeschichte des Lukas*, KNT 5/2 (Leipzig: Deichert, 1921), 681–82, as quoted in Hans-Josef Klauck, *Magic and Paganism in Early Christianity: The World of the Acts of the Apostles*, trans. Brian McNeill (Minneapolis: Fortress, 2003), 98.
4. The Acts account antedates by several centuries the story of the Mandylion, a "little towel" bearing an image of Jesus' face. According to legend it was sent by

This account of Jesus' healing through Paul's sweat, causing "evil spirits" to come out of people, is the first part of a frame around the story of the "sons of Sceva," base and phony would-be counterparts to Paul who, like Simon in Acts 8 and Bar-Jesus in Acts 13, are trying to take advantage of the successes of the Movement. "Itinerant exorcists" was a phrase equivalent to "charlatans" in Lukas's milieu, and he makes them "Jewish" as well, identifying them as seven sons of a "high priest" named Sceva—a Latin stage-name; there was no such person.[5] This tale is clearly a fabrication.[6] It has three purposes: to entertain, to exalt Paul as a genuine miracle-worker, and to give incentive for new believers to repent of their magical practices at great expense to themselves. (Books were extremely valuable.) Renunciation of possessions is of the highest importance to Lukas, as we have seen: the dirtiest word he knows is "rich." He presses that point by citing a huge sum of money as the supposed value of the magical papyri.[7] The audience is captivated by the hilarious scene, which prepares hearers and readers to absorb the point of the story—a technique all good preachers and teachers know.

Hence the repentant magicians and exorcists (including the sons of Sceva?) learn that (a) it is unwise to try to compete with the Movement by pretending to adopt its terminology and ideas and to wield its power, so that (b) the only solution is to abandon magic and lead a pure life free from lust for possessions or power of one's own.[8]

Evidently the message did not "take" (as those who have witnessed the wiles of televangelists will know). Magical papyri were treasured for

---

Jesus himself to King Abgar of Edessa. Abgar had written Jesus to come to Edessa to heal him of an unknown disease, but Jesus replied that he must complete his mission in Israel and then be taken up to heaven. Eusebius of Caesarea was the first to tell of the supposed correspondence, in the fourth century CE; the legend of the Mandylion, which substituted for Jesus' presence and healed the king, is not known to have been recorded before the sixth century. The account of healings accomplished by Paul's laundry is one forerunner of that story as well as of Veronica's veil and the Shroud of Turin.

5. See Klauck, *Magic and Paganism*, 100.

6. Charles Talbert, in *Reading Acts: A Literary and Theological Commentary on the Acts of the Apostles* (New York: Crossroad, 1997), treats it as a parody of a miracle story.

7. The amount is by no means exaggerated. Cf. Pervo, *Acts*, 480: "The chief sins of which [Lukas] takes countenance are those involving money and/or magic." Differently from Paul and the post-Paulines, sexual sins interest Lukas not at all.

8. See Klauck, *Magic and Paganism*, 102, and cf. Susan R. Garrett, *The Demise of the Devil: Magic and the Demonic in Luke's Writings* (Minneapolis: Fortress, 1989), 89–99.

centuries to come, and whatever power seemed useful was exploited. Hans-Josef Klauck cites one text from the sixth century CE: "By the God of the Hebrews, I adjure you, Jesus, you who appear in fire, you who are in the midst of field and snow and mist; may your inexorable angel descend and bind fast the wandering demon of this creature."[9] The modern quasi-religious "self-help" industry is not far removed.[10]

Lukas's dig at the Jewish community in Ephesus as having spawned Sceva and his sons seems symptomatic of the friction beginning to develop between Jesus-believers and other Jews in Ephesus by his own time, as the numbers of Jesus-followers there were increasing. The Jewish community at Ephesus was one of the oldest and best-established in the Greco-Roman world. At the time Lukas depicts (mid-first century CE) there had apparently been Jews in the city for at least three hundred years.[11] By that time the Jews there had the rare privilege of calling themselves "Ephesians" along with everyone else.[12] Their community evidently had a coherent organizational form, which enabled them to maintain a united front against their pagan neighbors as well as interlopers like Paul and his friends. Jews in Ephesus probably numbered in the many hundreds in Paul's time or soon after.[13]

Our only sources for Jewish interaction with the members of the Movement are Christian, and particularly the stories in Acts. Lukas's claim that Paul taught for three months in the synagogue (well, *a* synagogue; there must have been many to house several thousand Jews!) is striking when compared to his previous stays in Thessalonica and Corinth (to say nothing

9. Karl Preisendanz, ed. and trans., *Papyri Graecae Magicae: Die griechischen Zauberpapyri*, 2 vols. (Stuttgart: Teubner, 1973–74), 4:3007–27, quoted in Klauck, *Magic and Paganism*, 99–100.

10. An online search reveals titles that include *Pray Your Way to Breakthroughs*; *The Power of a Praying Wife*; *Praying for Your Husband from Head to Toe* (do we sense a theme here?); *Pray Your Way to Happiness*; *211 Powerful Night Prayers That Will Take Your Life to the Next Level*; *21/40 Nights of Decrees and Your Enemies Will Surrender* ("A simple audacious prayer manual contains biblical decrees that help courageous Christians to confront Satan and all his works") . . . *ad infinitum*.

11. An indispensable summary account is Paul Trebilco, "The Jewish Community in Ephesus and Its Interaction with Christ-Believers in the First Century CE and Beyond," in *The First Urban Churches*, vol. 3: *Ephesus*, ed. James R. Harrison and L. L. Welborn, WGRWSup 9 (Atlanta: SBL Press, 2018), 93–126.

12. Josephus, *C. Ap.* 2.39.

13. Paul Trebilco considers the minimum probable number to have been around four thousand.

of Athens). Perhaps Prisca and Aquila, who were already fixtures in synagogal life, helped him "put a lid on" his enthusiasm for a while. Even after
leaving the synagogue (19:9) he and his followers maintained contact with
its members, and undoubtedly there were many Jews who went to hear
Paul in his role as "philosopher" in the lecture hall of Tyrannus. (Here
Paul is shown attaining the status he had tried and failed to establish in
Athens.) When the silversmiths' riot breaks out, the Jewish leaders push
forward Alexander, one of their own, no doubt in a vain attempt to protect
the Jews from being lumped together with the rabble-rouser Paul.[14]

Lukas is writing at least half a century after the time he depicts and some
thirty years before the composition of the Deutero-Pauline letters. Their
author paints his opponents (who are within his own community) as, for
example, "paying attention to Jewish myths" (Titus 1:14; cf. 1 Tim 1:3-4)
and desiring to be "teachers of the law" (1 Tim 1:6-11). As Paul Trebilco
writes: "Perhaps the significant and sizeable Jewish community in Ephesus
may have exerted an influence on the opponents as they developed their
views, *as well as* their teaching reflecting the fact that they themselves were
probably Jewish Christians within the Christian community."[15]

In all this we may be tempted to see an inexorable and inevitable "development" of distancing, an unstoppable trajectory toward a "parting
of the ways" between Judaism and Christianity as well as between both
of them and paganism. We need instead to be cautious and self-critical
and to avoid monolithic models of relationships between "Judaism" and
"Christianity," taking into account that both together were a tiny minority
in the city of Ephesus with its population of some two hundred thousand,
and considering the effect of cultural context, locale, social class, and other
factors that may not be evident to us at this remove. Ephesus is just one
place where we get a brief glimpse of some interactions;[16] if we think we
know too little about what happened here we should be cautious about
generalizing to what "might have" or "must have" transpired elsewhere.

14. See Trebilco, "Jewish Community," 105n35.
15. Ibid., 109.
16. In the next generation Justin, writing in Rome, set his *Dialogue with Trypho* in
Ephesus. Whether that was factual or not, as Trebilco observes (ibid., 115–16), "both
Justin and his readers could well have seen Ephesus as a suitable and realistic venue
for a debate between a learned Christian and a learned Jew concerning matters such
as Jesus and the law."

Acts 19:21-41

Artemis of the Ephesians

The next transition is somewhat confusing: Paul decides it is time to leave Ephesus, to revisit Macedonia and Achaia and then go to Jerusalem once more, after which he "must also see Rome" (19:21). The passage seems to be an attempt to summarize Paul's projected itinerary in 2 Corinthians and also to prepare for the action to come in Acts 20–28. The conclusion that "[Paul] himself stayed for some time longer in Asia" (v. 22) after having sent Timothy and Erastus to Macedonia to prepare for his coming is vague: Paul may still be in "Asia" (i.e., Asia Minor), but is he in Ephesus? He is not present in the story in verses 23-41 except for his alleged intention to "go into the crowd" in verse 30, and even there his location is unclear. The only apparent reason for his being in the story at all is so that the Asiarchs[1] will show favor to him and shield him from the mob, thus enhancing his status in the eyes of Acts' audience. The same favor does not accrue to the other Christian missionaries, as Paul's companions, Gaius and Aristarchus, are dragged off by the mob. Alexander, representing the Jewish community (who would be equally opposed to the worship of an idol but did not try to disrupt the sale of copies), fares no better, and it falls to the city clerk

---

1. NRSV "officials of the province of Asia" (τινὲς δὲ καὶ τῶν Ἀσιαρχῶν). The function of these officials is not clear; hence the paraphrase in the translation. They did exist; they are mentioned in numerous inscriptions and on coins.

²¹Now after these things had been accomplished, Paul resolved in the Spirit to go through Macedonia and Achaia, and then to go on to Jerusalem. He said, "After I have gone there, I must also see Rome." ²²So he sent two of his helpers, Timothy and Erastus, to Macedonia, while he himself stayed for some time longer in Asia.

²³About that time no little disturbance broke out concerning the Way. ²⁴A man named Demetrius, a silversmith who made silver shrines of Artemis, brought no little business to the artisans. ²⁵These he gathered together, with the workers of the same trade, and said, "Men, you know that we get our wealth from this business. ²⁶You also see and hear that not only in Ephesus but in almost the whole of Asia this Paul has persuaded and drawn away a considerable number of people by saying that gods made with hands are not gods. ²⁷And there is danger not only that this trade of ours may come into disrepute but also that the temple of the great goddess Artemis will be scorned, and she will be deprived of

(γραμματεύς) to remind the mob that rioting is something likely to bring Roman disfavor and discipline down on the city.

Acts 19 seems to be a chapter completely devoid of the presence of women (unless we are to imagine Prisca toiling over the laundry tubs²)— but in fact its second half is completely dominated by the presence of a female figure: Artemis of Ephesus.

The Artemis proper to Ephesus (and in fact the dominant Artemis figure in the Greco-Roman world) was the key symbol with which the city of Ephesus and its inhabitants identified. In a sense she *was* Ephesus, and an assault on her was an attack on the identity of the city itself and all who dwelt within it.³ According to one series of legends Artemis, the daughter of Leto and Zeus, was born, with her twin brother Apollo, very near the site of Ephesus and was the founder of the city. Older tradition held that the city site was the home of Amazons, who built the first temple to Artemis.

The statue of Artemis, supposedly sent from heaven by Zeus, was not a meteorite, as "fell from heaven" might seem to imply. It was a wooden figure, smaller than life-size, darkened by constant anointings with nard

2. Those familiar with Rom 16:3-4 might wonder whether it was on this occasion that Prisca and Aquila "risked their necks" for Paul; surely a description of that would enliven the story!

3. The essays in *The First Urban Churches*, vol. 3: *Ephesus*, ed. James R. Harrison and L. L. Welborn, WGRWSup 9 (Atlanta: SBL Press, 2018) are extremely helpful for an understanding of Judaism and emergent Christianity in that ancient city.

her majesty that brought all Asia and the world to worship her."

²⁸When they heard this, they were enraged and shouted, "Great is Artemis of the Ephesians!" ²⁹The city was filled with the confusion; and people rushed together to the theater, dragging with them Gaius and Aristarchus, Macedonians who were Paul's travel companions. ³⁰Paul wished to go into the crowd, but the disciples would not let him; ³¹even some officials of the province of Asia, who were friendly to him, sent him a message urging him not to venture into the theater. ³²Meanwhile, some were shouting one thing, some another; for the assembly was in confusion, and most of them did not know why they had come together. ³³Some of the crowd gave instructions to Alexander, whom the Jews had pushed forward. And Alexander motioned for silence and tried to make a defense before the people. ³⁴But when they recognized that he was a Jew, for about two hours all of them shouted in unison, "Great is Artemis of the Ephesians!" ³⁵But when the town clerk had

to preserve the wood. The many supposed "breasts" of the figure are actually attached to a breastplate; no one is sure exactly what they represent (perhaps fruits?). Artemis, after all, was a virgin huntress. She was a patron of young girls and women but also of their later lives, including especially protecting them during childbirth. (It was said that, having been born first, she assisted her mother in birthing Apollo.) At the same time she could be regarded as representative of a chaste and ascetic life for women.

Close readers of Acts would understand that Demetrius's argument in verse 26 that "this Paul" is "saying that gods made with hands are not gods" is perfectly true: Paul had said precisely that in his speech at the Areopagus ("we ought not to think that the deity is like gold, or silver, or stone, an image formed by the art and imagination of mortals," 17:29). But Artemis of Ephesus is not a gold, silver, or stone image made by human hands: she is προπετές, the one "fallen" from heaven and therefore quite plausibly the subject of worship. Hence Paul's attack on idols is not relevant to the cult of Artemis, but it is very bad for those who *do* make images of her!

Although Lukas pictures the revolt of the silversmiths as purely a matter of greed (v. 25) he is closer to the mark when he has Demetrius threaten that "she will be deprived of her majesty that brought all Asia and the world to worship her" (v. 27).[4] Lukas is intimately familiar

---

4. See the contemptuous remark in Acts of John 33, referring to John's supposed destruction of her temple: "Artemis should have helped herself."

quieted the crowd, he said, "Citizens of Ephesus, who is there that does not know that the city of the Ephesians is the temple keeper of the great Artemis and of the statue that fell from heaven? [36]Since these things cannot be denied, you ought to be quiet and do nothing rash. [37]You have brought these men here who are neither temple robbers nor blasphemers of our goddess. [38]If therefore Demetrius and the artisans with him have a complaint against anyone, the courts are open, and there are proconsuls; let them bring charges there against one another. [39]If there is anything further you want to know, it must be settled in the regular assembly. [40]For we are in danger of being charged with rioting today, since there is no cause that we can give to justify this commotion." [41]When he had said this, he dismissed the assembly.

with the life and character of Ephesus. At about the time when he would have been writing, the cult of Artemis was at its zenith. Inscriptions from 104 CE tell of gifts from C. Vibius Salutaris of a whole series of statues to be carried in procession through the streets of the city, probably in connection with the annual celebration of the month of Artemision, accompanied by games and drinking. Artemis's devotees quite naturally attributed their city's fame and prosperity to the nurturing care of their goddess.

At the same time these celebrations expressed and further cemented the firm adherence of Ephesus to Rome and its emperors. The close connection dated to the reign of Augustus, and by the time of the events pictured in Acts 19 the whole world was aware that reverence for Artemis of Ephesus was homage to the Roman imperial family and cult, and vice versa. Ephesus had the privilege of minting coins; two from the Claudian era show the emperor (or the emperor and his wife) on one side and Artemis on the other, showing the close tie between the imperial power and that of the goddess. This explains why Lukas keeps Paul out of the scene and has the city clerk reproach the silversmiths with making false accusations. Tension between the Movement and the Roman imperial system was something to be avoided at the beginning of the second century if the Movement were to grow and flourish "under the radar," as it were.

An awareness of the importance of Artemis of Ephesus is a key factor in appreciating what it meant for women in Lukas's time to attach themselves to the Movement and to claim salvation from a male savior rather than a female—for Artemis was emphatically acclaimed as "savior." Women in labor called on her especially as "eternal Savioress of all," and during pregnancy they were expected to go to her priestess and donate an animal, or its feet, head, and skin—that is to say, the spoils of the hunt, for Artemis is the huntress.[5] Poets and playwrights used this imagery, and Plutarch, in commenting on the marriage ritual, speaks of childbirth as the domain of Artemis.[6] She figures in novels as well: so (of course) in *An Ephesian Tale* it is during a festival of Artemis that the handsome but misogynistic hero Habrocomes is overcome by the beauty of Anthia, who is so lovely she is frequently mistaken for the goddess herself.[7] The processional rites during her month were mating festivals, and when the couple pledge themselves to one another they make their vows in the name of Artemis.

Mary Galvin summarizes:

> The image prevalent in myth associates Artemis personally with re-maining steadfastly single and rejecting sexual union of any kind. Conversely the rites associated with Artemis involved the preparation of the young for that very transition, the journey from childhood to adulthood via puberty; and one of the consequences of adulthood was the responsibility for bearing the next generation who would likewise come under the protection of Artemis.[8]

Last but certainly not least, the temple of Artemis at Ephesus, begun in 323 BCE and enduring for six hundred years, was one of the Seven Wonders of the Ancient World and thus a source of enormous pride to the residents of her city. Obviously, persuading the Greek women of Ephesus from all classes[9] as well as those of other nationalities to abandon Artemis

---

5. Some authors have tried to associate the worship of Artemis the huntress with Paul's statement that he "fought with wild beasts at Ephesus" (1 Cor 15:32). Thus Morna Hooker, "Artemis of Ephesus," *JTS* 64 (2013): 37–46; Daniel Freyer-Griggs, "The Beasts at Ephesus and the Cult of Artemis," *HTR* 106 (2013): 459–77.

6. Plutarch, *Mor.* 263f–64b.

7. *Ephesian Tale* 1.2. So also Callirhoe stuns the public "just as when Artemis ap-pears to hunters in the wilderness. Many of those present even fell to their knees in reverence" (*Callirhoe* 1.2).

8. Mary Galvin, *Life, Death and Artemis*, vol. 2: *Artemis and the Ritual Process* (eBook, Smashwords, 2017), 71. The Christian apocrypha from the second century onward, by contrast, encouraged women to emulate the posited virginity of Jesus' mother and of Jesus himself.

9. Persons exposed in the marketplace for sale were sometimes dedicated to the *Artemision*. A decree of 44 CE shows that this was frowned upon by the authorities: "Likewise, it is my pleasure that public slaves [δημοσίους δούλους], who are said to

for a Jewish male savior was a tall order and one Lukas seems not to have wanted to suggest. Hence Paul's focus on the well-established and numerous Jewish population of the city, first in the synagogue and then next door, and his absence from the fray with the silversmiths.

Artemis has not retired gently from the field; on the evidence she may indeed be immortal. Think of the bold and independent artist Artemisia Gentileschi (1593–ca. 1654), "a sort of proto-feminist heroine, the queen bee of female empowerment."[10] Jean Shinoda Bolen wrote of Artemis as "the indomitable spirit in Everywoman."[11] Undoubtedly her strength and independence appealed to women then, much as they have in later centuries. A program group of the National Wildlife Federation, "bold, impassioned sportswomen who are out to change the face of conservation," bears the name "Artemis," and because Artemis, as huntress, is also goddess of the moon, NASA's project to return astronauts to the moon by 2024 bears her name.

Christianity found a way to cope. By the time the *Artemision* was destroyed in the fourth century CE, Christians had established a counter-myth and a substitute they considered far better: that of Mary, the mother of Jesus. The process developed thus: the apocryphal Acts of John, some parts of which probably date to the second century CE, contain tales of the apostle John in Ephesus, where, among other miracles, he destroys Artemis's temple (a couple of centuries before it actually happened). Irenaeus (*Adv. Haer.* 3.3.4) tells a story of John clashing with the heretic Cerinthus in Ephesus, and Eusebius (*Eccl. Hist.*) repeats some of the same information. At some point Mary, Jesus' mother, was added to the picture: on the basis of John 19:27 she was supposed to have been taken under the protection of the Beloved Disciple (= "John") and traveled with him to the island of Patmos and thence to Ephesus, where she died. Devotion to Mary did grow strong in Ephesus at a relatively early time:

purchase infants at whatever price and to dedicate them to Artemis that their slaves [οἱ δοῦλοι αὐτῶν] might be raised from her revenue, provide for their own slaves [τοῖς ἰδίοις δούλοις]." Hermann Wankel, et al., eds., *Die Inschriften von Ephesos*, 8 vols. in 11, IK 11–17 (Bonn: Habelt, 1979–1984). Abbreviated *IEph*. Quoted in James R. Harrison, "An Epigraphic Portrait of Ephesus and Its Villages," in Harrison and Welborn, *The First Urban Churches*, 3:1–67, at 39.

10. Alistair Sooke, as quoted from *The Telegraph* at https://www.bbc.com/news/entertainment-arts-54338537 (September 29, 2020). Artemis was sometimes associated with bees.

11. Jean Shinoda Bolen, *Artemis: The Indomitable Spirit in Everywoman* (San Francisco: Conari Press, 2014).

Ephesus was the scene of the church council in 431 CE at which Nestorius and the Antiochene faction on the one side clashed with Cyril of Alexandria and his associates on the other over the title *Theotokos* (God-birther) for Mary, rather than *Christotokos* (Christ-birther). Cyril and the *Theotokos* side were supported by Memnon, the bishop of Ephesus, and he in turn had the strong backing of his flock. The first known claim that Mary had lived in Ephesus is in the synodal letter of the Council of Ephesus, which speaks of "the city of the Ephesians, where John the Theologian and the Virgin Mother of God St. Mary [lived and are buried]." The evidence for either one having been there is nonexistent, but in its time it was very significant indeed: if Artemis had to go, there was a powerful need for a replacement, and who better to supplant the daughter of the most high God (Zeus) than Mary, the mother of God (Jesus)?

Acts 20:1-38

Paul Completes His Mission

"Paul sent for his disciples" (from where?). Two of them have just been abused by the mob in Ephesus (19:29), with Paul nowhere in sight! Paul's itinerary in the first part of the chapter seems intended to match what he writes in 2 Corinthians about his intentions. According to his letters he was collecting money from his western, Romanized missions to present as a gift to the community in Jerusalem, and in doing so he was juggling rivalries among Macedonia, Achaia, and the western coastal cities of Asia Minor. Lukas never says a word about the collection, probably because he knew that, as a reconciling gesture toward the Jerusalem church, it had been a failure. Although we can read from his depiction of the events in Jerusalem that Paul was coldly received by James and the Jerusalem community, Lukas tries to avoid admitting division, just as he does not emphasize (while not denying) community disharmony earlier (thus 6:1; 9:26-30; 11:1-3; 15:1-5, 36-40).

Instead, at 20:7-12 he inserts a story of a community assembly in Troas (near the site of ancient Troy) that, without characterizing the members of that community as Jewish or gentile, shows them engaging in the kind of common celebration of preaching and Eucharist that was both rooted in Jewish practice and becoming the typical model for Christian worship in centuries to come. The scene is framed by references to Paul and his companions' having "sailed from Philippi after the days of Unleavened Bread" (v. 6)—that is, they had celebrated Passover in Philippi (with

Acts 20:1-38

20:1After the uproar had ceased, Paul sent for the disciples; and after encouraging them and saying farewell, he left for Macedonia. 2When he had gone through those regions and had given the believers much encouragement, he came to Greece, 3where he stayed for three months. He was about to set sail for Syria when a plot was made against him by the Jews, and so he decided to return through Macedonia. 4He was accompanied by Sopater son of Pyrrhus from Beroea, by Aristarchus and Secundus from Thessalonica, by Gaius from Derbe, and by Timothy, as well as by Tychicus and Trophimus from Asia. 5They went ahead and were waiting for us in Troas; 6but we sailed from Philippi after the days of Unleavened Bread, and in five days we joined them in Troas, where we stayed for seven days.

7On the first day of the week, when we met to break bread, Paul was holding a discussion with them; since he intended to leave the next day, he continued speaking until midnight. 8There were many lamps in the room upstairs where we were meeting. 9A young man named Eutychus, who was sitting in the window, began to sink off into a deep sleep while Paul talked still longer. Overcome by sleep, he fell to the ground three floors below and was picked up dead. 10But Paul went down, and bending over him took him in his arms, and said, "Do not be alarmed, for his life is in him." 11Then Paul went upstairs, and after he had broken bread and eaten, he continued to converse with them until dawn; then he left. 12Meanwhile they had taken the boy away alive and were not a little comforted.

Lydia and the community there, we assume)—and to Paul's eagerness to reach Jerusalem by Pentecost (v. 16). In other words, the ending of Paul's missionary activity shows him still embedded in Jewish life.[1]

The story of the assembly in Troas matches remarkably with the account written by Pliny the Younger to the emperor Trajan describing his procedures with regard to "Christians" at roughly the same time when Lukas was writing. He describes his efforts to snuff out these subversive groups, though evidently he found the work rather distasteful. In one letter describing his way of proceeding he writes:

> They were accustomed to meet on a fixed day before dawn and sing responsively a hymn to Christ as to a god, and to bind themselves by oath, not to some crime, but not to commit fraud, theft, or adultery, nor falsify their trust, nor to refuse to return a trust when called upon to do

---

1. For a full examination of Acts 20:6-12 from this and related perspectives see Julie A. Glavic, "Eutychus in Acts and in the Church: The Narrative Significance of Acts 20:6-12," *BBR* 24 (2014): 179–206.

¹³We went ahead to the ship and set sail for Assos, intending to take Paul on board there; for he had made this arrangement, intending to go by land himself. ¹⁴When he met us in Assos, we took him on board and went to Mitylene. ¹⁵We sailed from there, and on the following day we arrived opposite Chios. The next day we touched at Samos, and the day after that we came to Miletus. ¹⁶For Paul had decided to sail past Ephesus, so that he might not have to spend time in Asia; he was eager to be in Jerusalem, if possible, on the day of Pentecost.

¹⁷From Miletus he sent a message to Ephesus, asking the elders of the church to meet him. ¹⁸When they came to him, he said to them:

"You yourselves know how I lived among you the entire time from the first day that I set foot in Asia, ¹⁹serving the Lord with all humility and with tears, enduring the trials that came to me through the plots of the Jews. ²⁰I did not shrink from doing anything helpful, proclaiming the message to you and teaching you publicly and from house to house, ²¹as I testified to both Jews and Greeks about repentance toward God and faith toward our Lord Jesus. ²²And now, as a captive to the Spirit, I am on my way to Jerusalem, not knowing what will happen to me there, ²³except that the Holy Spirit testifies to me in every city that imprisonment and persecutions are waiting for me. ²⁴But I do not count my life of any value to myself, if only I may finish my course and the ministry that I received from the Lord Jesus, to testify to the good news of God's grace.

---

so. When this was over, it was their custom to depart and to assemble again to partake of food—but ordinary and innocent food. . . . I judged it all the more necessary to find out what the truth was by torturing two female slaves who were called deacons (*ministrae*). But I discovered nothing else but depraved, excessive superstition.[2]

The nocturnal assembly Lukas describes fits this picture very well, as does the indication that enslaved women exercised διακονία in the community, because the key figure in the scene is an enslaved boy or man, Eutychus ("Lucky," a common slave name). We have seen that Lukas regularly refers to enslaved persons (and to Jesus) with the Greek word παῖς (feminine παιδίσκη), and Eutychus is first called a teenager (νεανίσκος, v. 9) and then a παῖς (v. 12).[3]

---

2. Pliny, *Letters* 10.96-97.

3. Παῖς is used for Jesus in Acts 3:13, 26; 4:27, and for Eutychus in 20:12. The feminine, παιδίσκη, describes Rhoda in 12:13 and the prophetic woman in Philippi at 16:16. In the last case it may also imply "prostitute" (that is, she was offered to other men by her owners, in exchange for payment—to themselves).

Acts 20:1-38 (cont.)

[25]"And now I know that none of you, among whom I have gone about proclaiming the kingdom, will ever see my face again. [26]Therefore I declare to you this day that I am not responsible for the blood of any of you, [27]for I did not shrink from declaring to you the whole purpose of God. [28]Keep watch over yourselves and over all the flock, of which the Holy Spirit has made you overseers, to shepherd the church of God that he obtained with the blood of his own Son. [29]I know that after I have gone, savage wolves will come in among you, not sparing the flock. [30]Some even from your own group will come distorting the truth in order to entice the disciples to follow them. [31]Therefore be alert, remembering that for three years I did not cease night or day to warn everyone with tears. [32]And now I commend you to God and to the message of his grace, a message that is able to build you up and to give you the inheritance among all who are sanctified. [33]I coveted no one's silver or gold or clothing. [34]You know for yourselves that I worked with my own hands to support myself and my companions. [35]In all this I have given you an example that by such work we must support the weak, remembering the words of the Lord Jesus, for he himself said, 'It is more blessed to give than to receive.'"

[36]When he had finished speaking, he knelt down with them all and prayed. [37]There was much weeping among them all; they embraced Paul and kissed him, [38]grieving especially because of what he had said, that they would not see him again. Then they brought him to the ship.

We learn, then, (a) that as has been evident throughout, the institution of enslavement was not questioned by Jesus-followers as depicted by Lukas (though there is indication in Paul's letters that some enslaved persons, at least, hoped to see themselves freed by their baptism)[4] and (b) that persons held in servitude could be, and often were, members of the Jesus communities, at least in these early days. Whether they were on an equal footing with other members remains open to question.[5]

4. Cf. 1 Cor 7:21, where Paul either advises the enslaved to take the opportunity to obtain their freedom, if offered, or else to make use of it for spiritual benefit. The Greek is utterly ambiguous. The author of the "letters of Ignatius," writing some decades after Acts, disapproves of the use of community funds for manumission of slaves, an indication that some communities were purchasing their freedom, or perhaps that enslaved members of the community were asking that they do so.

5. On the subject of slavery see esp. Jennifer A. Glancy, *Slavery in Early Christianity* (Minneapolis: Fortress, 2006); eadem, *Slavery as Moral Problem: In the Early Church and Today* (Minneapolis: Fortress, 2011).

The evening assembly takes place "on the first day of the week," which for Lukas means Sunday, as he tends to use a Roman calendar; the Sabbath celebration has been completed, a day's work accomplished,[6] and now the people of the Movement in Troas have gathered in one or more houses. The meeting room, in the third story of a tenement, could not have been large; given the crowd, the large number of "lamps" or torches, and a slave's weariness after a day's work, it is no wonder that Eutychus, who could not assume one of the (probably sparse) seats in the room and so was sitting in the window, fell asleep. With the audience's attention riveted on the speaker, no one noticed him slipping; he fell to the ground and lay unmoving. As happens on such occasions, the sermon was interrupted and Paul joined others in rushing to the aid of the boy. Lukas tells us that Paul bent over him and embraced him—echoing Peter's embrace of Tabitha. His assurance, "Do not be alarmed, for his life is in him" (v. 10), is deliberately ambiguous; those who want to believe Paul has performed a miracle of raising the dead may do so; those who do not can take it that the boy only had the wind knocked out of him. We might be curious to know whether he had any broken limbs and would thereafter be considered "worthless" by his owners—a status that for slaves was often a fate worse than death—but perhaps the fact that the people who picked him up and carried him away were "not a little comforted" (v. 12) is intended as a reassurance of community care.

Eutychus (Acts 20:7-12)

As explained in this commentary, both Eutychus's name ("Lucky") and his designation as a "boy" (παῖς) (v. 12) indicate a slave. The name is both apt (he's lucky that Paul was around to revive him) and ironic (he's unlucky to have fallen out of a window). Here the term "boy" does not necessarily mean that he was young but simply points to his low status; however, the use of νεανίσκος (v. 9) indicates youth. This nuance is lost in the NRSV translation, which masks his slave status by using "young man" and "boy" synonymously. Other names in this chapter, like Secundus, Tychicus, and Trophimus (v. 4), might indicate slave status or more likely that of a freedman.

Within Acts the story of the resuscitation of Eutychus shows two Lukan devices: a gender pairing with the story of the raising of Tabitha/Dorcas

---

6. Probably the Sunday begins at sundown on the Sabbath; see Pliny's letter.

(9:36-43) and a raising from the dead parallel with a similar story about Peter, the apostle who raises Tabitha. Here Paul, Peter's counterpart in the second half of Acts, raises a male character. There are, however, some telling differences between the Tabitha and Eutychus episodes. Tabitha is a woman, probably a widow (9:39), whose works of charity were well known and whose abilities as a seamstress were highly valued by the circle of widows to whom she belonged—possibly because her work helped to support them financially. The disciples in Joppa (of whom Tabitha is one, 9:36) are so distressed by her death that they send two of their number to Peter in nearby Lydda to tell him about it. The widows are weeping over her loss when Peter arrives, and he prays alone over her body before he commands her to arise (9:40).

Eutychus is a much more marginal figure. As noted in this commentary, he is seated in the window probably because he doesn't rate a better place in the assembly: after all, he is young and a slave. The scene of him nodding off as Paul drones on and on is consistent with ancient stereotypes of slaves as lazy and unreliable (cf. Matt 25:26) and may even have been perceived as comical by the intended audience, despite its (near-fatal) consequences (cf. Matt 24:51).[7] Compared to the scene of Peter praying over Tabitha, Paul's treatment of Eutychus seems almost offhand; he embraces him, proclaims that he is alive (and perhaps even uninjured, thus assuring the others of his continued utility as a slave), and goes back to the assembly (20:10-11).

Was Eutychus a member of the ἐκκλησία at Troas on the same footing with the others? Possibly he had been baptized along with other members of a believing household (cf. Acts 10:48; 16:15, 31-34; 18:8; 1 Cor 16:15), with or without his consent or understanding, or he might simply have been brought to the gathering to serve the needs of his owner. It is also possible that he was a believer who was attending the meeting with permission or that he sneaked out to hear Paul's preaching after a long day of hard work— no wonder he fell asleep! At any rate, the story ends well for both Eutychus and the assembly: "Meanwhile they had taken the boy away alive and were not a little comforted" (9:12).

Mary Ann Beavis

---

7. See Mary Ann Beavis, "Ancient Slavery as an Interpretive Context for the New Testament Servant Parables with Special Reference to the Unjust Steward (Luke 16:1-8)," *JBL* 111 (1992): 37–54, at 41–42.

There may be another reflection of the story of Tabitha, on a symbolic level: is the slave Eutychus also an important representative of the Spirit's presence, so that the community's being "comforted" results from the healing of a breach, as the result of Paul's preaching and also of his presence among them? Or is it a veiled warning about the danger to any community if it treats some members as "other" or "less than"?

Paul returns upstairs without further ado and finishes his all-night sermon. The incident seems to have occurred around midnight (see v. 7); after the eucharistic meal (v. 11), Paul goes on speaking until dawn. This was certainly, in Lukas's intention, a farewell discourse, but readers are not privy to it. There will be only one such speech, a model for all those not recorded, and it will be delivered at Miletus (20:18-35). The scene at Troas seems instead to be a paradigm for community life in the diaspora, with Paul the model for the traveling prophet or missionary.[8]

The detailed itinerary from Troas to Miletus seems rather pointless: for example, the statement that Paul bypassed Ephesus because he was in a hurry makes no sense if, afterward, he has to stop at Miletus, send a messenger to Ephesus, and then wait for the *presbyteroi* and *presbyterai* from there to join him in Miletus. Lukas's audience perhaps had good information about why Paul did not want to revisit Ephesus and did not need to have the story repeated; ours not to know.

That the "elders" of the Movement in Ephesus were a mixed group of women and men seems beyond dispute. After all, Prisca and Aquila were the real founders of the first house community in Ephesus (see 18:19-21), and it is unlikely that if any prominent women who had belonged to the Artemis cult had joined the Movement they would have been content to accept a lesser status than the cult had afforded them. The words Lukas puts in Paul's mouth here should be read in that light.

Unlike the Areopagus speech, then, and like the classical and biblical examples on which it is modeled, the address to the elders at Miletus is a

---

8. See the *Didachē* for instructions about how to receive traveling preachers (or not!): "Let everyone who comes in the name of the Lord be received, and then, when you have taken stock of [her/him], you will know—for you will have insight—what is right and false. If the person who comes is just passing through, help [her/him] as much as you can, but [s/he] shall not stay with you more than two or three days—if that is necessary. If [s/he] wants to settle in with you, though, and is a craftsperson, let that one work and eat. If [s/he] has no craft, take care in your insight that no Christian live with you in idleness" (Did. 12.1-4, in Kurt Niederwimmer, *The Didachē*, trans. Linda M. Maloney, Hermeneia [Minneapolis: Fortress, 1998]).

handing-on of authority to the next generation. It differs from its literary models in one major respect: the death of the speaker does not follow immediately (or ever, in the context of Acts). Lukas has more work for Paul to do vis-à-vis the Roman world in particular, but here he concludes his mission to spread the Movement through the diaspora and commissions others to carry it on. The author's knowledge of his death is signaled, however, in verse 25: "I know that none of you . . . will ever see my face again." The consolation of the soon-to-be-bereaved that would naturally follow is largely supplanted by warnings against external and internal attacks on the faith and exhortations to "support the weak."[9]

There is a sharp contrast here with Paul's hitherto jealously guarded prerogative (even more visible in his letters) as *the* messenger to the diaspora world of Jews and gentiles. The Lukan Paul is surrendering his missionary authority—but to elders on the synagogue model, not to a hierarchy such as will appear a few decades later in real time, by the mid-second century. Lukas uses the word ἐπίσκοπος, ancestor of "episcopal" but in that time and context meaning something like "overseer," as in NRSV. It is the elders themselves whom the Holy Spirit has made overseers. This reflects early usage in which "elder" (πρεσβύτερος) and "overseer, guardian" (ἐπίσκοπος) were generally equivalent. If a community was large enough to have two persons in those respective offices the ἐπίσκοπος would be the "business manager" or "treasurer" in charge of the community's material welfare. Something of that sort is probably what underlies Acts 6:1-6 as well.[10]

A vital aspect of farewell discourses in the Hebrew Bible and Jewish literature is the naming of a successor to the one departing,[11] but nothing of the sort happens here. The transition in leadership for the Ephesian community and its neighbors is not from one named individual to another but from one embodiment of the leadership role to a group. Lukas knows from his own experience that the passing of the apostolic generation will be marked by conflicts over leadership and the authority to teach, and he lays down his own marker here.[12]

9. For a thorough treatment of this subject see Zane B. McGee, "Transitioning Authority and Paul's Farewell Address: Examining the Narrative Function of Acts 20," *Stone-Campbell Journal* 20 (2017): 203–14.

10. For a thorough exploration of the various church "offices" in the first several centuries CE see Ute E. Eisen, *Women Officeholders in Early Christianity: Epigraphical and Literary Studies*, trans. Linda M. Maloney (Collegeville, MN: Liturgical Press, 2000).

11. E.g., Moses to Joshua (Deut 31:7-8); David to Solomon (1 Kgs 1:32-37).

12. Zane McGee writes: "As the Ephesian church is placed into the hands of the πρεσβύτεροι . . . Luke speaks not to them alone but to all those in the young, devel-

The dual theme of the speech is both definitive absence and pastoral fidelity. Paul's predicted absence (v. 28) necessitates the preparation of the elders for life without him and their commissioning to "keep watch over the flock" (v. 28). Finally, he "hands them over" to God and the word (v. 32), replicating an expression that appears five times in 1 Corinthians, three of them with direct reference to the handing on of tradition (1 Cor 11:2, 23; 15:3) and once (1 Cor 15:24) about Jesus' "handing over the kingdom" to the Father. So here the tradition is handed over to the elders who, in turn, are placed in the hands of God and of the message they have received, to guard it from corruption until the end.[13]

The exhortations in verses 26-35 support two Lukan themes: the community-oriented character of the Way and abhorrence of materialism in the form of greed. Hence "Paul" insists that he "coveted no one's silver or gold or clothing" and that he has worked to support himself and his companions, a statement at least partially belied by the authentic Pauline letters.[14] Still, Paul's (i.e., Lukas's) audience would have found here an edifying echo of the words of Socrates: "Who among humankind is as free as I, for I take no money or payment from anyone?"[15] The "words of the Lord Jesus" in verse 35 are recorded nowhere else; they could be from Jesus or Paul, but they are certainly Lukan in spirit. The remainder of Acts will illustrate Paul's Socratic freedom, even though—or precisely because—he will become and remain a captive.

---

oping church who read this first church history. It serves as the only direct example of 'succession' in the nonepistolary literature of how the church is to function in the absence of the leadership of the apostles. . . . Luke seeks to reassure the church that the present leadership has been rightly established" ("Transitioning Authority," 213–14). It is important to see here a mark of continuity, not a caesura between an "apostolic age" and a subsequent less-normative era.

13. John J. Kilgallen, "Paul's Speech to the Ephesian Elders: Its Structure," *ETL* 70 (1994): 112–20.

14. See esp. Phil 4:15-18; 1 Thess 2:9. Stephen J. Walton, "Paul in Acts and Epistles: The Miletus Speech and 1 Thessalonians as a Test Case" (PhD thesis, University of Sheffield, 1997); précis in his "Leadership and Lifestyle: Luke's Paul, Luke's Jesus and the Paul of 1 Thessalonians," *TynBul* 48 (1997): 377–80, addresses numerous parallels between the Miletus speech and 1 Thessalonians. But see Marlene Crüsemann, *The Pseudepigraphal Letters to the Thessalonians*, trans. Linda M. Maloney (New York: Bloomsbury T&T Clark, 2019).

15. Xenophon, *Apol.* 16.

Acts 21:1-17

Going up to Jerusalem

The opening of the chapter gives us a clear picture of the circumstances of sea travel in the early centuries CE ("When we found a ship bound for Phoenicia . . . and landed at Tyre, because the ship was to unload its cargo there," vv. 2-3). Everyone but those who owned their own trading or war vessels was at the mercy of commerce. If there was a ship bound for your destination, you were in luck; if not, you waited until one appeared or else made your way by land. Hence the helter-skelter itinerary, which may have been recorded in a letter or journal written in connection with the "collection." Either the haste to reach Jerusalem has vanished or there was no southeasterly bound ship at Tyre; Paul and companions spend a week in that place before being sent off by the members of the Way they have searched out there: men, women (γυναιξὶ, not "wives"), and children.

The people of the Way at Tyre become powerfully attached to Paul in the course of the week, so much so that they receive a word from the Holy Spirit showing them what is about to happen to him in Jerusalem and they "tell" him (ἔλεγον), *through the Spirit*, not to go there. So far as the text is concerned, Paul gives them no answer. The next stop is Ptolemais, and a day later the group proceeds to Caesarea. Here they, and the audience, again encounter Philip, and we are reminded that he is an "evangelist" and "one of the seven." For the audience this draws to

21:1When we had parted from them and set sail, we came by a straight course to Cos, and the next day to Rhodes, and from there to Patara. 2When we found a ship bound for Phoenicia, we went on board and set sail. 3We came in sight of Cyprus; and leaving it on our left, we sailed to Syria and landed at Tyre, because the ship was to unload its cargo there. 4We looked up the disciples and stayed there for seven days. Through the Spirit they told Paul not to go on to Jerusalem. 5When our days there were ended, we left and proceeded on our journey; and all of them, with wives and children, escorted us outside the city. There we knelt down on the beach and prayed 6and said farewell to one another. Then we went on board the ship, and they returned home.

7When we had finished the voyage from Tyre, we arrived at Ptolemais; and we greeted the believers and stayed with them for one day. 8The next day we left and came to Caesarea; and we went into the house of Philip the evangelist, one of the seven, and stayed with him. 9He had four unmarried daughters who had the gift of prophecy. 10While we were staying there for several days, a prophet named Agabus came down from Judea. 11He came to us and took Paul's belt, bound his own feet and hands with it, and said, "Thus says the Holy Spirit, 'This is the way the Jews in Jerusalem will bind the man who owns this belt and will hand him over to the Gentiles.'" 12When we heard this, we and the people there urged him not to go up to Jerusalem. 13Then Paul answered, "What are you doing, weeping and breaking my heart? For I am ready not only to be bound but even to die in Jerusalem for the name of the Lord Jesus." 14Since he would not be persuaded, we remained silent except to say, "The Lord's will be done."

15After these days we got ready and started to go up to Jerusalem. 16Some of the disciples from Caesarea also came along and brought us to the house of Mnason of Cyprus, an early disciple, with whom we were to stay.

17When we arrived in Jerusalem, the brothers welcomed us warmly.

a close the story that began with the Twelve and then the Seven; none of them will be found in Jerusalem when the company arrives there.[1]

Philip, we learn, has four daughters who are prophets. Why, then, does a male prophet have to come from Judea to speak to Paul? Why are the prophesying daughters silent? The obvious answer would seem to be that they were not at home: they were on the road prophesying in other communities. Why not? They lived long and active lives in early church legend, but evidently Lukas thinks that describing their activities would dampen the excitement of the story he is building.

1. As noted above, Lukas seems to have "parked" Philip in Caesarea for this purpose (cf. 8:40).

The Prophetic Daughters

Legend names the four prophetic daughters Hermione, Eutychia or Eukhidia, Irais, and Chariline. The first received the most attention and is the only one to be featured in a separate hagiography; she is celebrated as "Martyr Hermione" by the Orthodox Church. Eusebius speaks of them (without names) in his *Ecclesiastical History*.[2] According to him Philip moved to Hierapolis, and it was from Papias of Hierapolis that Eusebius learned about him and his daughters. Supposedly (in some traditions) two of them (Irais and Chariline?) remained with Philip and cared for him, and the three are all buried at Hierapolis. Hermione is supposed to have moved to Ephesus, where she was a healer of renown, devoting herself to the poor and homeless. She was persecuted by both Trajan and Hadrian but survived a variety of gruesome tortures, including being put in a cauldron filled with boiling tar, lead, and brimstone and being fried naked in a skillet. After converting the last of her would-be executioners "she also fell asleep in the Lord."[3]

The New Prophecy movement and related groups that stressed women's equality appealed to Philip's daughters as an example; judging by the violence of the attacks on them by the fourth-century heresy-hunter Epiphanius, they must have enjoyed considerable success in Asia Minor.[4]

Agabus seems to have been based in Jerusalem and periodically sent by the Spirit on assignment: we met him at Acts 11:27, where he was one of a group of prophets who "came down from Jerusalem to Antioch" to predict the famine that was about to take place, causing Barnabas and Saul to be dispatched to Jerusalem with aid. It could be that Lukas means his reappearance to signal to readers in the know that Paul is again bound to Jerusalem on a mission of mercy (with the not-to-be-mentioned collection). This time, however, Agabus speaks only of what is about to happen to Paul there: the "Jews" will bind him and hand him over to the "Gentiles." (In fact, it is rather the other way around in Lukas's story; it is the Romans who take Paul into custody and keep him there, foiling the attempts of the Jewish authorities to kill him.)

---

2. *Eccl. Hist.* 3.31.3; 3.39.9.

3. https://www.oca.org/saints/lives/2010/09/04/102492-martyr-hermione-daughter-of-saint-philip-the-deacon. Did Lukas know her in Ephesus?

4. Epiphanius, *Panarion* [*Refutation of All Heresies*] 4.28, 29 (fourth century CE).

Again Paul's companions and the disciples in Caesarea plead with Paul not to go to Jerusalem; this time Paul responds in a way that makes it clear what Lukas has in view: the paralleling of Paul's journey to his "passion" with that of Jesus. This time the Holy Spirit has prophesied what will happen and has not advised Paul to avoid it. The disciples' response, "The Lord's will be done [Τοῦ κυρίου τὸ θέλημα γινέσθω]," echoes Jesus' words in Gethsemane[5] and shows how fully, by this date, Jesus' followers identified his will with that of God.

So the travelers set out again, this time not stopping before they reach the home of Mnason (which is presumably in or very near Jerusalem, given what transpires the following day). Mnason is a Cypriote, but a believer from the "early days," as Peter referred to the time of Pentecost (11:15). Perhaps he was present on that occasion; he might even have brought news of the Way to Barnabas on his return home. He is one of the *first* believers in Jerusalem, one who remembers the apostles. Even so, he and his household and perhaps other believers[6] offer a warm welcome to the travelers, in contrast to what Paul will encounter the next day.[7] This (with vv. 18-20a) is the final repetition of a pattern of

---

5. Luke 22:42: "not my will but yours be done." "The Lord" in Acts 21:14 means Jesus.

6. It is a mystery why the NRSV reverts to the literal translation of ἀδελφοί ("brothers") here when elsewhere, except in direct address, the preferred translation has been "believers" (see, e.g., 17:10, 14; 18:27).

7. The Greek grammar of v. 16 is difficult, and the "Western" text represented by Codex Bezae (D), always eager to *verschlimmbessern* its source/model (improve it by making it worse), inserted language to "clear up" the verse by adding "and when we came to a certain village, we stayed with Mnason. . . . And when we had left there, we came. . . ." It seemed to the D redactor that in the received text the party arrived twice in Jerusalem, so Mnason got a new home "on the way." Stylistically speaking, the D reading is an improvement, but it changes the content. Modern commentators explained their choice of the D reading by observing that the distance between Caesarea and Jerusalem would make an overnight stop necessary; hence Mnason's "Christian roadhouse" (Henry Cadbury and Kirsopp Lake, *The Beginnings of Christianity* [London: Macmillan, 1933], 4:269–70). Scholars who took a dim view of the D-text in general rejected that solution, observing that it seems to have been created specifically to iron out the difficulties in the text (so Alfred Loisy, *Les Actes des Apôtres* [Frankfurt am Main: Minerva, 1973], 790–91). Further confusion was created by the Vulgate, which read the Greek to mean "they brought *with them* one Mnason [*adducentes . . . Mnasonem*]." The Authorized Version followed, and so did English translations for centuries. The RSV and NRSV at least leave Mnason at home, but the NABRE (2012) finally gets it right: "Some of the disciples from Caesarea came along *to lead us* to the house of Mnason." There would have been no need for Paul and his companions to bring an "early believer"

arrival of apostles or missionaries, communication of good news, and warm reception by the community. That Paul's news overall would be thought "good" by the Jerusalem community may seem questionable but it is, after all, "the Lord's will," as we have seen.

---

as witness *to* Jerusalem, whereas a base in the home *of* such a believer in the city was important, given the reception Paul expected (and received) from the "Pillars." For a full discussion of the issues posed by the text here, see Linda M. Maloney, *"All That God Had Done with Them": The Narration of the Works of God in the Early Christian Community as Described in the Acts of the Apostles*, AUS ser. 7: Theology and Religion 91 (New York: Lang, 1991), *ad loc.*

Acts 21:18-36

"Jerusalem, Jerusalem, the City That Kills the Prophets . . ."
(Luke 13:34)

This final scene featuring a missionary's communication of good tidings, affirmed by the community (vv. 18-20), marks the last appearance of the Jerusalem community in Acts. Within the space of a single verse "they" abandon their praise of God for the success of Paul's mission and instead warn him of its dangerous repercussions in the Holy City. With considerable hyperbole "they" tell him of the "many thousands of believers" among the Jews, all zealous for the law. In other words, the Jerusalem community under James's leadership has remained entirely Jewish and law-observant and has grown mightily thereby. But the first-century version of "fake news" about Paul's actions (v. 21) has agitated them, and they therefore pose a danger to Paul. He is advised to give a double demonstration of his continued fidelity to the law: first, to finance the purification of four Nazirites who are completing a vow, and second, to join them in the rite of purification, even though Paul has no need of it. Almost as an aside, the decree of the apostolic council is reiterated, as something that applies to "the Gentiles who have become believers." The statement that "we have sent a letter to them" seems out of place, since that action took place years previously according to story time, and Paul was personally involved with it. Is the intention here to reinforce an "us and them" dichotomy whereby gentile believers are

295

296 Acts of the Apostles

[18]The next day Paul went with us to visit James; and all the elders were present. [19]After greeting them, he related one by one the things that God had done among the Gentiles through his ministry. [20]When they heard it, they praised God. Then they said to him, "You see, brother, how many thousands of believers there are among the Jews, and they are all zealous for the law. [21]They have been told about you that you teach all the Jews living among the Gentiles to forsake Moses, and that you tell them not to circumcise their children or observe the customs. [22]What then is to be done? They will certainly hear that you have come. [23]So do what we tell you. We have four men who are under a vow. [24]Join these men, go through the rite of purification with them, and pay for the shaving of their heads. Thus all will know that there is nothing in what they have been told about you, but that you yourself observe and guard the law. [25]But as for the Gentiles who have become believers, we have sent a letter with our judgment that they should abstain from what has been sacrificed to idols and from blood and from what is strangled and from fornication." [26]Then Paul took the men, and the next day, having purified himself, he entered the temple with them, making public the completion of the days of purification when the sacrifice would be made for each of them.

to remain in the diaspora and not profane the city of Jerusalem and its temple (a moot point, at any rate, by the time Acts was written)?

The subsequent description of Paul's actions is confusing. The NRSV has rejected the RSV reading of verse 26, "he purified himself *with them* and went into the temple," and instead writes, "having purified himself, he entered the temple with them." Do the seven days of purification for the Nazirites, and the required sacrifice, still lie ahead (v. 27)? The RSV reading makes more sense: "Jews from Asia" who saw Paul at the beginning of the week create a disruption about a week later ("when the seven days were almost completed") after having seen Paul in the city accompanied by Trophimus, a gentile believer from Asia (cf. 20:5) who may even be known to these "Jews from Asia" who are raising the alarm.[1]

1. "Asia" (Minor) may in both cases stand for its principal city, Ephesus, since in 20:4 Paul's companion is called "Trophimus from Asia" and in 21:29 he is "Trophimus the Ephesian" (so not necessarily of Greek ethnicity). Was he perhaps enslaved, or even a eunuch?

²⁷When the seven days were almost completed, the Jews from Asia, who had seen him in the temple, stirred up the whole crowd. They seized him, ²⁸shouting, "Fellow Israelites, help! This is the man who is teaching everyone everywhere against our people, our law, and this place; more than that, he has actually brought Greeks into the temple and has defiled this holy place." ²⁹For they had previously seen Trophimus the Ephesian with him in the city, and they supposed that Paul had brought him into the temple. ³⁰Then all the city was aroused, and the people rushed together. They seized Paul and dragged him out of the temple, and immediately the doors were shut. ³¹While they were trying to kill him, word came to the tribune of the cohort that all Jerusalem was in an uproar. ³²Immediately he took soldiers and centurions and ran down to them. When they saw the tribune and the soldiers, they stopped beating Paul. ³³Then the tribune came, arrested him, and ordered him to be bound with two chains; he inquired who he was and what he had done. ³⁴Some in the crowd shouted one thing, some another; and as he could not learn the facts because of the uproar, he ordered him to be brought into the barracks. ³⁵When Paul came to the steps, the violence of the mob was so great that he had to be carried by the soldiers. ³⁶The crowd that followed kept shouting, "Away with him!"

Here again the issue of circumcision arises: an uncircumcised man[2] would pollute the temple. In a way this is a fitting introduction to the remainder of Acts: an issue of no relevance to women becomes the crux for Paul's incarceration and his subsequent years as a prisoner. At the time described (the 50s CE) the Romans were interested in keeping Judea pacified and therefore were quite willing to punish people who offended the Sadducean leadership. Josephus tells of a Roman soldier who tore up and burned a Torah scroll. The popular outcry led Cumanus to order the soldier brought to him and executed.[3] The point here is that Paul, as a Jew, was already subject to Roman jurisdiction and could be tried by the Roman officialdom for offending Jewish law, or he could agree to be tried by the Sanhedrin. The choice for him was obvious; if he were condemned by the Sanhedrin, the Romans might well execute him as Cumanus had done to the soldier. But his being tried under Roman law and thus being able to appeal to the emperor had nothing to do with

2. Simply referring to a man as a "Greek" would signify that he was not circumcised.
3. *J.W.* 2.228-31.

his being a Roman citizen or not (though his *not* being one doubtless rendered his imprisonment longer and less pleasant than it might have been). What really happened to Paul in Jerusalem was of no real interest to Lukas; the shape of his trial scenes is standard fare from the historical and novelistic literature of the period except that these trials feature the eloquence of the Lukan Paul.

Lukas colors Paul's arrest with reminiscences of the death of James some six years later; according to tradition James was arrested by the high priest Ananus, tried, and executed, either by stoning (so Josephus, *Ant.* 9.1.200) or by being thrown from the roof of the temple (cf. Luke 4:9). Like James, Paul addresses the mob from an elevated place (the top of the staircase rather than the "pinnacle" of the temple; see 21:35-36); like Jesus, he is pursued by a crowd shouting "Away with him!" Thus Paul, like Stephen and the apostle James (cf. 12:2) before him, follows in the footsteps of Jesus—except that Paul escapes, for now.

Acts 21:37–23:11

Jerusalem Attempts to Kill Another Prophet

Paul makes use of his Greek to waylay the tribune, who is shocked to learn that he is dealing with an educated man. Lukas draws the "mistaken identity" of the Egyptian rebel from Josephus.[1] Paul, once he has the tribune's ear, introduces himself as "a Jew, from Tarsus in Cilicia," and claims to be a citizen of that city, whose importance he stresses.[2] Paul may well have been a native of Tarsus, which had a large Jewish community, and he could likewise have been educated there, for Tarsus was a center of Hellenistic culture and philosophy. But Tarsus demanded that a man wishing to be a citizen must possess five hundred drachmae

---

1. "But there was an Egyptian false prophet that did the Jews more mischief . . . for he was a cheat, and pretended to be a prophet also, and got together thirty thousand men that were deluded by him; these he led round about from the wilderness to the mount which was called the Mount of Olives, and was ready to break into Jerusalem by force from that place . . . but Felix prevented his attempt" (*J.W.* 2.261-63). Lukas reduces the force to a more believable four thousand.

2. As indicated previously, the *litotes* οὐκ ἀσήμου πόλεως πολίτης was a familiar Greek idiom; the change from RSV "no mean city" to NRSV "important" is not an improvement. NABRE restores the idiom.

³⁷Just as Paul was about to be brought into the barracks, he said to the tribune, "May I say something to you?" The tribune replied, "Do you know Greek? ³⁸Then you are not the Egyptian who recently stirred up a revolt and led the four thousand assassins out into the wilderness?" ³⁹Paul replied, "I am a Jew, from Tarsus in Cilicia, a citizen of an important city; I beg you, let me speak to the people." ⁴⁰When he had given him permission, Paul stood on the steps and motioned to the people for silence; and when there was a great hush, he addressed them in the Hebrew language, saying:

²²:¹"Brothers and fathers, listen to the defense that I now make before you."

²When they heard him addressing them in Hebrew, they became even more quiet. Then he said:

³"I am a Jew, born in Tarsus in Cilicia, but brought up in this city at the feet of Gamaliel, educated strictly according to our ancestral law, being zealous for God, just as all of you are today. ⁴I persecuted this Way up to the point of death by binding both men and women and putting them in prison, ⁵as the high priest and the whole council of elders can testify about me. From them I also received letters to the brothers in Damascus, and I went there in order to bind those who were there and to bring them back to Jerusalem for punishment.

⁶"While I was on my way and approaching Damascus, about noon a great light from heaven suddenly shone about me. ⁷I fell to the ground and heard a voice saying to me, 'Saul, Saul, why are you persecuting me?' ⁸I answered, 'Who are you, Lord?' Then

he said to me, 'I am Jesus of Nazareth whom you are persecuting.' ⁹Now those who were with me saw the light but did not hear the voice of the one who was speaking to me. ¹⁰I asked, 'What am I to do, Lord?' The Lord said to me, 'Get up and go to Damascus; there you will be told everything that has been assigned to you to do.' ¹¹Since I could not see because of the brightness of that light, those who were with me took my hand and led me to Damascus.

¹²"A certain Ananias, who was a devout man according to the law and well spoken of by all the Jews living there, ¹³came to me; and standing beside me, he said, 'Brother Saul, regain your sight!' In that very hour I regained my sight and saw him. ¹⁴Then he said, 'The God of our ancestors has chosen you to know his will, to see the Righteous One and to hear his own voice; ¹⁵for you will be his witness to all the world of what you have seen and heard. ¹⁶And now why do you delay? Get up, be baptized, and have your sins washed away, calling on his name.'

¹⁷"After I had returned to Jerusalem and while I was praying in the temple, I fell into a trance ¹⁸and saw Jesus saying to me, 'Hurry and get out of Jerusalem quickly, because they will not accept your testimony about me.' ¹⁹And I said, 'Lord, they themselves know that in every synagogue I imprisoned and beat those who believed in you. ²⁰And while the blood of your witness Stephen was shed, I myself was standing by, approving and keeping the coats of those who killed him.' ²¹Then he said to me, 'Go, for I will send you far away to the Gentiles.'"

²²Up to this point they listened to him, but then they shouted, "Away with such a fellow from the earth! For he should not be allowed to live." ²³And while they were shouting, throwing off their cloaks, and tossing dust into the air, ²⁴the tribune directed that he was to be brought into the barracks, and ordered him to be examined by flogging, to find out the reason for this outcry against him. ²⁵But when they had tied him up with thongs, Paul said to the centurion who was standing by, "Is it legal for you to flog a Roman citizen who is uncondemned?" ²⁶When the centurion heard that, he went to the tribune and said to him, "What are you about to do? This man is a Roman citizen." ²⁷The tribune came and asked Paul, "Tell me, are you a Roman citizen?" And he said, "Yes." ²⁸The tribune answered, "It cost me a large sum of money to get my citizenship." Paul said, "But I was born a citizen." ²⁹Immediately those who were about to examine him drew back from him; and the tribune also was afraid, for he realized that Paul was a Roman citizen and that he had bound him.

³⁰Since he wanted to find out what Paul was being accused of by the Jews, the next day he released him and ordered the chief priests and the entire council to meet. He brought Paul down and had him stand before them.

²³:¹While Paul was looking intently at the council he said, "Brothers, up to this day I have lived my life with a clear conscience before God." ²Then the high priest Ananias ordered those standing near him to strike him on the mouth. ³At this Paul said to him, "God will strike you, you whitewashed wall! Are you sitting there to judge me according to the

in property, and that seems unlikely for the tentmaker Paul.[3] The claim is enough to move the tribune to let Paul speak to the crowd, and when he manages to achieve silence he begins to address them (not in Greek, of course, but in Aramaic). So begins the second recounting of Saul's vision before Damascus and its consequences.

Lukas is clearly the author of all three versions of the story of Saul's encounter with the risen Lord. The first, in chapter 9, was directed to the audience of Acts; this one is shaped to appeal to the supposed crowd of angry Jews confronting Paul on the temple steps but also (as always) beyond them to readers and hearers as much as half a century later.

The speech in Acts 22 begins with a *captatio benevolentiae* as Paul addresses the mob as "brothers and fathers," the same words (ἄνδρες

---

3. See Richard I. Pervo, *Acts*, Hermeneia (Minneapolis: Fortress, 2009), 554. In the subsequent speech Paul asserts that he was born in Tarsus but brought up and educated in Jerusalem, which seems unlikely but further negates the idea of Tarsian citizenship, much less Roman.

Acts 21:37–23:11 (cont.)

law, and yet in violation of the law you order me to be struck?" ⁴Those standing nearby said, "Do you dare to insult God's high priest?" ⁵And Paul said, "I did not realize, brothers, that he was high priest; for it is written, 'You shall not speak evil of a leader of your people.'"

⁶When Paul noticed that some were Sadducees and others were Pharisees, he called out in the council, "Brothers, I am a Pharisee, a son of Pharisees. I am on trial concerning the hope of the resurrection of the dead." ⁷When he said this, a dissension began between the Pharisees and the Sadducees, and the assembly was divided. ⁸(The Sadducees say that there is no resurrection, or angel, or spirit; but the Pharisees acknowledge all three.) ⁹Then a great clamor arose, and certain scribes of the Pharisees' group stood up and contended, "We find nothing wrong with this man. What if a spirit or an angel has spoken to him?" ¹⁰When the dissension became violent, the tribune, fearing that they would tear Paul to pieces, ordered the soldiers to go down, take him by force, and bring him into the barracks.

¹¹That night the Lord stood near him and said, "Keep up your courage! For just as you have testified for me in Jerusalem, so you must bear witness also in Rome."

ἀδελφοὶ καὶ πατέρες) with which Stephen addressed the council at 7:2; similarly, Peter spoke to the first post-ascension meeting (1:12) and the crowd on Pentecost (2:29) as ἄνδρες ἀδελφοί. In fact, that phrase appears fourteen times in Acts, but only twice (7:2 and 22:1) with the added "and fathers." We are alerted immediately to the parallel with Stephen.

From beginning to end "Paul" is intent to show his audience that he is one of them—a Jew from the diaspora but brought up in Jerusalem "at the feet of Gamaliel," the famous rabbi (and, be it noted, a Pharisee; cf. 23:6-7) who has already appeared speaking on behalf of the Jesus-followers in 5:34. Lukas does not allow Paul to deny the charge that he has been "teaching everyone⁴ everywhere against our people, our law, and this place" (21:28; such a denial would be at least partly untrue for the historical Paul, though not for the Paul of Acts). Instead he has him speak of his strict education in the law and his being "zealous for God" (22:3). Paul goes on to describe in gruesome detail his persecution of the people of the Way, including women as well as men (v. 4; cf. 8:2). The mission to Damascus and the scene on the road are almost the same as in chapter 9 except that this time Saul's companions see the light but do

4. Cf. 22:15.

not hear the voice, whereas the reverse was the case in chapter 9. "High noon" for dramatic events of conversion or commissioning was as much a cliché in the first and second centuries as in the twenty-first.

Missing from this account is Ananias's vision and the instruction given him. By the third recounting in chapter 26 Ananias will have vanished altogether. The focus narrows inexorably to the pairing of Saul and the risen Lord. In this second account, with its Jewish focus, Jesus identifies himself as "the Nazorean." Likewise Ananias is described not, as in chapter 9, as a "disciple" (i.e., of Jesus) but as "a devout man according to the law and well spoken of by all the Jews living there" (v. 12). He addresses Saul not on behalf of Jesus but on behalf of "the God of our ancestors" who has chosen Saul to see the Righteous One—the Pharisees, at least, would interpret this to mean the Messiah—and to be a witness. This is very much like the call of a prophet.[5] In the same vein, Saul is called on to be baptized "and have your sins washed away," which was the purpose of John's baptism, whereas the baptism of those who followed the Way was for receiving the Holy Spirit and power (cf. 9:17).

The vision thus denied to Ananias is bestowed instead on Saul, in the temple in Jerusalem. Jesus appears to him with the message: "Get out of town; they're going to kill you!" In chapter 9 Ananias was told that Saul/Paul was to preach to the gentiles, but he did not reveal that news to Saul. Here Jesus himself conveys the message,[6] but only in the very last word of the speech: "Go, for I will send you far away to the Gentiles" (v. 21)—and as soon as Paul speaks that word all hell breaks loose.

We should always remember that the "bad guys" in these Jerusalem scenes are not Jews in general; they are Jerusalem Jews, "Hellenists," and above all Sadducees, the upper-crust collaborators with the Romans, as the people of the land thought of them (with a great deal of justification).[7] They cooperate with the Romans for their own benefit, but they hold themselves superior to them, those filthy polytheistic gentiles. For Lukas the love of wealth condemns, no matter one's nationality or religion.

Once again the tribune is forced to intervene; he rescinds his permission for Paul to speak to the crowd and orders him brought into the barracks and flogged. To increase the dramatic tension, Paul waits until

---

5. Cf., e.g., Exod 3:10-12; Isa 6:1-7; Jer 1:10.

6. Richard I. Pervo writes: "The speech ends on an ironic note. The one accused of introducing gentiles into the temple had been instructed in the temple to leave it and approach the gentiles" (*Acts*, 566).

7. See, e.g., Josephus, *Ant.* 13.297–98.

the whip is ready to fall before warning the centurion that he is about to infringe the rights of a Roman—again speaking of an ἄνθρωπος Ῥωμαῖος, not a πολίτης.[8] The Vulgate renders accurately in verse 25: it has Paul ask about the fate of a *homines Romanus*, but in verse 26 the alarmed centurion is made to say *civis Romanus* (Greek original: Ῥωμαῖος). The tribune (in v. 27) asks Paul if he is a Ῥωμαῖος (Vulgate: *Romanus*). Thus the exchange is really: "Tell me, are you a Roman? And he said, 'Yes.' " The tribune (whose name, we learn in 23:26, is Claudius Lysias) is amazed that a lowly Jew such as Paul appears to claim Roman citizenship, and his reaction betrays his own low character: "It cost me a large sum of money to get my citizenship." Purchase of Roman citizenship was possible—on the black market, so to speak—but it was an illegal action done for personal gain, and thus to Lukas (and, he hopes, to his audience as well) it was abhorrent. Paul's own claim is again ambiguous: that he was "born so" (not, as in the NRSV, "born a citizen"). In any case, his true status is not based on material wealth or its uses.[9]

Jennifer Glancy has shown that the whole exchange is all but impossible: the minute Paul's back was bared and the marks of the lash or the rod appeared it would be clear to everyone that he was certainly not a citizen; if he were, his having been beaten rendered him so debased as to be beneath consideration.[10]

> Citizen or not, free or slave, a beaten body was a dishonored body; any free person who was publicly stripped and battered with rods suffered an effective reduction in social status. Even a single occasion of flogging dishonored a man; multiple occasions of flogging would raise questions about the character of a man unable or unwilling to guard his body against violation, who might even be perceived to invite such treatment.[11]

8. See the excursus, "Did Paul Claim to Be a Roman Citizen?" at Acts 16. "Citizen" is not in the Greek original. Flogging a Roman citizen was forbidden *tout court*; even condemnation to death did not alter that rule.

9. Many authors read this to mean that Paul was born the son of a manumitted slave; such persons were often granted Roman citizenship, particularly if their fathers were wealthy, e.g., former slaves of Roman emperors or other high officials. But if Paul was also born a Jew such a situation is highly unlikely. Besides, for Lukas it is a plot device and he is not interested in whether it is true or not. Such concerns are peculiar to modern historians.

10. We have been told of Paul's and Silas's being beaten with rods in Philippi (16:22-23). Paul himself chose to *boast* of being beaten over and over again: see 2 Cor 11:23-25.

11. Jennifer A. Glancy, "Boasting of Beatings (2 Corinthians 11:23-25)," *JBL* 123 (2004): 99–135, at 124.

Obviously the Corinthians to whom Paul wrote had been disgusted at the sight of Paul's flagellated flesh.[12] There is no reason to suppose that Roman officers would be less so. Nevertheless, in the story Lysias's fear of insulting a Roman citizen leads him to release Paul from the whipping post. Evidently, though, he still regards Paul's primary status as "Jew" because he retains him in custody and brings him before the "chief priests and the entire council" on the following day.

As the encounters continue, violence begets more violence. Paul declares he has a clear conscience and is struck in the face. He responds with verbal abuse of the high priest and a threat of divine vengeance. This is a reversal of the Stephen story, in which the high priest asks the accused, "Are these things so?" (7:1), and Stephen then makes his long speech, at the end of which he accuses the council of breaking the law, whereupon they seize him and stone him. Here Paul begins with the standard address "Men, brothers" (cf. 2:29) and declares he has a clear conscience, whereupon the high priest orders him to be struck on the mouth (cf. Luke 6:29, with the same verb, τύπτω).[13] Paul's venomous response is (supposedly) shocking to those who hear it, and his excuse is patently disingenuous: "I did not realize, brothers, that he was high priest." Previously (22:4-5) he has defended himself by saying that the *high priest* and council can testify to his youthful zeal in persecuting the people of the Way. Although those events are some twenty years in the past, Saul's apostasy from their group would scarcely have been forgotten, as the council's attitude toward him attests. Moreover, the high priest he supposedly does not recognize, Ananus ben Nebedeus,[14] was a notorious figure. Arrogant, cruel, and corrupt, he had been accused by the then-governor of Syria, Quadratus, of fomenting violence and was sent to Rome in 52 CE, but he was acquitted by Claudius and restored to his office. His fame (or notoriety) was undiminished.[15]

How might Lukas's audience have reacted to this scene? The enslaved among them, as well as many of the free women, would have had plenty of experience of being scorned and even struck in the face by

---

12. Cf. 1 Cor 4:10-13.

13. Paul certainly does not react in the spirit of the injunction given there: "If anyone strikes you on the cheek, offer the other also."

14. "Ananias" in Acts 23.

15. Cf. Josephus, *J.W.* 20.124-33. For a recent affirmation of the accuracy of the Acts portrayal of the Sadducees see Lester L. Grabbe, "What Did the Author of Acts Know about Pre-70 Judaism?," in *Wisdom Poured Out Like Water: Studies on Jewish and Christian Antiquity in Honor of Gabriele Boccaccini*, ed. J. Harold Ellens, et al. (Boston: deGruyter, 2018), 450–62, at 451–52.

their "superiors." Hearing that this treatment, this shaming, had been meted out to Paul had to have been painful. Were they also "put off" by having to listen to this tale of quarreling among men, or would they have admired Paul's stratagem of setting the Pharisees and Sadducees against one another?[16]

Paul makes the issue "the hope of the resurrection of the dead" (v. 6)—not the resurrection of Jesus, which was the belief that really set the followers of the Way against the Jewish leadership. Since belief in the resurrection of the dead was a prime divider between the Sadducees (no) and the Pharisees (yes), this sowed division among the members of the council and steered hostility away from Paul.

This tried-and-true tactic has been used for millennia, and continues to be used, to repress minorities: divide women against women, "straight" against LGBTQIA+, Black against Brown, *ad infinitum*. It usually works, as it does in this scene even among upper-class men. Lukas inserts the issues of "angels" and "spirits" alongside resurrection,[17] and even has the "scribes of the Pharisees" suggest that Paul has received a revelation from "a spirit or an angel" (vv. 8-9). Now for the third time violence erupts and the tribune has Paul brought back into the barracks. There Paul does indeed receive a revelation, not from a spirit or an angel but from the Lord (Jesus), and the revelation conveniently moves the plot forward: "so you must bear witness also in Rome" (v. 11).

---

16. If Lukas was familiar with Josephus's *Antiquities* (as now seems likely; cf. Richard I. Pervo, *Dating Acts: Between the Evangelists and the Apologists* [Santa Rosa, CA: Polebridge, 2006] and his "In the Suburbs of the Apologists," in *Contemporary Studies in Acts*, ed. Thomas E. Phillips [Macon, GA: Mercer University Press, 2009], 17–34), he would have found there another reason to despise the Sadducees. Josephus writes: "The Sadducees are able to persuade none but the rich . . . but the Pharisees have the multitude on their side" (*Ant.* 13.10.6, 298).

17. Josephus emphasizes the conflict between Sadducees and Pharisees over the issue of resurrection (*Ant.* 18.11-17; *J.W.* 2.8.14, 162-66). The Sadducees' doctrine that God is indifferent to humans would imply their denial of the existence of angels ("messengers") conveying God's will to humans; similarly, the denial of resurrection seems to mean that there is no "spirit" in humans animating the body or separable from it.

Acts 23:12-35

The Plot against Paul

This last part of chapter 23 is the counterpart to chapter 12: Paul's narrow escape from assassination parallels Peter's. Acts 23 is even better suited to film treatment than is Acts 12 since it contains more dialogue and more action. It opens with a thrilling conspiracy: "the Jews" (obviously not the Pharisees who, in verse 9, had declared Paul innocent, perhaps even angelically inspired[1]) vow to fast until they have killed him. As Richard Pervo points out, this is not a good tactic for people aiming to carry out a violent action,[2] and there are evidently too many involved[3] for the secret to stay hidden.

Sure enough, the word gets out, and a young man appears at the prison, asking for Paul. It turns out that he is Paul's nephew, his sister's son. (Paul has a family? a sister in Jerusalem with a family of her own? This is news to everyone! Perhaps the audience is to infer that he, like Uncle Paul before him, is studying Torah with Gamaliel and so is privy to rumors circulating in the temple precincts.)

---

1. Richard I. Pervo notes (*Acts*, Hermeneia [Minneapolis: Fortress, 2009], 581n12) that Lukas avoids speaking here of "the Sanhedrin" because that group includes Pharisees.

2. Cf. 1 Sam 14:24-26.

3. Forty, according to v. 21.

Acts 23:12-35

¹²In the morning the Jews joined in a conspiracy and bound themselves by an oath neither to eat nor drink until they had killed Paul. ¹³There were more than forty who joined in this conspiracy. ¹⁴They went to the chief priests and elders and said, "We have strictly bound ourselves by an oath to taste no food until we have killed Paul. ¹⁵Now then, you and the council must notify the tribune to bring him down to you, on the pretext that you want to make a more thorough examination of his case. And we are ready to do away with him before he arrives."

¹⁶Now the son of Paul's sister heard about the ambush; so he went and gained entrance to the barracks and told Paul. ¹⁷Paul called one of the centurions and said, "Take this young man to the tribune, for he has something to report to him." ¹⁸So he took him, brought him to the tribune, and said, "The prisoner Paul called me and asked me to bring this young man to you; he has something to tell you." ¹⁹The tribune took him by the hand, drew him aside privately, and asked, "What is it that you have to report to me?" ²⁰He answered, "The Jews have

On hearing of the plot, Paul summons (προσκαλεσάμενος)[4] a centurion and orders him to take the youth[5] to the tribune to repeat his story. Suspense increases: Will the tribune take this boy seriously? Will he set an investigation of the plot in motion, or will he just dismiss the youth and haul his prisoner before the Sanhedrin again?

Certainly not: the tribune Lysias is impressed with Paul. He treats the nephew with the utmost kindness (takes him by the hand, v. 19)[6] and speaks with him privately—a good idea, after all; it would not be appropriate to have rumors of a conspiracy circulating in the barracks. He believes every word of the report (which again speaks of "the Jews" as the perpetrators; Lukas knows that Romans, like colonizers before and since, have trouble telling provincials apart), and he springs into action.

The tribune's attitude is to be understood, of course, as providential in the literal sense. It is God's will that Paul be rescued (διασῴζω, v. 24).[7] Alert listeners will enjoy the suspense because they know Paul will not

---

4. The same verb, προσκαλέω, in v. 23 describes the tribune's summoning of his centurions. In the Lukan corpus it always describes the address of a superior to an inferior. Paul the prisoner has clout!

5. Νεανίας, equivalent to νεανίσκος, the descriptor used for Eutychus at 20:9.

6. For a similar scene see Chariton, *Callirhoe* 1.4.5.

7. NRSV "take him safely." The same verb describes Paul's being "saved" from the shipwreck in 27:43-44; 28:1, 4.

agreed to ask you to bring Paul down to the council tomorrow, as though they were going to inquire more thoroughly into his case. ²¹But do not be persuaded by them, for more than forty of their men are lying in ambush for him. They have bound themselves by an oath neither to eat nor drink until they kill him. They are ready now and are waiting for your consent." ²²So the tribune dismissed the young man, ordering him, "Tell no one that you have informed me of this."

²³Then he summoned two of the centurions and said, "Get ready to leave by nine o'clock tonight for Caesarea with two hundred soldiers, seventy horsemen, and two hundred spearmen. ²⁴Also provide mounts for Paul to ride, and take him safely to Felix the governor." ²⁵He wrote a letter to this effect:

²⁶"Claudius Lysias to his Excellency the governor Felix, greetings. ²⁷This man was seized by the Jews and was about to be killed by them, but when I had learned that he was a Roman citizen, I came with the guard and rescued him. ²⁸Since I wanted to know the charge for which they accused

be assassinated in Jerusalem. He *has to* "see Rome" (19:21); the Lord Jesus has said so (23:11).

The escort provided for Paul is a royal one[8] and improbably large (470 men): nearly half the nominal strength of the cohort under Lysias's command![9] The tribune is protecting himself as well as Paul: he wants to save Paul from the Jewish leadership, but he also wants to save himself from criticism (or worse) if anything should go wrong. Both the immense military force and his letter to the governor make that abundantly clear. The journey must be made on horseback; mounts are to be provided for Paul. Apparently the two hundred soldiers (on foot) will accompany the first part of the journey, as far as Antipatris.[10] Speed is not of the essence for this stretch, since the foot soldiers and spearmen can fight off any assassins' attacks. Beyond Antipatris the mounted troops will escort the prisoner to Caesarea at the gallop.

Paul on horseback? One wonders if he knew how to ride: he may have been in more danger from the galloping horses than from the assassins.

8. See John Chrysostom, *Hom.* 50: Paul is escorted "like a king."
9. Pervo, *Acts*, 583nn27, 28. A model garrison would number one thousand (ten detachments of one hundred, each headed by a centurion).
10. Antipatris, in the Sharon plain, was located about halfway between Jerusalem and Caesarea. No doubt Paul would have passed through it, and perhaps spent the night there, on his way to Jerusalem only a couple of weeks earlier.

Acts 23:12-35 (cont.)

him, I had him brought to their council. ²⁹I found that he was accused concerning questions of their law, but was charged with nothing deserving death or imprisonment. ³⁰When I was informed that there would be a plot against the man, I sent him to you at once, ordering his accusers also to state before you what they have against him."

³¹So the soldiers, according to their instructions, took Paul and brought him during the night to Antipatris. ³²The next day they let the horsemen go on with him, while they returned to the barracks. ³³When they came to Caesarea and delivered the letter to the governor, they presented Paul also before him. ³⁴On reading the letter, he asked what province he belonged to, and when he learned that he was from Cilicia, ³⁵he said, "I will give you a hearing when your accusers arrive." Then he ordered that he be kept under guard in Herod's headquarters.

In spite of the beautiful horses in artists' depictions of Paul's vision on the Damascus road there is nothing in the text of Acts, or in Paul's letters, to intimate that he traveled on horseback (or by donkey) at any time. The artists could be correct, but Lukas does not use any language to indicate mounted travel by Paul or his companions except here.

The tribune's letter justifies his actions on the grounds that Paul is a "Roman" (NRSV inserts "citizen"; the Greek has only Ῥωμαῖός) who is being unfairly persecuted by "the Jews" (wrongly presented as a unified body). The argument, as he perceives it (just as Gallio did at 18:15), is about matters of Jewish law and not really under his jurisdiction, but he is sending the prisoner to Felix to prevent his being subjected to extrajudicial murder.[11] The letter omits to mention Paul's supposed Tarsian citizenship, so the governor has to ask about it after Paul arrives. Citizens of Tarsus, a free city, were not really subject to the jurisdiction of other provinces (another reason to suspect that Paul was not a citizen of Tarsus, even if he came from there).[12] Nevertheless, the governor decides to hear the case as soon as accusers from Jerusalem arrive.

11. An audience familiar with stories of the high priest Ananus's actions against James and the Jerusalem community of the Way would have found this entirely plausible. (See at 23:1-5 above.)

12. Thorough discussion can be found in Adrian N. Sherwin-White, *Roman Society and Roman Law in the New Testament* (Oxford: Clarendon, 1963), in critical dialogue with Theodor Mommsen, "Die Rechtsverhältnisse des Apostels Paulus," *ZNW* 2 (1902): 81–96.

Acts 24:1-27

Paul before Felix

$\mathbf{A}$cts 24 presents the only real "trial scene" involving Paul, and it is truncated in the extreme, "an untechnical account with apologetic motive."[1] Lukas's purpose is both to reiterate Paul's defense of his mission and to create a suspenseful narrative out of a process depicted as lasting several years and surely marked for the most part by sheer tedium. There is no clear statement of the charges being brought, or of how they would have related to Roman law. Had Paul actually brought gentile men into the temple, under Roman procedure those violators would have been subject to summary execution—but only they, and not Paul. Hence the accusers seek throughout the story to have Paul turned over to the Sanhedrin for judgment, with the expectation that his fate would be the same as Stephen's.

The counter-speeches from Tertullus and Paul follow a pattern familiar to the audience from contemporary popular literature, opening with a proem, or preface with a *captatio benevolentiae*, a rhetorical technique aimed to capture the goodwill of the audience at the beginning of a speech or appeal. For example:

1. Henry J. Cadbury, "Roman Law and the Trial of Paul," in Kirsopp Lake and Henry J. Cadbury, *Additional Notes to the Commentary*, ed. Henry J. Cadbury and Kirsopp Lake, vol. 5 of *The Beginnings of Christianity*, ed. Frederick J. Foakes Jackson and Kirsopp Lake (New York: Macmillan, 1920–1933; repr. Grand Rapids: Baker, 1979), 297–338, at 298.

²⁴:¹Five days later the high priest Ananias came down with some elders and an attorney, a certain Tertullus, and they reported their case against Paul to the governor. ²When Paul had been summoned, Tertullus began to accuse him, saying: ³Your Excellency, because of you we have long enjoyed peace, and reforms have been made for this people because of your foresight. We welcome this in every way and everywhere with utmost gratitude. ⁴But, to detain you no further, I beg you to hear us briefly with your customary graciousness. ⁵We have, in fact, found this man a pestilent fellow, an agitator among all the Jews throughout the world, and a ringleader of the sect of the Nazarenes. ⁶He even tried to profane the temple, and so we seized him.* ⁸By examining him yourself you will be able to learn from him concerning everything of which we accuse him.

* The Western text (D) inserts: "and we would have judged him according to our law. But the chief captain Lysias came and with great violence took him out of our hands, commanding his accusers to come before you."

Chariton, *Callirhoe* 5, 6	Acts 24:2-4	Acts 24:10
[Proem: *captatio benevolentiae*]:	[Proem: *captatio benevolentiae*]	[Proem: *captatio benevolentiae*]
[6] . . . it was Dionysios who spoke first: "I am grateful to you, sire, for the honor you have paid to me, to the faithfulness of this woman here, and to the marriages of all. You did not look the other way when a private citizen was the object of a plot by a man in a position of power. No, you summoned that man to trial so you could punish his immorality and depravity in my case, and provide a deterrent in other cases."	[Tertullus] "Your Excellency, because of you we have long enjoyed peace, and reforms have been made for this people because of your foresight. We welcome this in every way and everywhere with utmost gratitude. But, to detain you no further, I beg you to hear us briefly with your customary graciousness."	[Paul] "I cheerfully make my defense, knowing that for many years you have been a judge over this nation."

Each text then offers the *narratio*, an exposition of the charges and circumstances. The speeches close with a *peroratio*:

⁹The Jews also joined in the charge by asserting that all this was true.

¹⁰When the governor motioned to him to speak, Paul replied:

"I cheerfully make my defense, knowing that for many years you have been a judge over this nation. ¹¹As you can find out, it is not more than twelve days since I went up to worship in Jerusalem. ¹²They did not find me disputing with anyone in the temple or stirring up a crowd either in the synagogues or throughout the city. ¹³Neither can they prove to you the charge that they now bring against me. ¹⁴But this I admit to you, that according to the Way, which they call a sect, I worship the God of our ancestors, believing everything laid down according to the law or written in the prophets. ¹⁵I have a hope in God—a hope that they themselves also accept—that there will be a resurrection of both the righteous and the unrighteous. ¹⁶Therefore I do my best always to have a clear conscience toward God and all people. ¹⁷Now after some years I came to bring alms to my nation and to offer sacrifices. ¹⁸While I was doing this, they found me in the temple, completing the rite of purification, without any crowd

Chariton, *Callirhoe*, 5, 6	Acts 24:8-9	Acts 24:20-21
"I will end by reading the letter that this man sent from Caria to Miletos with his own slaves. Take it and read what it says: 'From Chaireas. I am alive.' Let Mithridates exonerate himself by proving *that*. Consider, sire, just how brazen an adulterer has to be when he is even willing to forge a letter from a dead man." Dionysios' speech moved his listeners, and right away he had their vote.	[Tertullus] "By examining him yourself you will be able to learn from him concerning everything of which we accuse him." The Jews also joined in the charge by asserting that all this was true.	[Paul] "Or let these men here tell what crime they had found when I stood before the council, unless it was this one sentence that I called out while standing before them, 'It is about the resurrection of the dead that I am on trial before you today.'" But Felix . . . adjourned the hearing.

Verisimilitude is not in order in either text. Richard Pervo remarked of Tertullus's speech, "This prosecution would have been no more incompetent had it been designed by the defense—as it in fact was."[2]

2. Richard I. Pervo, *Acts*, Hermeneia (Minneapolis: Fortress, 2009), 595.

or disturbance. ¹⁹But there were some Jews from Asia—they ought to be here before you to make an accusation, if they have anything against me. ²⁰Or let these men here tell what crime they had found when I stood before the council, ²¹unless it was this one sentence that I called out while standing before them, "It is about the resurrection of the dead that I am on trial before you today."

²²But Felix, who was rather well informed about the Way, adjourned the hearing with the comment, "When Lysias the tribune comes down, I will decide your case." ²³Then he ordered the centurion to keep him in custody, but to let him have some liberty and not to prevent any of his friends from taking care of his needs.

²⁴Some days later when Felix came with his wife Drusilla, who was Jewish, he sent for Paul and heard him speak concerning faith in Christ Jesus. ²⁵And as he discussed justice, self-control, and the coming judgment, Felix became frightened and said, "Go away for the present; when I have an opportunity, I will send for you." ²⁶At the same time he hoped that money would be given him by Paul, and for that reason he used to send for him very often and converse with him.

²⁷After two years had passed, Felix was succeeded by Porcius Festus; and since he wanted to grant the Jews a favor, Felix left Paul in prison.

Felix supposedly prolongs Paul's imprisonment by ordering that the trial resume when the tribune, Claudius Lysias, shows up to make his affidavit—which he never does. Lukas alleges that Felix's real reason is that he hopes, by means of successive interrogations, to squeeze Paul for a bribe to obtain his release. Even though we are told that Paul's custody is governed by a centurion rather than a common soldier and his custodian was "to let him have some liberty and not to prevent any of his friends from taking care of his needs" (including, perhaps money for his release?) no funds are forthcoming, nor do we read of any friends' visits.

In fact, throughout time a friendless prisoner has been and is in dire straits indeed; until very recently she or he would have needed at least one attendant to fetch food, water, and probably fuel for heating and cooking—all at the prisoner's expense, of course. Charles Dickens's *Little Dorrit*, set in the mid-nineteenth century in England, paints the picture eloquently, and in antiquity circumstances were even more straitened. One wonders: where, indeed, are Paul's friends? He is in Caesarea, after all. Cornelius must long since have retired and moved back to Rome or to one of the *colonia*, but are there no descendants of the community that formed in his household who are still in Caesarea? Still more pertinent:

the evangelist Philip (plus or minus his daughters) was living in the city only a few weeks previously and presumably is still there. Why do we hear nothing of his ministry to Paul? Why is Paul so much more isolated in his own (adopted) country than he will later be in Rome (see Acts 28:30-31)?

Any such scenes, however, would anticipate the *denouement* in Rome and detract from the ending. Instead we hear of Paul being summoned to speak privately with the governor himself, together with his wife Drusilla who, we are told, was Jewish. Given that we learned in verse 22 that Felix "was rather well informed about the Way," we might hope that Drusilla herself was a follower and that Felix, like Sergius Paulus (13:7-12), will be moved by Paul's teaching to join the Movement. But that is not in Felix's character.

Felix, as followers of the television series *I, Claudius*[3] may remember, was formerly enslaved, possibly in the emperor's household. At any rate his brother Pallas was also a former bondsman who (as was not unusual in imperial Rome) ranked very high among Claudius's administrators and also for a time in Nero's; he plays a prominent if unsavory role in the television series. Such formerly enslaved persons might achieve considerable wealth and power, but they were always seen by the Roman upper classes as "climbers" and were resented by people in the lower social orders. Tacitus's account of Felix reflects the attitude of the elite and must be read in that light.[4] According to Josephus, Felix was hated for his cruelty (and was thus a fine partner for the high priest Ananus).[5] Felix had three wives in succession, and the first two were both named

3. The series *I, Claudius* (A BBC Television Production in Association with London Film Productions Limited, by Arrangement with Gerry Blattner Productions, Ltd., ©BBC 1976) was based on the novels of Robert Graves (*I, Claudius* and *Claudius the God* [London: Penguin, 1934]).

4. According to Tacitus, Pallas was responsible for a law enacted under Claudius providing that a free woman who married a slave would herself be enslaved, but could retain her freedom if the slave's master approved. The honors and monetary rewards bestowed on Pallas seem to indicate the action was not entirely altruistic on his part. (Tacitus, *Annals* 12.53, in *Complete Works of Tacitus*, trans. Alfred John Church, William Jackson Brodribb, and Sara Bryant [New York: Random House, 1942]).

5. See at 23:1-5 above. Tacitus also writes that Felix had, in fact, acquired a distinguished connection through his marriage to Drusilla: "Antonius Felix indulged in every kind of cruelty and immorality, wielding a king's authority with all the instincts of a slave. He had married Drusilla, a granddaughter of Antony and Cleopatra, so that he was Antony's grandson-in-law, while Claudius was Antony's grandson" (Tacitus, *Hist.* 5.504-6).

Drusilla. The one who appears in Acts is Drusilla the second. She was a daughter of Herod Agrippa I and had formerly been married to the king of Emesa, whom she divorced to marry Felix. Evidently Felix was a better catch. Given her membership in the Herodian family and her politico-marital maneuvering, it is unlikely that Drusilla had any interest in Paul or his ideas.[6]

The topics on which Paul is said to have addressed Felix ("justice, self-control, and the future judgment") were uninteresting, not to say uncomfortable, to the governor—all the more so because they are prime topics not for Paul but for the pseudo-Paul of the Pastoral Epistles. "Justice" is a poor translation for δικαιοσύνη, which more properly means "righteousness," including righteous deeds such as charity and living in right relationship with others. Paul's use of it in his authentic letters (fifteen times, nine of them in Romans) is not about what we call "justice" but instead refers to the quality praised in the Gospels, e.g., "Seek first the kingdom of God and his righteousness" (Matt 6:3). In Luke's Gospel we meet several "righteous" people: Zechariah and Anna (1:6); Simeon (2:25); Joseph of Arimathea (23:50).[7]

"Self-control" is also a modern euphemism for ἐγκράτεια, which usually has a sexual reference and in the Apocryphal Acts and later writings meant celibacy—not something that would have interested Felix (or Drusilla) in the least. "Self-control" in the broader sense was clearly not among Felix's virtues either. Tacitus (admittedly not a neutral observer), after the description of Pallas's actions quoted above, devotes a full para-

---

6. Josephus reports: "But for the marriage of Drusilla with Azizus, it was in no long time afterward dissolved, upon the following occasion: While Felix was procurator of Judea, he saw this Drusilla, and fell in love with her; for she did indeed exceed all other women in beauty, and he sent to her a person whose name was Simon, one of his friends; a Jew he was, and by birth a Cypriot, and one who pretended to be a magician; and endeavored to persuade her to forsake her present husband, and marry him; and promised, that if she would not refuse him, he would make her a happy woman. Accordingly, she acted ill, and because she was desirous to avoid her sister Bernice's envy, for she was very ill treated by her on account of her beauty, was prevailed upon to transgress the laws of her forefathers, and to marry Felix; and when he had had a son by her, he named him Agrippa" (*Ant.* 20.141-43). Berenice, Drusilla's older sister, may not have matched Drusilla in looks (though she too was admired for her beauty), but she far outstripped her in brains and influence. (See the excursus on Berenice at 25:23 below.)

7. In Matt 1:19 Joseph, the husband of Mary, is "righteous." So, in Luke's Gospel, is the other Joseph, the one from Arimathea, who is "good and righteous" rather than being "rich," as he is in Matt 27:57.

graph of his *Annals* to an account of Felix's administration of Judea, beginning: "Not equally moderate was his brother, surnamed Felix, who had for some time been governor of Judæa, and thought that he could do any evil act with impunity, backed up as he was by such power. . . . Felix . . . stimulated disloyal acts." He goes on to describe how Felix partnered with Ventidius Cumanus in promoting war and plunder between the two parts of their province and then, when the emperor Claudius intervened, saw to it that the whole blame fell on Cumanus.[8]

Lukas says nothing at all of the turmoil in Galilee and Samaria during these years, at a time when Paul has supposedly traveled tranquilly and unhindered from Caesarea to Jerusalem and then back again (this time under guard, but for fear of the gang of forty from Jerusalem, not of the warring factions). The whole focus is on Paul and his apparently tranquil—if unproductive—relationship with the governor who was perpetrating such violence on his fellow Jews.

Contemplating Paul in his state of relatively comfortable imprisonment might lead us to compare his situation with conditions of imprisonment in the twenty-first-century world, and especially in the United States, the "land of the free," which as of this writing imprisons more persons (not only proportionally, but in actual numbers) than any other nation on earth.[9] In the time of Paul and Felix, and for most of recorded history thereafter, imprisonment for crime was of relatively short duration: once brought to trial, an accused person was ordinarily acquitted, fined, or executed. (Imprisonment in the form of exile was sometimes imposed.) Given the existence of the prison-industrial complex (the

---

8. Tacitus, *Annals* 12.54. There is nothing unfamiliar about such practices: setting minority populations against one another for the sake of monetary gain is quite the current thing in the twenty-first century, as it has been throughout the history of colonialism. Thus the interests, and the very lives, of indigenous peoples are placed in opposition to those of miners and the workers who build pipelines; "white" people are frightened out of their homes by the "threat" that Black people are moving in, yielding a lavish profit to those who foment the rumors in order to "buy low, sell high"; unions were smashed in the 1980s to enable owners to pay lower wages and fewer benefits. Notoriously, women have been pitted against men in the wage-race-to-the-bottom, another tactic for dividing people whose economic interests are, in fact, identical.

9. A recent US president and his attorney general systematically executed all those under capital sentence in the federal prisons shortly before leaving office so that their sentences might not be commuted by his successor, who had promised to abolish the federal death penalty. One of the prisoners thus executed was the only woman to suffer that fate for a federal crime in seventy years.

system of privately owned, for-profit prisons) in the United States, we are scarcely in a position to condemn Felix for trying to extract money from Paul and his supporters. Even if we regard Paul and others who suffered for their faith as innocent victims or martyrs, the evidence that equally innocent persons are imprisoned and executed in modern America is too ample to be ignored.[10] That non-elites, and primarily women and men of color, suffer far more frequently from such injustice than the moneyed and powerful, now as then, goes without saying.

10. See esp. Bryan Stevenson, *Just Mercy: A Story of Justice and Redemption* (New York: Spiegel & Grau/Random House, 2014); Michelle Alexander, *The New Jim Crow: Mass Incarceration in the Age of Colorblindness*, 10th anniv. ed. (New York: New Press, 2020).

Acts 25:1–26:32

Paul before Festus, Agrippa, and Berenice

A new procurator arrives in Judea and the same cycle begins again: the "chief priests and leaders of the Jews" demand that Paul be brought to Jerusalem for trial (but really in order to be assassinated); the procurator says he will try him in Caesarea; the Jewish leaders travel there and accuse Paul; the procurator offers Paul the choice of being tried in Jerusalem. This time, in order to avoid being handed over to the Sanhedrin, Paul goes a fatal step further. He insists he has committed no offense against the emperor and appeals to the imperial jurisdiction. Festus seizes on that as an out: he interprets Paul to be requesting trial before the emperor himself, therefore in Rome. Lukas brings the scene to a climax with a flourish: "You have appealed to the emperor; to the emperor you will go" (v. 12).

There is no basis in the historical record for this procedure. It could have happened that way, but it is equally possible that Paul escaped from Judea unscathed and unjudged and traveled to Rome of his own volition, as he hoped to do when he wrote Romans (cf. Rom 1:15). Lukas knows, but does not tell the audience, that Paul very much needed to get out of Judea, voluntarily or no. Within four years after the supposed date of this trial (ca. 58–59?) Festus died unexpectedly, and during the interregnum before the arrival of his successor the high priest Ananus summoned

319

25:1Three days after Festus had arrived in the province, he went up from Caesarea to Jerusalem 2where the chief priests and the leaders of the Jews gave him a report against Paul. They appealed to him 3and requested, as a favor to them against Paul, to have him transferred to Jerusalem. They were, in fact, planning an ambush to kill him along the way. 4Festus replied that Paul was being kept at Caesarea, and that he himself intended to go there shortly. 5"So," he said, "let those of you who have the authority come down with me, and if there is anything wrong about the man, let them accuse him."

6After he had stayed among them not more than eight or ten days, he went down to Caesarea; the next day he took his seat on the tribunal and ordered Paul to be brought. 7When he arrived, the Jews who had gone down from Jerusalem surrounded him, bringing many serious charges against him, which they could not prove. 8Paul said in his defense, "I have in no way committed an offense against the law of the Jews, or against the temple, or against the emperor." 9But Festus, wishing to do the Jews a favor, asked Paul, "Do you wish to go up to Jerusalem and be tried there before me on these charges?" 10Paul said, "I am appealing to the emperor's tribunal; this is where I should be tried. I have done no wrong to the Jews, as you very well know. 11Now if I am in the wrong and have committed something for which I deserve to die, I am not trying to escape death; but if there is nothing to their charges against me, no one can turn me over to them. I appeal to the emperor." 12Then Festus, after he had conferred with his council, replied, "You have appealed to the emperor; to the emperor you will go."

13After several days had passed, King Agrippa and Bernice arrived at Caesarea to welcome Festus. 14Since they were staying there several days, Festus laid Paul's case before the king, saying, "There is a man here who was left in prison by Felix. 15When I was in Jerusalem, the chief priests and the elders of the Jews informed me about him and asked for a sentence against him. 16I told them that it was not the custom of the Romans to hand over anyone before the accused had met the accusers face to face and had been given an opportunity to make a defense against the charge. 17So when they met here, I lost no time, but on the next day took my seat on the tribunal and ordered the man to be brought. 18When the accusers stood up, they did not charge him with any of the crimes that I was expecting. 19Instead they had certain points of disagreement with him about their own religion and about a certain Jesus, who had died, but whom Paul asserted to be alive. 20Since I was at a loss how to investigate these questions, I asked whether he wished to go to Jerusalem and be tried there on these charges. 21But when Paul had appealed to be kept in custody for the decision of his Imperial Majesty, I ordered him to be held until I could send him to the emperor." 22Agrippa said to Festus, "I would like to hear the man myself." "Tomorrow," he said, "you will hear him."

23So on the next day Agrippa and Bernice came with great pomp, and they entered the audience hall with the military tribunes and the prominent men of the city. Then Festus gave the order and Paul was brought in. ²⁴And Festus said, "King Agrippa and all here present with us, you see this man about whom the whole Jewish community petitioned me, both in Jerusalem and here, shouting that he ought not to live any longer. ²⁵But I found that he had done nothing deserving death; and when he appealed to his Imperial Majesty, I decided to send him. ²⁶But I have nothing definite to write to our sovereign about him. Therefore I have brought him before all of you, and especially before you, King Agrippa, so that, after we have examined him, I may have something to write—²⁷for it seems to me unreasonable to send a prisoner without indicating the charges against him."

²⁶:¹Agrippa said to Paul, "You have permission to speak for yourself." Then Paul stretched out his hand and began to defend himself:

²"I consider myself fortunate that it is before you, King Agrippa, I am to make my defense today against all the accusations of the Jews, ³because you are especially familiar with all the customs and controversies of the Jews; therefore I beg of you to listen to me patiently.

⁴"All the Jews know my way of life from my youth, a life spent from the beginning among my own people and in Jerusalem. ⁵They have known for a long time, if they are willing to testify, that I have belonged to the strictest sect of our religion and lived as a Pharisee. ⁶And now I stand here on trial on account of my hope in the promise made by God to our ances-

tors, ⁷a promise that our twelve tribes hope to attain, as they earnestly worship day and night. It is for this hope, your Excellency, that I am accused by Jews! ⁸Why is it thought incredible by any of you that God raises the dead?

⁹"Indeed, I myself was convinced that I ought to do many things against the name of Jesus of Nazareth. ¹⁰And that is what I did in Jerusalem; with authority received from the chief priests, I not only locked up many of the saints in prison, but I also cast my vote against them when they were being condemned to death. ¹¹By punishing them often in all the synagogues I tried to force them to blaspheme; and since I was so furiously enraged at them, I pursued them even to foreign cities.

¹²"With this in mind, I was traveling to Damascus with the authority and commission of the chief priests, ¹³when at midday along the road, your Excellency, I saw a light from heaven, brighter than the sun, shining around me and my companions. ¹⁴When we had all fallen to the ground, I heard a voice saying to me in the Hebrew language, 'Saul, Saul, why are you persecuting me? It hurts you to kick against the goads.' ¹⁵I asked, 'Who are you, Lord?' The Lord answered, 'I am Jesus whom you are persecuting. ¹⁶But get up and stand on your feet; for I have appeared to you for this purpose, to appoint you to serve and testify to the things in which you have seen me and to those in which I will appear to you. ¹⁷I will rescue you from your people and from the Gentiles—to whom I am sending you ¹⁸to open their eyes so that they may turn from darkness to light and

from the power of Satan to God, so that they may receive forgiveness of sins and a place among those who are sanctified by faith in me.'

[19]"After that, King Agrippa, I was not disobedient to the heavenly vision, [20]but declared first to those in Damascus, then in Jerusalem and throughout the countryside of Judea, and also to the Gentiles, that they should repent and turn to God and do deeds consistent with repentance. [21]For this reason the Jews seized me in the temple and tried to kill me. [22]To this day I have had help from God, and so I stand here, testifying to both small and great, saying nothing but what the prophets and Moses said would take place: [23]that the Messiah must suffer, and that, by being the first to rise from the dead, he would proclaim light both to our people and to the Gentiles."

[24]While he was making this defense, Festus exclaimed, "You are out of your mind, Paul! Too much learning is driv-ing you insane!" [25]But Paul said, "I am not out of my mind, most excellent Festus, but I am speaking the sober truth. [26]Indeed the king knows about these things, and to him I speak freely; for I am certain that none of these things has escaped his notice, for this was not done in a corner. [27]King Agrippa, do you believe the prophets? I know that you believe." [28]Agrippa said to Paul, "Are you so quickly persuading me to become a Christian?" [29]Paul replied, "Whether quickly or not, I pray to God that not only you but also all who are listening to me today might become such as I am—except for these chains."

[30]Then the king got up, and with him the governor and Bernice and those who had been seated with them; [31]and as they were leaving, they said to one another, "This man is doing nothing to deserve death or imprisonment." [32]Agrippa said to Festus, "This man could have been set free if he had not appealed to the emperor."

the Sanhedrin (illegally) and held a trial of the Jerusalem leadership of the Way. The whole group, including James, were sentenced to death by stoning,[1] so that many suffered the death depicted in Acts 7:59-60 for Stephen. In Lukas's view of the story Ananus's attack on James and his companions was carried out in frustration at the Sanhedrin's failure to do the same to Paul, but nothing is said of it in Acts because the focus in these final chapters must remain on Paul.

Porcius Festus was a member of the equestrian order and was thus spared the scorn heaped on his freedman predecessor, Felix, by Roman authors. Josephus, for example, wrote approvingly of Festus's moves

---

1. Josephus, *Ant.* 20.9.1.200. See above in the description of Paul's first trial.

to suppress the *sicarii* (assassins, so called because they used knives resembling Roman sickles or *sicae*). Still, unrest continued in Caesarea and beyond because, far from punishing Felix's cruelties, Nero decided to limit the privileges of the Jewish inhabitants of the province of Syria (which included Judea). Festus also alienated the Jerusalem authorities by siding with Agrippa II in a dispute over an addition to the latter's palace in Jerusalem that overlooked the temple court, which moved the temple authorities to build a countering wall in the temple precincts to block Agrippa's view (and that of the garrison, whose quarters adjoined the palace). Festus did permit a Jewish embassy to Nero that secured a ruling in favor of the Jerusalem leadership (supposedly to gratify Nero's wife Poppaea, who was said to be sympathetic to the Jews), but by the time the embassy returned with the good news Festus had died. His successor, Albinus, was even more hostile to the Jews than Felix had been, and *his* successor, Gessius Florus (also a client of Poppaea),[2] was so much worse that, according to Josephus, people began to think fondly of Albinus. Within two years (in 66) the Jewish War had begun.[3]

Lukas remembers correctly that Festus was friendly with Agrippa II and his sister Berenice,[4] but they are introduced here chiefly for story purposes; that Paul ever met Agrippa II or Berenice is highly unlikely. Their presence in the story of Acts gives Festus a chance to present *his* version of Paul's arrest, trials, and imprisonment and to justify his own actions in passing the problem to the emperor. It also allows Paul to tell the story of his encounter with the Risen One a third time, with new and more vivid detail, affirming that Paul's appeal to a decision from the imperial jurisdiction (i.e., Festus's court) amounted to a request to be sent before the emperor himself. That was a convenient interpretation for Festus but historically it is improbable that Paul chose to be transported to Rome as a prisoner. Still, it serves the plot of Acts very nicely. It also applies the authority of the last Herodian king (and of the queen of Chalcis and—for a time—of Paul's home province, Cilicia) in support of the decision.

Lukas gives this, Paul's final and climactic oration, a suitably regal setting (though Berenice serves primarily as window dressing). Compare Chariton's introduction to a trial in the Persian court:

---

2. See Josephus, *Ant.* 20.11.252.

3. The principal source for these details is Josephus, *J.W.* 20.182-258.

4. Her name is variously spelled Bernice (so NRSV), Berenice (from Greek *pherenike*, "bearing victory"), or (following the Hebrew) Beroenice; the name is cognate with Veronica.

When the designated day arrived, the king took his seat. In the palace
there is a special chamber, distinguished both in size and appearance,
which is set aside as a courtroom. In the middle of this sits a throne for
the king, and on either side of him chairs for his friends and all those
who, by virtue of their rank and services, are leaders of leaders. In a
circle around the throne stand captains, commanders, and the most
highly valued of the king's freedmen. As a result, in speaking of this
council one might well say, "and the gods seated by Zeus' side met in
council." Those on trial are brought in amidst an atmosphere of fearful silence.[5]

Lukas's scene is less elaborate; after all, this is a provincial setting, lacking the full personnel of an imperial court. Still, it is impressive, as fits
the occasion.[6]

Of the three presentations of Paul's conversion and mission, this is
Lukas's *chef d'oeuvre*, with as much style and rhetorical nicety as he could
muster; the strain on his craft is visible from time to time. Again there are
few traces of an authentic judicial proceeding; here, unlike in the previous "trials," there are no charges laid, nor does Paul answer any. He refers
to belief in the resurrection, which was a point of contention in earlier
scenes but is scarcely a matter for adjudication. Paul is safe in speaking
of that belief as if it were the offense of which he is accused, since no
Jewish or Roman court could see it as grounds for capital punishment.

The speech itself is crafted as instruction for "insiders," since its theology would be virtually incomprehensible to anyone but a member
of the Movement (as Festus's exclamation in 26:24 underscores). It is
also for "insiders" in the sense that its context is "Jewish," and, despite
the explicit indication of Berenice's presence, it is directed entirely to
Agrippa, thus reinforcing that the upper-class women mentioned in Acts
are props and nothing more; it is working-class and enslaved women
who are important in the book!

The threefold narrative of the "conversion" scene also moves in the
direction of individualizing Paul, contrary to the picture of the Way that
was painted in the early chapters: as a community of communities, members of which receive their assignments and roles from the Spirit *through
the community*. This was still true for Paul in the third-person account
in Acts 9, in which Jesus' will for Paul is communicated by Ananias as

5. Chariton, *Callirhoe* 5, 4.

6. It is also the second scene of Herodian grandeur in Acts: cf. 12:21-22. Evidently
Berenice is the only woman present; the "leading men" are indeed ἄνδρες.

representative of the Damascus community. Likewise, at 13:2 it is in the context of community worship that the Spirit directs the "setting apart" of Barnabas and Paul for "the work to which I have called them." The apostolic council and its aftermath show Paul cutting ties with Barnabas and with the Antioch community. The second and third accounts of Paul's encounter with the risen Jesus are placed on Paul's own lips; in Acts 22 the call is still mediated through Ananias but Paul also receives a special vision of Jesus, who tells him explicitly, "*I* will send you far away to the Gentiles." Now, in Acts 26, the call comes directly from Jesus on the Damascus road—Ananias has vanished and Jesus chides Saul for persecuting *him*, not the members of the Way,[7] then promises to "rescue you [Paul] from your people and from the Gentiles." Paul does not learn from the community in Damascus but instead preaches repentance to them and "then in Jerusalem and throughout the countryside of Judea, and also to the Gentiles" (v. 20). From this point on we will hear nothing more of the communities of the Movement except for a brief appearance of some of the members who greet Paul at Puteoli and on the outskirts of Rome. Whether community members are among those "who came to him" at his Roman lodgings (28:30) we are not told; the focus of the chapter is on Paul's preaching to the Jewish local leaders, whom he addresses, in the usual fashion, as "brothers" (ἄνδρες ἀδελφοί).

Paul asserts that the form of Judaism he represents (centered on the words of "the prophets and Moses" and thus, implicitly, Pharisaic in nature) is in no way aberrant, nor has it been practiced in secrecy, as if it were a mystery cult.[8] The normativity of "the prophets" alongside the Torah was still uncertain and, as we have seen, was rejected by the Sadducees. Lukas may have been aware of a tendency in the newly emerging rabbinic Judaism he knew to make Torah alone the measure of belief and to "build a fence" around it with rules to prevent violation of its fundamental laws. Paul's appeal to Agrippa in this scene ("King Agrippa, do you believe the prophets? I know that you believe") is pregnant with meaning. The words of the prophets were essential to the new movement's understanding of events ("that the Messiah must suffer, and that, by being the first to rise from the dead, he would proclaim light

---

7. The AV translated Acts 26:14 as "it is hard for thee to kick against the pricks," which has occasioned some feminist ribaldry—for example, a suggested adaptation as a title for a commentary such as this one.

8. Mystery cults were "private" devotions that offered their initiates more personal and individual solace in need than did the official religions of the state.

both to our people and to the Gentiles," vv. 22-23). It is clear throughout Acts that *Moses is included among the prophets* (3:22; 7:20-44; cf. Luke 24:27), and since Moses is credited as the author of Torah the "words of the prophets" include both Torah and Nevi'im (Prophets; in the Tanakh these are the books of Joshua, Judges, 1 and 2 Samuel, 1 and 2 Kings [the "Former Prophets"] as well as the major prophets Isaiah, Jeremiah, and Ezekiel, and the Book of the Twelve).

Festus doesn't get the point at all; he thinks Paul is crazy. King Agrippa understands (and so, assuredly, does Berenice), but it is not in his interest to assent. In the story time the members of the Way are indeed a minor sect "in a corner," but by the time Lukas was writing, "Christian" (appearing here for the second and last time in Acts) had become a label for people subject to persecution and even execution (see 1 Pet 4:16, the only New Testament passage to use the word apart from the two in Acts: "Yet if any of you suffers as a Christian, do not consider it a disgrace, but glorify God because you bear this name").

This scene is key to Lukas's intent: Agrippa and Berenice, being Jews, "get it." They comprehend what Paul is saying: that the Movement is for the definitive rescue and renewal of Israel, just what the prophets have always promised. In the ongoing story Agrippa represents the Jewish leaders who understand but do not agree. Festus, who thinks Paul is "crazy," stands in for all the gentiles who simply do not understand, including those who think this Movement is something they can control and even enter into in order to take advantage of it. The scene is a warning both to resistant Jews that, if they waste the opportunity, gentiles will take advantage of it to Israel's detriment, and to gentiles that for them to do so will be contrary to God's will.

The scene ends with a solemn retiring procession. There have been no charges, no accusations, and no rebuttals. Festus professes to be utterly baffled about what to write to the emperor regarding Paul. All are agreed: Paul is innocent of any and all charges (of which, so far as this scene is concerned, there are none), but, regrettably, neither Festus nor Agrippa (nor Berenice) can or must take responsibility for releasing him because he has supposedly "appealed to the emperor." To Rome he must go—as the plot demands.[9]

---

9. We could enjoy imagining a scene in which Berenice asserts her authority over Cilicia and lets Paul go, to the consternation and outrage of her brother and Festus! Indeed, what if that really happened? Would Lukas or any other male chronicler have wanted to admit it?

Berenice

References to Berenice in Acts 25 and 26 and to her sister Drusilla in Acts 24 would have triggered interest especially among women in Lukas's audience who might have known something of their story, which is all but lost to today's readers. Drusilla, Berenice, and (Herod) Agrippa II were all siblings, children of Agrippa I (see Acts 12) and his cousin/wife Cypros.

Cypros apparently bore her first son, Marcus Julius Agrippa, in 27 CE and her first daughter, Berenice, in 28. It is possible (since the birthdates are uncertain) that the two were twins; certainly they were close companions in the nursery and the bond they forged there endured throughout their lives. Agrippa II was still a teenager when his father died in 44 CE (see Acts 12:20-23), by which time Berenice had already been married (at fifteen) to Marcus Julius Alexander, a nephew of Philo of Alexandria and thus member of a very prominent Jewish family. Marcus's brother, Tiberius Julius Alexander, was procurator of Judea from 46 to 48 (at the time of the famine). From 66 to 69 he became prefect of Egypt and used his Roman legions to crush the Jewish community in Alexandria before becoming right-hand man to Vespasian and then to Titus in the siege of Jerusalem. Even though Marcus Alexander died within a year of the marriage, Berenice and Agrippa evidently retained ties to her brother-in-law Tiberius Julius.

Soon after Marcus Alexander's death, Agrippa II affianced his widowed teenage sister to their own uncle, Herod of Chalcis, and she bore two sons before he too died in 50 CE. Berenice was on her own again, Queen of Chalcis, twenty-two years old with very young children. Her brother Agrippa, having achieved his majority, received the kingdom of Chalcis as an addition to his territories, so that brother and sister were respectively tetrarch and queen of that small territory located in the Beqaa Valley (now in eastern Lebanon). An inscription found in Beirut testifies that Berenice was indeed "Queen."

An unmarried brother and sister living and reigning together—there had to be gossip, and there was. Josephus reported that

> As for Bernice, she lived a widow a long while after the death of Herod [king of Chalcis],[10] who was both her husband and her uncle. But, when the report went that she had criminal conversation with her brother, she persuaded Polemo, who was king of Cilicia, to be circumcised, and to marry her, as supposing,

---

10. "Herod" is the family name.

that by this means she should prove those calumnies upon her to be false; and Polemo was prevailed upon, and that chiefly on account of her riches. Yet did not this matrimony endure long; but Bernice left Polemo and, as was said, with impure intentions [ἀκολασία]. So he forsook at once this matrimony, and the Jewish religion.[11]

The king of Cilicia could only be won over to accepting Judaism, with all its requirements, by money, so it seems—despite the fact that Bernice was still in her twenties and evidently very beautiful. But, as will appear, she was also a "strong-minded," that is, intelligent, woman who asserted her authority.[12]

It seems highly likely that Agrippa II (who never married or fathered children) was gay and that his sister, close friend from the cradle, gave him "cover" as he precariously balanced the roles of Jewish king and Roman vassal.

During the procuratorship of Gessius Florus (64–66), whose barbaric actions provoked the Jewish revolt, Bernice was far more active than her brother in trying to shield the Jewish people from Florus's barbarity. She repeatedly implored Florus to stop his soldiers from mistreating the people of Jerusalem; his only response was to turn the soldiers on the queen herself. Agrippa was resident in Rome, but Bernice was then living in Jerusalem, performing a vow. She stood before Florus with shaven head, begging him to spare her people, "yet could she neither have reverence paid to her, nor

---

11. Josephus, *Ant.* 20.145-47. The reference to ἀκολασία (also translated "inappropriate sexual desire" in this context) is ambiguous. Whose intentions are in view? Ἀκολασία is defined in *DBL* as "debauchery, licentiousness, sinfulness" and (of course!) seems to be attributed to Berenice, not to Polemo, but could it be an oblique acknowledgment that her purpose was to shield her brother? Or did Polemo take his revenge for having to submit to circumcision by forcing Berenice to perform repugnant sexual acts? At any rate Josephus's account of his subsequent defection from Judaism is independent witness to the poor prospects of persuading gentile men to accept circumcision in order to join the Movement.

12. The calumny lived on, combined with contempt for Judaism, in Juvenal's *Satire* 6.229-34, which refers to an object for sale in a Roman shop:

"That far-famed gem which Berenice wore,
The hire of incest, and thence valued more;
A brother's present, in that barbarous State,
Where kings the sabbath, barefoot, celebrate;
And old indulgence grants a length of life
To hogs, that fatten fearless of the knife."

The gem seems to have lost its fame; in 1817 William Gifford speculated that it may have been an agate, then goes on to retail the canard about Berenice, adding: "The in-

could she escape without some danger of being slain herself."[13] In other words, Berenice suffered from Florus and his crew much the same treatment as Paul had received from the Jewish authorities![14] Josephus does not offer information about the reason for Berenice's vow, but her pleading barefoot (and literally bareheaded) before Florus could mean that she was seeking mercy from the God of Israel for her beleaguered people.

When news of the uprising in Judea reached Rome, Agrippa quickly returned to join Vespasian; both he and Berenice supported Roman military actions to subdue the revolt. Berenice charmed Vespasian,[15] and in the course of the war she met his son and successor, Titus, who fell in love with Berenice, and she with him.[16] The now stateless king and queen returned to Rome with Titus, and, according to Dio Cassius, Berenice lived there in every respect as if she were Titus's wife, as she certainly hoped to be. But the Roman aristocracy had no intention of allowing another "Cleopatra," a strong and assertive royal woman from the East—and a Jew, besides—to rise to such status in their society. Poppaea had been bad enough, favoring the Jews as she had, but it would be much worse to have Berenice, who *was* a Jew, at Titus's side. She was forced to leave Rome, but she returned when Titus succeeded Vespasian as emperor, hoping at last to become Titus's wife. The mighty general nevertheless bowed to the pressures of the Roman elite and sent her away.[17]

---

cidents that enhanced the value of this ring, convey a forcible picture of the capricious and profligate extravagance which distinguished the women [!] of Juvenal's time." The libel against Judaism is simply taken for granted as appropriate. See William Gifford, *The Satires of Decimus Julius Juvenalis, and of Aulus Persius Flaccus Translated into English Verse*, 2 vols. (London: Nicol, Cadell, Davies, and Evans, 1817), 1:220–21.

13. Josephus, *J.W.* 2.15, 308-14.

14. Paul should probably be pictured as having a shaven head when he was attacked, since he was fulfilling a vow (cf. 18:18).

15. According to Tacitus, "[Berenice] was then in the flower of her youth and beauty, and her munificent gifts to Vespasian quite won the old man's heart" (*Hist.* 2.81).

16. "The young man's fancy was attracted by Berenice, but he did not allow this to interfere with business. Still his youth was a time of gay self-indulgence, and he showed more restraint in his own reign than in his father's" (Tacitus, *Hist.* 2.2).

17. Ross S. Kraemer writes: "Bernice's support for Josephus's political opponent, Justus of Tiberias, may have affected his judgment. But Josephus may also have found offensive the ability of Bernice (and other elite Herodian Jewish women) to circumvent the strictures of gender to live relatively autonomously and to play significant roles in first-century affairs. Such an interpretation accords well with his more favorable treatment of women like [Cypros], Bernice and Drusilla's mother, who conformed more closely to ancient expectations for elite women" ("Ber[e]nice," in *Women in*

Lukas introduces Berenice (and mentions her name three times) without comment and without any allusion to her remarkable history, which he probably knew from reading Josephus. He says nothing at all about her, not even her relationship to Agrippa—readers might well suppose that she is his wife, as the likewise silent Drusilla is Felix's—nor is she given her title as queen. She is merely a passive observer who, in the end, evidently adds her assent to the common opinion that Paul is innocent (not that Lukas thought a woman's assent counted for anything in the context).

Berenice thus serves as the last example in Acts of an aristocratic woman sympathetic to Paul— this time an elite *Jewish* woman. Here nonconformance with ancient conventions of gender falls out of the picture. The elite gentile women previously mentioned in Acts[18] were receptive to Paul's message, but possibly Berenice might be like the "devout [Jewish] women of high standing" at Pisidian Antioch who rejected him, so she is left speechless. "She functions all the more effectively as an elite Roman-allied vindicator of Paul if her judgment is clearly impartial."[19]

Berenice vanishes from Lukas's story at Acts 26:30, but she does not depart from the historical record until the year 79, when Titus became emperor, and she may have left traces beyond that time. Some second-century papyri mention an elite woman landowner named Julia Crispina. Her father was named Berenicianus—an unusual name that had belonged to Berenice's son by Herod of Chalcis. The assertiveness of Julia Crispina revealed by the documents could well be an inheritance from her grandmother. What if Titus and Berenice had in fact married— would Berenicianus have been made heir to his father's Herodian province, or that of his uncle Agrippa II? Could the Herodian dynasty then have continued, perhaps as guardians of a state reserved for Jews exiled from Palestine? How different history might have been![20]

Scripture: A Dictionary of Named and Unnamed Women in the Hebrew Bible, the Apocryphal/ Deuterocanonical Books, and the New Testament, ed. Carol Meyers, Toni Craven, and Ross S. Kraemer [Boston: Houghton Mifflin, 2000], 165–70, at 169).

18. See, e.g., 17:4, 12, 34, but cf. 13:50.

19. Kraemer, "Ber[e]nice," 170.

20. Ibid. Kraemer's article is the best and most accessible source for Berenice's story to date.

Acts 27:1–28:10

Paul at Sea

A cts cannot end without one last great adventure story, illustrat- ing the extremes of missionary peril. In 2 Corinthians, Paul mentions having been shipwrecked (three times, in fact: 2 Cor 11:25), and Lukas, having also told of the other vicissitudes Paul mentions there— being beaten with rods (once: Acts 16:22) and stoned (once: Acts 14:19)— finishes with one rip-roaring sea adventure. The "we" narrator returns, causing many scholars to search for details to corroborate the account of the voyage.[1] There are faint echoes of a number of popular romances and even of the *Odyssey* (the standard model for the perils and adventures of voyaging),[2] and sailors' "yarns" were as numerous and popular then as now.[3] Ultimately, though, this is a Lukan composition throughout.

---

1. A proposed "diary" as the basis for this story and other "we" passages is con- sidered by, e.g., Henry J. Cadbury, "We and I Passages in Luke-Acts," *NTS* 3 (1956): 128–32; Joseph A. Fitzmyer, *Luke the Theologian: Aspects of His Teaching* (New York: Paulist Press, 1989), 16–22; Colin J. Hemer, "First Person Narrative in Acts 27–28," *TynBul* 36 (1985): 79–109; J. M. Gilchrist, "The Historicity of Paul's Shipwreck," *JSNT* 61 (1996): 29–61. In the nineteenth century, when sailing ships were still plying the seas, James Smith devoted an entire monograph to *The Voyage and Shipwreck of St. Paul*, 4th ed. (London: Longmans, Green, 1880).

2. Dennis R. MacDonald, "The Shipwrecks of Odysseus and Paul," *NTS* 45 (1999): 88–107 claims that the *Odyssey* is the only source used for Acts 27. That is more than a stretch, but similar identifications are MacDonald's *métier*.

3. Susan M. Praeder, "Acts 27:1–28:16: Sea Voyages in Ancient Literature and the Theology of Luke-Acts," *CBQ* 46 (1984): 683–706, notes: "It is apparent that Luke is

²⁷:¹When it was decided that we were to sail for Italy, they transferred Paul and some other prisoners to a centurion of the Augustan Cohort, named Julius. ²Embarking on a ship of Adramyttium that was about to set sail to the ports along the coast of Asia, we put to sea, accompanied by Aristarchus, a Macedonian from Thessalonica. ³The next day we put in at Sidon; and Julius treated Paul kindly, and allowed him to go to his friends to be cared for. ⁴Putting out to sea from there, we sailed under the lee of Cyprus, because the winds were against us. ⁵After we had sailed across the sea that is off Cilicia and Pamphylia, we came to Myra in Lycia. ⁶There the centurion found an Alexandrian ship bound for Italy and put us on board. ⁷We sailed slowly for a number of days and arrived with difficulty off Cnidus, and as the wind was against us, we sailed under the lee of Crete off Salmone. ⁸Sailing past it with difficulty, we came to a place called Fair Havens, near the city of Lasea.

⁹Since much time had been lost and sailing was now dangerous, because even the Fast had already gone by, Paul advised them, ¹⁰saying, "Sirs, I can see that the voyage will be with danger and much heavy loss, not only of the cargo and the ship, but also of our lives." ¹¹But the centurion paid more attention to the pilot and to the owner of the ship than to what Paul said. ¹²Since the harbor was not suitable for spending the winter, the majority was in favor of putting to sea from there, on the chance that somehow they could reach Phoenix, where they could spend the winter. It was a harbor of Crete, facing southwest and northwest.

¹³When a moderate south wind began to blow, they thought they could achieve their purpose; so they weighed anchor and began to sail past Crete, close to the shore. ¹⁴But soon a violent wind, called the northeaster, rushed down from Crete. ¹⁵Since the ship was caught and could not be turned head-on into the wind, we gave way to it and were driven. ¹⁶By running under the lee of a small island called Cauda we were scarcely able to get the ship's boat under control. ¹⁷After hoisting it up they took measures to undergird the ship; then, fearing that they would run on the Syrtis, they lowered the sea anchor and so were driven. ¹⁸We were being pounded by the storm so violently that on the next day they began to throw the cargo overboard, ¹⁹and on the third day with their own hands they threw the ship's tackle overboard. ²⁰When neither sun nor stars appeared for many days, and no small tempest raged, all hope of our being saved was at last abandoned.

²¹Since they had been without food for a long time, Paul then stood up among them and said, "Men, you should have listened to me and not have set sail from Crete and thereby avoided this damage and loss. ²²I urge you now to keep up your courage, for there will be no loss of life among you, but only of the ship. ²³For last night there stood by me an angel of the God to whom I belong and whom I worship, ²⁴and he said, 'Do not be afraid, Paul; you must stand before the emperor; and indeed, God has granted safety to all those who are sailing with you.' ²⁵So keep up your courage, men, for I have faith in God that it will be exactly

as I have been told. [26]But we will have to run aground on some island."

[27]When the fourteenth night had come, as we were drifting across the sea of Adria, about midnight the sailors suspected that they were nearing land. [28]So they took soundings and found twenty fathoms; a little farther on they took soundings again and found fifteen fathoms. [29]Fearing that we might run on the rocks, they let down four anchors from the stern and prayed for day to come. [30]But when the sailors tried to escape from the ship and had lowered the boat into the sea, on the pretext of putting out anchors from the bow, [31]Paul said to the centurion and the soldiers, "Unless these men stay in the ship, you cannot be saved." [32]Then the soldiers cut away the ropes of the boat and set it adrift.

[33]Just before daybreak, Paul urged all of them to take some food, saying, "Today is the fourteenth day that you have been in suspense and remaining without food, having eaten nothing. [34]Therefore I urge you to take some food, for it will help you survive; for none of you will lose a hair from your heads." [35]After he had said this, he took bread; and giving thanks to God in the presence of all, he broke it and began to eat. [36]Then all of them were encouraged and took food for themselves. [37](We were in all two hundred seventy-six persons in the ship.) [38]After they had satisfied their hunger, they lightened the ship by throwing the wheat into the sea.

[39]In the morning they did not recognize the land, but they noticed a bay with a beach, on which they planned to run the ship ashore, if they could. [40]So they cast off the anchors and left them in the sea. At the same time they loosened the ropes that tied the steering-oars; then hoisting the foresail to the wind, they made for the beach. [41]But striking a reef, they ran the ship aground; the bow stuck and remained immovable, but the stern was being

---

familiar with several literary models or styles from sea voyages in ancient literature and is following some more closely than others" (705). Charles Talbert and J. H. Hayes, "A Theology of Sea Storms in Luke-Acts," SBLSP 1995 (Atlanta: Scholars Press, 1995), 321–36, offer a multitude of examples of this type-story, and a list of motifs can be found in Richard I. Pervo, *Profit with Delight: The Literary Genre of the Acts of the Apostles* (Philadelphia: Fortress, 1987), 156n89. These include late departure, passengers with superior knowledge, jettisoning cargo, friendly (or hostile) barbarians. Readers of Agatha Christie may recognize a number of them. The latest and most thorough examination of the account is by Marius Reiser, "Von Caesarea nach Malta. Literarischer Charakter und historische Glaubwürdigkeit von Apg 27," 49–74. In F. W. Horn , ed., *Das Ende des Paulus. Historische, theologische und literaturgeschichtliche Aspekte.* BZNW 106 (Berlin and New York: de Gruyter, 2001). Reiser, who has an encyclopedic knowledge of ancient literature, shows that the account of the sea voyage adheres closely to a form used by a number of authors who were Lukas's near contemporaries in which they gave personal accounts of their own experiences at sea.

broken up by the force of the waves.
[42]The soldiers' plan was to kill the prisoners, so that none might swim away
and escape; [43]but the centurion, wishing to save Paul, kept them from carrying out their plan. He ordered those
who could swim to jump overboard first
and make for the land, [44]and the rest to
follow, some on planks and others on
pieces of the ship. And so it was that
all were brought safely to land.

[28:1]After we had reached safety, we
then learned that the island was called
Malta. [2]The natives showed us unusual
kindness. Since it had begun to rain
and was cold, they kindled a fire and
welcomed all of us around it. [3]Paul had
gathered a bundle of brushwood and
was putting it on the fire, when a viper,
driven out by the heat, fastened itself
on his hand. [4]When the natives saw the
creature hanging from his hand, they
said to one another, "This man must
be a murderer; though he has escaped

from the sea, justice has not allowed
him to live." [5]He, however, shook off
the creature into the fire and suffered
no harm. [6]They were expecting him to
swell up or drop dead, but after they
had waited a long time and saw that
nothing unusual had happened to him,
they changed their minds and began to
say that he was a god.

[7]Now in the neighborhood of that
place were lands belonging to the leading man of the island, named Publius,
who received us and entertained us
hospitably for three days. [8]It so happened that the father of Publius lay sick
in bed with fever and dysentery. Paul
visited him and cured him by praying
and putting his hands on him. [9]After
this happened, the rest of the people
on the island who had diseases also
came and were cured. [10]They bestowed
many honors on us, and when we were
about to sail, they put on board all the
provisions we needed.

Lukas extended himself (not always altogether successfully) to display
his best Greek style here. His audience would have recognized allusions
to the story of Jonah. In fact, Paul appears here as a kind of anti-Jonah: he
takes ship not to escape God's command but to obey it; he does not sacrifice himself to save the crew but instead saves himself *and* the crew: like
Jesus, he allows none to perish (cf. Luke 8:24; 19:10, and note especially
the parallel in verse 34, "none of you will lose a hair from your heads"
with Luke 21:18, "not a hair of your head will perish"); like Jonah, he will
reach the great capital city and preach to the people there. The story of
Jesus' calming the storm at sea in Luke 8 is also background for Paul's
battle with the elements.

Paul (the prisoner) is in charge throughout. Julius, the centurion commissioned to take command (one more Roman official sympathetic to
Paul), exists mainly to keep Paul safe. He permits him to visit his friends

(i.e., members of the Movement) at Sidon (v. 3), and he stops the soldiers under his command from killing the prisoners because he wants "to save Paul" (vv. 42-43). Lukas gives the back of his hand to the ship's owner and captain, who in his view are motivated by greed in forcing the winter voyage.[4] They persuade the centurion to accept their orders rather than Paul's (vv. 10-11!), the only time Julius puts a foot wrong. The result is that both ship and cargo are lost, which in the author's opinion serves them right.

Lukas is careful to signal Paul's continued Jewish observance by dating the voyage in terms of "the Fast" (i.e., Yom Kippur, which would probably have fallen in September or October, though dating is not certain). The end of the sailing season was usually the Feast of Booths; Pervo remarks that "[n]ot until the introduction of the compass was sailing in the Mediterranean between October and March a routine activity."[5] This underscores the rashness and rapacity of the owner and captain: they pay no heed to the times God has appointed for certain activities, as marked by the Jewish festal calendar. (They were almost certainly gentiles, of course.)

The subsequent voyage is indeed a perilous one; the ship is effectively "at sea" in both the literal and the figurative senses. The northeast wind drives the vessel, steadied only by a sea anchor (v. 17), inexorably toward "Syrtis," the Gulf of Sidra in modern-day Libya, but at some point the wind evidently shifts, now coming from the southeast, so that the vessel turns into the open Mediterranean; fetching up on Malta is a piece of good luck—and, of course, convenient for the development of the story.[6]

The original audience would have understood the episode on "the fourteenth day" to herald a happy outcome:[7] after urging the company to take food and assuring them that he has received a divine message promising their safety, Paul "took bread; and giving thanks to God in the presence of all, he broke it and began to eat" (v. 35). This implicitly eucharistic meal, celebrating Jesus' death and resurrection, encourages

4. If one of the periodic grain shortages was occurring in Rome their motive might just as well have been fear of reprisal. See the excursus "Bread and Circuses," at Acts 11:19-30 above.

5. Richard I. Pervo, *Acts*, Hermeneia (Minneapolis: Fortress, 2009), 656n125.

6. Northrop Frye, *The Secular Scripture: A Study of the Structure of Romance* (Cambridge, MA: Harvard University Press, 1976), 4, discussing the Greek novel, remarks that "the normal means of transportation is by shipwreck."

7. They would have recognized a reference to Sunday, the day for eucharistic celebration, as signified also by Paul's action.

336 Acts of the Apostles

"all of them," who also eat.[8] The ship runs aground and breaks up, but all on board make it safely to shore.

Our purpose in this commentary calls us to consider the anonymous sufferers in the story: the prisoners and the ship's crew. Paul is a prisoner, but a very privileged one. As for the others, we never learn how many they were or what fate might await them in Rome. It would seem that their offenses must be heavy if the empire is spending resources to bring them there. They serve no particular purpose in the story except to highlight that Paul is one of them. The plight of prisoners has not improved much (if at all) in the intervening centuries; the very sight of them is abhorrent to most people, and compassion is rarely the reaction to their presence when they are seen toiling in fields or on roadsides. Preferably they remain out of sight and out of mind.

It seems the prisoners in the ship must have been shackled; ordinarily they would have been kept in the hold, but they seem to be present as part of the company Paul addresses (vv. 21-26, 33-38). The total of 276 persons (it is hard to imagine that any of them were women) seems very high for a ship of the period, but evidently grain ships carried big crews.[9] It seems very probable that some, if not all, of the sailors were enslaved; no wonder they tried to escape in the ship's boat (vv. 30-32). For the sake of the story they must not separate from the whole company, for it is necessary that *all* on board be rescued by divine mercy. Whether the enslaved sailors would have been content to be thus rescued rather than having the chance to escape and possibly gain their freedom would not have occurred to Lukas, but we have enough examples from the history of enslavement in the Americas to know that captives very frequently chose death over slavery.

In Lukas's story all persons on board—prisoners, guards, crew, and masters—are "brought safely to land" (v. 44), but then all except Paul effectively disappear from view. We are left to wonder what being "saved" signified for them.[10]

---

8. This is evidently another allusion to the all-inclusiveness of the eucharistic feast.

9. Pervo notes the full crews in grain ships and considers that the smaller numbers given in some of the many variants on the text were probably attempted corrections of a total that seems too large.

10. During the three centuries of the Atlantic slave trade many African captives chose suicide over enslavement; even more died in the fetid holds of the ships and were buried at sea; still other hundreds died when their ships were wrecked or sank in storms. A twenty-first-century initiative called "Diving with a Purpose" trains and supports African American divers to search for such wrecks and to preserve the remains of the dead with dignity.

Thus the dreadful sea adventure ends in tranquility; all 276 passengers, prisoners, soldiers, and crew come safely to land and instead of hostile "natives" (βάρβαροι[11]) ready to plunder them and the wreck they find magnanimous hospitality, including a fire (actually there would have to have been many fires to warm and dry several hundred people). According to MacDonald the scene depends heavily on Homer's *Odyssey*.[12]

On Malta we see Paul ceasing to identify with colonized people and entering fully into the sphere of the colonizers. Settlement of Malta had begun very early, somewhere around 5900 BCE. Its historical period begins with settlement by Phoenicians around 700 BCE. The island fell under Carthaginian domination in 480 BCE and served Carthage as an important naval base until it was occupied by Rome in 218 BCE, during the Second Punic War.

Thus the people Paul and his companions first encountered on Malta (or one of its offshore islands) were primarily Phoenician in origin; though they had been granted municipal privileges by Rome in 41 CE and the "leading man" Publius was probably the governor, the general population still spoke the native Semitic language of the place and were regarded as a colonized people.

What is so striking about Lukas's account is how, in the person of Paul, he steps so matter-of-factly into the role and space of the Roman colonizers. The greater number of the shipwrecked crowd disappear. The native population are amazed when, against their expectations, Paul is uninjured by the viper; they pronounce him a god but he seems not to know it, as there is no repetition of his protest in Lystra (14:14-18). Even so, word of Paul's character is evidently conveyed to Publius, who receives "us" (how many?) and offers shelter for three days. Paul, showing honor to his benefactor, heals Publius's father of fever and dysentery, maladies evidently common in Malta at that period. Differently from previous healings, Paul both prays over and lays hands upon the man.[13] When word of this gets around, the rest of the island's sick are

---

11. Βάρβαροι (literally "barbarians") appears only here in Acts, in vv. 2 and 4. In Pauline and Deutero-Pauline usage (e.g., Rom 1:14; Col 3:11) it means "not Greek," but in Acts 28 it is more: barbarous, uncivilized, lacking any real culture.

12. See MacDonald, "The Shipwrecks of Odysseus and Paul," 88–107.

13. Unlike Jesus and Peter (cf. Acts 3:7), Paul has been previously shown healing by command only (14:9) or by the touch of cloths that have been in contact with his body (19:11; cf. Peter's shadow, 5:15). He embraces Eutychus (20:10), but Eutychus is supposed to be dead. Otherwise Paul lays hands on people only to convey the Holy Spirit (19:6), as do others (6:6; 8:17, Peter and John; 9:17, Ananias; 13:3, the community at Antioch).

brought to Paul and he heals them too. We are probably to understand that Paul and his group of companions remain guests of Publius in the magnificent *Domus Romana*.

But Paul is a missionary of the good news (in his own eyes *the* missionary *par excellence*), and he preaches the message wherever he goes—except on Malta. Why not here? Surely the population would be receptive after all those healings! In fact, Maltese legend holds that Paul converted Publius, who became Malta's first bishop and evangelized the population. Lukas knows nothing about that. Paul is a respected guest and a welcome healer, despite being a prisoner, but evangelization is not in the picture.

Why this sudden change from Paul's previous practice? Perhaps Paul could not communicate with the native population because of their different language?[14] Somehow he and Barnabas had preached to the people of Lystra, though their language was Lycaonian and more foreign to them than Maltese, the Semitic speech of Malta. How, after all, did Publius convey his wishes to the population? Interpreters there were, surely. Lystra is a further parallel because there was no synagogue there either, and Paul customarily begins his mission in every locality by preaching in the synagogue. The text of Acts 14 speaks of the missionaries' difficulty in preventing the Lycaonians from treating them like gods, but somehow their missionizing there drew the ire of the Jews from Antioch and Iconium, so it must have consisted of something more than merely fighting off divinization.

The key probably lies in the word used at the very beginning of the Malta episode to describe the local population: they were βάρβαροι, barbarians.[15] Such people were of no account. As Pervo puts it: "[The incident with the viper] has no influence on the course of the story and was witnessed by persons who could not report it—and whose credibility stood no higher than that of the 'hysterical women' who first witnessed

14. See 1 Cor 14:11, "If . . . I do not know the meaning of a sound, I will be a foreigner to the speaker and the speaker a foreigner to me." There, however, Paul is referring to "speaking in tongues."

15. Here, as so often, the Authorized Version uses plain language, translating "barbarous people" and "barbarians" in Acts 28:2, 4, while modern translations write "natives." Mikeal C. Parsons and Martin M. Culy, *Acts: A Handbook on the Greek Text* (Waco, TX: Baylor University Press, 2003), *ad loc.*, translate "local inhabitants," but in the note on βάρβαροι they specify "Lit. 'the foreigners.'" We are looking here at a prime example of the effects of Enlightenment-era definitions of "race" on language usage: people become "foreigners" in their own land when the colonizers arrive.

Jesus' return from the dead."[16] He thinks, however, that Lukas's audience would have found "these witnesses . . . credible and their character commendable, as their hospitality demonstrated."[17] That may be true insofar as the audience were of the colonizer class. Colonized people might have had other feelings. In Maltese tradition Paul did not treat these people as "barbarians" unworthy of being taken seriously but instead evangelized them all—though Lukas may be closer to the truth, historically speaking. Physical evidence for Jewish and Christian presence in Malta dates to the fourth and fifth centuries CE.

The Paul of Acts, like the Paul of history, is a Jew, a Pharisee, and if not a Roman citizen at least well educated and fit to move in polite society. His mission is "to the Jew first" (Rom 1:16; 2:9, 10), then to the Greek, but his work is primarily in cities; country "barbarians" are beyond his sphere of perception. He is a man of words; a craftsman he may be, but hard physical labor is beneath him. The people who do it are (as throughout most of history) out of sight and out of mind. How thoroughly removed Lukas also is from that world is obvious when he refers to the "natives," the indigenous people of the island, as "foreigners."

"Barbarian" was also firmly associated with chattel slavery by the first centuries CE. The Greek word derives from Sanskrit *barbaras*, "stammering." In Greek it came to mean someone who did not speak Greek. The use of the term correlates with the development of chattel slavery in Greek society, especially Athens, which banned the enslavement of Greeks under Solon in the sixth century BCE.[18] The myopia of non-enslaved persons toward our own institutions is revealed in the fact that Lukas (together with the other New Testament writers, as well as many readers to this day) applauds the incorporation of enslaved persons into the early Jesus communities, their heroism as martyrs, their rise to high offices in the church—and yet we read right past the non-evangelization of the "barbarians" of Malta, who as such are somehow unworthy of our attention. Is it because they are a free people who have not been inculturated to Greco-Roman societies (most often by becoming enslaved persons) and so remain "uncivilized"?

16. Pervo, *Acts*, 675 and n. 50: "Celsus characterized Mary of Magdala (evidently) as 'a hysterical woman,' according to Origen, *Cels.* 2.55; cf. 2.59."

17. Ibid., n. 50.

18. This is analogous with the historical use of the word "black" as equivalent to "slave" in the United States.

Acts 28:11-31

"And So We Came to Rome"

Paul finally reaches his divinely determined destination, and there he remains, not exactly living happily ever after, but as in Grimms' fairy tales "if he has not died, he is living there still." What happens next (or various versions thereof) one may read in the apocryphal Acts of Paul, but for Lukas the story he is telling ends with Paul living and teaching in Rome. His active mission has ended, but his work of teaching has not. "All who came to him" may include members of the communities of the Way in Rome, which were surely known to Lukas, at least through Paul's letter to the Romans. While they are explicitly mentioned only in verse 15 as coming to meet Paul outside the city, the words that Lukas has Paul address to those who come to hear him are thoroughly in harmony with that letter. The group may include "Gentiles," since Paul says (v. 28) that God's salvation has been sent to them, but he does *not* say explicitly that he himself is turning to the gentiles, as he has in the past (cf. 13:46; 18:6). "They will listen" is a prediction, not a threat. As in every place, those who come to Paul most certainly include Jews. The "great numbers" in verse 23 are different from "all who came to him" in verse 30; while the latter may include Jews, the former are specifically the "local leaders of the Jews" (v. 17) who have arranged to meet with Paul.

This scene differs from previous instances of Paul's interaction with his fellow Jews in that none actually rejects Paul or attempts violence

[11]Three months later we set sail on a ship that had wintered at the island, an Alexandrian ship with the Twin Brothers* as its figurehead. [12]We put in at Syracuse and stayed there for three days; [13]then we weighed anchor and came to Rhegium. After one day there a south wind sprang up, and on the second day we came to Puteoli. [14]There we found believers and were invited to stay with them for seven days. And so we came to Rome. [15]The believers from there, when they heard of us, came as far as the Forum of Appius and Three Taverns to meet us. On seeing them, Paul thanked God and took courage.

[16]When we came into Rome, Paul was allowed to live by himself, with the soldier who was guarding him.

* Lit. "Dioscuri," i.e., Castor and Pollux.

[17]Three days later he called together the local leaders of the Jews. When they had assembled, he said to them, "Brothers, though I had done nothing against our people or the customs of our ancestors, yet I was arrested in Jerusalem and handed over to the Romans. [18]When they had examined me, the Romans wanted to release me, because there was no reason for the death penalty in my case. [19]But when the Jews objected, I was compelled to appeal to the emperor—even though I had no charge to bring against my nation. [20]For this reason therefore I have asked to see you and speak with you, since it is for the sake of the hope of Israel that I am bound with this chain." [21]They replied, "We have received no letters from Judea about you, and none of the brothers coming here has reported or spoken

against him. Paul tries, throughout an entire day, to convince the assembly about "the kingdom of God"—which, according to the Gospel authors, was Jesus' whole aim and the subject of all his preaching. Some are convinced; others are not (v. 24). They leave, still disputing with one another—and the modern Jewish saying that "where there are two Jews there are three opinions" is praise, not blame! Paul sends them off with a final statement that is *not* a dismissal, as so many interpreters have presumed it to be.

In my reading, verse 28 is key to understanding Lukas's scene, but in a way opposite to what was posited by so many commentators in the past (see below): namely, that it represents a rejection of the Jewish people. This event is pictured as taking place in *Rome,* and it was to the community of the Way in *Rome* that Paul had written the letter in which he most eloquently pleaded with gentile believers to understand that they are only secondarily the heirs of God's promises to Israel: *the covenant with Israel remains unbroken.* The gentiles are instruments as once Pha-

anything evil about you. ²²But we would like to hear from you what you think, for with regard to this sect we know that everywhere it is spoken against."

²³After they had set a day to meet with him, they came to him at his lodgings in great numbers. From morning until evening he explained the matter to them, testifying to the kingdom of God and trying to convince them about Jesus both from the law of Moses and from the prophets. ²⁴Some were convinced by what he had said, while others refused to believe. ²⁵So they disagreed with each other; and as they were leaving, Paul made one further statement: "The Holy Spirit was right in saying to your ancestors through the prophet Isaiah,

²⁶'Go to this people and say,
You will indeed listen, but never
    understand,
    and you will indeed look, but
        never perceive.
²⁷For this people's heart has

grown dull,
    and their ears are hard of
        hearing,
    and they have shut their eyes;
    so that they might not look with
        their eyes,
and listen with their ears,
    and understand with their heart
        and turn—
    and I would heal them.'
²⁸Let it be known to you then that this salvation of God has been sent to the Gentiles; they will listen."*

³⁰He lived there two whole years at his own expense and welcomed all who came to him, ³¹proclaiming the kingdom of God and teaching about the Lord Jesus Christ with all boldness and without hindrance.

*The Western (D) text adds v. 29: "And when he had said these words, the Jews departed, arguing vigorously among themselves."

---

raoh had been (Rom 9:17), so that the message of salvation may reach "the ends of the earth" (Acts 1:8; cf., *inter alia*, Pss 22:27; 46:9; 65:5; 67:7; 98:3; Isa 24:16, all predicting that the praise of Israel's God will sound from the farthest reaches of the world) and Israel will be aroused and "made jealous" (Rom 11:11, 14); only then can the world's salvation be fulfilled, for the grafted-in branches cannot flourish unless the root is sound (Rom 11:16). After all, "the gifts and the calling of God are irrevocable" (Rom 11:29).

This is the very opposite of "supersessionism." When Paul calls on his gentile audience in Romans to be a "living sacrifice" he is effectively calling them to surrender themselves to following the Way *for the sake of Israel.* It is not the people of Israel who must abandon the Torah; they are called, as always, to fulfill it, and the gentiles must serve them by living fully what Torah demands of them as gentiles. That was the instruction of the apostolic council (see Acts 15:19-21; cf. Lev 17–18).[1]

The Prophetic Witness

Until recently the attention of most exegetes has concentrated on Paul's quotation of Isaiah 6:9-11 (LXX) as representing Lukas's final rejection of the Jews. In the last decade that conclusion has been firmly rejected—most significantly by Jewish scholars,[2] who know that context matters. It is simply wrong to isolate a verse or a few words of Scripture, or even a pericope, and interpret it as if it stands alone. The word of God is one, just as God is One.

Isaiah 6:9-11 was very popular with the evangelists. It appears in Matthew 13:15 in the identical wording found here in Acts. John 12:40 has a much harsher version, making the people's hardening the work of God: "He has blinded their eyes and hardened their heart, so that they might not look with their eyes, and understand with their heart and turn—and I would heal them." In Matthew the quotation is part of Jesus' answer to the disciples' question about why he teaches in parables: understanding the message requires work, commitment, and, above all, a willingness to listen. John laments that the people did not believe Jesus despite the many "signs" he did among them and cites Isaiah as the prophecy thereby fulfilled. For Lukas it is hearing and accepting the word of Jesus that matters most, not fascination with "signs and wonders," which can be faked by magicians (as demonstrated in Acts 8:9-11; 13:6-12; 19:11-16).

---

1. Richard I. Pervo, *Acts*, Hermeneia (Minneapolis: Fortress, 2009), 377, writes of Acts 15:19-21: "Something of this sort could have been developed as a guide for Jews about interaction with gentiles in the Diaspora that was then taken up by early Christians." Thus the decree itself, as Lukas uses it, may well have been derived from Jewish *halakah* rather than the reverse.

2. The best summary treatment of this subject I have seen is Isaac W. Oliver/de Oliveira, "The 'Historical Paul' and the Paul of Acts: Which Is More Jewish?," in *Paul the Jew: Rereading the Apostle as a Figure of Second Temple Judaism*, ed. Gabriele Boccaccini and Carlos A. Segovia (Minneapolis: Fortress, 2016), 51–71, in which he compares the Paul of Acts with the Paul of Romans. Oliver has given a full, book-length explanation of his perspective on the meaning of Luke and Acts in his *Luke's Jewish Eschatology: The National Restoration of Israel in Luke-Acts* (New York: Oxford University Press, 2021). I am grateful to Dr. Amy-Jill Levine for directing me to this resource, even though I know she does not fully share its perspective.

Mark has a part of the quotation, likewise in the context of parables (in his case the Parable of the Sower). Mark's version ("in order that 'they may indeed look, but not perceive, and may indeed listen, but not understand; so that they may not turn again and be forgiven,'" 4:12) makes the conclusion negative, and it is evidently closer to the Hebrew text. Mark was writing in the immediate context of the fall of Jerusalem in 70 CE. Matthew has made the outcome more hopeful. His version hews to the Septuagint, as does the one in Acts.

In Luke's Gospel the people are much more receptive to Jesus' teaching and healing, so it is only in Acts that the book of Isaiah is brought into the picture. It appears at the very end of Acts, but it has been hovering in the background, especially in the accounts of Saul's vision. So we have to consider the context in Isaiah. Chapter 6 begins:

> In the year that King Uzziah died, I saw the Lord sitting on a throne, high and lofty; and the hem of his robe filled the temple. Seraphs were in attendance above him; each had six wings: with two they covered their faces, and with two they covered their feet, and with two they flew. And one called to another and said:
> "Holy, holy, holy is the LORD of hosts;
>   the whole earth is full of his glory."
> The pivots on the thresholds shook at the voices of those who called, and the house filled with smoke. And I said: "Woe is me! I am lost, for I am a man of unclean lips, and I live among a people of unclean lips; yet my eyes have seen the King, the LORD of hosts!"
> Then one of the seraphs flew to me, holding a live coal that had been taken from the altar with a pair of tongs. The seraph touched my mouth with it and said: "Now that this has touched your lips, your guilt has departed and your sin is blotted out." Then I heard the voice of the Lord saying, "Whom shall I send, and who will go for us?" And I said, "Here am I; send me!" (Isaiah 6:1-8[3])

Paul has not been as eager and forthcoming as Isaiah, but he has certainly had a powerful experience of being chosen and sent. His words to the people Israel have been as welcome as were those of prophets in the past—which is to say, the call to turn to God has never been well received (in any society!) by those for whom it is inconvenient, those who are comfortable with things as they are, while the poor listen with open ears. That is why in Lukas's portrayal Paul, like Stephen, meets with opposition from the leadership in the temple and in the synagogues

---

3. There was already an echo of this scene at 7:55-56 (Stephen's vision).

and yet continues to teach and prophesy and to gain followers from among the less well-situated and even from a few of those in positions of authority, as in Cyprus, Beroea, and Corinth.

Lukas is fond of the prophetic model. It was the central characterization of Jesus in Luke's Gospel (see, e.g., 4:16-30; 6:23, 26; 7:16; 9:8, 19; 11:49-50; 13:33-34; 24:19). In Acts, Peter (3:22-25) and Stephen (7:37, 52) allude to Jesus as one of the prophets, and Saul himself is said to be a "prophet and teacher" (13:1), though last on the list of those at Antioch. Those who read the prophetic books of the Hebrew Scriptures know that prophets always speak the truth, even (or especially?) when it hurts. So in Acts 28 Paul shows himself to be in the line of Israel's prophets, doing what they all have done and expecting the fate that awaited them—but, like the prophets of old, offering a hope to cling to when times are at their worst. He speaks in the spirit of the rabbis in Auschwitz who put God on trial, pronounced that God owes (*ḥayav*) God's people, and continued to worship God nevertheless.[4] He shows himself a true Pharisee by holding to the truth and authority of the prophets, whereas the Sadducees relied on Torah alone and so denied the hope of repentance and of resurrection and thus of the healing promised through Isaiah.

The Isaiah passage continues (vv. 9-10):

> And he said, "Go and say to this people:
> 'Keep listening, but do not comprehend;
> keep looking, but do not understand.'
> Make the mind of this people dull,
>   and stop their ears,
>   and shut their eyes,
> so that they may not look with their eyes,
>   and listen with their ears,
> and comprehend with their minds,
>   and turn and be healed."

That is the NRSV translation, corresponding to the Hebrew, but Isaac Oliver has shown that Lukas's use of the LXX (almost always) points to a different conclusion. The Greek version in Isaiah LXX and in Acts 28 ends with καὶ ἰάσομαι αὐτούς: "and I will heal them"—future indicative—while the preceding verbs in the verse are in the subjunctive. Thus the Greek of Isaiah and of Acts reads *"lest they see with their eyes and hear*

---

4. See *The JC*, September 19, 2008, at https://www.thejc.com/news/uk/wiesel-yes-we
-really-did-put-god-on-trial-1.5056, and cf. BDB חוב. The usage of *ḥayav* is cognate with German "Schuld, schuldig," which can mean either guilt or indebtedness.

with their ears and understand with their heart and turn, and I will heal them." Ἰάσομαι is in the first-person singular, in contrast to the previous third-person-plural references (whereas the Hebrew of the MT references Israel in the singular: יראה, "lest it sees"). "Thus, by switching the mood, number, and person in the very last clause of Isa 6:10, the Septuagint signals that *God will heal Israel*."[5]

There were many Jews who saw the destruction of Jerusalem in 70 CE as another instance of God's punishment for Israel's infidelity. The communities of Jesus' followers would have hoped that the message of forgiveness and redemption they preached would help their fellow Jews meet the crisis in hope. Instead, the rabbinic movement saw themselves called to emphasize a different part of the prophetic message: that Israel's destiny depends on the keeping of Torah, which is Israel's unique and proper duty—and the reason why gentile inclusion was a nonissue. The healing promised in Isaiah 6 is for Israel; it is both identical with and the fruit of keeping Torah.[6]

Even in the first and second centuries the message of redemption preached by the members of the Way could sound like "cheap grace," and the struggle between those within Christianity who assert that salvation is without preconditions and those who affirm what the first group calls "works righteousness" has endured through the centuries. That is much less a problem in Judaism, which rightly maintains that the two parts of the *Shema*—"Hear, O Israel . . . therefore you shall . . ."—are one and inseparable.

The rest of Isaiah 6, verses 11-13, shows the prophetic pattern:

> Then I said, "How long, O Lord?" And he said:
> "Until cities lie waste
>   without inhabitant,
> and houses without people,
>   and the land is utterly desolate;
> until the LORD sends everyone far away,
>   and vast is the emptiness in the midst of the land.

5. Oliver, *Luke's Jewish Eschatology*, 206–7. Italics in original.

6. Isaac Oliver also references a telling rabbinic discussion on the question of whether Israel must keep Torah in order to be healed or whether the Lord will accomplish that healing without any kind of repentance or obedience on Israel's part. For details of how Codex D and other manuscripts altered the Greek text of Isaiah here (and also in Acts 2 and 26) to make it condemn Israel see esp. Paul Metzger, "Zeitspiegel: Neutestamentliche Handschriften als Zeugnisse der Kirchengeschichte," in *The Book of Acts as Church History*, ed. Tobias Nicklas and Michael Tilly, BZNW 120 (Berlin: de Gruyter, 2003), 241–62.

> Even if a tenth part remain in it,
>   it will be burned again,
> like a terebinth or an oak
>   whose stump remains standing
>   when it is felled."
> The holy seed is its stump.

There can be little doubt that the Jews of Lukas's time applied that prophecy to themselves and clung to the thread of promise at the end: "The holy seed is its stump."[7] Even with the devastation visited upon the land in 70 CE, and again half a century later, the holy seed of hope endures, because God is faithful to God's promises.

Walter Brueggemann writes of Isaiah 6 that

> If . . . we take this oracular announcement in the context of the entire book of Isaiah, we already know that the long-term vision of the book concerns the deep loss of Jerusalem *and its fragile restoration.* . . . It is clear in this hard saying, even if much else is not clear here, that the purposes of God are at work in the midst of severe human obduracy. There are no easy healings. There are no ready turnings. The healings are not readily available, and the turnings are too demanding. . . . [T]here is comfort at the end of the oracle. But it is only late, a seeming afterthought. . . . The prophetic drama does not permit a rush to postexile, even as the gospel does not permit a rush past Friday to arrive too early and too easily at Sunday.[8]

A "Parting of the Ways"?

In the wake of the Holocaust many Christian scholars sought to exculpate themselves and others who had either cooperated in or stood aside during the slaughter of Jews in Europe by pointing to the supposed anti-Semitism of their own Scriptures ("Luke made me do it!"). Most prominent among them was J. T. Sanders, who joined his predecessor Ernst Haenchen[9] in concluding that "Luke has written the Jews off." Sanders

---

7. See Romans 9–11, especially the metaphor of Israel the root and gentiles as branches grafted in.

8. Walter Brueggemann, *Isaiah 1–39*, WBC (Louisville: Westminster John Knox, 1998), 61–63.

9. Ernst Haenschen, "The Book of Acts as Source Material for the History of Early Christianity," in *Studies in Luke-Acts*, ed. Leander E. Keck and J. Louis Martyn (Philadelphia: Fortress, 1966), 258–78, at 278. Sanders quotes the statement repeatedly. See James D. G. Dunn, "The Question of Anti-Semitism in the New Testament," in *Jews*

went even further, writing that "Luke" produced a "final solution of the Jewish problem."[10] At about that same time the Roman Catholic scholar John Pawlikowski was writing that "Acts is by far the most anti-Jewish book in the New Testament"[11] and Rosemary Radford Ruether was asking: "Is it possible to say 'Jesus is Messiah' without, implicitly or explicitly, saying at the same time 'and the Jews be damned'?"[12]

A turn in scholarship began in the last decades of the twentieth century with applications by various authors of James D. G. Dunn's idea of a largely (though not entirely) peaceful "parting of the ways" between Judaism and Christianity.[13] The twenty-first century has seen the emergence of a wide-ranging critique of previous theories based on increased access to and evaluation of first- and second-century texts, both Jewish and "Christian"—including a debate about which writings belong to which category and what the overlap signifies.[14] Some Jewish scholars, capitalizing on the new attention to such texts, have led the way in challenging older ideas of an early and hostile split between what they regard (rightly, in my opinion) as plural nascent Christianities and Judaisms. A pioneer in this regard was Daniel Boyarin, who, together with Peter

---

and Christians: The Parting of the Ways, A.D. 70 to 135, ed. J. D. G. Dunn (Grand Rapids: Eerdmans, 1999), 177–211.

10. Jack T. Sanders, "The Salvation of the Jews in Luke-Acts," in *Luke-Acts: New Perspectives from the Society of Biblical Literature*, ed. Charles H. Talbert (New York: Crossroad, 1984), 115, quoted in Oliver, *Luke's Jewish Eschatology*, 201. It is incomprehensible, to say the least, that a Christian author could write those words in 1984.

11. John T. Pawlikowski, review of Norman A. Beck, *Mature Christianity*, CBQ 49 (1987): 138, cited in Oliver, *Luke's Jewish Eschatology*, 201.

12. Rosemary Radford Ruether, *Faith and Fratricide: The Theological Roots of Anti-Semitism* (New York: Seabury, 1974), 246.

13. James D. G. Dunn, *The Partings of the Ways: Between Christianity and Judaism and Their Significance for the Character of Christianity* (London: SCM, 1991). See also his contribution to the "New Perspective on Paul" debate over justification in his *Jesus, Paul, and the Law: Studies in Mark and Galatians* (Louisville: Westminster John Knox, 1990). For a Jewish critique see Daniel Boyarin, *A Radical Jew: Paul and the Politics of Identity* (Berkeley: University of California Press, 1994).

14. A useful collection for understanding this new movement in thought is *The Ways That Never Parted: Jews and Christians in Late Antiquity and the Early Middle Ages*, ed. Adam H. Becker and Annette Yoshiko Reed (Minneapolis: Fortress, 2007). For a summary of the "Parting(s)" versus "Never Parting," debate, see Jonathan Gorsky, "The Parting of the Ways—A Review Essay," *HeyJ* 50 (2009): 996–1005, available at https://onlinelibrary.wiley.com/doi/full/10.1111/j.1468-2265.2009.00519.x (also downloadable as .pdf).

Schäfer and others, has "convincingly established that the 'Council of Yavneh' was a much later construct, rather than an historical event."[15]

Both Jewish and Christian scholars remain divided on the issues surrounding New Testament—and particularly Lukan—attitudes toward Jews and Judaism. Gary Gilbert, in his notes on Acts 28:28 in *The Jewish Annotated New Testament*, wrote in the first edition that "at least by anticipation of what developed later, if not in reality by the time represented in the narrative (mid-60s CE), the mission to the Jews is over."[16] In the revised edition of 2017 the wording is exactly the same. Yet Isaac Oliver's book (see n. 2 above), with extensive reference to rabbinic literature, argues just the opposite, and more such studies continue to appear.[17] The ways have not parted: they have braided themselves in interesting twists and coils.

That, as Walter Brueggemann writes, "the purposes of God are at work in the midst of severe human obduracy" is, in fact, the heart of the lesson Lukas wishes to leave with his audience, both Jewish and gentile. As he writes, the storm of rebellion is already astir among Jews in Egypt and in Palestine. Unrest will lead ultimately to the expulsion of Jews from Judea and its renaming as "Palestine," the home of the Philistines whom Israel had ousted long ago, and with the reconfiguration of Jerusalem as Aelia Capitolina, in which the only temples are for pagan gods. At the same time it will bring persecution on the heads of those beginning to be called "Christians," both Jew and gentile, for refusal to honor the divine emperor in Rome. A tax levied on Jews serves to drive a wedge: one must identify as a Jew

---

15. Adam H. Becker and Annette Yoshiko Reed, "Introduction" to *The Ways That Never Parted*, 5; see also nn. 13 and 14 above. See especially Daniel Boyarin, *Border Lines: The Partition of Judaeo-Christianity* (Philadelphia: University of Pennsylvania Press, 2004); Peter Schäfer, "Die sogenannte Synode von Jabne," *Judaica* 31 (1975): 54–64, and the other literature cited in n. 13. My personal acquaintance with Daniel Boyarin, a former colleague at the Graduate Theological Union in Berkeley, leads me to share his view.

16. Gary Gilbert, "Acts," in *The Jewish Annotated New Testament*, ed. Amy-Jill Levine and Mark Zvi Brettler, 2nd ed. (Oxford: Oxford University Press, 2017), 252.

17. See, e.g., the essays in *Wisdom Poured Out Like Water: Studies on Jewish and Christian Antiquity in Honor of Gabriele Boccaccini*, ed. J. Harold Ellens, Isaac W. Oliver, Jason Von Ehrenkrook, James Waddell, and Jason M. Zurawski (Boston: deGruyter, 2018). These include Lester L. Grabbe, "What Did the Author of Acts Know about Pre-70 Judaism?," 450–62; Mark S. Kinzer, "Sacrifice, Prayer, and the Holy Spirit: The Tamid Offering in Luke-Acts," 463–75; Isaac W. Oliver, "Are Luke and Acts Anti-Marcionite?" 499–525; Anders Klostergaard Petersen, "Unveiling the Obvious—Synagogue and Church: Sisters or Different Species?" 575–92.

and pay the tax or else refuse to do so and thereby repudiate the root of one's identity. In doing so one would also lose the advantage of the permission granted to Jews not to sacrifice to the emperor, and many a Christian paid the price for refusing to do so.

Certainly we now know that the depiction of Paul living in Rome for two years with such freedom and in a rented space[18] "at his own expense" bears little resemblance to the realities of that time. Lukas's contemporaries would have had a better picture; they would have known that "living by himself, with the soldier that was guarding him" meant he was chained to his guard (cf. v. 20) and certainly not in commodious quarters. That he had to pay for his keep is likely. (See above at Acts 24.) Lukas prefers that we think of Paul, as he himself had boasted, as not dependent on support from anyone.[19]

The audience for Acts may, at the time of writing, be still basking in the glow of being relatively undisturbed, of being able to teach "about the Lord Jesus Christ with all boldness and without hindrance" (28:31)—or some of them may already have suffered the scourge of Nero's persecution and the pressure of Roman governors under Trajan, as exemplified by Pliny. Lukas has told them a dramatic and hopeful story of the Way's beginnings to bolster their courage for the present and the future, ending with a caution from the past. It is meant both to guard against complacency and to reaffirm that both the warnings and the promises given to Israel apply to followers of Jesus also.[20] It also leaves open the question whether Paul died in Rome under Nero or whether he won his freedom (or was exiled) and continued his work in Spain.[21]

---

18. Μίσθωμα (v. 30) and ξενία ("lodgings," v. 23) are synonyms referring to rented quarters. In the Acts of Paul 11 the place is a "barn." Later writers speculated on whether Paul earned the rent by his labor or whether he sold his clothes and books (as might be inferred from 2 Tim 4:13). See Pervo, *Acts*, 687n70.

19. Cf., e.g., Acts 20:34; 2 Cor 11.

20. In her *Hearing Between the Lines: The Audience as Fellow-Worker in Luke-Acts and Its Literary Milieu*, LNTS 425 (London: T&T Clark, 2010), Kathy Maxwell quotes William S. Kurz (*Reading Luke-Acts: Dynamics of Biblical Narrative* [Louisville: Westminster John Knox, 1993], 31): "Ending the story of Acts with Paul's unhindered preaching 'propels the narrative toward the future and the time of the intended [audience]'" (*Hearing*, 174).

21. The author of 1 Clement (which could have been known to the author of Acts) thinks Paul left Rome and went to Spain. (1 Clem 5: "having taught righteousness to the whole world, and come to the extreme limit of the west.") The "Muratorian Canon" or "Muratorian Fragment," supposedly the first canonical listing of books of the New Testament, may have been created as early as 170 or as late as the fourth

It seems appropriate to conclude with some words from Maia Kotrosits. I agree wholeheartedly with her when, in her book *Rethinking Early Christian Identity: Affect, Violence, and Belonging*, in the chapter "Reading Acts in Diaspora," she writes:

> I bring an affective reading to bear on the Acts of the Apostles to entertain the book as something other than a highly elaborate imagination of Christian origins, charter document for Christianity, or a construction of Christian identity—all of which assume Christian-belonging to be the central social interest of the book. . . . In my reading, Acts is a diasporic account of the very strange confederations and rivalries constitutive of colonial life, and a melancholic epic of imperial romances and disappointments. . . .
>
> Acts is not only a story of epic significance or utopian or counter-cultural impulses, but also a story of arrested possibility, of regrettable coalitions with dominant structure and systems, of sighs and reflections that it should have been some other way. . . . I additionally want to suggest that the affective drifts in our renderings of Acts actually bring us to considerations of belonging within and around the text that are more pressing than "Christian identity": the strange gatherings and haunted sociality of life within empire.[22]

Kotrosits's previous chapter was titled "On the Historical Queerness of Christianity,"[23] and in it she likewise identifies what came to be called *Ioudaismos* as "a negotiation of diaspora-belonging."[24] We have noted how Lukas queers his most important characters (Jesus, Peter, Lydia,

---

century. (See the text at https://www.bible-researcher.com/muratorian.html, and studies such as Joseph Verheyden, "The Canon Muratori: A Matter of Dispute," in *The Biblical Canons*, ed. Jean-Marie Auwers and Henk Jan De Jonge, BETL 163 [Leuven: Leuven University Press, 2003], 487–556.) In lines 36–39 the text says of Acts: "For 'most excellent Theophilus' Luke compiled the individual events that took place in his presence—as he plainly shows by omitting the martyrdom of Peter as well as the departure of Paul from the city [of Rome] when he journeyed to Spain." Lukas nicely avoids the issue, thus not allowing the message of his book to be obscured by it.

22. Maya Kotrosits, *Rethinking Early Christian Identity: Affect, Violence, and Belonging* (Minneapolis: Fortress, 2015), 86, 89.

23. Ibid., 47–83.

24. Ibid., 73, with reference to Judith Lieu, *Neither Jew Nor Greek? Constructing Early Christianity* (London: Bloomsbury T&T Clark, 2003; 2nd ed. 2016), and also to Boyarin's *Border Lines*; Steve Mason, "Jews, Judeans, Judaizing, Judaism," *JSJ* 38 (2007): 457–512; and Philip Esler, *Conflict and Identity in Romans* (Minneapolis: Fortress, 2009), all expressing challenges to faith-based identity, "suggesting that it disembeds cultic practice from geographic, ethnic, and cultural contexts."

Paul) in subtle ways. Taking a feminist perspective on and seeking continuity with writings whose authors were trying to come to terms with new social and cultural identities is inevitably an experience of queering our own perspectives by moving out of what we think we know about ourselves and those writings to a place where we acknowledge that we do not know either of them. I wrote at the beginning that my preferred approach to any subject has always been "What if it did not happen as we thought it did? What if it was this way instead?" Given enough time and strength, I might begin again at the beginning and question my own analysis in the same way; since I cannot, I invite my readers to do so. I myself can only say, "Here ends the reading."

Afterword

Liquid God

Willie James Jennings

mpire has been cracked open. The book of Acts begins the draining of a world filled with patriarchal power and masculinist privilege. Linda Maloney captures this truth beautifully in this work. The plug has been pulled and slowly but surely the hope of a particular kind of power is dissipating into the nothingness where lurks the demonic. It is a power rooted in the hope for the rise of the great man, the one that will lead us into a glorious new future. Histories have been too often told to encircle the great men, moving constantly around their bodies, their behaviors and moods, their actions and genius from which the world enters its maturity. The book of Acts will have none of that. Jesus will not be the great man. He will be the community formed in his name. Jesus will not be the genius whose cunning reason becomes the paradigm for global victory or domination. He will be the giver of connecting life that binds and elevates all to a shared vision.

The book of Acts is a people's history of God that directly challenges masculinist historiography and the pedagogies of history that continue to teach people to read the world through the actions of great men. In fact, we cannot escape those ways of reading and teaching history simply by rejecting them, because the great men are too strong to be denied in that way. They can only be denied by following the one who killed the great man on the cross and rose from the dead for the sake of the many. Jesus will be known in the many. History must be seen from the many. The future envisioned by the many will be the future of God. Eschatology is always communal if it is indeed God's last things. Yet the steps of escape from the great man that Jesus provides mark a radical and dangerous egalitarianism. This egalitarianism is deadly, killing equally the ambitions of men and women and all those caught up in masculinist desire to be remembered as the movers and shakers of history, the builders of worlds, and the heroes of change.

If the world of man—patriarchal, kyriarchal, longingly masculinist—is being drained, then what is emerging in Acts? A world filled with the flows of God: Acts gives witness to Israel's liquid God, and this will be the beginning of a new kind of witness, the witness to life after death, the victory over violence without violence—all of it found in the flow. This means that the followers of the risen Jesus will be called to enact a different kind of *Kyrios*, an anti-lord Lord of the flow. Like the effects of a flood, the kyriarchal structures of society will now begin to crumble from the rising flow of the Spirit moving through the Jesus followers.

This will be uncharted territory inside an unfathomed identity for these disciples. It is an identity we are yet to fathom, its depths calling to us. But not for Mary, the mother of Jesus. Mary is the first true witness. Our witness is anchored in Mary's reality and truth. Mary's decisive position as the bearer of witness and, as later theology will declare, as *Theotokos*, God-bearer, teaches us the truth of the flow, its uncontainability, its uncontrollability, and its inextricable connection to new life, revolutionary life. Mary shows us what is at stake in this liquid witness—a life out of place, a life out of phase with the prevailing patriarchal order, out of phase with heteronormative marriage, and out of phase with safe and quiet existence in a social order. To speak Mary's name is to speak the revolutionary difference of being the witness to her son. The flow of God through Mary will become the flow of God through her son Jesus, and now in the book of Acts that flow will move through the disciples of Jesus.

The disciples of Jesus are seeking to discern this new reality of witness while yet participating in the old ways of witness. A man speaks the truth of another man—this is the old way, an old way rooted in patriarchal power and kyriarchal vision. Such vision convinces people that a sure account, a trustworthy account of the past that will orient us rightly to the future may come only from men. Yet the Spirit comes, and the disciples speak, all of them. Those gathered will, like newborns, utter a marvelous sound: the sound of life. The book of Acts gives us a birthing scene that indicates the opening of the divine womb. God our mother rejoices in giving the gift of God's self. The Spirit wills newness, and we will know this desire of God for us. Through the joining of flesh and Spirit, God aims at permanence. The Spirit will speak, hovering in, on, under, over, between, and through, permeating creaturely life like liquids that cover the birthing process. Water and Spirit are now forever joined.

It makes sense to associate the Spirit with the feminine, but it makes even more sense to allow God's release as seen in the book of Acts to free what is meant by the feminine from androcentric captivity. What later theologians will recite as a trinitarian axiom—that the external operations of the Trinity are without division (*opera Trinitatis ad extra sunt indivisa*)—has its home here in Acts' beautiful moments of divine birthing. The triune God pours out holy juices that will never dissipate, and in them and with them a child cries out wonderfully and power-fully, showing new life. Liquid Spirit, Liquid God—new wine is being poured out on flesh. God our mother pours out God's own life, and the disciples will speak.

The liquid God is flowing. Beginning at Pentecost and throughout the narrative of Acts we learn that God cannot be captured but only wit-nessed, in the profundity of divine freedom in liquidity—drenching all children and those who have yielded their life in service to God. There is an equality formed in this liquidity—of water and Spirit. We are yet in the work of divine birthing and the releasing of the creative juices of God. God has come full term—the fullness of time—and the earth herself will signal this moment of the mother. It is therefore no stretch to see in Acts the enacting of the Mother-Daughter-Spirit moment of God, the flows of God that moved through this child of Nazareth and through whom flows the power of God to resurrection now flowing through the disciples of Jesus. There is great danger and power in a released body and a yielded spirit. Its image can and has easily served as the basis for a religious politics of subjugation, especially for women. Too often those longing for power have used that image to establish their willing and wanting as the willing and wanting of God. Yet the releasing in Acts car-ries narrative and temporal specificity—it is the moment of birthing, the moment when our bodies yield to the new life that must come forward, pressing through the pain that will not, that must not be the last word for our existence. The Mother-Daughter-Spirit God releases and yields: here is the deepest truth of this new faith in Jesus. It was the path of his resurrection, and it will also mark our path in and with Jesus. We release ourselves to the power of God found in Jesus and we yield to the Spirit.

What will this mean? Many things might be said about this yielding shown in the book of Acts, but two matters noted in this commentary must be given pride of place because they are so close to the heartbeat of this text and to the life of God witnessed through it.

First, releasing ourselves to the flow of God means being drawn toward a new common life rooted in sharing our lives. Sharing has often existed in a malignant and nefarious site where slaves, and women, and children are further established within a patriarchal and androcentric fantasy as collectible commodities. This would be a corrupted common, resisting the new of the Spirit. Yet the sharing formed in Jesus' resurrected body and enacted by the Spirit suggests something far different from and far more radical than the sharing formed of empire. It suggests sharing the body's needs and the body's plight in traversing an oppressive society. Everyone counts—this is the democratic spirit we find in Acts—and everyone has needs. Between the everyone who counts and the everyone who needs flows the radicality we find at the beginning of Acts: of selling possessions and goods and distributing the proceeds to the needy. Both churches and societies have struggled with this radicality because it speaks of endless flows. Such flows erode social and economic hierarchies and weaken the foundations of hoarding societies built on uneven exchange, wealth accumulation, cheap labor, ecclesial coercion, and governmental corruption.

Jesus-disciples, however, leak. Goods, possessions, money do not stagnate in them or with them, because they move from place to place, home to home through a politics of generosity that is both beautiful and unnerving, especially for those whose power and position are threatened by such leaky people.

Such sharing is a direct attack on the hierarchies that constitute social life. Empire is in trouble in the book of Acts: not just the Roman Empire, with its codified and canonized slavocracy and patriarchy, but also its economically structured visions of gender and sexuality. The Spirit is flowing through those not seen as human, not acknowledged as having voice, and bound to the market with prices on their heads. This is extraordinary, and it is also a much needed and much longed-for word for the Jewish diaspora. Diaspora living—alien, exile, stranger, foreigner, marginal—is already life in the cracks, cuts, and rips of a society, and ironically these are exactly the spaces where liquidity is most powerful as it seeps into everything that is stable, central, fixed, and absolute. There the liquid starts to crumble things from within.

Divine liquidity is inescapably and irrefutably good news for women. As Maloney writes powerfully in this commentary, we cannot overemphasize the significance of women in the narrative sweep of Acts, not first because they are given "prominent roles" in the book, though some have such roles. We must note this significance because women are seen, their invisibility erased by the Spirit of God. Such visibility does not require heroic gestures or masculinist displays of power or cunning actions of statecraft. All that is necessary is yielding to the Spirit. The humanity of women that has always been there, always been seen by God, now has pneumatological bright light cast on it and on lives deeply loved by God. Women will be at the heart of the new joining that is gestured in the book of Acts, the bringing together of Jew and Gentile, the breaking down of the walls of hostility and fear, and the weaving together of Jewish diaspora hope with Gentile longing for thriving life. Yet the yielding to the Spirit requires what both diaspora citizens and empire subjects cannot fathom: moving toward one another in life together, sensing the pull of the currents that are drawing them toward each other.

Chapters 10–15 show us that sensing, and these chapters also show us the beginning of a failure, an understandable one, but a failure none the less. Diaspora cannot imagine what God was imagining: the people of Israel joining the Gentiles in ways of life without adopting those ways of life and without losing faithful identity rooted in Torah. Empire subjects cannot imagine what the God of Israel was imagining: abandoning the gods of their peoples without losing themselves and their hope for a future because they would soon learn that their true Creator deeply loved them, all the way down to the dirt on which they stood, all the way down to the plants and animals they ate, all the way down to the stories they told, all the way down to the shape of their bodies and the contours of their loves—and that, together with Israel, with diaspora, this God found in Jesus would drench them in the divine juices and lead them into a more excellent way to know and love who they are and love the One who is the life-giver.

This good news, however, is a revolution that would touch the routine, and for doing such a revolutionary thing the disciples must suffer. This is the second matter in the book of Acts that must be highlighted. No commentary that is true to the story of Acts can ignore the centrality of the prison, of incarceration and punishment. All will bear the pain of the prison, of loss and absence, of death and torture, but women will bear it acutely as they watch the disciples they know—brothers, and partners, and children, and friends—imprisoned. For many women and children what will come with the imprisonment of loved ones will be the loss of protection and support. But we should not imagine, because the book of Acts gives us no reason to do so, that women were not imprisoned, not tortured or beaten, not thrown out of places both sacred and profane, not discarded by family and friends and branded as diaspora traitors and theological heretics. Women were imprisoned and women are imprisoned at rates that make no sense for their crimes and for the nonsense that mocks a real understanding of criminality. Women are imprisoned for trying to survive, trying to protect themselves, trying to make life possible in a world that kills them for nothing, brutalizes them for sport, and ignores their well-being as a matter of course.

Under the conditions of empire the prison is always close, nearby in the shadows. Thus to speak the revolutionary name of Jesus, to announce his way, and to yield to the Spirit's flow is to bring the prison out of the shadows looking for its next body to consume. We should understand the prison in Acts (and prisons now) as a technology wielded by the powerful and the resentful to thwart the Holy Spirit by seeking to kill the human spirit. The prison has always been about a way of disciplining the body by means of death for the purpose of creating docile subjects who would live forever marked by death, showing forth its wounding as a sign of death's claim on a life. The prison is death's agent, helping death to mark bodies for an early exit. In this way the prison seeks to stop the flow of the Spirit by ending the flow of life. The resurrection of Jesus, however, breaks the power of the prison and the finality of violence.

The disciples of Jesus in the book of Acts know this. They understand, albeit not fully, the power of his resurrection: here is one who survived a successful assassination and exposed the stratagems of the principalities and powers. Those scare tactics and threats, those operations of physical coercion, those practices of torture, even the deployment of death through murder will not destroy the human spirit because it is vivified by the Holy Spirit. Yet, lest we sound too triumphalist about what we read in Acts, we must remember the life on the ground in that book, where people are on the run for their lives, where they are in hiding, drawing on all the wisdom and practice of diaspora living. This is flow work and flow life, and the women in the book of Acts know it extremely well. As Maloney shows us throughout this commentary, the church forms in homes, in women-space, where the power of the Spirit is in domestic space but never ever domesticated. So too with the women in these spaces who foment and format revolutionary life in the Spirit.

And so it begins in the book of Acts. Disciples will be prisoners. Prisoners will be disciples. Incarceration will mark the journey of holy flesh, redeemed flesh, and the life of witnesses to Jesus. Yet incarceration can never stop the flow of the Spirit, and therefore we cannot be stopped.

The book of Acts, however, shows two ways of not being thwarted. The first is the way of empire that bends and breaks all who oppose its will. Empire will not only destroy life to sustain its life and its way of life but it will seduce all who are near the sound of its voice to believe that this is the only way to sustain life. Empire will not be thwarted even if it must destroy everything in sight: buildings, peoples, animals, plants, crops, land, water, earth, and sky. Empire will not be thwarted even if it must create compounded lies and constellations of falsehoods, even if it must manufacture religions and schools of thought at tremendous expense and over long periods of time. The disciples of Jesus are always close to being seduced by this way of not being thwarted, because it feels so close at hand, so easy to touch. The second way of not being thwarted is precisely seen and felt inside forms of captivity, inside the logics of incarceration, within the strategies used to silence voices, and it is the way of water and wind and drumbeat and song and memory. These are the realities that echo holy flow.

The Spirit can be resisted but not thwarted, and those who live by the Spirit share in the same reality. There is resistance that seems impenetrable. There is blockage that seems permanent. There is opposition that seems endlessly clever and quick. But here is the Spirit of the living God who works through tiny holes, cuts, small seeds, quiet voices that say yes to God. The disciples of Jesus will not be thwarted, because he is risen indeed. And the Spirit flows. This is the good news both to diaspora Israel and Gentile nations: both may share in the divine juices and both may know the power of God to build up through pulling down.

What is the pulling down? The pulling down is being brought all the way down to a rejected cornerstone. This downward motion does not reinforce hierarchies. It exposes their hubris when articulated as divinely ordered by God. Such hierarchies are formed by builders aiming toward a tower of Babel in hopes of establishing godlike existence and pretending to know the divine mind. These builders rejected the true cornerstone and thereby rejected a building project rooted in the divine life. God would build life with us by building up life in and through us by the Spirit. This would be life that draws the poor and the rejected, the outcast and the tormented into the shared work of envisioning and building the new. Jesus is the cornerstone of a new habitation, and he is the only one who rises, above and beyond the ruling class and above and beyond their judgments. Christians have often failed to get this movement correct in the way we understand social life and the way we build life. Too often we have imagined our presence with the powerful and even the quest to be the powerful as stepping up, using our voices and the cunning of reason to establish a masculinist visibility.

The Spirit of God aims to release us from the stupidity of Babel, where human hubris in the rush to seize power always tramples over human need. We rise with Christ into the commons. We exalt the one who is for the many, and we begin the life of faith precisely in the call to gather together. We are called to gather (*ekklēsia*), and we are called to become gatherers. Indeed, the book of Acts ends where we begin. We are there with Paul at the site of incarceration, watching the fear and apprehension of Jewish diaspora in Rome and seeing Paul turn outward in his imperial captivity, welcoming all who would come to him and sharing the good news of Jesus Christ. Even in Rome, even under house arrest, even with an uncertain future, even surrounded by fear and disbelief, the Spirit of God yet releases; the juices yet flow. Paul knew this, and so must we.

Works Cited

Aaron, David H. "Shedding Light on God's Body in Rabbinic Midrashim: Reflections on the Theory of a Luminous Adam." *HTR* 90 (1997): 299–314.

Aguilar, Grace. *The Women of Israel*. England, 1845; New York: D. Appleton, 1872.

Albrecht, Ruth. "Jungfrau/Witwe." In *Wörterbuch der Feministischen Theologie*, edited by Elisabeth Gössmann and Beate Wehn, 207–10. Gütersloh: Mohn, 1991.

Alexander, Loveday. "Chronology of Paul." In *Dictionary of Paul and His Letters: A Compendium of Contemporary Biblical Scholarship*, edited by Gerald F. Hawthorne, Ralph P. Martin, and Daniel G. Reid, 115–23. IVP Bible Dictionary Series. Downers Grove: Intervarsity, 2015.

———. *The Preface to Luke's Gospel: Literary Convention and Social Context in Luke 1.1-4 and Acts 1.1*. SNTSMS 78. Cambridge: Cambridge University Press, 1993.

Alexander, Michelle. *The New Jim Crow: Mass Incarceration in the Age of Colorblindness*. 10th anniv. ed. New York: New Press, 2020.

Anderson, Janice Capel, and Stephen D. Moore, eds. *Mark and Method: New Approaches in Biblical Studies*. 2nd ed. Minneapolis: Fortress, 2008.

Aquino, María Pilar, and María José Rosado-Nunes, eds. *Feminist Intercultural Theology: Latina Explorations for a Just World*. Studies in Latino/a Catholicism. Maryknoll, NY: Orbis Books, 2007.

Aquino, María Pilar, Daisy L. Machado, and Jeanette Rodríguez, eds. *A Reader in Latina Feminist Theology*. Austin: University of Texas Press, 2002.

Astell, Mary. *Some Reflections upon Marriage*. New York: Source Book Press, 1970. Reprint of the 1730 edition; earliest ed. 1700.

Bach, Alice, ed. *Women in the Hebrew Bible*: A Reader. New York: Routledge, 1999.

Badley, Jo-Ann. "What Is Mary Doing in Acts? Confessional Narratives and the Synoptic Tradition." In *Rediscovering the Marys: Maria, Mariamne, Miriam*, edited by Mary Ann Beavis and Ally Kateusz, 47–58. LNTS (= JSNTSup) 620. London: Bloomsbury T&T Clark, 2020.

Bal, Mieke. *Lethal Love: Feminist Literary Readings of Biblical Love Stories*. Bloomington: Indiana University Press, 1987.

Balch, David L. "Women Prophets / Maenads Visually Represented in Two Roman Colonies: Pompeii and Corinth." In *Contested Ethnicities and Images: Studies in Acts and Art*, 259–78. WUNT 345. Tübingen: Mohr Siebeck, 2015.

Barreto, Eric D. *Ethnic Negotiations*. WUNT 294. Tübingen: Mohr Siebeck, 2010.

Barrett, Charles Kingsley. *A Critical and Exegetical Commentary on the Acts of the Apostles*. Vol. 1. ICC. London: T&T Clark, 1994.

Baskin, Judith R. "Women and Post-Biblical Commentary." In *The Torah: A Women's Commentary*, edited by Tamara Cohn Eskenazi and Andrea L. Weiss, xlix–lv. New York: URJ Press and Women of Reform Judaism, The Federation of Temple Sisterhoods, 2008.

Bauer, Shane. *American Prison: A Reporter's Undercover Journey into the Business of Punishment*. New York: Penguin, 2018.

Beavis, Mary Ann. "Ancient Slavery as an Interpretive Context for the New Testament Servant Parables with Special Reference to the Unjust Steward (Luke 16:1-8)." *JBL* 111 (1992): 37–54.

———. " 'If Anyone Will Not Work, Let Them Not Eat': 2 Thessalonians 3.10 and the Social Support of Women." In *A Feminist Companion to Paul: Deutero-Pauline Writings*, edited by Amy-Jill Levine with Marianne Blickenstaff, 29–36. FCNTECW 7. London: T&T Clark International, 2003.

———. *Jesus and Utopia: Looking for the Kingdom of God in the Roman World*. Minneapolis: Fortress, 2006.

Beavis, Mary Ann, Irmtraud Fischer, Mercedes Navarro Puerto, and Adriana Valerio, eds. The Bible and Women: An Encyclopaedia of Exegesis and Cultural History. https://www.bibleandwomen.org.

Béchard, Dean P. "Paul Among the Rustics: The Lystran Episode (Acts 14:8-20) and Lucan Apologetic." *CBQ* 63 (2001): 84–101.

Becker, Adam H., and Annette Yoshiko Reed, eds. *The Ways That Never Parted: Jews and Christians in Late Antiquity and the Early Middle Ages*. Minneapolis: Fortress, 2007.

Bertram, Georg. ὠδίν, ὠδίνω, *TDNT* 9 (1974): 667–74.

Bhabha, Homi. *The Location of Culture*. New York: Routledge, 1994.

Bird, Phyllis A. *Missing Persons and Mistaken Identities: Women and Gender in Ancient Israel*. Minneapolis: Fortress, 1997.

Böhler, Dieter. *1 Esdras*. Translated by Linda M. Maloney. IECOT. Stuttgart: Kohlhammer, 2016.

Bolen, Jean Shinoda. *Artemis: The Indomitable Spirit in Everywoman*. San Francisco: Conari Press, 2014.

Bollók, János. "The Description of Paul in the Acta Pauli." In *The Apocryphal Acts of Paul and Thecla*, edited by Jan N. Bremmer, 1–15. Kampen: Kok Pharos, 1996.

Børresen, Kari Elisabeth, and Adriana Valerio, eds. *The High Middle Ages*. The Bible and Women: An Encyclopaedia of Exegesis and Cultural History. Atlanta: SBL Press, 2015.

Bovon, François. "Beyond the Book of Acts: Stephen, the First Christian Martyr, in Traditions Outside the New Testament Canon of Scripture." *PRSt* 32 (2005): 93–107.

Boyarin, Daniel. *Border Lines: The Partition of Judaeo-Christianity*. Philadelphia: University of Pennsylvania Press, 2004.

———. *A Radical Jew: Paul and the Politics of Identity*. Berkeley: University of California Press, 1994.

Brandenburger, Egon. "Taten der Barmherzigkeit als Dienst gegenüber dem königlichem Herrn (Mt 25,31-46)." In *Diakonie: biblische Grundlagen und Orientierungen. Ein Arbeitsbuch*, edited by Gerhard K. Schäfer and Theodor Strohm, 297–325. 2nd ed. Heidelberg: HVA, 1994.

Brantenberg, Gerd. *Egalia's Daughters: A Satire of the Sexes*. Translated by Louis Mackay. Emeryville, CA: Seal Press, 1985.

Brock, Sebastian J. *Holy Spirit in the Syrian Baptismal Tradition*. Syrian Churches Series 9. 2nd ed. Pune, India: Anita Printers, 1998.

Brooten, Bernadette J. *Love Between Women: Early Christian Responses to Female Homoeroticism*. Chicago: University of Chicago Press, 1996.

———. *Women Leaders in the Ancient Synagogue: Inscriptional Evidence and Background Issues*. BJS 36. Chico, CA: Scholars Press, 1982.

Brooten, Bernadette J., ed., with Jacqueline L. Hazelton. *Beyond Slavery: Overcoming Its Religious and Sexual Legacies*. Black Religion/Womanist Thought/ Social Justice. New York: Palgrave Macmillan, 2010.

Brown, Lucinda A. "Tabitha." In *Women in Scripture: A Dictionary of Named and Unnamed Women in the Hebrew Bible, the Apocryphal/Deuterocanonical Books, and the New Testament*, edited by Carol Meyers, Toni Craven, and Ross S. Kraemer, 159–60. Grand Rapids: Eerdmans, 2001.

Brown, Raymond E., and John P. Meier. *Antioch and Rome: New Testament Cradles of Catholic Christianity*. Mahwah, NJ: Paulist Press, 1983.

Brueggemann, Walter. *Isaiah 1–39*. WBC. Louisville: Westminster John Knox, 1998.

Burke, Sean D. *Queering the Ethiopian Eunuch: Strategies of Ambiguity in Acts*. Emerging Scholars. Minneapolis: Fortress, 2013.

Butler, Judith. *Gender Trouble: Feminism and the Subversion of Identity*. New York: Routledge, 1990.

Cabrol, Fernand, and Henri Leclercq, eds. *Dictionnaire d'archéologie chrétienne et de liturgie*. Paris: Letouzey et Ane, 1907–1953.

Cadbury, Henry J., and Kirsopp Lake. *The Beginnings of Christianity*. London: Macmillan, 1933.

———. "We and I Passages in Luke-Acts." *NTS* 3 (1956): 128–32.

Cannon, Katie G. "The Emergence of Black Feminist Consciousness." In *Feminist Interpretation of the Bible*, edited by Letty M. Russell, 30–40. Philadelphia: Westminster, 1985.

Carter, Warren. *The Gospel of Matthew in Its Roman Imperial Context*. London: T&T Clark, 2005.

———. *The Roman Empire and the New Testament: An Essential Guide*. Nashville: Abingdon, 2006.

Castelli, Elizabeth. "*Les Belles Infidèles*/Fidelity or Feminism? The Meanings of Feminist Biblical Translation." In *Searching the Scriptures: A Feminist Introduction*, vol. 1, edited by Elisabeth Schüssler Fiorenza with the assistance of Shelly Matthews, 189–204. New York: Crossroad, 1993.

Chambers, Kathy. " 'Knock, Knock—Who's There?' Acts 12:6-17 as a Comedy of Errors." In *A Feminist Companion to the Acts of the Apostles*, edited by Amy-Jill Levine with Marianne Blickenstaff, 89–97. FCNTECW 9. Cleveland: Pilgrim Press, 2004.

Charles, Ronald. *The Silencing of Slaves in Early Jewish and Christian Texts*. Routledge Studies in the Early Christian World. London: Routledge, 2020.

Church, Alfred John, William Jackson Brodribb, and Sara Bryant, trans. *Complete Works of Tacitus*. New York: Random House, 1942.

Claassens, L. Juliana, and Carolyn J. Sharp, eds. *Feminist Frameworks and the Bible: Power, Ambiguity, and Intersectionality*. LHBOTS 630. London: Bloomsbury T&T Clark, 2017.

Claassens, L. Juliana, and Irmtraud Fischer, eds. *Prophecy and Gender in the Hebrew Bible*. The Bible and Women: An Encyclopaedia of Exegesis and Cultural History. Atlanta: SBL Press, 2021.

Cohen, Shaye J. D. "Judaism without Circumcision and 'Judaism' without 'Circumcision' in Ignatius." *HTR* 95 (2002): 395–415.

———. "Was Timothy Jewish (Acts 16:1-3)? Patristic Exegesis, Rabbinic Law, and Matrilineal Descent." *JBL* 105 (1986): 251–68.

———. *Why Aren't Jewish Women Circumcised? Gender and Covenant in Judaism*. Berkeley: University of California Press, 2005.

Collins, John J. *Daniel, with an Introduction to Apocalyptic Literature*. FOTL 20. Grand Rapids: Eerdmans, 1984.

Consolino, Franca Ela, and Judith Herrin, eds. *The Early Middle Ages*. The Bible and Women: An Encyclopaedia of Exegesis and Cultural History. Atlanta: SBL Press, 2020.

Conzelmann, Hans. *Acts of the Apostles: A Commentary*. Translated by James Limburg, A. Thomas Kraabel, and Donald H. Juel. Hermeneia. Philadelphia: Fortress, 1987.

Corley, Kathleen E. *Private Women, Public Meals: Social Conflict in the Synoptic Tradition*. Peabody, MA: Hendrickson, 1993.

Crüsemann, Marlene. *The Pseudepigraphal Letters to the Thessalonians*. Translated by Linda M. Maloney. New York: Bloomsbury T&T Clark, 2019.

D'Angelo, Mary Rose. "The *ANHP* Question in Luke-Acts: Imperial Masculinity and the Deployment of Women in the Early Second Century." In *A Feminist Companion to Luke*, edited by Amy-Jill Levine with Marianne Blickenstaff, 44–69. FCNTECW 3. London: Sheffield Academic, 2002.

———. " 'Knowing How to Preside over His Own Household': Imperial Masculinity and Christian Asceticism in the Pastorals, *Hermas*, and Luke-Acts." In *New Testament Masculinities*, edited by Stephen D. Moore and Janice Capel Anderson, 265–95. SemeiaSt 45. Atlanta: SBL, 2003.

———. "Women Partners in the New Testament." *JFSR* 6 (1990): 65–86.

Daly, Mary. *Beyond God the Father: A Philosophy of Women's Liberation*. Boston: Beacon, 1985.

Davis, Angela Y. "Racialized Punishment and Prison Abolition." In *The Angela Y. Davis Reader*, edited by Joy James, 96–109. Malden, MA: Blackwell, 1998.

Denaux, Adelbert, Rita Corstjens, and Hellen Mardaga. *The Vocabulary of Luke*. BTS 10. Leuven: Peeters, 2009.

DeSilva, David A. *The Letter to the Galatians*. NICNT. Grand Rapids: Eerdmans, 2018.

Dibelius, Martin. *Studies in the Acts of the Apostles*. Edited by Heinrich Greeven. Translated by Mary Ling. London: SCM, 1973.

Dinkler, Michal Beth. *Literary Theory and the New Testament*. AYBRL. New Haven: Yale University Press, 2019.

Dmitriev, Svlatoslav. *City Government in Hellenistic and Roman Asia Minor*. Oxford: Oxford University Press, 2005.

Drijvers, Han J. W., trans. "The Acts of Thomas." In *New Testament Apocrypha* 2, edited by Wilhelm Schneemelcher, translated by R. McLean Wilson, 322–411. Rev. ed. Cambridge: James Clark, 1992.

Dube, Musa W. "Batswakwa: Which Traveller Are You (John 1:1-18)?" In *The Bible in Africa: Transactions, Trajectories and Trends*, edited by Gerald O. West and Musa W. Dube, 150–62. Leiden: Brill, 2000.

———, ed. *Postcolonial Feminist Interpretation of the Bible*. St. Louis: Chalice, 2000.

Dunn, J. D. G. "The Ascension of Jesus: A Test Case for Hermeneutics." In *Auferstehung—Resurrection: The Fourth Durham-Tübingen Research Symposium; Resurrection, Transfiguration and Exaltation in Old Testament, Ancient Judaism and Early Christianity*, edited by Friedrich Avemarie and Hermann Lichtenberger. WUNT 135. Tübingen: Mohr Siebeck, 2001.

———. *Jesus, Paul, and the Law: Studies in Mark and Galatians*. Louisville: Westminster John Knox, 1990.

———. *The Partings of the Ways: Between Christianity and Judaism and Their Significance for the Character of Christianity*. London: SCM, 1991.

———. "The Question of Anti-Semitism in the New Testament." In *Jews and Christians: The Parting of the Ways, A.D. 70 to 135*, edited by J. D. G. Dunn, 177–211. Grand Rapids: Eerdmans, 1999.

Dupont, Jacques. "L'Union Entre les Premiers Chrétiens dans les Acts des Apôtres." In *Nouvelles Études sur les Acts des Apôtres*, 296–318. LD 118. Paris: Cerf, 1984.

Eagleton, Terry. *Ideology: An Introduction*. London: Verso, 2007.

———. *Literary Theory: An Introduction*. 3rd ed. Minneapolis: University of Minnesota Press, 2008.

Eisen, Ute E. *Die Poetik der Apostelgeschichte: Eine narratologische Studie*. NTOA 58. Fribourg: Academic Press; Göttingen: Vandenhoeck & Ruprecht, 2006.

———. *Women Officeholders in Early Christianity: Epigraphical and Literary Studies*. Translated by Linda M. Maloney. Collegeville, MN: Liturgical Press, 2000.

Elliott, John H. *A Home for the Homeless: A Social-Scientific Criticism of 1 Peter, Its Situation and Strategy*. Minneapolis: Fortress, 1990.

Elliot, Neil. *The Arrogance of Nations: Reading Romans in the Shadow of Empire*. Minneapolis: Fortress, 2008.

———. "The 'Patience of the Jews': Strategies of Resistance and Accommodation to Imperial Cultures." In *Pauline Conversations in Context: Essays in Honor of Calvin J. Roetzel*, 32–41. JSNTSup 221. Sheffield: Sheffield Academic, 2002.

Ellis, Linda. "A Brief Look at the Juvenal's 'Bread & Circuses,'" at https://drlindaellis.net.

Ephræm Syri: Commentarii in Epistolas D. Pauli: Nunc Primum Ex Armenio in Latinum Sermonem a Patribus Mekithartistis. Venice: Typographia Sancti Lazari, 1893.

Eskenazi, Tamara Cohn, and Andrea L. Weiss, eds. *The Torah: A Women's Commentary*. New York: URJ Press and Women of Reform Judaism, The Federation of Temple Sisterhoods, 2008.

Esler, Philip. *Conflict and Identity in Romans*. Minneapolis: Fortress, 2009.

Exum, J. Cheryl. "Second Thoughts about Secondary Characters: Women in Exodus 1.8–2.10." In *A Feminist Companion to Exodus to Deuteronomy*, edited by Athalya Brenner, 75–97. FCB 6. Sheffield: Sheffield Academic, 1994.

Exum, J. Cheryl, and David J. A. Clines, eds. *The New Literary Criticism and the Hebrew Bible*. Valley Forge, PA: Trinity Press International, 1993.

Fell, Margaret. *Women's Speaking Justified, Proved and Allowed by the Scriptures*. London, 1667.

Feminist Biblical Interpretation: A Compendium of Critical Commentary on the Books of the Bible and Related Literature. Translated by Lisa E. Dahill, Everett R. Kalin, Nancy Lukens, Linda M. Maloney, Barbara Rumscheidt, Martin Rumscheidt, and Tina Steiner. Edited by Luise Schottroff and Marie-Theres Wacker. Grand Rapids: Eerdmans, 2012.

Fewell, Danna Nolan, and David M. Gunn. *Gender, Power, and Promise: The Subject of the Bible's First Story*. Nashville: Abingdon, 1993.

Fischer, Irmtraud, and Mercedes Navarro Puerto, with Andrea Taschl-Erber, eds. *Torah*. The Bible and Women: An Encyclopaedia of Exegesis and Cultural History. Atlanta: SBL, 2011.

Fitzmyer, Joseph A. *Luke the Theologian: Aspects of His Teaching.* New York: Paulist Press, 1989.

Foakes Jackson, Frederick J., and Kirsopp Lake, eds. *The Beginnings of Christianity.* 5 vols. New York: Macmillan, 1920–33; repr. Grand Rapids: Baker, 1979.

Folger, Arie. "Eine unwahrscheinliche Reise." In *Ebrei e Cristiani: Eine jüdisch-christliche Begegnung an der Lateran-Universität in Rom am 16. Mai 2019. Theologica 7/2.3* (2019): 9–21.

Foxhall, Lin. *Studying Gender in Classical Antiquity.* New York: Cambridge University Press, 2013.

Franco, Cristiana. *Shameless: The Canine and the Feminine in Ancient Greece.* Translated by Matthew Fox. Berkeley: University of California Press, 2014.

Fredriksen, Paula. Review of Joshua D. Garroway, *The Beginning of the Gospel: Paul, Philippi, and the Origins of Christianity.* Cham, Switzerland: Palgrave Macmillan, 2018. In *RBL* (June 2020), online at https://www.bookreviews .org.

Freyer-Griggs, Daniel. "The Beasts at Ephesus and the Cult of Artemis." *HTR* 106 (2013): 459–77.

Frye, Northrop. *The Secular Scripture: A Study of the Structure of Romance.* Cambridge, MA: Harvard University Press, 1976.

Frymer-Kensky, Tikva. *Reading the Women of the Bible.* New York: Schocken Books, 2002.

Galinsky, Karl. "The Cult of the Roman Emperor: Uniter or Divider?" In *Rome and Religion: A Cross-Disciplinary Dialogue on the Imperial Cult,* edited by Jeffrey Brodd and Jonathan L. Reed, 1–22. Atlanta: SBL, 2012.

Galvin, Mary. *Life, Death and Artemis.* Vol. 2: *Artemis and the Ritual Process.* eBook: Smashwords, 2017.

Garrett, Susan R. *The Demise of the Devil: Magic and the Demonic in Luke's Writings.* Minneapolis: Fortress, 1989.

———. "Exodus from Bondage: Luke 9:31 and Acts 12:1-4." *CBQ* 52 (1990): 656–89.

Getty-Sullivan, Mary Ann. *Women in the New Testament.* Collegeville, MN: Liturgical Press, 2001.

Gifford, William. *The Satires of Decimus Julius Juvenalis, and of Aulus Persius Flaccus translated into English Verse.* 2 vols. London: Nicol, Cadell, Davies, and Evans, 1817.

Gilbert, Gary. "Acts." In *The Jewish Annotated New Testament,* edited by Amy-Jill Levine and Marc Zvi Brettler, 219–80. 2nd ed. Oxford: Oxford University Press, 2017.

Gilchrist, J. M. "The Historicity of Paul's Shipwreck." *JSNT* 61 (1996): 39–61.

Glancy, Jennifer A. "Boasting of Beatings (2 Corinthians 11:23-25)." *JBL* 123 (2004): 99–135.

———. *Slavery as Moral Problem in the Early Church and Today.* Minneapolis: Fortress, 2011.

—. *Slavery in Early Christianity*. Minneapolis: Fortress, 2006.

Glavic, Julie A. "Eutychus in Acts and in the Church: The Narrative Significance of Acts 20:6-12." *BBR* 24 (2014): 179–206.

Gonzalez, Michelle A. "Latina Feminist Theology: Past, Present, and Future." *JFSR* 25 (2009): 150–55.

Good, Deirdre J. "Reading Strategies for Biblical Passages on Same-Sex Relations." *Theology and Sexuality* 7 (1997): 70–82.

Goodman, Martin. *Rome and Jerusalem: The Clash of Ancient Civilizations*. New York: Vintage, 2008.

—. *The Ruling Class of Judaea: The Origins of the Jewish Revolt against Rome A.D. 66–70*. Cambridge: Cambridge University Press, 1987.

Gorsky, Jonathan. "The Parting of the Ways—A Review Essay." *HeyJ* 50 (2009): 996–1005.

Grabbe, Lester L. *Judaic Religion in the Second Temple Period: Belief and Practice from the Exile to Yavneh*. London: Routledge, 2000.

—. "What Did the Author of Acts Know About Pre-70 Judaism?" In *Wisdom Poured Out Like Water: Studies on Jewish and Christian Antiquity in Honor of Gabriele Boccaccini*, edited by J. Harold Ellens, Isaac W. Oliver, Jason von Ehrenkrook, James Waddell, and Jason M. Zurawski, 450–62. Boston: de-Gruyter, 2018.

Graves, Robert. *Claudius the God*. London: Penguin, 1934.

—. *I, Claudius*. London: Penguin, 1934.

Gregory, Andrew. *The Reception of Luke and Acts in the Period Before Irenaeus: Looking for Luke in the Second Century*. WUNT 169. Tübingen: Mohr Siebeck, 2003.

Gregory, Andrew F., and C. Kavin Rowe, eds. *Rethinking the Unity and Reception of Luke and Acts*. Columbia: University of South Carolina Press, 2010.

Grimké, Sarah. *Letters on the Equality of the Sexes and the Condition of Woman*. Boston: Isaac Knapp, 1838.

Gruca-Macaulay, Alexandra. *Lydia as a Rhetorical Construct in Acts*. Atlanta: SBL Press, 2016.

Guest, Deryn. *When Deborah Met Jael: Lesbian Feminist Hermeneutics*. London: SCM, 2005.

Habel, Norman C., and Peter Trudinger. *Exploring Ecological Hermeneutics*. SBLSymS 46. Atlanta: SBL, 2008.

Haenchen, Ernst. "The Book of Acts as Source Material for the History of Early Christianity," in *Studies in Luke-Acts*, edited by Leander E. Keck and J. Louis Martyn, 258–78. Philadelphia: Fortress, 1966.

Hakola, Raimo, Nina Nikki, and Ulla Tervahauta, eds. *Others and the Construction of Early Christian Identities*. Publications of the Finnish Exegetical Society 106. Helsinki: Finnish Exegetical Society, 2013.

Hanson, John. "Dreams and Visions in the Graeco-Roman World and Early Christianity." *ANRW* 2. *Principat*, edited by Wolfgang Haase, 23.2 (1980): 1395–1427.

—. "The Dream/Vision Report and Acts 10:1–11:18: A Form-Critical Study." PhD diss., Harvard, 1978.

Harnack, Adolf von. "The Authorship of the Epistle to the Hebrews." *LCR* 19 (1900): 448–71.

Harrill, J. Albert. "The Dramatic Function of the Running Slave Rhoda (Acts 12.13-16): A Piece of Greco-Roman Comedy." *NTS* 46 (2000): 150–57.

Harrison, James R. "An Epigraphic Portrait of Ephesus and Its Villages." In *The First Urban Churches*, vol. 3: *Ephesus*, edited by James R. Harrison and L. L. Welborn, 1–67. WGRWSup 9. Atlanta: SBL Press, 2018.

Harrison, James R., and L. L. Welborn, eds. *The First Urban Churches*. Vol. 3: *Ephesus*. WGRWSup 9. Atlanta: SBL Press, 2018.

Harvey, Susan Ashbrook. "Feminine Imagery for the Divine: The Holy Spirit, the *Odes of Solomon*, and Early Syriac Tradition." *SVTQ* 37 (1993): 111–39.

Hauser, Alan J., and Duane F. Watson, eds. *A History of Biblical Interpretation*. Vol. 1: *The Ancient Period*. Grand Rapids: Eerdmans, 2003.

Hearon, Holly E., and Philip Ruge-Jones, eds. *The Bible in Ancient and Modern Media: Story and Performance*. Eugene, OR: Cascade Books, 2009.

Hemer, Colin J. "First Person Narrative in Acts 27–28." *TynBul* 36 (1985): 79–109.

Hens-Piazza, Gina. *The New Historicism*. GBS, Old Testament Series. Minneapolis: Fortress, 2002.

Heym, Stefan [Helmut Flieg]. *The King David Report*. London: Hodder & Stoughton, 1973.

Hicks-Keeton, Jill, Lori Baron, and Matthew Thiessen, eds. *The Ways That Often Parted: Essays in Honor of Joel Marcus*. Atlanta: SBL Press, 2018.

Hill, Craig C. *Hellenists and Hebrews*. Minneapolis: Fortress, 1992.

Hogeterp, Albert, and Adelbert Denaux. *Semitisms in Luke's Greek*. WUNT 2.401. Tübingen: Mohr Siebeck, 2018.

Hooker, Morna. "Artemis of Ephesus." *JTS* 64 (2013): 37–46.

Hoppin, Ruth. *Priscilla's Letter: Finding the Author of the Epistle to the Hebrews*. Fort Bragg, CA: Lost Coast Press, 1997.

Hornsby, Teresa, and Ken Stone, eds. *Bible Trouble: Queer Readings at the Boundaries of Biblical Scholarship*. Atlanta: SBL, 2011.

Ilan, Tal, Lorena Miralles-Maciá, and Ronit Nikolsky, eds. *Rabbinic Literature*. The Bible and Women: An Encyclopaedia of Exegesis and Cultural History. Atlanta: SBL Press, 2022.

Isaac, Benjamin. *The Invention of Racism in Classical Antiquity*. Princeton: Princeton University Press, 2004.

Isasi-Díaz, Ada María. *Mujerista Theology: A Theology for the Twenty-First Century*. Maryknoll, NY: Orbis Books, 1996.

James, M. R. *The Apocryphal New Testament*. Oxford: Clarendon, 1924.

Jeffers, James S. *The Greco-Roman World of the New Testament Era: Exploring the Background of Early Christianity*. Downers Grove: InterVarsity Press, 1999.

Jennings, Willie James. *Acts*. Belief: A Theological Commentary on the Bible. Louisville: Westminster John Knox, 2017.

Jobling, David. *The Sense of Biblical Narrative: Three Structural Analyses in the Old Testament*. JSOTSup 7. Sheffield: University of Sheffield Press, 1978.

Jobling, David, and Tina Pippin, eds. *Semeia* 59: *Ideological Criticism of Biblical Texts*. Atlanta: Scholars Press, 1992.

Johnson, Elizabeth A. "God." In *Dictionary of Feminist Theologies*, edited by Letty M. Russell and J. Shannon Clarkson, 128–30. Louisville: Westminster John Knox, 1996.

———. *She Who Is: The Mystery of God in Feminist Theological Discourse*. New York: Crossroad, 1992.

Johnson, Luke Timothy. *The Acts of the Apostles*. SP 5. Collegeville, MN: Liturgical Press, 1992.

———. *The Literary Function of Possessions in Luke-Acts*. SBLDS 39. Missoula: Scholars Press, 1977.

Joshel, Sandra. *Work, Identity, and Legal Status at Rome: A Study of the Occupational Inscriptions at Rome*. Norman: Oklahoma University Press, 1992.

Junior, Nyasha. *An Introduction to Womanist Biblical Interpretation*. Louisville: Westminster John Knox, 2015.

Kateusz, Ally. *Mary and Early Christian Women: Hidden Leadership*. New York: Palgrave Macmillan, 2019.

Kee, Howard Clark. *To Every Nation under Heaven: The Acts of the Apostles*. New Testament in Context. Harrisburg, PA: Trinity Press International, 1997.

Keener, Craig S. *Acts: An Exegetical Commentary*. Vol. 1: Introduction and 1:1–2:47; Vol. 2: 3:1–14:28; Vol. 3: 15:1–23:35; Vol. 4: 24:1–28:31. Grand Rapids: Baker Academic, 2012–2015.

Kennedy, George A. "The Speeches in Acts." In *New Testament Interpretation through Rhetorical Criticism*, 114–40. Chapel Hill: University of North Carolina Press, 1984.

Kilgallen, John J. "Paul's Speech to the Ephesian Elders: Its Structure." *ETL* 70 (1994): 112–20.

Kinzer, Mark S. "Sacrifice, Prayer, and the Holy Spirit: The Tamid Offering in Luke-Acts." In *Wisdom Poured Out Like Water: Studies on Jewish and Christian Antiquity in Honor of Gabriele Boccaccini*, edited by J. Harold Ellens, Isaac W. Oliver, Jason Von Ehrenkrook, James Waddell, and Jason M. Zurawski, 463–75. Boston: deGruyter, 2018.

Kittredge, Cynthia Briggs. "Hebrews." In *Searching the Scriptures*, vol. 2, edited by Elisabeth Schüssler Fiorenza, 428–54. New York: Crossroad, 1984.

Kitzberger, Ingrid Rosa, ed. *Autobiographical Biblical Interpretation: Between Text and Self*. Leiden: Deo, 2002.

Klassen, William. *Judas: Betrayer or Friend of Jesus?* Minneapolis: Fortress, 2005.

Klauck, Hans-Josef. "Junia Theodora und die Gemeinde von Korinth." In *Religion und Gesellschaft im frühen Christentum*, 232–50. WUNT 152. Tübingen: Mohr Siebeck, 2003.

———. *Magic and Paganism in Early Christianity: The World of the Acts of the Apostles*. Translated by Brian McNeil. Minneapolis: Fortress, 2003.

Knust, Jennifer. "Enslaved to Demons: Sex, Violence and the Apologies of Justin Martyr." In *Mapping Gender in Ancient Religious Discourses*, edited by Todd Penner and Caroline Vander Stichele, 431–55. Leiden: Brill, 2007.

Kotrosits, Maya. *Rethinking Early Christian Identity: Affect, Violence, and Belonging*. Minneapolis: Fortress, 2015.

Kraemer, Ross S. "Ber[e]nice." In *Women in Scripture: A Dictionary of Named and Unnamed Women in the Hebrew Bible, the Apocryphal/Deuterocanonical Books, and the New Testament*, edited by Carol Meyers, Toni Craven, and Ross S. Kraemer, 165–70. Boston: Houghton Mifflin, 2000.

Kraemer, Ross Shepard, and Mary Rose D'Angelo, eds. *Women and Christian Origins*. New York: Oxford University Press, 1999.

Kurz, William S. *Reading Luke-Acts: Dynamics of Biblical Narrative*. Louisville: Westminster John Knox, 1993.

LaCugna, Catherine Mowry. *God for Us: The Trinity and Christian Life*. San Francisco: HarperCollins, 1991.

Lake, Kirsopp, and Henry J. Cadbury. *Additional Notes to the Commentary*. Vol. 5: *The Beginnings of Christianity*, ed. Frederick J. Foakes Jackson and Kirsopp Lake. New York: Macmillan, 1920–33; repr. Grand Rapids: Baker, 1979.

Lerner, Gerda. "One Thousand Years of Feminist Bible Criticism." Chap. 7 (pp. 138–66) in *Creation of Feminist Consciousness: From the Middle Ages to Eighteen-Seventy*. New York: Oxford University Press, 1993.

Levine, Amy-Jill. "The New Testament and Anti-Judaism." In *The Misunderstood Jew: The Church and the Scandal of the Jewish Jesus*, 87–117. San Francisco: HarperSanFrancisco, 2006.

Levine, Lee I. "The Synagogue." In *The Jewish Annotated New Testament*, edited by Amy-Jill Levine and Marc Zvi Brettler, 662–66. 2nd ed. New York: Oxford University Press, 2017.

Lieu, Judith. *Neither Jew Nor Greek? Constructing Early Christianity*. London: Bloomsbury T&T Clark, 2003; 2nd ed. 2016.

Liew, Tat-Siong Benny. "Acts of the Apostles." In *Global Bible Commentary*, 419–28. Nashville: Abingdon, 2004.

Lohfink, Gerhard. "Compliment and Return Compliment." In *Between Heaven and Earth: New Explorations of Great Biblical Texts*, translated by Linda M. Maloney, 49–53. Collegeville, MN: Liturgical Press, 2022.

———. *Die Himmelfahrt Jesu: Untersuchungen zu den Himmelfahrts- und Erhöhungstexte bei Lukas*. Munich: Kösel, 1971.

———. "How the Church Grows." In *Between Heaven and Earth: New Explorations of Great Biblical Texts*, translated by Linda M. Maloney, 326–30. Collegeville, MN: Liturgical Press, 2022.

———. *Paulus vor Damaskus: Arbeitsweisen der neueren Bibelwissenschaft dargestellt an den Texten Apg 9, 1-19; 22, 3-21; 26, 9-18*. SBS 4. Stuttgart: Katholisches Bibelwerk, 1966. English: *The Conversion of St. Paul: Narrative and History in*

Acts, translated and edited by Bruce J. Malina. Chicago: Franciscan Herald Press, 1976.

Lohfink, Norbert. *The Covenant Never Revoked: Biblical Reflections on Christian-Jewish Dialogue*. Translated by John J. Scullion. Mahwah, NJ: Paulist Press, 1991.

Loisy, Alfred. *Les Actes des Apôtres*. Frankfurt am Main: Minerva, 1973.

Longenecker, Richard N. *Galatians*. WBC 41. Dallas: Word Books, 1990.

Loraux, Nicole. *The Experiences of Tiresias: The Feminine and the Greek Man*. Translated by Paula Wissing. Princeton: Princeton University Press, 1995.

Louw, Johannes P., and Eugene A. Nida, eds. *Greek-English Lexicon of the New Testament Based on Semantic Domains*. 2 vols. New York: United Bible Societies, 1988.

Lüdemann, Gerd. *Early Christianity according to the Traditions in Acts*. Translated by John Bowden. Minneapolis: Fortress, 1989.

MacDonald, Dennis R. "The Shipwrecks of Odysseus and Paul." *NTS* 45 (1999): 88–107.

MacDonald, Margaret Y. *Early Christian Women and Pagan Opinion: The Power of the Hysterical Woman*. Cambridge: Cambridge University Press, 1996.

Macmullen, Ramsay. *Enemies of the Roman Order: Treason, Unrest, and Alienation in the Empire*. London: Routledge, 1992.

Maier, Christl M., and Nuria Calduch-Benages, eds. *The Writings and Later Wisdom Books*. The Bible and Women: An Encyclopaedia of Exegesis and Cultural History. Atlanta: SBL Press, 2014.

Maier, Cristl M., and Carolyn J. Sharp. *Prophecy and Power: Jeremiah in Feminist and Postcolonial Perspective*. London: Bloomsbury, 2013.

Maloney, Linda M. *"All That God Had Done with Them": The Narration of the Works of God in the Early Christian Community as Described in the Acts of the Apostles*. AUS ser. 7. Theology and Religion 91. New York: Lang, 1991.

Marchal, Joseph A. "Queer Studies and Critical Masculinity Studies in Feminist Biblical Studies." In *Feminist Biblical Studies in the Twentieth Century: Scholarship and Movement*, edited by Elisabeth Schüssler Fiorenza, 261–80. The Bible and Women: An Encyclopaedia of Exegesis and Cultural History. Atlanta: SBL Press, 2014.

Mason, Steve. "Jews, Judeans, Judaizing, Judaism." *JSJ* 38 (2007): 457–512.

Matthews, Shelly. *First Converts: Rich Pagan Women and the Rhetoric of Mission in Early Judaism and Christianity*. Stanford: Stanford University Press, 2001.

———. *Perfect Martyr: The Stoning of Stephen and the Construction of Christian Identity*. New York: Oxford University Press, 2010.

Maxwell, Kathy. *Hearing Between the Lines: The Audience as Fellow-Worker in Luke-Acts and Its Literary Milieu*. LNTS 425. London: T&T Clark, 2010.

McFague, Sallie. *Models of God: Theology for an Ecological, Nuclear Age*. Philadelphia: Fortress, 1987.

McGee, Zane B. "Transitioning Authority and Paul's Farewell Address: Examining the Narrative Function of Acts 20." *Stone-Campbell Journal* 20 (2017): 203–14.

McKinlay, Judith E. *Reframing Her: Biblical Women in Postcolonial Focus*. Sheffield: Sheffield Phoenix, 2004.

McKnight, Edgar V., and Elizabeth Struthers Malbon, eds. *The New Literary Criticism and the New Testament*. Valley Forge, PA: Trinity Press International, 1994.

Mealand, D. "The Seams and Summaries of Luke and Acts." *JSNT* 38 (2016): 482–502.

Metzger, Bruce. *The Canon of the New Testament: Its Origin, Development, and Significance*. New York: Oxford University Press, 1987.

Metzger, Paul. "Zeitspiegel: Neutestamentliche Handschriften als Zeugnisse der Kirchengeschichte." In *The Book of Acts as Church History*, edited by Tobias Nicklas and Michael Tilly, 241–62. BZNW 120. Berlin: de Gruyter, 2003.

Meyers, Carol. *Discovering Eve: Ancient Israelite Women in Context*. New York: Oxford University Press, 1991.

Meyers, Carol, Toni Craven, and Ross S. Kraemer, eds. *Women in Scripture: A Dictionary of Named and Unnamed Women in the Hebrew Bible, the Apocryphal/Deuterocanonical Books, and the New Testament*. Boston: Houghton Mifflin, 2000/Grand Rapids: Eerdmans, 2001.

Milavec, Aaron. *The Didachē: Text, Translation, Analysis, and Commentary*. Collegeville, MN: Liturgical Press, 2003.

Milgrom, Jacob. *Leviticus: A Book of Ritual and Ethics*. Continental Commentary. Minneapolis: Fortress, 2004.

Mills, Sara. "Gender and Colonial Space." In *Feminist Postcolonial Theory: A Reader*, edited by Reina Lewis and Sara Mills, 692–719. Edinburgh: Edinburgh University Press, 2010.

Moessner, David. *Lord of the Banquet: The Literary and Theological Significance of the Lukan Travel Narrative*. Minneapolis: Fortress, 1989.

Mommsen, Theodor. "Die Rechtsverhältnisse des Apostels Paulus." *ZNW* 2 (1902): 81–96.

Moore, Stephen D. *The Bible in Theory: Critical and Postcritical Essays*. Atlanta: SBL, 2010.

———. *Poststructuralism and the New Testament: Derrida and Foucault at the Foot of the Cross*. Minneapolis: Fortress, 1994.

Morris, Benny. *The Birth of the Palestinian Refugee Problem, 1947–1949*. Cambridge Middle East Library. Cambridge: Cambridge University Press, 1987.

Munro, Ealasaid. "Feminism: A Fourth Wave?" *Political Insight* (September 2013). https://journals.sagepub.com/doi/pdf/10.1111/2041-9066.12021.

Murray, Robert. *Symbols of Church and Kingdom: A Study in Early Syriac Tradition*. Cambridge: Cambridge University Press, 1975.

Navarro Puerto, Mercedes, and Marinella Perroni, eds.; Amy-Jill Levine, English ed. *Gospels: Narrative and History*. The Bible and Women: An Encyclopaedia of Exegesis and Cultural History. Atlanta: SBL Press, 2015.

Newman, Barbara. *Sister of Wisdom: St. Hildegard's Theology of the Feminine*. Berkeley: University of California Press, 1987.

Niditch, Susan. *"My Brother Esau Is a Hairy Man": Hair and Identity in Ancient Israel*. Oxford: Oxford University Press, 2008.

Niederwimmer, Kurt. *The Didachē*. Translated by Linda M. Maloney. Hermeneia. Minneapolis: Fortress, 1998.

Nowell, Irene. *Women in the Old Testament*. Collegeville, MN: Liturgical Press, 1997.

Oakes, Peter. *Galatians*. Paideia. Grand Rapids: Baker, 2015.

Oliver/de Oliveira, Isaac W. "Are Luke and Acts Anti-Marcionite?" In *Wisdom Poured Out Like Water: Studies on Jewish and Christian Antiquity in Honor of Gabriele Boccaccini*, edited by J. Harold Ellens, Isaac W. Oliver, Jason Von Ehrenkrook, James Waddell, and Jason M. Zurawski, 499–525. Boston: deGruyter, 2018.

———. "The 'Historical Paul' and the Paul of Acts: Which Is More Jewish?" In *Paul the Jew: Rereading the Apostle as a Figure of Second Temple Judaism*, edited by Gabriele Boccaccini and Carlos A. Segovia, 51–71. Minneapolis: Fortress, 2016.

———. *Luke's Jewish Eschatology: The National Restoration of Israel in Luke-Acts*. New York: Oxford University Press, 2021.

———. *Torah Praxis after 70 CE: Reading Matthew and Luke-Acts as Jewish Texts*. WUNT 2.355. Tübingen: Mohr Siebeck, 2013.

Painter, John. *Just James: The Brother of Jesus in History and Tradition*. Columbia: University of South Carolina Press, 1997.

Parsons, Mikeal C. *Body and Character in Luke and Acts: The Subversion of Physiognomy in Early Christianity*. Waco, TX: Baylor University Press, 2011.

Parsons, Mikeal C., and Heather Gorman. Review of Walters, *The Assumed Authorial Unity of Luke and Acts: A Reassessment of the Evidence. Neot* 46 (2012): 139–52.

Parsons, Mikeal C., and Martin M. Culy. *Acts: A Handbook on the Greek Text*. Waco, TX: Baylor University Press, 2003.

Parsons, Mikeal C., and Michael Wade Martin. *Ancient Rhetoric and the New Testament: The Influence of Early Greek Composition*. Waco, TX: Baylor University Press, 2018.

Parsons, Mikeal C., and Richard I. Pervo. *Rethinking the Unity of Luke and Acts*. Minneapolis: Fortress, 1993.

Pavolini, Carlo. "A Survey of Excavations and Studies on Ostia (2004–2014)." *JRS* 106 (November 2016): 199–236.

Pawlikowski, John T. Review of Norman A. Beck, *Mature Christianity. CBQ* 49 (1987): 138.

Penchansky, David. "Deconstruction." In *The Oxford Encyclopedia of Biblical Interpretation*, edited by Steven McKenzie, 196–205. New York: Oxford University Press, 2013.

Penner, Todd. *In Praise of Christian Origins: Stephen and the Hellenists in Lukan Apologetic Historiography*. Emory Studies in Early Christianity 10. New York: T&T Clark, 2004.

Penner, Todd, and Caroline Vander Stichele. "Gendering Violence: Patterns of Power and Constructs of Masculinity in the Acts of the Apostles." In *A Feminist Companion to the Acts of the Apostles*, edited by Amy-Jill Levine with Marianne Blickenstaff, 193–209. FCNTECW 9. Cleveland: Pilgrim Press, 2004.

———, eds. *Mapping Gender in Ancient Religious Discourses*. Leiden: Brill, 2007.

Pervo, Richard I. *Acts*. Hermeneia. Minneapolis: Fortress, 2009.

———. *Dating Acts: Between the Evangelists and the Apologists*. Santa Rosa, CA: Polebridge, 2006.

———. "In the Suburbs of the Apologists." In *Contemporary Studies in Acts*, edited by Thomas E. Phillips, 17–34. Macon, GA: Mercer University Press, 2009.

———. *The Making of Paul: Constructions of the Apostle in Early Christianity*. Minneapolis: Fortress, 2010.

———. "My Happy Home: The Role of Jerusalem in Acts 1–7." *Forum* 3 (Spring 2000): 31–55.

———. *Profit with Delight: The Literary Genre of the Acts of the Apostles*. Philadelphia: Fortress, 1987.

Peters, Edward M. "Prison before the Prison: The Ancient and Medieval Worlds." In *The Oxford History of the Prison: The Practice of Punishment in Western Society*, edited by Norval Morris and David J. Rothman. New York: Oxford University Press, 1998.

Petersen, Anders Klostergaard. "Unveiling the Obvious—Synagogue and Church: Sisters or Different Species?" In *Wisdom Poured Out Like Water: Studies on Jewish and Christian Antiquity in Honor of Gabriele Boccaccini*, edited by J. Harold Ellens, Isaac W. Oliver, Jason Von Ehrenkrook, James Waddell, and Jason M. Zurawski, 575–92. Boston: deGruyter, 2018.

Philostratus. *The Life of Apollonius of Tyana*. LCL 16. Cambridge, MA: Harvard University Press, 1912.

Pilch, John J. *Stephen: Paul and the Hellenist Israelites*. Collegeville, MN: Liturgical Press, 2008.

Plaskow, Judith. "Anti-Judaism in Feminist Christian Interpretation." In *Searching the Scriptures: A Feminist Introduction*, vol. 1, edited by Elisabeth Schüssler Fiorenza with the assistance of Shelly Matthews, 117–29. New York: Crossroad, 1993.

Portefaix, Lillian. *Sisters Rejoice: Paul's Letter to the Philippians and Luke-Acts as Seen by First-Century Women*. Stockholm: Almqvist & Wiksell, 1988.

Portier-Young, Anathea E. *Apocalypse against Empire: Theologies of Resistance in Early Judaism*. Grand Rapids: Eerdmans, 2011.

Praeder, Susan M. "Acts 27:1–28:16: Sea Voyages in Ancient Literature and the Theology of Luke-Acts." *CBQ* 46 (1984): 683–706.

Preisendanz, Karl, ed. and trans. *Papyri Graecae Magicae: Die griechischen Zauberpapyri*. 2 vols. Stuttgart: Teubner, 1973–1974.

Prince, Deborah Thompson. "Exploring the Visions of Acts in Their Narrative Context." In *Bible as Never Seen Before: Analyzing Dreams and Visions in Ancient Religious Literature*. SemeiaSt. Atlanta: SBL Press, forthcoming.

Pui-lan, Kwok. *Postcolonial Imagination and Feminist Theology*. Louisville: Westminster John Knox, 2005.

Rampton, Martha. "Four Waves of Feminism." October 25, 2015. https://www.pacificu.edu/magazine/four-waves-feminism.

Reid, Barbara E. "An Overture to the Gospel of Luke." *CurTM* 39 (2012): 428–34.

———. "The Power of Widows and How to Suppress It (Acts 6:1-7)." In *A Feminist Companion to the Acts of the Apostles*, edited by Amy-Jill Levine with Marianne Blickenstaff, 71–88. FCNTECW 9. New York: T&T Clark, 2004.

Reid, Barbara E., and Shelly Matthews. *Luke 1–9*. WCS 43A. Collegeville, MN: Liturgical Press, 2021.

———. *Luke 10–24*. WCS 43B. Collegeville, MN: Liturgical Press, 2021.

Reif, Stefan C. *Judaism and Hebrew Prayer*. Cambridge: Cambridge University Press, 1993.

Reimer, Ivoni Richter. "Acts." Translated by Nancy Lukens. In *Feminist Biblical Interpretation: A Compendium of Critical Commentary on the Books of the Bible and Related Literature*, edited by Luise Schottroff and Marie-Theres Wacker. Grand Rapids: Eerdmans, 2012.

———. "Apostolado, diaconia e missão de mulheres nas origens do cristianismo: rever tradições para empoderar e promover cidadania plena." *Revista Pós-Escrito* 4 (2011): 110–26.

———. "A Discípula Tabita Vive! O poder do mito na reorganização da vida comunitária." In *Anais do III Congresso Internacional em Ciências da Religião. Mitologia e Literatura Sagrada*, edited by Ivoni Richter Reimer, Haroldo Reimer, and Joel Antônio Ferreira, 173–82. Goiânia: Ed. da PUC Goiás, 2010.

———. *Milagre das Mãos: curas e exorcismos de Jesus em seu contexto histórico-cultural*. Goiânia: Ed. da UCG; São Leopoldo: Oikos, 2008.

———. *Women in the Acts of the Apostles: A Feminist Liberation Perspective*. Translated by Linda M. Maloney. Minneapolis: Fortress, 1995.

Reinhartz, Adele. "From Narrative to History: The Resurrection of Mary and Martha." In *"Women Like This": New Perspectives on Jewish Women in the Greco-Roman World*, edited by Amy-Jill Levine, 161–84. EJL 1. Atlanta: Scholars Press, 1991.

Reiser, Marius. "Von Caesarea nach Malta. Literarischer Charakter und historische Glaubwürdigkeit von Apg 27." In *Das Ende des Paulus. Historische, theologische und literargeschichtliche Aspekte*, edited by F. W. Horn, 49–74. BZNW 106. Berlin and New York: de Gruyter, 2001.

Ress, Mary Judith. *Ecofeminism in Latin America*. Women from the Margins. Maryknoll, NY: Orbis Books, 2006.

Riesner, Rainer. *Paul's Early Period: Chronology, Mission Strategy, Theology*. Translated by Douglass Stott. Grand Rapids: Eerdmans, 1998.

Ringe, Sharon H. "When Women Interpret the Bible." In *Women's Bible Commentary*, edited by Carol A. Newsom, Sharon H. Ringe, and Jacqueline E. Lapsley. 3rd ed. Louisville: Westminster John Knox, 2012.

Rosenfeld, Ben-Zion. *Torah Centers and Rabbinic Activity in Palestine, 70–400 CE: History and Geographic Distribution*. Translated by Chava Cassel. Leiden: Brill, 2010.

Rothschild, Clare K. "Perfect Martyr? Dangerous Material in the Stoning of Stephen." In *Delightful Acts: New Essays on Canonical and Non-canonical Acts*, edited by Harold W. Attridge, Dennis R. MacDonald, and Clare K. Rothschild, 177–91. WUNT 391. Tübingen: Mohr Siebeck, 2017.

Rowe, C. Kavin. *World Upside Down: Reading Acts in the Graeco-Roman Age*. Oxford: Oxford University Press, 2009.

Ruether, Rosemary Radford. *Faith and Fratricide: The Theological Roots of Anti-Semitism*. New York: Seabury, 1974.

———. *Sexism and God-Talk: Toward a Feminist Theology*. Boston: Beacon, 1993.

Rutledge, David. Reading Marginally: *Feminism, Deconstruction and the Bible*. BibInt 21. Leiden: Brill, 1996.

Ryan, Jordan J. *The Role of the Synagogue in the Aims of Jesus*. Minneapolis: Fortress, 2017.

Sakenfeld, Katharine Doob. *Just Wives? Stories of Power and Survival in the Old Testament and Today*. Louisville: Westminster John Knox, 2003.

Salmon, Marilyn. "Insider or Outsider? Luke's Relationship with Judaism." In *Luke-Acts and the Jewish People*, edited by Joseph B. Tyson, 76–82. Minneapolis: Augsburg, 1988.

Sanders, Jack T. "The Salvation of the Jews in Luke-Acts." In *Luke-Acts: New Perspectives from the Society of Biblical Literature*, edited by Charles H. Talbert, 104–28. New York: Crossroad, 1984.

Schäfer, Peter. "Die sogenannte Synode von Jabne." *Judaica* 31 (1975): 54–64.

Schiffner, Kerstin. "Solidarität." In *Entdeckungen. Ungewöhnliche Texte aus dem Neuen Testament*, edited by Dietlinde Jessen and Stefanie Müller, 83–92. Stuttgart: Katholisches Bibelwerk, 2003.

Schneiders, Sandra M. *The Revelatory Text: Interpreting the New Testament as Sacred Scripture*. Rev. ed. Collegeville, MN: Liturgical Press, 1999.

Scholz, Susanne, ed. *Feminist Interpretation of the Hebrew Bible in Retrospect*. Recent Research in Biblical Studies 7, 8, 9. Sheffield: Sheffield Phoenix, 2013, 2014, 2016.

———. "From the 'Woman's Bible' to the 'Women's Bible,' The History of Feminist Approaches to the Hebrew Bible." In *Introducing the Women's Hebrew Bible*, 12–32. IFT 13. New York: T&T Clark, 2007.

Schottroff, Luise. "DienerInnen der Heiligen: der Diakonat der Frauen im Neuen Testament." In *Diakonie: biblische Grundlagen und Orientierungen. Ein Arbeitsbuch*, edited by Gerhard K. Schäfer and Theodor Strohm, 222–42. 2nd ed. Heidelberg: HVA, 1994.

———. "'Holy in Body and Spirit' (1 Cor. 7:34): The Forms of Women's Lives in Early Christianity." Chapter 7.3 in part 3 of Luise Schottroff, Silvia Schroer, and Marie-Theres Wacker, *Feminist Interpretation: The Bible in Women's Per-*

spective, translated by Martin and Barbara Rumscheidt, 190–96. Minneapolis: Fortress, 1998.

———. *Lydia's Impatient Sisters: A Feminist Social History of Early Christianity*. Translated by Barbara and Martin Rumscheidt. Louisville: Westminster John Knox, 1995.

———. "Part 3: Toward a Feminist Reconstruction of the History of Early Christianity." In Luise Schottroff, Silvia Schroer, and Marie-Theres Wacker, *Feminist Interpretation: The Bible in Women's Perspective*, translated by Martin and Barbara Rumscheidt, 177–254. Minneapolis: Fortress, 1998.

Schreiner, Thomas R. *Galatians*. ECNT 9. Grand Rapids: Zondervan, 2010.

Schrenk, Gottlob. "διαλέγομαι, διαλογίζομαι, διαλογισμός." *TDNT* 2 (1964): 93–98.

Schuller, Eileen, and Marie-Theres Wacker, eds. *Early Jewish Writings*. The Bible and Women: An Encyclopaedia of Exegesis and Cultural History. Atlanta: SBL Press, 2017.

Schüssler Fiorenza, Elisabeth, ed. *Feminist Biblical Studies in the Twentieth Century: Scholarship and Movement*. The Bible and Women: An Encyclopaedia of Exegesis and Cultural History. Atlanta: SBL Press, 2014.

———. *In Memory of Her: A Feminist Theological Reconstruction of Christian Origins*. New York: Crossroad, 1983/1994.

———. *Jesus: Miriam's Child, Sophia's Prophet; Critical Issues in Feminist Christology*. New York: Continuum, 1994.

———. "Miracles, Mission, and Apologetics: An Introduction." In *Aspects of Religious Propaganda in Judaism and Early Christianity*, edited by Elisabeth Schüssler Fiorenza, 1–25. Notre Dame, IN: University of Notre Dame Press, 1976.

———. *The Power of the Word: Scripture and the Rhetoric of Empire*. Minneapolis: Fortress, 2007.

———. *Wisdom Ways: Introducing Feminist Biblical Interpretation*. Maryknoll, NY: Orbis Books, 2001.

Schutte, P. J. W. "When *They*, *We*, and the Passive Become *I*—Introducing Autobiographical Biblical Criticism." *HTS Teologiese Studies / Theological Studies* 61 (2005): 401–16.

Schwartz, Daniel R. "Jewish Movements of the New Testament Period." In *The Jewish Annotated New Testament*, edited by Amy-Jill Levine and Marc Zvi Brettler, 526–30. 2nd ed. Oxford: Oxford University Press, 2017.

Schwartz, Saundra. "From Bedroom to Courtroom: The Adultery Type-Scene and the *Acts of Andrew*." In *Mapping Gender in Ancient Religious Discourses*, edited by Todd Penner and Caroline Vander Stichele, 267–311. Leiden: Brill, 2007.

Seeman, Chris. "Trading Places: Luke's Big Omission and Acts 10." In *Reading a Tendentious Bible: Essays in Honor of Robert B. Coote*, edited by Marvin Chaney, et al., 155–65. Sheffield: Sheffield Phoenix, 2014.

Seim, Turid Karlsen. *The Double Message: Patterns of Gender in Luke-Acts*. Edinburgh: T&T Clark, 1994.

Shapiro, Dani. *Devotion: A Memoir*. New York: HarperCollins, 2010.

Sharon, Nadav. *Judea under Roman Domination: The First Generation of Statelessness and Its Legacy*. EJL 46. Atlanta: SBL Press, 2018.

Sherwin-White, Adrian N. *The Letters of Pliny*, edited by A. N. Sherwin-White. Oxford: Oxford University Press, 1966.

———. *Roman Society and Roman Law in the New Testament*. Oxford: Clarendon, 1963.

Sherwood, Yvonne. *A Biblical Text and Its Afterlives: The Survival of Jonah in Western Culture*. Cambridge: Cambridge University Press, 2000.

———. "Introduction." In *The Bible and Feminism: Remapping the Field*. New York: Oxford University Press, 2017.

Sievers, Joseph, and Amy-Jill Levine, eds. *The Pharisees*. Grand Rapids: Eerdmans, 2021.

Smith, Daniel Lynwood. *Into the World of the New Testament: Greco-Roman and Jewish Texts and Contexts*. London: Bloomsbury, 2015.

Smith, David. "Luke, the Jews, and the Politics of Early Christian Identity." PhD diss., Duke University, 2018.

Smith, James. *The Voyage and Shipwreck of St. Paul*. 4th ed. London: Longmans, Green, 1880.

Smith, Mitzi J. *The Literary Construction of the Other in the Acts of the Apostles: Charismatics, the Jews, and Women*. Eugene, OR: Pickwick, 2011.

———. "Paul, Timothy, and the Respectability Politics of Race: A Womanist Inter(con)textual Reading of Acts 16:1-5." *Religions* 10 (March 13, 2019).

Snyder, Graydon F. *Ante-Pacem: Archaeological Evidence of Church Life before Constantine*. Macon, GA: Mercer University Press, 1985.

Soards, Marion L. *The Speeches in Acts: Their Content, Context, and Concerns*. Louisville: Westminster John Knox, 1994.

Sohn-Kronthaler, Michaela, and Ruth Albrecht, eds. *Faith and Feminism in Nineteenth-Century Religious Communities*. The Bible and Women: An Encyclopaedia of Exegesis and Cultural History. Atlanta: SBL Press, 2019.

Sojourner Truth. "Ain't I a Woman?" Modern History Sourcebook. https://sourcebooks.fordham.edu/mod/sojtruth-woman.asp.

Spellers, Stephanie. *The Church Cracked Open: Disruption, Decline, and New Hope for Beloved Community*. New York: Church Publishing, 2021.

Spencer, F. Scott. "Neglected Widows in Acts 6:1-7." *CBQ* 56 (1994): 715–33.

Standhartinger, Angela. "Better Ending: Paul in the Roman *Colonia Philippi* in Acts 16." In *Delightful Acts: New Essays on Canonical and Non-canonical Acts*, edited by Harold W. Attridge, Dennis R. MacDonald, and Clare K. Rothschild, 227–43. WUNT 391. Tübingen: Mohr Siebeck, 2017.

Stegemann, Ekkehard W., and Wolfgang Stegemann. *The Jesus Movement: A Social History of its First Century*. Translated by O. C. Dean Jr. Minneapolis: Fortress, 1999.

Stevenson, Bryan. *Just Mercy: A Story of Justice and Redemption.* New York: Spiegel & Grau/Random House, 2014.

Strait, Drew J. *Hidden Criticism of the Angry Tyrant in Early Judaism and the Acts of the Apostles.* Lanham, MD: Lexington Books/Fortress Academic, 2019.

Sundberg, Albert C., Jr. "Canon Muratori: A Fourth-Century List." *HTR* 66 (1973): 1–41.

Taitz, Emily, Sondra Henry, and Cheryl Tallan, eds. *JPS Guide to Jewish Women 600 B.C.E.–1900 C.E.* Philadelphia: JPS, 2003.

Talbert, Charles. *Reading Acts: A Literary and Theological Commentary on the Acts of the Apostles.* New York: Crossroad, 1997.

Talbert, Charles, and J. H. Hayes. "A Theology of Sea Storms in Luke-Acts." *SBLSP* 1995 (Atlanta: Scholars Press, 1995): 321–36.

Taylor, Gary. *Castration: An Abbreviated History of Western Manhood.* New York: Routledge, 2000.

Taylor, Marion Ann, and Agnes Choi, eds. *Handbook of Women Biblical Interpreters: A Historical and Biographical Guide.* Grand Rapids: Baker Academic, 2012.

Theissen, Gerd. *The Social Setting of Pauline Christianity: Essays on Corinth.* Translated and edited by J. Schütz. Philadelphia: Fortress, 1982.

Theobald, Michael. *Israel-Vergessenheit in den Pastoralbriefen: ein neuer Vorschlag zu ihrer historisch- theologischen Verortung im 2. Jahrhundert n. Chr. unter besonderer Berücksichtigung der Ignatius-Briefe.* Stuttgart: Katholisches Bibelwerk, 2016.

Thiessen, Matthew. *Contesting Conversion: Genealogy, Circumcision, and Identity in Ancient Judaism and Christianity.* Oxford: Oxford University Press, 2011.

———. "Luke 2:22, Leviticus 22, and Parturient Impurity." *NovT* 54 (2012): 16–29.

Thompson, Glen L. "What We Have Here Is a Failure to Communicate: Paul and Barnabas at Lystra—Seen from Wauwatosa." In *Heritage and Hope: Essays in Honor of the 150th Anniversary of Wisconsin Lutheran Seminary,* edited by Kenneth A. Cherney, 105–34. Milwaukee: Wisconsin Lutheran Seminary Press, 2013.

Thurston, Bonnie B. *Women in the New Testament: Questions and Commentary.* Companions to the New Testament. New York: Crossroad, 1998.

Tolbert, Mary Ann. "Social, Sociological, and Anthropological Methods." In *Searching the Scriptures: A Feminist Introduction,* vol. 1, edited by Elisabeth Schüssler Fiorenza with the assistance of Shelly Matthews, 255–71. New York: Crossroad, 1993.

Torrey, Charles C. *The Lives of the Prophets.* Greek text and translation. Eugene, OR: Wipf & Stock, 2020.

Trebilco, Paul. "The Jewish Community in Ephesus and Its Interaction with Christ-Believers in the First Century CE and Beyond." In *The First Urban Churches,* vol. 3: *Ephesus,* edited by James R. Harrison and L. L. Welborn, 93–126. WGRWSup 9. Atlanta: SBL Press, 2018.

———. "The Significance of the Distribution of Self-designations in Acts." *NovT* 54 (2012): 30–49.

Trible, Phyllis. *God and the Rhetoric of Sexuality*. OBT. Philadelphia: Fortress, 1978.

Trzaskoma, Stephen M., trans. *Callirhoe and an Ephesian Story: Two Novels from Ancient Greece*. Indianapolis: Hackett, 2010.

Tyson, Joseph B. *Marcion and Luke-Acts: A Defining Struggle*. Columbia: University of South Carolina Press, 2006.

Vander Stichele, Caroline. "Gender and Genre: Acts in/of Interpretation." In *Contextualizing Acts: Lukan Narrative and Greco-Roman Discourse*, edited by Caroline Vander Stichele and Todd Penner, 311–29. SymS 20. Atlanta: SBL, 2003.

Vander Stichele, Caroline, and Todd Penner, eds. *Contextualizing Acts: Lukan Narrative and Greco-Roman Discourse*. SymS 20. Atlanta: SBL, 2003.

———. *Contextualizing Gender in Early Christian Discourse: Thinking Beyond Thecla*. London: T&T Clark, 2009.

———. *Her Master's Tools? Feminist and Postcolonial Engagements of Historical-Critical Discourse*. Atlanta: SBL, 2005.

———. *Mapping Gender in Ancient Religious Discourses*. BibInt 84. Leiden: Brill, 2007.

———. "Scripturing Gender in Acts: The Past and Present Power of *Imperium*." In their *Mapping Gender in Ancient Religious Discourses*, 231–66. BibInt 84. Leiden: Brill, 2007.

van Dijk-Hemmes, Fokkelien. "Traces of Women's Texts in the Hebrew Bible." In *On Gendering Texts: Female and Male Voices in the Hebrew Bible*, edited by Fokkelien van Dijk-Hemmes and Athalya Brenner, 17–112. Leiden: Brill, 1993.

Verheyden, Joseph. "The Canon Muratori: A Matter of Dispute." In *The Biblical Canons*, edited by Jean-Marie Auwers and Henk Jan De Jonge, 487–556. BETL 163. Leuven: Leuven University Press, 2003.

Vlassopoulos, Kostas. "Athenian Slave Names and Athenian Social History." *ZPE* 175 (2010): 113–44.

Walker, Alice. *In Search of Our Mothers' Gardens: Womanist Prose*. New York: Harcourt Brace Jovanovich, 1967, 1983.

Walters, Patricia. *The Assumed Authorial Unity of Luke and Acts: A Reassessment of the Evidence*. SNTSMS 145. Cambridge: Cambridge University Press, 2009.

———. Response to review of book by Mikeal Parsons and Heather Gorman (*Neot* 46 [2012]: 139–52), *Neot* 52 (2018): 489–95.

Walton, Stephen J. "Leadership and Lifestyle: Luke's Paul, Luke's Jesus and the Paul of 1 Thessalonians." *TynBul* 48 (1997): 377–80.

———. "Paul in Acts and Epistles: The Miletus Speech and 1 Thessalonians as a Test Case." PhD thesis, University of Sheffield, 1997.

Wankel, Hermann, et al., eds. *Die Inschriften von Ephesos*. 8 vols. in 11. IK 11–17. Bonn: Habelt, 1979–1984.

Weems, Renita J. *Just a Sister Away: A Womanist Vision of Women's Relationships in the Bible*. San Diego: Lura Media, 1988.

White, L. Michael. *From Jesus to Christianity: How Four Generations of Visionaries and Storytellers Created the New Testament and Christian Faith.* New York: HarperCollins, 2004.

Wilckens, Ulrich. *Die Missionsreden der Apostelgeschichte: Form- und traditions-geschichtliche Untersuchungen.* WMANT 5. 2nd ed. Neukirchen-Vluyn: Neukirchener Verlag, 1963.

Wilkerson, Isabel. *Caste: The Origins of Our Discontents.* New York: Random House, 2020.

Wilson, Emily. "A Doggish Translation," review of Barry B. Powell, *The Poems of Hesiod* (Berkeley: University of California Press, 2017). *NYRB* 65 (January 18, 2018): 35–36.

Wilson, Mark. "The Social and Geographical World of Thyatira." In *Lexham Geographic Commentary on Acts through Revelation*, 655–64. Bellingham, WA: Lexham, 2019.

Winter, Bruce. "Acts and Food Shortages." In *The Book of Acts in Its Graeco-Roman Setting*, edited by David W. J. Gill and Conrad Gempf, 59–78. BAFCS 2. Grand Rapids: Eerdmans, 1994.

Wire, Antoinette C. *2 Corinthians.* WCS 48. Collegeville, MN: Liturgical Press, 2019.

———. *The Corinthian Women Prophets: A Reconstruction through Paul's Rhetoric.* Minneapolis: Fortress, 1990.

Witherington, Ben, III. *The Acts of the Apostles: A Socio-Rhetorical Commentary.* Grand Rapids: Eerdmans, 1998.

Wordelman, Amy L. "Cultural Divides and Dual Realities: A Greco-Roman Context for Acts 14." In *Contextualizing Acts: Lukan Narrative and Greco-Roman Discourse*, edited by Todd Penner and Caroline Vander Stichele, 205–32. SymS 20. Atlanta: SBL, 2003.

Wyschogrod, Michael. *Abraham's Promise: Judaism and Jewish-Christian Relations.* Edited by R. Kendall Soulen. Grand Rapids: Eerdmans, 2004.

Yee, Gale, ed. *Judges and Method: New Approaches in Biblical Studies.* Minneapolis: Fortress, 1995.

Zahn, Theodor. *Die Apostelgeschichte des Lukas.* KNT 5/2. Leipzig: Deichert, 1921.

Index of Scripture References and Other Ancient Writings

Index of Names and Subjects

Authors

Linda Mitchell Maloney received her PhD in American studies from St. Louis University (1968) and her ThD in New Testament from the Eberhard-Karls-Universität Tübingen (1990), with Prof. Dr. Gerhard Lohfink as her Doktorvater. She is the first woman in the history of the Roman Catholic faculty at Tübingen to earn the ThD in Scripture. Having taught American history at several universities in the 1970s (and cofounded the Women's Studies Program at the University of South Carolina), she joined the faculty of the Franciscan School of Theology at the Graduate Theological Union from 1989 to 1995. Thereafter, until 2007, she was academic editor at Liturgical Press. She was ordained to the Episcopal priesthood in 2003. Since 2005 she has served churches in the Diocese of Vermont and in the Anglican Church of Canada, Diocese of Montreal. She has been active since 1986 as a translator of books on Scripture, theology, and liturgy, mainly from German to English, including four volumes in the Hermeneia series from Fortress Press.

Ivoni Richter Reimer is a native of Brazil. She earned her ThD at the University of Kassel in Germany in 1990, working with Luise Schottroff. Her dissertation, translated into English (1995) as *Women in the Acts of the Apostles: A Feminist Liberation Perspective*, has been published in four languages. Since 1991 she has been a professor of theology and religious studies, in Rio de Janeiro at the Universidade Metodista and Faculdade Teológica Batista do Sul do Brasil, and then in Goiânia/Goiás at the Pontificia Universidade de Goiás, influencing three generations of students of feminist liberation theology and exegesis; she is also a Lutheran pastor, active in community building and developing leadership. Her books include *Maria, Jesus e Paulo com as mulheres: Textos, interpretações e História* (2014), which she describes as a book "about Jesus and Paul in . . . relationships that are built from and together with women"; also *Santa Praxedes: uma jovem com funções eclesiais e sociais em Roma* (2016), on St. Praxedes in the context of women in house communities and active sociopolitical work in the first century CE.

Volume Editor

Mary Ann Beavis, contributor to and editor of this volume, is professor emerita of religion and culture at St. Thomas More College in Saskatoon, Canada. She is the coauthor, with HyeRan Kim-Cragg, of two volumes in this Wisdom Commentary series, *Hebrews* (2015) and *1–2 Thessalonians* (2016), and has written *What Does the Bible Say? A Critical Conversation with Popular Culture in a Biblically Illiterate World* (Eugene, OR: Cascade, 2017), and *The First Christian Slave: Onesimus in Context* (Eugene, OR: Cascade, 2021). Her current research interest is in the area of slave religiosity in early Christianity.

Series Editor

Barbara E. Reid, general editor of the Wisdom Commentary series, is a Dominican Sister of Grand Rapids, Michigan. She is the president of Catholic Theological Union and the first woman to hold the position. She has been a member of the CTU faculty since 1988 and also served as vice president and academic dean from 2009 to 2018. She holds a PhD in biblical studies from The Catholic University of America and was president of the Catholic Biblical Association in 2014–2015. Her most recent publications are *Luke 1–9* and *Luke 10–24*, co-authored with Shelly Matthews (WCS 43A, 43B; Liturgical Press, 2021), *Wisdom's Feast: An Invitation to Feminist Interpretation of the Scriptures* (Eerdmans, 2016), and *Abiding Word: Sunday Reflections on Year A, B, C* (3 vols.; Liturgical Press, 2011, 2012, 2013).